# WOMEN OF BYZANTIUM

# WOMEN
## *of*
# BYZANTIUM

*Carolyn L. Connor*

YALE UNIVERSITY PRESS
NEW HAVEN & LONDON

Designed by Nancy Ovedovitz and set in Adobe Garamond
Oldstyle type by Tseng Information Systems, Inc. Printed in the United
States of America by Sheridan Books.

Library of Congress Cataloging-in-Publication Data
Connor, Carolyn L. (Carolyn Loessel)
Women of Byzantium / Carolyn L. Connor.
p. cm.
Includes bibliographical references and index.
ISBN 0-300-09957-6 (alk. paper)
1. Women—Byzantine Empire.   2. Women—History—
Middle Ages, 500–1500.   I. Title.
HQ1147.B98C66 2004
305.4′09495—dc22      2004001540

A catalogue record for this book is available from the British Library.

10   9   8   7   6   5   4   3   2   1

*To my students*

# CONTENTS

# ACKNOWLEDGMENTS

I would like to acknowledge the financial assistance of the University Research Council at the University of North Carolina in helping subsidize the production of color plates. At Yale University Press I would like to thank Harry Haskell in particular for his patience, understanding, and helpful good humor in seeing this book through to completion. Without him it never would have completed the journey. I also cordially thank Larisa Heimert, Keith T. Condon, and Lawrence Kenney for their editorial assistance.

# INTRODUCTION

Everyone has a story. Given a chance to tell it, most people will recount the events that shaped their lives in explaining how they arrived at where they are. At any given time one's life-story is necessarily a composite view of his or her life up to that time, seen from a perspective that defines successes and failures, choices and chance happenings, hopes and realities, all of which composes a more or less coherent picture. When a person's story is told by others as remembered after his or her life is completed, sometimes by a friend or sometimes someone far removed in time, with that person motivated by certain agendas, it inevitably becomes more selective, with the advantages of hindsight shaping the author's memory and intent. It is with an awareness of these various patterns and origins of our personal histories and the ways in which memory functions that I now approach the stories of Byzantine women, seemingly so far removed in time and culture—or are they?

Histories of the early Christian and medieval East, the lands now occupied by the modern states of Greece, Turkey, and the Near East, once the heartland of Byzantium, have dealt primarily with political events, administrative decisions, and military conquests. It is no wonder that women are barely mentioned in these accounts, for men held the offices, led the armies, and made most of the decisions that shaped the political map during the first millennium and a half of the common era. The absence of women in the historical records of a patriarchal, postclassical civilization would not be surprising. Is the history of Byzantine women therefore unrecoverable? Beyond their biological roles as bearers and nurturers of children, women played different roles from men, sometimes less visible in public life but nonetheless crucial in the operation and makeup of society. Their occupations, beliefs, and social roles significantly shaped the culture and sometimes intersected with spheres of male activity. They could and did rule the empire in their own right; their choices in marriage often determined male rulers, and their influence and leadership affected matters of state. Hence an alertness to issues of gender is essential in understanding Byzantine society as a whole as well as the place women held in that society. By gender I mean, above all, the social roles ascribed to men and women. Gender, and what happens when gender roles are bent, will play an important part in the work of writing women back into the histories of Byzantium.[1]

As it turns out, women are very much present in the abundant surviving sources: saints' lives, chronicles, polemical treatises, biographies, legal records, among many others. In addition, art, artifacts, and buildings hold important testimonies about women. Byzantinists have demonstrated just how numerous and meaningful these records are. In this book I have tried to assimilate and build upon the broad experience and interdisciplinary range of my colleagues in Byzantine studies, to all of whom I am greatly indebted. Recent advances and new directions in scholarship in a number of fields and involving a range of approaches have shown there is actually much more information about Byzantine women than one would imagine. In the past several decades Byzantinists have delved into archives and legal and monastic records and made considerable progress in gathering and quantifying statistics and in revealing patterns of women's lives. Literary, historical, and religious documents are being read in new ways, thanks in part to the heightened awareness brought about by the application of some theoretical approaches. Archaeological and art historical evidence—from buildings and their decoration in sculpture, mosaics, and frescoes to jewelry, enameling, illuminated manuscripts, and small artifacts—is being analyzed with a new eye to women's objectives and connections to symbolic expression. Thanks to recent exhibitions and the publication of catalogues of Byzantine art the public at large can now visualize the material splendor and everyday objects of that civilization as never before. Society is in a different place too because of the maturing of the feminist movement. Commentators have moved beyond documenting their exclusion and oppression to showing the achievements and importance of women's contributions historically. Many scholars have responded with new kinds of studies of texts and images. This book is part of that response to a perceived need to frame and situate the women who were integral to Byzantine culture within their various contexts, in their many roles.

Scholars of Byzantine studies have been inclined to publish more for the academic or the specialist than for a broad readership. This is understandable since Byzantium and its ancient roots are not as well known as, say, the history of western Europe in the Middle Ages, and a certain amount of background and technical expertise is required, as in gaining the skills necessary to read ancient and foreign languages. It is also a field in which scholars habitually work across a number of disciplines and fields: history, philology, art history, archaeology, literary criticism, numismatics, religion, classical studies, medieval studies, women's studies, and others. Although some efforts have been made to alleviate the problem of speaking to a wider audience, studies of Byzantine women still present barriers in the foreignness of terms and in assumptions that readers are acquainted with the customs and the ways the society functioned. What is still needed is to draw together and present in a clear, contextualized, and accessible way the stories of the women of Byzantium, for if one looks first at key concepts and defines essential terms, this exciting material can be dealt with firsthand, opening a door to modern readers. Making accessible the rich material on Byzantine women is my first concern in this book.

Because women played such a vital part in Byzantine civilization, from its origins in the first centuries of the common era to the conquest of Constantinople in 1453, it is important to look at the whole spectrum of Byzantine history. In this way one sees women as situated firmly within Byzantine culture as a whole and as central rather than peripheral to the society—aims which are reflected in this book's structure. Organization is by part and chapter and follows a chronology of the civilization, from its classical roots in late antiquity, around 250 to 500 CE, to the late Byzantine period, between 1204 and the end of the Byzantine Empire in 1453. For convenience, the parts correspond to four successive periods. An introduction to each part outlines major events, issues of transition, dynastic lines, or short case studies by way of example. Within each of the four parts, individual chapters take up a series of topics, such as women and pilgrimage, imperial marriage, patronage, monasticism, etc. As I introduce background in that topic, along with terms, major issues, and the approach to be taken in that chapter, I pose questions which naturally arise in connection with the topic. In the second part of each chapter, a case study focuses on a historical woman, as I explore the primary text or texts most revealing about that person, in conjunction with telling images.

Nothing speaks more directly of the past than contemporary texts and images. I make abundant use of quotations and also frequently bring into the discussion visual materials pertinent to women, interpreting both for the messages they might have conveyed to contemporaries. Many quoted passages catch the voices of Byzantine women themselves or narrate the situations to which they reacted; some reveal the expectations to which they were subject; and others reflect the gendered biases of male authors. Primary texts in the best English translations available and images in a variey of media are the critical evidence for my study of women of Byzantium. Throughout the book readings that are especially recommended in connection with a section or chapter are listed immediately following the text of that section. All works cited are included in the bibliography. The later parts of the book are intended to build on earlier ones. References to prior examples help relate earlier to later trends, demonstrate continuity, or illustrate changes occurring over time. By dealing with different media in the context of each chapter and by varying the approaches and disciplines utilized in the thirteen chapters, I hope to challenge and encourage readers to pursue their own studies of Byzantium or to expand their inquiries into areas that have sparked their interest. For this, the chapter bibliographies and general bibliography are intended to serve as tools, as are the glossary of terms, map, plan, genealogical tables, and list of rulers. My other major concern in this book is thus its utility.

Among the subjects of this book are some extraordinary women, women who already have books or articles written about them and are well known, for example, the empress Theodora, the wife of Justinian; Galla Placidia; Anna Komnene; and Zoe, the wife of three emperors. I also discuss ordinary women, who for the most part are nameless participants in events or members of crowds or groups whose activity is recorded. Evidence of the lives of these ordinary mothers, daughters, wives, and sisters must be teased out of texts in order to get a sense of their presence, for although they composed half of the society, they have often been forgotten or ignored. Broadening the net to include all levels of society and the details and nuances in the ways authors refer to them in their texts, I show that the evidence of those ordinary women of Byzantium is rich and exciting.

I have not assumed that readers will know Greek, the primary language of the Byzantines, and have for the most part used common spellings and transliterations for the readers' convenience. Greek names and terms are transliterated by means of conventional or familiar spellings which Latinize or Anglicize the original. For example, Constantinos Porphyrogennetos becomes Constantine Porphyrogennitus, Maria becomes Mary, and Elene becomes Helen or Helena. Even when this method is used, one will still discover variations in spellings, a situation inherent in changing scholarly practices. For example, Anna Comnena, as she used to be called, is now Anna Komnene, as most scholars presently refer to her; names are thus Hellenized in chapter 11, "The World of Anna Komnene," but most of these are easily recognizable, with only word-endings changing and *K*'s being used instead of *C*'s. Such Hellenizing also applies to the most helpful reference publication for the material discussed in this book, the *Oxford Dictionary of Byzantium*, referred to in notes as *ODB*. It is a recommended complement to the chapter readings and is a reliable, highly informative reference tool and source of further information and bibliography.

Finally, while trying to see men and women in complementary relationships, I focus primarily on women on this journey into Byzantium, as I seek out what women's views of themselves might have been: their self-definition, or consciousness of the self, to put it in modern, psychological terms. This intent has been usefully defined by Angeliki Laiou, and I will apply it to my understanding of women whenever possible. Laiou defines establishing a perception of female ideology as essential in discovering Byzantine women:

> The role of ideology must be clarified; in particular, it seems essential to study the perception women had of themselves as females, and the degree to which this perception may have diverged from male ideology on this issue.[2]

Laiou suggests that ideology applies not so much to a modern understanding and categorization of Byzantine women, in present terms and according to current methodologies, as to their understanding of themselves within their own social context and in relation to male ideology within that context. Pursuit of Byzantine women in this mode is indeed most interesting and productive. Although Laiou claims that the recapturing of women's self-perception is most valuable, in most cases we do not have works produced by them or voicing their opinions. Instead scholars must rely on narratives written by males, reflecting their own agendas, some of which do not deal primarily with women at all but only mention them in passing, between the lines. All such testimony holds great value and authenticity, as we will see.

It is time to look at the women of Byzantium on their own terms and to engage with contemporary authors and their process of shaping, remembering, and recounting the narratives from which we draw women's stories. In conjunction with the literary record, it is important not only to scrutinize images of women in art in an attempt to imagine what Byzantines saw when they viewed these same images but also to visualize the lost products of women's creativity. Using an integrative and eclectic method, I deal with a broad range of issues of consequence to women from all levels of society throughout the long and fascinating history of Byzantium. Part of the delight in making such an inquiry lies in the questions that it raises. For even though some of these will remain unanswerable, the imaginative pursuit of the diverse evidence for women and their lives, roles, and attitudes about themselves should reward us for many years to come.

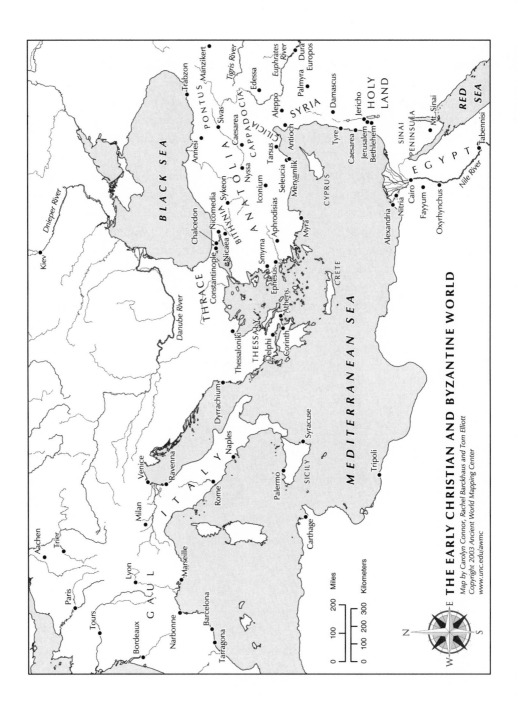

**THE EARLY CHRISTIAN AND BYZANTINE WORLD**

Map by Carolyn Connor, Rachel Barckhaus and Tom Elliott
Copyright 2003 Ancient World Mapping Center
www.unc.edu/awmc

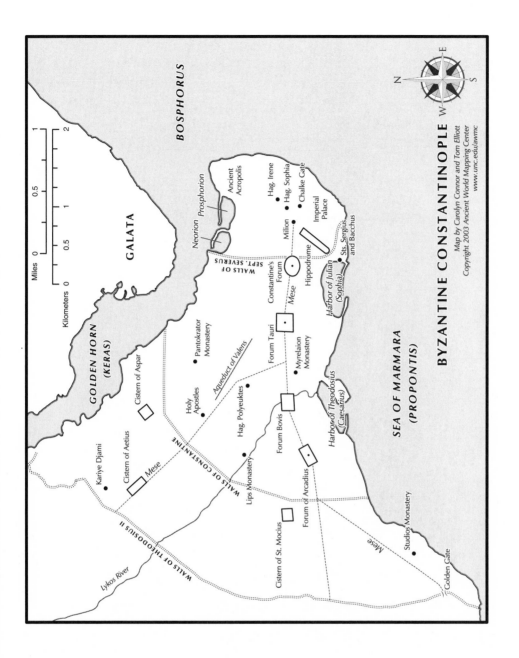

# BYZANTINE CONSTANTINOPLE

Map by Carolyn Connor and Tom Elliott
Copyright 2003 Ancient World Mapping Center
www.unc.edu/awmc

*Part I*

# LATE ANTIQUITY (250–500 CE)

*Introduction: Thekla*

Situated in a time of fundamental change, Thekla's story characterizes a shift away from the old norms of antiquity. Her resolve leads to a new kind of paradigm and helps prepare the way for the new directions that thousands of women's lives would take as, from the time of the first Christian conversions of the first century CE, Christianity opened up the options and goals available to women and men. From its beginnings in the Near East, the new religion with its daring and radical claims affected people and societies in profound ways, not only in terms of converts finding fulfillment in a spiritual dimension, but especially in the choices and changes they could and did make in their lives.

Christianity was only one of many religions taking in converts and propounding various beliefs and patterns of worship, and the reasons for its extraordinary success are still only partially understood. As the movement gained momentum around the Mediterranean world in the first centuries, women may have recognized the potential offered them by a new kind of religious life, but any consequent change was neither abrupt nor calculated by them. A highly patriarchal society does not give up traditions easily, and gendered expectations of women's and men's roles were engrained from classical as well as biblical precedent. In this early period of Christianity, changes took place gradually, and the opportunities and channels for women's active participation slowly had the effect of transforming their lives, as we will see in the first three chapters of this book.[1]

Thekla's story demonstrates more dramatically than any abstract description of social change during the first two centuries of the common era what it meant for a woman to face a new set of religious choices. Her conversion and its consequences have long held a fascination for readers and hearers of the story, from her own time through the Middle Ages, in Byzantium and the Latin West, and up until today. As an associate of Saint Paul, she would have lived in the mid–first century; her life was written in the second century and then rewritten in the sixth and again in the tenth. It was translated from the original Greek into Latin by the early Middle Ages. She was honored as a saint, and a cult of veneration grew up from an early date at her reputed place of burial near Seleucia in Asia Minor and at other sites associated with her. She was and is still remembered on her feast day of September 24.[2]

Accounts of Christian conversion were a natural outgrowth of the Acts of the Apostles and Epistles, in which Saint Paul relates his evangelizing efforts, travels, and trials. While based on the theme of Paul's teaching and preaching, the apocryphal *Acts of Paul and Thekla,* also known simply as the *Acts of Thekla,* composed anonymously, probably in the mid–second century, illustrates the dilemma created for women by the new faith and its impact on families and the state. This work was one of a number of apocryphal texts of the second to fourth centuries in which women are actively described. The *Acts of Thekla* is the principal and earliest source of information about this woman, and I believe there is a grain of truth in it, a real person named Thekla, on which the story was based. But as with all such written Lives of saints, the accounts are more revealing about the contemporary desire to formulate paradigms or inspire faith than about an actual historical person and her experiences. Thus the *Acts of Thekla* is of greater significance because it is symptomatic of the interests of its writers and readers than because it might be related to a real person. With these interpretive problems in mind, based on internal evidence of the text, one can surmise the circumstances under which it was written.

Writings concerning women, fictional or historical, are extremely rare in antiquity, and there is no established literary model the author might have used to describe a woman's life and activity. The story initially resembles a popular romance, with Thekla as the heroine, for it is adventure-filled and entertaining. Factual and direct in its expression, it reveals, for example, the unequal treatment of women under Roman law. It also yields information about the expectations placed on ancient women by their families and communities. While some scholars have doubted the historicity of the account, its value as testimony is undeniable. Approached contextually, it can be seen as the literary product of a time which found the story meaningful enough to set down in writing. Art historical evidence helps broaden our perception of what must have been a widespread cult of the saint.

Thekla is the protagonist in a dramatic story concerning a young woman of marriageable age, probably around twelve or thirteen, living in Iconium, present-day Konya, in Turkey, at the time of the first apostolic missions. Drawn to Paul's teachings on celibacy, she thwarts her family's plans for her marriage to her fiancé by announcing that she will follow the apostle Paul and the tenets of his new faith. Facing harsh censure in her home town, she travels to Antioch and experiences close escapes from death in a series of tests in the arena. Unconcerned with bodily adornment and feminine appearance, she is convinced through Paul's preaching that virginity and self-denial are the way to self-fulfillment and a new identity, and she perseveres to preach and carry on the mission of Paul in Asia Minor. The text responds to anxieties and needs in that society and establishes Thekla as a martyr of the church and the first female apostle.[3]

Such a theme represents an unconventional and bold step taken by a woman at this time, long before Christianity's general acceptance in the Roman Empire. While the tests she endures represent standard means of punishing criminals, her survival verges on the miraculous, and the support she receives from other women resembles a form of female solidarity. Granted this paradoxical and gripping story, told simply and factually, gathered great popularity, why did it have such wide appeal? and for whom? Who was the author of this text? How did women see themselves at this time?

As the account begins, Thekla appears transfixed as she listens to Saint Paul preaching:

> And while Paul was speaking so in the middle of the assembly in the house of Onesiphorus, a certain virgin named Thecla (her mother was Theocleia) who was engaged to a man named Thamyris, sat at a nearby window in her house and listened night and day to what Paul said about the chaste life. (*Acts of Thekla,* 7)[4]

Enclosed in her own house, Thekla becomes engrossed in Paul's preaching, which she can hear from her window. In general women did not appear in public in antiquity but were usually kept occupied inside their homes, for reasons of safety and propriety. Thekla's first experience of Paul's preaching is thus aural, not visual. Theocleia, alarmed and uncomprehending of her daughter's behavior, addresses the girl's fiancé:

> Thamyris, this man is shaking up the city of the Iconians, and your Thecla too. For all the women and the young men go in to him and are taught by him that it is necessary, as he says, "to fear one single god only and live a pure life." And my daughter also, like a spider bound at the window by his words, is controlled by a new desire and a terrible passion. For the virgin concentrates on the things he says and is captivated. (9)

Paul's preaching poses a threat by advocating a break with traditions connected with young people's conduct and with marriage. The "new desire" and "terrible passion" referred to by Theocleia define reactions that must have affected many inhabitants of the Roman Empire at this time. The engagement of a woman was a legal and binding contract and to break it a serious affront to society.

The rapt fascination inspired by Paul's words is comparable to the attraction of a spider to the light of a window opening where it can spin its web. His words appear to have a supernatural power over her; they affect her like a cast spell. Belief in magic was integral to ancient society, and the possibilty that someone was under the power of a magic spell would have inspired fear in those who observed such behavior. Thamyris, lamenting the potential loss of his fiancée, incites the Iconians to arrest Paul, which meets with support from bystanders: "And the whole crowd shouted, 'Away with the magus! for he has corrupted all our women'" (15). A magus, or sorcerer, would have had the power to bind people in servitude to the forces of evil, and this concern naturally makes Thamyris and Theocleia fearful for Thekla. A crowd of witnesses voices its approval, challenging this dangerous influence.

When brought before the proconsul for judgment, Paul proclaims his mission of preaching salvation and is thrown into prison. Thekla follows him, still determined to be his adherent:

> But during the night Thecla removed her bracelets and gave them to the doorkeeper, and when the door was opened for her she headed off to the prison. Upon giving a silver mirror to the jailer, she went in to Paul and sitting at his feet she heard about the mighty acts of God. And Paul feared nothing but continued to live with full confidence in God; and her faith also increased, as she kissed his fetters. (18)

Giving away possessions associated with luxury and feminine adornment, Thekla goes to Paul at night in his prison. Her actions break basic social rules and reverse traditional roles, as she symbolically gives up the things of the world to humble herself before this charismatic teacher. Her commitment to her new faith preempts any other concerns.

When Paul is led away to be tried, Thekla reacts by making physical contact with the place where he had been sitting: "She rolled around in the place where Paul was teaching as he sat in the prison" (20). Rolling on the spot demonstrates her wish for further identification with this man and his powerful message. Bizarre and impulsive as this action may seem, such a physical connection with the place fills a need in Thekla. Her action must have been understood by the audience hearing this story. Any location sanctified by contact with a holy individual gains in importance as the cults of the saints and holy places become established in the early centuries of Christianity.

When Thekla herself is also tried before the governor he asks her, "Why do you not marry Thamyris according to the law of the Iconians?" He is questioning not so much her renunciation of marriage and breaking of a civil law as her presumption at putting the rest of society at risk by setting a dangerous example, so dangerous that Thekla's own mother cries out, "Burn the lawless one! Burn her who is no bride in the midst of the theater in order that all the women who have been taught by this man may be afraid!" (20) To Theocleia a marriage contract arranged among parents has such binding force that if her daughter repudiates it she deserves to die. Obeying her natural instincts, a mother would normally do all that was possible to preserve a child's life, but in this case it is Theocleia who suggests that her daughter be punished by burning, in order to serve as an example to other women. Society's expectations about women overrule all other considerations, even the strong ties of mother to child. This extreme case of objectification of the young Thekla illustrates how strictly gender roles regarding women were prescribed in this society and how vital it was to maintain women's subservience to authority.

The pyre is to be laid by young men and virgins, the very age group to which Thekla and Thamyris belong. When the governor who sentenced her to burning sees Thekla at the execution, he reacts in a show of mixed emotions: "And as she was brought in naked, the governor wept and marveled at the power in her" (22). Her faith makes her strong enough to face death by burning, embodying a new kind of power which is recognized by the governor in his autocratic power. He admires her beauty and courage while lamenting her destruction, but proceeds with the execution as planned. The outcome, however, is Thekla's liberation, as supernatural events save her: an earthquake shakes the town, and a hailstorm extinguishes the fire. Thekla's first test is over, and she leaves Iconium, an exile, to search for Paul.

On discovering Paul at a tomb outside the city with some of his Christian followers she makes her request:

> And Thekla said to Paul, "I shall cut my hair short and follow you wherever you go."
> But he said, "The time is horrible, and you are beautiful. May no other temptation
> come upon you worse than the first and you not bear up but act with cowardice." And
> Thecla said, "Only give me the seal in Christ, and temptation will not touch me." And
> Paul said, "Have patience, Thecla, and you will receive the water." (25)

Condemning Thekla because she is beautiful and, he believes, incapable of resisting sexual temptation and marriage, Paul puts off her request and refuses to baptize her. Even her willingness to take the unconventional and symbolic step of cutting her hair and thereby renounce her femininity is insufficient for Paul to trust her commitment. Handicapped by her beauty, discriminated against because of her sex, she must carry on without receiving the sacrament of baptism she desires.

Having refused Thekla's request for baptism, Paul complies with her second request and permits her to accompany him to Antioch. There, however, when she is accosted on the street by an important official of the city named Alexander, Paul denies any connection with her. Since women traveling alone or without protectors were considered to be of dubious morals, Paul's disassociation with her at this moment leaves her vulnerable. When Alexander embraces her she again receives no help from Paul and defends herself, saying,

> "Force not the stranger, force not the servant of God!" . . . And grabbing Alexander,
> she ripped his cloak, took the crown off his head, and made him a laughingstock. (26)

Acting in self-defense, Thekla upsets Alexander's appearance, causing him to look foolish. This is judged an offense by the governor, and she is again sentenced to death, this time to the wild beasts in the arena or amphitheater. Gladiatorial shows or wild beast shows in the arenas of Roman cities often included the pitting of Christians condemned for their faith against impossible odds. The passage shows that the laws in effect at this time did not treat women and men equally. A man who transgressed the bounds of social norms might be imprisoned or exiled, while a woman who refused marriage, declared herself a Christian, or publicly embarrassed a man, even to defend herself, suffered torture and death.

As Thekla is sentenced, a new element enters the scene, as women voice their objection to the proceedings: "But the women were horrified and cried out before the judgment seat, 'An evil judgment! An impious judgment!'" (27). No mention is made of women being involved in Thekla's trial in Antioch, but suddenly, as in a Greek chorus, there is a group of women who come to her defense. Such acclamations by the public were part of civic appearances of officials and governors and could cause civic instability or erupt into violence. An unexpected show of resistance to Thekla's sentencing is staged by "the women," but to no avail. She is, however, granted one plea:

> Thecla begged the governor that she might remain pure until her battle with the beasts. And a wealthy woman named Tryphaena, whose daughter had died, took her into custody and found comfort in her. (27)

Thekla asks for protection because she knows that rape is part of the customary treatment of women condemned to death. Thekla is therefore put into the custody of Tryphaena to protect her while awaiting her punishment.

Thekla then faces her second ordeal:

> When the beasts were led in procession, they bound her to a fierce lioness, and the queen Tryphaena followed her. And as Thecla sat upon the lioness's back, the lioness licked her feet, and all the crowd was astounded. Now the charge on her inscription was Sacrilegious. But the women with their children cried out from above, saying, "O God, an impious judgment is come to pass in this city!" (28)

For a second time supernatural forces intervene. A lioness upon whose back Thekla was tied licks her feet instead of mauling her. Again "the women" have a voice and protest her charge, written on a placard or perhaps on her body, of "Sacrilegious." Who are these women? Are we to assume that there were Christians living in Antioch and that the women seated "above" or at the back of the amphitheater, in the uppermost tiers, are Christian women? Or are they average Roman citizens expressing moral outrage that Thekla's punishment is too severe? Female resistance to Thekla's execution takes the form of a submissive lioness and the acclamations of women.

Yet another punishment is planned for the following day. This time Thekla is to be thrown to wild beasts. The scene is vividly described:

> Then there was a clamor, a roaring of the beasts, and a shouting of the people and of the women who sat together, some saying, "Bring the sacrilegious one!" But the women were saying, "Let the city perish for this lawlessness! Slay us all, Proconsul! A bitter spectacle, an evil judgment!" (32)

With each new public appearance, Thekla is more vociferously defended by a majority of "the women who sat together," who now condemn the whole city in response to the governor's unjust sentence. The rhetoric of dissent becomes more and more elevated with each of Thekla's trials, as the events become an increasing threat to civil authority. This time, although pitted against bears and lions, Thekla survives thanks to a lioness who fights to the death to protect her from the other beasts and thanks also to another, more unusual form of protest:

> Now, the women, as other more terrible beasts were thrown in, wailed, and some threw petals, others nard, others cassia, others amomum, so that there was an abundance of perfumes. And all the beasts, overcome as if by sleep, did not touch her. (35)

This time the women intervene by throwing fragrant substances into the ring which tranquilize the wild beasts and render them harmless.

After this last reprieve, Thekla sees a ditch full of water and accomplishes her aim:

> She said, "Now is the time for me to wash." And she threw herself in, saying, "In the name of Jesus Christ, I baptize myself on the last day!" . . . about her there was a cloud of fire so that neither could the beasts touch her nor could she be seen naked. (34)

Since women were not allowed by the early church to baptize, Thekla's daring self-baptism establishes a dangerous precedent, one that would be difficult to defend.[5] Her nakedness, the cloud of fire, and her subsequent liberation and presentation with clothes by the governor of the city (38) can also be read as a symbolic parallel to early Christian baptism; the initiate stripped, entered the font, and was baptized through immersion and on leaving the font was reclothed in white robes, in a symbolic rebirth.

After the failure of all the attempted punishments, the governor realizes that the situation is getting out of hand. Fearing the disapproval of Caesar, he releases Thekla. Again, the women have their say:

> All the women cried out with a loud voice and as with one mouth gave praise to God, saying, "One is God who has saved Thecla!"—so that all the city was shaken by the sound. (38)

The city was "shaken by the sound" of the women's acclamation. Thekla's survival and acquittal demonstrate the power of the Christian God, and the women now acclaim him for providing her salvation. The women not only express approval of the outcome, but also relief that the city has not made a mistake and through an unjust punishment brought down some form of retribution on itself, perhaps some disaster.

Why were the women able to have a voice in this case, and how often would such a public demonstration by women have taken place? How is it that they could disagree publicly? Were't there risks involved in such outspokenness against civil authority? This depiction of the women of Antioch poses questions while also representing a remembered instance of women united in their support of a Christian convert and virgin. The passage records a rare instance of female solidarity.

After her liberation, Thekla converts Tryphaena to Christianity along with the rest of her household, who become her new family, and she continues in pursuit of Paul, following him to Myra on the southern coast of Anatolia: "So taking male and female servants, she got herself ready, sewed her chiton into a cloak like a man's, and headed off to Myra" (40). Continuing to break the rules, Thekla now dresses as a man. Cross-dressing is documented in later saints' lives and must have occasionally been a practical necessity when a woman wished to travel in disguise for greater safety. But a band of men and women traveling together, with Thekla wearing men's clothing, represents yet another act of defiance.

When she finds Paul and recounts her means of survival to him, he finally capitulates. She had conducted her own baptism, but Paul makes her an apostle:

> So Paul said, "Go and teach the word of God!" Now Tryphaena sent her a lot of clothing and gold, so it could be left behind for Paul for the ministry of the poor. (41)

At last Thekla is able to pursue her mission and departs on her own to preach and spread Christianity. Paul's ministry to the poor is enriched by Tryphaena's gifts—an early indication of female patronage of Christian ministry.

Thekla eventually settles on the coast of Asia Minor to the east of Myra, near Seleucia:

> And when she had given this witness she headed off to Seleucia, and after enlightening many with the word of God, she slept with a fine sleep. (43)

Thekla's later activity as an apostle, her residence near Seleucia, and her death are dealt with succinctly. Death is referred to, as is customary in the Orthodox Church, as a going to sleep.

There is no internal evidence here or elsewhere in the text of who the author was or why the story was written down. In the oddness and uniqueness of its details, Thekla's story would appear to derive from actual events or reporting of events. The text must have served a didactic purpose and was used to encourage women to enter into baptism and to participate in the church's efforts to rally converts. The description of the women of Antioch has suggested to some it may have been written by a woman—perhaps one of the women who witnessed Thekla's trials or heard of them from a witness.[6] It seems likely it could have been written by a female follower or convert or by one who visited her either while she was alive or at her presumed burial place in Seleucia.

Evidence of the early cult of Saint Thekla can still be seen at the site of her residence and death at the settlement called Meryamlık, or Hagia Thekla, in the arid countryside not far from the coast, to the south of Seleucia (modern Silifke, Turkey; see map on page xvi).[7] This site apparently functioned as a hub of the cult of Thekla and attracted pilgrims from all over the Mediterranean world. Today, the ruins of

*Fig. 1. Roundel: Saint Thekla with Wild Beasts and Angels, limestone, found in Egypt, diam. 64.8 cm, Nelson-Atkins Museum of Art, Kansas City, Mo., fifth century. (Copyright Collection of the Nelson-Atkins Museum of Art, Kansas City, Missouri [Purchase: Nelson Trust] 48–10)*

an extensive settlement including three basilicas and a bath may still be seen. A very large basilica church eighty meters in length was built in the fifth century over a site sacred to her, testifying to the great prosperity and enormous wealth of this place sanctified by Thekla's presence. The basilica, of which only fragments of the east end survive, was probably built by the emperor Zeno around 476. A crypt beneath the church may still be visited, on the south side of which is a large shelf or niche cut into the rock and which is said to be Thekla's burial place. A cross-shaped font is cut into the rock floor of the north side of the crypt; here the faithful must have come to receive baptism. The church is surrounded as far as the eye can see by monastic dwellings of dry stone masonry whose walls are in various stages of collapse, evidently built through the centuries by people wishing to live in proximity to the place associated with Thekla and her mission. The site is impressive testimony to the popularity of the cult of Saint Thekla.

The cult was popular also in Syria and Egypt, and by the seventh century it was also established in Constantinople.[8] Images of Thekla indicate the dissemination of her story in the Near East. Two such images were discovered in Egypt. On a limestone roundel carved in high relief and dated to the fifth century, Thekla is shown surrounded by a laurel wreath (fig. 1).[9] She stands haloed, with hands behind her back and wearing a thin garment, and appears as a sensuous young woman. She is framed to the left and right by a lion and lioness, and two angels hover above. The style is bold and naturalistic, while the design is symmetrical and the figures hieratically arranged. Her miraculous salvation in her tests with the beasts is evoked by this emblematic depiction. The roundel probably served as part of the architectural decoration in a church or shrine at which Thekla was venerated.

Clay ampullae, small two-handled containers for holy oil, were found in Egypt at a site commemorating Saints Menas and Thekla, for the saints are depicted on the two sides of the vessels and labeled. Such ampullae were commonly produced and made available at sites dedicated to holy personages and contained small quantities of a substance associated with the place. The substance, oil, water, or dust, was believed to carry powers of healing. These small containers, ranging from 7.5

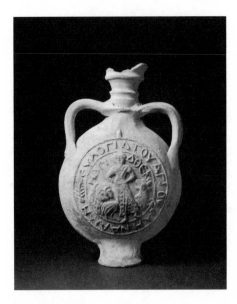

*Fig. 2. Ampulla with Saint Thekla Between Beasts, terracotta, from Egypt, h. 27 cm, diam. 17.5 cm, Paris, Louvre, seventh century. (Copyright Réunion des Musées Nationaux/Art Resource, N.Y.)*

to 17.5 cm (3 to 7 in.) in diameter, were made available as souvenirs. On one ampulla dated to the seventh century, Thekla is depicted within a circle in a schematic rendering standing with hands behind her back, framed by two beasts, a lion and a lioness or bear (fig. 2).[10] The rendering is linear and crude, but the essentials, which are comparable to the roundel discussed above, can still be discerned. Around the image is inscribed E HAGIA THEKL[A] (Saint Thekla), and in an outer band EULOGIA TOU HAGIOU MENA, AMEN (Blessing of Saint Menas, Amen). The ampulla illustrates how a small object seen in conjunction with beliefs promulgated through a literary narrative could establish a connection with the divine and even a potential for miracles. The material evidence of such ampullae provides a link between seventh-century practices associated with Saint Thekla's memory and the second-century text on which our evidence depends.

Whether Thekla's story is truth or legend is not as significant as the reasons for its long-lasting appeal. People must have known it, discussed it, named their children after Thekla, and visited places associated with her. Its appeal may have been greater for women than for men in encouraging them to break with societal norms and convert to Christianity. It also exemplified more generally the heroic dedication of Christian martyrs, who maintained their faith in the face of adversity in the persecutions of the second to fourth centuries. According to the Church Fathers, martyrdom offered an opportunity for women to demonstrate that their faith made them the equal of men. Many converts of both sexes were not saved miraculously but were tortured and suffered hideous deaths. For example, another remarkable early martyrs' narrative, dating to the early third century and written largely by the martyr herself, Perpetua, describes her dilemmas and tortures and those of the slave Felicatas and their fellow Christians who are put to death most cruelly in the arena.[11] Thekla, although she did not die in the arena, is the first female martyr to be recognized as a saint. Her story of rebellion and defiance both entertained and served as a source of inspiration and an example of feminine advancement.

The *Acts of Thekla* encouraged women's celibacy and piety. By broaching issues of parental expectations and filial obligations and conflicts with civil law it gave new or potential converts a precedent in making the break from tradition. The most important break was the refusal of marriage and maintenance of virginity. Although on the one hand celibacy posed a threat to society and countermanded scriptural teaching by withdrawing men and women from the process of procreation, on the other hand, it was, according to Christian belief, a sanctifying of the human body in the service of Christ. The virgin life, which I will discuss in chapter 1, made the adherent into one of the angels and was encouraged by teachers like Paul and by the church fathers. In the first centuries, however, such a choice was still revolutionary.

A later version of Thekla's story appears in the *Life and Miracles of Thekla,* written in the mid–fifth century, probably in the vicinity of Seleucia. A section concerning the end of Thekla's life has been added to this text; a collection of forty-six miracle accounts stems from an oral tradition that must have been established by that time. The accounts testify to pilgrims' experiences at the shine in Seleucia and in particular to the active participation of women in the cult.[12] Two tenth-century versions of the Thekla story are drawn from the second-century *Acts* and the fifth-century *Miracles.* The Metaphrastian Menologion, a calendar of abbreviated saints' lives, narrates a version of Thekla's life which follows the *Acts* closely but appends a section based on the *Miracles.* This version includes the story of her death at age ninety. According to the Menologion, when attacked by violent men she prayed and was admitted to a rock which closed after her. The Synaxarium of Constantinople, a compilation of notices for use in the liturgy, paraphrases the Metaphrastian text and adds a note that her synaxis, or remembrance, is carried on at her martyrium in Chrythopoleia.[13]

The paradoxes within the narrative are evident. Thekla's story is about a successful revolutionary, but it is also about suffering and hardship. It advocates women supporting other women and retaining their virginity, but it also justifies breaking laws, family ties, and dress codes. Based on the realities of a woman's choices, it nevertheless depends on the supernatural and the miraculous to ensure salvation. Although her story has immense appeal and served a social function far outliving the milieu in which it originated, it still remained an anomaly, for not many late ancient and Byzantine women succeeded as dramatically as Thekla.[14]

Themes related to the example of Thekla appear in part 1 of this book. The first three chapters, on late antiquity, deal with various kinds of evidence of women's determination to follow the dictates of their convictions. In chapter 1, I discuss ascetic women and the settings within which they could be found in the early church; the example of Macrina is vividly recorded in her Life, written by her famous brother Gregory of Nyssa. In chapter 2, I show how female pilgrimage becomes intelligible through an extraordinary text written by a fourth-century woman, Egeria, about her travels in the East. Chapter 3 brings three imperial women of the Theodosian dynasty into focus; among them, Galla Placidia serves as a case study of what an imperial princess of the fifth century could and did accomplish. Thekla's empowering paradigm makes a fitting start to this book, for she inspired women to imitate her moral role and helped shape women's leadership over the next twelve hundred years.

## Associated Readings

"Thekla of Iconium: An Ascetic Christian and the Prototypical Convert," in *Maenads, Martyrs, Matrons, Monastics,* ed. Ross S. Kraemer (Philadelphia, 1988), 280–88, for the English translation of the *Acts* used here.

*The Apocryphal Gospels,* M. R. James, ed. and trans., *The Apocryphal New Testament* (Oxford, 1924), *Acts of Paul and Thekla,* 272–81.

Gillian Clark, *Women in Late Antiquity: Pagan and Christian Life-styles* (Oxford, 1993).

Stephen J. Davis, *The Cult of Saint Thecla: A Tradition of Women's Piety in Late Antiquity* (Oxford, 2001).

Ross S. Kraemer, *Her Share of the Blessings: Women's Religions among Pagans, Jews, and Christians in the Greco-Roman World* (New York, 1992).

*One*

# ASCETIC WOMEN AND RELIGIOUS LIFE
# IN EARLY CHRISTIANITY: MACRINA

The emperor Constantine's adoption of Christianity signaled by his Edict of Milan of 313 issued in a period of momentous change. The edict ordained that Christianity would now be tolerated among the people of the Roman Empire, which at that time included much of Europe, the Middle East, and North Africa. Accordingly, Christians would no longer suffer persecution and martyrdom because of their beliefs.[1] It also meant a decisive shift in politics, for now the highest authority in the state acknowledged the yet higher authority of God, forming one of the most effective alliances in history. As the statues of the old gods were pulled down, the church and its bishops assumed responsibility for the souls of all the faithful. With imperial support, what had been a religion of secrecy now headed toward consolidation as a church whose power would rival that of the state. It is difficult to envision the full extent of the transformations brought about by this movement of Christianization of the Roman Empire. Between the Edict of Milan and the antipagan legislation of Theodosius I in 391–92, the ancient world changed rapidly, even though it took decades, even centuries, for some areas, with their entrenched systems of the old pantheon of gods and of imported eastern religions, to become predominantly Christian.[2]

Integral to the religious shifts of the fourth century was a shift in the role of women in society, which was closely knitted to their membership in the church. In this chapter I will focus on changes that affected women's lives from the period of persecutions of the second and third centuries, in which women formed a substantial proportion of those martyred in the arena, to the establishment of religious institutions and ascetic lifestyles in the fourth and fifth centuries. With these patterns came a new kind of autonomy for women. No longer was it necessary for them to die for their faith, but instead they could adopt a celibate life dedicated to the church and maintain lives as respected and protected members of a town or community. Just as women's activities in the service of the church were important to the success of Christianity, the possibilities opened to women through Christian patterns of life were empowering for them. The language of martyrdom remained part of the characterization of the self-denial espoused by both men and women. The "athlete of Christ" now struggled to win the war against temptation and attacks of the demons of desire in order to serve effectively in this life as well as to prepare for the next. Women found diverse careers in religion in a variety of contexts, rural and urban, private and public, solitary and communal. They took up religious lives for varied reasons, often different from those affecting men. For a surprising number, the life in Christ constituted the focal point of their lives.[3]

A lifestyle adopted by many Christians, men and women alike, was that of ascetic renunciation. *Ascesis,* coming from the Greek word for athletic or military training, meant denial of worldly pleasures and comforts as well as dedication to prayer and humility, as a form of service to Christ. Asceticism is usually associated with tonsured monks and nuns but was actually more widely and flexibly practiced among lay individuals and groups. In some forms of asceticism, mortification of the body and emotional duress could be severe and might include fasting, standing vigils, sleeping on the ground, going barefoot, wearing a single tunic, hair shirt, or chains; some ascetics practiced continuous prayer, isolation, celibacy, absolute obedience to a monastic superior, manual labor, and poverty. At its core asceticism emphasized the spiritual life and rejected the fleshly aspect of humanity, which manifested itself in strict control of the body.[4] Some ascetic men and women exhibited miraculous powers of healing or foresight; others served as counselors or caregivers for the poor. Particularly dedicated or charismatic ascetics sometimes achieved sainthood.

The fourth-century *Lives of the Desert Fathers* and *Lausiac History of Palladius* narrate the stories of exemplars of the ascetic life, of men and women in the desert communities of Egypt.[5] The model for these lives was the *Life of Anthony,* written by Athanasius of Alexandria around 357, describing the ideal ascetic and his retreat into the desert. These texts recount the practices taken up by Christian believers in an attempt to simplify their lives and to become closer to God. Life in the desert was characterized by the pursuit of piety through good works, prayer, and fasting. Vegetables raised in small gardens and bread were the staple diet.[6] Adherents lived in small mud-brick cells or one- or two-room dwellings, sometimes in more permanent buildings with many cells surrounded by walls, such as at Tabennisi and Oxyrhynchus. At the latter community, for example, the narrator recalls, "As far as we could ascertain from the bishop of that place, we would say that he had under his jurisdiction ten thousand monks and twenty thousand nuns."[7] Although this estimation of numbers of Egyptian desert ascetics may be an exaggeration, it is clear this was a mass movement involving more than a few dozen solitaries. These written lives described such a vivid pattern of asceticism that the subjects were seen to mirror the texts they had studied.[8] The result was the development of several types of monasticism.

Monasticism, from the Greek *mone,* to live alone, first practiced by Christians in fourth-century Egypt, became a standard form of asceticism with two types of practice. Anthony exemplified the eremitic, or solitary, lifestyle, and Pachomius, the cenobitic or communal. From Egypt these two types of monasticism spread to Palestine and Gaul and beyond. Pachomius's sister, Maria, founded a communal monastery for women near her brother's at Tabennisi, which indicates that women's communities were developed from the start of the movement alongside men's. Of course men's communities were in principle aimed at escaping proximity to women and thereby temptation, but in many cases cenobitic houses for men and women were near each other, as in this example. The Egyptian desert of the fourth and fifth centuries saw numerous visitors who drew inspiration from the experience, some of them highly influential, such as Basil the Great, Melanie the Younger, Jerome, Evagrius, Paula, and John Cassian.[9]

During this period women began to participate in society on a new basis, no longer constrained and controlled, invisible and housebound, but with the capability of interacting with men and with other women in the public sphere. Perhaps most significantly, they could choose to marry or not to marry. By taking up lives as holy virgins or brides of Christ they had access to friendships, learning, and travel formerly all but denied to women. Although naturally there were still constraints imposed on women, this new religiously determined status redefined their positions in society in important ways. Literary works of this time deal with women by name rather than anonymously, and although there are no preserved texts known to have been written by women, it is clear that they were writing letters because we have preserved the responses of their male colleagues. In other texts, women are described by male writers as their equals. Such is the case with the fourth-century *Life of Macrina,* to be explored in the second part of this chapter. Macrina is an example of a woman who participated in the ascetic movement of the fourth century and served as an example to succeeding generations of ascetic women.[10]

The question of exceptional women versus ordinary women must be raised. The records mostly concern extraordinary or highly motivated women and women well endowed financially, but their more ordinary, unprivileged sisters also were part of this new personal freedom accessible to women. Although they themselves probably did not stop to reflect on the changes they were experiencing, their lives were different from those of women in more ancient societies or in the Roman society into which Thekla was born. Because women of varying social status were active participants in this movement I will consider aspects of life and practice which can be associated with ordinary as well as extraordinary women.

All women, whether rich or poor, princesses or slaves, had to deal with conflicting and polarized stereotypes imposed by the church, from seductress (Eve) to paragon of purity and virtue (the Virgin Mary). These conflicts inherent in their sexual identities were inescapable. For example, for a woman to be a virgin might be pleasing to God but displeasing to her parents, who might wish her to marry and procure beneficial alliances with other families or produce children to inherit their property or care for them in their old age.[11] The pressures felt by wealthy women of course differed from those of poor women or slaves, for they had greater visibility and influence under the law. Put another way, it was important for society to control them, for they could use their wealth to affect social change and sway public opinion. Women's traditional sexual and gender roles complicated the choices open to women in late antiquity, for their status as Christians gave them possibilities as never before.

Biblical and patristic writings based on interpretations of Scripture marginalized women. Church fathers were ambivalent about women because they were seen both as God's creation and gift to men and also as the curse of the world. Confusion naturally arose because of the precepts of Old Testament narrative. Genesis 2 says Eve was created from the rib of Adam and was therefore second in importance, while Genesis 1 says both were created at the same time and were therefore equal. Saint Paul calls men "the image of God" but women, "coworkers." Some church fathers, for example, Jerome and Tertullian, used Scripture to denigrate women generally, but women were met with approval if they dedicated their lives to religious activities. The church advocated celibacy as a way for women to win through asceticism the status lost through the Fall and through marriage.[12] Thus while asceticism for women was encouraged, ironically it gave women greater freedom and therefore men had less control over them, thereby posing a threat. While men's and women's asceticism was accepted from the third and fourth centuries on, women gradually achieved through it greater self-determination and autonomy than if they married conventionally.

Marriage was the traditional role of women, and through marriage they consolidated the status, wealth, and power of families. A girl could be engaged while still a baby but usually married around age twelve.[13] Upon her marriage, the control over her exerted by her father passed to her husband. Through much of her life, however, a woman's father retained his legal rights over her, since her birth status was more important than her married one.[14] Marriage was seen as an expedient for money to change hands in the form of the dowry or to populate the state.[15] Love in marriage or a companionable relationship was a stroke of good fortune, not the basis for the institution.[16] Childbearing was the most dangerous part of marriage, as large numbers of women died in childbirth. Society needed as well as expected women to marry and produce children to make up for losses in the high mortality rates of women and children.

In view of the social necessity of marriage, a momentous shift was enacted when celibacy became a principal feature of Christian piety. As was generally thought, Adam and Eve had sex only after their expulsion from Eden, and therefore celibacy was good and marriage a lesser, sinful state. Renunciation of their sexual function as allayers of male lust and bearers of children thus raised women to a new kind of personhood.[17] Some ordinary women chose the virgin life as young girls in order to escape unwanted marriages, whereas others were dedicated as brides of Christ by parents who could not provide them with doweries. They joined monastic communities or remained at home. From the fourth century on, virginity replaced martyrdom in demonstrating superior commitment to Christ. Female celibacy broke the pattern of subjugation to men but was also a threat to family order, the church, and the state because of the rules pertaining to property and its inheritance.[18]

Virgins were referred to by Athanasius, the fourth-century archbishop of Alexandria in Egypt, as "Brides of Christ."[19] These women were protected by the church from at least this time and were a source of pride in a Christian community. The decision to be a "sacred virgin" was made by sixteen- to seventeen-year-old girls themselves or by their parents, since parents controlled marital prospects. The child was sometimes an unwanted baby and was given to the church instead of being exposed and left to die. The girl became a human offering, a sacred vessel dedicated to Christ. Girls could be withdrawn from dedication by their parents if they were sought in a marriage that could be profitable for the family. In the words of Peter Brown, "Women, like wealth, were there to circulate."[20] Dedicating a virgin has been compared to freezing a community's assets. As sacred virgins, women were highly objectified in being seen as part of the wealth controlled by the early church.

The Virgin Mary as dedicated to the temple served as a model for virgins. Sacred virgins as brides of Christ were, in principle, unavailable to another marriage partner and were thought to live in the company of Christ and his angels. Women who took the vow of virginity and then decided to marry were excommunicated and were seen as *bigamoi,* or those who marry twice.[21] Virginity as a form of asceticism gave special value to women in two strata of society: first, upper-class women could have an impact on a household or even on an entire city by becoming ascetic leaders and sponsors; second, average women of ascetic leanings could become brides of Christ. What was the life of a sacred virgin in these two categories like?

Sacred virgins, or *parthenoi,* remained in seclusion in the ordinary Christian household, in their parents' homes, and left only for services in the church. It was believed that a *parthenos* protected her house and even the locality in which the family lived. Sometimes these women were organized in pairs or groups or gathered around a rich widow.[22] They sometimes went into the desert like male ascetics and could even enjoy friendships with males. However, live-in relationships between men, monks, or clergy and these virgins was frowned upon, and for the most part men and women ascetics were kept apart. A person who protected sacred virgins was called *philoparthenos,* a friend of virgins, and this role was considered a charitable activity. A virgin's awareness of her sexuality made her constantly vigilant and anxious; she controlled her diet and often fasted. Control of her body gave a sacred virgin a new kind of power. When a young woman symbolically went "into the desert," it could mean an isolated hermitage, the privacy of her own chamber or household, a city nunnery or group retreat, or a rural monastic community.[23]

Sacred virgins did not always remain at home or within an urban community. Sometimes they circulated. They advised, ministered to, protected, and taught other women. Their lives were sheltered, uninterrupted by marriage or childbearing, and their physical integrity was deeply respected. They were associated with cities, and monks with the desert. Within the city, shrines and churches were gathering places for holy virgins. When they went on pilgrimage in order to venerate relics of martyrs or visit living holy men at their hermitages, they were hospitably received at female monasteries and hospices along the way. Literacy and learning, otherwise reserved to males, were made accessible to sacred virgins, and the Scriptures were their schoolbook. In contrast to ordinary virgins, aristocratic virgins had unusual and widespread influence in the early church, as in the cases of the great virgin "activists."[24]

Aristocratic women who were ascetics or who were deeply religious enjoyed a freedom similar to that of men. Women with birth, wealth, and learning often became celibate after they had been widowed or sometimes while still married. They left husbands and families to join communities or travel on pilgrimage; sometimes family members followed their example and also entered religious institutions. There are numerous examples of these well-traveled, well-heeled benefactresses of the poor. There was no set pattern for their pursuits, for they retained their wealth and controlled how it was spent. The establishment of religious foundations by fourth-century aristocratic women is well documented, as in the cases of Melania the Elder, Paula, Olympias, and Macrina. These women maintained control over the institutions they founded and led a flexible and self-determined existence in spite of the antifemale patristic discourse of the fourth and fifth centuries.[25]

"House asceticism," practiced in Rome and Jerusalem by the mid–fourth century, was available to the wealthy although it involved a change in attitude to comforts and wealth. This private form of renunciation was pursued by women who wished to dedicate themselves to God but in a private rather than public setting. While remaining at home, they demonstrated that property did not cause pride or undue attachment to worldly possessions. They did no physical labor but had a daily routine restricted to prayer, study, writing, and contemplation. They often had servants on whom they relied. They could travel and go on pilgrimage to holy sites, a possibility not open to married women, who were for the most part confined to traditional patterns of life involving house and family. Learning was praised and admired as a studious activity, especially becoming conversant with the writings of the church fathers. On occasion such women were known to debate or edify emperors. Fostering conversion of non-Christians was also an accepted occupation of women of means.

Society depended on the generosity of wealthy women who used their wealth for the public good, whether serving as sponsors of building projects such as churches, monasteries, hospices, and hospitals, or distributing alms to the poor. They could take up life in the monasteries they founded or remain in their palatial homes. Some wore chains or hair shirts under their clothing as part of their ascetic denial of bodily comforts. Self-determination characterized their lives. They used their influence and family names to protect people who were being unjustly treated. Their social utility was vital, and some of these women achieved considerable fame. Widows, normally expected to remarry, now took the option to remain celebate, even if widowed at a young age. Their use of their wealth sometimes caused alarm, as in the case of Olympias. Having borne children, they were now free to go on pilgrimage, found monasteries, and visit learned men and other women. The widow's vow of celebacy was a significant social reordering.

For aristocratic women of late antiquity, the religious life was the only career outside the domestic sphere open to them, and they lent substantial power to the early church. Their assertiveness was accepted by the society, and they enjoyed a social liberation that may be considered the "best of both worlds."[26] Christians differentiated themselves from pagans in their sexual discipline, which, for women, meant considerable freedom. The sexes mingled easily in the great churches, and all were subject to the bishop and to God in a public environment. Women participated in the life of the church, practiced asceticism at home, or made their own decisions about withdrawl to monastic life.[27]

While new avenues were opened to women in the fourth century, the priesthood was closed to them. They were, however, ordained as deaconesses from the fourth century on and aided the bishop with pedagogic and ritual functions pertaining to women. It is clear from the *Apostolic Constitutions* of the fourth century that women's roles in the church were limited and circumscribed by male authority and that women were increasingly segregated from men.[28] Nuns were encouraged to go on pilgrimage and traveled in groups, stopping at other nunneries for food and shelter along the way. Women not only found possibilities for new lifestyles in the first Christian centuries, but also helped decisively in the success of the new religion. They could make choices and as virgins, widows, or nuns take up a life dedicated to an ideal of virtue and purity, a life "pleasing to God." In spite of the suspicion and taboos placed on women who did not serve society in ways deemed acceptable, they persisted in taking control of their bodies and in pursuing various forms of religious dedication.

Although rhetoric and learning were considered part of a man's masculine privilege, and women were thought unfit for learning, according to John Chrysostom, women obtained an education and participated in intellectual debate with men from this time on. For ordinary women, this meant treading a fine line between activities which would be socially accepted and those that would not. One example can be seen in John Chrysostom's and Jerome's rebukes of the female ascetics who lived in close proximity with male ascetics, the women called *subintroductae,* in what was deemed highly inappropriate behavior.[29] The case of Macrina, an early female ascetic, demonstrates the climate of this time of shifting patterns and taboos in women's roles.

## Macrina

The Life, or *Vita,* of Macrina was originally written in the form of a letter from her brother Gregory to a friend. It represents a unique combination of epistle, biography, and an early form of hagiography, a highly constructed genre of writing filled with a variety of *topoi* or repeated patterns that reiterated the main themes of a saint's life. In the case of Macrina, her brother Gregory wishes to preserve the memory of his sister, whom he greatly loved and admired, and so undertakes to write her life story. The Life is a vivid description of a woman in the century of Constantine who chose a religious calling to the exclusion of marriage. In a sequence starting with her birth and childhood, it describes Macrina's character, her decisions, relationships with family members, and acts of piety, up to her death. All are recounted by Gregory in a highly personal and subjective vein which often verges on encomium. The text is usually referred to as the *Vita Macrinae Junioris,* for she was called Macrina the Younger to distinguish her from Macrina the Elder, her paternal grandmother. Another of Gregory's writings, the *De Anima et Resurrectione,* or *On the Soul and the Resurrection,* concerns her theological views in more detail, but for our purposes I will rely on the *Vita.*[30]

Macrina's life, unlike Thekla's, is situated firmly in the world of early Christianity. Her family was descended from a distinguished line of Cappadocian landowners who experienced the period of persecutions, for they had already converted to Christianity by the third century. Her grandfather died under Licinius for his Christian beliefs, and her grandmother was martyred defending hers under Maximinus Daia. We know little of her parents except that her father's death left the family well off and headed by Macrina's mother, Emmelia.

Macrina's generation produced three brothers who were bishops, Gregory, who became known as Saint Gregory of Nyssa, Basil, who became Saint Basil the Great, and Peter, known as Saint Peter of Sebaste. Along with Gregory of Nazianzus, Basil and Gregory of Nyssa were known as the Cappadocian Fathers, the men who helped lay the theological foundations of the Orthodox Church. Among Basil's writings, his Great Rule set down the regulatory system used in monasteries in the Christian East for the next millennium and beyond. Basil was much influenced by his sister, but Macrina's primary roles were that of strong leader within her family and founder and first abbess of a nunnery. Throughout her life she served as a teacher and practitioner of Christian philosophy. She was made a saint after her death and is commemorated in the church on the anniversary of her death, her feast day, July 19.

The *Life of Macrina* offers a perspective on men's and women's lives in fourth-century Cappadocia and primarily describes a woman who, according to Gregory, fulfilled the roles of mother, father, teacher, and pedagogue to her siblings as the eldest daughter in the family. Her brother reveals her life as identified with that of Thekla from the time of her birth, and he represents her as a dedicated virgin as well as a teacher and "apostle." Gregory wishes to demonstrate her extraordinary piety and intelligence, both in nurturing the family and in guiding a community of nuns. To him, she is the model of the virgin life and of human virtue, considerations of gender aside. In his portrait of her, Gregory declares that in "Christ there is no male or female, but in Him all are one."[31] He depicts her as a "Christian Socrates," a seeker after truth and believer in the immortality of the soul. Gregory treats the death of his sister as parallel to that of Socrates, but only after affirming the necessity of linking body to soul rather than the body divesting itself of its soul in death. Macrina's life fulfills both pagan and Christian ideals of wise philosopher. The *Life of Macrina* was written shortly after her death in 379, probably between 380 and 383.[32]

The text of the letter, which I will refer to as the Life, begins with Gregory recalling a meeting with the letter's recipient, in Antioch on his way to Jerusalem, and a conversation they had about Macrina:

> It was a woman who prompted our narrative, if, that is, we may call her a woman, for I do not know if it is appropriate to apply a name drawn from nature to one who has risen above nature. (1.14–17; 26)

In Gregory's view, Macrina has transcended any characterization of a woman according to gender. This comment prepares the reader for the elevated philosophical values Gregory places on his sister, her qualities of soul and the nature of their close personal and intellectual relationship. It is because of her extraordinary qualities that Gregory decides to write her Life:

> And so, since you were convinced that the story of her good deeds would be of some use because you thought that a life of this quality should not be forgotten for the future and that she who had raised herself through philosophy to the highest limit of human virtue should not pass along this way veiled and in silence, I thought it good to obey you and tell her story, as briefly as I could, in a simple, unaffected narrative. (1.24–31; 26–27)

Gregory is fully aware that his letter will serve as Macrina's biography and be used to relate her virtuous example to others. He has made a value judgment, that hers is a superior life, acknowledging too that women do not ordinarily gain recognition, but "pass along this way veiled and in silence." Most women of his acquaintance probably did wear veils over their heads, and their modesty of appearance conformed with their quiet modesty of comportment. But Macrina is different, and Gregory is responding to his own definition of the good in preserving Macrina's story. Knowing the strength of his own convictions and affection for his deceased sister, he asserts that this will be not an encomium, using conventional exaggeration, but a straightforward and truthful account.

In the first part of the narrative Gregory describes supernatural events which surrounded Macrina's birth:

> And when the time came when she [Emmelia] was to be freed from her labour pain by giving birth to the child, she fell asleep and seemed to be carrying in her arms the child still embraced by her womb, and someone in suprahuman majesty of form and shape appeared to address the little child by the name of Thekla, that Thekla of great fame among maidens. After doing this three times and calling upon her to witness it, the person disappeared from her sight and gave ease to her labor pains so that as soon

as she woke up from her sleep she saw that the dream was reality. And so that was Macrina's secret name. In my view, however, the figure who appeared declared this not so much to guide the mother in her choice of name as to foretell the life of the child and to point out, by the identity of name, a similarity in their choice of life. (2.21–34; 27–28)

A vision associates the unborn child with Thekla. Thekla must have been regarded by Gregory, who knew her life from the *Acts of Thekla*, as admirable for making unconventional decisions in determining her own life as a virgin and an apostle. To him, even more in retrospect, Thekla was the appropriate model for the patterns of life adopted by his sister, Macrina. The secret naming of Macrina after Thekla is also a form of prophecy about the kind of life his sister would lead. Similar visions or supernatural events became associated with the birth stories at the beginnings of saints' lives or other events in their lives, constituting one of the many kinds of literary tropes and topoi encountered in the vitae.

Macrina was nursed as a child by her own mother, Emmelia, an option available only to the upper classes in Roman society, and was schooled by her as well, according to the Life. Gregory points out his sister's intelligence and excellent education in the subjects of study appropriate for a girl, which emphatically did not include ancient drama or comedy:

> For she held that it was shameful and altogether unfitting to teach a tender and easily influenced nature either the passions of tragedy—those passions of women which have given the poets their sources of inspiration and their plots—or the indecent revels of comedy, or the causes of the evils which befell Troy, definitely spoiling the child's nature with the really rather irreverent tales about women. (3.9–15; 28)

Classical texts are seen as a source of corruption. By reading about women who were uncontrolled in their passions, she might receive a bad example, for such a lack of control represented bad morality. Appropriate texts for her study were deemed to be Scripture or "whatever was conducive to the moral life." Macrina studied the Wisdom of Solomon and knew the Psalter by heart.

The skills proper for the young Macrina were those associated with the working of wool, textile production being a traditional occupation of women within their homes from ancient times. This was, like reading, a housebound activity. As she matures it becomes apparent that she is not only intelligent and skillful but also beautiful:

> Growing up with these and similar occupations and having become especially skilled in the working of wool, she attained her twelfth year, the age in which the bloom of youth starts to radiate more than at any other time. Here it is indeed worth marvelling how the beauty of the young girl, although concealed, did not remain unnoticed. There did not seem to be any such marvel in the whole of that country which could compare with her beauty and gracefulness, so that not even painters' hands could come close to her fresh beauty; and the art which engineers everything and which dares even

to wrestle with the greatest subjects, going so far as to fashion in imitation images of the planets themselves, did not have the power to render a true likeness of her blessed beauty. (4.1–13; 29)

Macrina did not venture into public, and so her beauty remains "concealed." Nonetheless, when she reaches the age of twelve, the usual age of betrothals and marriage for women, Macrina's beauty catches the attention of potential suitors. According to Gregory, neither skillful painters nor nature, "the art which engineers everything," could imitate Macrina's beauty, a topos indicating that all beauty was seen as an emanation of the divine. A betrothal to a young lawyer is arranged by her father, but the young man dies prematurely, at which point Macrina makes a decision:

> When the young man's death had broken off what had been decided for her, she called her father's decision a marriage, as if what had been decided upon had in fact really happened, and she determined to remain by herself for the rest of her life, a decision which was more firmly rooted than one might have expected in one of her age. (5.1–5; 30)

Unpersuaded by further offers of marriage, Macrina insists that she will rejoin her fiancé at the Resurrection and that it would be "improper and unlawful" for her to marry another man, invoking the Roman state of *univira*, or the right to one marriage and refusal of a second.[33] As noted in Thekla's story, an engagement as an intention of marriage had binding power and legal force. It could even be, as in this case, the reason for not taking up another engagement. Macrina chooses this interpretation, and the decision is "safeguarded," for she lives close to her mother and shares her life in a mutual exchange. The need for safeguarding or protection stemmed from instances of men carrying off women by force, since a beautiful virgin would be especially vulnerable.[34]

From this time on, Macrina's life becomes increasingly ascetic. While her mother continues to be her teacher, who "cares for her soul," the daughter performs the menial duties of their daily life, including preparing their bread "with her own hands." Another of Macrina's roles is to help with financial concerns of paying taxes, for her mother had not only four sons and five daughters to care for, but also responsibility for the family bookkeeping. They were well off, as is indicated by the comment that they were paying taxes on property in three provinces. Macrina directs the lives of both women, for it is she who tries to guide her mother in a philosophy of denial of the body and elevation of the soul in the search for a "more perfect life."

On Basil's return to the family Macrina becomes his mentor and wins him over to the same ideal of philosophy, one in which he too assumes a life of self-deprivation and poverty. A further stage of austerity is reached when Macrina turns their house into a house of ascetics:

> Macrina persuaded her mother to give up their accustomed way of life, their rather ostentatious life-style and the services she had previously been accustomed to receive

from her maids, and she also persuaded her to put herself on an equal footing with the many in spirit and to share a common life with all her maids, making them sisters and equals instead of slaves and servants. (7.2–8; 32)

We must imagine a band of women who no longer live in a master-servant relationship, but instead one of equality and life in common. Such a restructuring of a household must have been rare at this time. Female slaves were sometimes given their freedom and a dowry upon a master's death, but the scenario described in the Life is more difficult to imagine. The final step involves moving from their home to an estate far away. After the large family of children has been brought up, the father has died, and the family resources have been distributed among the children, Macrina sets up an ascetic community at Annesi, on family land far to the north, in Pontus:

She prepared her [mother] to put herself on an equal footing with the community of maidens, so as to share on equal terms with them one table, bed and all the needs of life, with every difference of rank eliminated from their lives. And such was the order of their life, such was the high level of philopsophy and the holy conduct of their living by day and by night that it exceeds the power of words to describe it. . . . [They lived] in harmonious imitation of the life of the angels . . . Their only care was for divine realities and there was constant prayer and the unceasing singing of hymns. (11.8–20, 29–30; 35–36)

This ideal ascetic community founded by Macrina at Annesi probably depended on the rule established by her brother, Saint Basil, and was similar to the type of ascetic life described in the *Lives of the Desert Fathers*. Macrina has given up the world to imitate the life of the angels.[35]

While leading this community Macrina takes on the upbringing and education of her youngest brother, Peter: "She became everything for the child, father, teacher, guide, mother, counselor in every good, and she perfected him." Following her example, he later becomes a caretaker for the poor who have been attempting to escape a famine in the land. Peter is present with Macrina at the death of their mother, who proclaims on her deathbed, "So may sanctification come to this my first and to this my tenth born." She foretells the sanctification of both Macrina and Peter, for the making of a saint or saints is a process which must start with the recognition of good deeds.

At the death of her brother Basil, Macrina's strength of spirit inspires another literary image, that of the athlete. She remained tranquil and, according to the Life, "stood her ground like an undefeated athlete, who does not cringe at any point before the onslaught of misfortune" (14.27–28; 39). The athlete of Christ, a topos encountered in the earliest Christian writings, persists into late medieval Lives of saints. The suffering of saints and martyrs as they strive to avoid temptation and signs of weakness is compared to the efforts of the ancient athlete.

A vision in a dream alerts Gregory that Macrina, whom he has not seen in eight years, is very ill, and so he travels to the remote community at Annesi, where she lives as abbess among the nuns of the monastery she founded:

> An entire contingent of men poured forth from the monastic enclosure . . . and a group of maidens from the convent awaited our coming by the church in good order. (16.3–6; 40–41)

The passage indicates that this is a double monastery, the two communities retaining separate enclosures but sharing the use of the church.[36] When Gregory encounters Macrina she is near death but maintains her ascetic lifestyle:

> She was resting not on a bed or a couch, but on the ground, on a plank covered with sack-cloth, with another plank supporting her head and designed to serve instead of a pillow, lying under her neck muscles at a raised angle and giving the right amount of support to her neck. (16.14–19; 41)

Unconcerned with bodily comforts, the dying Macrina converses with Gregory, offering expressions of her beliefs, of strength and selflessness. She is compared by Gregory to a holy martyr and then to the runner who

> has overtaken his rival and is already close to the finish of the race-course, when he draws near to the prize and sees the victor's crown, rejoices in his heart, as though he had already won the prizes which lie before him, and proclaims his victory. (19.24–29; 44)

The athlete of Christ image, echoed in Timothy 4, "I have fought the good fight," is used to describe her life near its conclusion. She relates events of her own life, utters a long prayer concerning the immortality of the soul, which Gregory transcribes in the Life, and dies peacefully. In recounting a good life and a good death, the text of the life establishes a paradigm of female sanctity and ensures that this victorious athlete will attain salvation, the sought-after "victory."

When the body is laid out and the nuns give voice to their laments, the roles Macrina has played for these women become clear:

> From the girls who called her by the name of mother and nurse, their grief flared out more passionately than from the rest. They were those who had been left prostrate along the roadways at the time of the famine; and she had picked them up, nursed them, brought them back to health and guided them personally to the pure, uncorrupted life. (26.29–34; 51)

Certain women in her community had been abandoned during a famine by fleeing families in search of sustenance. The harsh realities faced by ordinary women, the poor, and those on the fringe of society become vivid in passages such as this. Women came to the aid of other poor women when all else had failed.

Women of high status had also come to Macrina's monastery. A woman named Vetiana, the daughter of a senator, had been widowed very young but chose to join this community rather than remarry. A deaconess, Lampadion, is also named; she points out to Gregory the extent of Macrina's ascetic poverty:

> You have in your hands everything she put away. Look at her cloak, look at the veil on her head, the worn sandals on her feet; this is her wealth, this her fortune. Apart from what you see there is nothing laid by in hidden chests or chambers in reserve. She knew only one repository for her own wealth, the treasury of heaven. (29.14–20; 53)

Lampadion affirms Macrina's vow of poverty on earth and preoccupation with the life after death. On preparing Macrina's body for burial, Vetiana and Gregory discover a simple iron chain around her neck, from which are suspended a simple cross and an iron ring. The ring bears a hollow stone in which is a fragment of "the Wood of Life," or the True Cross. From the time of its discovery by the Augusta Helena around 326, the cross on which Christ was crucified made its way in smaller and larger pieces around eastern Christendom. Apparently Macrina had acquired a small fragment of this precious relic and had worn it hidden inside her ring.

Macrina's burial garment is provided by Gregory, a red dress, the dress of a bride. This is covered by the black cloak of a monastic, as it is deemed inappropriate for the sisters to see their abbess dressed as a bride. In spite of the drab exterior, her appearance on the bier is brilliant:

> She shone even in the dark mantle; God's power, I think, added even such grace to her body that, exactly as in the vision I had while dreaming, rays of light seemed to shine out from her beauty. (32.8–12; 55)

The shining bodies of saints, another frequently encountered topos in vitae, express optically and aesthetically the power of their virtue. As we will see, light is expressive symbolically of holiness and divine grace throughout Byzantine culture. The rite of passage from life to death is a dynamic one, as the funeral is celebrated in the monastic church, the men and monks separated from the women and maidens in different parts of the church. A long procession with candles and singing accompanies the body to the family mausoleum, where it joins those of her parents. At the end of the Life is a series of accounts of miracles reported by common people: the healing of a little girl's eye disease, accomplished by a healing salve given by Macrina; a farming miracle of superabundant grain; several others involving exorcisms, prophecies, and curses are alluded to by Gregory:

> All of these are believed to be true by those who knew the details of them, even if they are beyond belief. But for those who are more bound to this world of flesh, they are considered to be outside the realm of what can be accepted, that is by those who do not know that the distribution of grace is in proportion to one's faith. (39.13–15; 61–62)

Miracles and affirmation of the importance of faith conclude this extraordinary text. Miraculous healing by faith as described here will also have a long career in saints' lives over the next millennium, for a catalogue of miracles is customarily appended to hagiographical accounts. As already noted, miraculous interventions helped Thekla survive close escapes from death. Expectation of an experience of the miraculous was always present in the early Christian and Byzantine world.

Both Thekla and Macrina gained their power from ascetic renunciation, celibacy, and the pursuit of a pure and useful Christian life, one as an apostle in southern Anatolia, the other as a monastic in the countryside of Pontus. Both refused marriage, Macrina claiming the right of univira and Thekla refusing to marry her fiancé. That Thekla was an inspiration for Macrina is not surprising, as there were few role models for women outside the traditional family ones of late ancient society. The group of women who voiced their feelings at the injustices done Thekla rallied as if in support of one who shared their lot. The poor women who had been left by the road when fleeing from a famine were thankful for their rescue by Macrina and her nuns. Sympathy and support of women by other women are recurring patterns in both the *Life of Macrina* and the *Acts of Thekla*. Women helped each other survive; those with means helped those without.

Gregory's testimony is a persuasive piece of writing on behalf of his deceased sister. In the Life we find his depiction of a woman as an equal, even a superior, to men. Macrina's voice is heard through Gregory's in an account that is gendered not in the sense of negative male bias, as is encountered in many medieval writings on women,[37] but gendered by a male writer in support and praise of a woman. A woman's life within the domestic sphere becomes important for the first time, for Gregory respects her as a shaper of her family's future and a wise and stable leader of nuns based on the family model. Sons normally took over the leadership of a family on the death of the father, but in this case it was Macrina. Even as she assumes this responsibility she retains her identity as a woman among women, or as one scholar describes her, "a composite of and perfect synthesis between the male and the female, familial and the ascetic, the public and the private."[38] She is simultaneously an example of the ideal female and a real person who chose an ascetic life before this had become a recognized practice. Through her brother's text, Macrina's memory is preserved and shaped into a sweeping statement on women's potential in early Christian society.

## Associated Readings

*The Life of Saint Macrina by Gregory, Bishop of Nyssa,* trans. Kevin Corrigan (Toronto, 1989).
*Grégoire de Nysse, Vie de Sainte Macrine,* ed and trans., Pierre Maraval (Paris, 1971) for the Greek text.
Peter Brown, "Daughters of Jerusalem: The Ascetic Life of Women in the Fourth Century," in *The Body and Society: Women and Sexual Renunciation in Early Christianity* (New York, 1988), 259–84.
Elizabeth A. Clark, *Women in the Early Church* (Wilmington, Del., 1983).

Gillian Cloke, *"This Female Man of God": Women and Spiritual Power in the Patristic Age AD 350–450* (London, 1995).

Susanna Elm, *Virgins of God: The Making of Asceticism in Late Antiquity* (Oxford, 1994).

Patricia Wilson-Kastner, "Macrina: Virgin and Teacher," *Andrews University Seminary Studies* 17 (1979): 105–17.

*Two*

# PILGRIMAGE: EGERIA

People were on the move in the early centuries of the Christian era to an extent which is difficult to imagine, and the realities of long-distance travel are hard to reconstruct. One important motivation for travel was the desire to go on religious pilgrimage, to venerate holy places, to see and walk where the saints and personnages from Scripture had walked, lived, performed miracles, and died. The Holy Land, including Jerusalem and the sites surrounding it, was the main locus of pilgrimage. Men and women left their homes and journeyed overland or by sea, in large and small groups, over great distances, often over a number of years, seeking contact with particular sites. Among the pilgrims were holy virgins or nuns who had chosen a religious life, and others who had determined because of a vow or other personal wish to make the sacrifice and effort. Some were wealthy enough to travel in comparative comfort with an entourage of servants and family members; others traveled painfully, on foot. Everyone, from emperors and empresses to ordinary people, pious husbands and wives, went on pilgrimage and joined the singing crowds which ebbed and flowed through the streets of Jerusalem.

In this chapter I turn to the goals and experiences of the pilgrim in late antiquity. What did it mean for a woman to go on pilgrimage as opposed to a man? what were her objectives? and what kinds of experiences were women likely to have had? The writings of the nun Egeria bring us into immediate contact with female pilgrimage in the East. As self-motivated and dedicated to achieving her goals as Macrina, this late fourth-century pilgrim recorded her thoughts and experiences in a work known as *Egeria's Travels*.

People embark on pilgrimages out of a desire to visit a place to venerate the holy persons, objects, or events associated with it. Holy men and women living at their hermitages deep in the Egyptian desert were also visited by pilgrims, as noted in chapter 1. The practice was not mandated in Scripture or by the patristic writers but nevertheless developed into a notable Christian religious phenomenon in the Mediterranean world, especially from the fourth century on.[1] Since it was an option open to all, pilgrimage exemplified the Christian model of equality before God and constituted a leveling force within society. Spiritual pilgrimage could also take place, in the mind or imagination alone. All kinds of wandering, whether actual or spiritual, arose from the same need: perfection as a journey toward the divine and the heavenly Jerusalem.[2]

Pilgrimage was mainly focused on the holy places, or *loca sancta*, of Israel-Palestine, Syria, present-day Turkey, and Egypt as well as Rome and Constantinople. Old and New Testament sites alike were visited because events of the Old Testament were seen as prefiguring those associated with Christ's miracles and events in his life and Passion. Many sites were held sacred and visited by both Jews and Christians.[3] Also venerated were tombs of saints and places where relics of martyrs were deposited, often huge churches associated with an event or with a saint who "bore witness" to the grace of God; hence they were called *martyria,* from the Greek *marturevo,* to bear witness.[4]

Many loca sancta were sites of miraculous healing, such as those of Saint Menas at Abu Mena in Egypt and of Saint Thekla near Seleucia. In some respects martyr shrines of Christian times replaced shrines of ancient pagan heroes and gods; the processions and offerings to honor the saint followed similar patterns and filled similar needs to those of classical antiquity.[5] Physical contact with Christian holy places offered concrete testimony to the truth of Scripture; it intensified faith and promoted healing. Suppliants came to pilgrimage sites not only to pray, offer thanks for a safe journey, and join in liturgical observances, but also to seek miraclous cures, advice, and inspiration and to do penance. Those who lived at or maintained such holy sites, monks, clerics, or local guides, played a role in the pilgrims' experience as well, helping to evoke the person or events associated with the place through readings and stories.

The most popular goal of pilgrimage was the site of Christ's Crucifixion and burial marked by the church of the Holy Sepulcher in Jerusalem. Other locations in and around the city were the house of Caiaphas, Garden of Gethsemane, Pool of Siloam, and Tower of David, where David composed the Psalms; also the church of the Nativity in Bethlehem and the site of Christ's baptism in the Jordan River, among many others. Mount Sinai on the Sinai Peninsula, with its associations of Old Testament theophany, was one of the most challenging sites to visit because of its remoteness and rugged terrain.

The remains of some famous pilgrimage sites survive today, for example, the impressive monastery of Saint Symeon Stylites, which stands in ruins in the Syrian desert near Aleppo, and the basilica at Ephesus, Turkey, which was once the repository of the bones of Saint John the Evangelist. In Rome, the shrine containing the bones of Saint Peter was visited in the catacombs under the Constantinian basilica of Saint Peter's from late antiquity throughout the Middle Ages; the shrine is still one of the most visited and venerated places in the world. In the majority of cases a holy site retained its significance even after all traces of structures or repositories had disappeared. Sometimes a site is documented but its location is unknown. In most cases, both monuments and relics have long since disappeared, as in the churches of Constantinople, the church of the Holy Apostles being the greatest loss. The Byzantine capital was once filled with palaces and chapels housing collections of precious relics which were still a goal of pilgrims in the Middle Ages; almost none survive today.[6] One can imagine that simply reaching these pilgrimage destinations was a momentous accomplishment and a deeply moving experience.

The journey was usually arduous and filled with risks. Along the way, lodging for pilgrims was provided in hospices or guest houses; some *xenodocheia,* literally, places for strangers, offered room and board free of charge and were a form of philanthropy sponsored by private patrons or the state; in some cases they provided care for the sick. Often such institutions were attached to monasteries.[7] Nunneries furnished shelter for women, and male monasteries for men. Women needed to take care to remain in groups and to avoid travel by night and were well advised to travel in the company of their husbands or of men who were armed for protection. Transport for pilgrims was on horse, mule, or donkey, sometimes in drawn carts; many traveled on foot. By far the fastest and easiest mode of travel was by ship, but on water as well as on land dangers were present in the form of pirates or brigands.[8] Thieves, shipwreck, disease, and a host of discomforts and dangers characterized the journey. The ancient system of Roman roads could make overland travel somewhat easier and more direct. Army garrisons positioned along the roads afforded some protection to travelers. Local residents or guides assisted pilgrims in finding their way as well as provided additional information on the region. What happened when the long-anticipated goal was in sight?

Acts of reverencing the goal of a pilgrimage took several forms: the place or object was kissed; prayers of thanks were said; passages from Scripture relating to the site were read aloud. A private reenactment of the event associated with the site might be performed; public rituals involving processions, hymning, and blessing by a priest accompanied mass movements of pilgrims. Tokens, or *eulogiae,* collected at pilgrimage sites were thought to be vested with the power of the place from which they had come. These so-called blessings could take the form of fruit, dust from the site, oil from lamps at the site, or water and were carried away in containers, often boxs or vials; small ampullae made of clay or lead traveled home with the pilgrim. These portable objects often were inscribed and carried artistic depictions connected with the pilgrimage site, as in the ampulla from the site of Saints Thekla and Menas in Egypt (see fig. 2).[9] Some carried apotropaic, or evil-averting, signs or inscriptions, and, as one scholar described them, eulogiae were "carriers of portable, palpable sanctity."[10] One of the most potent tokens to be acquired was a piece of the wood of the True Cross.

Helena, the mother of Constantine the Great, was probably the first and most famous Christian pilgrim. As a woman, she set a powerful example for other women. Named Augusta, or coruler, with her son in 324, she went to Jerusalem in 326–27.[11] There she identified the holy sites associated with the Crucifixion and Resurrection of Christ, which soon became goals of pilgrimage.[12] She is most famous for having discovered the True Cross upon which Christ was crucified and the tomb from which he arose. The church of the Holy Sepulcher, sponsored by the emperor Constantine, transformed these sacred places into a complex of courtyards, a basilica, a rotunda over the shrine of the sepulcher itself, and a mound of Calvary recognized as Golgotha.[13] The embellishment of these sites helped fuel interest in pilgrimage, for they were very richly endowed with the most costly materials and ornaments. Pilgrimage increased dramatically from Helena's time on, and the Holy Land became a geographical focus for Christian piety.

Helena's role in identifying these places set an early and authoritative precedent for female pilgrimage, for she was the first long-distance pilgrim known.[14] Constantine and his successors continued to provide funds for the building of lavish churches as one way of furthering their political aims; these included the church on the Mount of Olives at the place of the Ascension and in Bethelehem at the place of the Nativity, as well as over the tombs of saints around the empire. The *Life of Constantine* by Eusebius promotes the eight splendid churches built by the emperor, in a campaign to affirm the victory of Christianity. His narrative also served as propaganda for the new alliance between the emperor and the Christian God.[15] A whole group of great churches and shrines grew up on the circuit of sites to be visited by pilgrims in the Holy Land.

Other locales visited by pilgrims were of specific interest to women. According to the account of the Bordeaux Pilgrim, who traveled to the Holy Land around 333, there were many sites concerned with women, for example, the spring on Mount Syna, where women who wished to become pregnant washed, or the well at Sychar, where the Samaritan woman spoke with Christ, or the tomb of Rachel near Bethlehem, and tombs of other Old Testament figures and their wives at Hebron.[16] Women had already assumed a significant role in the New Testament, and the places associated with them inspired contemporary women. Awareness and imitation of these women's roles drew women to sites in and around Jerusalem.

In addition to the Holy Land, female pilgrims went to Egypt, arriving at the port of Alexandria. By the mid–fourth and well into the fifth centuries women were visiting the desert fathers along with sites in the Holy Land, among them Poemenia, Silvia, Paula and her daughter Eustochium, Marcella, Melania the Elder and Melania the Younger, and Eudocia Augusta; Eudocia's pilgrimage was modeled on that of Helena.[17] These female pilgrims were elite women; they traveled in groups for safety, and in style.[18]

In the *Life of Melania the Younger,* her extensive pilgrimages to North Africa,

Egypt, Jerusalem, and Constantinople in the years between 406 and 439 are described.[19] Melania's lifestyle in Jerusalem was that of an ascetic:

> Thus Melania and her mother lived together by themselves. Melania was not quick to see anyone except the holy and highly reputed bishops, especially those who stood out for their doctrine, so that she might spend the time of the conferences inquiring about the divine word. As we said before, she wrote in notebooks and fasted during the week. Every evening, after the Church of the Holy Sepulcher was closed, she remained at the Cross until the psalm-singers arrived. Then she departed for her cell and slept for a short while.[20]

All-night vigils at the church of the Holy Sepulcher and days devoted to learning about Scripture were typical of female ascetics, as discussed in chapter 1. After her mother's death, Melania acquired a surrogate family in the form of a community of nuns which she founded:

> She spent that year in great grief, ascetic discipline, and fasting, and at the end of it she had a monastery built for herself and decided to save other souls along with herself. She asked her brother to gather some virgins for her. So there arose a monastery of ninety virgins, more or less, whom she trained as a group from the first not to associate with a man.[21]

When in Jerusalem she was not content to venerate pilgrimage sites but also founded a monastery for ninety virgins. One function of such a monastery is suggested in a document called "the Letter to the Virgins who went to Jerusalem to Pray and have Returned," written by Athanasius in the 350s to 370s. It is addressed to a commnunity of virgins who had completed a successful pilgrimage to the "holy places."[22] In Jerusalem they stayed with fellow virgins, which indicates that women in religious communities made it a practice to offer hospitality to female pilgrims.

On Melania's pilgrimage to Egypt she visited male and female ascetics: "They arrived in Egypt and toured the cells of the holy monks and the very faithful virgins, supplying to each as he had need, for they were indeed wise administrators."[23] Pilgrims helped support existing monastic communities, making donations of money to aid these pious people in their self-exile from the world, for many lived in the desert. At one such desert retreat Melania was received without regard to her gender:

> Leaving Alexandria, they came to the mountain of Nitria and to the place called "The Cells," in which the fathers of the most holy men there received the saint as if she were a man. In truth, she had been detached from the female nature and had acquired a masculine disposition, or rather, a heavenly one.[24]

Here the author, Gerontius, pays Melania the ultimate gendered compliment: that she was worthy of being treated as if she were a man or, alternatively, that she was sexless, like an angel in heaven.

Sometimes, however, even the desexing of a female visitor was not enough. The holy man Arsenius was living at Canopus in Egypt when he had a visit from an aristocratic woman. The encounter is worth quoting in full:

> When Abba Arsenius was living at Canopus a very rich and God-fearing virgin of senatorial rank came from Rome to see him. When the Archbishop Theophilus met her, she asked him to persuade the old man to receive her. So he went to ask him to do so in these words, "A certain person of senatorial rank has come from Rome and wishes to see you." The old man refused to meet her. But when the archbishop told the young girl this, she ordered the beast of burden to be saddled saying, "I trust in God that I shall see him, for it is not a man whom I have come to see (there are plenty of those in our town), but a prophet." When she had reached the old man's cell, by a dispensation of God, he was outside it. Seeing him she threw herself at his feet. Outraged, he lifted her up again, and said, looking steadily at her, "If you must see my face, here it is, look." She was covered with shame and did not look at his face. Then the old man said to her, "Have you not heard tell of my way of life? It ought to be respected. How dare you make such a journey? Do you not realise you are a woman and cannot go just anywhere? Or is it so that on returning to Rome you can say to other women: I have seen Arsenius? Then they will turn the sea into a thoroughfare with women coming to see me." She said, "May it please the Lord, I shall not let anyone come here; but pray for me and remember me always." But he answered her, "I pray God to remove remembrance of you from my heart."

Later when she lies ill and in distress the local archbishop explains Arsenius's ways to her:

> The archbishop said to her, "Do you not realise that you are a woman, and that it is through women that the enemy wars against the Saints? That is the explanation of the old man's words; but as for your soul, he will pray for it continually." At this, her spirit was healed and she returned home joyfully.[25]

Women were not always encouraged to go on pilgrimage, and when they did the way was not always made easy for them, for the prevailing view was that women should not venture from home. Holy men shunned women by retreating to the desert, regarding them as a potential source of temptation and evil, and some, regardless of the woman's status, refused to see or associate with them.

In spite of the pitfalls of pilgrimage, these elite women set the trend for women in late Roman society and lent a new slant to what it meant to be a pious Christian. The empress Eudocia (see chapter 3) went on pilgrimage to Jerusalem and built a church to house the relics of Saint Stephen and a nunnery nearby. She was buried there, as she had requested, near the relics of the saint. As a result of pilgrimage, women sponsored major buildings at holy places, built monasteries, and proved important benefactors of existing monastic houses and charitable institutions.[26] These in turn provided a place for other women to lodge or remain for extended periods when on pilgrimage. A vivid impression of the experience of an early pilgrim is preserved in Egeria's firsthand account of her pilgrimage to the East.

## Egeria

The pilgrim Egeria is known to us through her Latin account of her pilgrimage of the years 381 to 384, about one-third of which survives.[27] She is thought to have come from the western Mediterranean or perhaps the Atlantic coast of Gaul or Spain. She appears to have been the wealthy and educated superior, or abbess, of a convent of nuns. She addresses her writings in the form of a letter, serving as a kind of memoir to the "venerable ladies my sisters," the nuns of her convent back home. Her writings are valuable as an early description of Christian pilgrimage by a woman in the East. *Egeria's Travels* describes the practices, rituals, buildings, vegetation, and topography of the sites and surroundings she encountered, from Constantinople across Turkey and Syria to Palestine and Egypt. One of the most important contributions of Egeria's account is its description of the buildings on Golgotha founded fifty years earlier by Constantine the Great in Jerusalem and of the services and liturgies celebrated there and at the surrounding loca sancta. Especially vivid and precisely described are the Easter services.[28]

The fragmentary manuscript containing the surviving portions of Egeria's account is a copy made in the eleventh century. This in turn was lost for seven hundred years and rediscovered in 1884 bound into a codex in a monastic library in Arezzo. The first English translation from the Latin was made in 1891.[29] Aside from the internal evidence of the text we have no information on who Egeria was and why she traveled to the East. In addition to its rich information on liturgical observances at Jerusalem and other sites, it gives us a view of a religious woman, her approach to pilgrimage, including her thoughts when summing up her own experience, and her relationship with those she encounters on her journey. The Bible is her main reference guide at the sites she visits, and she often quotes biblical passages and describes the readings at the holy places. Egeria's voice and point of view transmit a rare and precious report from the past.

Egeria is a curious and eager visitor, and she is passionately interested in places and practices connected with her faith. She visited four kinds of sites: places associated with Old Testament theophanies, caves and houses connected with Old and New Testament figures, tombs and churches commemorating martyrdoms of saints, and places associated with Christ's ministry and miracles. These holy places provide visible and tangible proof of the truth of biblical narrative and cause Egeria to break into exclamations of praise, wonder, and prayer.

According to Egeria, travel from her port of origin was by ship to Constantinople, and from there by donkey south through Asia Minor and Syria-Palestine. She often walked when the terrain was too rough for a mount, as at Mount Sinai, but mostly she traveled on major roads riding a donkey. Ascetic monks offer hospitality, guidance, and news. Egeria is constantly in the company of both men and women, all of whom share the bond of their dedication to the spiritual life. She and they together read appropriate passages from Scripture and share meals and conversations; the experience involved much sociability. There is a pattern to her stops and visits which is implied in her references to the "customary things," that is, prescribed or ritualized observances that are followed at pilgrimage sites. She does not seem to fear for her safety or specifically seek protection from anyone or anything. The reader can visualize Egeria both as an honored guest at individual sites and as part of the milling crowds of participants in processions and services in Jerusalem. The efforts she expended on her pilgrimage were not merely to satisfy her curiosity but to inform herself about the holy places and to bring her spiritually closer to God, deeds which she believed would have their own reward in heaven.[30]

Egeria writes with freshness and enthusiasm in the first person. Her style is straightforward and unembellished; she sometimes repeats herself but is always spontaneous and informative. She seems accustomed to expressing herself in narrative or epistolary form. She rarely complains but does refer to the harshness of the environment, for example, in climbing Mount Sinai. She must have been in excellent health and extremely hardy and resilient physically to endure four years of strenuous travel. Most of all, one gets a clear sense of her dedication. This was not a bland or passive personality, but a forceful and self-determined woman. There must have been hundreds, or more likely thousands, of men and women pursuing similar goals at the time Egeria traveled, but among them she was the only woman to write a document that survived.

The fragmentary account takes up as Egeria approaches Mount Sinai. She starts the climb on a Sunday morning:

> These mountains are climbed with infinite labor, because you do not go up them very slowly in a circular path, as we say "in a spiral," but you go straight up the whole way as if climbing over a wall. Then one must directly descend each one of these mountains until you reach the very base of the central mountain which is called Sinai. So by the will of Christ our God, helped by the prayers of holy men who were going up with us, and with great labor, it was done. I had to go up on foot because one cannot go straight up riding. Nonetheless one does not feel the labor, because I saw the desire which I had being completed through the will of God. (3.1–2)[31]

Uncomplaining, Egeria comments on the effort required to climb on foot and at a steep ascent, attributing her ability to do so to God's help. This is hard work, both ascending and descending, which she may not have anticipated. She must also have been subjected to extreme exposure to the elements on such a climb, to sun and wind and therefore dehydration and sunburn. These cannot have been circumstances to which she was accustomed. Regardless, it is, in her words, "the desire which I had" that enables her to make the climb. It was also helpful to be part of a group of mutually dedicated believers. The "prayers of the holy men who were going up with us" aided her in enduring the physical hardships of the journey. Who her traveling companions were we are never told explicitly. Were they fellow nuns or female pilgrims? or was she the only woman, accompanied by a male entourage?

The holy men she mentions are escorts from the locale who were serving as guides to her party. Other monastics meet them on the summit. She refers to the customary procedures on arrival:

> In fact no one stays on the summit of the central mountain, for there is nothing there except the church and the cave where Saint Moses was [Ex. 33:22]. The reading in this place was all from the book of Moses, the Oblation was made in due order and here we communicated. Now as we left the church the presbyters gave us eulogia from this place, fruits which grow in this mountain. (3.5–6)

Reading from Exodus, the Book of Moses, the passages relating Moses' receiving of the Law is central to her observances, and this occurs in a chapel on the summit. Other monastics who live in the area join in. Communion is celebrated, after which Egeria is presented with eulogia of fruit raised in orchards on the mountain itself, again part of a habitual ritual. Some physical form of connection with the site—in this case fruit—makes the visit complete and satisfying to her.

The greatest impression, however, is made by the extraordinary scope and scale of the setting:

> But I would like you to know, venerable ladies my sisters, that from the place where we were standing, the area around the church, the summit of the middle, it seemed to us that those mountains which we had first ascended with difficulty were like little hills. Nonetheless they seemed boundless and I do not think that I have seen any higher, except for the middle mountain which greatly exceeds them. From that place we saw Egypt, Palestine, the Red Sea, and the Parthenian Sea which goes all the way to Alexandria, and finally the infinite Saracen lands. It is scarcely possible to believe it, but these holy men pointed out each place to us. (3.8)

There is no comparable landscape in her homeland to which Egeria can equate Mount Sinai. Egeria's expressions of wonder refer to the immensity of the mountain, which far exceeds any surrounding terrain in scale, and the view it affords, which she tries to convey through repeating the indications of her guides; they must have gestured in various directions and said, "This way lies X, this way Y . . ." Egeria interprets this as actually seeing those areas, which would of course have been impossible. She is, however, prepared to assume such a superhuman capacity. Here we have a glimpse not so much of her credulity or naiveté, as of her state of mind. She is totally caught up in experiencing the place.

After making a tour of other holy sites on the mountain, in a tireless show of inquisitiveness and determination, she descends to the place of the burning bush:

After descending the mountain we arrived at the bush at about the tenth hour. This is the bush I spoke of before, from which God spoke to Moses in the fire, and in that place there are many monks' dwellings and a church in the head of the valley. In front of the church is a most agreeable garden, with an abundance of the best water. In this garden the bush grows. They point out the place adjoining it, where Saint Moses stood when God said to him, "Loosen the strap of your sandal," and so forth. By the time we had come into the place, it was about four in the afternoon, and thus because it was already evening, we could not make Oblation; but we prayed in the church and also in the garden where the bush was; the reading was also from the book of Moses according to our custom. Thus because it was late we ate with the holy men in the garden before the bush, and so we made there our resting place. Early the next day we arose and asked the presbyters if they would make the Oblation, and so they did. (4.7–8)

The burning bush mentioned in Exodus 3:1 is on the return route of Egeria's pilgrimage to Mount Sinai. In a fashion similar to her arrival at the summit, she now prays at the church near the site of the bush and at the bush itself, pursues a reading from the Bible, and finally takes holy communion. Again, the holy men who reside in the area gather to respond to the needs of the pilgrims. One must imagine an open-air evening meal in which Egeria joins with the monks, and that she camped or was given shelter at a cell or a hospice in the area for the night.

Certain prescribed practices seem to take place at evey site she visits. As Egeria says in one passage, "Indeed I have always wished that when we come to a particular place, a passage from Scripture is read about it" (4). She also expects to take communion at each site, and this happens just before they depart from the site of the bush. The local hermits, priests, or other monastics join in receiving her and her party and in feeding and informing them. The usual culinary fare of these holy men would probably have been a vegetarian diet. Was Egeria accustomed to eating meat, at least occasionally? One wonders how Egeria's evening meal would have differed if it had not been so late.

Here, then, in the Sinai episode we have the essentials of pilgrimage according to the description of a participant. There does not seem to be any tension in the fact that she is a woman; on the other hand, we do not hear of any other women travelers or hosts until later in her narrative. Egeria expects to set the agenda, to be shown and have celebrated what she wishes. Only a person of some authority and wealth could command such regular performance of what is "their custom" at each juncture. Her importance is suggested by the farewell from Sinai:

But I also cannot thank enough all those holy people who were so kind as freely to receive me in their dwellings and even lead me to all the places that I always sought from Scripture. Many of the holy men who lived on or about the mountain, and were strong enough in body, were kind enough to guide us all the way to Pharan. (5.12)

Not only were Egeria and her party well received, but on their departure they were accompanied not by a guide but by "many of the holy men." This was more than a common courtesy for, as we learn in the next paragraph, Pharan is twenty-five miles from the mountain. Egeria is no ordinary pilgrim, and neither is she an ordinary woman. Because women led relatively more sheltered lives than men, it is a wonder that Egeria had the strength to tolerate the hardships she encountered on her pilgrimage to Sinai.

Egeria's position in the group is suggested in the description of her visit to the land of Goshen called Arabia:

> It is four days through the desert from Clysma, that is, from the Red Sea, to the city of Arabia, and even though it is through the desert, each resting place has a fort, with soldiers and officers, who always led us from fort to fort. . . .
>
> During this journey the holy men who were with us, the clergy and monks, showed us every single thing which I was seeking from the Scriptures. (7.2)

Soldiers and officers provide safe passage for Egeria's party from site to site, until local holy men take over to guide them around the sites. The Roman military machine was evidently at the service of important pilgrims like Egeria and her traveling companions, who were, according to this passage, holy men, clergy, and monks. Holy men could have been laymen, but clergy would have been priests and therefore of comparable status and importance to Egeria. Hence she was routinely in the company of men, but she is the one who is being shown "every single thing which *I* was seeking." She specifies what she wants to do and see and is accommodated.

On her way north, at Edessa in Syria, Egeria is hospitably received by the bishop, the most important ecclesiastical official of the area. Here she is shown all the Old Testament sites connected with Abraham, takes special interest in Rebecca and her well, and has a learned discussion with the bishop on the meaning of certain passages in Genesis:

> Then the holy bishop of the city, a truly religious monk and confessor, having hospitably received me, told me: "Because I see, daughter, that you have taken such a great work upon yourself, because of your piety coming even from the ends of the earth to these places, we will show you whatever you want, whatever it would please Christians to see." (19.5)

The bishop's statement, while somewhat patronizing, indicates that he recognizes Egeria's exceptional zeal and is therefore respectful of her desires. It also implies that special factors are what make him willing to be of service to her. She is led around the palace of King Abgar by him, is shown the letters of Abgar and Jesus, and even given copies to bring home. Then she is shown a portrait of Abgar:

> He first led me to the palace of King Abgar, and showed me there a large portrait of him, quite like him, they say, and as lustrous as if it were made of pearls. Looking at

Abgar face to face, he seems to be truly a wise and honorable man. Then the bishop said to me: "Here is king Abgar, who before he saw the lord believed in him as truly the son of God." (19.6)

For Egeria to be shown such a precious image, one which was thought to protect the city of Edessa, is special treatment indeed. Furthermore, Egeria approaches the image as if it were a double of its prototype. Looking "at Abgar," not "at the portrait of Abgar," indicates Egeria approaches the image as a vehicle of direct communication, in accordance with attitudes to icons in the Christian East.

After praying at the church built near the site of Rachel's well, Egeria visits the eremitic monks who live in cells nearby:

> Then, having prayed in the church, I went up with the holy bishop to the holy monks in their dwellings, and I gave thanks to God and to those who deigned to receive me when I had come there, and to tell me things worthy to come from their mouths. Then they kindly gave me eulogia and to everyone who was with me, as is the custom of the monks to give to those whom they freely receive in their cells. (21.1)

Egeria's party is received in the monks' cells, in a gesture of exceptional hospitality, and given the customary eulogia.

In the next leg of her journey she takes a detour to Seleucia, calling on the local bishop before venturing out to visit the nearby shrine of Saint Thekla:

> Because it is about a mile and a half from the city to Saint Thecla's martyrium, on a flatish hill, I decided to go out there and stay overnight. . . .
>
> At the holy church one finds nothing except numberless monastic dwellings for men and women. I discovered there my very dear friend the holy deaconess Marthana, to whose life everyone in the East bears testimony, whom I had gotten to know in Jerusalem, where she had gone up to pray. She rules these monastic dwellings of apotactites or virgins. When she saw me, how can I tell you what joy it was to her or to me? (23.2–3)

Egeria's friend, Marthana, the deaconess at Saint Thecla's, is a welcome sight. This deaconess and abbess may be for the East a counterpart of what Egeria was in the West. Her exclamation of joy is unusually enthusiastic, and her curiosity to learn about religious life at this famous shrine is evident. The community consists of religious men and women—*apotactae,* or those who are set apart—who have renounced life in the world. As at so many sites a "very beautiful church" is noted by Egeria. She visits the church:

> When I had come there in the name of God, prayer was made at the shrine and the reading was from the Acts of Thecla. I gave thanks to God who deigned to fulfill all my desires, though I am unworthy and undeserving. (23.4–5)

Egeria's visit to the shrine at Thekla's burial place is accompanied by a reading from the *Acts of Thecla,* discussed in the introduction to part 1. This text is appropriately read at Thekla's shrine just as biblical passages were read at other sites. Thekla must have served as a paradigm for women monastics like Marthana and Egeria, whose travels "imitated" those of the apostle Thekla.

Later in her voyage Egeria takes special pains to visit the shrine of another female saint and martyr, Saint Euphemia, whose huge martyrium was in Chalcedon, across the Bosphoros from Constantinople: "I came to Chalcedon, where I stayed because of the very famous martyrium of Saint Euphemia, which I have heard about for a long time" (23.7). Egeria has either read or heard about the church of Saint Euphemia, with its basilica, courtyard, and rotunda over the reliquary with the body of the saint.[32] Through the language one senses her anticipation and enthusiasm at seeing this site, qualities she has exhibited at many other junctures. Such zeal renders her narrative intensely human.

After her safe return to Constantinople she also visits martyria and relics in and around the capital city, for which she again expresses thanks, grateful to have seen what she wished. She speaks of her plans to visit Ephesus and possibily other sites, if, that is, she survives the journey:

> If after this I am in the body, if I have come to find out about other places, either I will speak of them in the presence of your affection, or certainly, if anything else occurs to me, I will write you. You indeed, ladies, my light, deign to remember me, whether I be in the body or out of the body. (23.10)

Egeria promises to recount her coming experiences to her sister nuns firsthand, if possible, or by letter, even if she herself does not return. The present missive is to be sent before she embarks on these further travels. Her tone is warm and affectionate; her concern is that she be remembered kindly. This first half of her narrative takes the journalistic form of a long letter to the nuns of her monastic community. Her account probably traveled on shipboard over the long distance back to Spain or Gaul. Repeatedly addressing the ladies as "my light," Egeria clearly feels a close bond in human as well as vocational terms with these distant nuns, her sisters in religion.

In the second half of the preserved narrative, Egeria launches into a very different kind of description: a technical, almost pedantic, and quite repetitive account of the Jerusalem liturgies, based on the three years she had spent in Jerusalem.[33] Her stay in Jerusalem took place before her return to Constantinople, and so is included in this missive. The account is filled with references to singing, walking in processions, watching as lamps are lit in lavish, incense-filled interiors, evoking a highly sensuous experience. The parthenae or apotactae, virgin women, and their counterparts the *monazontes,* or men who live alone, are laypeople who are associated with the individual churches or sites and who lead visitors in the daily observances at the holy sites. Their role consists largely of singing. Most descriptions focus on the Anastasis, a great rotunda sheltering the tomb of Christ, and the services revolving around it. Here Egeria is one of the many hundreds of worshipers. She does not appear to be accompanied by bishops or other members of a party but seems to be a single agent.

Having outlined the customary readings and processions she focuses briefly on the setting:

> The decoration on that day in the church of the Anastasis, the Cross and Bethlehem is beyond words. You see there is nothing but gold and gems and silk; if you look at the curtains, they are also of gold-striped silk. All of the church furnishing used that day is gold encrusted with gems. How can I describe or estimate the numbers and weight of candelabra, candles and lamps and other furnishings? What can I say about the decorating of the building itself, which Constantine, under his mother's supervision, honored as much as his empire permitted with gold, mosaics, and precious marble, not only at the [Great Church], but as well at the Anastasis and the Cross and other holy places at Jerusalem? (25.8–9)

Here Egeria puts into words that which is "beyond words," in a rare firsthand description of the splendor of Constantine's great basilica and other foundations. Helena, mother of Constantine, is credited by Egeria with the planning of such splendor. The decorations are rich enough to impress even one who has seen a great deal of worldly splendor, including the churches of Constantinople. It is not clear whether she has visited Rome, which might be a competitor. Egeria's spontaneous excitement shows she is moved, as was intended, by the public display of wealth of church and state combined which was poured into these monuments.[34]

Historical details about processions, liturgies, and their setting are included in this portion of the account. While the Piacenza Pilgrim's account of the sixth century confirms some of these details, such as the teaching of catechumens and their preparation for baptism, Egeria describes in greater detail ceremonies of the display and kissing of the relic of the True Cross and the veneration of relics at the feast of the dedication of the church of the Holy Sepulcher. Cautionary measures are taken when the most precious relic is brought out of safekeeping during the ceremony:

> Then the bishop's chair is set up on Golgotha behind the Cross, which now stands there; the bishop is seated on the chair, and before him is placed a table covered with a linen cloth. The deacons stand in a circle around the table and the silver casket decorated with gold is brought in, in which is the holy wood of the Cross. It is opened and taken out, and both the wood of the Cross and the title are placed on the table. While it is on the table, the bishop sits and grasps the ends of the holy wood with his hands, and the deacons, who are standing around him, keep watch. Here is why they guard it so. It is the custom that all of the people here come one by one, the faithful and the catechumens, bowing before the table, kissing the holy Cross and moving on. I was told that because someone (I do not know who) bit off and stole some of the holy Cross; now it is guarded by the deacons so that it dare not be done by someone again. (37.1–2)

The story of this theft was no doubt circulated among those present at the ceremony of the veneration of the wood of the cross.

The religious festival of the dedication was attended by crowds of visitors from the provinces and "forty or fifty bishops." The dedication coincided with the commemoration of Helena's finding of the True Cross, which must have been especially meaningful to female pilgrims who looked to Helena as a role model. The constant press of eager crowds of men and women and monastics in this part of Egeria's account gives some indication of the volume of traffic through the holy city, the majority of which must have consisted of ordinary people. This second half of her journal is unlike the first in repeatedly evoking the presence of great masses and movements of humanity, and of the diversity of crowds participating in the processions of Easter Week and beyond.

Egeria's account represents her as a person as well as a pilgrim with a mission. She is alert and perceptive about her physical environment. Objects and landscapes draw enthusiastic responses and aesthetically sensitive descriptions. She is emotionally attuned to her experiences, always eager to see more, while her warmth of personality and humanity allow her to engage easily with those she meets. Her faith, humility, and dedication are expressed at every turn. She applies an almost academic precision to her descriptions of the Jerusalem liturgies, conscious of using proper terms and including details of language and expression.

Pilgrimage clearly had intense meaning for Egeria: the journey, the companionship, the rituals and rhythm of observances and movements, the sensory experience. Although she must have enjoyed some wealth and status, this does not prevent her from participating fully in the strenuous aspects of travel and attending observances at all hours of the day and night. Throughout the narrative there is a constant association of sites with holy texts, mainly Old and New Testament scripture and lives of saints, indicating the significant mimetic aspect of pilgrimage. Through readings and paraphrasing of texts she duplicates or relives the events associated with those places and spaces.[35] Her intent is often to understand exactly how the site coordinates with Scripture, for she has read about and heard reports of the sites from other pilgrims; she must have informed herself carefully about the prescribed list of sites of interest to pilgrims. Places associated with women are of interest to Egeria, and she includes in her itinerary Saint Thekla's burial chamber near Seleucia, Saint Euphemia's martyrium in Chalcedon, and the church of the Holy Sepulcher with its associations with Helena, mother of Constantine, along with sites associated with Old Testament women at Edessa. These paradigms of female virtue or sanctity form a part of her broad, inclusive agenda. Egeria visited a diverse group of locales for a variety of reasons, one of which was her gender.

For Egeria, seeing the places, standing on "the very spot," and experiencing landscapes, buildings, and interiors fulfills a personal need and more than compensates for the efforts of the journey. The system and practice of pilgrimage are recognized and respected by all whom she meets along the way, showing that by the year 380, only sixty-seven years after the Edict of Milan, the practice of Christian pilgrimage was well established. Even for a Latin speaker traveling mainly in lands where Greek,

Aramaic, Hebrew, or local dialects were spoken, the pilgrim in the East could participate fully in rituals and visits to numerous sites, benefiting from the help and protection of local monks and Roman soldiers. Egeria's account of her pilgrimage provides us with a foundation for understanding the practice as it would be followed for the next one thousand years in the medieval world and even up until today. It is also authentic and moving testimony to a remarkable woman's experience of pilgrimage and to her ability to write a lucid and compelling narrative account.

## Associated Readings

John Wilkinson, ed. and trans., *Egeria's Travels,* 3d ed. (Warminster, England, 1999).

Patricia Wilson-Kastner, "Egeria: Introduction" and "The Pilgrimage of Egeria" (English translation), in *A Lost Tradition: Women Writers of the Early Church,* ed. Patricia Wilson-Kastner (Washington, D.C., 1981), 71–134.

Elizabeth A. Clark, *The Life of Melania the Younger: Introduction, Translation, and Commentary* (New York, 1984).

Susanna Elm, *Virgins of God: The Making of Asceticism in Late Antiquity* (Oxford, 1994).

E. D. Hunt, *Holy Land Pilgrimage in the Later Roman Empire, AD 312–460* (Oxford, 1982).

Robert Ousterhout, ed., *The Blessings of Pilgrimage,* Illinois Byzantine Studies I (Urbana, 1990).

## Three

# FEMALE IMPERIAL AUTHORITY:
# EMPRESSES OF THE THEODOSIAN HOUSE:
# GALLA PLACIDIA

The stolid profiles of the women of the Valentinian and Theodosian dynasties as they appear on coins minted during the late fourth and fifth centuries offer slight hints at some of the issues behind these images. Coinage was a traditional mode of projecting emperors' images throughout the empire, indicating in its formulaic portraits and inscriptions who was in charge, who provided military protection, the importance of divine protection, and the hope for longevity and stability of rule; coins also noted where they were minted. The messages conveyed by coins bearing images of empresses, however, were somewhat different from those of emperors, and these images underwent revealing changes over a short period of time in connection with pertinent issues. The changes reveal the evolving roles of the female rulers of the fourth and fifth centuries, who were actually in the process of carving out for the first time a female image of imperial rule and authority. Stiff, official, and abbreviated though these images and associated symbols appear, the coins provide an entrée into understanding the lives and concerns of these women. Thanks to their high visibility, they are known to us today, albeit in varying degrees of detail, through a variety of contemporary sources, artworks, and recent scholarship. What were the roles and influence of these Theodosian empresses?

In the public eye from the moment of her marriage, a late Roman or Byzantine empress found that much of her life was determined by protocol. In spite of the demands of the position, however, she could retain her individuality as well as her capacity to influence the emperor's decisions, for she made her own decisions and took actions which were significant for the empire. The greatest visibility applied to female children or to the empress herself, when elevated by the emperor to the rank of Augusta. Corresponding to the emperor's rank of Augustus, this rank indicated that its female counterpart shared the position of ruling with the emperor; they became corulers, or Augusti. Having considered women and the religious life and women as pilgrims in the two preceding chapters, I will now explore what it meant for a woman to be an Augusta. While this time was still very much the twilight of Roman antiquity, internal forces were forging a new mode of Byzantine rule which would rely on the active presence of imperial women. Circulating throughout the empire, images of women on coins were both proof and the product of the formulation of a new kind of female rule.

With the demise of Constantine's line in the mid–fourth century, the empire was again divided into an eastern and a western branch, restoring the strategy developed by Diocletian in his tetrarchy of 293 to 305. Valentinian I ruled the western half of the empire from his capital in Milan, while his counterpart in the East, Valens, ruled from Constantinople. Theodosius I, Valens's successor, was brought to power in 379, and under him the center of gravity continued to shift to the East as this capable ruler shaped his own system of political and military administration. Under the Theodosian dynasty, which lasted until 455, the change in the way the imperial family projected its image to the public was based on the paradigm which Constantine and his mother, Helena, had founded of Christian piety. I want to focus on this new and meaningful role and emphasis on female identity during the Theodosian dynasty. The empress Galla Placidia, with one foot in the East and the other in the West, cogently illustrates a dynamic case of the new imperial ideal. Artistic endeavors sponsored by her shed light on her agendas and help clarify some ways in which she was seen by contemporaries. Her remarkable story deserves to be better known.

The concept of New Rome characterized the shift of power from Rome to Constantinople, when the old capital was definitively superseded in the last decades of the fourth century. While Rome continued to function as a garrisoned and walled city, and as the episcopal see of Saint Peter, with the popes residing at the Lateran palace, the new eastern center of power, Constantinople, was from the time of its founding and dedication by Constantine in 330 gradually invested with the idea of sacred Christian rule and of a God-guarded city. The patriarch, head of the Orthodox Christian Church, resided there in his palace adjacent to the imperial palace. Within the fortified city of Constantinople, the imperial palace occupied a large area to the east and south of the hippodrome on ground which was terraced and gradually sloped down to the sea walls; this palace became increasingly the seat of authority, both physical and conceptual, of the empire (see plan on page xvii).

Begun by Constantine, this imperial residence was by the late fourth century a sprawling complex of great halls, courtyards, and palaces within the palace. Imitating its counterpart, the palace of the Roman emperors on the Palatine Hill in Rome, in imagery and splendor, the Constantinopolitan palace was imbued with a new association: the glory of heavenly Jerusalem. The relics of martyrs and saints assembled in its churches rivaled even those of the Holy Land. Little remains of the imperial palace of the Byzantine emperors today, for though it was in use down to the eleventh century, it was eventually abandoned. Impressive fragments of walls, terraces, architectural elements, and mosaic floors survive, but the most informative testimony on the palace is found in texts rather than in the archaeological reports.

The sacred authority of the emperor was represented by the palace with its lavish trappings and enhanced by a system of elaborate ceremonial and of attire of all those serving and protecting the royal personages and their family members. A complex hierarchy of attendants and officials developed, with the empress, like the emperor, having her own separate quarters and entourage consisting of eunuchs and aristocratic women; she also had her own wealth to use as she saw fit, although, as we shall see, expectations of her philanthropy and generosity evolved into an established set of roles. Empresses of late antiquity gradually achieved a great deal of autonomy and exerted influence akin to corule, an unheard-of concept for women in ancient Greece and Rome or in any Western medieval state.[1]

In the West, the Valentinian dynasty maintained its seat in Milan and secondarily at Trier and then, after 402, at Ravenna. Even then, it was barely able to govern the vestiges of the old Roman Empire in what is now Italy, France, Germany, Spain, and North Africa (Algeria, Tunisia). As in Constantinople and Rome, traces also remain in Trier, Milan, and Ravenna of imperial residences and attached buildings and walls. On the migratory paths of Gauls, Germans, Huns and Goths, Alans and Franks, the western lands took the brunt of the "barbarian invasions" pressing on the empire's frontiers. Rome itself was sacked three times in the first half of the fifth century. Women who were born or married into the Valentinian or Theodosian dynasty often found that diplomacy, and even marriage with these barbarians, was fundamental to their survival and that of their children.

In sharp contrast to the lifestyle of an ascetic leader like Macrina or a dedicated pilgrim like Egeria, that of a Byzantine empress was dominated by the complex etiquette and rituals surrounding every aspect of daily life. The women's quarters of the palace, called the *gynaeceum* or *gynaikonitis* consisted of suites of grand rooms where she was served by officials and attendants: the *praepositus,* grand master, chief taster, and grand mistress or patrician of the girdle. Eunuchs, men who were beardless because they had been castrated in childhood, were the constant companions of imperial women, often acquiring positions of great power in the palace hierarchy.[2] A principal preoccupation was with the imperial wardrobe, for it was as important for the empress as it was for the emperor to be impressively attired for all occasions. Some empresses were extraordinarily devoted to their prayers and religious activities. Others were learned, for they had access to a superior education and to books, which was not the case with the average woman. An empress had her own private wealth to use as she saw fit, even her own politics and religious leanings. For she was in a position to exert considerable influence on those who were given secular or ecclesiastical power in the bureaucracy that operated within church, government, and administration.

Empresses were chosen by various means. Sometimes there was a "brideshow," in effect a beauty and talent contest, which attracted applicants from around the empire.[3] In this way, based largely on her external appearance, a young woman could suddenly find herself and her family famous and wealthy. Betrothals of imperial couples also took place when they were still infants; the marriage was celebrated at around age twelve or at puberty for the woman, while the husband was usually older. The coronation of an empress, which took place before her marriage, was in the palace, whereas the marriage took place in the great principal church of the empire, Hagia Sophia.

The marriage of an emperor and empress and the birth of heirs were important events for the whole empire. Royal children were referred to as the *porphyrogennetus,* for a male, or *porphyrogenneta,* for a female, meaning "purple-born." This epithet derived from the Porphyra, the chamber within the palace lined with porphyry stone. This deep-purplish-red stone quarried in Egypt was generally reserved for use by the imperial family; the color deep crimson when applied to other substances, from shoes or elaborate silk robes to ivory diptychs or manuscript pages, was also associated with imperial or high-status use. The birth of a child in the Porphyra was an event heralded and attended by the entire court. These and other occasions—official dinners, particularly for the wives of court officials and for visiting diplomats' wives, processions, awarding of honors, and attendance at sports events in the hippodrome—were honed into a highly complex ceremonial in which the presence of the empress was crucial. In effect, a substantial portion of court life revolved around the empress.

The public nature of an empress's role meant she was not sequestered and out of sight in the palace. Hers was not a life of seclusion and restraint, but one of strategic visibility, for it was her public duty to circulate, participate in civic events, and be seen. Also central to her image was the role of mother and bearer of children to perpetuate the family line. An empress sometimes educated her children herself before handing them over to tutors. Empresses also served as regents for their sons after an emperor's death and until the child reached majority at age eighteen. During a regency she played a direct role in government by ruling the empire while her son was being prepared to rule. The widow, or sometimes the daughter, of a deceased emperor was entitled by right to rule in her own name. If there were no children, it was her option (or duty) to choose a husband who would rule the empire effectively.

An emperor who did not succeed to the throne through birth, adoption, or inheritance could attain the position only through a coup—or through marriage to the previous emperor's widow. Sometimes a usurper who had internal support would force the widow of his predecessor to marry him, knowing the power vested in the position of empress would provide continuity for his rule. Holding of the position of emperor and empress was deemed to be ordained by God, which lent a formidable power to dynastic succession or to those guarding it—and an onus to those threatening it. Ariadne Augusta, daughter of Leo I who had no son to inherit the throne, married Zeno in 466, who became emperor by virtue of this marriage in 474.

They ruled until his death in 491, when Ariadne convened a court to deliberate on her choice of a new husband. She married Anastasius, who became Anastasius I and ruled until 518.[4] As in the case of Ariadne, the succession of imperial rule could, and often did, depend on an empress's choice of husband.

If one relied solely on histories of the political events and military conquests of the later fourth and fifth centuries one would hardly be aware that powerful, dynamic women were playing a crucial role over this critical period in the formation of a Christian Byzantine state. In 381, at the Council of Constantinople, the second Oecumenical Council of the church, convoked by Theodosius I, Nicene Orthodoxy was confirmed and Christianity was given an increased visibility and authority. In 391 the same emperor, while simultaneously prohibiting pagan sacrifice, declared by edict that Orthodox Christianity was the true faith and thus the official religion of the empire. It was important for both empress and emperor to maintain this religious aspect of imperial ideology. A study of the imperial women of this time and their range of backgrounds, personalities, and causes lends a broader understanding to the foundations of Byzantine civilization.

I now turn to an account of events and actions from the empresses' viewpoint. I will look primarily at the women associated with Theodosius I, his first wife, Aelia Flaccilla, in power from 378 to 387, and second wife, Galla, 387 to 395; also Theodosius II, his sister Pulcheria, 408 to 455, and his wife, Athenais Eudocia, 421 to 460, and their relations with their western counterparts of the house of Valentinian, including primarily Galla Placidia, who ruled from 425 to 450 (see list of emperors and empresses on page 319 and genealogical table of the Theodosian dynasty on page 317). Theodosian and Valentinian family lines intermingled through marriage, resulting in close contacts between the eastern and western parts of the empire. For although rule was divided between East and West, throughout the period under consideration the fiction of a united empire was maintained. This bond was weakening, in particular during the regency of the empress Galla Placidia, when the final split and disintegration of the western branch were imminent. As we shall see, portraits of women on coinage reflect their roles and also suggest some of the changes taking place because of female influence. Figural sculpture, the authoritative public medium of antiquity, still served to evoke and project the female image of imperial authority.

The Theodosian house came to power unexpectedly. Valentinian I had been named to succeed the last of Constantine's line, after the short reign of Jovian, in 364, and he energetically tackled the daunting prospect of bringing order to the West, in what is now Central Europe, while naming his brother Valens to rule in the East. When Valens was killed in a catastrophic defeat by the Visigoths and Ostrogoths at Adrianople in 378, Valentinian's son and successor, Gratian, found himself sole ruler of the Roman Empire. Gracian named Theodosius in 379 as his counterpart in the East to enable him to concentrate on maintaining order in the Rhineland. Thus the Valentinian line spawned the new Theodosian dynasty, which would remain in power for almost another century and whose descendants would live well into the sixth century.[5]

Theodosius had attained a high position in the army, where his father had also made his career, and had retired to his estates in Spain when he was called by Gratian to take up rule of the East. This army man, proving to be highly capable and a brilliant tactician, administrator, social reformer, and diplomat, molded a difficult situation into one of stability and promise. Perhaps his greatest accomplishment was to continue to provide Constantinople with buildings connoting its greatness and further marking it as the successor of Rome. He also carried on the process initiated by Constantine of collecting ancient statuary and monuments to embellish public places in Constantinople; in addition, he continued to collect the protective relics of saints. He installed the severed head of Saint John the Baptist at a new church in the suburb of Hebdomon, thereby identifying the city with sacred as well as secular imperial ideals.

Sharing in these undertakings was Theodosius's wife, Aelia Flavia Flaccilla, a member of the Spanish aristocracy who married him around 377, just before he assumed the rule of the East. Until her death in 387 she represented qualities about which we learn from her funeral speech by the great theologian, Gregory of Nyssa, who also, we will remember, wrote the Life of his sister, Macrina. These qualities served to define a new and enduring female image of authority which would support the emperor in his efforts and emphasize the familial side of rule: concerns for children, wifely loyalty, piety, and dynastic continuity.[6]

The concepts of female virtue which are laid out in Gregory's florid speech are associated with Flaccilla's *basileia,* or imperial dominion, and helped construct a new imperial image for women.[7] First mentioned is her piety, *eusebeia,* referring to her dedication to the Orthodox faith and repudiation of idolotrous practices; devotion to relics and willingness to go on pilgrimage, like a new Helena, characterized the empress's piety. Humility, *tapeinophrosyne,* was maintained in Flaccilla's willingness to abase herself in service to the poor and sick and in her carrying out menial chores when visiting the hospitals of the capital. Such a quality brought the imperial personage closer to the people of the city, even into direct contact with them. Flaccilla's philanthropy, *philanthropeia,* or love of mankind, was demonstrated by her generosity in making expenditures for the destitute and the needy and the pardoning of criminals. She also used her influence to persuade her husband to her point of view when making decisions involving shows of clemency. Finally, her wifely love, *philandria,* meant in effect her fecundity or ability to bear children, specifically male children, to perpetuate the dynastic line. Flaccilla was indeed successful in this respect and won approval for giving birth first to Arcadius and later Honorius, both of whom ruled as emperors. Just after the birth of Arcadius, in 383, Flaccilla was made Augusta. What did this title imply?

Proclaiming Flaccilla Augusta meant she became an official colleague of Theodosius. In 383 the young child Arcadius was raised by Theodosius to the rank of

*Fig. 3. Coin of Aelia Flaccilla, gold solidus, Hunter Coin Cabinet, Glasgow, UK, 379–83. (Copyright Hunterian Museum, University of Glasgow)*

Augustus, formally declaring him the heir to imperial succession. Indeed, both of her sons by Theodosius lived to attain imperial rule, Arcadius in the East and Honorius in the West. The convergence of the child's birth and elevation and the elevation of Flaccilla demonstrates that one criterion for being granted full partnership in rule was producing a dynasty-perpetuating baby. Although Flaccilla was not the first Roman empress to be named Augusta (Constantine's mother, Helena, and wife, Fausta, had been Augustae) and although not all empresses who bore male children were automatically given the title, she was the first in the Theodosian dynasty. She would epitomize the various capacities and qualities mentioned above as a paradigm of excellence for future empresses, all in the span of a short reign of eight years.[8]

Coins struck in the years between her elevation in 383 and death in 387 reflected this momentous change in status by indicating her name and title. For example, a gold solidus minted in Constantinople has on the front, or obverse, her portrait with the Latin inscription AEL[IA] FLAC-CILLA AUG[USTA] (see fig. 3).[9] First is her family name, Aelia, then her given name, Flaccilla, and then her title, Augusta, using standard abbreviations. On the reverse is a seated personification of Victory, portrayed as a winged, seated woman who writes Chi-Rho on a shield, the first two letters of Christ's name in Greek. Victory is labeled SALUS REI PUBLICAE, or "well-being of the commonwealth." This formula is used almost exclusively on coins of Augustae from this time on. In addition, no Christian symbol appears on coins of Theodosius, only on those of the empress Flaccilla. The mint is indicated in the lower zone beneath Victory: in this case CON refers to Constantinople and OB to obryzum, or pure gold. The notion of Christian victory is conveyed in highly classicizing allegorical terms on the reverse, but let us consider her portrait on the obverse in more detail.

The portrait of Aelia Flaccilla takes a bust form, with the shoulders and torso turned slightly to the right and the head in profile. The trappings of imperial rule are depicted according to a code which must have been easily decipherable to contemporaries. The empress wears her hair in a complex style, with a braid or braids forming a raised spine from the back up over the top of her head. A diadem consisting of a band studded with precious stones in rosette settings and a large center jewel in a setting encircles her head below the top of the braid and is held in place by a number of short strands of pearls maintaining the locks of hair around her temples close to the head. Pearl-headed pins line the edge of the braid. At the nape of the neck is a loop of hair contained at the lowest point of the diadem just above its three waving

*Fig. 4. Statuette of Aelia Flaccilla (?), marble, from Constantinople (?), h. 78 cm, Paris, Bibliothèque nationale, Cabinet des Médailles, late fourth century. (Copyright Bibliothèque nationale de France, BnF)*

fillets, or tie-strings, also made up of strands of smaller pearls. A pearl necklace and pendant pearl earrings complete the strictly feminine elements of the costume.

Other aspects of the costume stem from male attire. Over her tunic with shoulder ornament is worn a mantle, the *paludamentum,* which is pinned at the right shoulder by a brooch, or *fibula,* consisting of a large center stone in a setting with three pendant strands of large pearls. This ultimately military garb is customarily seen in emperors' portraits on coins and other ceremonial images but eventually refers to a costume worn by both emperors and empresses on state occasions and signifying the highest earthly authority. While earlier coin types with female Augustae showed them in female costume, Flaccilla's coins show an Augusta for the first time wearing items of ceremonial garb appointed for males.[10] The break in tradition can be interpreted as indicating that from this time on the empress assumed the new and more prominent status and public role as sharer of imperial rule.

Cities in Asia Minor such as Ephesus, Aphrodisias, and Antioch are known to have placed portraits of Aelia Flaccilla in public places after her elevation to Augusta. Theodosius also commissioned a statue of the empress for the senate house in Constantinople.[11] A striking portrait, now in the Cabinet des Médailles in Paris, has been tentatively identified as Flaccilla (fig. 4).[12] The half-life-size marble statuette, 78 cm high, depicts a slender woman whose movement is arrested in midstride, as the flexed left leg and slightly turned body suggest. She wears a tunic, or dalmatic, with two *clavi,* or applied ornamental stripes, down the front; the clavi were apparently filled with another substance, perhaps colored wax or gold. Over this is a dalmatic of slightly heavier fabric with intricate creases and folds delineating its corkscrew motion as it fits tightly around her body, and in which her left arm and shoulder are enveloped. The left hand holds a diptych, or ceremonial tablet, at her side, and the right, now missing, presented an object forward of the torso. The left foot is concealed behind folds of drapery but the right, now missing, was carved in another substance, perhaps porphyry, and attached.

There is no doubt the statuette represents an empress, for she wears the imperial diadem and has a hairstyle, with pronounced roll or chignon above the diadem, and jewelry similar to the coin type discussed above. The neck was once encircled with a necklace, probably made from precious metals and gems; holes below the edge of the hair indicate pendant earrings were affixed. The smooth face with its deep-set eyes and pursed mouth appears somewhat dreamy and contemplative. Although the statue cannot be identified with certainty, its feeling of monumentality suggests a larger double, perhaps one of the statues like those mentioned above known to have been set up in cities in the Near East. The same statue type is probably depicted in coins of Flaccilla which have reverses showing her graceful, draped, and standing figure.[13] The Paris statuette probably stood in a niche because the back is roughly carved and was not meant to be seen. Its strong sense of presence is extraordinary in such a small piece, and it is unequaled in artistic quality in late antiquity. The function of such images in evoking personal authority can be better understood if one considers that statues of Theodosius and his sons and wife were attacked and damaged in Antioch in 387 as a form of protest of the emperor's taxation policy.[14] Statues and coins were not just an effective means of conveying a likeness, but a succinct means of deploying imperial propaganda, and Flaccilla's set a new standard for female rank and authority.

On the death of Aelia Flaccilla, Theodosius married Galla, daughter of the western emperor Valentinian I, in 387. This union drew Theodosius into the politics and ambitions of the Valentinian house, for he was now obliged, through the unwritten rule of kinship, to name not Maximus, a capable and Orthodox pretender, but Galla's brother, Valentinian II, to the position of next Augustus in the West (see genealogical table on page 317). While the seven-year marriage of Theodosius I and Galla produced one royal child, Galla Placidia, Galla was never given the title Augusta. I will return to Galla Placidia later in this chapter. As we will see, her career reveals the sudden turns the life of a Theodosian princess could take.

At his death in 395, Theodosius was succeeded by his son Arcadius, while Honorius, his younger son, succeeded Valentinian II in the West. Arcadius did not prove a strong ruler, but his wife, Eudoxia, daughter of a Roman mother and a Frankish general, Bauto, maintained the female image of imperial authority set by Flaccilla. Her piety she demonstrated by founding numerous churches and in particular through the translation, or transferal to a new location, of the relics of saints. Exhibiting another important trait, humility, the empress appeared without her imperial insignia among the throngs of townspeople, including women and virgins, who turned out to accompany processions with relics.[15] Her devotion to relics of saints and martyrs served to promote the notion of the protection of the rulers and the people by these powerful talismens. Her wifely love she demonstrated by bearing five children: Flaccilla, Pulcheria, Arcadia, and Marina, and, in 401, the desired male heir, Theodosius, later Theodosius II. Eudoxia died in childbirth along with her sixth child in 404. The perils of childbirth, always the highest cause of mortality among women, did not make exception for the highest ranks of society.

Eudoxia was elevated to Augusta in 400, and from then until her death coins were minted with her portrait.[16] On the obverse was her profile, appearing much like Flaccilla's. Like Flaccilla also, she was given the first name, Aelia, but since this was not a family name as it had been for Flaccilla, it must be regarded as an honorific title passed down among Augustae after Flaccilla. The reverses of her coins depicted, just as on Flaccilla's, the seated Victory inscribing a shield. A significant innovation on her coinage, however, is the appearance on the obverses of a hand with a wreath hovering above her head, a divine crowning motif found occasionally on earlier coins of emperors. From this time on it becomes standard for portraits of Augustae on coins, for apparently the designation by God was part of the preferred ideological apparatus associated with empresses. Thus, beginning in this generation, the Augusta borrowed from the Augustus one further attribute, the crowning hand.

Eudoxia's well-reported "imperious attitude," which irritated the charismatic bishop of Constantinople, John Chrysostom, caused a rift to develop out of all proportion between rulers and people.[17] Their sparring was exacerbated by the installation of a silver statue of Eudoxia near the church of Hagia Sophia, the noisy dedication of which was said to have disturbed the bishop. In addition, he disapproved of her lifestyle—and of females in general—which resulted in his outbursts of categorical denunciation, in public, such as the following in one of his sermons:

> You who are in the flesh make war against the incorporeal one. You who enjoy baths and perfumes and sex with a male do battle with the pure and untouched church. But you too will find yourself a widow, although your man still lives. For you are a woman, and you wish to make the church a widow. Last evening you addressed me as the thirteenth apostle, and today you call me Judas. Yesterday you sat with me as a friend, but now you spring on me like a wild animal.[18]

The quarrel in which they were embroiled proved disastrous for both individuals and for the city. Mobs burned the church of Hagia Sophia in protest when the popular preacher was exiled at Eudoxia's request. Eudoxia, however, is thought to have paid with her life, for she went into premature labor a few months later and died.[19] Arcadius, an ineffectual ruler, died soon after in 408. With dissent occupying so much of Eudoxia's short life, it is no wonder that two of their children, Pul-

cheria and Theodosius II, also led tumultuous lives, in both the public and private spheres.

Distinct personalities characterized the next generation of Theodosian Augustae, in particular the sister of Theodosius II, Pulcheria, and his wife, Athenais Eudocia. Theodosius II, who had an unusually long rule, from 408 to 450, was brought up in the palace and and groomed for rule by his older sister, Pulcheria. In 412 she officially assumed the role of guardian, training him in the necessary deportment. Under the early influence of Eudoxia, Pulcheria had inclined to extreme piety, and her religious training of her brother and their two sisters resulted, it was said, in the palace taking on the atmosphere of a monastery. In 413 at the age of fourteen, rather than seek marriage she dedicated, in a public ceremony in Hagia Sophia, an altar to her virginity and to God; her two surviving sisters, Arcadia and Marina, followed suit.[20] The political implications of these dedications were evident: the possibility of competition caused by other males marrying into the family was excluded, and Theodosius II was assured of undisputed power as emperor. They also made the claim that the holy vows of Pulcheria and her sisters guarded the emperor from threats or harm. Palace intrigues were not stopped by this assumed piety of the royal family, and the historians Sozomon, Socrates, and Theodoret leave us much to illuminate Pulcheria's confrontations with others who threatened interference with her control of the government and of her brother. At age fifteen, in 414, Pulcheria was granted the title of Augusta by her brother. She was reputed to have taken control of the government, while her bookish brother spent his time in more scholarly pursuits. Her portrait joined those of other Augusti in the Senate house as well as on issues of coins.

Coins minted with Pulcheria's portrait reveal an innovation. While solidi minted in Constantinople early in Pulcheria's career, from around 414 to 420, show her profile on the obverse in much the same manner as Eudoxia's, after 420 a new reverse comes into usage. Instead of the seated Victory inscribing the Chi-Rho on a shield, we find a standing Victory holding a tall cross with jeweled border (fig. 5).[21] The extreme piety of the Theodosius–Pulcheria household was complemented by military victory in order to promote the image of strong authority. Pulcheria maneuvered to combine these by calling for a campaign against the Persians to provide the needed ingredient of a military victory over the infidel.[22] To commemorate this victory, coin issues of 420 to 422 changed the obverse type to a Victory holding a long-shafted cross. Here is graphic evidence of a change in the image of the sovereign, a politi-

*Fig. 6. Translation of Relics, ivory plaque, Cathedral Treasury, Trier, Germany, fifth century. (Copyright Trier, Domschatz, Foto: Ann Münchow)*

cal move aimed to emphasize the help of God in gaining victory for the Augusti. The change in coin types of Pulcheria from those minted in 414 to 420 to the "long cross solidi" minted in 420 to 422 reflects a change in roles of Augustae. Coins of Pulcheria now have the same reverses as those of Theodosius II, whereas before this time, female Augustae never share the same reverses as male Augusti.[23]

Imagery of Theodosian women continues to appropriate features seen on emperors' coinage, indicating the agenda of promoting the image of Christian victory. The long crosses refer not only to a jeweled cross set up on Golgotha in Jerusalem, the gift of Pulcheria, but to imperial victory in the Persian war, reinforcing the connection between the victory of the emperor and that of Christ.[24] Pulcheria's coins for the first time in any coin issue have Christian symbols on both obverse and reverse: the hand of God crowning the Augusta on the obverse and the long-shafted cross held by Victory on the reverse. Another aspect of Pulcheria's campaign consisted of associating relics of saints with the imperial persons, as in the case of the transfer of the relics of Saint Stephen from Jerusalem to the imperial palace in Constantinople. For as if in return for the imperial gift of the jeweled cross on Golgotha, the bishop of Jerusalem presented the Augusti with a precious token, in itself symbolic of victory, the relics of Saint Stephen; the name Stephen, from the word for crown, *stephanos,* was identified with his Christian triumph in dying the first martyr's death. The arrival of this relic was commemorated by the church and was no doubt part of Pulcheria's planned identity as victorious eminence and friend of holy relics.

Pulcheria's efforts to identify imperial victory with sacred protection are brought together iconographically in a remarkable artwork, an ivory plaque preserved in the cathedral treasury in Trier, Germany (fig. 6).[25] While this ivory has been the subject of much speculation, Kenneth Holum and Gary Vikan have argued convincingly

*Fig. 7. Ivory Leaf with Ariadne,
Bargello, Florence, Italy, ca. 500.
(Copyright Scala/Art Resource, N.Y.)*

that it depicts the translation or moving of the box containing the right arm of Saint Stephen to a new church built by Pulcheria within the confines of the imperial palace in Constantinople in 421.[26] If this is correct, it represents a rare artistic portrayal of a historical event sponsored by Pulcheria.

The large size of this ivory distinguishes it initially: it is 13.1 cm high by 26.1 cm wide by 2.3 cm thick; it is not known for certain to what type of object it belonged, but it was probably a side panel of a box. The panel has been minutely carved in high relief with much undercutting over its entire surface. Most prominent are two clerical figures on the left who are holding a box and sitting in a cart drawn by two mules. The cart follows in a procession consisting of figures carrying candles and led by a person who can only be an emperor because of his costume. He, in turn, stands before the diminutive figure of an Augusta, again identifiable through her dress. She wears the long chlamys with jeweled border, a diadem and pendilia, all articulated as rows of pearls, a costume closely resembling that of the empress Ariadne in ivories of ca. 500 (fig. 7).[27] In the ivory diptych panel, Ariadne is enthroned beneath a balda-chin framed by eagles, and the similarities of jeweled costume identify both women unmistakably as empresses. In the Trier ivory, the empress gestures with her right hand as if welcoming the cart and its occupants; with her left she holds a long-shafted cross like the cross on coins of Pulcheria mentioned above. Behind her is a basilical church, identifiable through its long roof and prominent apse; the doors are open on the left end and also on the near side, where an oblong chamber is appended to the chapel proper. Carpenters are at work on the roof, completing the building; one hails the approaching procession.

Behind and above the figures of the clerics is an arched gateway supported on two tiers of columns, and with a tympanum containing a bust-length image of Christ. This has been identified as the Chalke gate in Constantinople, the entranceway to the imperial palace through which a procession into the palace would have passed.[28] The scenario takes place inside the parameters of the palace, where we see a three-tiered architectural facade with arcades carried by piers on the lowest level, within which stand spectators or attendant figures. Censor-swinging figures who gesture to indicate they are singing or acclaiming lean out of the trabiated second story. A row of busts lines the uppermost level before a blind arcade. All would have been part of an ornamental facade; the ivory uniquely records the actual appearance of the interior of the imperial palace. Greeting the entry procession are the emperor Theodosius and the Augusta Pulcheria, who plays the central role of sponsor. A text attributed to Proclus, successor of John Chrysostom, convincingly evokes the scene in the ivory, the translation of Saint Stephen's relics, and the implications of the event: "The crown/Saint Stephen is in the palace, for the virgin empress has brought him into her bridechamber."[29] The acclamation scene and the prominently located church in the ivory must represent, as in comparable depictions of translations of relics in manuscripts, the final phase of the translation and arrival of the box of relics at its newly constructed repository. The long-shafted cross held by the empress defines the event as a victorious arrival identified with Christ's victory on the cross and is in keeping with Pulcheria's agenda and assumed iconography.

Later sources, the earliest of which is the *Chronicle of Theophanes Confessor* of the ninth century, describe the translation in greater detail. In the chronicle, Pulcheria's role of receiving the relics of Saint Stephen in the palace and placing them in a splendid chapel which she had built for the purpose provides a direct parallel to the narrative content of the ivory.[30] Thus the coins and the Trier ivory link these rulers with the long-shafted cross. This attribute has been read even further by scholars as asserting that the so-called Cross of Constantine, an ancient object kept in the palace, was after this time kept in the same chapel as the relics of Stephen, also at Pulcheria's instigation.[31] Pulcheria enlarged on the female imperial virtue of piety established by Flaccilla and maintained by Eudoxia, and she exploited her position as Augusta to become the central figure in the religious politics of the time.

Although women had assumed a religious identity in the early Christian centuries, they were always subordinate to men in the eyes of the church. This subordination found expression, for example, in the relegation of the women to the galleries, called the *gynaikeia,* or women's place, in the Great Church of Hagia Sophia. Women's religious identity changed under Pulcheria's influence, an important manifestation of which was the elevation of the Virgin Mary to a special relationship with people and city. Pulcheria identified herself with contemporary preaching on the purity of the Virgin Mary and became not only a paradigm of ascetic renunciation within the palace, but assimilated herself to Mary as a paradigm of perfect womanhood. She "embraced Mary as a paradigm for her own asceticism."[32] Later in life she founded the three great churches of the Virgin Theotokos in Constantinople: the Blachernai, Hodegoi, and Chalkoprateia. These large public churches, in a distinctly different milieu from that of Saint Stephen's within the palace, demonstrated to the wider populus an association between Mary, the mother of God, and imperial rule.[33] This was an important step in forging the city's identity as divinely allied and guarded and founded the notion, ensconced by the late sixth and early seventh centuries, that the Virgin was the protector of not only rulers but the city of Constantinople and all its inhabitants.[34]

The Augusta Pulcheria not only educated the young emperor, governed in his place, and pursued a politics of Christian ideology, but when the time came for him to marry she almost certainly participated in the process of finding him a wife. The circumstances leading to Theodosius's marriage are reported only in later sources, but nonetheless they probably contain a grain of truth.[35] The story starts with Leontius, a sophist and professor at the university in Athens who had two sons and a daughter; all were well-educated pagans. At his death his sons inherited all his wealth, and so the daughter, Athenais, went to Constantinople to seek help against this unjust settlement. Pulcheria, impressed by this intellectually accomplished and beautiful woman, introduced Athenais to her brother, and they soon fell in love. After converting to Christianity and being baptized with the Christian name Eudocia, she married Theodosius.

That Athenais Eudocia married the emperor in 421 is undisputed. The background and circumstances, including Pulcheria's role in engineering the marriage, however, are more controversial. Whatever the circumstances of the choice of this professor's daughter as empress, the advantage to both Pulcheria and Theodosius lay in the fact that she could not have produced a link with possible usurpers to Theodosius's throne; she was, in effect, a "nobody."[36] Fulfilling her important role as consort, in 422 she bore him a daughter, Licinia Eudoxia, the first of three children. In 423 Eudocia was given the title of Augusta, thus becoming equal in rank with Pulcheria.

The two Augustae differed in their inclinations and political aims, and not surprisingly there is said to have ensued a long battle between the two women for control of the weak Theodosius II. Coins minted in that year in Constantinople had obverses showing the new Augusta, Athenais Eudocia, with the epithet Aelia and the hand of God holding a crown over her head, just as in those of Pulcheria and Eudoxia before her. She shared the long-cross obverses with Pulcheria and also had a cross-within-a-wreath type (fig. 8).[37] The simultaneous presence in the palace of two Augustae,

*Fig. 8. Coin of Athenais Eudocia, gold solidus, Dumbarton Oaks Collection, Washington, D.C., 423–50. (Courtesy Dumbarton Oaks, Byzantine Photograph and Fieldwork Archives, Washington, D.C.)*

the sister and the wife of the emperor, implies if not conflict at least the need for negotiated roles. Concern for the educational curriculum was one role that fell to Eudocia.

In 425 Athenais Eudocia was probably instrumental along with her husband in refounding the university of Constantinople. The new curriculum included the classical education formerly found only outside of the capital at Antioch, Athens, and Alexandria as well as Christian theology and ethics. Her influence may have helped in the "Graecizing" of the empire, which increasingly spoke and wrote in Greek in the East, while in the West, Latin took precedence and Greek disappeared altogether.[38] The university significantly had ten chairs of Greek and ten of Latin grammar, five for Greek and three for Latin rhetoric, with one for philosophy and two for law. Eudocia's fostering of classical education must have played a role in edicts issued by Theodosius in the same year leading to the advancement and privileging of professors in the society.[39] This was an education geared primarily to the bureaucracy serving the state, thus producing within the network running the empire a combination of classical and Christian culture, a feature which was to define Byzantine civilization throughout its history. Eudocia's learnedness in itself, however, is a subject of study.

While empress, Athenais Eudocia continued to pursue her intellectual bents and wrote a number of works of hagiography and biblical paraphrase, mostly while she was living in the Holy Land after 439.[40] The earliest of these, written shortly after her marriage to Theodosius, is an encomium in hexameters commemorating the Byzantine victory over the Persians in 421. She wrote this in heroic Homeric language and meter (dactylic hexameter), as was the custom among classically trained writers. Five other works are ascibed to her: poetic paraphrases of the Octateuch and the "Prophecies of Daniel and Zachariah," a speech to the people of Antioch, a "Homeric Cento of the life of Christ," and the "Martyrdom of Saint Cyprian." Of these none is precisely dated except for the encomium of 421 and the "Martyrdom" of around 440.[41]

The "Martyrdom of Saint Cyprian" is known primarily from a fragmentary text in the Laurentian library in Florence;[42] the story falls into two parts. In the first, Cyprian, a magician, is hired by a young man smitten with lust for a virgin, Justa, in order to win her over through tricks and incantations. She takes refuge in the sign of the cross and avoids Cyprian's traps. Cyprian confesses his error, and he "burnt to ashes the forms of his feeble wooden images."[43] After apprenticing himself to the bishop Anthimos, he eventually takes the bishop's place as head of the Christian community in Antioch. But Justa, whose virtue is depicted in opposition to Cyprian's machinations throughout book 1, appears at the end of the chapter:

> Cyprian, now in charge of the glorious sanctuary of God, welcomed the virgin, honoring her with a deaconship and changing her name from Justa to Justina the Blameless; and he made her mother of all tender girls who were handmaids of the Great God.[44]

Eudocia's hagiography concerns not only the convert Cyprian, but also a heroine who withstands temptations to pursue her career as a deaconess and whose mission is to minister to and protect young girls in the care of the church, its "virgins of God."

The second book pursues an entirely different line in tracing the early career of Cyprian, when he was still a pagan, and his visions of evil spirits. Narrated by the reformed Cyprian himself, it is a propagandistic retelling of the victory of Christianity over ignorant paganism and Cyprian's struggles with Satan. How this pair of surviving books was related to Eudocia's literary and religious interests is difficult to ascertain in the absence of more of her oeuvre. Regardless of its shortcomings, which scholars are quick to point out, the "Martyrdom" is a rare representative of a work written in a sophisticated literary genre by a fifth-century woman. In spite of her classical education and dedication to ancient language and literature, however, it is clear she remained a devout Christian.[45] Eudocia's writings represent an important phase in the utilization of ancient and pagan meters and literary forms in Christian works. It is no wonder she was a well-known literary figure in her time.[46]

In 431 Eudocia attended the Ecumenical Council of Ephesus at which she supported Pulcheria. At this council, the Orthodox position overruled that of Nestorius, archbishop of Constantinople, who insisted on the distinctiveness of the humanitiy and divinity in Christ. The result of the council was the establishment of the doctrine of Mary as Theotokos, or Mother of God, an important inference of the assertion of the combined human and divine natures of Christ.[47] Theodosius convened this important council, which was no doubt attended and supported by the two Augustae.

The religious life of Athenais Eudocia is known to us mainly from her later career. In thanks for the marriage of her daughter Licinia Eudoxia to Valentinian III she traveled to the Holy Land on pilgrimage in 437–38, accompanied by her friend Melania the Younger, later Saint Melania. She acquired important relics, some [more] of the bones of Saint Stephen and the chains of the apostle Peter, and brought them to Constantinople where they were housed in the church of Saint Lawrence, founded by Pulcheria.[48] Eudocia and Pulcheria, rivals though they may have been, shared a devotion to relics of saints and cooperated in certain acts of Christian piety.

An adultery scandal followed Eudocia's return from Jerusalem, and, at least according to some sources, this was the reason for her later, self-imposed exile. The sixth-century "Chronicle of Malalas" relates the main events.[49] Theodosius gave Eudocia a large, beautiful apple. Paulinus, a close friend of both Theodosius and Eudocia, was ill, and Eudocia gave him the apple as a get-well present. When Paulinus then gave what was obviously the same apple as a gift to Theodosius, the emperor

*Fig. 9. Coin of Pulcheria and Marcian, gold solidus, Hunter Coin Cabinet, Glasgow, UK, 450–57. (Copyright Hunterian Museum, University of Glasgow)*

became suspicious and questioned his wife about what she had done with the apple he had given her. Eudocia said she had eaten it, even when asked to swear an oath. The symbolism of apples and gifts aside, Theodosius suspected Paulinus of having an adulterous relationship with his wife and had him executed in 440. Soon after, Eudocia returned to Jerusalem and remained there in what has been termed voluntary exile for the next eighteen years, until her death in 460.[50]

Eudocia, while in Jerusalem, for a time became associated with the Monophysites, a group practicing a heretical brand of Christianity which rivaled Orthodox Christianity throughout the fifth and sixth centuries.[51] In this she appeared to spar with Pulcheria in a kind of politico-religious battle, but not for long. Eudocia returned to Orthodoxy after 450. She also outlived Theodosius II, who died in that year, but she remained in Jerusalem. During her continued residence there she founded many churches and monasteries and was a generous benefactor of the poor. Among her foundations there were churches to Saint Sophia, Saint Peter, Saint John the Baptist, Saint Stephen, a church at Siloam, the archbishop's residence, her own palace, a hostel for pilgrims, the walls of Jerusalem, and many monastic enclosures and hospices for the poor in and around the city. She lived in Jerusalem for eighteen years. On her death in 460, Eudocia was buried in the church of Saint Stephen which she had founded, in a tomb near the saint's relics, as she had planned.[52] The professor's daughter from Athens maintained the ideals of a pious empress, but on her own terms, to the end.

The death of Theodosius II posed a problem of succession. Pulcheria ruled briefly alone but soon named the soldier Marcian as her consort. She personally conferred on him the diadem and paludamentum, badges of imperial rule, in an unusual instance of a woman performing the ceremony of the elevation of an emperor to power.[53] Pulcheria's determination to maintain the dynasty overruled her avowal of chastity. Their celibate marriage began in 450, and in a coin minted in that year, Christ is depicted as sponsoring the union (fig. 9).[54] The reverse shows three standing figures, all haloed; the figure on the left, Marcian, joins his right hand to that of the small figure on the right, Pulcheria, while in the center, Christ puts his arms around their shoulders. The inscription is FELICITER NUBTIIS (felicitous the marriage!); the joining of right hands in marriage (*dextratum iunctio*) is shown as divinely sponsored by Christ.

Together Marcian and Pulcheria convened the Council of Chalcedon in 451, the

*Fig. 10. Coin of Licinia Eudoxia, gold solidus, Dumbarton Oaks Collection, Washington, D.C., 439. (Courtesy Dumbarton Oaks, Byzantine Photograph and Fieldwork Archives, Washington, D.C.)*

Fourth Ecumenical Council of the church. The council met initially in the church of Saint Euphemia, a large martyrium housing the repository of the saint's relics, near Chalcedon, chosen because of Pulcheria's confidence in the salutary power of this female saint.[55] The council affirmed the relationship among the persons of the Trinity and again proclaimed Mary as Theotokos, or Mother of God. At this council the heresy of Nestorianism, mentioned above, was definitively denied. Just as Marcian was called New Constantine, Pulcheria was acclaimed as the New Helena, in yet another personification of the female imperial ideal. She died in 455 and Marcian in 457, and they were buried in the church of the Holy Apostles in Constantinople. The Augusta Pulcheria was the last member of the Theodosian dynasty to rule in the East.

In the western part of the empire, Licinia Eudoxia, daughter of Athenais Eudocia and Theodosius II, had married the young heir to the throne, Valentinian III, in 437 in order to bring about the much-desired union between the Valentinian and Theodosian houses. This was an opportunity to unite the eastern and western halves of the empire, as coins minted for the occasion express. At the time of the marriage of the eighteen-year-old Valentinian III to the fifteen-year-old Licinia Eudoxia, coins were struck in Constantinople showing the senior emperor, Theodosius II, between the newlyweds, indicating the ultimate source of Valentinian's power.[56] On the reverse was the inscription FELICITER NUBTIIS, (felicitous the marriage!). Two years later coins were also struck with Licinia Eudoxia's portrait labeled SALUS ORIENTIS FELICITAS OCCIDENTIS (well-being [or salvation] of the East, felicity of the West), emphasizing union and harmony between the two parts of the empire.[57]

On some western issues of 439 in Rome and Ravenna, however, a new type of frontal portrait bust, the first of its kind for an Augusta, appears. Licinia Eudoxia wears a radiating, spikey crown with six pinnacles, at the center of which is a cross (fig. 10).[58] Pendilia of pearls hang from crown to shoulders, and she wears a necklace of three strands of pearls; the diadem, paludamentum, and brooch identify her as empress. Around the rim is the inscription LICINIA EUDOXIA AUGUSTA. On the reverse is a type seen only in medallions minted for Galla Placidia, the mother of Valentinian III: Licinia Eudoxia sits frontally, enthroned on a jeweled throne, and holds the *globus cruciger* and a cross scepter; although very small in scale, her diadem and pendilia can once more be discerned. The now customary inscription reads SALUS REI PUBLICAE.

The children of Licinia Eudoxia and Valentinian III were both girls, Eudocia and Placidia, and in keeping with a now well-established tradition, Licinia Eudoxia was given the rank of Augusta in 439 after the birth of the first daughter. In the years ahead she would be forced to marry her husband's murderer, Maximus, and she and her two daughters would be carried off to Carthage in North Africa as hostages of the Vandal king Gaiseric.[59] In the 460s, she would return to Constantinople to live out her life. One of her daughters, Eudocia, would marry Gaiseric's son, Huneric, who also became king of the Vandals. On his death she would rejoin her grandmother and namesake, Athenais Eudocia, in death, for she retired to Jerusalem and at her request was buried next to Athenais at the church of Saint Stephen. The other daughter, Placidia, would marry Olybrius, emperor in the West in 472 (see genealogical table of these Theodosian women, page 317 below). The woman who helped perpetuate this line of empresses in the West was the daughter of Theodosius I by his second wife, Galla, named Galla Placidia. She accomplished this through acting as regent for her son Valentinian III in a tireless attempt to promote both her son and daughter-in-law.

## Galla Placidia

Galla Placidia was born in either Thessalonika or Constantinople in 388 or 389.[60] She was of imperial lineage on both her parents' sides and, more important, represented a link between the western Valentinian dynasty and the eastern Theodosian dynasty. Although she remained for a time at the court in Constantinople, she spent most of her life in the West. Her second husband, Constantius III, ruled briefly as coemperor of the West. After his death in 421 she was forced by her half-brother Honorius to flee but returned two years later and ruled as regent for her son and as Augusta of the western Roman Empire during much of the period from 423 to 450, at the western capital of Ravenna. Galla Placidia's life, even more than those of Pulcheria and Athenais Eudocia, illustrates conflicts and changes at a turning point in history. What was a united eastern and western Roman Empire during Galla Placidia's childhood was by the end of her life decisively divided, marking the beginning of diverging outlooks and cultural patterns in the two halves of the empire that persist until today.[61]

The marriage of Theodosius I to Galla, sister of Valentinian II, in 387 meant a political alliance with Valentinian's family was part of the bargain, for Galla was the daughter of Valentinian I and sister of Valentinian II, both emperors in the West. While awaiting the outcome of Theodosius's campaign in the West against the usurper Maximus, Galla gave birth to Galla Placidia.[62] Arcadius, ruling in Theodosius's absence, did not get along with his stepmother, and it was not until Theodosius's triumphal entry into Constantinople with Honorius that Galla and her daughter, who had never been seen by her father, joined the imperial retinue. At this time, in view of the enmity between Galla and Arcadius, a House of Placidia was established in the city, which probably included a private residence and land as well as an endowment. Galla Placidia's future as an imperial princess was thus provided for by her father when she was still a baby.[63]

Her first years were a time of momentous events. When Galla Placidia was two, in 391, her father proclaimed Christianity the sole religion of the Roman state. When she was four years old, in 393, her half-brother Honorius was proclaimed Augustus of the West by Theodosius. A display of pomp and ceremony took place, of which she was a part and which must have made an impression on the princess as she rode in robes of gold in the procession.[64] It is probable that at this time Galla Placidia received the title of *noblissima puella* (most noble girl), which was customarily conferred on young princesses. When Galla Placidia was five years old, in 394, her mother died in childbirth with her fourth child. Galla Placidia was the only child of Theodosius's second marriage to survive. The following year, when her father was again occupied with securing the western empire, he died in Milan. His two children, Honorius and Galla Placidia, were brought to Milan, then the western capital, to see him on his deathbed, where he died in the spiritual comfort of the great bishop Ambrose of Milan.[65] He was the last emperor to rule the united Roman Empire. After lying in state in Milan, the body of Theodosius the Great, as he was already called, was carried to Constantinople for burial at the Church of the Holy Apostles in the mausoleum containing the body of Constantine.[66] His six-year-old daughter, Galla Placidia, was surely present at the services in Milan, and from this time on she spent most of her life in the West.

The upbringing of both Galla Placidia and Honorius was entrusted to the general Stilicho and his wife, Serena, niece of Theodosius I. Under the supervision of her cousin Serena, and in the company of Serena's daughter Maria, Galla Placidia was given a traditional Roman education in literature, both Greek and Latin, in the homely virtues of weaving and embroidering cloth; she was also trained as a pious Christian with a thorough grounding in the Scriptures.[67] Honorius was nominal ruler of the western empire, first in Milan and then, after 402, in Ravenna. He constructed in the ancient capital, Rome, a circular mausoleum attached to the south transept of Saint Peters's, later known as Saint Petronilla. This was intended to serve as the burial place for the western members of the Theodosian and Valentinian houses.[68] It was long before Honorius's death in 423, however, that Galla Placidia learned what it was to be a major player in the theater of empire.

Galla Placidia remained unmarried for a longer time than was usual for girls of this time, and it has been surmised that the powerful Stilicho was waiting for the right moment to marry her to his son, Eucherius. During a period of chaos in 408 when Stilicho and his son were murdered in Ravenna for their supposed pro-German sympathies, Galla Placidia was residing in Rome at an imperial residence. In the same year Serena was put to death with the concurrence of Honorius and Galla Placidia, who, although raised by her, must have thought her guilty of treason against the state. In 410 when Galla Placidia was twenty-one years old, Visigoths led by Alaric took Rome. Honorius, then residing at Ravenna, was unable to stop the invasion and could do nothing to prevent the princess from falling into Visigothic hands. After a three-day sack of Rome they left, taking with them Galla Placidia, who witnessed great destruction of the ancient repository of Greek and Roman culture and art. By the end of the year, Alaric himself was dead, his armies were on the march along the west coast of Italy, and his successor, Athaulf, was in charge. At some point in the journey northward and westward toward Gaul, Athaulf must have considered marrying Galla Placidia.

In marrying the daughter of Theodosius I, Athaulf would become an agent of the Romans or at least would enter into an alliance which would benefit his people. This was an alliance which Honorius and his second in command and power behind the throne, Constantius, would have to accept. While traveling with Athaulf, Galla Placidia, one can surmise, convinced him of the greatness and impermeability of Roman civilization. Because of the Gothic army's need for food, however, a treaty was signed in 413 under which the Romans would supply grain in return for the release of the princess to Honorius. A pawn in a game of bartering for grain, Galla Placidia awaited the outcome.

During this time, however, Athaulf apparently fell in love with her and reneged on the grain agreement. His tactic changed to one of mollification of the Romans, through whom he hoped to gain a peaceful settlement, which would be symbolized by his union with Galla Placidia. His change of heart toward the Roman state and his appreciation of its accomplishments were apparently due to the influence of Galla Placidia.[69] After reaching Narbonne (Narbo Martius) in southern France, the Goths made it their headquarters, and in 414 Athaulf and Galla Placidia were married there. She may also have persuaded him to convert from Arianism to Orthodox Christianity at this time. Ironically, among Athaulf's wedding gifts to his new wife were gold treasures and jewels plundered from Rome.[70]

Forced by the Romans to withdraw into Spain, the Goths settled at Barcelona, where in 415 Galla Placidia gave birth to a son and named him Theodosius. The name itself reveals the aspirations of Galla Placidia and Athaulf: they hoped he would be emperor of both the Romans and the Goths. But the baby lived only a short time, and his silver coffin was deposited in an oratory near Barcelona. Soon after, in 415, Athaulf was murdered by a treacherous groom. In five years, from age twenty-one to twenty-six, Galla Placidia had experienced the sack of Rome, travel with the Goths all over the Italian peninsula, southern France, and into Spain, marriage to their king, and finally the loss of both husband and baby. In a humiliating ritual, she was forced to walk in front of the horse of Segeric, the usurper, along with other Roman prisoners.[71] As he was dying, Athaulf had requested that Galla Placidia be returned to the Romans, for he must have thought his marriage to the princess was a cause of enmity between his subjects and the Romans, and so he hoped to secure peace for the Goths through her return. In order to placate the Romans and become their allies, and in order to obtain enough grain to survive, the Goths handed over the imperial princess to the Romans in 416.

Bringing with her a household of Gothic supporters, Galla Placidia returned to Honorius in Ravenna. Not long afterward, in spite of her protests, she was ordered by him to marry his general Constantius, who sought this marriage, for her lineage would be an asset to his ambitions to rule the Roman Empire. Among her reasons for resisting the marriage was probably the misery he had caused the Goths, but nonetheless, in 417 they were married. In the coming years she proved to be a capable manager of money as well as an astute politician, as her influence over Constantius in settling a dispute over papal elections in 419 showed.[72]

A second child was born to Galla Placidia in 419 in Ravenna. Named Flavius Valentinian III, he lived to be emperor of the western empire. She also had a daughter, Justa Grata Honoria. In naming her children, Galla Placidia made explicit not only her imperial claims on both sides of the family but also her determination that these claims were to be inherited by the children.[73] From this time on she was caught up in her ambitions for her son, and as a first step, she had her brother name him *noblissimus puer* (most noble boy), in 421. But the principal step to securing her son on the path to the throne was yet to come. In 421 Honorius, realizing he owed his security to his colleague, conferred on him the rank of Augustus, making him Constantius III. Shortly afterward, the two jointly conferred the rank of Augusta on Galla Placidia. Relations with the East did not proceed easily from this time on, as Theodosius II and Pulcheria did not recognize the titles conferred on Constantius or Galla Placidia by Honorius. But Constantius III did not have time to enforce recognition of himself or his wife, for he died of pleurisy in 421, leaving Galla Placidia with two young children.

Honorius did not prove to be as malleable as Constantius, for he banished Galla Placidia from Ravenna in 423 on charges of treason. Taking her household staff with her, she and her children sought asylum in Constantinople, a city she had not seen since she was six years old. En route, the ship in which they were traveling encountered a severe storm, and Galla Placidia vowed that she would sponsor a church to Saint John the Evangelist if they reached their destination safely. The storm abated, and the ship arrived safely in Constantinople. While living at the palace provided her by her father, it must have rankled Galla Placidia that her nephew, the emperor Theodosius II, did not honor her as an Augusta, a title which his sister Pulcheria and wife Eudocia both held. She took up the chaste and pious life that Pulcheria had espoused but did not have to wait long for recognition.

In 423 Honorius died without a successor, and in 424 the threat of a usurper stepping into his place made it expedient for Theodosius to recognize Galla Placidia as Augusta and her son as Most Noble. His next task was to restore them to the palace in Ravenna. First, however, there were negotiations which must have included Galla Placidia's proposal that the infant daughter of Theodosius II and Athenais Eudocia, Licinia Eudoxia, be betrothed to her five-year-old son, Valentinian. This would ensure the support of the East and further link the eastern and western branches of the family. In return, Galla Placidia agreed to turn over eastern Illyricum to the jurisdiction of the eastern emperor, a case in which marriage and territorial division were

*Fig. 11. Coin of Galla Placidia, gold solidus, Dumbarton Oaks Collection, Washington, D.C., 426–30. (Courtesy Dumbarton Oaks, Byzantine Photograph and Fieldwork Archives, Washington, D.C.)*

mutually reinforcing, the beginning of a long tradition in Byzantium. An expedition was organized to reclaim the West and to reinstate the legitimate and only true heir to the throne, the young boy Valentinian. In 425 Valentinian III was elevated to Augustus in the ancient capital of Rome with a splendid procession and ceremonies. The six-year-old child became emperor of the West, and not long afterward, in 426, he was made to confer the title of Augusta on his little sister, Honoria. At last Galla Placidia and her children were situated as she had hoped.

Coins minted around this time reveal the delicate politics of accession. Coins of Galla Placidia minted in the East between 424 and 425 styled her as Aelia Placidia, leaving out the Galla and thus emphasizing her ties to the eastern branch; these are assumed to have been minted at the time that Theodosius II decided to recognize Galla Placidia's legitimacy as Augusta.[74] Later exammples celebrate the Augustae Galla Placidia and her daughter, Justa Grata Honoria, as seen, for example, in a gold solidus of Galla Placidia of 426–30 (fig. 11).[75] Obverses of these coins minted in the West left out the family name Aelia, inserting instead the title D[OMINA] N[OSTRA], our royal lady, perhaps in deference to the superiority of the eastern Augustae or perhaps to proclaim some degree of individuality.[76] Also distinguishing these obverses was the appearance of an inscribed Chi-Rho on the empress's shoulder, as if to confirm the Christian symbolism of the crowning hand of God above her head. On the reverse is a Victory with a long-cross, imitating those struck for Pulcheria and Theodosius in the wake of the Persian campaign. The *vota* series with such legends as VOTXX MULTXXX, commemorating twenty years of rule, as seen here, were also brought to the West by Galla Placidia. Her awareness of precedent at the eastern court, shown by her adoption of types from Constantinople, indicate her wish for continued association between herself and the eastern empire and house of Theodosius.[77] On the other hand, during her first years as Augusta a medallion was minted at Ravenna showing her profile portrait on the obverse, and on the reverse she appears seated on a high-backed throne and haloed, with the legend SALUS REI PUBLICAE, the first instance of a late ancient or Byzantine empress to be represented on coinage enthroned; this type was later taken up in coins minted for her daughter-in-law, Licinia Eudoxia, as mentioned above.[78]

Galla Placidia's acceptance as ruler was bolstered by the images she had struck on her coins. The hand of God crowns her on the obverses of her coins, and wreathed crosses or Victories holding long-crosses appear on the reverses, showing the continuing determination that an image of female authority appear as pious and aligned with the church. Her image as mother also contributed to her legitimacy, indicating that gender roles were continuously at the root of female power.[79] The tradition described in this chapter of empresses of the Theodosian dynasty having coins minted in their own names died out after the mid–fifth century and returned only sporadically after that. Although the subject merits more than this summary review, one may conclude that the practice was associated with the formulation of new roles and responsibilities inherent in the position of women as empresses and Augustae.

Galla Placidia ruled as regent for Valentinian III in Ravenna from 425 to 437 and jointly from 437 until her death in 450; she was always, according to contemporary sources, "zealous for the welfare of her son."[80] Her decisions were followed in government and diplomacy, for she was well prepared to take the role of ruler; the degree to which she ruled after 437, the year of Valentinian's eighteenth birthday and his marriage to Licinia Eudoxia, is controversial, but up to this time she was undisputed ruler.[81] Escalating problems within the structure and administration of the empire, pressures from barbarian neighbors, and economic decline were all undermining the possibility of smooth or successful rule, no matter how great her aptitude. Military capacity was less accessible to her, and her efforts to play generals off against one another were only partially successful, Aetius being the most powerful general with whom she had to contend. Declining populations made the maintenance of standing armies even less feasible than during Honorius's reign. As a ruler she was attentive to all these fronts; her stay among the Goths had given her a useful understanding of their outlook and tactics.

The famous Theodosian Law Code, or *Codex Theodosianus,* theoretically jointly sponsored by the emperors in both East and West, was an undertaking in which Galla Placidia very likely had a hand.[82] For example, she is known to have sponsored a law giving a mother the right to inherit the estate of a deceased child. The completed code was promulgated by the Roman senate under Valentinian III in 438 with celebrations and acclamations, the same year as its promulgation by Theodosius II in Constantinople.[83] The fact that laws accepted in the East were sent to and promulgated in the West, but not the other way around, however, indicates increasing division between the two parts of the empire. The code was to have far-reaching importance in the West, not for the western empire, which ceased to exist forty years later, but for western Europe until well into the Middle Ages. Although governing the western empire became increasingly difficult and its survival doubtful, Valentinian's legislation of the 440s showed he tried to rule responsibly.[84]

In matters of religion, Galla Placidia sympathized with the Arians, a heretical branch of Christianity which did not believe in the equality of the elements of the Trinity or Christ's full divinity. Arianism was the traditional religion of the Germanic tribes in the West, including the Goths among whom she had lived. Galla Placidia, however, was herself Orthodox, and in sympathy with the West she maintained the tradition of female eusebeia. After Constantius's death in 421, under Pulcheria's influence she likely entered upon a life of chastity.[85] After her son's marriage to Licinia Eudoxia in 437 she retired somewhat from direct rule and devoted herself increasingly to works of piety. One of these was the great Roman basilica of San Paulo fuori le mura, which was restored between 440 and 461; her major role in the project was commemorated in a mosaic inscription in the triumphal arch.[86] She also provided mosaic decoration for the church of Santa Croce in Gerusalemme in 438. Her daughter-in-law, Licinia Eudoxia, also sponsored churches in Rome, following her mother-in-law's example. Galla Placidia's only known secular commission was the Porticus Placidiana in the port of Rome.

While Valentinian III preferred to live in Rome, Galla Placidia preferred Ravenna, and she beautified that city as well with church buildings, using her accumulated, very considerable wealth. Although now destroyed, a number of churches in Ravenna benefited from Galla Placidia's sponsorship. The church of Saint John the Evangelist was built by her as a result of her vow when nearly shipwrecked en route to Constantinople. She decorated it with mosaics, including portraits of multiple generations of the Theodosian and Valentinian branches of her family, which appeared on a ceiling vault.[87] One mosaic showed Saint John saving her ship from disaster. Inscriptions in the church mention Constantine the Great in connection with the family's tradition of Christian faith and rule, indicating the church was meant as dynastic propaganda as well as her generous gift to the city.[88] The cathedral of Ravenna, the Basilica Ursiana, was also built by her. The most ambitious project undertaken by Galla Placidia, however, was the church of Santa Croce, decorated or built by Galla Placidia as the church for the imperial palace in 417–21. Attached to the narthex of this church, which survives only in ruins, was the so-called Mausoleum of Galla Placidia, which survives beautifully intact.

The chief tangible association with Galla Placidia today is this little chapel known as the Mausoleum of Galla Placidia, built in Ravenna some time between 425 and 450. It is thought the chapel may have been part of a monastery dedicated to Saint Lawrence, one of the popular saints in Italy, but more likely it was attached to the narthex of the church of S. Croce. Although Galla Placidia died in Rome and was buried there, it is believed she originally commissioned the mausoleum to hold the remains of herself and her family.[89] This small building is the most extraordinary legacy of Galla Placidia.

The little cross-shaped building is perfectly preserved. Its red brick exterior presents a severe profile with gabled roofs abutting a short tower at the center. Ornamentation takes the form of recessed arches and windows of alabaster (fig. 12). Judging from other buildings in Ravenna preserved by Galla Placidia, this too was a personally supervised project, incorporating ideas of the donor in its interior decoration as well as its general design. Indeed, the appearance on the interior, in which mosaics cover all available arches and vaults above the dado in matched marble slabs, is entirely appropriate for an imperial princess with experience of the finest artworks of Rome and Constantinople. From the mosaic lunettes showing Christ as Good

*Fig. 12. Mausoleum of Galla Placidia, Ravenna, Italy, 425–50.*
*(Copyright Alinari/Art Resource, N.Y.)*

Shepherd and the Martyr Saint Lawrence boldly stepping on his grill of martyrdom, to the starry sky of the pendentive dome with evangelist symbols hovering in the clouds, the program of decoration evokes the theme of salvation through the Word (see pls. 1 and 2).[90]

Harts drink from the Fountain of Life, and doves drink from bowls beneath the figures of apostles illuminated metaphysically with light from the alabaster windows. Rich patterns of ornament cover barrel vaults and framing arches at all points of architectural transition. The imagery refers to the sacraments, teachings of the apostles and martyrdom of the saints, all under the protection of Christ. The depictions can also be seen to reflect a funeral prayer, the *commendatio animae,* or committing of the spirit, which was used in western ritual from the third century on; the prayer has thirteen petitions on the model of "Free this soul, Lord, as you freed Daniel from the lion's den."[91] The ornamental motifs used in the borders and frames imitate patterns found in late ancient Roman polychrome floor mosaics, such as the perspective meander, perspective ribbon, and grapevine.

The sensitive blending of themes, motifs, and artistic skill can be attributed to the determination of Galla Placidia to have a thoroughly Roman resting place for herself, or, according to recent scholarship, a temporary resting place for the silver coffin of her baby, Theodosius. It has been suggested that after her enforced travels among the Goths she brought the coffin back to Ravenna and that this is where it resided until mother and baby were buried together in Rome in 450 in the mausoleum of the western dynasty, Saint Petronilla, in Saint Peter's.[92] This uniquely well-preserved mausoleum reflects the style and taste of the Theodosian empress who planned and supervised its execution.

The material splendor of the Mausoleum of Galla Placidia gives some sense of the dazzling qualities of the many lost interiors with their mosaic decoration that she commissioned around this time. It is also in keeping with a description of her actual burial place in Rome. A Renaissance journal is the unlikely source of such a description: in 1458, Nicolo della Tuccia writes of a discovery in the Honorian mausoleum in Saint Peter's (Saint Petronilla):

> A marble sarcophagus of great beauty was found, enclosing two cypress-wood coffins, one large, and the other small, and each sheathed in silver, with a combined weight of metal of 832 pounds. The bodies in the coffins were covered with fine cloth of gold, weighing a total of sixteen pounds.[93]

Although it was initially suspected that the bodies were those of Constantine and one of his infant children, this did not prevent the pope from sending the precious materials—both gold and silver—to his mint. Nicolo's brief notice is the sole record we have of this remarkable discovery.[94]

It is highly probable that the bodies were those of Galla Placidia and her baby son. Galla Placidia kept the image of imperial pride and piety before her, as was appropriate for the daughter of Theodosius the Great. Inscribed on the triumphal arch of San Paolo fuori le mura in Rome was just that sort of reminder: "The pious [or faithful] mind of Placidia rejoices that the whole beauty of her father's work is resplendent through the zeal of the pontiff Leo."[95] Beauty, like piety, endured through visual splendor. Galla Placidia knew well the evocative power of precious, well-crafted materials to support her own and her family's public image.

## Associated Readings

Alan Cameron, "The Empress and the Poet: Paganism and Politics at the Court of Theodosius II," *Yale Classical Studies* 27 (1982): 217–83.

Kenneth G. Holum, *Theodosian Empresses: Women and Imperial Dominion in Late Antiquity* (Berkeley, 1982).

Gillian Mackie, "The Mausoleum of Galla Placidia: A Possible Occupant," *Byzantion* 65 (1995): 396–404.

Stewart Irvin Oost, *Galla Placidia Augusta: A Biographical Essay* (Chicago: 1968).

Gary Vikan and Kenneth G. Holum, "The Trier Ivory," *DOP* 33 (1979): 115–33.

*Part II*

# EARLY BYZANTIUM (500–843)

*Introduction: The Problematic for a Study of Byzantine Women*

In an article published in 1983 Judith Herrin sums up the state of inquiry on Byzantine women and the most productive approaches for assessing women's place in Byzantine society in the period of the sixth to twelfth centuries.[1] Herrin is quick to revise the assumption that only matters pertaining to men are of significance in the writing of histories: "It is now widely recognised that the analysis of male-dominated societies should not be undertaken as if men alone counted in their histories."[2] She also advocates casting a broad net in order to glean information that will lead to a more complex and integrated understanding of women: "The nature of the source material means that this will have to be a collective effort, mounted on the basis of different specialist contributions."[3]

Herrin acknowledges the many problems involved in the pursuit of information about women, and the fact that while women in other medieval societies have been the subject of scholarly inquiry for generations, little had yet been done to promote an understanding of women of Byzantium. Although the subject has received increasing attention since 1983, with a number of titles published in the past twenty years, residual barriers remain, approaches are limited, and certain avenues of access to women bear revisiting and enlargement.[4]

Female contributions are neglected partly because of the nature of Byzantine society: it was a military entity in which men exercised administrative, political, and legislative power. Religious authority was also inaccessible to women, except in minor roles. It is no wonder then that only exceptional women for sensational or other eccentric reasons have entered the histories. Herrin proposes three "avenues" to identify the positions, activity, and authority of women in Byzantine society. First, sources written by men are often biased according to gender and express a point of view in keeping with male priorities or agendas; in addition, mentions of women and how they lived, reacted, and worked tend to be incidental rather than central to their accounts. Through close readings of these sources, nonetheless, one discovers useful information about the patterns of women's lives. Second, legal documents make it possible to examine under what circumstances women received recognition under the law, as can be demonstrated in specific cases. Third, the analysis of ecclesiastical institutions and women's relationships to the church, its strictures, and women's reported or approved religious pursuits is instructive. Herrin's approaches, while still viable, require revision in the light of recent work in the wider field of medieval studies.

A difficulty with all of these approaches is that texts may be read in a number of ways. For one, they may be seen as reflecting an ideal rather than the contemporary reality. For another, texts should be considered as literary works in their own right, belonging to distinct genres and therefore representative of differing styles and intended to appeal to different audiences. In any case, texts alone no longer suffice, for the testimony of archaeological and art historical evidence opens new and important vantage points into women's priorities and concerns. Ordinary women are the most silent and faceless group, for records rarely deal with them outright, commonly choosing to mention or depict them only in passing. The synthesis of evidence and materials in part 2 attempts to break new ground in assessing not only what information can be teased out of texts and images but also how one treats that source of insight as a vehicle of expression. As a guide, I refer to Angeliki Laiou's suggestion mentioned in the introduction, that the most fruitful approach to women's roles tries to ascertain how the women themselves thought and on what basis they acted. I will thus continue to be attuned to women's points of view whenever possible.

In a search for Byzantine women, women in city life are still easier of access than those living in the country. For example, we know the realities of hunger and poverty forced some city women to seek basic sustenance by entering professions meeting with society's disapproval, such as acting or other entertainment professions, and prostitution. Others made a living as shopkeepers or midwives. As we have seen from earliest times, the basis of women's status was the family and marriage, and since marriage was thought of as being for the procreation of children, state and church protected this institution.[5]

Overall, society placed great emphasis on marriage for women in order that they fulfill normative expectations; through marriage they remained in the domestic sphere in which they themselves were raised. In her home, a married woman's activities were primarily childbearing, the rearing and education of children, and the weaving of cloth for the family's use as well as running of the household. As in antiquity, only through marriage could women maintain a place in society as well as financial security.[6] Widows occupied an important position, for they often controlled the wealth of a family in addition to their own dowries. Wealth passed from generation to generation through the female family members, and dowries were protected by law, giving women substantial power through control of assets. Wills give us one of the clearest indications of how women acquired and disposed of their goods. At best, Herrin concludes, women could be considered at risk, that is, very vulnerable, if they did not fulfill prescribed gender roles in this society.[7]

Beyond the domestic sphere a great deal of women's activity in Byzantium centered on the church. An important part of a woman's identity revolved around her religious convictions, which could be expressed in a variety of ways. Within the church, the order of deaconesses was a serious commitment for women, but their authority was limited by male members of the clergy, and their roles became increasingly limited.[8] Wealth was chaneled into monasteries through female adherents, making the church a major financial repository as well as a center of the orbit of many women's lives. Through these religious structures women gained new possibilities for expressing their piety, even within marriage. Increasingly, women found ways to influence religious ideology and practice.[9] Thus, even though they had little or no political influence, they were able to express themselves in cultural terms and attain a high degree of self-definition through involvement with domestic affairs and the church. Many women became nuns by choice or entered into celibate marriages. Those who found companionship and solace in the sisterhood of a religious community were especially attracted to the cult of the Virgin Mary, who represented the ideal of womanhood and sanctity.

The nature of the influence of the cult of the Virgin on women's religious life continues to be a controversial topic, in part because it is difficult to disentangle imperial edict and canon law from actual practice. As we saw in chapter 3, the empress Pulcheria was especially devoted to the Virgin and did much to promote her cult in Constantinople, most visibly through the building of large public churches. Three major foundations were dedicated to the Virgin: the Chalkoprateia, which housed her girdle, the Blachernai, which housed her robe, and Hodegon, which housed the icon of the Virgin and Child painted by Saint Luke. Other foundations within the imperial palace possessed her shroud and the swaddling clothes of Jesus with the stains of her milk.[10] The Virgin was said to have protected the city of Constantinople from the Avar seige of 626 after her icons were carried along the walls and placed on the gates of the city. She was seen in a vision on the waters of the Golden Horn wielding a sword and encouraging the people to "redden the waters of the imperial city with the blood of Avars and Slavs"; the khan of the Avars reported seeing a veiled lady lady walking on the walls of the city, all of which convinced the Avars to retreat.[11] Even well before this event, however, Mary was represented increasingly as the special protectress of Constantinople. She was venerated through relics and icons, and hymns were composed by the great hymnographer Romanos the Melodist and sung in her praise. The cult of the Virgin flourished in early Byzantium.[12]

Women's subjective identification with and veneration of the Virgin also increased in this period, for she was seen not only as rescuing women from the sins of Eve, but also as the paradigm of virginal purity and of motherhood. Through her women sought solace and hoped for salvation through her intercession with Christ on their behalf. Men and women both saw the Virgin as an ally and friend and prayed for her help, forgiveness, and intercession. The rise of icons has been associated with the popularity and sponsorship of the Virgin's cult by women, and this rich topic for debate has been under frequent discussion to the present day.[13] The period we are dealing with here, early Byzantium, was culturally one of intense faith in which the most basic values of society were understood as religious ones. I will venture to define women's place in this society, taking up three areas of influence: women's sinfulness, women's patronage, and women's roles in elite urban, versus rural, settings.

In chapter 4, I broach the question of female sinfulness and sanctity, a paradoxical linkage which appears most frequently in the genre of hagiography. Women's gender roles and limited rights help one understand the appeal of hagiographical accounts of repentant harlots and women who disguised themselves as men. Saint Mary of Egypt, the case study for this chapter, pursued a life which surprisingly took her from being a lascivious woman to a saintly ascetic. In this chapter I will look at her story for what it tells us about women as part of its own agenda and on its own terms. Her story reveals not only some realities behind prostitution and poor women who found themselves without families, but also that moral attitutes allowed for acceptance of the repentant harlot.

Chapter 5 concerns artistic patronage, which was occasionally undertaken by aristocratic women in whom wealth, pride, and taste converged. Numerous examples of women's patronage can be cited, for media ranging from floor mosaics to liturgical silver. In early Byzantium the possibility also existed for an ambitious woman to leave her mark in the form of major buildings. I examine through archaeological and literary testimony the aims and achievements of the princess Anicia Juliana in early sixth-century Constantinople.

Chapter 6 deals with contemporary Byzantine writings and artistic evidence on probably the most famous of all Byzantine women, the empress Theodora, wife of the emperor Justinian I from 527 to 548. Scholars have expressed diverse views of this controversial woman, as have writers of drama and fiction down to the present day. Artistic images of Theodora and her attendants represent a rare opportunity to observe the actual appearances, dress, and adornment of the empress and of women associated with her and to reassess the messages inherent in these images. Although Theodora was undoubtedly one of the most extraordinary women of Byzantium, her inaccessability as a real person presents a challenge in dealing with Byzantine women generally.

In chapter 7 I respond again to Theodora's challenge by seeking out her ordinary counterparts, or opposites in status, among women of the rural countryside as they appear in the *Life of Theodore of Sykeon*. This chapter treats polarities in juxtaposing contemporary women of the rural provinces and their lifestyle and activities with Theodora and her palace associates, as observed in the preceding chapter. Through this hagiographic account, ordinary women reveal their dilemmas, choices, and concerns with startling and moving clarity.

As in part 1, the four chapters in part 2 will first build a frame of reference around a particular theme in order to introduce general issues and types of evidence. Following these topical essays are studies of known individuals using approaches appropriate to the surviving evidence. Through an integration of literary and artistic material one acquires a nuanced view of the subjects in a cross-section of society. Keeping in mind a spectrum of women's needs, from the spiritual to the physical, I will in this section apply some new ways of synthesizing and configuring evidence, in order to gain insights about those women with power and those ordinary women of the crowd whose scant testimony is significant too.

## Associated Readings

James A. Brundage, *Law, Sex and Christian Society in Medieval Europe* (Chicago and London, 1987), chap. 3, "Sex and the Law in the Christian Empire, from Constantine to Justinian," 77–123.

Averil Cameron, "The Theotokos in Sixth-Century Constantinople: A City Finds Its Symbol," in A. Cameron, *Continuity and Change in Sixth-Century Byzantium* (London, 1981), 79–108.

Judith Herrin, "In Search of Byzantine Women: Three Avenues of Approach," in *Images of Women in Antiquity,* eds. A. Cameron and A. Kuhrt (Detroit and London, 1983) 167–89.

Alice-Mary Talbot, "Women," in *The Byzantines,* ed. Gugliolmo Cavallo, trans. Thomas Dunlap, Teresa Lavender Fagan, and Charles Lambert (Chicago and London, 1997), 117–43.

# Four

# SAINTS AND SINNERS:
# WOMEN AT RISK: MARY OF EGYPT

Behind much of the literature of conversion is the great New Testament penitent, Mary Magdalene, the repentant prostitute who bathed Jesus' feet and was later present at his burial.[1] The sinful woman who repents and is saved is a theme which recurs in stories about saints. Popular in the early Byzantine period, the theme became a powerful vehicle for messages of redemption and salvation. Hagiographic writings about the redemptive lives and miracles of saints, with their obviously proselytizing tone, hold up a mirror of society that reveals much about ordinary women, even women of the lowest echelons of society, including lascivious women and prostitutes. Accounts like the Lives of Thekla or Macrina, discussed in chapter 1, were concerned with the "intersection of the human and the divine."[2] The next generation of writers of *Vitae,* that is, of the fifth to seventh centuries, describe saintly women who in some cases were born to lives of privilege, as were Thekla and Macrina, but in others describe extreme cases in which poor or degenerate women find illumination and salvation, even sanctity. This chapter will deal with women of the lower classes whose paradoxical recognition as saints presents unexpected insights into early Byzantine society.

These often bizarre stories describe a segment of society sharing an emotional burden with which a substantial number of people could identify: people who considered themselves unworthy of forgiveness because of their past sins. The stories of sinful women had as their fundamental purpose the edification and instruction of the faithful within their own social context. As Susan Ashbrook Harvey aptly writes,

> We may or may not be able to identify the actual persons and events behind the stories. But the stories themselves are pieces of history. To be meaningful to the society for

which they were written, the stories had to share the values and assumptions of that society. They had to be true to the thought world of their time, as well as to the ordinary manner of peoples' lives, their way of doing things and seeing things. So these stories reveal to us not the individuals of their day but rather something of the world in which they lived and moved. From this view these stories offer us a rich harvest of historical depth.[3]

I will consider Byzantine women on the fringes of society, women whose lives became paradigms of sanctity through the most extraordinary reversals. They both repel and fascinate us by their degeneracy, or by their daring. The puzzling dichotomy between the most reviled and the most revered, and the playing out of the differences between women's and men's gender roles, sets up a tension that explains society's interest in the repentant harlot and in the woman disguised as a man. These stories are indeed meaningful "pieces of history."

Two collections of female saints' lives in translation have recently enlarged and extended our notions of female sanctity in their blend of the romantic and the legendary, the biographical and the historial.[4] The diverse patterns among these lives reflect the wide variety of human experience and response. The real-life origins of these stories demonstrate what must have been their appeal: that within the ordinary life is the potential for the extraordinary as well as the good. Byzantine saints' lives are not biography or history in the contemporary sense, but instead illustrate the workings of the divine in the lives of ordinary people. They interpret or explain what happened or was remembered to have happened, based on an incident at a given point in time, and the oral tradition that followed.[5] Hagiography is filled with historical detail and can be a rich source for illustrative material and factual details associated with known events and places, and just as often with social and familial customs of a routine nature, such as relationships between mothers and daughters.[6] These Lives are also highly formulaic, with topoi, or patterns of lifestyle and behavior, reappearing with regularity among them. These topoi frequently rely on events in the Gospels as their models.

In the early Lives, persecution and its results in hideous punishments, such as crucifixion or brutality (flagellation or stoning), has its model in Scripture, just as does the performance of miraculous deeds. In later Lives, the miraculous becomes a fundamental expectation in the identification of saints, such miracles as the person's exceptional foresight, power of healing, detection of unseen things, and ability to levitate while praying, to name just a few. To many Lives are appended series of miracle stories, illustrating their subjects' extraordinary powers and modes of posthumous healing, often centered on the tomb, icon, or shrine of the saintly person. Although forms of penitence and ascetic denial seem far removed from the hardships of gladiatorial combat in the amphitheater or contests in Olympic and other athletic games, the toils of saints continued to be referred to through the topos of the performance of athletic feats. Women as well as men are referred to as athletes of Christ.[7]

Authorship of lives of both male and female saints is almost wholly the work of men, some of whom are identified and some not. Most were or professed to be near-contemporaries of their saintly subjects.[8] In the case of a male writer of a female saint's life, the mind and attitude of the writer cannot be divorced from the manner in which a story is told, provoking an important question of how gender relates to history writing.[9] Indeed, some writers appear to contradict themselves in recounting events as having one result, while personnages within the story react in a way that is opposed to the author's interpretation. Women's expected gender roles are often denied in the course of a female saint's career, since a male author probably held conflicting personal views when writing an account of a female saint's actions. As Harvey notes, "The stereotype of pious women as passive, subservient and unobtrusive is simply unfounded in the face of these women whose actions are acclaimed as inspired even while they disconcert the popular sensibilities."[10] If women could not be valued as women within their own societies, they could at least be valued as reflections of God.[11] Indeed, in many instances, the highest praise offered by a male author for his female subject was to describe her as having manly courage or determination or as excelling in virtue in spite of her sex.

The written Lives of these women, whether factual or semilegendary, depict their subjects as developing their own personal version or vision of the work they feel compelled to do, sometimes at a crucial turning point in the narrative, as in a flash of illumination, and sometimes in a pattern of behavior already established from childhood. The denouement allows for wildly eccentric careers to resolve themselves into an instructive story. The hagiographical account itself was crucial in the making of a saint, providing testimony to the tangible results of this person's successful mission, as we will see throughout medieval Byzantium. The writer's goal may thus be seen as both edification of the public and propaganda for the furthering of the saint's cult.[12] The writing process is also a pious action in itself. Within the text, however, is the male writer's own aim or agenda, which challenges us to read these texts very closely, as, for example, in the story of Pelagia.

The Life of Pelagia of Antioch, written in the fifth century, was translated first from the original Syriac into Greek and then, as her story became popular in the West, into Latin and other languages, a common pattern for the transmission of saints' lives in the Middle Ages. As the Life begins in fifth-century Antioch, the author, Jacob, introduces himself and states his purpose in writing the account:

> I wanted to write to you, my holy fathers and brethren, about the conversion of the prostitute Pelagia, in the hopes that you might find great benefit in hearing and learning of it, and accordingly give praise to your merciful Lord God who does not wish anyone to perish, but rather that all sinners should be saved and return to the knowledge of truth. (1; 41)[13]

According to Jacob, his account of Pelagia's conversion is meant to serve as an example that no matter how sinful a person, salvation is always possible. A female subject can serve this purpose as well as a male one, and the genre is addressed to male as well as female listeners.

Extolling Nonnos, the bishop whom he serves, Jacob then describes the encounter of Nonnos and Pelagia in the streets of Antioch, in one of the great passages in hagiographic literature:

> This prostitute then appeared before our eyes, sitting prominently on a riding donkey adorned with little bells and caparisoned; in front of her was a great throng of her servants and she herself was decked out with gold ornaments, pearls, and all sorts of precious stones, resplendent in luxurious and expensive clothes. On her hands and feet she wore armbands, silks, and anklets decorated with all sorts of pearls, while around her neck were necklaces and strings of pendants and pearls. Her beauty stunned those who beheld her, captivating them in their desire for her . . . she went by with her head uncovered, with a scarf thrown round her shoulders in a shameless fashion, as though she were a man; indeed in her haughty impudence her garb was not very different from a man's apart from her makeup, and the fact that her skin was as dazzling as snow. To put it briefly, her appearance incited everyone who set eyes on her to fall in love with her. (4,6; 42–43)

The seductive beauty of the prostitute is not lost on the monastic author any more than it is on the bishop, and he prays fervently, asking God to turn this "baited snare" and "stumbling block for mankind" toward a life of truth and chastity. The encounter is deeply moving and a cause for self-examination for the bishop.

In this description, the warning to men and monks is explicit, but at the same time, her conduct is seen as resembling that of a man, making clear the opposing rules of conduct assigned to men as opposed to women. It did not make her any less appealing as a woman that she was bareheaded and had fine clothes like a man, for these qualities were negative only for conventional male expectations of how a proper woman would comport herself. Respectable women apparently covered or veiled their heads and wore modest clothes to avoid inspiring temptation in males, whereas it was acceptable for men to go about bareheaded in public and dressed in jaunty cloaks or garb appropriate to their status.[14] Pelagia is thus described as being out of step with the gender roles assigned to proper women, even though this comportment was expected in one of her profession. The bishop's plea plays on the concept of adornment of the soul in making oneself pleasing to God versus the physical adornment of the prostitute.

Just as Pelagia had attracted admirers or clients by her appearance, now she is ensnared by the bishop's words, presenting yet another reversal. She decides to repent in order to attain salvation and accordingly addresses Nonnos:

> "Make me into a Christian this very day—for I am a sea of sins. Take me, sir, and make me holy by means of your pure instruction—for I am an abyss of evils. Take from me my sins and wickednesses today, and through your prayers cast them away from me in the cleansing bath of your God's baptism. Stand up, I beg you, my lord, and in-

voke over me the name of the holy Trinity; baptize me for the remission of my sins. Stand up, my lord, and strip off from me the dirty clothing of prostitution; clothe me with pure garments, the beautiful dress for the novel banquet to which I have come. . . . Make me a bride of Christ this very day, giving me rebirth by saving baptism and offering me up to your God." (24,26; 50–51).

In this remarkable speech, Pelagia establishes a relationship with Nonnus; in her request there is irony too. She asks to be stripped of her clothing, not as a prostitute for male sexual enjoyment, but as preparation for baptism. The symbolism of the wearing or shedding of clothing sharpens the contrast between the adornment in worldly riches and depravity, as she abandons the world and takes up the simple garments of the baptized who is reborn in Christ. Pelagia's petition is granted, and she receives baptism with the sponsorship of a deaconess, Romana. Romana's role can be seen as characteristic of one function of deaconesses in the early church: they assured women's modesty on undergoing the customary baptism by immersion.

After giving her wealth to the church of Antioch for relief for the poor, Pelagia then secretly dresses as a man and travels from Antioch to Jerusalem, where she enters a monastery and becomes renowned as the eunuch monk Pelagius. Like Thekla, she assumes male clothing for greater security when traveling, but Pelagius retains this garb. Her external beauty fades as she adopts a harsh, ascetic life in a male monastery. In order to become holy, she must become unrecognizable as a woman. After her death, her sex is revealed when the holy men set about anointing her body for burial and exclaim, "Praise to you, Lord, how many hidden saints you have on earth—and not just men, but women as well!" (49; 61). Only by becoming a virtuous man can Pelagia be a saintly woman.

The paradoxical images in the Life of Pelagia have been compared with Old and New Testament confrontations between sinful women and types of Christ, as, for example, in such dramas as 2 Chronicles 9.1–4, between Solomon and Sheba, and the whore of Babylon in Revelation. She is at once the fallen Eve and the immaculate Mary. She is a snare for men and a holy eunuch. Pelagia, with Nonnus as the holy conduit, reflects biblical depictions of debased women who are rehabilitated through the mediation of spiritual men."[15]

The hagiographical character who dresses herself as a monk is popular in Byzantium but disappears from the literature in the ninth century. Evelyn Patlagean has studied the cases of women disguised as men and considers this evolution a reflection of needs within the society.[16] She places Pelagia in an extreme position, for she is not attached to or dependent on any man for her survival and is living off her wits and her seductive beauty. As a prostitute, she is the opposite of the feminine norm, who is controlled and dominated by her husband. As the eunuch Pelagius, she also transgresses monastic norms but succeeds in adopting this life only at the expense of her femininity. She succeeds and becomes holy only by abolishing the external differences between men and women.[17]

The story of the repentant harlot Pelagia not only provides entertaining reading or listening, but is revealing about the actual state of many women in Byzantine society, whose choices lay between marriage or the convent. Pelagia's profession, prostitution, was a common one for women who lacked the families, dowries, or inheritance needed to make a marriage alliance.[18] Commercial centers were places where the commerce in women thrived too: Antioch, Alexandria, Beruit, Edessa, and, of course, Constantinople. Some were daughters of poor artisans and workers lured by pimps' descriptions of luxuries; others were prisoners kidnapped by pirates or captives of wars. These women were purchased and kept in brothels or kept by individuals as slaves, living with their owners or benefactors as concubines. Parents sold their daughters into prostitution, or girls signed on voluntarily. Although forbidden by law, the trade flourished. Pimps, or *pornoboskoi,* would claim their workers were volunteering their services to escape punishment. Female children who were not part of a family structure, illegitimate children, and those born in poverty were not eligible for marriage. These were women at risk, for their choices often came down to prostitution or starvation.

Prostitution was also a counterpart of other professions, such as acting; mime, musician, or dancer; flute girls and singers were expected, just as in ancient Greece and Rome, to offer sexual favors to those assembled at a party. Until the second quarter of the sixth century under legislation enacted by Justin and Justinian, actresses could not marry. After this time, conversion and repentance of a former actress made it possible for her to marry; Justinian's own marriage to Theodora was reputedly behind this legislation (see chapter 6). Innkeepers were akin to brothel keepers in making prostitutes available to their clients, and for this reason monks on pilgrimage kept to monastically run hostels and were forbidden the use of commercial way stations and inns. While rich prostitutes like Pelagia may have been notorious, the majority were no doubt desperate and ordinary. Copper coins, those of lowest monetary value, are mentioned as forms of payment.[19] Prostitutes often became beggars or shared the streets with other beggars; poor diet and disease often led to their early deaths. Emperors specifically gave alms to these most impoverished members of society. Charitable institutions and the church also concerned themselves with their care.

If prostitutes, while common, were outside societal norms, under what circumstances were women protected by the law?[20] In early Byzantium, the law was primarily concerned with safeguarding property in families grounded in marriage. Men and women, however, were treated differently. Married men could engage in sex with their slaves or with prostitutes without penalty, but women, if married, could suffer dire punishment if adultery was discovered.[21] Women were bound to chastity in marriage in order to ensure the legitimacy of children who would inherit property. Men were exempt from prosecution in matters of marital infidelity, unless the infidelity was with a married woman. Adultery was a major crime when committed by a woman; the penalty could be torture and death.[22] In Athenais Eudocia's suspected adultery with Paulinus, (see chapter 3), the real concern was that Eudocia's son might not have been the legitimate son of Theodosius II and therefore unacceptable as heir to the throne. Concubines were a middle category, for they served as companions and often nurturers of children if they were of too low a class to be married to their partners. Concubines were the acceptable alternative to married wives, and the law recognized their rights.[23]

Poor women, because they were subject to a double standard under the law, had few ways to escape from poverty and prostitution. One escape was to proclaim their intent to become Christians, to renounce their former ways, and to assume celibate and pious lives, presumably within the context of a monastic institution in which they would receive food and shelter. In spite of the advantages of such a refuge many women were placed in monastic institutions against their will as a form of punishment. According to a law of Justinian, a repentant adulteress must spend two years in a convent, where she could elect to stay unless her husband took her back.[24] Justinian and Theodora were known to have founded a monastic institution called *Metanoia*, or Repentance, for the rehabilitation of prostitutes, but some of its residents apparently preferred death to monastic enclosure.[25] In spite of the law's and the government's concern about what women did with their bodies, many women who were poor and had turned to prostitution were overlooked.

As we saw in the story of Pelagia/Pelagius, along with Lives' familiar theme of the repentant prostitute was that of the woman disguised as a man. This too dealt with women left with few choices who found themselves, for a number of reasons, at risk or on the fringes of society. This theme became popular in early Byzantium, although no known civil laws deal with this particular behavior, and the church banned the practice. The life of Mary/Marinus will serve as a further example of this particular hagiographic theme. This seventh-century text, like that of Pelagia, was translated into a number of languages and became popular in later medieval times.[26] Mary, the daughter of a pious, widowed man, Eugenios, could not bear to be separated from her father and left alone when he retired to a monastery late in life. In order to make it possible for them to remain close to one another, Eugenios cuts off Mary's hair, dresses her like a man, and calls her Marinos, and they enter a monastery together. While in service for the monastery Mary has to travel away from the community and is lodged at an inn. Another lodger, a soldier passing through, sleeps with the innkeeper's daughter, who becomes pregnant. The girl is persuaded to place the blame on the young monk, Marinos.

Ostracized from the monastery he/she is given the girl's child to bring up. Later, Marinos is readmitted to the monastery, where the boy-child also takes the habit. Only on Marinos's death is it discovered that he is really a woman. Mary becomes renowned for her endurance and patience, and she is considered a saintly woman. As a sequel to the story, the lying innkeeper's daughter is cured of possession by a demon when visiting the tomb of the holy woman Mary. The lesson is one primarily addressed to women:

Let us then, beloved, zealously emulate the blesed Mary and her patient endurance, so that on the day of judgment we may find mercy from our Lord, Jesus Christ."[27]

Patient endurance was the only alternative for some women. As we glean from this Life, the reality was that poverty forced women who were alone and vulnerable into roles which, unconventional though they were, solved an immediate problem of security or safety. The alternatives for a girl deprived of family were few. Avoiding the negative image surrounding any woman who deviated in behavior from the norm was difficult if a woman's means were limited. Women were always at risk of losing their stature as vessels of devotion, and combating these difficult circumstances was the greatest challenge to a woman.[28] Stories of repentant harlots and transvestite nuns were thus read for edification, and women were urged to emulate Mary; the problem must have been universal. Transvestism was one means of escaping their condition in life, an empowering alternative that bent normative gender roles.[29] In such dramatic reversals of circumstances, however, women could still be seen as exemplifying the working of God.[30]

As godly exemplars, women like Pelagia/Pelagius and Mary/Marinus whose stories were reported and recorded underwent sanctification. The process of sanctification is still not clearly understood, but it is thought to have taken place as a result of gradual recognition of the extraordinary qualities of a person, both during and after her life-time, sometimes because miracles occurred, usually because a tomb became a place of pilgrimage and cult activity. Commemoration took the form of gatherings and the reading of the life of the individual on his or her saint's day, usually the anniversary of the day of death. When the feast day was assimilated into the principal ecclesiastical calendar, the *Synaxarium of Constantinople,* a collection of abbreviated lives used as liturgical readings and arranged according to the days of the liturgical year, then canonization was complete. It is unclear whether the impulse grew out of a popular tradition or from pronouncement by local or patriarchal ecclesiastical authorities. Thus we are not necessarily dealing with elites in the writing of some of these stories, but with popular or grassroots needs and beliefs which became exemplars for the Orthodox Church.

Attitudes toward women were misogynistic, despite Christian teachings, and fewer women than men were recognized as saints. The greatest number of women who were recognized as saints and made their way into the church calendar were martyrs of the early Christian period, and after this time their numbers declined steadily. For example, there were fifty-five holy women recorded in the church calendar who were martyred during the persecutions of the third and early fourth centuries, fourteen of the fourth and fifth, four from the sixth, none from the seventh, and eight from the iconoclastic era of the eighth and ninth. In contrast, there were sixty-four male saints for the iconoclastic period. There were five female saints' lives recorded in the tenth century, one each for the eleventh, twelfth, thirteenth, and fourteenth centuries, none for the fifteenth.[31] In the centuries following the early

Christian martyrdoms, female saints came from the ranks of nuns, abbesses, wives, empresses, and even prostitutes. There is consistently an imbalance between not only written lives of female versus male saints but also women who took up ascetic lives as nuns versus men who became monks. Can we deduce from this that women simply had less freedom than men to determine the courses of their lives, or that their lives were of less interest to society?

Whether undervalued or not in relation to men, women receive spectacular treatment in church art of the sixth century. As evocative as are the descriptions of the harlot Pelagia in her Life, with her rich jewels, silks, and makeup, the vision of the saint in her robes in heaven as captured in the art of mosaic is even more powerful. Some of the most visually striking mosaic wall decorations from early Byzantium are the processions of saints in the church of Sant' Apollinare Nuovo in Ravenna, Italy (see pl. 3); the mosaics date to around 550.[32] On the north, or left, side of the nave as one enters, twenty-two richly clad, haloed women move in a stately procession led by the three Magi toward the enthoned Virgin and Child at the eastern end of the nave. The figures stand almost life size, and their names are inscribed in Latin above each of their heads; the second of these women is Saint Pelagia.

The impression made by these processions is almost hypnotic, for they move with the observer, who walks parallel to their path, mirroring the newly baptized along with the clergy who led them toward the altar as newly reborn to Christ.[33] Dressed as brides of Christ these women represent the unity of the cities of Italy: Rome, Ravenna, and Milan, and other regions and cities of the Christian world. Like the others, Pelagia wears finery consisting of a heavily embroidered dalmatic over her white tunic. Over the dalmatic is a lorum, or shawl. She wears a diadem with a large central jewel and other jewelry, including a necklace, jeweled collar, and wristlets. All of the women wear red shoes and carry jeweled crowns in their outstretched and veiled hands. Between the figures are date palms in which hang ripe fruit, and at the foot of each tree trunk is a garden motif, lilies or other flowers and, in one instance, a lamb.

Recalling the virgins of the parable of the wise and foolish virgins (Matt. 25:1), the virgin martyrs are mentioned in the diptychs of the canon of the liturgy of Milan. They serve as a visual counterpart of the text of the Mass and function liturgically. The procession is lead by Saint Euphemia, the patron saint of the Second Ecumenical Council held at the church dedicated to her in Chalcedon in 451 and one of the chief eastern martyr saints. Her presence expresses the Italian adherence to Chalcedonian Orthodoxy. She is followed by Pelagia, who likewise confirms the ties between her city, Antioch, one of the great sees of Christendom, and Ravenna. The other twenty saints are Roman, Ravennate, and North African. The virgin martyrs are depicted on the left side of the church because this was the side on which women stood during the liturgy; across from them is a corresponding procession of male martyrs, on the right, or south, side where men stood. The mosaics and their liturgical and human context worked together in a mystical and profound way.[34]

In this sense the virgins are not simply part of the decoration of the church, as in a stage set. They offer crowns just as the participants offer the elements for the oblation—the bread was shaped like a crown in reality, symbol of immortality as well as of victory in the divine fight. The female martyrs, like the Magi at the head of their procession, offer their gifts to the Virgin Mary and Christ. Since the processions are gender specific, one can reasonably associate the female martyrs with the experience of women and the male martyrs with that of men. The bridal image, which applies to both processions, is an ancient one for those dedicating themselves to Christ. According to Otto Von Simson, the converging processions represent the liturgy as an anticipation of the Second Coming; he explains the meaning of the female martyrs as virgins who meet the Divine Spouse on the Day of Judgment:

> The procession of virgin martyrs in Sant' Apollinare Nuovo presents the eschatological meaning of the liturgy as a bridal vision, inviting the women of Ravenna to approach the sanctuary as the wise virgins who go out to meet the Spouse on the Day of Judgment. This appeal to feminine experience, this divination of an insight of which perhaps only the feminine psyche is capable, occurs occasionally also in the ancient homiletical literature. The mosaics in Sant' Apollinare Nuovo are the most beautiful artistic evidence of the active share which Christian worship assigned to every member of the ancient church.[35]

According to Von Simson, the female martyrs depicted at Sant' Apollinare had special meaning for women participating in the procession of the baptismal liturgy, or in the celebration of any other liturgy. The mosaics represent a heavenly parallel with or paradigm for their earthly lives as exemplary women.

The popularity of the early female saints and martyrs remains entrenched throughout the history of Byzantium. Their lives were known and read, and their images appear as monumental icons in the fresco and mosaic decoration of churches from the sixth to the fourteenth centuries and in post-Byzantine art as well. Among the stories of the mortification of the flesh, those of repentant prostitutes are classified as "literature of conversion" because of their common theme.[36] I now turn to an example of this theme, Mary of Egypt, who represents an extreme case of reversal of normative patterns for women. She attained sanctity not only through repentance but also through espousal of the harshest form of ascetic discipline: life as a solitary living naked in the desert. Her story and her sanctification hold out unique possibilities for understanding attitudes and roles of women in early Byzantine culture.

## Mary of Egypt

One of the great stories of a repentant sinner is that of Mary of Egypt. Differing from Pelagia, she exemplifies even more complete depravity, for she prostituted herself not for money but for lust, and in so doing debauched or led astray the young men who were her victims. She falls into the category of harlot, a sexually loose or immoral woman; thus, all prostitutes are harlots, but not all harlots are prostitutes.[37] The earliest surviving version of the Life of Mary of Egypt dates from the mid-sixth century.[38] A longer, more detailed one dating from the early seventh century was written by Sophronios, the patriarch of Jerusalem (560–638). Because there were female solitaries in both the Egyptian and Syrian deserts it is possible that the strange story of Mary of Egypt was based on one of them.[39]

The Life written by Sophronios, as well as being an edifying tale of penitence written, like that of Pelagia, for a monastic audience, has elements which give it an emotional appeal or appeal as popular entertainment.[40] The Greek original was translated into Latin in the eighth century and in addition into Syriac, Armenian, Ethiopic, and Slavonic. Among her various feast days in the Orthodox East are April 1 and the fifth Sunday of Lent. Sophronios's Life is distinguished from the earlier version in its first person accounts by Mary of her sinful youth.

Sophronios's account begins with the retreat of an ascetic monk named Zosimas to fast in the desert during Lent.[41] In his search for perfection, Zosimas, the ideal monk, retreats deep into an inaccessible part of the desert and then later recounts his unexpected encounter with a naked, sun-blackened woman there. Her initial questions to him are, "Why did you come to see a sinful woman? Why did you wish to see a woman who is deprived of every virtue?" (14; 78).[42] Initially Mary questions Zosimas and indicates she knows who he is. She also conveys her willingness to be obedient to his wish. Trembling and in awe, Zosimas observes that she is levitating "about one cubit above the earth, hanging in the air, and praying in this way" (15; 79).

The ability to levitate, which is characteristic of holy men and women, symbolizes their extraordinary powers and is a frequent topos in saints' lives. This sure mark of holiness causes Zosimas to beg her to relate the details of her life so that others, as he claims, may profit from the lesson. At this point Zosimas's retreat turns into a journey which ends only after her death, when he shares the secret of the exotic story of Mary's life with his fellow monks. Sophronios recounts the story as his received version of Mary's own words to Zosimas as she describes her childhood:

> "My homeland, dear brother, was Egypt. When my parents were still alive and I was twelve years old, I rejected my love for them and went to Alexandria. I am ashamed to think about how I first destroyed my own virginity and how I then threw myself entirely and insatiably into the lust of sexual intercourse. But now I feel it is more decent for me to speak openly what I shall briefly describe, so that you may become aware of my lust and love of pleasure. For more than seventeen years—please forgive me—I was a public temptation to licentiousness, not for payment, I swear, since I did not accept anything although men often wished to pay me. I simply contrived this so that I could seduce many more men, thus turning my lust into a free gift. You should not think that I did not accept payment because I was rich, for I lived by begging and often by spinning coarse flax fibers. The truth is that I had an insatiable passion and uncontrollable lust to wallow in filth. This was and was considered to be my life, to insult nature with my lust." (18; 80)

A runaway at age twelve, Mary for seventeen years seduced men to satisfy her lust. The danger of this sort of prostitute was doubled, as she did not charge the customary fee and could therefore lure the innocent. Men are portrayed as her unsuspecting victims, rather than she being portrayed as victimized by them. She eked out the necessities by begging in the street and by working in the traditional woman's role, spinning for the production of woven fabrics. Her life of depravity continued until she joined a group of young men who were sailing from Alexandria en route to Jerusalem for the Feast of the Exaltation of the Holy Cross. She decides to join them and uses her body to buy her passage, as Zosimas reports, using Mary's own words:

> "How can I possibly describe to you what followed, my dear man? What tongue can declare, or what ears can bear to hear what happened . . . during the journey that followed and the acts into which I forced those wretched men against their will?" (21; 81)

The theme of entrapment of men is stressed again, as it was in the story of Pelagia, a warning to the male monastic listener of the dangers of the lustful woman. This stereotype contributed to the male bias against women typical of the time.

On their arrival in Jerusalem she wanders around "hunting the souls of young men," describing herself (in Zosimas's voice) as a predator. She finds herself in a crowd entering the courtyard and approaching the church of the Holy Sepulcher:

> "When the time came for the divine Exaltation of the Cross, I tried to join the crowd and force my way to the entrance, pushing my way forward but being pushed back. Eventually, with great trouble and grief—wretched woman that I am—I approached the door through which one entered the church where the life-giving cross was displayed. But as soon as I stepped on the threshold of the door, all the other people entered unhindered, while some kind of divine power held me back, not allowing me to pass through the entrance of the church." (22; 82)

When this happens repeatedly she realizes that her sinfulness is preventing her from entering, and she prays to an icon of the Virgin Mary for help, begging the Virgin to serve as guarantor in a vow:

> "I name Thee before God, Who was born from Thee, as a worthy guarantor, that I shall no longer insult this flesh by any shameful intercourse whatsoever but from the moment I look upon the wood of Thy Son's cross, I shall immediately renounce the world and all worldly things, and I shall go wherever Thou shalt instruct and guide me, as the guarantor of my salvation." (23; 83)

In her prayer before the icon, Mary promises to change her life if she is permitted to see the wood of the cross. She again joins those entering the church:

> "No longer did anyone push me this way and that, nor did anyone prevent me from approaching the door through which they entered the church. Indeed, I was filled with a shivering fear and astonishment, shaking and trembling all over. Then I reached the door that until then had been barred to me, as if all the force that previously held me

back was now preparing the way for my entrance. In this way I entered the church without any effort. Thus I found myself inside the Holy of Holies, and I was deemed worthy to see the life-giving cross and saw the mysteries of God and knew that He is always ready to accept our repentance." (24; 83)

Recounted in Mary's voice, the didactic purpose of this conversion story is evident; it demonstrates as well the efficacy of icons. Those reading or hearing the story would gain confidence in the possibility of leading a new life, whatever their transgressions had been. If a prostitute of the worst kind, or any lascivious or sinful woman, could attain salvation through repentance, then here was a paradigm to provide hope. The "life-giving Cross" is glorified as a symbol of hope.

Hope is also offered to the unworthy who can find acceptance through the intercession of the Virgin Mary. Mary of Egypt asks the Virgin for direction:

> "It is now time, my Lady, to fulfill what was agreed in Thy act of guarantee. Guide me now wherever Thou dost command. Be the teacher of my salvation and guide me toward the path which leads to repentance. While I was saying these words, I heard someone crying aloud from afar, 'If you cross the river Jordan, you shall find a fine place of repose.'" (25; 84)

A mysterious voice instructs her on what to do next and promises relief from her anxiety. She follows the voice's directive.

Mary goes to the spot by the Jordan River where John the Baptist baptized Christ. She washes in the river, in what is equivalent to self-baptism, for she then takes holy communion at the church there. Crossing the Jordan, she takes up life as a solitary in the desert. This regime has lasted forty-seven years by the time Zosimas finds her. Self-deprivation and mortification of the flesh are extreme in this ascetic withdrawal, for she has not seen a person during all this time and has no clothing at all.[43] Although she does not know how to read, she recites extensive verses from Scripture. Her request to Zosimas is that he tell no one of their encounter until after her death: "Pray to the Lord for me, the prodigal woman" (31; 87). She begs him to return to the Jordan in one year, during Lent, and to bring her the sacraments.

A year later, as Zosimas stands at the Jordan, she appears on the far side of the river, and a miracle occurs:

> Then he saw her making the sign of the holy cross over the Jordan—for, as he told us, there was a full moon that night—and at the same time she set foot on the water and walked on it, approaching him. (35; 89)

The parallel with Christ walking on the sea of Galilee is one of many scriptural parallels found in the Life. She receives the eucharistic sacraments from Zosimas and extracts a promise: that he return to the place of their first meeting the following year.

A year later, he returns and finds her lying dead on the ground, facing east. Having no tools to dig a grave, Zosimas addresses a huge lion which appears standing by: "Do what is necessary with your claws, so that we may return to the earth the body of the blessed woman." (39. 92) The lion digs a pit deep enough to bury the body, indicating the collusion of nature in attending to the saintly woman's burial.

On his return to his monastery Zosimas recounts his experience to the monks. He then proceeds to live out a long life at the monastery, his need for enlightenment fulfilled. The importance of an oral tradition passed down by word of mouth to the current author, Sophronios, is stressed at the end of the account:

> The monks continued to pass on these events by word of mouth from one generation to the other, presenting them as a model of ascetic life, to benefit those who wish to listen. However, to this day they have never heard that anyone else has set this story down in writing. Thus I have put down in this written narrative what I had heard by word of mouth. (41; 92)

His prayer indicates that he hopes for a reward in heaven for his truthful recounting of Mary's story and aspires to the same sanctity as the subject of his account:

> I wrote this story to the best of my ability, desiring to prefer nothing but the truth. May God, Who rewards with great gifts those who take refuge in Him, grant me as a reward the benefit of those who read this story, and may He grant it as well to the one who commanded that this work—I mean this narrative—be handed down in writing. And may God deem us worthy of the state and position of this blessed Mary, the subject of the story, along with all those individuals who ever pleased Him through their contemplation and acts. Let us, too, therefore, give glory to God, the universal King of ages, so that He may deem us worthy of mercy on the day of judgment, in the name of Jesus Christ our Lord, to Whom belongs all glory, honor and reverence forever, together with His eternal Father and the all-holy benevolent, and life-giving Spirit, now and forever and to the ages of ages. Amen.[44]

The authority of the written word is understood by this seventh-century author, and he performs this task in the knowledge that it is a holy act for which he hopes to benefit at the Last Judgment. Both author and audience thus stand to gain from the production and dissemination of the story of Mary of Egypt. Expressions of humility like those of Sophronios are a common topos in saints' lives. Preservation of an oral tradition is the motivating force of which a bishop would be well aware in writing down or dictating this account.

Although to modern readers this may seem a bizarre tale, those for whom the account was intended—monks, nuns, those hearing it read during Lent—were affected, one can imagine, in various ways. The long-standing appeal of this Life, for it was highly popular in the later Middle Ages in France, Italy, and Spain, testifies to the universal interest in paradoxical and exotic subject matter.[45] Mary was most immediately associated with the customary fasting and penitence during Lent. Her feast is celebrated on several days during the church calendar year, as mentioned above, one of which, the fifth Sunday in Lent, is known as the Sunday of Our Holy Mother Mary of Egypt.[46]

Exactly why and to whom did this Life have such great appeal? Does the account of a promiscuous woman excite particular attention? Does it offer hope for people, especially women who might have led sinful lives and thus provide a paradigm? Can those who have never experienced the desert identify with the reality of such self-imposed, solitary exile? Do listeners/readers undertake a vicarious jouney into the desert through imagining the circumstances of Mary's ascetic life? To what extent is the story legendary? and would this matter if it were so? Was part of its purpose to promote pilgrimage to Jerusalem? Does it offer an incentive for women to take control of their bodies? The fact that the account is about an ordinary woman experiencing the plight faced by many ordinary women forced into prostitution led to its special appeal to men and women throughout Christendom.

In attempting to respond to these and other questions, I turn to a group of depictions of Mary of Egypt in art dating much later than the story. While images of this ascetic woman appear in fresco decoration in churches in the Balkans and in Cappadocia in Turkey of the tenth through twelfth centuries, by far the most numerous depictions are found in medieval churches on the island of Cyprus, dating from the twelfth to the sixteenth century. The monk Zosimas appears paired with Mary of Egypt at least fourteen times in the small, post-Byzantine churches of the Troodos Mountains.[47] Mary is usually seen on the sofit or intrados of an opening, a window, door, or apse, with Zosimas facing her on the opposite sofit, as, for example, in a fresco in the church of the Panaghia Phorbiotissa at Asinou dated to 1106 (fig. 13).[48] She holds her hands up toward Zosimas on the opposite wall; he offers a chalice and is about to administer communion to her with a liturgical spoon. Mary appears as an almost skeletal figure with a ragged hair shirt about her hairy, seminude body. The hair on her head is white and disheveled, showing the effects of long neglect in a harsh environment. She is very different in appearance from the saints who appear around her at Asinou or those in the earlier wall mosaics of Sant' Apollinare Nuovo discussed above.

These depictions, in showing the hideous external results of sin and of self-deprivation, are meant as a visual deterrent. Other women who ignored society's rules, Saint Athanasia, for example, are also shown in many of these churches, but not in the extreme imagery of Mary of Egypt.[49] Women's fasting during Lent encourages an identification with her, as an enactment or mimesis of the harsh penitential regime which ultimately led to her salvation. The viewer cannot avoid being struck by Mary's appearance and empathizes with its impact on Zosimas, thereby imitating his experience and reaffirming his or her own faith. Mary's story and emaciated appearance convey a theological truth about salvation.[50]

These interpretations of Mary's story in conjunction with artistic representations allow one to better understand a prayer in the Lenten Triodion which is read at Saturday vespers before the Sunday of Saint Mary of Egypt. Her story, including that of

*Fig. 13. Saint Mary of Egypt, fresco, west face of wall
between apse and prothesis, Church of Panagia Phorbiotissa,
Asinou, Cyprus, 1106. (Photo by author)*

her salvation, is included in the yearly celebration of the Lenten cycle, read repeatedly
during the recitation of the liturgy:

> The pollution of past sins prevented thee from entering the church to see the elevation
> of the Holy Cross; but then thy conscience and the awareness of thine actions turned
> thee, O wise in God, to a better way of life. And, having looked upon the ikon of the
> blessed Maid of God, thou hast condemned all thy previous transgressions . . . and so
> hast gone with boldness to venerate the precious Cross (said twice).
>     . . . The power of thy Cross, O Christ, has worked wonders, for even the woman
> who was once a harlot chose to follow the ascetic way. Casting aside her weakness,
> bravely she opposed the devil; and having gained the prize of victory, she intercedes
> for our souls.[51]

Through visually striking transformations of their bodies sinful women become re-
cipients of God's grace, and their stories are forcefully presented to readers/viewers
as a series of paradoxes and reversals with a divine purpose.

## Associated Readings

"Life of St. Mary of Egypt," trans. Maria Kouli, 64–93, and "Life of St. Mary/Marinos,"
    trans. Nicholas Constas, 1–12, in *Holy Women of Byzantium: Ten Saints' Lives in English
    Translation,* ed. Alice-Mary Talbot (Dumbarton Oaks, 1996).
"Pelagia of Antioch," introduction and translation, in Sebastian P. Brock and Susan A. Har-
    vey, *Holy Women of the Syrian Orient* (Berkeley, 1987), 40–62.
Susan A. Harvey, "Women in Early Byzantine Hagiography: Reversing the Story," in Lynda
    L. Coon, Katherine J. Haldane, and Elisabeth W. Sommer, eds. *That Gentle Strength:
    Historical Perspectives on Women in Christianity* (Charlottesville and London, 1990).
Benedicta Ward, "St. Mary of Egypt; The Liturgical Icon of Repentance," in *Harlots of the
    Desert: A Study of Repentance in Early Monastic Sources,* Ward, ed. (Kalamazoo, 1987).

# Five

# WOMEN AND ARTISTIC PATRONAGE:
## ANICIA JULIANA

Just as ancient texts provide constant challenges of determining authorship and interpretation, so buildings and other works of art in Byzantium present an analogous problem: that of determining their sponsorship or patronage. It is particularly problematic to determine women's initiative in projects, for women were less frequently in positions of authority from which they could commission substantial works than were men. Under what circumstances were women responsible for the erection of buildings or the fabrication of various kinds of material production? and what were their objectives in such creative endeavors? How does one know of women's involvement in sponsorship, ranging from the the construction of tombs to the dedication of floor mosaics? what assumptions can one make about the commissioning of jewelry they wore? For scholars studying the Italian Renaissance, patronage has long been a fruitful avenue of pursuit, for that field is particularly rich in evidence for identifying the people and motivations behind building projects and of works of art.[1] But in Byzantium, agency is rarely recorded and even rarer in the case of women's agency than men's.

The specifics of female sponsorship are sparsely documented in the sources, although empresses, often in conjunction with emperors, and some private citizens are named in connection with particular projects. Buildings that are attributed in historical testimonies are naturally more numerous than surviving structures, making it difficult to gauge the nature of the involvement of the patron in the majority of cases. For smaller, more personal and portable possessions, we usually have only the object itself to bear witness to its origins and purpose, as in the case of ivories. Sometimes an inscription or other form of signature or monogram helps clarify an object's origins, but uncertainties always remain. In considering the broad question of female patronage, can we detect an area or areas in which women were especially active? What were the circumstances under which Byzantine women commissioned ambitious enterprises that were meant to last, like those of male patrons, works of the finest quality and craftsmanship?[2]

In this chapter, *patronage* will refer to the activity of an individual or individuals who paid for an enterprise or had a major role in its conception and design and/or attached their name(s) to it in some physical form. This is to distinguish the work of patrons from that of architects and the actual builders or craftsmen, whose names are even more rarely recorded. When I refer to a person as having built a church, I mean that person paid for it and probably had some say in its planning or design. I will also consider various media and categories of objects for which such evidence exists for private and personal sponsorship by ordinary people, for, as we will see, even ordinary citizens could participate in joint sponsorship on a modest scale. Large-scale building activity, however, normally the purview of emperors and empresses, as in the projects of Galla Placidia (see chapter 3), was also occasionally undertaken by wealthy or aristocratic women.[3] What were the concerns of female patrons and what motivated their choices in prescribing the character of an artwork or a building? Were women's reasons for sponsoring artistic endeavor different from those of men?

Motivations for sponsorship might cover a range of possibilities. Given Byzantine society's predilection for ornate, colorful, and precious surfaces and materials, it is clear that conspicuous expenditure was one way to reflect one's social and economic status. The more bright, costly, and beautifully crafted the artwork, the more important the associated individual(s). Furthermore, beautifully crafted artworks were valued and admired by all categories in Byzantine society, rich and poor, men and women, young and old. A creative project was a contribution to society and therefore linked to the patron's place in society; the more visible the commission, the more powerful and elevated the patron's position would appear.

Just as it was possible to pay for a major and very visible project if a patron was very wealthy, it was possible to pay a great deal for a luxury object that would be seen only by a selected few. In the case of a less visible or public person, fewer people would appreciate a small foundation or gift to a church made by, say, a provincial landowner, but this did not mean the patron would not gain in local status. Patronage must therefore be considered in relation to its intended viewer or public, for only through the reception and acknowledgment of a patron's commission was status conveyed to the individual.

Responsibility was inherent in the Byzantine system, as it was in ancient Greece and Rome, to provide the public with amenities which connoted not only the importance, but also the generosity and social consciousness of a particular emperor, empress, or court official. Local reputation, likewise, could be enhanced by donations of governors, local officials, or even ordinary people or groups of ordinary individuals, through patronage of material objects that would be seen and admired by the community. Female initiatives involving small-scale or locally significant objects or artworks are indicative of the social role of more ordinary women.

Lavish display could also reflect the piety of the individual or collective group, as we deduce from the many large-scale projects in architecture and mosaic decoration undertaken by emperors and the church in late antiquity and early Byzantium.[4] The equation between preciousness and holiness, an ideology of aesthetics, extends throughout Byzantine culture. Personal piety, vows, and prayers of thanks are often the stated motivation behind individual donations or creations which are dedicated to God or the saints. The more beautiful and expensive imperial commissions affirmed the ruler's relationship with God and position as his representative on earth. The custom of dedicating churches and ecclesiastical complexes such as monasteries to a saint thus enables the individual patron to build an association with that holy person. In return, it was believed, the saint conveyed his or her holy power to the donor by interceding on behalf of that individual before God. It is therefore not unusual to discover religious motivations in the sponsorship of beautiful structures and decorations.

Religious piety and social status stand behind examples of patronage by men and women, but what are the primary concerns behind female artistic patronage? To respond to this question I will first consider examples of women's roles in connection with liturgical silver or silver objects manufactured for use in churches. Jewelry associated with marriage can also be connected in some cases with the sponsorship of women. Mosaics decorating the floors and walls of churches were often paid for by families and individuals, including women who are named. Cases exist in which buildings associated with women, both standing and no longer extant but recorded, carried messages revealing the intents of their donors, messages which take various symbolic forms, as in the case of Anicia Juliana.

The case study for this chapter will focus on a Byzantine princess, Anicia Juliana, who lived ca. 461 to 528, and two projects she sponsored for which evidence survives: a large church and a deluxe edition of a book. Both were produced owing to her initiative and financing, and her personal role is clearly documented through dedicatory texts, inscriptions, and a portrait. A synthesis of textual, archaeological, and artistic evidence elucidates the nature and meaning of this patron's activity. Anicia Juliana was a wealthy, influential woman with taste, pride, ambition, and a sense of religious duty. She used her money in ways appropriate to her status, but not without risk, for she was caught in the dangerous web of sixth-century politics. I will begin the discussion of women's patronage, however, with smaller objects.

Portable objects offer some typical ways of establishing patronage. Patrons usually identify themselves and state their aims by inscribing their donations with their names and some kind of explanation or comment. Such is the case, for example, with a gilt silver plate from Tomis on the Black Sea, on exhibit at the Hermitage Museum in Leningrad, dating to ca. 518. In a band around the inside of the plate is inscribed in Latin, "This plate was renovated from the old [that is, out of old objects or from old materials] by Paternus, our venerable bishop. Amen."[5] The bishop Paternus tells us he commissioned the plate as part of a process of renovation, perhaps involving recasting of older, damaged pieces of church silver. This plate was meant to be used and seen in the celebration of the liturgy, as a paten to hold the eucharistic bread. The bishop's generous gesture would have been highly visible to his congregation. The appearance of such inscribed names with accompanying explanations is usually the only way of attributing patronage, while the dating and place of production are attested through silver stamps.[6]

The patrons of buildings are often recorded in texts read at the building's dedication or in panegyrical or poetic texts describing the foundations, as in Procopius's mid-sixth-century treatise *On the Buildings*. In book 1 he describes at length the emperor Justinian's ambitious project, the church of Hagia Sophia, beginning with the following: "The Emperor, disregarding all considerations of expense, hastened to begin construction, and raised craftsmen from the whole world."[7] Procopius makes the point that expense was no object for the emperor in reconstructing the empire's Great Church, destroyed in the Nika riots of 532. The author also states that Justinian was personally involved in the project and goes on to describe in lofty, archaizing prose the structure and its furnishings. The church still stands, allowing us to correlate Procopius's description with the building itself. The monograms of Justinian and Theodora appear carved in roundels on the front faces of the marble capitals of the columns, on both main and gallery levels, identifying and repeatedly reminding the viewer of those responsible for the building of the edifice.[8] The patrons' piety, generosity, and power are recorded in texts and engraved on the building's fabric.

In other cases the patrons' names are set in mosaics, painted in frescoes, or carved in stone in inscriptions on the exterior or interior of a building. Sometimes city gates or other civic monuments, such as the Obelisk of Theodosius in Constantinople, still exhibit inscriptions crediting specific individuals with their construction; in other cases, the inscriptions have been recorded but the monument has disappeared. In yet others, a major monument partially survives, but there is no conclusive evidence for its patronage or date, as in the fascinating case of the Imperial Palace Floor Mosaic in Constantinople. Circumstantial evidence is provided by coin finds, brick stamps, and pottery; in addition, stylistic and iconographic analyses of elements of the decoration offer clues to the dating and thus clues to the identity of the patron.[9]

With these general considerations in mind, I will consider some examples of female patronage or involvement, starting with liturgical silver, sometimes referred to as church treasure. Much of this silver was part of hoards discovered by accident in Syria and Turkey and then sold illegally to collectors and dealers; in some fortunate cases the treasures remain largely intact. Such hoards represent the accumulated wealth of a church, hidden away at some point in order to keep it from falling into the hands of invaders and then never reclaimed. The accumulated silver objects of a given church could be melted down in times of crisis and then restored or renewed at a later time, thus making this category of objects a kind of liquid wealth whose exact worth was calculated in terms of the weight of the vessels. Inscribed silver objects made for use in church services in the early Byzantine period, of which we have a large number, still speak to today's observer, just as they were intended to speak to their beholders at the time of their production, about the hopes and intentions of those who had them made. Sometimes women were the dedicatees and sometimes they were the dedicators, as we will see in the following examples.

The Sion treasure, a collection of silver church furnishings and implements, is a rare survivor from the third quarter of the sixth century.[10] Discovered in southern Turkey, it is now divided between the archaeological museum in Istanbul and the Dumbarton Oaks Collection in Washington, D.C. The portion on display at Dumbarton Oaks has been beautifully restored and comprises the most impressive group of associated Byzantine church objects on display in this country. Among the liturgical vessels and implements are monumental patens, chalices, amphorae, censers, book covers, and a variety of lighting furnishings: candelabrae and standing and hanging lamps. All are inscribed with names and short explanations of the givers' intentions. For example, a large paten with cusped border is engraved in large block letters with the inscription, "For the memory and repose of John, of God-loving memory, and Procle his daughter."[11] Some unidentified individual dedicated this paten to John and his daughter, Procle, in order that a tangible reminder of these deceased persons would persist in the church community where it was used. An openwork lamp is inscribed, "For the memory and repose of the most blessed Himeria."[12] Again, a dedication to a deceased woman is anonymous. Another paten is inscribed, "For the memory of Maria the Illustrious"; her title, *clarissima,* originally referred to the wives and daughters of men of senatorial rank and indicates that Maria was of high birth and social status.[13] A silver-clad book cover is inscribed, "For the memory and repose of Prinkipios, deacon, and Stephane and Leontia," perhaps a wife and daughter."[14] Of the twenty names of individuals which appear inscribed on the objects, five are of women. The objects offer unique insights into the community in which they originated.

Objects such as these which are inscribed in memory of one or more individuals who have died were probably donated by a surviving family member, a person who is sometimes but not always identified.[15] The other common type of inscriptions refer to the living, for example, "Eutichianus, most humble bishop, presents this to the Lord for the forgiveness of his sins."[16] In such a case it is clear not only who was responsible, but also that the patron, Eutichianus, was alive when his gift was offered to the church. Four clerical donors and a bishop are documented as having presented most of the objects to the Church of Holy Sion. No women are cited explicitly as donors of the Sion Treasure, and we are left wondering how often women bought and dedicated spectacular silver treasure.

Families from country villages, on the other hand, were responsible for many of the donations in another treasure, the Kaper Koraon Treasure, consisting of approxi-

*Fig. 14. Riha Paten, silver, Dumbarton Oaks Collection, Washington, D.C., 577 (Courtesy Dumbarton Oaks, Byzantine Photograph and Fieldwork Archives, Washington, D.C.)*

mately two dozen objects originating around the village of Kaper Koraon in Syria and now located primarily in the Walters Art Gallery in Baltimore but also at Dumbarton Oaks in Washington.[17] Here, four or five families evidently gave silver implements to their church over the years between 540 and 640. Only four of the fifty individuals mentioned in inscriptions have titles; the rest were middle-class property owners, merchants, and artisans who contributed piecemeal toward overall costs of objects.

This manner of subscription donors has been identified not only for liturgical silver but also for components of church decoration, such as mosaics and columns. In these cases a large number of individuals each donated a relatively small amount toward the costs of the overall project.[18] For a modest object such as a silver chalice weighing one pound, the cost of the silver would have been equivalent to the purchase of a section of mosaic pavement, a small book, or a camel, indicating that even the poorest member of a community could donate some part of a liturgical object.[19] Women's names appear frequently in the sometimes long inscriptions on the liturgical objects in the Kaper Koraon Treasure. One of the most elaborately decorated gilded and nielloed patens, the Riha Paten, in the Dumbarton Oaks Collection, dates to around 577 (fig. 14). On the inner surface is a relief depicting the Communion of the Apostles, and around the flat rim is an inscription:

"For the repose of the soul of Sergia, daugher of John, and of Theodosius, and for the salvation of Megas and of Nonnous and of their children."[20]

Sergia and Nonnous were women who belonged to a family whose members joined forces to make up the necessary funds for the paten. The inscription is ambiguous as to whether Megas and Nonnous are alive and were the sponsors. Through such inscriptions on pieces found in the same localized area scholars have been able to reconstruct a genealogical tree for the names and relationships derived from the inscriptions on the objects in the treasure.[21]

*Fig. 15. Gold pectoral with Annunciation, from Constantinople (?), Berlin State Museums, Germany, early seventh century. (Copyright, Antikensammlung, Staatliche Museen zu Berlin, Preussischer Kulturbesitz)*

Other objects in the Kaper Koraon treasure were dedicated by women. A gilded silver flask in the Walters Art Gallery is inscribed, "In fulfillment of a vow and for the salvation of Megale, and of her children and her nephews and for the repose of Heliodoros and Akakios."[22] Megale vowed that she would dedicate a vessel in her church for some unknown reason, perhaps her recovery from a disease or the recovery of a loved one. A chalice now in the Boston Museum of Fine Arts is inscribed around the rim, "Having vowed, Sara offered this chalice to the First Martyr."[23] The chalice was commissionsed by a woman, but, again, we cannot know why she dedicated it to Saint Stephen. An armband with medallions dating to the sixth century is inscribed, "Holy, Holy, Holy, Lord"; "Health"; and "Theotoke, help Anna. Grace."[24] Anna either wore or dedicated her personal ornament as a form of prayer to the Theotokos, or Virgin Mary, perhaps for her health in childbirth or some other danger which she was about to encounter or perhaps simply as a wish for protection. Jewelry, amulets, silks, and other items of adornment worn by women had symbolic or protective meanings too.[25]

Like liturgical silver, women's jewelry, which also survives in some abundance, gives us information about its wearers and originators if it is inscribed. While the problem of agency is impossible to resolve in most cases, it is still informative to consider the issues reflected in inscribed pieces. A spectacular gold pectoral now in the Berlin state museums was part of a treasure found in Egypt and is dated to the early seventh century (fig. 15).[26] Set between terminals of the neckring is an assemblage of twelve gold coins in which is set a medallion with the bust of an emperor. Inscribed in Greek around this portrait is, "Lord, help the wearer"; the words for *wearer* are in the feminine gender. A pendant medallion set in a broad openwork roundel shows the Annunciation to the Virgin Mary on the obverse, and the Miracle at Cana on the reverse inscribed "first of the signs." This large, brilliant piece of jewelry was worn by a woman, although it cannot be ascertained whether a woman commissioned it. The scenes on the pendant medallion are consistent with examples of Christian iconography depicting events from New Testament and apocryphal accounts. They had special meaning for a woman, in connection with the themes of divine motherhood,

Fig. 16. Gold marriage belt, Dumbarton Oaks Collection, Washington, D.C., late sixth to early seventh century. (Courtesy Dumbarton Oaks, Byzantine Photograph and Fieldwork Archives, Washington, D.C.)

angelic protection or grace, or miraculous intervention by Christ. New Testament scenes also had protective powers of association with sites in the Holy Land where they took place, as pilgrim artifacts indicate.[27] Christian beliefs regarding the divine protection of women are behind the anonymously commissioned gold pectoral.

More specifically related to marriage, a gold marriage belt of the late sixth or early seventh century in the Dumbarton Oaks Collection has an inscription similar to that on the pectoral.[28] A series of twenty-one roundels with portraits of pagan deities, identified as Dionysus, Hermes, Asclepius, and Poseidon, connects two large, hollow roundels showing a man and a woman on either side of Christ, who joins their right hands (fig. 16). The identical inscriptions on the two large roundels read, "From God, concord, grace, and health." This luxurious piece of marriage jewelry was probably worn by the bride after being presented as a gift to her and expresses the wish or prayer to God for matrimonial harmony, felicity, and health. The marriage ceremony is depicted with Christ rather than a priest performing the "joining of right hands," or *dextrarum iunctio*, symbolizing the wish for divine protection of the marriage. The unusual inclusion of pagan gods in a piece meant for Christian usage denotes that the ancient gods still provided symbolic protection in accordance with a set of earlier but not yet entirely exhausted beliefs. Health, as in the armband mentioned above, is a prime preoccupation, for illness and complications associated with childbirth were the greatest threats to mature women's lives. Like the pectoral, the belt is anonymous in its sponsorship. Because it also was made to be worn by a woman it was commissioned by someone sharing a woman's interests.

A similar set of interests is expressed by a marriage ring on which appears a scene comparable to the marriage belt's joining-of-right-hands. On the bezel of an octagonal ring in the Dumbarton Oaks Collection dated to the seventh century is a tiny engraved scene inlaid with niello of Christ and the Virgin Mary, who raise their arms to bless the groom at the left and bride at the right; below the group is inscribed "concord" (fig. 17).[29] The cusped bezel with its blessing scene is set on the eighth side

*Fig. 17. Octagonal marriage ring, gold with niello, from Syria-Palestine, Dumbarton Oaks Collection, Washington, D.C., seventh century. (Courtesy Dumbarton Oaks, Byzantine Photograph and Fieldwork Archives, Washington, D.C.)*

of an octagonal ring with seven abbreviated scenes of the life of Christ engraved on its facets. Iconographically the scenes may be identified with sites in the Holy Land which were visited by pilgrims, for similar representations appear on pilgrims' souvenirs, such as ampullae, and on the Fieschi-Morgan Reliquary in the Metropolitan Museum in New York.[30] The scenes are thought to have an apotropaic function and thus express the wish for divine protection. A prayer is inscribed around the edge of the bezel: "Lord, help Thy servants, Peter and Theodote," and on the edges of the shank is an inscription from John 14:27: "My peace I leave with you; my peace I give unto you." These inscriptions complement the evocative visual messages of the incarnation scenes of reassurance and of hope for divine protection and salvation. The amuletic quality of these assembled visual and inscribed messages would grant the ring's wearer, whether it was Peter or his wife, Theodote, a divinely protected marriage; it is unclear which of them commissioned the ring.

Two other rings at Dumbarton Oaks also carry inscriptions asking for help for their female wearers. A gold ring with an openwork hoop has an inscription between its two borders: "Lord, help Mary" and carries an amethyst in a lotus flower setting.[31] Another gold ring, also dating to the seventh century, has a flat bezel with an engraved inscription in reverse: "Mother of God, help Helen." Another similar ring in the Louvre Museum in Paris has the following inscription on the band: "Mother of God, come to the aid of your servant Giora" (feminine ending).[32] Such rings were worn by women and could well have been commissioned by them. These rings, unlike church silver, were constantly visible, part of everyday life, and made of durable materials. They afford an intimate glimpse of the beliefs women invested in small objects, in particular hopes for health and divine protection.

Further examples of commissions in which women were involved and which in some cases they may have initiated are represented by floor mosaics. In most such cases the buildings have long disappeared, but their floors have survived and been excavated intact. A group of mosaic floors in Jordan has abundant inscriptions worked into the decorative patterns and records families and individuals responsible for their production; in a number of instances even the names of the mosaicists survive.

Mosaics have a long history of usage to embellish floors, usually of important buildings, because of the expense of materials and installation. Figural mosaics appeared on the floors of dining rooms in palatial structures in the late fourth-century-

BCE residences at Pella, the Hellenistic capital of Macedon in northern Greece. The tradition continued through Roman times, the most spectacular ensembles being those at Antioch and in the towns of North Africa, which date to the second through fourth centuries. In some cases, the name of the owner of the house is known or the patron is named in inscriptions in the mosaics. Numerous churches were also given mosaic floors around this time, many of which survive in North Africa, the Near East, and the Holy Land. Inscriptions in Greek or Latin sometimes identify their artists or patrons but more often label the subject matter.[33] In early Christian floors, inscriptions were used primarily to identify the donors; sometimes a group of subscription sponsors is identifiable through these inscriptions placed prominently within the designs.

An exceptionally rich group of mosaic floors survives in churches in Jordan, and many preserve dedicatory inscriptions in which women figure.[34] For example, in the Church of the Apostles in Madaba, a roundel depicting a personification of the sea appears in the center of the nave surrounded by a field of pairs of affronted, beribboned birds. Around the edge of the roundel appears the following inscription in Greek: "O Lord God who has made the heavens and the earth, give life to Anastasius, to Thomas and Theodora. This is the work of Salaman the mosaicist."[35] Thomas and Theodora may be the children of Anastasius, or they may be a married couple related to him. Theodora was part of the group commissioning the mosaic, the artist of which they were proud to name. Also in Madaba, a chapel of the Twal family has an inscription in Greek on the step between nave and chancel: "With the offering of your servant Aitha, this holy place was paved with mosaics."[36] In this case a woman was solely responsible for the decoration of the mosaic floors.

In many cases women are named in the prayers inscribed in mosaic in the separate portions of a building in which they sponsored the mosaic floors. For example, the mosaics of the south side-aisle in the Church of the Holy Martyrs Lot and Procopius in the Mount Nebo region in modern-day Jordan, dating to the mid–sixth century, mention three women in their dedicatory inscriptions.[37] At the center of the nave in a composition of fruit trees, animals, and altars is the Greek inscription, "Then they shall offer calves upon Your altar [Psalm 51:21]. Lord have mercy on the lowly Epiphania." In the south aisle of the same church is a *tabula ansata,* or framed insert, at the end of a long mosaic carpet of leaves in diagonal squares with the inscription, "O Saint Lot, receive the prayer of Rome and Porphyria and Mary, your servants." These examples are just a few of many mosaic ensembles, mostly of the fifth to seventh centuries, which record family and individual dedications in which women play a prominent role as patrons.

Women also appear prominently along with their families in the wall mosaics of the Church of Saint Demetrius in Thessaloniki, Greece, built in the mid–fifth century. In the spandrels of the north aisle was a series of depictions of saints and donors, which now survives only in photographs and watercolors because they were destroyed in a fire in 1917.[38] This once-splendid series can be dated probably some time in the late fifth or sixth century. The mosaics have not been sufficiently studied for their implications about women's roles and patronage in the church.

The scenes in the spandrels include episodes involving the child, Maria, who appears with her mother, perhaps offered as a votive for her cure or protection by the saint. In one scene the mother holds up her baby girl to Saint Demetrius, who is seated before his ciborium and who gestures toward images of Christ and the Virgin Mary as if conveying the mother's prayers to these divine personages. The child is swaddled as a baby and has a cross inscribed on her forehead, as she does throughout the series. The mother wears a long maphorium, or mantle, with a veil covering her head. In the adjacent spandrel the mother appears again with the child, now grown larger, and supplicates the Virgin Mary, who appears standing between two angels and who in turn addresses a medallion portrait of Saint Demetrius. In a third scene, the mother presents her child to a standing figure of Saint Demetrius, to whom they hold out votive candles. And in a fourth the child appears with her parents and two other women standing before the saint; the child, now clad in a dark mantle, offers the saint two doves, perhaps indicating she has died and visits the saint in Paradise or that she has been otherwise dedicated to God. Perhaps she is shown with her mother and female family members as a young novice taking the veil in thanks for her healing by the saint. A segment just to the right of this final scene has been too badly damaged to decipher.

The series appears among isolated scenes of prayer or commemoration, scenes in which the donors of the mosaics are sometimes identified, but no such inscriptions explain this mysterious series. Because the mother appears so prominently with the child Maria she might logically be identified as the donor of the series, except that we do not know her name. The mosaics, which may be read from left to right, perhaps were offered periodically over a span of years and served as a witness to her donations to the Church of Saint Demetrius. The mosaics probably commemorate gifts to the church beyond and in addition to donations of the mosaics themselves, donations made initially in the hope of securing the saint's protection or healing, and the mosaics given in gratitude for her child's safety up until her dedication to God or her death. Only a very wealthy woman or family represented by women, for their are a number of other accompanying women shown in the series, could have afforded such extensive and expensive mosaic projects. In the absence of any but short identifying inscriptions Maria's story may never be known, but the mosaics are indicative of the patronage of a woman or family of women who wished to have their concern for a female child who is marked as God's durably and prominently recorded.

A few surviving or partly surviving building projects were associated with women or their sponsorship in the fourth and fifth centuries, as we have already noted, especially buildings with funerary associations. The Mausoleum of Helena in Rome, built between 315 and 327 still bears her name, but it is of uncertain origin; the *Liber Pontificalis* records it as the commission of her son, Constantine.[39] The Mausoleum of Constantina, daughter of Constantine, now known as the Church of Santa

Costanza, on the Via Nomentana outside Rome is a similar case.[40] According to the most recent scholarship on the buildings at the site, there was originally a large basilica dedicated to Saint Agnes and next to it a baptistery; these were commissioned by Constantine's daughter, Constantina, around CE 330, near her villa on the Via Nomentana. Constantina is named as the patron of the complex in an acrostic inscription which was once over the door of the basilica.[41]

The baptistery was replaced after Constantina's death in 354 by the present mausoleum, in 360 or 361. It was probably commissioned by the emperor, Julian the Apostate, to be the tomb of his wife, Helena, younger sister of Constantina and was intended from the start to be the burial place of both women.[42] Portraits of two women appear in two segments of the preserved mosaic decoration of the annular vault, surrounded by elaborate fields of randomly scrolling grapevines, harvesting putti, and other harvest imagery (see pl. 4).[43] A porphyry sarcophagus taken from the mausoleum also bears scrolling grapevines and harvesting putti, confirming both its connection with the decorative program and its origin as an imperial commission, for porphyry was used only by the imperial house. Thus, although the mausoleum's association with Constantina and Helena is likely and the decorative imagery is funerary, with both pagan and Christian connotations, there is no evidence that Constantina paid for the mausoleum. There is, however, evidence that she financed the now-ruined Church of Sant' Agnese.

In the same tradition as Constantina, Galla Placidia's building projects in Rome and Ravenna (see chapter 3) were some of the most lavish of the time, and she was was known both for her activities as a builder of churches and sponsor of their adornment. Unfortunately, none survive except the Mausoleum of Galla Placidia.[44] Other lost products of female patronage are too numerous to name. Among them are the churches and monasteries sponsored by Olympias and Melania the Younger in the early fifth century and the numerous foundations sponsored by the Augusta Athenais Eudocia in the mid–fifth century in Jerusalem and the Holy Land, notably the church and monastery of Saint Stephen where she was buried. Palaces were built by the Augusta Pulcheria in the fifth century and by Theodora in the sixth as places of retreat or relaxation, but none of these survive to substantiate the textual references or give some impression of the character of the buildings that these women's imperial taste and means could produce. Noteworthy exceptions, however, are attributable to Anicia Juliana, an aristocratic patron of the arts whose role can be amply demonstrated.

## Anicia Juliana

The imperial princess Anicia Juliana, born in Constantinople around 461, resided in a palace that had belonged to her father, Olybrius, in a district of the city named after him, "ta Olybriou."[45] She was wealthy and distinguished, for Olybrius had been emperor in the West in 472, and her mother, Placidia, was the daughter of the emperor Valentinian III and hence a descendant of the house of Theodosius I (see genealogical table on page 317). She would have had the best education available and was also, no doubt, well read and highly literate. Because of her imperial lineage she held the title at the imperial court of *Patricia,* which meant she was a member of the elaborate ceremonies surrounding the emperor and empress in their palace. She must have had what we would consider today high public visibility.

In 478 Anicia Juliana married the general Areobindus, whose military campaigns on the eastern frontier aided in buffering the empire from the Persians. A movement to make him emperor in 512 failed. Their son, named Flavius Anicius Olybrius after his grandfather, achieved the high civil honor of being named consul when still very young, in 491. He married Irene, the niece of the emperor Anastasius I, and they had two children, both girls, whose names are unknown. Juliana's pride in such a family would be understandable, and she used her great wealth accordingly. Her most notable civic role continued a tradition going back to her maternal great-grandmother, Athenais Eudocia, wife of the emperor Theodosius II. Like Eudocia, Juliana was a devout Orthodox Christian and a builder of churches, as ambitious and costly an undertaking then as it would be today or at any time.[46]

The time in which Anicia Juliana lived combined intense Christian religiosity with traditional Roman values, for these were still the early centuries of Christianity. A staunch Chalcedonian, Juliana helped end the Akakian schism between Rome and Constantinople in 519 through her alliance with the Palestinian holy man Sabas and their joint correspondence with Pope Hormisdas.[47] These times also witnessed crass efforts to achieve upward mobility. The new rulers, although Christian, were from a class different from the old Roman nobility to which Anicia Juliana belonged. Justin I and his nephew Justinian I belonged to this new generation of untitled autocrats from a provincial peasant background. During Justin I's rule, from 518 to 527, Justinian wielded the real power behind the throne and at his death became emperor. Like Justin, Justinian rose by means of the military, a good education, cleverness, and, when necessary, violence.[48] The aristocratic and by now aging Anicia Juliana no doubt both envied and resented these men's ascent to power (and that of their equally untitled wives) in the second and third decades of the sixth century, probably thinking her husband or her son or she herself would have made a more fitting ruler. Justinian likely thought this wealthy old woman's church building a challenge to his imperial supremacy, for only the most powerful members of society took on this public role—especially when she built her final church.

From 524 to 527 Anicia Juliana sponsored the building of what was probably the most lavish ecclesiastical foundation to appear in the imperial capital up to that time, the church of Hagios Polyeuktos.[49] This church, which housed a long carved inscription praising Anicia Juliana and her family, confronted the young Justinian with a problem. Who would raise greater monuments to the glory of God, this woman or himself? Of course we now know that after becoming sole emperor in 527 Justinian proved to be one of the greatest builders in history. It is thought that he commissioned his greatest work, the cathedral of Hagia Sophia in Constantinople, built during 532–37, as a response to Anicia Juliana's challenge.[50] But she did not live to see her church outdone by Hagia Sophia. She died within a year of the completion of Hagios Polyeuktos, probably in 528.

Given the evidence which has recently come to light, I would argue that her magnificent church was built not primarily to commemorate her family, fame, and status or to demonstrate her piety and generosity or to rival Justinian—all of which may have been the case. Her primary motivation in building this church adjacent to her palace was to provide her final resting place, through which she intended to claim an enduring place in history, to achieve immortality. The beautifully crafted poetic inscription in the church stressing her lineage and pride and the great variety of Hellenizing and Persian-inspired sculptural motifs of its ornate decoration strongly indicate that this was her aim.[51] Anicia Juliana and her accomplishments represent a case of female patronage worth examining within the context of her time.

Miraculously, the Byzantine Empire's principal church, Hagia Sophia, now more than fourteen hundred years old, has survived dozens of earthquakes and fires which periodically affect the city of Constantinople. Changed into a mosque with added minarets after the Ottoman conquest of Byzantium in 1453, the great building has endured. In its present state as a museum, it still reflects its premier status in both cultures. But this was not the only magnificent church in sixth-century Constantinople, difficult as it is to imagine buildings which have disappeared, and even though surviving evidence reveals they must have rivaled those that remain. Only a disciplined imagination can reconstruct another prominent building, Anicia Juliana's church of Hagios Polyeuktos. It collapsed in an earthquake in the twelfth century and is known today only through its archaeological remains, excavated only some forty years ago.

In 1960 an extraordinary discovery was made in the heart of Istanbul. Bulldozers preparing the ground for a new city hall in the Saraçhane district started encountering massive foundations of brick and stone and blocks of carved marble. Soon archaeologists were excavating the site in an effort to determine the building's identity. Architectural fragments of cornices, moldings, piers, and columns emerged, some carved with exotic designs and others bearing fragments of a Greek inscription. Ihor Ševčenko recognized in these fragments parts of inscribed words that were part of a long metrical poem preserved in an anthology of Greek inscriptions, the *Greek Anthology*. As the poem stated, it was carved on a church dedicated to the martyr-saint Polyeuktos, a foundation sponsored by the princess Anicia Juliana. Although references to a church of Hagios Polyeuktos appeared in a number of Byzantine texts, its location was unknown. Recognition that the inscribed blocks were part of the same poem as preserved in the *Greek Anthology* meant that church and poem could now be reintegrated and studied. The discovery also created a rare opportunity to more fully understand Anicia Juliana's role as a patron of church building and the arts.[52]

As excavations continued under Martin Harrison through the 1960s, the extraordinary, even revolutionary, nature of the church was gradually revealed. In scale it was

*Fig. 18. Peacock niche with grapevines in spandrel, marble, sculptural fragment from Church of Hagios Polyeuktos, Istanbul Archaeological Museum, Istanbul, Turkey, 525–27. (Photo courtesy Meganne Raines)*

huge, almost square, 51.45 m long by 51.90 m wide. Its tall foundations elevated the main floor level 5 m above ground level. Underneath the sanctuary was a large crypt with access via a long passage under the nave.[53] Fragments of cornices and moldings carrying highly abstract designs resembling motifs found in Sassanian Persian sculpture were found where they had fallen nearly a millennium ago. Stylized fruit trees, date palms, pomegranate trees, and palmettes appeared on capitals. Strapwork and lattice-like designs covered pier capitals in a style otherwise unknown in Byzantium. Columns inlaid with semiprecious stones—amethists, turquoise, lapis lazuli—had supported the ciborium canopy over the altar. Numerous mosaic fragments indicated that the nonsculpted surfaces had been decorated with figural compositions on a gold background in the apse and with abstract designs on other surfaces, the predominating colors of the mosaics being dark blues and greens.[54]

Most extraordinary among the remains were blocks of the entablature with its carved inscription. These were covered with a deeply undercut design consisting of a twisting vine stem with grapes and grape leaves carved in minute detail, showing even the veins of the leaves in delicate relief (fig. 18). These naturalistic elements appeared in conjunction with bold letters of the inscription carved in high relief, an enormous extravagence, since relief carving is far costlier than engraving. Many fragments of the inscription came to light where they had fallen from the entablature of the building when it collapsed. The irregular shapes and turnings of the inscribed blocks indicated that the long, seventy-six-line poem had run in a band clockwise around the entire interior of the church, starting at the southeast corner of the nave. Scholia in the *Greek Anthology* recorded that sections of the poem also appeared in the atrium and outside the entrance gate.[55]

Inside the church the poem ran in a band along the entablature, which contained a series of niches. Inside the niches stood carved peacocks, with raised or spread tails, the remains of which were found on the site. A number of carved peacock bodies were also excavated, and it was clear from their broken supports how they occupied each niche (see figs. 18 and 19). It was determined by the excavators that there were originally thirty peacocks around the interior of the church. Pigment traces were discovered on enough of the fragments to reconstruct the original appearance of birds

*Fig. 19. Peacock body, marble, sculptural fragment from Church of Hagios Polyeuktos, Istanbul Archaeological Museum, Istanbul, Turkey, 525–27. (After R. M. Harrison, Temple for Byzantium, fig. 91)*

and surrounding vine scrolls and inscriptions. The backgrounds of vines and letters were painted in a bright blue made of ground lapis lazuli, and the birds and feathers were colored in green, blue, and gold. Each bird wore a necklace carved in relief, had inlaid green glass eyes, and held in its beak a chain for suspension of some object, perhaps a lamp. These life-size birds must have made a striking impression as they confronted the viewer from their perches around the church's main interior. In order to decipher the messages of these singular decorative motifs and their connection with the patron I will consider their iconography.[56]

In antiquity the peacock was associated with Hera, the haughty wife of Zeus. Once Hera had one of Zeus's paramours, Io, turned into a heifer, and set Argus, a monstrous dog with many eyes, to guard her. When Ares killed the beast, its eyes were said to have been made part of the design of a peacock's tail. Peacocks traditionally symbolized royalty and, in later Roman times, the apotheosis of empresses. Early Christian art took over the peacock to symbolize the beauty of God's creation. The bird also refers to nature's powers of renewal, because it loses and regrows its feathers every spring and thus became a symbol of resurrection and immortality.[57] In Christian tombs and on sarcophagi the peacock was frequently depicted as a symbol of eternal life, as on the Sarcophagus of Constantina in the Vatican museum of around 350, on the wall of a painted tomb in Nicaea,[58] and on funerary sculpture in Egypt.[59] Examples show the peacock served as a Christian symbol of eternal life.

When peacocks appear with grapevines, as they do in the entablature of Hagios Polyeuktos, one might suspect a calculated juxtaposition of motifs with mutually reinforcing meanings. Grapevines are associated in ancient art with the god of wine, Dionysus. His revels, frequently depicted on Greek vases, are surrounded by grapevines, and therefore any depiction of grapevines is usually associated with Bacchic pursuits. Like peacocks, however, grapevines acquired Christian meaning and were appropriated as one way to refer symbolically to the wine of the eucharist or to the renewal of life in Christ.[60] For example, grapevines surround a fourth-century mosaic composition of Christ-helios in the vault of the Tomb of the Julii in Rome.[61] Portraits of deceased women in the Mausoleum of Santa Costanza are also surrounded with a field of grapevines, harvesters, and scenes of grape pressing (see pl. 4), and grape-harvesting imagery also appears frequently on early Christian sarcophagi, such as the Three Shepherds Sarcophagus in the Vatican museum.[62] Peacocks appear in a field of spiraling grapevines on the sixth-century sarcophagus of Archbishop Theodore in Ravenna.[63]

The grapevine is a polyvalent image used in literature to allegorize other concepts, for example, in the patristic writings on the Hexaemeron by Basil the Great in the fourth century. Basil expounds on the passage in John 15:1, "Christ is the vine." He states, "Human souls . . . are Christ's vine, those which He has surrounded with the security that His precepts give, as if with a fence and with the guard of His angels."[64] In this way the vine becomes a metaphor not only for the soul but also for the church. Seen in the setting of a large church, extensive decoration that employs peacocks and grapevines conveys a funerary theme of immortality as its principal message. Related messages and content are found in another luxury medium, an illuminated manuscript, now located in the Austrian national library in Vienna.

Until the discovery of the remains of Hagios Polyeuktos, the prime association with Anicia Juliana was a handsome, lavishly illustrated volume of the the writings of the ancient doctor Dioscurides.[65] His first-century treatise *De Materia Medica* (On medicinal substance[s]) instructs how to utilize plants, herbs, and roots for medicinal purposes. The work was a basic medical and pharmacological resource in late antiquity and Byzantine times; the Vienna edition has been dated to 512. That it was a deluxe edition is clear in its size: the pages measure 38 by 33 cm, and the book contains some 498 painted illustrations of plants and animals, including 5 frontispieces. Bound into this luxurious book are ancient works on animals and insects, including a treatise on birds known as the "Ornithiaka." Like the treatise on plants, it is a work of scientific accuracy and analytic intent, the oldest existing guide to the birds.

One of the frontispieces of this volume, folio 6 verso, is the oldest surviving dedication page in a bound book, and it depicts the patron, Anicia Juliana (see pl. 5). In a ceremonial portrait, Juliana, clad in the golden gown of the Patricia and holding a diptych, sits on a golden throne flanked by female personifications labeled in Greek: Magnanimity holds gold coins on her lap, and Prudence a bound book; these personifications allegorically tell of Juliana's generosity and her wise conduct. A winged putto holding an open book onto which the princess scatters gold coins is labeled, "Desire of the Woman devoted to Building," and another small figure labeled "Gratitude of the Arts" bows deeply. In these two allegorical figures further aspects of Juliana's agenda are defined: her dedication to building projects and her patronage of the arts. The portrait with its accompanying labeled figures creates a composite image of Juliana's principal role in Byzantine society, but the messages of the dedication page continue.

On close examination, the rich, deep blue field has an octagonal frame made of an intertwined, twisted rope of applied gold leaf, and within it on a narrow black band is a metrical inscription in tiny Greek letters. In the spandrels formed by the rope where it meets an outer circle of rope are impressionistically painted miniature scenes of little figures engaged in various activities against a blue ground. In the magenta fields in the tips of the star are eight gold letters spelling the name IOULIANA, Juliana. While the group in the middle of the composition depicts visually and allegorically Juliana's character and preoccupations, the rope frame with its octagonal inscription and scenes tells us more about her specific role. The Greek inscription begins in the segment above Juliana's head, and the eight lines of the poem run around the octagon:

> Behold with all good praises, Queen, Honoratis hymns you and praises you. The magnanimity of the Anicii, of which family you are a member, goes forth into all the world to speak your praises. For you built the church of the Lord, towering beautifully on high.[66]

The poem is an acrostic, the first word of each successive line starting with a letter of Juliana's name. Its style is highly embellished and formal. The verses indicate that Juliana, a member of the distinguished family of the Anicii, is noted for building a church at Honoratis, a fact that is formally celebrated in this frontispiece.

The scenes painted in the spandrels are equally revealing as a complement to the poem. In spite of abrasion of these areas, we can distinguish in one scene figures fitting blocks of building stone into place, in another figures standing on scaffolding and pulling on ropes; in another the putti-workmen hammer wooden beams, and in yet another they are engaged in painting. All eight scenes refer to stages involved in the construction and decoration of a building. The spandrels illustrate literally what the poem proclaims: "You built the church of the Lord, towering beautifully on high."

The frontispiece indicates that the book was commissioned by Anicia Juliana. It was probably kept in her personal library in her palace and was probably used for display as well as for a source of information.[67] No expense was spared in the production of this luxurious manuscript, and considering the elegant and refined classical style of the miniatures and use of valuable pigments, it must have been made by the most skilled artisans in book production available. In commissioning this portrait at the front of her book, she also commemorates her notoriety as the builder of a church.[68] Unfortunately, this church and another which she had rebuilt, the church of Saint Euphemia in Constantinople, have disappeared without a trace. Even their locations are unknown.[69] Testimonies thus exist that Juliana built and decorated at least two other churches in addition to Hagios Polyeuktos.

The Vienna Dioscurides also presents a puzzle that has intrigued scholars. Painted in the center of the first page, folio 1 verso, is a large peacock in bright colors and painstaking detail (fig. 20). Because it is so unlike the other frontispieces, scholars have thought its placement was a mistake in rebinding and that it had originally appeared in the section on birds. Although the page is damaged, we can clearly see a peacock standing with fanned tail and strutting pose. On close examination it can be seen that the feathers are painted entirely in gold with the blue pigment applied over it, in a use of pigments and gold leaf not found on the other illustrations of birds. There is no detectable inscription remaining on the page. Is this depiction of a peacock really bound out of order, as has been conjectured, or was it placed here intentionally as a symbol or "signature bird" of the patron of the manuscript? Do the

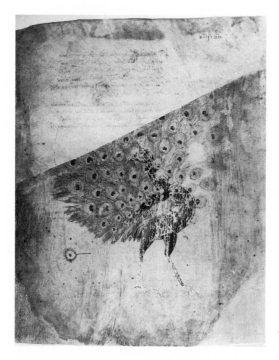

*Fig. 20. Peacock, Manuscript of Dioscurides, De Materia Medica, Vienna, Österreishische Nationalbibliothek, cod. med. gr. 1, fol. 1v, ca. 512. (Copyright Austrian National Library, Bildarchiv)*

peacocks of the niches around the church function similarly as signatures of Anicia Juliana, assigning dual meanings to this prominent iconographic element?[70]

The analogies between book and church, in which we encounter peacocks and panegyrical texts praising Anicia Juliana, are evident, but how can these converging features be interpreted in discerning Juliana's agenda in building Hagios Polyeuktos? The metrical inscription in the church may point toward a solution. The poem's first forty-one lines, which were carved on the entablature surrounding the main interior space of the church, refer to Juliana's illustrious family, beginning with an allusion to her great-grandmother, Athenais Eudocia, wife of Theodosius II:

> The empress Eudocia, in her eagerness to honor God, was the first to build here a temple to the divinely inspired Polyeuktos; but she did not make it as fine or as large as this, not from any restraint or lack of resources—for what can a queen lack?—but because she had a divine premonition that she would leave a family which would know well how to provide a better embellishment. (lines 1–6)[71]

According to the epigram, the first church on this site was sponsored by the empress Eudocia, wife of Theodosius II, discussed in chapter 3. After a trope claiming that supernatural powers of foresight were involved in her ancestor's building scheme, the epigram continues,

> From this stock Juliana, bright light of blessed parents, sharing their royal blood in the fourth generation, did not disappoint the hopes of that queen, but raised this building

from its small original to its present size and form, increasing the glory of her many-sceptered ancestors. (6–11)

It is clear from this passage that Juliana's enlarged church is intended as a dynastic statement and a claim to royal status going back four generations (see genealogical table on page 317).[72] The epigram also alludes to other churches she has built:

Even you do not know how many houses dedicated to God your hand has made; for you alone, I think, have built innumerable temples throughout the world, always revering the servants of the heavenly God. (30–33)

In this archaic conceit addressing the builder herself, the poem claims that she sponsored so many churches to the saints that even she has lost count of the number. Finally, the segment of the epigram located inside the church ends with a prayer for the protection and immortality of herself and her family:

[Juliana] gave birth to a family which is immortal, always treading the full path of piety . . . Protect her readily, along with her son and his daughters . . . And may the unutterable glory of the most industrious family survive as long as the Sun drives his fiery chariot. (35–41)

This invocation in full-blown epic style puts her family's memory in a cosmic context. For all its hyperbole and exaggeration, the poem represents a recapping of Juliana's lineage and life's work as well as a prayer for God's protection of her family, for which she claims immortality.[73]

The next thirty-four lines, which were inscribed around the atrium in front of the church, further glorify her through an *ekphrasis,* or rhetorical description, of the impression made by the church's interior and by a mosaic composition in the church. This segment ends with a prayer for the souls of Juliana's parents and for her own life and the lives of her children and coming generations. The emphasis in this section is on the church building itself and the integrity of Juliana, who was the planner behind it. Prior great builders, Constantine I and Theodosius I, are evoked, and the claim is made that Juliana surpasses even the biblical king Solomon:

She alone has conquered time and surpassed the wisdom of celebrated Solomon, raising a temple to receive God, the richly wrought and graceful splendour of which the ages cannot celebrate. (47–50)

Through her building of the church of Hagios Polyeuktos she claims a place among those immoralilzed through their building accomplishments: Constantine, Theodosius I, and even Solomon. By surpassing them, the poem says, she "conquers time," another way of again claiming immortality.

The grandiose statements made by the epigram were surely included in the patron's instructions to the author, assuming the author was commissioned to put into poetic form Juliana's desired content. Or, as I prefer to believe, Juliana followed in the tradition of her great-grandmother Athenais Eudocia not only in her predilection for church building but also as a scholar and writer. Eudocia's literary accomplishments, discussed in chapter 3, were considerable, and with Juliana's privileged upbringing she too must have had access to the best tutors and training in rhetoric and composition. She could well have been the author of her own epigrams, in Hagios Polyeuktos and on the frontispiece of the Vienna Dioscurides, among others.[74] Even in its archaic, highly formal and rhetorical phrases and lofty claims, the epigram in Hagios Polyeuktos speaks to us in the voice of a proud and determined woman.

As her final church was being completed around 527, Juliana was surely aware that a new order was taking shape under the young emperor Justinian. This church posed a clear challenge to him and therefore a danger to her children and grandchildren, for whom she voices concern in the epigram.[75] This danger may be the reason she chose to apply her gold to the ceiling of Hagios Polyeuktos, as we hear in the story told by the Frankish historian Gregory of Tours (ca. 540–94) of the meeting between Anicia Juliana and the emperor Justinian. As the historian recounts, knowing that Justinian was keen on seeing her wealth deposited in his treasury, she put off a meeting he proposed and deluded him into thinking it was because she was occupied in gathering her riches together to present to him. Instead she gave the order to her workmen:

> "Go and, having made plates according to the measurements of the beams, decorate the roof of the church of the holy martyr Polyeuktos with this, lest it reach the hand of our avaricious Emperor." They prepared everything as the lady had instructed, and fitted the plates to the roof and covered it with purest gold.

When Justinian met with her, thinking he would receive a large portion of her wealth, he was led into the church and shown the gold in the roof. Juliana said to him,

> "Look up, I beseech you, at the roof of this church, most glorious Emperor, and know that my poor resources are contained in this work. You must now do what you want. I offer no opposition."[76]

Justinian then realized his position, for he could not confiscate gold from the fabric of a holy church. As a conciliatory gesture she presented him with an emerald ring of great size and beauty, which she claimed was worth more than all her gold. Gregory of Tours's account of the emperor's failure to confiscate Juliana's wealth signals that Hagios Polyeuktos and its builder were famous even as far away as Gaul, present-day France. The story of Juliana's clever device to retain a portion of her wealth in the ceiling overlaid with gold fits the voice and image of a woman who lived in a world of greed and deception but managed to survive.

Within a year of the completion of the church of Saint Polyeuktos Anicia Juliana was dead. In the next generation her family fades from history, after her palace and wealth were taken over by Justinian. She had been well aware of the pressures on the old aristocracy in the face of Justinian's rapacious confiscations of property. While alive, she managed to preserve and continue her family's tradition of church building and to keep her wealth out of Justinian's hands.[77] She thereby succeeded in accomplishing the equivalent of the deeds of a reigning empress, for she took her imperial lineage seriously and believed in exercising her royal prerogative as a princess.

Juliana's patronage follows the pattern of patronage of her great grandmother, Athenais Eudocia, builder of the first church of Saint Polyeuktos, who spent the last fourteen years of her life in Jerusalem. Juliana may well have traveled to Jerusalem herself and seen her great-grandmother's foundations and her tomb (see chapter 3). Eudocia's primary building project had been a huge, very elaborate church dedicated to Saint Stephen, whose relics were enshrined there. As she had planned, at her death in 460 she was buried in a tomb located under this church, near the bones of Saint Stephen.[78] Other women of the Theodosian dynasty who reined as empresses were buried with their husbands either in the Honorian mausoleum, Saint Petronilla at Saint Peter's in Rome, or in the imperial mausoleum built by Constantine at the church of the Holy Apostles in Constantinople.[79] With Eudocia's example in mind, Anicia Juliana, who did not qualify for burial at the church of the Holy Apostles, rebuilt Eudocia's church of Hagios Polyeuktos in Constantinopole as her own burial church. The meanings of the peacocks and the vines, symbolizing resurrection, the soul, and salvation through the eucharist, converge when juxtaposed with the inscription and its assertion of immortality for the builder. The church's funerary and commemorative function would explain the extraordinarily long dynastic statement and prominent sculptural imagery.

Anicia Juliana, the patron of two very different artworks discussed here, can thus still, to some degree, be known today. Her book of herbal medicine conveys a sense of her learnedness and her taste for the luxurious copying and illustration of an important scientific treatise. The remains of her extravagant church of Hagios Polyeuctos are echoes of the beautifully carved and once brightly painted entablature with its funerary iconography of peacocks and vines as the setting for her panegyrical poem extolling her generosity and her lineage. As its patron she must have gloried in participating in the church's dedication ceremonies, probably looking much like her portrait in the Dioscurides manuscript seen in plate 5, finally satisfied that she had made her ultimate statement.

Although she could not have known it at the time, through this monument she revolutionized architectural sculptural decoration and domed church design, and through her epigram she set a new standard for poetic praise of a building and its patron. These works can still be imagined as Anicia Juliana planned them and as she saw and experienced them. Likewise it is through them that we gain a sense of the woman, made even more vivid by experiencing the products of her sponsorship. The church continued to serve as an image and reminder of who she was for the next six hundred years, standing high in the middle of the imperial city. If she couldn't rule as empress of Byzantium, this proud woman could still claim immortality through burial in a church which surpassed those of her predecessors. The evidence associated with Anicia Juliana's patronage transmits a powerful sense of who she was.

## Associated Readings

The epigram from Hagios Polyeuktos: *Greek Anthology,* Loeb Classical Library Edition, vol I, trans. W. R. Paton (1916; repr. Cambridge, 1993), book 1, epigram 10 (Greek text with facing English translation).

Carolyn L. Connor, "The Epigram in the Church of Hagios Polyeuktos in Constantinople and Its Byzantine Response," *Byzantion* 69 (1999): 479–527.

Martin Harrison, *A Temple for Byzantium: The Discovery and Excavation of Anicia Juliana's Palace Church in Istanbul* (Austin, 1989).

Martin Harrison, *Excavations at Saraçhane in Istanbul,* vol. 1: *The Excavations, Structures, Architectural Decoration, Small Finds, Coins, Bones, and Molluscs* (Princeton, 1986).

*Six*

# THE CHALLENGE OF THEODORA

The empress Theodora (527–48), wife of the emperor Justinian I, confronts us with a calm stare in her portrait in mosaic in the sanctuary of the church of San Vitale in Ravenna, Italy (fig. 22 and pl. 6).[1] Her imperial attire of gold, silks, and jewels is captured down to the last detail. While Theodora is perhaps the best-known woman of Byzantium, she is also the least well understood. The scandal associated with her life as an actress before she rose dramatically to become empress made her notorious in her own time, and she remains a mysterious figure up until the present. Information about her comes almost entirely from a biased contemporary source, the writings of the historian Procopius in his account the *Secret History*.[2] This text of the mid–sixth century purports to be an unburdening of Procopius's concerns about the damage caused the empire by the emperor and empress and by two people close to them, the general Belisarius and his wife, Antonina. His attacks on them, especially Theodora, are vicious and unremitting.

Understanding Theodora within the context of her time is a challenge because of the difficulty of putting the *Secret History* into perspective, separating the gossip and hearsay from the facts and insights about her life and character. Matching the person described by the historian with some degree of reality requires a close, cautious reading of the *Secret History*, above all the passages that treat Theodora and her activities. Who was Theodora and what aspects of her life define her character as the wife of Justinian? What can one discover of her real actions and choices? How did she fulfill her role as empress of Byzantium? In this chapter I will attempt to disentangle the person from the web of allegations surrounding her.[3]

Theodora's challenge also extends to her famous portrait in San Vitale. In her outward gaze she invites the viewer to interpret the unspecified drama taking place in the mosaic as well as to take in her regal appearance and that of her companions. Procopius's *Secret History* suggests an interpretation of the scene which fits some events of the 540s. In addition, material aspects of the women in the mosaic lead us to seek concrete examples of the types of insignia, jewelry, and clothing worn by them, in order further to understand the meaning of their splendid appearance. Art helps evoke aspects of Theodora and her world which cannot be expressed or gleaned through texts. Seen in conjunction with each other, these two kinds of imagery, literary and artistic, elaborate what one can learn about the empress.

The reign of Justinian (527–65) and the empress Theodora (527–48) was ostensibly a prosperous one in terms of the number of buildings that rose during those years all over the Byzantine Empire, the extensive legal codifications sponsored by Justinian, and the writings in historical, poetic, and hymnographic genres which date to this time. The rebuilt church of Hagia Sophia, in Constantinople, completed in 537, was the architectural masterpiece of this reign. Dozens of other churches and utilitarian buildings rose in the imperial city, and such engineering projects as jetties and harbors were undertaken. Most have left no trace. In places as remote as Mount Sinai in the Sinai Peninsula of Egypt and along the frontier with the Sassanian Persians, whole cities, forts, and monasteries were built to accommodate Justinian's plans. Dazzling ensembles of mosaics, of which only a handful survive, decorated churches around the empire.

The era was undeniably one of harsh repression, as the Nika riots of 532 illustrate. It is said that during this uprising thirty thousand people were cut down by Justinian's soldiers when they attempted to oust him as emperor. Religious disputes, characteristic of this age, as of all periods of Byzantine history, not only shook the church but split the imperial pair. This brilliant and fascinating period has been the subject of much scholarly research and popular writing.[4] But not only the actions of men determined its character. One of the most prominent and elusive subjects in any account of the period is the empress Theodora, but it is mainly through the eyes of Procopius that modern views of her have formed.

Procopius, the court historian during the reign of Justinian, was well situated to depict events of the time. Little is known about his background except that he came to Constantinople from Caesarea in Palestine, was well educated, and considered himself the upper-class ally, if not the equal, of those with senatorial rank. He probably came from a family of the old Roman aristocracy.[5] He wrote his first work, the *Wars,* a secular, classicizing history in eight volumes, while on campaign with the great general Belisarius. *Wars* details military and political events, while observing places and people key to Justinian's vision of a reconstituted Roman Empire. The emperor hoped to recreate the old Roman Empire, which had been largely lost to the barbarians in the West by the early sixth century. As secretary and legal advisor to Belisarius from around 527 to 540, Procopius accompanied the general and his armies in the eastern wars against the Sassanian Persians, in Africa in wars to subdue the Vandals, and in the West during the reconquest of Italy from the Ostrogoths.

Another of his works, the *Buildings,* a panegyric and also an imperial commission, praises the numerous construction enterprises undertaken by the emperor around the empire, but mostly in the East, from churches to bridges, forts to cisterns.[6] Although not as lengthy as the *Wars,* the *Buildings,* in six books, shows Procopius's firsthand acquaintance with the monuments as well as his training in the art of elaborate rhetorical description. Part of his agenda is stressing Justinian's closeness to God. In his capacity as court historian and encomiast he must have spent much of his life close to those with great power, the imperial family and that of Belisarius and his wife, Antonina, for Antonina often accompanied Belisarius on campaign. Both works were written as panegyrics, praising the emperor and his general through accounts of events and deeds, and were published in the 550s.

X The *Secret History* was probably written at the same time as the first seven books of the *Wars,* in 550–51, and before the *Buildings,* of 554, but it differs radically from these works.[7] The *Wars* and the *Buildings,* however, bear consideration in relation to the *Secret History* for their corroboration of facts or, in some cases, for divergent views of Theodora. Also, as we will see, certain elements of the *Secret History* are confirmed in the contemporary writings of such historians as Malalas, Theophanes, and John of Ephesus. Considering Procopius the person, his other works, and the histories of other writers helps one assess the tone and content of the *Secret History.*

The *Secret History* was not intended, at least initially, for publication, as can be judged from its Greek title, *Anekdota,* or "things not for dissemination," as well as from its preface. An eleventh-century copy of the work was discovered by chance in the Vatican library bound into an unrelated volume, and it was finally published in 1623. This "unpublished" work is the most detailed extant account of people and events connected with the imperial pair and their immediate associates in Constantinople, and it includes many references to women. The genre is more accurately classified as invective than history. In invective, the reader learns as much about the author as about his subjects, as his bias reveals itself as a reaction to the subject. It is therefore worthwhile to try to detect the author's personal attitude, taking into account both his relationship with the subjects and his literary models. If one considers Procopius's possible motives for wishing to slander his subjects, along with characteristic features of invective, it is possible to distinguish what is closest to factual detail from what is fiction or gross exaggeration.

The extreme, exaggerated statements in Procopius alert the reader that he was writing in a genre that entails, even requires, outrageous criticism of public figures.[8] In a tradition going back at least to the fourth century BCE, Athenian orators such as Demosthenes and Aeschines knew how to slander and demean their opponents using conventions that gave them a moral advantage. For example, they would elaborate on any hint that a person's career might have included an unsavory episode or that his parentage or occupational history was humbler than presumed. The conventions of invective did not work as well with more recent events, but the farther back one went, the more inventive and farther from the truth statements could be.

When the author's source relied on rhetorical abuse or gossip, accounts tended to be interlarded with expressions like, "People say that . . ." or some other vague locution, as a preface to malicious comments. Invective is a known rhetorical strategy dating to classical times in which the speaker or writer aimed to gain an advantage over his opponent. The *Secret History* functions within this genre, thus comprising a highly contrasting counterpart to Procopius's other works in his trilogy.

What are Procopius's stated aims and motives in writing the *Secret History?* In his Preface, the author emphasizes his intention to write a different type of account from the *Wars,* in which he chronicles events in a standard manner. Here, instead, he plans to tell "the truth" about Justinian and Theodora:

> What I shall write now follows a different plan, supplementing the previous formal chronicle with a disclosure of what really happened throughout the Roman empire. You see, it was not possible, during the life of certain persons, to write the truth of what they did, as a historian should. If I had, their hordes of spies would have found out about it, and they would have put me to a most horrible death. (*Secret History* 1.1)[9]

From the start Procopius's relationship with Theodora has an effect on this work. For the "certain person" can be referring only to the empress, who died in 548, as the person who would have hunted him down through her "hordes of spies." He then states that although it may be difficult for readers to accept his account as probable, he feels that it is his duty to disclose the "wickedness and deeds" of the sovereigns and that this information will not go uncorroborated by the testimony of others. Although he still claims to be a writer of history because he is disclosing the truth, his agenda is revealed in the Preface: "First I shall reveal the folly of Belisarius, and then the depravity of Justinian and Theodora" (1.10). His attitude is clearly one of outrage, as he prepares the reader to assume his views—but what were his motives? Although he is aware of the risks and knows that the work must remain under wraps during his lifetime, he does intend that it be read and is fully aware of the power of his pen:

> Furthermore, the disclosure of these actions and tempers will be published for all time, and in consequence others will perhaps feel less urge to transgress. (1.8)

His stated motive is that the work will profit others who suffer similar hardships. The reader can also gauge, however, that it serves as a form of revenge and personal catharsis, helping purge his resentment for his own sufferings at the hands of the rulers.

The work starts by describing the parentage of Antonina, wife of the general Belisarius, and their marital problems. Antonina, the daughter of a charioteer and an actress, is described as unfaithful, cruel, and scheming. Her adulterous affair with an adopted son takes place practically in public, while her natural son is ignored. Procopius's description of Antonina fits the genre of invective in referring to her low-class origins, and it is through Antonina that we are introduced to Theodora, for the two women are friends and confidants:

> Now the Empress gave evidence to all mankind that for every murder to which she was indebted, she could pay in greater and even more savage requital. For Antonina had betrayed for her one enemy, when she had lately ensnared the Cappadocian; but she ruined, for Antonina's sake, a number of blameless men. (3.6–7)

The two women cooperate in betraying or murdering each others' enemies, as in their plot to get rid of John the Cappadocian, Justinian's notorious minister of finance. Thus allusions to Antonina's degeneracy and complicity with the empress serve as a preamble to the reader's first encounter with Theodora, when she surprises Antonina by having her adopted son and lover, Theodosius, brought to Constantinople. A little drama such as in an ancient comedy ensues:

> On the day after his arrival [Theodora] sent for Antonina. "My dearest lady," she said, "a pearl fell into my hands yesterday, such a one as no mortal has ever seen. If you wish, I will not grudge you a sight of this jewel, but will show it to you." Not knowing what had happened, her friend begged Theodora to show her the pearl; and the Empress, leading Theodosius from the rooms of one of the eunuchs, revealed him. For a moment Antonina, speechless with joy, remained dumb. Then she broke into an ecstasy of gratitude, and called Theodora her saviour, her benefactress, and her true mistress. Thereafter, the Empress kept Theodosius in the palace.(3.16–19)

Theodora rewards her friend for her loyalty by aiding her in a dissolute love affair.

This story illustrates what Procopius must have observed firsthand of the relationship between the two women, exchanges of favors and complicity in plots to remove obstacles or aid one another. Depicting Antonina as immoral and promiscuous also serves a rhetorical strategy in preparing for Procopius's equally damaging and discrediting presentation of Theodora in chapter 9. By disparaging Antonina and Theodora, Procopius also demeans their husbands, Belisarius and Justinian, suggesting that the men were emasculated by their wives.[10] Why would he wish to write in this vein? The answer confronts us on every page of his work: He was himself the victim of abuse, neglect, or derision by these powerful women. They also, in his view, caused the degradation of Belisarius, whom he had greatly admired. The women represent the opposite of what he and his educated, aristocratic class of society would associate with proper womanhood. Procopius feels threatened by Antonina and Theodora, and so he exaggerates their scheming and lack of restraint, using the literary genre available to him.

If one disregards the more outrageous examples of Procopius's bias or rhetorical strategy, the *Secret History* more nearly approaches a social history of that time, rather than an event-based documentary history in the modern sense. The themes he deals with represent the very fabric of society, its dangers, pitfalls, patterns, and injustices.

Marriage, for example, a prime concern of Procopius, is taken up frequently. Arranged marriages were the accepted social norm, especially for upper-class women, but in many instances, according to Procopius, the traditional pattern is set awry by Theodora, who manipulates marriages for her own ends.[11] Her own marriage to Justinian in 523 or 524 came about as a result of a change in laws pertaining to an actress's marrying one holding senatorial or higher rank. A law was codified not only to permit Justinian's marriage to Theodora, but was custom-made to rehabilitate the children of ex-actresses, namely, Theodora's illegitimate daughter.[12] Justinian's legislation did little to revise the old Roman asymmetrical view, which gave men more latitude in definitions of adultery and grounds for divorce than women, nor did it make possible marriages for prostitutes.[13] The prime function of marriage continued to be procreation and protection of family assets. Theodora is depicted by Procopius as micromanaging or interfering in marriages in a number of episodes in which assets of the parties involved are her real concern.[14] One such scenario, again, involves Antonina and Theodora.

In what is apparently an attempt by Theodora to acquire the wealth Antonina and Belisarius had accumulated in the course of his military campaigns, she betrothes her own grandson, Anastasius, to Belisarius and Antonina's only child, their daughter Joannina: "To tie him further to her, she betrothed Joannina, Belisarius's only daughter, to Anastasius her grandson" (4.37). If this marriage were in effect, Joannina would inherit her parents' fortune, and it would eventually fall into the hands of Theodora's family. Antonina resisted the marriage, however, and she and Belisarius delayed the wedding ceremony, saying they wished to be present in Constantinople for the celebration. The betrothal, however, did take place. Although the marriage would not be performed as long as the parents of the bride were in Italy, Theodora had an alternate plan:

> But the Queen was still determined her [grandson] should be master of Belisarius's wealth, for she knew his daughter would inherit it, as Belisarius had no other child. Yet she had no confidence in Antonina; and fearing that after her own life was ended, Antonina would not be loyal to her house, for all that she had been so helpful in the Empress's emergencies, and that she would break the agreement. (4.18–20)

Theodora's intuition tells her, according to Procopius, that if she herself were to die, the marriage would lose its appeal for Antonina and that she would seek a more prestigious union for her daughter, in spite of her demonstrated loyalty to the empress. The underlying mistrust, hypocrisy, and cynicism in the women's relationship is depicted by Procopius. While parental determination of marriage ties of their children is the social norm, Theodora is credited with manipulating the process in the following way:

> Theodora did an unholy thing. She made the boy and girl live together without any ceremony. And they say she forced the girl against her will to submit to his clandestine

embrace, so that, being thus deflowered, the girl would agree to the marriage, and the Emperor could not forbid the event. (5.21)

Although Justinian apparently also was against the marriage, Theodora encourages the young couple to live together, assuming that once Joannina is no longer a virgin she will not be a marriage prospect for any other man. In this episode Theodora is trying any means to ensure the prosperity of her own line. Because the boy's mother is her illegitimage child, and not hers with Justinian, Justinian does not have the same stake in the marriage that she does.

The maneuvering turns into a battle of wills between Theodora and Antonina and eventually takes on a cruel twist. After Theodora's death, Antonina separates the couple regardless of the fact that they were happy together. Antonina's determination to manage her daughter's marriage preempts any parental concern she might have had for her daughter's happiness and welfare:

> However, after the first ravishing, Anastasius and the girl fell warmly in love with each other, and for not less than eight months continued their unmarital relations. But when, after Theodora's death, Antonina came to Constantinople, she was unwilling to forget the outrage the Queen had committed against her. Not bothering about the fact that if she united her daughter to any other man, she would be making an ex-prostitute out of her, she refused to accept Theodora's [grandson] as a son-in-law, and by force tore the girl, ignoring her fondest pleadings, from the man she loved. For this act of senseless obstinacy she was universally censured. (5.22–24)

Whereas in the narrative in the *Acts of Thekla* (discussed in the introduction to part I above) Thekla's mother has the right to condemn her child to death for resisting an arranged betrothal, here, conversely, a mother has the right to countermand a betrothal agreement and prevent the marriage of her daughter in accordance with her own wishes and regardless of the feelings of the young woman. And her right applies even if the reputation of the woman is compromised.

Either Antonina thought that a superior marriage alliance could still be made for her daughter because of their considerable wealth or she was simply acting out of spite. Theodora is of no use to Antonina once she is dead, and Antonina moves decisively to disassociate her family from Theodora's. The incident as recounted by Procopius also degrades the husbands of the two women, for they appear powerless to influence their wives. Procopius indicates that in his view the proper course of action would have been to allow the couple to remain united. His upper-class sensibilities are ruffled in this as in many other instances of manipulated marriages in the *Secret History*. Some of the most sensitive social patterns on which Theodora evidently trespassed concerned betrothal and the connected issues of dowries and marriage.[15]

Having been introduced to Theodora through accounts of her scheming in the initial chapters, the reader finally learns, in chapter 9, some basic facts about her parents and childhood. Born ca. 497 either in Constantinople or in Paphlagonia, Theodora lost her father at a young age. Procopius begins his account of her with the period after the father's death when Theodora and her two sisters were put into the acting profession by their mother. To be an actress meant not only that a girl or woman performed in various dramas, mimes, and musical entertainments, but also that she was available for sexual exploitation. Here Procopius offers salacious details of Theodora's promiscuousness that are in keeping with the malicious intent of the conventions of invective. Also, since these events took place some thirty years before the writing, his inventiveness is savage. He knows the power of scandal to draw an audience, and the more prominent the subject, the greater the temptation to interject scandalous stories; hence the famous story about the geese:

> Often, even in the theater, in the sight of all the people, she removed her costume and stood nude in their midst, except for a girdle about the groin: not that she was abashed at revealing that, too, to the audience, but because there was a law against appearing altogether naked on the stage, without at least this much of a fig-leaf. Covered thus with a ribbon, she would sink down to the stage floor and recline on her back. Slaves to whom the duty was entrusted would then scatter grains of barley from above into the calyx of this passion flower, whence geese, trained for the purpose, would next pick the grains one by one with their bills and eat. (9.20–21)

Such performances, among others recounted by Procopius, must have been increasingly savored by the gossip mongers in retrospect, especially as the status of Theodora changed dramatically. The purpose of recapping such stories was to help make her into an object of derision and scorn in the eyes of Procopius's sympathizers:

> So perverse was her wantonness that she should have hid not only the customary part of her person, as other women do, but her face as well. Thus those who were intimate with her were straightway recognized from that very fact to be perverts, and any more respectable man who chanced upon her in the Forum avoided her and withdrew in haste, lest the hem of his mantle, touching such a creature, might be thought to share in her pollution. (9.24–26)

In this passage, Procopius seeks to inspire the reader's contempt for the subject.[16] Similar claims of female pollution are launched periodically throughout the *Secret History*, as Procopius repeatedly reminds his readers of Theodora's profession before becoming empress, in an attempt to extend the taint of her past into the present.

In his efforts to slander the empress he reveals his greatest bias as a historian: he fears strong women. He frequently imputes to Theodora and Antonina their character as "bad women," whereas more conventional upper-class women are "good women," and these latter, furthermore, are often the victims of bad women. In one example Procopius reveals what he considers to be a paradigmatic image of womanhood:

For no thought of shame came to Justinian in marrying [Theodora], though he might have taken his pick of the noblest born, most highly educated, most modest, carefully nurtured, virtuous and beautiful virgins of all the ladies in the whole roman Empire; a maiden, as they say, with upstanding breasts. Instead, he preferred to make his own what had been common to all men, and, careless of all her revealed history, took in wedlock a woman who was not only guilty of every other contamination but boasted of her many abortions. (10.2–3).

In this list of seven desirable attributes, Procopius presents us with his gendered stereotype of the good woman. And in juxtaposition he refers to Theodora's contamination, harping on her past as making her defective, guilty, and bad. In referring to Theodora's "revealed history," he countenances what must have been abundant gossip, in which he probably eagerly shared. Among the gossipy populus, however, the theme of the repentant harlot, as encountered in chapter 4, was surely well known. Taking up a virtuous and pious life and leaving one of dubious morality behind was probably a recognized pattern in early Byzantium. Thus, while some might have accepted her as reformed or as a rags to riches success story, Procopius maintains his views, associating her only with her past.

With regard to Theodora's appearance, not even Procopius can find much to criticize, and so he does not say much at all:

Now Theodora was fair of face and of a very graceful, though small, person; her complexion was moderately colorful, if somewhat pale; and her eyes were dazzling and vivacious. (10.11).[17]

This short, conventional, and fairly positive description is followed by a summary of the sovereigns' public lives together and their style of rule:

What she and her husband did together must now be briefly described: for neither did anything without the consent of the other. For some time it was generally supposed they were totally different in mind and action; but later it was revealed that their apparent disagreement had been arranged so that their subjects might not unanimously revolt against them, but instead be divided in opinion. (10.13–14)

. . . By such well-planned hypocrisies they confused the public and, pretending to be at variance with each other, were able to establish a firm and mutual tyranny. (10.23)

The clause "neither did anything without the consent of the other" denotes that, to all appearances, the pair governed jointly and in close mutual consultation. Their style of governing, on the other hand, involved a divided dynamic. This dynamic, which the public found confusing, Procopius asserts was the result of calculation and a clever strategy of deception. The couple's way of interrelating has been discussed by scholars as their "underlying interior dynamic," or their "Doppelspiel," a disingenuous policy of divide and rule.[18] Procopius notes that if the emperor entrusted any business to an official without first consulting Theodora, she made that person suffer.[19] Their standard way of governing was, then, that at her insistence all decisions be shared and that agreements be mutual. Regardless of what Procopius or anyone else thought about it or who was responsible for the pattern, the pair successfully shared genuine joint rule.

Their style of joint rule may be witnessed at a particularly dramatic turning point, as described by Procopius in the *Wars*. During the Nika riots of 532, when it looked as if the rulers were going to be ousted by a populus rebelling against their oppression, all were assembled in the hippodrome. Justinian had made arrangements for the escape of the imperial couple along with those closest to them. Procopius recaps a speech made by Theodora in which she disagrees with Justinian's plan to flee:

> May I never be without this purple, and may I not live on that day when those who meet me do not address me as mistress. If you now want to save yourself, Emperor, there is no problem. For we have a lot of money, and the sea and the boats are here. But consider the possibility that after you have been saved you might not happily exchange that safety for death. A certain ancient saying appeals to me that royalty [*baisileia*] is a good funeral shroud. (*Wars* 1.24–33)[20]

Although containing numerous topoi and having many possible slants in interpretation, the speech as reported may have a kernal of truth. After the days of rioting and the threat to their power, Justinian did not abandon the city and the crown. He instead ordered the slaughter of the dissenters, later had two pretenders executed, and remained in power. Justinian and Theodora ruled as a team, and at one critical juncture Theodora openly disagreed with her husband, with the result that they remained in power. That power was assailable by another means, however, and this was the most damaging threat of all: accusations of collusion with the supernatural.

Procopius appeals on numerous occasions to beliefs about the supernatural. His most serious allegations were that Justinian and Theodora were demons. In Byzantium, demons, or agents of the Devil, were believed to be perpetrators of temptation and destruction, sometimes in human disguise.[21] Only vigilance and adherence to a virtuous Christian life would protect from their evil influence. Demonic presence manifested itself, it was believed, by seizures or by self-destructive behavior or frenzy which today would be associated with types of insanity. Physical illness also was seen as caused by demons residing within the body, and exorcizing of demons was a sought-after cure brought about by holy men and saints. Other cataclysmic events, such as floods, epidemics, and earthquakes were seen as the work of demons or the displeasure of God. By associating the imperial couple with demons Procopius refers to the source of their powers of destruction:

> Wherefore to me, and many others of us, these two seemed not to be human beings, but veritable demons, and what the poets call vampires: who laid their heads together to see how they could most easily and quickly destroy the race and deeds of men; and assuming human bodies, became man-demons, and so convulsed the world. And one

could find evidence of this in many things, but especially in the superhuman power with which they worked their will. (12.14)

The allegation that the imperial pair are demons in human bodies is a deduction based on the way the couple worked together, often with devastating results for their victims. Examples of their greed, persistence, and cleverness in confiscating property, subverting justice, and causing hardship are enumerated as part of the workings of their evil will. Given the belief in demons, this was a type of gossip which was not merely malicious but played on real fears about supernatural powers and agents of the Devil. Such is the case with the anecdote about one of Theodora's lovers.

> Furthermore some of Theodora's lovers, while she was on the stage, say that at night a demon would sometimes descend upon them and drive them from the room, so that it might spend the night with her. (12.28)

To relate a sexual liaison between Theodora and a demon, a claim made by one of Theodora's lovers before her marriage to Justinian, is the worst Procopius can do. Theodora's association with demons, however, only applies to the years "when she was on the stage," or many years prior; this instance of invective has had ample time to inflate. Theodora is also associated with sorcery. In a statement about her participation in magic with her friend Peter Barsyames, she is said to have "consorted with magicians and sorcerers" from childhood and that she "believed in the black art and had great confidence in it." [22] Her power over Justinian is also attributed to sorcery. Procopius's statements concerning demons and sorcery are precededed by "Some say . . . ," betraying his reliance on hearsay and gossip. Belief in the supernatural was, however, common, and such accusations could therefore represent a serious threat to the couple's public image.

Another damaging complaint launched by Procopius against Theodora is that she spent much time enjoying luxuries, including taking baths:

> To her body she gave greater care than was necessary, if less than she thought desirable. For early she entered the bath and late she left it; and having bathed, went to breakfast. After breakfast she rested. At dinner and supper she partook of every kind of food and drink; and many hours she devoted to sleep, by day till nightfall, by night till the rising sun. Though she wasted her hours thus intemperately, what time of the day remained she deemed ample for managing the Roman Empire. (15.6–9)

Baths, long a form of recreation for the Romans, also had known medicinal or rehabilitative effects. Records of nunneries show more frequent baths were part of the care of women who were ill. It is possible that Theodora's relaxation and baths may have been part of a treatment for cancer, which was the cause of her death at around age fifty. If Theodora found it expedient to rest before the ceremonies and dining which were part of the expected routines of the sovereigns, Procopius accused her of wasting time when she should have been tending to governing the empire. This accusation by Procopius, however, cuts both ways, for it appears Theodora took her duties as ruler seriously enough to be well rested for the time she spent on governing and in public.[23]

Behind-the-scenes acts of aggression, according to Procopius, were also Theodora's prerogative. The murder of the beautiful, well-educated Ostragothic queen Amalasuntha is ascribed by Procopius to Theodora. Amalasuntha, the daughter of the Ostrogothic king Theodoric of Ravenna, was regent for her son Athalaric during his minority and ruled as queen after his death in 534. She was murdered while in exile in Italy, Procopius claims, because Theodora was fearful that she would come to Constantinople and pose a threat to her. Because of her jealousy and fear that Justinian might prove fickle, she persuaded Justinian to have the woman murdered.[24] Procopius states that in this case as in others it was nearly impossible to gain information about the empress's activities, which were closely guarded secrets:

> For if the Queen wanted to keep any of her actions concealed, it remained secret and unmentioned; and neither was any who knew of the matter allowed to tell it to his closest friend, or could any who tried to learn what had happened ever find out, not matter how much of a busybody he was.
>
> . . . No other tyrant since mankind began ever inspired such fear, since not a word could be spoken against her without her hearing of it: her multitude of spies brought her the news of whatever was said and done in public or in private. (16.12–14)

Procopius acknowledges that much of his information about Theodora is hearsay or invention, for her style of ruling involved strict confidentiality and secrecy. The statement offers insight into Procopius's own situation at court, and his resulting sense of frustration, anger, and fear: he was not privy to Theodora's affairs, which remained "secret and unmentioned," forcing him to rely instead on gossip. To an official who was used to being well informed and whose reputation probably depended on his access to information, this situation must have been deeply iritating.[25] His fear about being discovered writing the *Secret History* and persecuted, mentioned in the Preface, is embroidered here. Procopius had lived in fear that his writings would become known by Theodora. After her death he finally felt safe enough to circulate his story to trusted friends. On the other hand, without his deep fear of the empress, he might not have written the *Secret History* to vent his anger and frustration, and we would be without a valuable source.

Procopius was not known to have held any office at court after his return from Belisarius's campaigns. The reason is not hard to discern within the context of the *Secret History:*

> Theodora's idea was to control everything in the state to suit herself. Civil and ecclesiastical offices were all in her hands, and there was only one thing she was always careful to inquire about and guard as the standard of her appointments: that no honest gentleman should be given high rank, for fear he would have scruples against obeying her commands. (17.27–28)

As a self-proclaimed "honest gentleman," Procopius was probably overlooked because of Theodora's controlling style of rule. He no doubt shared this resentment with others of good birth and education who were similarly neglected by the empress, providing a sympathetic readership for the *Secret History* when it was finally circulated privately.

Social reform and philanthropy were part of Theodora's roles as empress, as tradition dictated. Her founding of monasteries, churches, and nunneries is recorded in the *Buildings* and also by Malalas in his *Chronicle,* regarding her church-building activities in Antioch and Jerusalem.[26] In the *Secret History,* Procopius describes, in a backhanded compliment, her founding of an establishment for wayward women:

> Theodora also devoted considerable attention to the punishment of women caught in carnal sin. She picked up more than five hundred harlots in the Forum, who earned a miserable living by selling themselves there for three obols, and sent them to the opposite mainland, where they were locked up in the monastery called Repentance to force them to reform their way of life. Some of them, however, threw themselves from the parapets at night and thus freed themselves from an undesired salvation. (17.5–6)

This ostensibly philanthropic act, in which Theodora takes dramatic action to help women forced into prostitution, backfires, according to Procopius. It is difficult, however, to believe some good was not achieved by her founding of the monastery of Repentance, for in the *Buildings* Procopius speaks of Justinina and Theodora "cleansing the state of the pollution of the brothels" by helping the women "who were struggling with extreme poverty" when they founded the monastery of Repentance.[27] Is the sovereigns' philanthropy a genuine effort to help women escape from prostitution? or is it a stopgap strategy that fails?[28] Which of Procopius's versions of the Repentance story are we to believe — or neither?

If her philanthropy was a failed gesture it would be commensurate with Procopius's claim that she undermined the morals of women of the court. Procopius states that "the ladies of the court at this time were nearly all of abandoned morals," and also that they "ran no risk in being faithless to their husbands, as the sin brought no penalty."[29] How should we interpret his claim that Theodora encouraged women in her circle to lead adulterous relationships? Is there some element of truth to this claim of free living among the court women? or is this an extension of his stereotyping of the empress as bad woman, derived from the stories of her immoral activity and company while still an actress?

Among the many themes of Procopius's criticisms of Theodora is her establishment of innovative patterns in court ceremony. The reception of visitors at court is of great concern to Procopius, as it probably was to Theodora, and receives the following commentary:

> Formerly, when the Senate approached the Emperor, it paid homage in the following manner. Every patrician kissed him on the right breast; the Emperor kissed the patri-

cian on the head, and he was dismissed. Then the rest bent their right knee to the emperor and withdrew. It was not customary to pay homage to the Queen.

. . . But those who were admitted to the presence of Justinian and Theodora, whether they were patricians or otherwise, fell on their faces on the floor, stretching their hands and feet out, kissed first one foot and then the other of the Augustus, and then retired. Nor did Theodora refuse this honor; and she even received the ambassadors of the Persians and other barbarians and gave them presents, as if she were in command of the Roman Empire; a thing that had never happened in all previous time.

. . . And formerly intimates of the Emperor called him emperor and the Empress, empress; and the other officials according to the title of their rank. But if anybody addressed either of these two as emperor or Empress without adding "Your Majesty" or "Your Highness," or forgot to call himself their slave, he was considered either ignorant or insolent, and was dismissed in disgrace as if he had done some awful crime or committed an unpardonable sin. (30.21–26)

In the eyes of a traditional, old school aristocrat any change or innovation is a threat. He therefore blames Theodora for initiating a new and demeaning ritual for court audiences, as in her requirement insisting on the title "Your Majesty." In addition, Justinian had been easy of access, and it had even been easy to converse with him in private, but the pattern changed under Theodora's influence:

But to the Queen's presence even the highest officials could not enter without great delay and trouble; like slaves they had to wait all day in a small and stuffy antechamber, for to absent himself was a risk no official dared to take. So they stood there on their tiptoes, each straining to keep his face above his neighbors's, so that eunuchs, as they came out from the audience room, would see them. Some would be called, perhaps, after several days; and when they did enter into her presence in great fear, they were quickly dismissed as soon as they had made obeisance and kissed her feet. For to speak or make any request, unless she commanded, was not permitted. (15.13–16)

Theodora insisted that the same ceremonial honor be shown her as was shown to Justinian. Not only did she increase the rituals of self-abasement but also replaced what had been the legal process of appeal with personal petition to the emperor and empress:

The magistrates of old had administered justice and the laws according to their conscience, and made their decisions while in their own offices, while their subjects neither seeing nor hearing any injustice, of course had little cause to trouble the Emperor. But these two, taking control of everything to the misfortune of their subjects, forced everyone to come to them and beg like slaves. (30.28–30)

The abandonment of old customs by which jurists had some degree of autonomy rankles Procopius, who must have been among those left standing on their tiptoes, waiting for an audience with the sovereigns, or who had to beg "like a slave."

The fear instilled in those doing obeisance is evidently part of Procopius's experience as well, for it is expressed intermittently throughout the work. He devotes a significant portion of the last chapter of the *Secret History* to a discussion of Theodora's insistence on being addressed and honored by prostration in the same fashion as the emperor, as can be seen from the passages in chapter 30. According to the earlier statement in chapter 15, this humiliating ritual was extended to both the sovereigns in audiences with everyone, even with their own courtiers. Such formalities and conventions of obeisance were associated with oriental kingdoms, such as Egypt and Persia. Now these ceremonies extended to imperial audiences in Constantinople, and the innovation took place under the influence of Theodora.

Only vague mention is made of Theodora's intervention in ecclesiastical affairs in the *Secret History,* whereas other sources note that this was an important part of her interests and activities. In the *Secret History* Procopius merely states,

> Theodora's idea was to control everything in the state to suit herself. Civil and ecclesiastical offices were all in her hands . . . (27.27)

He does not go into the intricate politics of the Monophysite controversy and Theodora's adherence to this heretical branch of Christianity as oppposed to Chalcedonian Orthodoxy, the accepted definition of Christianity. Justinian was Chalcedonian, but Theodora maintained her Monophysite leanings throughout her life, protecting Monophysite leaders who would otherwise have been persecuted. Her influence in church affairs was considerable, and the fact that she was able to support this opposing doctrine demonstrates her independence and ability to juggle such issues within her personal relationship with Justinian.[30] While Procopius stresses the couple's ability to appear to take opposing sides on many matters, as mentioned above, here is a case in which they actually differed. How do we explain the fact that Procopius never discusses Theodora's religious opposition to Justinian?

The best source on Theodora's espousal of the Monophysite cause appears in John of Ephesus, *Lives of the Eastern Saints.*[31] Theodora managed not only to protect important bishops, monks, and leaders of that sect, including Severus of Antioch, from persecution, but also to hide some of them in the Hormisdas Palace, adjacent to the imperial palace in Constantinople. She also sponsored proselytizing missions to Asia Minor and Africa. Her protection of this sect was felt even after her death, when Justinian respected her wishes that Monophysites be spared.[32] Diverging from Justinian, Theodora supported a heterodox religious sect with Justinian's knowledge but still appeared united with Justinian as upholder of Orthodoxy.[33] She was true to her own religious background and beliefs, even though her faithfulness meant a potentially serious rift might develop between her and her husband. Through her diplomatic skill, or skill in veiling her personal preferences, she succeeded in supporting the Monophysites, thereby perpetuating a rival and at times more powerful branch of Christianity than Orthodoxy. This division would never be entirely resolved, but the Iconoclast controversy finally produced a unified church three hundred years later.

After Theodora's death, Justinian's rule became less and less effective, for he had not only depended on her for help in ruling but also loved her; he often visited her tomb at the church of the Holy Apostles. In the *Wars* Procopius states, as if reiterating a known fact, that Justinian acted in harmony with Theodora's wishes "because of the extraordinary love which the emperor felt for her." In the *Novels,* a section of his Law Code, Justinian says, "For we know, though we are lovers of chastity, that nothing is more vehement than the fury of love."[34] In another Novel, he refers to Theodora as he states, "We have taken as partner in our counsels our most pious consort given us by God," indicating the degree to which he associates Theodora with the functions of his office.[35] Here he speaks according to his own feelings and respect for his wife.

Whatever else one can say about Theodora, she remained the faithful consort and partner of Justinian for twenty-five years, was never separated from him, and was loved and respected by him. A careful reading of Procopius's works reveals a brilliant, dedicated woman who once in power did what she had to to survive and to maintain a true joint rule. She went beyond the stereotypes set for female rule and adhered to her beliefs and personal interests, which apparently sometimes involved acts of cruelty and revenge. Because her strength and individuality were more than a traditionalist like Procopius could tolerate, he exaggerated and slandered her on the stereotypes she transgressed, thereby providing useful information about contemporary male and female gender biases and expectations. If we discount Procopius's exaggerations in accordance with literary formulae and take into account his personal attitudes and biases, the *Secret History* becomes an extraordinary well of information about Theodora's personality, style of joint rule, relationship with her husband, and innovative influence.

Betrayal, duplicity, and low morality are facets of Theodora's character to which Procopius refers most often. He no doubt experienced firsthand what her betrayal meant: her disregard for "honest men" in traditional official roles, such as senators. Theodora may have been given to pleasure and luxury, but for modern readers the most sensational aspects of Procopius's depiction are probably the sexual exploits of Theodora's early career. None of Procopius's many accusations, however, would have been taken as seriously as that of her collusion with demons.[36]

Like the Augustae of the Theodosian house, Flaccilla, Eudoxia, Pulcheria, Athenais Eudocia, and Galla Placidia, Theodora shaped a highly individual style of rule.[37] This role would be continued by Theodora's successor, the empress Sophia, who was her niece. Sophia's husband, Justin II (565–78), who was the son of Justinian's sister, Vigilantia, proved incapable of ruling because of madness, and Sophia capably filled the position, also influencing the choice of the next two emperors after him.[38] Theodora carved out a mode of operation according to which she followed her own preferences and inclinations, from charitable works to court ceremonial, and from bathing to religious adherence. The *Secret History's* indirect testimony to Theodora's strength and individuality is, ironically, contrary to Procopius's aim in composing the work, for it allows one to recapture her complex character and personality.

In Procopius's other works, *Wars* and *Buildings,* stereotypes of women appear more as a formality, for his main interest is in the "deeds of men."[39] The women who are depicted in *Wars* are passive, their importance to men lying in the financial and career benefits of a good marriage. Women are portrayed as victims in the falls of cities such as Rome and Antioch, although others fall victim to their own bad judgment when they act on the basis of their emotions. On the whole, women are dangerous if they are too independent, and the more prudent state of affairs is for them to be dependent and subservient to men. If there is a moral to Procopius's story, it is that privilege for women should not be equated with license and that imperial women should follow societal norms of the good woman too.[40] To illustrate his view of proper female morality he ruthlessly stereotypes Theodora and Antonina through slander, gossip, and invention to construct his bad woman images. His stereotyping and polarities of viewpoint, however, afford insights into contemporary expectations about female behavior. We can assume that citizens of Byzantium would have understood these assumptions similarly.[41] Elizabeth Fisher, in her interpretation of Theodora, characterizes the technique used by Procopius:

> The portrayals of Theodora and Antonina in the *Historia Arcana* [*Secret History*] are thus essential to its purpose. Procopius was himself subject to and conscious of the attitudes toward women typical of his times; in skillfully exploiting these attitudes to destroy the reputations of Justininan and Belisarius, he has created an extraordinarily effective work of slander.[42]

In her study, Fisher helps us see Theodora and Antonina, the prime female subjects of the *Secret History,* in a contemporary context and in relation to Procopius's purpose, as she cogently relates their characterizations to gendered stereotypes of women.

As empress, Theodora no doubt had a great deal of influence, but the nature of that influence has been filtered through the misogynistic and biased viewpoint of Procopius. Our challenge has been to discern something of the "real" Theodora in it, just as generations of scholars have and will continue to shed light on different aspects of this problem, using different approaches. On examining the *Secret History* from a feminist perspective, however, one cannot help yearning for a glimpse of the empress, Antonina, and the women who surrounded them in the palace. How did they look when they appeared at court ceremonies? What kinds of clothing and jewelry did they wear? In the bright, mysterious mosaics of the sanctuary of San Vitale in Ravenna, Italy, lie clues.

## Visualizing Theodora

The mosaic portrait of Theodora and her retinue at the church of San Vitale in Ravenna serves in one sense as a visual counterpart to the literary image of Theodora in Procopius's *Secret History.* It must be viewed, however, in conjunction with the Justinian panel paired with it on the opposite wall of the sanctuary (figs. 21 and

*Fig. 21. Justinian with his retinue, mosaic panel, north wall of sanctuary, San Vitale, Ravenna, Italy, ca. 545–47. (Copyright Scala/Art Resource, N.Y.)*

22), from which it differs in marked ways. Some scholars have been tempted to see in this dichotomy encoded messages about the gender roles of the sovereigns, about femininity and masculinity, and male and female imperial status.[43] The date of the panels has been determined as just before the dedication of the church in 547, and the action represented as the celebration of the Small Entrance of the liturgy, with the sovereigns' individual ceremonial roles symbolically situated in the church of Hagia Sophia in Constantinople.[44] On one level, the mosaics represent the sovereigns as patrons or donors in their mirrored gestures of gift giving, but they have also been shown to contain multiple levels of meaning within the context of the rest of the sanctuary decoration and contemporary political and religious issues.[45] I will focus first on a reading of the Theodora panel.

The empress stands to the left of center in the panel, extending a gold and jeweled chalice in both hands; two men are on the left, and seven women on the right.[46] There is a suggestion of stately movement from right to left, as the group passes through a curtained, architecturally defined space, toward a darkened doorway. The men who lead the procession, probably eunuchs, for they are beardless, have tableia on their cloaks, indicating they are court officials. The women can be divided into three groups: Theodora, an older and a younger woman who stand immediately on

*Fig. 22. Theodora with her retinue, mosaic panel, south wall of sanctuary, San Vitale, Ravenna, Italy, ca. 545–47. (Copyright Scala/Art Resource, N.Y.)*

her right, and five colorfully and elegantly clad and coiffed women who form a cluster farther to the right. Theodora's appearance (see pl. 6) almost matches the summary description by Procopius: "She was fair of face and of a very graceful though small person; her complexion was moderately colorful if somewhat pale; and her eyes were dazzling and vivacious."[47] Her pallor, as seen in the mosaic, has been associated with the illness which caused her death. Such an official portrait would, on the other hand, probably not have reflected any such specific traits but would have stemmed from a standard painted model brought from Constantinople to Ravenna. She did not, in other words, sit for this portrait, hence its slightly generalized and idealized quality. Still, such individual features as her long neck and somewhat sunken eyes may have corresponded to her actual appearance. Following ancient artistic conventions, the empress is depicted slightly taller than those around her to indicate her higher rank and importance. Her halo likewise indicates her imperial and therefore divinely ordained status. The symbolic features of her height and halo are combined with specific insignia of imperial rank seen in her splendid attire.

Theodora's voluminous, deep-purple cloak sweeps from shoulders to feet. Its gold embroidered border includes, along the hem, depictions of the three Magi, whose gestures of gift giving match her own. Just visible underneath the cloak is a long, white tunic with oval gold patch visible on her right shoulder and colorful embroidery on hem, side-slits, and wristbands. Her shoes are trimmed with gold and emeralds. Theodora's garb and adornment are even more elaborate than those of the emperor in the panel opposite and include the prominent attributes of power appropriated by empresses since Flaccilla, as noted in chapter 3. Her costume is most closely paralleled in an ivory diptych leaf of ca. 500 to 520 in the Kunsthistorisches Museum in Vienna showing the empress Ariadne (compare fig. 7 for a similar ivory). In this deeply carved and purple-stained ivory, jewels are abundantly applied to the person, insignia, and garments of the empress, and the pattern of ornament of her mantle is painted onto the surface of the ivory.[48]

The Ravenna mosaic's glass tesserae record the bright colors of fabrics and gems with striking fidelity. A heavily jeweled diadem encircles Theodora's tightly snooded hair bound with pearls. Pendilia consisting of long ropes of pearls hang from the crown on either side, the pearls indicated by round tesserae of mother-of-pearl. She also wears earrings consisting of gold hoops with pendant pearls, emeralds, and sapphires, and a short necklace of almond-shaped emeralds at the throat. A great jeweled ceremonial collar, or *maniakion,* lies about her shoulders, trimmed with pearls and large teardrop-shaped pendants and incorporating three large jeweled emblems. Her cloak is pinned with a large brooch or fibula of the bow type, with the loop, or bow, visible above her right shoulder, and its three large teardrop-shaped pendants hang just below the maniakion. Purple cloak, pendant brooch, and the basic form of the crown are juxtaposed in the facing portraits of emperor and empress, indicating that these are essential insignia of imperial power. This image of Theodora must correspond to the empress's appearance at the ceremonial occasions and audiences referred to in the *Secret History.* It also must have resembled her portrait in other mosaics and statues which are mentioned in the sources but have disappeared.

No other positively identified portrait of Theodora survives, although there are several sculpted heads which may have come from statues of the empress. We know of many statues of her in cities around the empire, including one on a porphyry column in a courtyard of the Arcadianne Baths on the coast of the Sea of Marmora just outside the walls of Constantinople.[49] We also know of a mosaic depicting Justinian's triumphs which once decorated the ceiling of the Chalke Gate, the vestibule of the imperial palace in Constantinople. Procopius describes it in his *Buildings:*

> In the center stand the emperor and the empress Theodora, both seeming to rejoice and to celebrate victories over both the King of the Vandals and the King of the Goths, who approach them as prisoners of war to be led into bondage. Around them stands the Roman Senate, all in festal mood. This spirit is expressed by the cubes of the mosaic which by their colors depict exultation on their very countenances. So they rejoice and smile as they bestow on the emperor honors equal to those of God, because of the magnitude of his achievements.[50]

The Ravenna mosaic invites comparison with this text emphasizing the brilliant, colorful effect of the cubes of mosaic. While Theodora stands opposite Justinian in the mosaics of San Vitale, each in a separate procession, in the Chalke Gate mosaic, on the other hand, she apparently stood immediately next to him. A liturgical procession and act of donation are distinguished in format from a secular celebration of military victory; the same concept of united sovereigns is presented in both instances, however, but employing a different arrangement. In the religious processions they are accompanied by associates, officials, and an honor guard, while in the state occasion they are accompanied by the senate.[51] The description of the lost Chalke Gate mosaic reinforces the likelihood that Theodora appeared there as at San Vitale, with the essential elements of the cloak, brooch, and crown, clearly representing the concept of joint rule of united sovereigns.[52]

The group of five women at the far right follow at the end of Theodora's train. They all look off to one side or the other, not engaging the viewer with their gazes. Their faces are depicted with similar, generalized traits, and they wear similarly bound hair; their hands are not visible, with the exception of one who holds a white scarf; two white scarves hang from their waists. Their jewelry is varied, and their tunics and shawls are of contrasting colors and patterns in bright shades of orange, green, white, beige, and gold. The first woman in line appears somewhat distinguished from the others, for she wears an elegant collarlike necklace of pearls and emeralds, a smaller version of the maniakion, and has medallions sewn onto her tunic and shawl. The others wear earrings and smaller necklaces. These five accompanying women in the train represent what was likely a much larger female retinue with specific roles in the public and private life of the empress. They afford a unique glimpse of her "ladies of the palace," referred to in derogatory terms by Procopius, as discussed above.[53] They would have been present to serve the empress in everyday life as well as to attend her at official ceremonies. But who are the two striking women in between?

The pair of women immediately to the right of Theodora have an individualized quality not found in the ladies in waiting and are allotted ample space in which to move and show themselves (see pl. 6). The one who stands next to Theodora is depicted as older, with pale, thin face, pointed chin, and deep blue eyes. The other, on the right, is young, of rosy complexion and with dark eyes, and of great beauty. Like the empress, they gaze straight out at the viewer. The face of the older woman, unlike the empress's, appears to be a keen likeness, as if it could have been done from life. This woman gestures with her right hand with its emerald ring toward the younger, who responds with a slight acknowledgment of her left hand, simultaneously presenting an emerald ring of even larger size on the third finger of her left hand. A relationship of mother and daughter is suggested by their relative ages, their gestures, and their overlapping attitudes in the mosaic. The women are of identical height and wear similar veiled hairstyles, one gray and the other gold. Their earrings, like those worn by Theodora, consist of gold hoops and pendant emeralds, pearls, and sapphires, although of smaller size than the empress's. Gold choker necklaces with pendants are worn by both, that of the younger woman having a single lozenge-shaped emerald at the center. Their similar green- and gold-striped wristbands edged with pearls further associate the women, linking them as a pair.

The older woman wears somewhat somber colors: a dark gray tunic with woven geometric designs and two wide gold vertical bands with zig-zag edges and decorated with embroidered flower-chains; her shawl is gray and white, also patterned with slightly smaller roundel designs than on the skirt. On her shawl is a prominent gold medallion shaped like a six-pointed star. The younger woman wears a violet tunic woven with blue bird motifs and with two gold medallions with central floral motifs. Her shawl is gold with similar floral motifs of bright green, orange, and red woven into the fabric throughout. For sheer brilliance of color and quantity of gold worn by any figure she is unsurpassed in both panels. Can these women be identified?

A pair of distinguished scholars has argued that they are Antonina, wife of Belisarius, and her only daughter, Joannina, and although this theory is impossible to prove, it is very likely for a number of reasons.[54] As discussed above, Procopius definitively associates Theodora and Antonina as friends, confidants, allies, and, to some extent, mutually dependent manipulators. No other woman is mentioned in any of the surviving sources who is as close to the empress as the wife of Belisarius, Justinian's general and the principal implementer of his ambitious policy of reconquest. Antonina, according to Procopius, "was on terms of closest friendship and intimacy with the empress."[55] Antonina is thus the first figure one would expect to find in a depiction of an individualized person in the empress's immediate female entourage. Antonina's connection through gestures with the younger woman next to her suggests that this is her daughter, Joannina, who was, as noted above, of particular interest to Theodora.

Joannina must have been one the great heiresses of the time. It stands to reason that Belisarius had acquired great wealth in the course of his campaigns, and the fact is also acknowledged by Procopius, who knew him well. Theodora arranged the betrothal between her grandson, Anastasius, and Joannina, as discussed above.[56] In the Justinian panel the rest of the personages involved in such a betrothal can be identified. To the left of Justinian is a mature man in court costume who has been identified as the general Belisarius, and next to him a handsome young man, beardless and similarly attired, who must be Anastasius, his future son-in-law. The personages in the two mosaic panels are juxtaposed in a mirror image with their spouses or future spouses: Justinian, followed by Belisarius and Anastasius are juxtaposed with Theodora, followed by Antonina and Joannina. The ring-displaying women share the center of Theodora's panel, just as Belisarius and Anastasius appear with Justinian.[57] The symmetry and juxtaposition of the two groups responds to an important motive behind the creation of the mosaic, a show of imperial solidarity through the visualization of a marriage alliance between two families.

The engagement has been dated to spring 544, and since Theodora died in 548,

I believe she must have used her authority some time between 544 and 547 when the church of San Vitale was consecrated, to have the hoped-for union commemorated.[58] Ravenna would have been an appropriate place to do this for political reasons, for just as the bishop Maximian was reenforcing Justinian's imperial ties to the city, the military presence in the city had as its focal and most visible figures the general Belisarius and Antonina, both of whom spent considerable time in Italy. Procopius mentions specifically that Belisarius and Antonina were in Italy, probably at the Byzantine capital, Ravenna, at the time Theodora was attempting to tie the knot:

> To avoid this alliance they delayed the ceremony "until they could both be present at it," and then, when the Empress summoned them to Constantinople, pretended they were unable at the time to leave Italy.[59]

The specificity of this passage and the ostensible excuse, that the bride's parents both wished to be present but were in Italy, correlate to indicate an important function of the mosaic.

These splendid mosaics are, I suggest, part of Theodora's plan to ensure that the marriage with her grandson would take place. The mosaics are also meant to be a public show of unity between the family of the imperial couple and that of Belisarius and Antonina, with the impending marriage about to seal the pact. Such a message was important in the reestablishment of Byzantine power in Italy, which had experienced serious setbacks.[60] Although we have already noted the unhappy outcome of the engagement of Joannina and Anastasius after Theodora's death, this mosaic was commissioned and executed at a moment when it functioned to enhance imperial power and solidarity in Italy. The presence of the two elegantly dressed women, mother and daughter, prominently showing their rings, visually evokes issues of wealth, alliances, and marriage at the highest level.

The large and prominently displayed emerald ring must refer to Joannina's engagement to Anastasius in 544, arranged by Theodora. It is tempting to associate this ring with that extraordinary emerald ring given by Anicia Juliana to Justinian as a token of her wealth in 527. In any case, such a large emerald as that seen here undoubtedly had imperial, if not dynastic, connotations. The dramatic showing of the ring reflects Theodora's wish to have the engagement of the pair depicted as irrevocable.

The mosaic serves as a record of a dynastic union with implications for the future of the empire. The two families are depicted as already joined in the mosaic panels—and perhaps also the next generation already in place to inherit power. Because Justinian and Theodora did not have children of their own, this was as close as they would come to providing a legacy from within their own family. By commissioning the mosaic panel as we see it, Theodora persuasively conveyed her intention of uniting the two families, in spite of the difficulties presented by the traveling distance between Ravenna and Constantinople and Antonina's excuses. If Italy would not come to Constantinople, then Constantinople would come to Italy.[61]

The Theodora panel in the sanctuary of San Vitale, with its counterpart the Justinian panel, reflects the empress's personal intentions for her grandson's marriage. The marriage alliance adds another layer of meaning to the already complex religious, political, and symbolic content of the mosaic panels. In connection with this discussion of the mosaics' extended meanings, I want to consider how the material splendor depicted in them might actually have appeared.

The dazzling colors of the Theodora mosaic at Ravenna correspond to precious fabrics and jewelry actually worn by women of this time. Many styles of dress and jewelry were carryovers from late antiquity, as seen, for example, in the portraits of women on mummy cases from Roman Egypt dating to the first through fourth centuries and in tomb sculptures from Palmyra dating to the third century.[62] The showiness or elaborateness of jewelry in the later Roman Empire varied according to the woman's status, but the trend of displaying jewelry as imperial insignia grew steadily.[63] The crown with pendilia is clearly the most prominent of Byzantine imperial insignia. Although no early Byzantine imperial crowns have survived, comparable examples of later date are preserved with their pendilia intact.[64] The Holy Crown of Hungary, for example, has a wide band ornamented with jewels and enamels with a wide strap arching over the top of the wearer's head and a gold cross set at the top. Gold chains from which hang clusters of jewels are suspended around the crown on two sides.[65]

The other ubiquitous sign of imperial power, the three-pendant brooch, survives in several examples. The brooch worn by Theodora is of a bow type with a large jewel on the arc of the bow and three pendant chains with terminal pearls. A gold brooch in the Kunsthistorisches Museum from the fourth century has varied stones in a triangular shape from which hang three gold chains ending in teardrop-shaped pendants set with stones.[66] Another fibula, on anonymous loan to the Metropolitan Museum in New York, has been called an "imperial fibula" because of its resemblance to that in the San Vitale panels; it too includes three loops for attachment of pendants.[67] The unmistakable presence of a loop or bow rising above the contour of Theodora's shoulder, however, indicates another type of fibula or brooch. An example in the Metropolitan Museum consists of a heavy gold catchplate once ornamented with a beaded ring, a bow, and, at the end of the bow, a crossbar of three globes with granulated gold collars (fig. 23).[68] This bow fibula, another characteristic design, is closer to the type worn by Theodora in the mosaic because it has the crucial detail of the loop or bow. Missing, however, is a place for attachment of the three pendants and the capping gem. No exact counterpart of the brooch used to hold Theodora's imperial chlamys survives, although the components are clearly recognizable in a number of examples.

Other pieces of jewelry worn by the women in the Theodora panel have close parallels in surviving examples. Earrings and necklaces similar to those worn by Theodora, Antonina, and Joannina are on display at Dumbarton Oaks. One such example, dating to the fifth century, has a gold hoop from which hang a pearl set in a gold ring, an emerald, and a pear-shaped sapphire.[69] Choker necklaces similar to that worn by

Theodora with gems threaded on a gold wire with looped links are displayed in the Cyprus museum, Walters Art Gallery in Baltimore, Dumbarton Oaks, and Metropolitan Museum. A set of earrings and necklace is on display at Dumbarton Oaks (see pl. 7).[70]

Finally, the heavy, jeweled collar worn by Theodora and the less ornate version worn by the first lady-in-waiting can be visualized through an extraordinary piece preserved in Berlin. Dating to the sixth or early seventh century, it probably was made in Constantinople (fig. 24).[71] This necklace, made up of eleven gold openwork plaques mounted with pearls and three rows of precious stones, has seventeen pendants composed of pearls and jewels on gold wires. Originally more than one hundred pearls, emeralds, and sapphires decorated this lunate-shaped necklace, making it extremely heavy and a considerable burden to wear. Last, bracelets such as those worn by Antonina and Joannina can be seen in a number of museums. For example, a pair at the Metropolitan Museum dating to the seventh century consists of two hoops which fasten close to the wrist and is studded with sapphires and emeralds bordered with strings of pearls on heavy gold wires (fig. 25).[72]

In addition to the ornate jewelry worn by the women, the jeweled hairstyles worn by empresses with their crowns can be reconstructed through observation of other media. The Castello Sforzesco head in Milan, thought to represent Theodora, serves better than any other example to illustrate how the diademed snood she wears in the San Vitale mosaic was constructed (fig. 26).[73] Carved in marble, this head with elaborate crown shows, in addition to a double row of pearls encircling the head, double strands of pearls crossing up and over the head between the two cloth-covered peaks of hair and single strands along the ridges of the peaks; a damaged area in the marble at the top of the head shows where an attachment has broken off. There are also fillet ties at the back and pendilia of pearls down the sides of the temples. A glance at this head shows how closely it corresponds to Theodora's portrait at San Vitale, with the peaked, snooded hairstyle and lavish use of pearls in diadem and

pendilia. The mosaic shows jewels set between the rows of pearls as well as a peak ornament rising from the top of the head.[74] If one takes into account evidence of the missing peak-ornament, Theodora's crown and hair ornaments correspond precisely to those of the Milan head.

As for the materials and types of fabric worn by the women in the mosaic, a passage from Procopius's *Buildings* is instructive in evoking the meaning of imperial garments and insignia when presented to Armenian satraps by Justinian and is also revealing about the eastern associations with such lavish adornment:

> They received the symbols of office only from the Roman Emperor. It is worthwhile to describe these insignia, for they will never again be seen by man. There is a cloak made of wool not such as is produced by sheep, but gathered from the sea. Pinnos the creature is called on which this wool grows. And the part where the purple should have been, that is, where the insertion of purple cloth is usually made, is overlaid with gold. The cloak was fastened by a golden brooch in the middle of which was a precious stone from which hung three sapphires by loose golden chains. There was a tunic of silk

*Fig. 26. Head of Theodora (?), marble, from Castello Sforzesco, Civico Museo d'Arte Antica, Milan, Italy, ca. 530–40. (Copyright Scala/Art Resource, N.Y.)*

adorned in every part with decorations of gold which they are wont to call plumia. The boots were of red colour and reached to the knee, of the sort which only the Roman Emperor and the Persian king are permitted to wear. (*Buildings* 3.18–23)

The finery described here as Byzantine gifts to the Armenian satraps is comparable to that seen in the Ravenna mosaics. The three-pendant brooch has the most conspicuous imperial connotation. The emphasis in the Procopius passage, however, is on fabrics: the wool cloak, dyed in precious purple dye, with gold *tableion*, a broad, ornamental fabric panel; the silk tunic with gold decorations; and, of course, the red boots. The colors of fabrics as well as the designs and precious materials were symbolic of status, for the wearing of purple and certain shades of red cloth of wool or silk was reserved for the emperor. Both the wearing and the giving of such garments and insignia, as we see in the Ravenna mosaics, were the prerogative of royalty.

Examples of fine, deeply dyed wool, linen, and silk fabric have survived from this period, coming mainly from Egyptian tombs and from the reliquary caskets in which saints were buried in the medieval West. Such uses indicate that the finest woven fabrics, received through trade or as diplomatic gifts, were highly prized in the West. Purple cloth, especially purple fabrics dyed several times—probably ranging in hue from an almost black-purple, like that seen in the sovereigns' robes in the Ravenna mosaics (pl. 6), to a bright purple-red, such as that seen in the Dumbarton Oaks Samson silk (pl. 8)—were of greatest value. The famous story of the theft of the secret of silk production—the silkworms themselves—by Justinian's monk-spies suggests the probable beginning of this industry during his reign.[75] Silk is currently the best preserved and studied of these high-status fabrics.[76]

Sassanian Persian silk was traded directly with Byzantium and served as a model for Byzantine silk production from the mid–sixth century on. The presentation of exceptionally fine and precious silk fabric was part of the ritual of reception and presentation of gifts between the two empires.[77] It is also clear that precious silks were worn by members of the palace hierarchy of officials and attendants as well as by the imperial family. Theodora's mantle with its gold pattern of magi offering gifts can be compared to woven figured silks. For example, a Dionysiac scene is depicted in brown on a deep purple ground in a silk from the treasury of Sens cathedral in central France.[78] Famous silks with New Testament scenes are preserved in the Museo Sacro of the Vatican and date to the sixth century.[79] The woven geometric patterns in the tunic and shawl worn by Antonina probably duplicate woven silks with typical Sassanian designs in roundels. Popular designs were the Senmurv, or half-lion, half-bird designs, lions, elephants, griffons, and horsemen, among others; examples of deep purple and yellow on green ground with inwoven roundels with Senmurvs survive with their bright colors intact.[80] Many examples of Byzantine figured silks can be seen in the Byzantine collection at Dumbarton Oaks, among them the famous Samson Panel dating to the sixth or seventh century (see pl. 8).[81] This exceptionally large fragment shows repeat motifs of a muscular man strangling a lion against a background of saturated red. The appliquéd oval patches in gold thread seen on Theodora's and Joannina's tunics also have counterparts in preserved linen tunics with applied wool patches and friezes; such patches were also made in silk with drawlooms.[82]

The dress with blue birds worn by Joannina is comparable to examples of silks preserved at Sens;[83] also, a striking example of a Byzantine silk with allover bird pattern in purple can be seen in the cathedral treasure of Sainte-Foy at Conques in France.[84] The frequency of such Sassanian-inspired ornamental motifs and designs on Byzantine silks requires explanation, and a partial one in fact occurs in Procopius's description of gifts to the Armenians. To present lavish gifts enhanced one's status as giver and was part of a ritual meant not only to gain but also to give respect. One could further interpret Byzantine use of Sassanian silk designs as the appropriation of a rival culture with the aim of assimilating its power through symbolic means and thereby asserting one's superiority. The language of fabrics, colors, and designs, so dynamically displayed in the Theodora panel, is inextricably interwoven with the language of Byzantine diplomacy and display of status characteristic of the time.

The Procopius passages on gifts of insignia and on the Chalke mosaics, in addition to the visual evidence of the San Vitale mosaics, have a bearing on Procopius's repeated descriptions in the *Secret History* of the increasingly elaborate court ritual which Theodora encouraged. The Byzantines shared with Persia a love of splendor and sumptuous jeweled adornment for sovereigns. During Theodora's reign the elaborateness of audiences and ceremonies of reception of visitors was heightened on the Persian model. Persian styles may have contributed to the tendency already present in late antique Rome to convey status of imperial figures and high-ranking associates through a conspicuous display of jewelry.[85] The Ravenna mosaics show, however, that Theodora claimed the right to wear the most heavily jeweled ornaments and rich fabrics along with her imperial insignia. She must have set the standard among women, with a carefully graduated system running from titled women, such as the Patricia, down through high-ranking women and ladies of the court, to wives of officials and women of lower rank to whom were prescribed less lavish jewels and fabrics. One can see this heirarchy of ornament illustrated in the mosaic.

Not only did Theodora personally increase the degree of abasement and formality of ceremony surrounding an imperial audience, so loudly decried by Procopius, but it follows that she also chose to heighten the richness of adornment of her own person and those attending her. Both of these innovations were inspired by oriental practices and material splendor which were being increasingly imitated in Byzantium. In visualizing Theodora through the mosaics and through surviving examples of jewelry and fabric, one can approximate the indelible impression left by her tastes and vitality on Byzantine material culture.

## Associated Readings

Procopius *Secret History,* trans. Richard Atwater (Ann Arbor, 1963).

———. *Secret History, Wars, Buildings,* trans. H. B. Dewing (1914–40; repr. Cambridge, Mass., 1998), for Greek and English translation.

Elizabeth A. Fisher, "Theodora and Antonina in the *Historia Arcana:* History and/or Fiction?" *Arethusa* 11 (1978): 253–79.

Lynda Garland, *Byzantine Empresses: Women and Power in Byzantium, AD 527–1204* (New York, 1999), esp. chap. 1, "Theodora, wife of Justinian (527–48)," 11–39.

Irina Andreescu-Treadgold and Warren Treadgold, "Procopius and the Imperial Panels of S. Vitale," *Art Bulletin* 79 (1997): 708–23.

*Seven*

# ORDINARY WOMEN IN THE
# ORBIT OF THEODORE OF SYKEON

While the *Secret History* is revealing about the "real" Theodora and women at the top of society in Constantinople, ordinary women of this time are also accessible in rare instances. Rare because in Byzantium, ordinary people's lives are not recorded per se, as in the oral histories that are becoming increasingly popular in American literary culture. An elevated form of biography existed in the compilations of the lives or, more precisely, deeds of rulers, as in the Life of the emperor Basil I written by his grandson, Constantine VII. Saints' Lives often have as their subjects people who start out as ordinary people but are made extraordinary through the exemplary way God is seen to work through them. No literary work resembling an autobiography or personal journal has survived to shed light on ordinary people in everyday life. Yet just as village women's names inscribed on silver objects and subscription mosaics indicate their role as patrons (see chapter 5), so a work written a little more than half a century after the *Secret History,* the *Life of Saint Theodore of Sykeon,* reveals the presence and activity of common women.[1]

The *Life of Theodore,* written by Theodore's disciple George, is an account of the life and miracles of a Byzantine monk who lived in Galatia, what is today north-central Turkey, in the last half of the sixth and early seventh centuries. Throughout, the work depicts women of the countryside who were associated with this holy man. Although Theodore travels to Jerusalem, Constantinople, and other cities of Asia Minor, most of the narrative concerns his activities within the agrarian society in and around the rural village of Sykeon. The work thus deals with a social milieu entirely unlike that of the *Secret History* and with country as opposed to city life; in addition, it is written in a different genre. Far from the imperial court and Theodora's circle was a community whose women are described by the monkish author in unpreten-

146

tious prose. They play a major part in the story of the saint's childhood, his support system in later life, and in the collection of accounts of miracles appended to the Life. The author describes women as they relate to Theodore within the context of his life story.

As in other hagiographic works about male saints written by men, women are mentioned in the narrative but are not a principal concern of the author. In this Life they emerge with some vividness and clarity in their daily occupations, relationships to one another, patterns of life, beliefs, and fates. George's testimony about women, although indirect and hidden between the lines, is abundant and functions as a subtext. To what extent can one rely on this genre—and in particular on this unlikely source of information—for factual indications of events and an accurate picture of the ways of life of the people concerned? Does this text contain a gender bias, like Procopius's *Secret History*?

George, as he himself states, grew up near Sykeon, was educated at the monastery founded by his subject, and lived there as a monk and disciple of Theodore from around 601 until the saint's death in 613. He started writing the *Life of Theodore* while serving as a monk and priest and completed it after becaming abbot, following Theodore's death. The saint was born during the reign of Justinian, so the main narrative takes place in the years from the 550s or 560s to 613. The Life is written in a decidedly popular style, for we are dealing with an author who did not have the rhetorical training and cosmopolitan background of a Procopius. He did have direct knowledge of and proximity to the subject of his narrative, a basic education, and a thorough knowledge of Scripture. He also knew the texts of other hagiographic works, which served as models, and he includes topoi characteristic of the genre. Like the Life of Saint Macrina (see chapter 1) and the Life of Mary of Egypt (see chapter 4), this one was intended to play an important role in the making of the saint.[2]

George gathered his material about Theodore carefully, and he explains his sources at various points in the narrative, as in the following passage:

> Now these doings of his childhood and youth have been written by me George, his unworthy servant and disciple; some of them I learnt from his contemporaries and schoolfellows, who lived and associated with him at that time and actually saw these things with their own eyes, but the majority of them I gathered from the lips of the holy and saintly man himself. (22.1–8)

He writes mainly for people who are acquainted with the individuals, families, and events he describes, and his recollections, which include a wealth of historical detail and social commentary on the contemporary scene, are based on firsthand observation. His tone is humble and sincere, but he writes knowledgeably and factually from within the sphere of his subject. His only bias is his eagerness to record what is perfect and godly in this man.

As abbot of the monastery, he is also fulfilling a religious duty, and his writing itself is an act of piety. As he makes clear in the Prologue, his aim is to inspire his readers with the supreme virtue of his predecessor, so that they may emulate his "angelic and blameless life."[3] No doubt the saint himself recounted to the author many of the early episodes, which prominently involve women of his family. Theodore's concern for them may be the reason for their frequent appearance in George's narrative. The Life deals with farmers, peasants, and villagers, those who viewed the emperor, empress, and court in Constantinople from a distance, physically and conceptually. The Life begins during the reign of Justinian with the birth of the saint and the circumstances of his childhood and upbringing.

Sykeon was located on a major route between Constantinople and Ancyra (present-day Ankara, Turkey), near the town of Anastasioupolis, and this is where the reader first encounters the women who give Theodore a start in life:

> The public highway of the imperial post ran through this village, and on the road stood an inn kept by a very beautiful girl, Mary, and her mother, Elpidia, and a sister Despoinia. And these women lived in the inn and followed the profession of courtesans. (3.4–10)

After the author's pious introduction, the saint's story begins with the matter-of-fact statement that the women who ran the inn at Sykeon were available sexually to male guests and are referred to by the author as *hetairai*, or courtesans. We already noted in the case of Theodora's early career that women who were actresses were also expected to serve as courtesans or prostitutes. According to expectations within the society, a courier traveling on the highway was given the customary treatment when he stayed at the inn at Sykeon:

> At that time when Justinian of pious memory was Emperor, certain imperial decrees were being dispatched from the capital, and thus it chanced that a certain well-known man, Cosmas by name, who had become popular in the Hippodrome in the corps of those who performed acrobatic feats on camels, was appointed to carry out the emperor's orders. (3.10–14)

Cosmas is a royal messenger and a popular performer in the hippodrome; the father-to-be of the saint comes from the same milieu as the empress Theodora. This former acrobat working as a messenger in the service of the emperor obtains the sexual services of Mary, the innkeeper, which results in her bearing an illegitimate child:

> On this man's journey to the East he stayed for some time in the inn, and seeing Mary and how fair she was, he desired her and took her to his bed. From this union she conceived and saw in a dream a very large and brilliant star descending from heaven into her womb. She awoke all trembling with fear and related the vision she had seen in the night to Cosmas, the imperial messenger, and he said to her, "Take good care of yourself, dear, for perchance God will watch over you and give you a son who will be deemed worthy to become a bishop." With these words he left her in the morning and went on his way rejoicing. (3.14–25)

Mary's dream is interpreted by Cosmas as a sign that her child will be extraordinary, even rising to the position of bishop. This sign of divine intervention is a familiar topos in other saints' Lives, and Cosmas's statement that the child might become a bishop is an after-the-fact recognition of his actual career as bishop of Anastasioupolis. Cosmas departs from the scene, and the women are left to cope with the outcome of his visit.

Mary then consults an old man known as a prophet in the region, and his prophecy is that the child will be a great man, "not as men hold greatness, but he will be well-pleasing to God."[4] Consulting a prophet was one way a woman would deal with the unknown and risky future of having a child out of wedlock. As for raising such a child, she relied on family and community, as we learn in the first part of the Life.

After his baptism, Theodore, whose name means "gift of God," is raised to the age of six by his mother, at which point she has ambitions for his future:

> When the child was about six years old, his mother wanted him to enter the emperor's service in the capital, so she made ready for him a gold belt and expensive clothes and everything else necessary, and then she prepared herself for the journey. (5.7–10)

Perhaps since Cosmas had been in the imperial service Mary hopes that her child might follow in his father's path, and she provides luxurious items to prepare her son for an audience at Justinian's court. With the income derived from her profession running the inn she is able to purchase a gold belt and expensive clothes for him. One can imagine this was not done without some personal sacrifice.

A vision in another dream discourages Mary from taking the boy to Constantinople, and instead she works tirelessly for his welfare at home:

> She wore herself away with increasing care of her son, and when he was eight years old she gave him to a teacher to be taught his letters. (5.16–19)

Even though Theodore does not live in a family headed by a man, his mother works to fulfill his needs. Even though she is a single mother in a disreputable profession, there is allowance within the society for her to have access to an education for her child.

Life at the inn is enhanced by the cook, Stephen, who is very skilled and whose meals draw important guests who pay well. The women proprietors and their cook prosper. Under the influence of Stephen, a pious man who leads a life of ascetic renunciation, their lives gradually change:

> The women by this time had become quite respectable, for they had abandoned their profession as prostitutes and followed the path of sobriety and godliness. (6.2–4)

How the women gave up their profession as prostitutes (for in this passage the term *pornai* is used) is not mentioned. Did they renounce their former pattern or repent in consultation with the local priest? The change is simply stated and was probably a familiar pattern within the society. Stephen the cook has an influence on Theodore, too, by inspiring him to take up the ascetic life. The child becomes dedicated to Saint George, whose shrine is located near the village. There the young Theodore spends parts of his days studying the Scriptures. He resists his mother's attempts to nourish him with food, and she worries about him with typical motherly concern. The author conveys the image of an extremely attentive and somewhat overprotective mother attempting to deal with a reclusive child.

After surviving a bout with the plague, Theodore becomes more devout and is even called in his sleep by visions. Saint George regularly awakens him at night in dreams and asks him to visit his shrine:

> When he began to adopt this habit, his mother and the women sleeping with her would wake up in the morning, and not seeing him in his bed they suspected that he had crept out and was spending the nights in the martyr's shrine; and they wondered how it was, since he slept between them, that he got out so successfully without anybody noticing it. . . .
>
> When the women did not find him in bed in the morning they became very angry and sent servants who brought him back dragging him by the hair. His mother whipped him and tied him to the bed with his arms behind his back, and gave him no food. (9.1–6, 10–15)

Theodore slept between his mother and another woman in one bed, probably in a room with several beds, in what must have been a dormitory-style arrangement. Children probably normally slept in the same bed or room with adults because it served practical needs of warmth and security. In Theodore's case, it facilitates the women's keeping track of Theodore's visits to the shrine. Severe corporal punishments result when the boy slips out to spend the night there, but in a vision Saint George rebukes the mother and puts an end to the punishments. Not only do the women release the boy to do as he wishes, but he is supported and joined in his ascetic practices by his younger sister, Blatta, who "sympathized with him and loved him dearly" (9.31). While the episodes are meant to illustrate Theodore's ascetic piety from an early age, the account is revealing about the practices used in rearing children. Women guard, nourish, and punish according to social norms and what they feel is best for their children.

Family tensions, battles of wills, and influence of the supernatural are all part of the relationship between mother and son. In one confrontation, Theodore demonstrates to his mother and grandmother that things of this world are of no value to him:

> He also regarded the wealth of the world as nought and wishing to get rid of it, he unbuckled his gold belt, took off his necklace and the bracelet from his wrist and threw them down in front of the women saying, "You suspect that these things may get lost and it is because of them you trouble me. Take them then and begone! for I will not leave this place." And the women took them and went as they could not persuade him. (12.9–16)

Symbolically Theodore relinquishes the ornaments that convey worldly status, accusing the women of self-interest. His mother's concern is natural, however, for she worked to provide such luxuries and now justifiably worries that he, in his unconventional withdrawal, might lose these valuable possessions. The rejection of worldly goods is also a literary convention meant not only to indicate that Theodore holds different ideas from the norm, but also to herald his life as an ascetic hermit. In this as in other episodes we observe how a mother with high hopes for a child might treat him in the course of his upbringing. Mothers apparently played a strong formative role in the careers of their children, unless forced to accept an alternative pattern.

This family gradually acquiesces and supports the child's leanings, for just as women are constantly vigilant and controlling in Theodore's early career, they are also seen as willing to adapt to his unusual patterns of life:

> By now he had reached the age of fourteen and decided within himself to bid a final farewell to his home and take up his abode in the martyr's oratory. And he did indeed bid farewell to the women, and went up to the oratory and lived there giving thanks to God; but as his mother and the women who lived with her still did not realize that he had irrevocably chosen his blessed mode of life and that his resolve was no youthful fancy, they used to carry up to him fresh white loaves, and divers kinds of boiled and roasted birds. Theodore took them all indeed in order to satisfy them and because his fasting was in secret; however, he never touched any of these things but after his mother and her sister had gone down he would come out of the chapel and throw all the food out on the rocks . . . and the birds and beasts ate it up. (15.1–14)

The process of gradually leaving Theodore to his own devices again indicates the protectiveness, even of young adults, by families anxious about their welfare. The women given him choice kinds of meat in order to tempt him to eat, pampering him with the best that was available. Such practices of protectiveness and pampering were probably current within the society, for there would be no point in the author's distorting such mundane details. The episode, however, also illustrates the lengths to which the young saint went to pursue his calling, a topos showing his designation as a man of God.

Theodore's grandmother, Elpidia, proves to be particularly devoted to him, especially when he takes up a harsh ascetic exercise: during Lent he lives in an underground cave he has dug in the chapel:

> Now his grandmother, Elpidia, truly sympathized with him and loved him more than her two daughters; and she came up to the chapel and stayed with him all the time of his silence and ministered to him and gave him a little nourishment of fruit or some vegetable salad. (16.28–32)

Elpidia recognizes Theodore's extraordinary nature and has a deeper understanding of the workings of the divine than her daughters. The more dedicated he becomes to his solitary, ascetic life, the more devoted she becomes. The women in the orbit of Saint Theodore supply his needs and furnish him with a support system, whether he accepts it or not. The mother, the aunt, the sister, and the grandmother all play important roles in his life. Of all the family members, the grandmother understands him best. The mother, Mary, however, when her role as nurturer of her son is satisfied, leaves her family at the inn.

Mary leaves Sykeon to get married and take up a life "of the flesh":

> Now his mother minded not the things of the Lord but the things of the flesh, and did not feel for her son that intense longing and affection for their children which like a fire consumes some mothers. She left her most holy son, took the portion of the inheritance due to her, and was joined in marriage to a notable man, David by name, a leading citizen in the metropolis of Ancyra. (25.1–7)

Mary wishes to leave Sykeon and live in the capital city of Galacia, Ancyra. Her stake in the inn, presumably provided by her mother, serves as her dowry, and she is enabled to rise in status through her marriage to a distinguished man, David. Without the dowry she could probably not hope to achieve a good marriage, or any marriage at all. The fact that she was a prostitute during her earlier days at the inn does not seem to interfere with her marriage prospects. The hagiographer presents her choice of married life and "the flesh" as a lack of affection for her son, indicating that the "good mother" should be completely devoted to or "consumed" by her duty to her child. Of course the point of view is expressed by one who has renounced the flesh as part of his calling and whose lack of sympathy for the mother's position is understandable.

A realistic decision is made by the mother, who has the prospect of security and a better life, and she accepts David's offer of marriage. In her place, the other female family members continue their support of Theodore:

> But her sister, Despoinia, and her mother Elpidia and the Saint's sister, Blatta, could not bear to be separated from him, but rather through observing his virtuous life they strove as far as possible to imitate him, purifying and ennobling themselves by sobriety and chastity, by almsgiving and prayers. (25.7–12)

The remaining women in the family rally around Theodore, even imitating his piety and generosity. At the death of Despoinia, his aunt, she bequeaths all her worldly goods to Theodore, enriching his chapel through gifts of land and currency. Having no children to inherit her possessions, Despoina endows her nephew's religious foundation rather than provide her niece, Blatta, with a dowry. Soon after, Blatta is taken from the family and deposited in a nunnery in Ancyra:

> And his sister, Blatta, a virgin of twelve years old, the most holy man took to the metropolis of Ancyra and placed her in the charge of the dedicated virgins in the convent called Petris; and after she had received the habit of a nun he dedicated her to the Lord, for she was winning many victories in her spiritual life. . . . His blessed sister lived three years and then passed to her rest having borne testimony by her good works;

when her most holy brother, who had also been her guide into the Kingdom, heard of her death, he sent her forth as a bride to the heavenly bridal-chamber and rejoiced in Christ. (25.14–24)

When their mother has left the family, Theodore has the authority as male guardian to place his twelve-year-old sister in a convent and does so against her wishes. Financial circumstances may have necessitated Theodore's act, or Blatta may have been inclined toward an ascetic life. She was fifteen years old at her death and is buried as a Bride of Christ, her brother officiating at the funeral.

The only close female relative who remains in Sykeon is Elpidia, the grandmother. Late in life, however, she also leaves the inn and Sykeon and is placed at a nearby convent as its abbess:

> His grandmother, the blessed Elpidia, loved him exceedingly and sympathized with him, and would often come up and view his ascetic contest and glority God who had made a rose-bearing, fruitful bough of piety to grow out of the thistles of harlotry and had raised up a child of Abraham out of useless stones. And stretching forth her hands to heaven she prayed for him that his mind should remain undisturbed and raised above material things ever giving glory to God and that he should keep his faith 'steadfast and unmoveable' unto the end.
>     . . . He asked her to come to the convent of Saint Christopher lying to the East and there he persuaded her to remain. And the children who came to him plagued by unclean spirits he used to send to her (especially if they were girls) to receive treatment and to be taught their duties by living with her and that those who wished to remain after they were cured might be enrolled among the nuns. (25.24–43)

Theodore is the only man in this three-generation family, and even in his withdrawal from the world he determines the fates of his sister and his grandmother, both of whom enter convents. His grandmother Elpidia devotes herself to philanthropy by helping primarily girls who are mentally or psychologically unwell. At the convent, the girls receive some basic education and are "taught their duties," presumably women's domestic chores of weaving, sewing, and cooking. Elpidia's role as abbess reveals the options open to women in these circumstances:

> She had carefully provided everything necessary for the suppport of the women under her care; some had renounced this world, others were ill, and she had already created a very fine convent. . . . She now came to the days in which she was to die and during this time because of an intense longing for him, but still more because she somehow foreknew that it would be a farewell visit, she stayed closely by him, praying with him and singing with him . . . Later after a slight illness she passed away peacefully in her sleep and was buried by Theodore with due honour. (32.3–25)

Unless they had the possibility of marrying or earning a living through a trade, women would remain in the convent of Saint Christopher as nuns until their deaths. Just as the empress Theodora founded the convent of Repentance for prostitutes,

Elpidia ran a convent to help local women deal with the limited resources available to them. Both examples confirm that women living in either the city or the country had few alternatives: either there was marriage if a dowry were provided, participation in a business, such as the inn run by the women, or entertainment, both of which involved prostitution and the possibility of illegitimate children. Women or girls who were mentally ill relied on charity, or, for those who were well but widowed, alone, or inclined to that vocation, there was life as a nun. Women's possibilities appear limited and harshly circumscribed by social conditions in these examples from within Theodore's family; women, however, consistently help and support other women.

Although she had run an inn in which she and her daughters served as prostitutes, Elpidia, by ending her life administering a charitable religious institution, was attaining a common goal of Orthodox Christians. She, like Theodora, could be called a reformed harlot or repentant sinner, which was accepted within the society as long as piety and a changed pattern of life ensued. The fate of a child born out of wedlock was probably a sober one under most circumstances. As we learn, however, it was possible for an illegitimate child to attain a godly life: a virtuous holy man could grow out of the "thistles of harlotry." Theodore is such an exception. The whole family is proud that Theodore proves extraordinary in his undertakings, and his needs are privileged over those of the women. When he no longer requires the services of the women of his family, he steers them toward lives of service within the church.

Mary reenters the narrative briefly when news arrives of her death:

> A man came from the metropolis of Ancyra and brought the news of the death of the Saint's mother, Mary, so that he might send and receive her dowry, as she had died childless . . . ; but [Theodore] made supplication to God on her behalf, while fasting for a week, imploring Him to grant her forgiveness for her failings. (33.1–12)

Because she did not have any children during her marriage to David, her dowry is returned to her only surviving child, Theodore. This important legal right of a woman to keep her financial resources in her family rather than having them pass to her husband or his family on her death is an instance of the actual application of the inheritance laws of the time. Theodore probably used the inheritance to endow his monastery. Mary's life as a prostitute is not forgotten even though she later marries, but the hope of eventual forgiveness "for her failings" and salvation for her soul is maintained through her son's prayers of intercession on her behalf before God.

The benefits of having an unusual child seem to be clearly understood by the family members from early on. The author records their initial lack of understanding of the boy's desires for self-denial as well as their later devotion to him, a topos frequently encountered in saints' lives. They nurture him and give him the best adornment, education, and nourishment that they can and foster and support his career as an ascetic and a holy man, since this is a recognized vocation within late ancient and Byzantine society; he eventually does become a bishop as prophesied.[5]

In this account of the life of a rural holy man, information about the roles and expectations of women appears throughout the text, between the lines, and interwoven with the saint's miracles. The agenda behind these miracle accounts is validation of the saint as a miracle-worker, and they are therefore valuable because they are not filtered by bias, only by enthusiasm and possible exaggeration. As we will see, gendered roles of women and expectations from within the society are apparent from these short narratives. Details and patterns of life probably represent actual situations. For example, gynecological problems are dealt with by Theodore: a woman with a "serious malady of the womb" in chapter 26 and a woman with a ten-year issue of blood in chapter 96 are cured by the saint's prayers.

Demon possession is a common problem of women, and the Life refers to a number of cases of illness among women attributed to demons. For example, a woman from the village of Kalpinon was being "evilly treated by a demon." In this strange episode Theodore first converses with it:

> When the Saint rebuked the demon, the latter cried out saying, "O! violence! do not be angry with me, iron-eater, servant of the Most High, do not send me away into the fire of punishment. For it is not I who am guilty, for I entered into this woman against my will, at the command of one Theodotus, surnamed Kourappus, of the village of Mazamia." The servant of Christ said to him, "Behold, I command you in the name of Jesus Christ, the Son of God, not to trouble her in her works from now on until she comes back here again." (35.3–11)

The demon is intimidated by Theodore's rebuke but gives as his excuse that he was coerced to enter the woman because of a curse by one Theodotus. We are not told why the woman might have been cursed, but the saint deals with the more immediate and practical need for a truce between demon and woman, which is to remain in effect until the woman has had a chance to do her manual work:

> They went home, secured their summer crops and their vintage and then went back again. As they entered into the church of the Archangel and saw the Saint's face, the demon began to torture the woman savagely; her husband declared on oath saying that she had not been troubled by the demon at all from the day that he received the Saint's command until that moment. They stayed there one week and as the demon could not bear the rebukes of him who was truly a worker of miracles, he cast the woman down at the feet of the Saint and went out of her. The woman was quite cured and departed with her husband for her home in great joy. (35.14–25)

The woman's husband affirms that the truce with the demon had indeed been effective, and the pair remain at the church until the desired cure is experienced. The husband who brought his wife to the saint initially is part of the process, for it is clear he needs his wife's help in the fields; without her, taking in the harvest would be difficult if not impossible. In such an agrarian setting women worked physically in the fields along with men, and for a woman to have a disability of any kind must have meant hardship in a family's economic survival. The cure is evidently a violent process, in which the woman is thrown to the ground as the saint scolds the demon into leaving her body. After the demon is convinced to leave, the woman is able to return to her role as a partner in farming with her husband.

Cures of demonic possession are the most numerous types of healing of women, with thirteen cases of miracles involving demon-possessed women.[6] These are accomplished by diverse means. In some cases, demons are shaken out of the victims when the saint seizes them by the hair as part of the process of exorcism (chapters 43 and 71). In a number of cases slave girls or women are brought to the saint for cures of demonic possession (chapters 84, 92, 94, 140). Female slaves were of concern to their masters and mistresses as they were necessary for the running of a household or managing of a farm or business; when they were incapacitated, their owners used any form of help available. In one cure, the saint puts his foot on the neck of a possessed slave girl and beats on her breast. "For some time the slave girl remained speechless," and then she was cured (chapter 140); her speechlessness describes an understandable physiological reaction to the treatment involved in the cure. Many afflictions of women are caused by demons living under stones which are dug up, allowing evil spirits to escape. Sometimes they harass a whole community, such as in chapter 115, in which six men and eight women from the village of Permetaia are attacked by demons. They are contained when the saint casts them out and replaces the stone.

A wide variety of types of healings of women occur in the Life. In yet another instance, the saint blows upon the tongue of an eight-year-old girl who is dumb, at which the malady leaves her body. Others are cured of paralysis when he anoints them with oil (chapter 68). Psychological counseling is offered a couple in need of marriage therapy in chapter 145. In the same chapter, childless couples are given the ability to conceive with the help of the saint's prayers. Women who depend on animals need them to be docile, as in chapter 99, in which the saint tames a woman's wild mule. Many of the miracles concern crops, livestock, and drought or famine, all problems encountered in farming districts such as that around Sykeon, and in which women share in agrarian pursuits.

In another episode, two women of senatorial rank travel some distance to seek out the saint's help for their children:

> Two ladies of senatorial rank belonging to the aristocracy of Ephesus came to Theodore's monastery; they were carried in litters with a large train of servants. They brought their children to the Saint to be healed; the one had a son Andreas, a young man of twenty who was dumb, and the other had a little girl of eight, who was paralysed. (summary of 110)

The little girl is cured, while the crowd which has assembled looks on; the young man is blessed and the saint tells his mother her son will speak on their journey home, which is reported to have indeed come about. These wealthy women traveled luxuriously into the poorer countryside on behalf of their afflicted children. Women of rank could apparently pursue their goals independently, crossing geographic and social boundaries as needed; in this instance of service to the upper class, the saint affects the cures, making no distinction between the aristocratic women and his accustomed clientele of peasants.

Women and women's lives, conditions of work, variations in means, and participation in family and community welfare play a significant part in the narrative of the *Life of Theodore*. In the early Life, we find a tight-knit, multigenerational family who are in business together keeping an inn and for whose female members the saint is an important influence throughout their lives.[7] From the miracle accounts, on the other hand, we obtain a vivid glimpse of the countryside with ordinary people working to make a living and remain in sound health. The saint has encounters with numerous poor women of the countryside, including female slaves, and less frequently with better off women from Ephesus or Ancyra. While the accounts serve to demonstrate the powers of miraculous healing and problem solving provided by the saint, they are also revealing about womens' beliefs, superstitions, and types of needs.

The profession of courtesan or prostitute is accepted as one of the options open to women, but they can also choose to exchange this way of life for either marriage or membership in a monastic community. The importance of women's dowries and how they can be used is a recurrent theme in the Life. The presence of women in the saint's "clientele" who are healed and who form a part of the crowds and processions who gather in the countryside, for example, to pray for the end of a drought, shows they were by no means silent or invisible participants in rural Byzantine society. The weather miracles of chapters 50 to 52, for example, include grateful women and their hymns of praise. While most of the women who appear in the *Life of Theodore* are not named, we still glean from this text a wealth of information about the lifestyles of ordinary women.

In these two chapters juxtaposing city life and country life, we move from images of imperial splendor in mosaic to the literary image of a bastard child's gold belt provided by his prostitute mother. Women within diverse milieux are encountered. The prominence and notoriety of the empress Theodora is balanced by a view of ordinary women like Mary and Elpidia of the village of Sykeon, whose lives are representative of a major part (about half) of the population of Byzantium. Concerns about Theodora's luxurious bathing habits are contrasted in the Life with women's concerns for their children's eating habits and for grain harvests. Heart-wrenching realities of the choices that had to be made between keeping a child within the family and putting her in a convent emerge through reading of these common dilemmas. In contrast to Procopius's bitter invective based among the elite of Byzantium, we ponder the earnest narrative of a monk through which we encounter those women who shared common beliefs and dangers in the harsh existence of the countryside.

## Associated Readings

*The Life of Theodore of Sykeon,* 88–185, in *Three Byzantine Saints,* Dawes and Baines, eds. (Crestwood, N.Y., 1977).

Peter Brown, "Arbiters of the Holy: The Christian Holy Man in Late Antiquity," in *Authority and the Sacred: Aspects of the Christianisation of the Roman World* (Cambridge, Mass., 1995), 55–78.

Susan A. Harvey, "Women in Early Byzantine Hagiography: Reversing the Story," in Lynda L. Coon, Katherine J. Haldane, and Elisabeth W. Sommer, eds., *That Gentle Strength: Historical Perspectives on Women in Christianity* (Charlottesville and London, 1990).

———. "Sacred Bonding: Mothers and Daughters in Early Syriac Hagiography," *Journal of Early Christian Studies* 4 (1996): 27–56.

*Part III*

# THE MIDDLE BYZANTINE PERIOD
# (843–1204)

*Introduction: Women, the Faith in Icons, and the Triumph of Orthodoxy*

On March 11, 843, a joyful procession filed through the streets of Constantinople led by the empress Theodora, widow of the emperor Theophilus and regent for the heir to the throne, Michael III. Carried in the procession was one of the holiest icons of Byzantium, an image of the Virgin Mary which had been kept at the Blachernae monastery, for the day celebrated the return of all icons and images to their place in daily life. The Triumph of Orthodoxy, as the occasion was called, has been commemorated on the first Sunday in Lent by the Orthodox Church ever since and is one of the most important liturgical feasts of the church calendar. What choices were made by the citizens of Byzantium during the time of iconoclasm, from 726 to 843, when religious images were banned? and how was a resolution to this political and religious crisis reached? In particular, what was the part played by women? and how would this affect their lives in the centuries following?

The triumph celebrated the successful reestablishment of the legitimacy of icons or images (*eikones*), meaning any religious images on wooden panels, mosaics or frescoes on the walls of churches, and paintings in books. It is only a more current definition that refers mainly to painted panels with portraits of saints or other holy figures. The triumph also marked the resolution of theological debates regarding the function and meaning of icons. The most essential pronouncement was that the tangible substance of an image was not itself worshiped, for worship (*latreia*) did not require any intermediary but was addressed directly to God and the saints. Worshiping an icon would thus be idolatrous and reminiscent of pagan practices. Instead, icons were venerated, that is, the person or event depicted was honored. Veneration (*proskynesis*), of which the outward sign was bowing before or kissing the image, was a form of respect, in which the icon served as a kind of telecommunication apparatus between the viewer and the model or prototype of the image.[1]

The icon thus served to remind the viewer of the truth behind the likeness or event depicted. Veneration was not a substitute for the worship due the prototype. In worship, a person addressed through prayer and contemplation the holy personage, the Virgin Mary, Christ, or a saint, without the intermediary of the icon. Through worship or through veneration using icons, the Orthodox believer aimed to establish a spiritual relationship with the saint, in the hope of receiving the kind of support and reassurance offered by a special friend or ally. Icons—all images—functioned in a meaningful, integral way to link believers to the ancient tradition of representation of religious truths in Scripture and to the example set by saints and martyrs. After this important dogmatic distinction between worship and veneration was defined, along with other issues of practice, the use of icons was again encouraged in churches and private residences or as part of one's personal possessions. The times of persecution of iconodules (literally, "slaves of images") were ended but only after complex arguments affirmed that icon veneration was not a breach of the Second Commandment, but instead a necessary expression of faith in the truth of the incarnation, when God became matter and took on substance in the person of Christ.[2]

Icons were initially banned by imperial decree under the emperor Leo III in 726, and a period of bitter persecution known as iconoclasm ensued. Families and whole populations were divided by the decree, just as in a time of civil war. The immediate causes of iconoclasm are obscure. There had been a perceptible undercurrent of scepticism on the use of images going back to the time of the founding of the empire in late antiquity. It may have been the disastrous seventh- and eighth-century defeats of Byzantine armies by the Moslems in the Near East, a people who banned all images, that led to a suspicion that God's anger was behind the losses. Icons had become too popular and influential and appeared in direct disobedience of the commandment in Exodus 20:4, "Though shalt not make unto thyself any graven images, nor shalt though bow down to them or worship them." The banning of images seemed a way to molify God. While the complex reasons behind the ban may never be completely understood, persecutions by the military followed Leo's edict, and all citizens were affected by them. Especially affected were monks and nuns and their monasteries, which were strongholds of images, as attested by the monumental decoration of monastic churches and illustrations of religious books. It has been claimed that women were special advocates of icons and that because of their housebound existence they were especially dedicated to private devotional practices involving icons. The two periods of iconoclasm were interrupted by a temporary restoration of images, from 787 to 815, and here I turn to the role of women.[3]

That women played a role in the reestablishment of icons in 843 is demonstrated by the lead taken by Theodora in celebrating the Triumph of Orthodoxy; but this was not the first termination of iconoclasm. An earlier empress, Irene, widow of the emperor Leo IV and regent for their son, Constantine VI, had in 787 also restored icon worship, bringing about a hiatus in iconoclasm.[4] The edicts of the Second Council of Nicaea convened by Irene remain an important set of definitions of what was intended in legitimizing images. Irene's dedication to icons was not shared by her son, whom she later blinded in order to achieve control of the empire. She was sole ruler from 797 to 802 and had gold coins struck with her portrait on both sides to emphasize her position. She was the initiator of philanthropic enterprises and restorer of churches in and around the capital, but Irene's rule did not last long, and she was exiled in 802 to the island of Lesbos, where she died in 803.[5] Iconoclasm was resumed in 815 under Leo V.[6] Irene is remembered along with Theodora as a champion of images, and both later had their Lives recorded and were made saints. Irene also had a famous image displayed over the gate to the imperial palace, the Chalke Gate, in 797 symbolizing the return to Orthodox protection through images of both palace and city. An inscription on this image stated:

> [The image] which Leo the emperor had formerly cast down, Irene has reerected here.[7]

The empresses Irene and Theodora in turn restored the cult of icons, but unlike Irene's restoration of 787, Theodora's proclamation of 843 was lasting and remained in effect through the final six hundred years of the Byzantine Empire.

Stories of women's secret veneration and efforts to preserve icons survive from the period of iconoclasm. For example, a story grew up that when Leo III first proclaimed a ban on images in 726 he sent a soldier to ascend a ladder and remove the icon of Christ on the Chalke Gate. An enraged group of women led by one Theodosia stormed the gate and killed the soldier but were themselves later executed for their deed.[8] Although the story is likely to be legendary and the women ficticious, it reflects a perception that women were so strongly attached to icons that they would have been willing to risk independent action to protect them.[9] Using the terms of one scholar, this text does not provide evidence for women, but for representations of women, probably by men, giving it value primarily as testimony about the gendered view of women.[10] In 814, Leo V actually did have the Chalke icon which had been installed by Irene in 797 destroyed. The notion of its former destruction by Leo III had been invented for political reasons under Irene.[11]

Dedication to the cause of icons at this time can be demonstrated by the life and production of Kassia, a noblewoman who was reputedly in the brideshow for the emperor Theophilus (829–42).[12] When Theodora was chosen over her, she became a nun, founded a monastery in Constantinople, and became known as the writer of numerous hymns. She had had a classical Greek education, and while her hymns are straightforward and forceful in their language, her learnedness is evident. She composed notices for the Menaia for feast days, especially those commemorating such female saints as Thekla, Pelagia, Barbara, Agatha, Mary of Egypt.[13] She was known for defying iconoclasm; enjoying an exceptional self-determination, she celebrated the release from persecution by becoming one of the famous hymnographers of Byzantium. She died as abbess of her monastery in 865.

Images were slow to make their reappearance after iconoclasm. The Chalke icon was restored by Theodora some time after the death of Theophilus in 842, when she took up rule as regent for Michael III, and before 847.[14] The other major image after iconoclasm was not installed until twenty years later. The mosaic of the Virgin and Child in the apse of the church of Hagia Sophia was dedicated in 867 during the brief joint rule of Theodora's son Michael III and his designated coemperor Basil I.[15] Although Theodora had been a capable administrator, Michael did not have similar capacities; he was murdered while still in his twenties by his coemperor in a sea of intrigue and treachery.[16] With this murder in 867, the long-lived and prosperous Macedonian dynasty was born.

Evidence for women's curtailed roles in the period after iconoclasm conflicts with the influential roles they had in connection with the reestablishment of icons. In her study of the increasing private religious roles of women, Judith Herrin questions the impact of the edict of the Council in Trullo of 692, which stated, among other precepts, that women should remain silent in church. If forced into silence and passivity by their exclusion from active roles in the church, women could still turn to icons for their own use in the domestic sphere. Because icons were accessible to rich and poor alike they became a common source of reassurance and focus for religious devotion of all women.[17] Women spent much time in the home, and there they became attached to portable icons of the type that one could handle and carry on one's person and that could be addressed, supplicated, and venerated at will.[18]

Monasteries were also places of refuge for the lovers of icons, and the Studios monastery in Constantinople was a famous outpost of resistance to iconoclasm. Female self-expression, however, was rare and regarded dubiously by the society:

> Within the Byzantine Christian tradition, women could be seen as paragons of virtue, virgins, saintly mothers and holy widows. But as prostitutes, licentious young girls who would seduce married men and monks, or ordinary women who simply enjoyed dancing in public, jumping over bonfires or cross-dressing, they represented what the church understood as a definite threat to its social control and order. Hence the double-edged appreciation of women in Byzantium.[19]

In spite of this curtailment of women's activity by the Council in Trullo, in the period following iconoclasm women were a force in the reestablishment of icon veneration and adherence to the resolutions celebrated at the Feast of Orthodoxy. During the middle Byzantine period, women played a public and determining role, as had the empresses Irene and Theodora, as well as a private, inconspicuous domestic one. In educating their children and grandchildren to share their beliefs, women continued to play a significant role within Orthodox culture. With the reinstatement of images, icons were increasingly integrated in middle Byzantine society, offering women and men vehicles for their prayers. Rich and poor women again had access to icons, constituting a leveling of social classes. Just as in late antiquity, with the birth of Christianity and female asceticism (see chapter 1), new possibilities were opened for women with the return of icons.

Changes occurred in the roles of women in the middle Byzantine period, some of which are associated with ecclesiastical edicts and some of which developed naturally as a reaction to their increased encloistering either within the nunnery or the home. Since the public role of women declined from the seventh century on and the positions of deaconess and holy virgin became rare, other outlets for women's religiosity appeared.[20] Nunneries created new opportunities for female leadership and piety, although they were not as well funded and long-lasting as male monasteries. Increasingly women who were married or widowed took up monastic vocations and became prominent within their communities.[21]

Gendered notions within the society continued to censure outspoken, strong-minded women.[22] A strict code of behavior applied to women of the aristocratic and upper classes: the veil was worn whenever a woman ventured into public, and women pursued, whenever possible, a modest and withdrawn lifestyle. Such stereotypes of women's behavior reveal that for them there was another reality. Women's most important roles continued to be within the confines of marriage and the family, where the only men they conversed with were their husbands and where devotion to their children's education and to running the household were their primary concerns. Behind this modest demeanor, however, there were women who were strong, active partners in marriages and who played major political roles through the influence they wielded over their husbands. Empresses determined the continuity of dynasties through their marriage decisions, and ordinary women worked in trade and managed economic and family affairs. As in the preceding sections, we remain attuned to the evidence for ordinary women, even though they often do not have names and appear only in allusions to groups with a specific cause or metier, as in the women who reputedly stormed the Chalke Gate. Although they are difficult to discover, they can still be accounted for and given credit for the role they played in Byzantine life and society.[23]

In the following four chapters I will follow different routes of access to information about women, as I observe options open to women and their own attitudes to the kinds of experience and lifestyle they led. In chapter 8, I look at the character of female monasticism in this period. As noted above, an increasingly important alternative to marriage, or a second marriage, was retreat to a monastery, especially for widows. Many routine household activities followed them behind monastic walls, such as spinning, weaving, and gardening, but, more surprisingly, their superstitions and magical practices continued to play a part in monastic life. The *Life of Irene of Chrysobalanton* is a revealing glimpse into the monastic lives of young women, and in particular the leadership role of its aristocratic heroine, Irene. In this carefully crafted Life, I follow the career of a young girl who came to Constantinople from Cappadocia and pursued a dynamic monastic career, couched within the now-familiar genre of hagiography.

In chapter 9 I take up the representation of women in art, observing how female bodies appear when artists depict them and their activities, and what the conventionalized character of these depictions means. A prime example of the highly constructed quality of artistic representation of women appears in series of depictions of female saints in the mosaics of churches, in particular the main church at the monastery of Hosios Loukas in Greece. From these images I move to a discussion of wider depictions of women and female saints in other churches of the middle Byzantine period and beyond, in the painted churches of medieval Cyprus. The study focuses on depictions of Saint Helena and the implications of the enduring popularity of her image in art. In considering the evidence of images, I question whether Byzantine viewers interpreted images of female saints in a gendered fashion. How did female agency affect the choice of images in church programs? and above all, what did images of female saints convey about and to women?

Chapter 10, a study of imperial marriage, evokes life in the women's quarters, or *gynaikonitis* (gynaeceum) of the imperial palace in the eleventh century. Practices and anomalies are seen from the point of view of an astute contemporary observer, Michael Psellos, as he comments on the activities, intrigues, dilemmas, and personal pursuits of a dynasty of imperial women. How and under what conditions did empresses determine the shifts of rule and power? The well-documented cases of Zoe and her sister Theodora, the last sovereigns of the Macedonian dynasty, present an intimate view of imperial marriage as well as the practice of concubinage within the palace.[24] This resilient dynasty had as its mainstays women who participated in public life and gloried in their use of power, but whose sense of duty took a personal toll.

In chapter 11, we enter the world of aristocratic women, including princesses, and their education. In examining the famous Byzantine practice of sending women out as brides for foreign princes, often as bargaining tools in games of power, we gain a sense of women's important diplomatic roles in representing Byzantium abroad. These women adopted other cultures and ways of life while maintaining their own identity as Byzantines, as circumstances dictated. As in the early centuries, aristocratic and imperial women had the most freedom of any to travel, converse, write, and study in the company of men and sometimes to conduct love affairs. Anna Komnene is a rare example of a well-educated Byzantine princess who wrote the history of her father's reign in her famous work, the *Alexiad*. In it she describes the extraordinary roles carried out by the imperial women, descriptions which are interwoven with her revelation of her own story. Social freedom of imperial women of this time was at its greatest of any time, as we see under the guidance of Anna in her narrative of her family's handling of diplomacy and warfare and of her own anguished acceptance of her fate.

In the middle Byzantine period, conventions and restrictions applied to women because of their sex; however, these were accepted by women generally.[25] Why? Because maintaining a stereotyped ideal of conventional appearances was necessary not only because of gendered norms too ancient to reject entirely, but also because it affirmed that the underlying reality was more flexible and wide-ranging in its possibilities:

Essential to women's outward appearance are the veil, the downcast eye, reluctance to speak before men, a devotion to household matters, if married, and to weaving and spinning in any case if not, and added to this, for Empresses at least, a certain resplendence of apparel and an untouchable dignity of demeanour. It is these characteristics which compose the conventional ideal of womankind.[26]

Outward show of forthrightness was shunned, but in fact managerial talents and communication skills such as Irene of Chrysobalanton's, the maintenance of a dynastic image such as Zoe's, and intelligence and writing ability such as Anna's were valued. Prescribed conventions of behavior actually obscure the underlying reality of a growing social freedom, economic autonomy, and independent thinking of medieval Byzantine women.

## Associated Readings

Judith Herrin, *Women in Purple: Rulers of Medieval Byzantium* (Princeton, 2001).

A. P. Kazhdan and Alice-Mary Talbot, "Women and Iconoclasm," *Byzantinische Zeitschrift* 84–5 (1991–2): 391–408.

Angeliki Laiou, "The Role of Women in Byzantine Society," *Jahrbuch der Österreichische Byzantinistik* (1981): 233–60.

*Eight*

# WOMEN'S MONASTICISM:
# IRENE OF CHRYSOBALANTON

The procession with icons through the streets of Constantinople on March 11, 843, signaling the Triumph of Orthodoxy was indeed a new beginning, not only for the Orthodox Church but for the Byzantine Empire. Theodora, empress of Byzantium, along with the patriarch led a throng from the imperial monastery at the Blachernai to the Great Church of Hagia Sophia, carrying the most venerated icons of Christendom and singing hymns of victory. A fourteenth-century gold-ground icon in the British Museum depicts this important event (see pl. 9).[1] Angel-deacons support a huge, crimson-draped icon of the Virgin and Child, while figures in procession are lined up on either side and in the register below. The crimson-clad, crowned figures of the empress Theodora and her young son, Michael III, stand on the left, and Patriarch Methodios appears with monks on the right. Below are saints, including, on the far left, a nun who holds a cross and an icon of Christ; she is labeled Theodosia.[2] Although the icon dates much later than the event it depicts, it reveals that over time significant associations remained connected with this pivotal event and the Triumph of Orthodoxy.

After the ban on icons was lifted, their use was again encouraged as part of the explicit legislation of the church. Now monastic communities in which iconophile monks and nuns venerated sacred images were safe from the persecutions they had undergone during the period of iconoclasm from 726 to 843. No longer would monasteries be pillaged, their books burned, and the images on their walls destroyed. No longer would monks and nuns who refused to give up their attachment to icons be punished by forced marriages.[3] Harsh reprisals must have taken place on both sides, for no doubt the iconoclasts, who had maintained that graven images were forbidden by God, suffered greatly too. The empire had survived a terrible religious and political struggle. The resulting restructuring of accepted dogma and strengthening of Orthodox religious convictions would help it to endure for another six hundred years.

In 855, twelve years after this procession, another, smaller procession entered the gates of Constantinople, as a ten-year-old girl named Irene, traveling from Cappadocia in the heart of Anatolia, arrived with her servants and baggage to compete in a brideshow. The empress Theodora had announced a competition to choose a bride for Michael, now aged fifteen. As was customary in brideshows, only the most beautiful and well-born women competed.[4] When Irene arrived, however, she found that a bride had already been chosen, and instead of marrying she decided to enter into the ascetic life at the convent of Chrysobalanton. Her exemplary life as abbess of the convent served to inspire other aristocratic women to join convents. Miraculous qualities were attributed to her during her life, and after her death she was recognized as a saint. Irene's story survives in an account, *The Life of Saint Irene, Abbess of Chrysobalanton,* which illuminates not only the religious and political climate of the capital city in the years following the Triumph of Orthodoxy, but also the monastic vocation for women as it prevailed in the middle Byzantine period of the ninth to twelfth centuries. It is also a fascinating and readable piece of Byzantine literature.

Women's monasticism had evolved and become more regularized in the five centuries since Macrina founded her community in remote Pontus. In this chapter I will first establish a basis for understanding the character of monasticism in this period, since scholarly writings in this field have been especially rich in recent decades. With this foundation, I will then consider the text of the Life with an eye to the way the genre of hagiography, saintly biography, performs its role of illustrating the manifestations of sanctity. Another intent on the part of the historian, however, is to glean what the conditions of life, practices, and concerns were of the women who lived at Chrysobalanton. How did Irene perform her role as abbess? and what were the patterns and assumptions within this community of women? Living behind locked gates and monastic walls, were they nonetheless in some ways engaged in the life of the capital? or were they totally isolated and living in a world apart? How did the women themselves react to this environment? The Life of Irene provides an illuminating view of the conditions of women's religious life in ninth-century Constantinople.

The ninth through the twelfth centuries saw the flourishing of monastic institutions, in particular an increase in the establishment of private foundations and small monasteries governed by the wishes of individuals and families. Small monastic churches gradually replaced the large, imperially sponsored public churches, and as the scale diminished, the number of foundations proliferated. The growth of a landed aristocracy alongside an urban elite fueled this trend, as more and more prosperous citizens sought to institute a religious haven both for their private worship during their lives and for the repose of their souls after death. Monastic establishments grew up in towns and countryside throughout the empire.

At this time the church also increasingly took over from the state many of its philanthropic and charitable roles. Monasteries, therefore, served all classes of individuals and in a variety of ways, from places of refuge to hospitals and from burial places to leadership opportunities, some foundations eliciting more fame and notoriety than others. As we have seen in the study of the early centuries, the social climate had a direct influence on how such institutions functioned. Hence we can best observe women's monasticism of the middle-Byzantine period by examining such questions as, Under what circumstances did women enter convents? was taking the veil always voluntary? did young women entering monasteries have to be virgins? how did male and female institutions relate to one another? how autonomous were women in the governing of their nunneries? what was life in a typical convent like and how was this determined? These and many other questions also furnish the basis for comparing monastic institutions in Byzantium with those in the medieval West.

Any person wishing, after a trial period, to take vows and undergo tonsure, or "take the veil" as the women's ceremony is sometimes called, could do so, for monasteries were open to all. For the rich, however, there were special prerogatives. Those who could offer generous donations to the institutions they joined were assured of a comfortable life, a place of burial, and perpetual prayers in their memory. The new name taken by a person at the time of tonsure usually started with the same letter or letters as his or her baptismal name. Hence, Theodore might become Theoleptus, or Kleone might become Katherine; they would then live out their lives as "Theoleptus the monk" or "Katherine the nun." The customary garb of a monk or a nun was a black tunic and outer cloak; a nun wore in addition a veil to cover her head, as depicted in the Triumph of Orthodoxy icon. There was a great variety in the size and nature of monastic institutions.[5] Some were small enclaves on the outskirts of poor and remote villages, others were wealthy intellectual centers in the capital city housing hundreds of monastics. Separate monastic orders like those found in the West did not exist in Byzantium. Some monasteries served as hospitals, others as orphanages or soup kitchens. Many housed relics or icons dedicated to a particular saint and were therefore places of pilgrimage.

Monastic life remained an important option for women in medieval Byzantium, just as it had in the early period. Although women tended to remain within the home, some volunarily opted for the religious life of nunneries, for which substantial and varied records survive. Because there were no monastic orders in Byzantium, each community had its own charter with individual specifications for its way of life, although many features were held in common. In the ninth century we begin to see surviving *typika*, or monastic charters, of which there were two types, founders' typika and liturgical typika.[6] Founders' typika dictated all aspects of daily life, according to the wishes of the founder or refounder of the monastery. These highly personal documents expressed the special wishes of the founder, down to such details as the frequency of distribution of food to the hungry at the monastery's gate. Philanthropic activity was part of the designated role of nuns; they helped the poor and sick, aiding the surrounding populus in various ways.[7] Special provisions were made in a founder's typikon for burial and commemoration of the founder and his or her family; endowments provided for vigils and memorial services celebrated at prescribed intervals, in perpetuity, and even the number of candles made of pure beeswax to be kept burning beside the tomb.

A second type, the liturgical typikon, was a schedule according to the calendar year (which started on September 1) of services, including daily prayers or celebrations and their conduct, even down to their lighting and ornament.[8] The patterns of life described in the typika varied but essentially consisted of work and prayer, and the avoidance whenever possible of contact between men and women. Women assumed some of the same responsibilities in nunneries that they had in the world, such as gardening, weaving, and cooking. The majority of typika that survive are for male institutions, but we can assume similar patterns for female ones, since borrowings are common among the existing typika. Out of the fifty surviving founders' typika, five were written by women for women's institutions.[9] It is possible many convents never had formal charters, or those they had did not survive. In some cases of surviving saints' Lives, such as the Life of Irene to be considered below, the vitae can be considered an indication of the way of life and regulatory principles that governed a given monastic institution, although, naturally, differing in character from the typika. Even though fewer records overall deal with women's monasticism than with men's, it is possible through these valuable documents to detect much about life in women's monasteries.

Monastic regulations presupposed separation of the sexes and permitted little visiting of nunneries by men; outside of the priest the only men admitted to a convent were spiritual confessors and doctors. The founding of double monasteries, that is, adjacent foundations for men and women administered by one superior, was banned in 787 to avoid sexual temptation, and in 810 all double monasteries were ordered closed. While nuns were not permitted, except in rare cases, to visit male monasteries, they managed to pursue some activities outside their monastic walls: visiting the sick, attending funerals, visiting spiritual confessors, and going on local pilgrimages.[10] In the early twelfth century the former empress Irene Doukaina Komnene refounded one of the richest monasteries of Constantinople, the Theotokos Kecharitomene (the Mother of God "full of grace"); the typikon, written by her, survives and is a fascinating source on female monastic life.[11] It stipulates, for example, that all priests and officials who entered the convent must be eunuchs, and that doctors be eunuchs or old men. It also specified that sick nuns could see their fathers only if taken to the gate on a stretcher, and that male relatives could not even attend memorial services for deceased nuns.[12]

In general, monastic regulations and stipulations for administration were more constricting for women's monasteries than for men's and represented forms of control of women.[13] Women's autonomy was also limited within them, as female monasteries were highly dependant on male authority. Since women could not be priests, nuns were dependent on a male to conduct the liturgy for the sacrament of holy communion, for last sacraments before death, and for burial. Men also served as guardians of nunneries. Women could be deaconesses, but this position was primarily honorific and did not include as much responsibility in the middle Byzantine period as it had in the early church; in the times of adult baptism, deaconesses were required to maintain female modesty, but after infant baptism prevailed from the sixth century on, their position lapsed. In any case, deaconesses could not administer the sacraments.

According to the typika, convents dispensed various social services to poor women taken in as orphans, widows, and the sick or elderly.[14] Orphaned girls and unwed mothers who were sheltered could make their decisions on whether or not to remain encloistered and take vows at the age of sixteen. Other women escaped abusive marriages by joining a convent. The largest category of women who found their way into nunneries were widows who through economic necessity or spiritual inclination joined these institutions. Care of widows often involved donation of their assets to the convent in return for a place to live and a proper burial.[15] Women afflicted with demons were cared for by nuns in convents, often in the hope that their illness would be cured through their prayers and those of the nuns; for this reason monasteries that housed healing shrines were frequently the retreat of mentally ill women.[16]

Overall, fewer women than men took up monastic life. In a register of monastic institutions in Constantinople in all eleven centuries of its history, for example, there were 270 male monasteries and 77 nunneries, that is, only 22 percent of the institutions were female. In the early centuries convents and monasteries are recorded in equal numbers, but in the middle Byzantine period the majority of religious institutions were for monks.[17] From this we can conclude that women who could not care for themselves were either cared for by their families or lived out their lives as beggars or in poverty. For those women who were affiliated with charitable insitutions attached to nunneries, much of their life was taken up with helping those less fortunate; philanthropy offered them a socially acceptable alternative to complete encloistering.

In the provinces there was an even lower percentage of nunneries than in the large cities. Although there was some degree of safety behind the walls of a nunnery, the frequent Arab, Slav, and other invaders' attacks made life in a provincial setting more dangerous than within a city. The size of a monastery could range from a dozen to several hundred individuals; most complexes accommodated from twenty to fifty. Male monasteries tended generally to be wealthier than female ones, with better endowments for maintenance of buildings and their furnishings.[18] Life in a monastery or nunnery was similar in many respects to life in the world, consisting of simple routines of daily chores as well as fasting and prayer. The community was divided according to the status of the entering nun: church nuns and choir nuns led a more privileged life, whereas laboring nuns tended to the gardens and kitchen, pursuing more manual labor than their choir nun sisters.[19] While it was a life lived in common with other monastics, it was one of comparative isolation and constraint in comparison with the range of activities of the community beyond the monastery's walls.

As one can see in drawings of Byzantine monasteries made, for example, by the eighteenth-century Russian pilgrim Barskij, monasteries were miniature walled cities, with gates that could be shut at night, cutting the monastic community off from its surroundings.[20] Structures within the walls usually comprised a church, individual cells for the monks or nuns, a refectory or dining hall, guest quarters, stables, and gardens. Remnants of a few monastic complexes survive today in Constantinople, and more in countries that were formerly provinces of the Byzantine Empire: Greece, Turkey, Syria, Israel, the former Yugoslavia, Bulgaria, Cyprus, and southern Italy. Some are preserved almost completely intact with gold mosaics and frescoes decorating the domes, vaults, and walls of their churches. The monastery of Hosios Loukas in Phocis, Greece, is a well-preserved example of a male monastery which could have housed up to one hundred monks. Its enclosing walls survive, along with corner towers and also monks' cells, stables, abbot's residence, refectory, warming house, and two churches. The larger of the two churches, the Katholikon, retains much of its mosaic and fresco decoration.[21] An extraordinary form of monastic complex is represented by the cave monasteries of Cappadocia in central Turkey, where the requisite spaces were created by hollowing out the living rock; many of these survive today in a semiruined state, for example, those in and around the Göreme Valley, some with their wall paintings partly preserved.[22]

Women who lived in monasteries came from many walks of life and took vows for many of the same reasons as in the late antique and early Byzantine periods. Impoverished parents might dedicate their young children to God, others in gratitude for divine intervention in a crisis. Young girls might make the decisions themselves in order to escape unwanted marriages or to honor a personal vow of virginity. Married women could choose a monastic retreat late in life after bearing, and often losing, a number of children. Their wish was to withdraw from worldly cares and dedicate themselves to a life of tranquility and prayer. Often several members of a family, parents and children, would take monastic vows at the same time, the women joining convents and the men monasteries located in proximity to one another, thus maintaining some sense of family unity even in their respective retreats.[23] In other cases, battered wives found refuge and protection behind monastic walls.[24] Poverty and their inability to support themselves drove many women to join monasteries. Widows made up the largest component among women monastics, as noted. In the middle Byzantine period the majority of nuns were not dedicated virgins but widows, young and old, and older women doing penance.[25]

Aristocratic or imperial women led a more flexible and comfortable monastic life than ordinary women. They could afford to build new institutions or renovate old ones and often lived as the abbess, or spiritual leader and chief administrator, of the institution they had founded. Theirs could also be a sociable retreat, with few responsibilities, as they enjoyed the comfortable surroundings and stimulation of intellectual pursuits and conversation. They could even bring with them female servants to provide for their needs.[26] In contrast, a whole group of noblewomen chose an ascetic lifestyle, wearing hair shirts under their clothing in secret and undergoing harsh fasting and self-deprivation in their diet. For other imperial women the monastery was a form of incarceration. Princesses and aristocratic daughters were sometimes forced to join nunneries before they were married, for it was inconvenient for the sisters of an emperor or heir to the throne to have husbands or offspring who might be potential competitors for power. At the death in 959 of the emperor Constantine VII, Porphyrogenitus, his widow, and five daughters were sent weeping to convents as his son Romanus II and the empress Theophano ascended the throne.[27]

Under certain circumstances, members of an imperial family might choose to go into exile at a monastery. If, for example, an imperial woman wished to escape arrest for her part in a plot against the emperor or another serious impropriety, she might voluntarily retreat to a monastery rather than risk execution. The beautiful Princess Islands off the eastern shore of the Sea of Marmora were dotted with monasteries known as places of refuge where royal or aristocratic miscreants lived out their lives as political prisoners under close surveillance and with little chance of escape. The princess Anna Komnene, as we will see in chapter 9, wrote the *Alexiad*, a learned history of her father's reign, while under house arrest in the Kecharitomene monastery in Constantinople, mentioned above, after she was implicated in a plot to murder her brother.

Female religious of the middle Byzantine period tended to stay within the monastic walls, while monks had more mobility, made frequent journeys, and went on pilgrimage. This feature presents an obvious contrast to the case of nuns like Egeria (see chapter 2) or the empress Athenais Eudocia (see chapter 3), who went on pilgrimage to Jerusalem and elsewhere and were frequently in the company of men. When women did travel to other nunneries or to visit a shrine, they sometimes assumed male garb for safety. As discussed in chapter 4, in rarer cases, they took the bold step of entering monasteries dressed as men in order to be near their tonsured husbands.[28]

Within the monastic system and organization, some women distinguished themselves for their exceptional virtue or intelligence; this led to their assuming positions of leadership and considerable power. In some cases the nuns or abbesses of monasteries led such exemplary lives and demonstrated such superior wisdom or insight that their fame spread. Some were made saints or canonized after their deaths.[29] Although the precise process is unclear, the writing down of the exemplary person's Life, or Vita, appears to have been the first step toward official sanctification by the church.

These compelling stories were written according to formulae established in the early period of hagiography, between the fourth and seventh centuries, and usually included proofs of extraordinary powers, by deeds or miracles, and a description of the social context or families connected to the saint and of the posthumous power of the saint; there was usually, but not always, some connection between the saint and imperial authority.[30] When the church recognized a saint, the individual's name was recorded in the Constantinopolitan calendar of the liturgical year, and she was honored on a specific day.[31] Although formulaic in many respects and filled with topoi, hagiographical accounts are usually based on the life of a real person. We have already encountered late ancient and early Byzantine ascetic women in the accounts of Macrina, Mary of Egypt, and Theodore of Sykeon. In this chapter we will become acquainted with the later development of the genre of hagiography as I focus on the text of a life dating to the tenth century, the *Life of Saint Irene Abbess of Chrysobalanton,* a work which is both entertaining and highly informative about one woman's monastic career.

## Irene of Chrysobalanton

The *Life of Irene of Chrysobalanton* speaks eloquently about the religious climate at a time when the iconoclastic controversy was still within living memory for many, as here in the opening chapter:

> The persecution of the venerators of the image of Christ had now come to an end. Overcome by the will of Him that scorneth the scorners and defeated, the senseless rush of the Iconoclasts' rabid arrogance had been abhorred, expelled, and destroyed, like the trailing tail, as it were, of a dragon. The Empress Theodora, who had been married to the Emperor although she was faithful to God, succeeded to his throne but not to his impiety. Already at the very beginning she gave mature and perfect life to the piety with which she in her fear of God had been pregnant, opening the way for all to revere and venerate the undefiled icons safely and candidly. God's church regained her adornment, the God-pleasing representations on icons, which were painted and venerated on walls and panels, in all kinds of material, bronze, silver, and gold. (1; 3–5)[32]

In this polemical statement, the anonymous author emphasizes the importance of this time immediately after the reinstatement of icons as one of triumph after a long period of difficulty. Rehabilitation of the iconoclast emperor Theophilus follows in chapter 2, reminding the audience of the political climate and delicate question of imperial involvement in the controversy. Since the subject of the Life is a woman, it is fitting to remind the audience of the roles of women during iconoclasm; the author mentions the iconodule empress Theodora and in the following paragraph the empress Irene before launching into the main narrative.

The brideshow announced by the empress Theodora to choose a suitable bride for her son introduces us to Irene as a young girl. The author describes the qualifications for the competition:

The girl should belong to the illustrious and outstanding, and to a pious family who took pride in the Orthodox faith, she should excel in moral beauty and spiritual nobility, and be distinguished by corporeal fairness so as to surpass all girls of her age. A proclamation about this was sent throughout all the land that was subject to the Empire of the Romans. . . .

People who reared such girls prepared them and had them escorted from their various lands to the Imperial City. Thus the admirable Irene, whose mode of life this writing will narrate from the beginning, a woman renowned for moral grace and corporeal beauty alike, was given a most rich and splendid outfit by her parents, who sent her to Constantinople from Cappadocia whence she drew her origin. (3; 9)

As a girl of ten years of age, Irene, probably the daughter of landowners with estates in the rich agricultural hinterland of Cappadocia in Asia Minor, was prepared by her parents and sent dressed in sumptuous clothes to enter the competition.

On the way she stopped to visit a holy monk of some fame, Ioannikios, who lived in the mountains of Bithynia. He greeted her with a puzzling declaration:

Welcome, Irene, servant of God! Hasten, my child, with joy to the Imperial City, hasten! The Convent of Chrysobalanton needs you to shepherd her virgins! (3; 11)

Arriving in the capital city, she discovered a bride had already been chosen for the emperor. After being welcomed by her aristocratic relatives, the Gouber family, Irene decided that instead of returning to Cappadocia or seeking an arranged marriage she would become a "bride of Christ, and always to satisfy Him alone."[33] Remembering Ioannikios's prophetic words, she took the veil at the monastery of Chrysobalanton, symbolically divesting herself of things of this world:

The necklaces and jewels she wore, and all other things that she kept as imperial gifts ever since she had been liberally received by the Empress, all these she willingly either distributed to the poor and to her own servants or brought to the convent as an offering to God. Then she had her hair shorn, and with it was shorn, too, all her mundane and earthly concern. She also changed her dress, arraying herself in a ragged hair-shirt, as she wished to wear out that tender and delicate body to have a soul that was renewed and flourished and approached God to the same extent as the body perished. (4; 15)[34]

The severance from a comfortable life in aristocratic society to take up one of self-denial is abrupt. Difficult as it is to imagine such decisive conduct in a young girl, the instructive purpose behind the narrative must be taken into account. For the author is fashioning the account to impress on the reader the self-determination and self-sacrifice necessary when a woman takes the veil. The ascetic practice of wearing coarse clothing and depriving the body of all comforts is a topos encountered here as in many Lives, since asceticism is an acknowledged part of dedicating a life to Christ. The harsher the ascetic regime, the worthier the monastic; to "perish" in the body was to have renewed life in the spirit, a principle derived from early Christian martyrdom. We might recall a paradigm of female asceticism encountered in chapter 2, Saint Mary of Egypt, who refused to wear any clothing, wandering the desert naked. Irene's story is manipulated subtly throughout by the author to fulfill its hagiographic function.

At times, the twenty-four chapters of the Life read like an adventure narrative, at others like a soap opera, but this too is characteristic of the genre. The writing of hagiography conformed to contemporary Byzantine expectations and was a stylized mode of illustrating the mystery of sanctity.[35] It is also designed to hold the attention of the reader/listener and therefore has entertainment as well as educational value. Already in chapter 7, Irene is selected to succeed the deceased abbess, but only after the patriarch Methodius has been consulted:

> Without delay the patriarch rose from his throne at once and asked for a censer. Burning incense and praising God he initiated a hymn befitting the occasion. Then he first ordained Irene deaconess of the Great Church—for through the Spirit in him he knew her purity—, and thereafter consecrated her with the seal of hegumenate. He spoke many words to her about leadership, but still more to the other nuns about faith and obedience, reminding them of the punishments and again of the good things that beyond await those who lead a virtuous or a vicious life here. After a prayer for concord and love among them he let them depart in peace. (7; 29)

The pattern of life and practices anticipated by nuns determines such didactic passages. This description of the ceremony of Irene's ordination as abbess also serves as valuable documentation of medieval church practice. Dependence on a male, the patriarch of the Orthodox Church, for the ordaining of an abbess indicates control by the church, at least of this aspect of a nunnery's existence. The text here is as useful as a social historical tool as it is representative of a literary genre.

Other episodes give a clearer picture of the social concerns and objectives of the narrative. One genre expectation is that demons will confront the saintly person in an attempt to deter her steadfastness. In chapter 11, Irene is attacked and set on fire by demons:

> Then the demon stretched out his hand and kindled a stick against the lamp-wick. He dropped it around the neck of the holy woman, and it burnt up as if fanned, violently inflaming her whole hood along with the scapular and the shift, and began even to lick her flesh. It went over her, scorching her shoulders, her breast, her spine, her kidneys, and her flanks. As it spread the fire would soon have encircled her body, had not one of the sisters, who was awake for the nocturnal prayers, smelled the smoke from her flesh and left her cell in fear, thinking, "In what part of the convent can the fire be?" Tracking the scent she followed the odour to the cell of the abbess and stopped there. Looking in and seeing that it was filled with smoke and steam she only just managed to fling the door open and entered. She found—a terrible sight!—Irene all in flames but standing immobile and unwavering and unconquered, paying no heed whatever to the fire. (11; 47)

The text vividly and painfully evokes the sight of the burning woman, calculating the reactions of the reader/listener as in a drama. Irene's reaction is described for its ironic effect: after the nun extinguishes the fire she is scolded by Irene for depriving her of attaining martyrdom, as she says, "I hate a gift that causes me a loss." The reversal of the reader's expectations is a device used frequently in the Life to stress the distancing of monastic ideals from worldly ones.

The extraordinary story of the possessed nun from Cappadocia in chapter 13 offers insights into ways in which a monastic community dealt with sexuality. A noblewoman who has entered the nunnery finds herself tormented by memories of a former suitor:

> The girl was unexpectedly attacked by a seething passion which maddened her with a frantic lust for her former suitor and did not allow her to control herself. Violently leaping, screaming, moaning, crying and calling out his name in a loud voice, she assured with fearful oaths that unless someone let her see him with her eyes and enjoy to excess his sight and conversation, she would hang herself. (13; 53–54)

Healing of the woman's "sickness" is facilitated when Irene is reassured by a vision of Saints Basil and Anastasia, who appear flying through the air and deliver a package to the convent:

> From the air there was let down a package weighing about three pounds, and this she received in her unfolded garment. Running together, excited at the wonderful occurrence, all the sisters beat their breasts and extolled the Mother of God. Lighting candles they began to undo the package which contained a variety of magic devices wrapped in it: two idols made of lead, one resembling the suitor, the other the sick nun, embracing each other and bound together with hairs and threads, then some other contrivances of malignancy, and inscribed on them the name of the author of the evil and appellations of his servant demons. (13; 62–63)

In the morning, as instructed in a vision, they take the afflicted woman to the church of Saint Anastasia. Going down to the saint's tomb under the church, the woman is anointed by the priest with oil from the lamps around the tomb, and the instruments of sorcery are burned:

> Now one miracle could be seen following the other. As the fire consumed each of the instruments of the sorcery, so the woman was liberated from her invisible ties and restored to soundness of mind, thanking and praising Him who had saved her. Reduced to ashes, all the objects were already disappearing into nothingness when screams resounded from the charcoals, like the squeals one may hear when swine are butchered in great numbers. (13; 63)

Belief in the power of demons was part of daily life in Byzantium, and what could not be attributed rationally was attributed to demons, including many kinds of sickness. The possessed or lovesick woman is cured by a mixture of procedures that we might characterize as faith healing, but more likely as witchcraft or voodoo. As in this story, the line between Christian miracle and pagan magic is sometimes very fine.[36]

One of the qualities demonstrated by Irene on several occasions is her ability to levitate, which culminates in the story of the mysteriously bowing cypress trees. As part of her ascetic regime Irene prays while standing with arms upstretched to heaven, and she prays over especially long periods during Lent, when she takes very little food and hardly sleeps. At such a time Irene is spied upon by one of the sisters, who is astonished

> to behold Irene hanging in the air about two cubits above the ground and praying with her hands extended towards heaven. Two lofty cypresses were standing on either side of the forecourt, reaching far up into the air. As Irene bent forward and prostrated herself before god, they trembled gently together and bowed their crowns to the ground along with her, waiting for her to rise. But even when the holy woman stood upright, the trees did not raise their crowns, until approaching she made the sign of the cross on each of them; then, as if blessed, they returned to their erect position . . . after a short time kerchiefs of silk-web were seen hanging in the crowns of the cypresses, bringing amazing delight to the spectators—surely Irene had fastened them with her all-holy hands, as the tree-tops often thus bowed before her. (16; 77–79)

In this picturesque description conjuring up an image of trees with brightly colored silk scarves tied around their peaks lies a story which is meant to demonstrate the power of the saintly woman to inspire the collusion of nature in her miracles. Irene swears the nuns to secrecy on the cause of the miracle, a frequently recurring topos in this life, as in many others, being a saint's insistence that his or her miraculous deeds remain hidden.[37] Modesty and humility accompany sanctity and are illustrated in such stories as the saint's levitation and the bowing cypresses.

Irene's miraculous powers of insight apply even to a mouse seen in the vicinity of the altar of the convent's church. Mere mention of this problem at dinner has the result that, after dinner is over, the saint's prayer has the desired result:

> After the meal, when they offered thanks to God together, she summoned the overseer of the church and said to her, "Go and take up the mouse which lies dead before the entrance to the sanctuary and throw it out on the dunghill." Meanwhile the priest had joined them to pray, and since he had seen that very mouse dead, he was amazed at the holy woman's command and went out crying, "Wonderful is God in his saints!" (17; 81)

Irene's foresight facilitates the detection and elimination of vermin threatening the communion bread and, presumably, the monastery's food supply. The story of the mouse probably refers to a serious concern to keep rodents in the nunnery's granary under control.

In chapter 21, Irene's relatives enter the picture when they supplicate her for help in the wrongful persecution of a kinsman. The author announces this miracle-story with some enthusiasm:

> One more of her wonderful deeds should be added to the narrative, a clear proof of her proximity to God and her freedom of speech before Him. (21; 89)

Not only is the abbess considered to be a friend of God but she exhibits the special quality of "freedom of speech," or *parresia,* with him. This means that God will listen to her prayers on behalf of people on earth. This ability of intercession characterizes the power instilled within a saint and demonstrates why saints were supplicated to convey the prayers of ordinary people to God. The story of Irene's powers on one occasion is worth relating in some detail.

We learn what occasioned the family to call on Irene's powers of intercession, for a titled man of the family has been accused by the emperor and is threatened with imprisonment or even summary execution. The result is a supernatural occurrence, and it occurs in a very different milieu from any encountered earlier in the Life:

> About midnight the Emperor, awake, not dreaming, seemed to see the holy Irene standing beside him, saying, "Emperor, stand up at once and release from prison the man you have unjustly confined." (21; 91)

The apparition, having come to the emperor's bedroom in the imperial palace, identifies herself as Irene, abbess of the convent of Chrysobalanton, and threatens him with divine judgment, pricks him in the side, and then leaves his chamber. The emperor, alarmed, calls on his bodyguards, who assure him that no one has entered the chamber; he concludes that the vision was divine. To test this theory he asks his prisoner if he knows this woman and where she can be found. The man tells the emperor that he does indeed know the abbess and that she never leaves her convent, located near the cistern of Aspar.[38]

The emperor reacts by organizing a visiting party of nobles to go to the convent, and among them he commissions a painter to paint her portrait. The party arrives at the convent, their arrival having been predicted by Irene, and to their surprise, before they can state their mission she confronts them with her command to release the man who is unjustly imprisoned. Her face flashes with lightning, and the painter surreptitiously paints an accurate portrait as they talk. On returning to the palace they show the image to the emperor:

> Then they showed him her image, and just as the Emperor cast his eyes on it, a flash of lightning suddenly sprang up from it, gleaming terribly before his eyes and made him cry aloud in terror, "Have mercy upon me, O God, according to Thy lovingkindness!" Greatly appalled he stood speechless for a long time, looking at the portrait in amazement that it showed exactly the woman who had threatened him in his dream. (22; 97)

In a time in which people still remember the impact of iconoclasm, the need to affirm the legitimacy of images is understandable. In this recognition episode the power of images is demonstrated, and the importance of their bearing a likeness that is recognizable and effective is emphasized.

As if to affirm the efficacy of icons, the story of the liberation of one of Irene's relatives through her intervention is brought about through the agency of an icon.

> No longer doubting his vision he led the prisoner out of his confinement, thanking God that He had prevented him from the unjust murder of the man and manifestly rescued him from the evils that would in consequence have behallen him. (21; 97–99)

Stressing that the ultimate justice is determined by God, the emperor gives thanks that the saintly Irene intervened on his behalf.

Irene's diverse and exceptional powers are illustrated throughout the collected stories found in the chapters of her Life. At the end, she prophesies her own death and is attended at her burial by the nuns of her convent. This touching scene likely evinces firsthand experience of such an event by the author. Although Irene's shining face in death, the sisters' laments, and description of the burial represent topoi, the passages reflect intimate knowledge of events affecting a sisterhood of nuns. Since the Life is so gender specific, it is entirely possible that it was written by a woman, for the author never identifies himself or herself, as in other vitae. If this were the case, the Life of Irene would be one of a handful of Byzantine hagiographic writings ascribable to a female author.

The final chapter affirms the connotations of the name Irene, which means "peace." This chapter describes her impact after her death:

> Even now her revered coffin is a source of every kind of benefit, and everyone approaching it in search of the cure of whatever his prayers include will find it ready and helpful. (24; 113)

Like many saints' tombs that became places of miraculous healing and responses to petitions, Irene's coffin evidently retained the power to give special benefits.

The Life is at times formulaic in its reenforcement of an ideal image of female piety, for all saints' lives are similarly shaped with societal agendas in mind. The very stylization of such Lives, however, helps us understand and interpret the society from which they spring. One might refer, for example, to her abundant tears of humility that require a well to contain them in chapter 14 and her attacks by the devil in chapter 6. Her acts of philanthropy, as noted above, acknowledge an acceptable preoccupation among Byzantine upper class and monastic women. The account of the spread of her fame is also a common topos found in saints' lives, as she is constantly consulted for advice. Her selection to succeed the dying abbess and replace her as *hegumene*, or abbess, appears as a prelude—or pretext—for a lengthy recitation on proper monastic conduct and the prescribed role of the abbess (chapters 7 and 8). Other episodes, however, such as the possessed nun who is being driven crazy by passion for her former suitor, no doubt reflect a reality with which communities of ascetics had to contend.

A variety of miracles are recounted, from the miracle of the deceased mouse to heavenly intervention in the form of a blinding flash of light when the abbess appears to the emperor of Byzantium, Basil I. The emperor obeys and later becomes a devotee of the saint, as we learn in chapter 21. The Life is filled with visions and prophecies, contacts with historical figures, and highly original details such as the bowing cypresses.

The Life has been assumed by some to be fiction,[39] but to define it as such neglects an understanding of the societally based literary genre it represents. In that it is full of details about ninth- and tenth-century events, customs, and monastic life and includes stories too bizarre to have been fabricated, even by an imaginative author, I believe it is based on fact. The text was written in the last decades of the tenth century, well after the saint's death around 940, possibly by a female ascetic who knew of Irene's exemplary life through stories collected by fellow monastics. Given this length of time before its writing down, the received stories would have had time to grow. The Life also could have been written by a male monastic intent on prescribing correct or admirable behavior for female monastics from a male point of view or even on representing repressive strategies aimed at controlling or circumscribing female roles. Given the emphasis on the Gouber family in the Vita, it was most likely composed by one of Irene's aristocratic and well-educated relatives. Irene is cast as the ideal female ascetic, a person with great talent as an administrator and leader as well as a captivating speaker. She held a special appeal for aristocratic women whom she inspired also to take the veil, and she even commanded the respect of and had access to the emperor of Byzantium.

Hagiography provides not just allusions to details of life, but also insights into otherwise unrecorded kinds of information for the middle Byzantine period. In its details, its descriptions, and its quirky stories, it sheds light on the thought world of medieval Byzantine society, and in this case on the monastic life of women. We also detect the hidden agendas, noting how the text was intended to function as a vehicle to demonstrate the subject's worthiness, to instruct potential monastics on correct behavior and patterns of life, and, most important, to help bring about the subject's eventual acceptance into the church calendar as a saint. The Life of a saint was habitually read aloud at the saint's tomb as part of the liturgy on the saint's feast day. Over the years until the fall of Constantinople, we can imagine believers gathered in the church at the monastery of Chrysobalanton to hear Irene's edifying Life read aloud every July 28 as they celebrated her feast day.

## Associated Readings

*The Life of Saint Irene Abbess of Chrysobalanton: A Critical Edition with Introduction, Translation, Notes and Indices,* Jan Olof Rosenqvist (Uppsala, 1986).

Alice-Mary Talbot, "Byzantine Women, Saints' Lives, and Social Welfare," in *Through the Eye of a Needle: The Judaeo-Christian Roots of Social Welfare,* ed. E. A. Hanawalt and C. Lindbergh (Kirksville, Mo., 1994), 105–22.

———. "A Comparison of the Monastic Experience of Byzantine Men and Women," *Greek Orthodox Theological Review* 30 (1985): 1–20.

———. "The Byzantine Family and the Monastery," *Dumbarton Oaks Papers* 44 (1990): 119–29.

*Nine*

# WOMEN IN ART: THE BYZANTINE IMAGE
# OF FEMALE SANCTITY: HELENA

In the middle Byzantine period of the ninth through twelfth centuries women appear in the visual arts in diverse media and represent a variety of figure types and messages. This chapter explores the appearance and meaning of depictions of women in art, and in particuar the implications of images of female saints found in church decoration of the ninth century on. To approach these images it is first necessary to define what we are seeing, and to do this it is useful to associate style with function as we distinguish three basic modes of representation. It becomes clear in scrutinizing these images that we are dealing with a distinctly Byzantine style, one which is recognizable at a glance but which encompasses a variety of modes of representation. These modes can be seen in a range of image types, from the formal portraits we associate with icons to ornamental motifs and figures to narrative scenes.[1] For example, in the portrait of the empress Zoe in an eleventh-century mosaic in the church of Hagia Sophia (fig. 27 and pl. 17), we see the crowned, richly clad holder of female power. As in the portrait of the empress Theodora (see chapter 6, fig. 22 and pl. 6), Zoe's facial features are somewhat individualized, referring to her actual appearance, but otherwise the portrait is stiff and two dimensional, meant to be read as a display of her insignia and her role as patron of the church (about which more will be said in chapter 10). The iconic mode of this portrait is the most familiar type of image in Byzantine art,

The iconic mode is also seen in conjunction with other stylistic genres. For example, on a mid-eleventh-century gold-and-enamel crown, the so-called Crown of Constantine IX Monomachos in the Budapest museum (fig. 28), a series of figures, one male and six female, appear on an ensemble of plaques which once were sewn onto fabric to make up an imperial crown; the plaques are executed in cloisonné

Fig. 27. The empress Zoe, detail of color plate 17, Empress Zoe and Emperor Constantine IX Monomachus with Christ, mosaic panel, Hagia Sophia, Istanbul, Turkey, 1028–42. (Courtesy Dumbarton Oaks, Byzantine Photograph and Fieldwork Archives, Washington, D.C.)

enamel with bright colors, predominently blue and red, juxtaposed with the gold of the cloisons and ground.[2] The emperor Constantine and two Augustae, Zoe and Theodora, wear imperial badges of power and carry scepters in the three central plaques, exhibiting the same iconic formality as the Zoe mosaic. To either side of the empresses, however, are plaques with a pair of dancing girls, seen turning and kicking their right legs out behind them in a lively dancing movement; they hold striped scarves billowing over their heads, and the proportions of their bodies are greatly distorted to emphasize their long legs. Various interpretations have been offered of who these spontaneous, expressive figures might be,[3] but what is clear is the contrast between the ornamental mode of representing the dancing girls and that of the figures with whom they appear. Turning to a third medium, we distinguish another stylistic mode.

In a rare scene from everyday life, a page from the twelfth-century Madrid Skylitzes manuscript shows an aristocratic female patron of the emperor Basil I, Danielis, seated in her sedan chair en route to the imperial city (pl. 10).[4] Danielis is wearing a long, pink cloak, and her head and neck are swathed in a light blue veil. She sits in a relaxed pose on a wicker seat in her elegant vehicle. The wooden frame of the litter is decorated with a meander pattern, the floor of the compartment is covered with a rug with an overall blue and red losenge design, seen in bird's-eye perspective, and the tentlike canopy is pink with red seams. Her eight carriers wear blue or pink tunics, red leggings, and black boots; eight other members of her entourage gesture as if acclaiming her appearance. Pared down to essentials, this scene probably approximates the way in which women of means traveled when covering long distances. In this case, Danielis, who lived in the vicinity of Patras in Greece, was on her way overland to Constantinople.

The bodies of all the figures in the Danielis scene are highly generalized; faces

*Fig. 28. Crown of Constantine IX Monomachos, gold and cloisonné enamel, Hungarian National Museum, Budapest, Hungary, 1042–50. (Copyright Erich Lessing/Art Resource, N.Y.)*

are delicately painted and expressive but not individualized. Clothing is articulated through swirl-patterns and repetitions of folds and highlights over thighs and elbows and is largely defined by color, contour, and geometric simplification rather than modeled in an integrated approach to the underlying body structure. In spite of the two-dimensional appearance of figures and setting, however, this stylistic mode has its roots in a long classical tradition; the emphasis has shifted away from illusionism or idealized representation to clear narration of the event being illustrated, in a narrative mode. After two lines of text, another band of illustration shows Danielis's arrival and presentation of gifts to the emperor, again, easily readable and with figures' names clearly written in red ink for the viewer's easy access to the content, for the scenes appear in a historical text for which the images function as illustration. The narrative mode shows an abbreviated scene depicted for clear legibility.

Having broadly outlined the iconic, ornamental, and narrative modes in Byzantine style, I will concentrate on the ways figures are depicted and the reasons behind

*Fig. 29. Tyche of the city of Gibeon, detail, Joshua Roll, Vatican Library MS Pal. gr. 431, sheet 12, mid–tenth century. (Copyright Biblioteca Apostolica Vaticana [Vatican])*

such depiction. For images in Byzantium work differently from those of other medieval or early modern cultures, and their character and function derive in part from the resolutions reached through iconoclasm (see introduction to part 3). Images were meant to function as a vehicle to convey meaning.[5] Byzantine imagery is also affected in large part by aesthetic values formulated in the classical antiquity out of which it grew, these values being later transformed through the use of imagery as an imperially or religiously sponsored form of expression. Whether seen in a secular or religious context, in an official or a more decorative application, or according to an abstract or more naturalistic conception, in Byzantium all images belong to a system in which cultural and aesthetic values are intermingled. A stage in the continuing process of relating and distancing from the classical ideal can be detected in images of the period of artistic revival in the century after iconoclasm.

During the flourishing of the arts under the Macedonian dynasty in the ninth and tenth centuries, antique-inspired forms experience a clearly discernible renewal. The stylistic character of this period provides a catalyst for observing the shifts in the treatment of human forms in succeeding centuries, helping explain, for example, the appearance of figures on the Danielis page of the Madrid Skylitzes. Two mid-tenth-century manuscripts, the Joshua Roll and the Paris Psalter, serve to demonstrate this classicizing revival in figure style. Female personifications are among the antique characteristics included in these manuscripts, and their classical antecedents are evident. The *tyche,* or allegorical representation, of the city of Gibeon seen on sheet 12 of the Joshua Roll, for example, sits in a naturalistically turned pose as she gestures in reaction to the battle taking place on her left (fig. 29).[6] Her arms and face

*Fig. 30. Israelite women dancing, Paris Psalter, Paris, Bib. Nat. Cod. gr. 139, fol. 5v, mid–tenth century. (Copyright Erich Lessing/Art Resource, N.Y.)*

are delicately modeled in ink wash, with shadows and highlights applied within the coutours of her body; drapery is bunched or pulled tightly over her limbs in a fashion that indicates their underlying structure.

In the famous Paris Psalter, the personification of Melody sits beside the Old Testament hero David as he composes the Psalms in an illusionistically painted, bucolic setting complete with attentive animals (pl. 11).[7] She too has an organically conceived body, with drapery falling in sharp folds with highlights emphasizing volume and body structure.

These two seated female figures, Gibeon and Melody personified, are obviously rendered in closer proximity to the antique-inspired ideal than the seated figure of Danielis on her litter. The explanation for this difference can be partly understood by observing another page of the Paris Psalter, the scene of the Israelite women dancing (fig. 30).[8] In this full-page painting, the body of the dancing woman in the foreground is contorted to convey movements of the dance. There is not the same sense of integration as in Melody on the David page but rather a double-jointed looseness and discontinuity of head, limbs, and torso. Whatever the variations in artistic practice or adherence to models reflected here, the result shows a relaxation of the need or the wish to depict physical integrity.

The distancing of Byzantine style from its ancient roots and the formulation of a distinctly less naturalistic appearance characterizes middle and late Byzantine art in all media, with intermittent instances of a return to more classicizing ideals. The resulting stylistic genre varies but retains a recognizable Byzantine character, defined by loose or highly stylized depictions of human bodies; linear, crisp drapery and highlights; scale and proportions which are not naturalistic; summary indication of settings or depth of picture field; formulaic facial types; labels within the picture field; and emphasis on clear representation of the narrative content of scenes. The ultimate

*Fig. 31. Adam and Eve, detail, ivory plaque on a casket with scenes from the stories of Adam and Eve, and Cain and Abel, Hessisches Landesmuseum, Darmstadt, Germany, tenth or eleventh century. (Copyright Hessisches Landesmuseun Darmstadt)*

dependence on antique models but with simultaneous linear and two-dimensional treatment of the human body and its pictorial setting constitute recognizable qualities of the Byzantine style. The three modes I have distinguished share elements of the same style but vary according to the function of the images: dogmatic representation, ornamentation, and narration.

Given these variations in mode, the ways in which women are shown physically in art may appear naive or awkward, in the odd shapes and proportions of their bodies, the lack of individuality in their facial features, and even the way their clothes fit.[9] Byzantine women in the middle period appear as strangely neutral beings, with more generalized features than feminine attributes. Even Adam and Eve in representations of the Fall, seen, for example, on a tenth- or eleventh-century ivory casket in the Hessisches Landesmuseum in Darmstadt, Germany, have the physique of puppets or dolls (fig. 31).[10] In the female nude, breasts are seen as bumps or circles, and male genitals are omitted or hidden behind the curve of a thigh. Depictions of men are just as broadly articulated as those of women, but when they are clothed, care is taken to indicate details of their dress which are emblematic of their status. There was apparently little interest in rendering women in a lifelike manner, but more care is taken to indicate attributes of rank or clothing typical of a particular category, for example, nuns versus dancers. Direct study of human anatomy is not a preoccupation of middle Byzantine artists.

The abstract element of Byzantine style regularizes and generalizes figures to a set of formulaic body types and proportions. These in turn are overlaid with conventional patterns of folds to give some impression of three-dimensionality or movement. Individuality and naturalism, however, including what we would consider portrait features, hardly exist except to a minor extent and in isolated cases. Although coloristically lively and visually readable, the figures are divorced from nature. Inscribed labels appear in all media and types of imagery and are crucial in identifying the individuals represented. The depiction becomes not a portrait but a signpost for that person—or does it? Let us consider one frequently encountered category: depictions of saintly or holy individuals.

According to the system of depiction I have described, labels indicating the identity of figures seem to substitute for likeness.[11] Combined with this standard practice, recognizable types are maintained for the most holy figures, such as the Virgin Mary and Christ, and some of the apostles, but for the most part what we would today consider a portrait quality is lacking. What the person means or represents in a symbolic or theological sense takes precedence over reality in a visual sense. Certain types of individuals are represented according to prescribed iconography, for example, hermits, who are depicted as thin ascetics by means of a linear technique, and warrior saints, who resemble ancient gods and heroes.[12] Colors of varied saturation and brightness take on the expressive role of suggesting tactile or essential qualities of the subject or her garments, including the symbolic use of gold as an emanation of the divine or blue for the virginity and sanctity of the Virgin Mary.[13] All these aspects of the image were taken in by the Byzantine viewer, but what, then, did the viewer gain through sight?

According to theologians making the case for images, sight was a more important faculty than hearing for acquiring enlightenment, as claimed in an oration of the fourth-century theologian Gregory of Nyssa: "For painting, even if it is silent, is capable of speaking from the wall and being of the greatest benefit."[14] After iconoclasm, the case is more persuasive. As Photius, the ninth-century patriarch of Constantinople, stated, images speak even more clearly than words when conveying the messages of divine truth: "Yet the comprehension that comes about through sight is shown in very fact to be far superior to the learning that penetrates through the ears."[15] Images are necessary, and the meanings made accessible through pictures take precedence over the written or spoken word.

A famous sermon preached by the patriarch Photius on the occasion of the dedication of the mosaic of the Virgin and Child in the apse of Hagia Sophia in Constantinople in 867 is a case in point. The mosaic shows Mary swathed in a voluminous blue robe, seated on a jeweled throne and holding the Christ Child, who wears a gold and silver tunic; both are silhouetted against the immense gold curve of the apse (pl. 12). The sermon claims that it has such lifelike qualities that it would seem to be "capable of speech" and that "the lips have been made flesh by the colors."[16] When we look at the mosaic today, however, it does not appear so convincing, and it is also out of scale and proportion in the vast space of the church. Instead of concluding, as some have, that the Byzantines could not draw skillfully, we learn that their notion of what constituted a likeness differed from ours.

The image in Hagia Sophia had a special authority, as the sermon further explains, for it confirmed the permissibility of icons, evoked the presence of the divine Mother, and expressed the doctrine of the incarnation of Christ. These symbolic meanings and associations made the image more "real" to the Byzantine viewer than even the most talented painter could render it. The apse image of Hagia Sophia set the standard for the apse decorations of Byzantine churches from this time forward, in which the Virgin was always labeled *Meter Theou*, or Mother of God. The viewer's attunement to the image from within the culture took precedence over how the traits were shown through lines or closeness to nature. Some were better executed and some less, but this was not what Byzantine viewers saw when they contemplated the image. Because the ideas instilled in the image were based on qualities and associations of the prototype, they saw the Mother of God herself.

Gradually programs of pictorial decoration began to appear again in churches around the empire. This public imagery represented in approved fashion theological truths at their most perceptible and universally understandable. The vast majority of Byzantine churches and their decoration in mosaics and frescoes have, of course, disappeared, although written descriptions give some idea of their character. A number of surviving examples, some remarkably intact, convey vividly the effects of the aftermath of iconoclasm when imagery was again free to proliferate. These survivors appear in disparate places, from remote Greek villages to the high plateau of Anatolia. Although little has survived in Constantinople, its numerous wealthy foundations dedicated to saints are recorded and must once have had decorated interiors similar in character to those that survive.

Images of female saints had their place within a system of decoration developed in the centuries after iconoclasm. This system had a distinct character, while being infinitely flexible.[17] The architecture and interior decoration are ideally suited to work together in evoking, in effect, a world somewhere between heaven and earth. In the dome, Christ as Pantocrator, or All-powerful One, looks down through a porthole-like rainbow symbolizing heaven, his face stern and judgmental while he gives a blessing with his right hand. On the curved vaults around the church's interior are the Virgin and Child in the apse, flanked by angels, and narrative scenes from the Life of Christ as found in the Gospels and Apocrypha. The curved surfaces on which appear the Annunciation, Nativity, Baptism, Transfiguration, among others, produce the effect of sharing the viewer's space, so that he or she symbolically participates as a witness at these sacred events celebrated liturgically throughout the year.

Lower down on the walls, in the chapels and narthex or in the crypt, are depicted other narrative scenes from the the life, miracles, and Passion of Christ, all executed in the narrative mode discussed above. Finally, on the walls and vaults just over the viewer's head are depicted individual images of saints: fathers of the church, holy bishops, monks and martyrs, doctors and miracle workers. These individual images are in the iconic mode, and among them are images of holy women: empresses, martyrs, nuns and abbesses, teachers, and repentant sinners.

Who are these women who have achieved sainthood? and what is their function in the interior decoration of Byzantine churches? Do they engage viewers in a responsive relationship with a special intent regarding their individuality or status as women? Is there a gender-specific relationship between female saints and their audience?

Holy personages, both men and women, appear individually in mosaics and frescoes on the walls of churches, as medallion busts, in round frames, half-length figures or standing full length, side by side. They appear in churches from the middle Byzantine period well into post-Byzantine times of the sixteenth century. Greek inscriptions identify the saints by name, and most can be localized in terms of when and where they lived. Yet these images in their iconic frontality and staring eyes remain mysterious, eluding interpretation. As part of a complex system, however, their selection is not random but must have had inherent meaning for contemporaries.[18] One popular image is that of Saint Helena, the mother of Constantine I, who appears frequently in these cycles and is always paired with her son, the emperor. What message was this imperial pair meant to convey? What do iconic images of female saints tell us about women and sanctity? What can we learn about women of Byzantium from the images of saints?

Representations of male saints predominate in church decoration in accordance with their importance in church history. As we have seen, women played only a marginal role in church administration and could not be members of the clergy. Misogynistic attitudes barred them from contact with monks, and they were thought to be the incaration of temptation and the devil. Bishops, warriors, patristic fathers, and holy abbots all shaped the fabric of the church and its practices and beliefs, women's influence being marginal. By the ninth and tenth centuries, however, a number of female saints, many of whom lived in late antiquity and the period of the early martyrs, were incorporated into the church calendar, which was revised and regularized at the end of the tenth century.[19] A selection of these saintly women appears in the monumental decoration of churches from this time on, although it is considerably smaller than the number of male saints regularly represented and has a less obvious rationale. Why did a small group of women find its way into church art? Were these the saints with the most appealing written Lives? or were they the saints to whom the most famous martyr-churches were dedicated and therefore had associations with their relics? Were female saints perhaps especially popular among women because of their protective or healing powers for female illnesses? Were they therefore favorite name-saints? Were they meant to represent a special set of qualities which were thought of as paradigmatic for women? Did women think of themselves as imitating certain qualities of saints? How do these images of female sanctity reflect women in Byzantine culture?

To explore the questions raised by the appearance of female saints in church deco-ration, I turn to the mosaics in the Katholikon at the monastery of Hosios Loukas in Greece. In this large, well-preserved monastic church is the most complete series of narrative scenes and individual portraits of saints of any surviving monument. The first church at the monastery was erected during the lifetime of its patron saint, Saint Luke of Steiris, a holy man who lived in the region between Thebes and Delphi and along the Bay of Corinth in the tenth century. According to the *Life and Miracles of Saint Luke of Steiris,* the first church at the monastery was dedicated to Saint Barbara through the patronage of the strategos, or military governor, of the theme of Hellas, Krinites.[20] Sometime after his death in 953 a larger and more magnificent church was built to accommodate the crowds of pilgrims coming to visit the site. Constructed of stone and brick and decorated lavishly throughout with colored marbles, gold mo-saics, and frescoes on the main level, in the galleries, and in the crypt, this church was probably built with combined local and imperial funds derived from a success-ful war with the Arabs on Crete. Scholars disagree on its date, but the late tenth or early eleventh century is likely.[21]

Portraits of female saints appear prominently in the mosaic decoration of the Katholikon. Twelve portraits of holy women appear localized on the west wall of the narthex, or porch, of the church (pls. 13 and 14). One hundred and ten individual portraits of male saints, including fathers of the church, apostles, and warrior saints, occupy other areas of walls and vaults throughout the church and its crypt. Narrative scenes appear on curved surfaces in the main nave and on the walls of the narthex; further narrative scenes appear in the frescoes of the side chapels and crypt. The iconic depictions of female saints in the narthex represent a practice without a theory. Only in the eighteenth-century *Painter's Manual* of Dionysius of Fourna is there a hint at a tradition of depicting female saints near the doors of churches.[22] One can surmise that within the flexible middle Byzantine program, donors' wishes and local concerns determined variations in artistic practices, but there is no standard prac-tice for the inclusion or selection of female saints. The procession of named female martyr-saints in the early Byzantine church of Sant' Apollinare Nuovo in Ravenna, discussed in chapter 4 (pl. 3), antedates the cluster in Hosios Loukas by more than 450 years and is an instance without a parallel. The presence of a concentration of portraits of female saints in the narthex of Hosios Loukas, a male monastery, is an example which requires explanation.[23]

Researchers know women were a strong and pious presence in the middle Byzan-tine period and that they became increasingly mobile and powerful, as both donors and coreligionists, but what accounts for this instance of women's images in the church? The great scholar of Byzantine monumental decoration, the late Doula Mouriki, said that to understand a Byzantine monument one had to "live inside" the culture, and she herself achieved that to an extraordinary degree. Yet for most people it is often difficult to understand how Byzantine art functioned as an expression of that society. It is particularly perplexing to imagine how these images of holy women at Hosios Loukas were perceived by contemporaries who saw them, both men and women. In an insightful study of the relationship between Byzantine church imagery and utilization of space, William Tronzo has shown that the image of Christ washing the disciples' feet was installed in direct proximity to the place where this ritual was carried out mimetically in monastic churches.[24] Alternative approaches have been taken by scholars studying Western medieval saints; by examining narratives written about female saints and medieval texts of their Lives, they have revealed much in terms of contemporary reflections of the gendered roles of women in society.[25] I will draw on both of these approaches to show how the imagery of female sanctity in art opens a new perspective on women of Byzantium.

The mosaics of female saints in the narthex at Hosios Loukas are arranged in two groups of six, each occupying an arched recess, or lunette, on the west wall of the north and south bays of the narthex. The saints appear as both standing figures and as busts in roundels, arranged in two registers separated by thin red lines. The upper zone allows for full-length standing figures and the lower, interrupted by windows, for horizontal rows of medallion portraits. All the saints are identified by inscriptions placed to either side of their heads or within the roundels. The grounds around figures and inside and outside the medallions are entirely filled with gold mosaic, and the surrounding intrados of arches and borders are decorated with ornate bands of floral and textile-inspired motifs.

In the center of the upper register of the south lunette Saints Helena and Constantine, dressed in imperial garments of jeweled loroi and crowns with pendilia, hold a tall patriarchal, or two-barred, cross between them while they gesture toward it with their free hands (pl. 13). This grouping had at least two prototypes in statues in Constantinople, according to an eighth-century text, which may account for the origins of the basic format.[26] Constantine is the only male figure appearing within the groups, and he appears in this context as a counterpart of Helena, whose primary association is the discovery of the True Cross and who is almost always associated with this attribute.[27] She has another patriarchal cross woven into the shield design, or *thorakion,* on her loros. Constantine is associated with his vision of the cross; after his famous dream it was established as a symbol of military victory as well as of victory over death.

On either side of this pair are large medallion busts of Saints Thekla and Agatha, who wear dark green and pink maphoria, respectively, and carry small white martyrs' crosses. Thekla of Ikonium, whom we encountered in the introduction to part I, is known from the *Acts of Paul and Thekla* as the first woman martyr and female apostle. She accompanied Saint Paul on his travels in the late first century CE and suffered trials when pitted against wild beasts in the arena; she founded a monastery near Seleucia in southern Asia Minor. She carries a book in reference to her invocation in the *Commendatio Animae,* the commending of the soul of the deceased, a prayer which forms part of the funeral service of the Orthodox Church.[28]

Agatha of Sicily, a noblewoman and virgin, was martyred in Catania under Decius in the third century. After rejecting the advances of the consul of Sicily, Quintianus, she was tortured and mutilated. In a hymn by Kassia she is remembered for the appearance of an angel at her tomb who placed a tablet on it inscribed, "Holy mind, possessed of free choice, honor from God, and deliverance of the country."[29] She is patroness of goldsmiths, weavers, and women with breast ailments and is invoked against outbreak of fire.[30]

In the register below are three holy women in monastic garb, Anastasia, Febronia, and Eugenia, who also carry small white crosses and raise their left hands in a blessing. They all wear black mantles covering their heads and are indistinguishable as facial types. The woman labeled Anastasia is likely to be Anastasia of Sirmium, who was martyred under Diocletian in 304. She was commemorated in a major church dedicated to her in Constantinople; her relics were deposited there in 457. Her name, a popular form of Anastasis, was meant to recall not only faith in the Resurrection but also the resilience of faith in icons during the period of iconoclasm.

Febronia was martyred at Nisibus, also under the emperor Diocletian, and a popular cult to her was established by the late sixth century. According to her Life, perhaps written by a fellow nun, she belonged to a convent at the time when persecutions were terrorizing the Syrian countryside. The virgin was seized but granted leniency on the condition that she marry the eparch, Lysimachos, for she was very beautiful. She refused and was tortured in a grisly fashion. A church dedicated to her was founded in Nisibus, and another in Constantinople.[31]

Eugenia of Alexandria was an aristocratic and learned virgin martyred under Valerian in the mid–third century in Rome. She was a representative of *monachopartheneia,* that is, she wore monks' clothing in order to join a Christian monastic community—even becoming an abbot.[32]

In the north bay in the upper register of the lunette (pl. 14) appear three regal standing figures: Saints Irene, Catherine, and Barbara, corresponding to Helena and Constantine in the south lunette. All three carry small white crosses. Irene, crowned and in imperial garb, holds an orb on which is engraved a cross on a stepped pedestal. On the font of her loros appears an icon in a roundel. She is the empress Irene who served as regent for her son Constantine VI and then ruled alone from 780 to 802, the first woman to rule the Byzantine Empire in her own right. She is best known for reinstating icons in the break in iconoclasm and for presiding over the Oecumenical Council of Nicaea II of 787.

Catherine of Alexandria is similarly attired, with the addition of a bright green sash and crown. A virgin and convert of imperial family, she debated with pagan philosophers in Alexandria and was martyred under Maxentius in the early fourth century for converting others to Christianity. She was tortured on a wheel and beheaded. She is patroness of learning and of noblewomen.[33]

Saint Barbara stands out for her exotic costume, a white tunic and veil, jeweled tiara, and deep blue cape. Martyred in Nicomedia under Maximian (286–305), this well-educated woman was imprisoned in a tower by her father because she was very beautiful but would not marry. When she would not renounce her Christianity she was tortured and finally beheaded, as ordered by her father. She is patroness of armorers, artillery, and fortifications and is invoked against sudden death or dying without the sacraments. The first church at Hosios Loukas was dedicated to her.[34]

In the lower register are roundels with busts of Euphemia, Marina, and Juliana. Saint Euphemia, daughter of a wealthy senator, was tortured by fire and wild beasts and martyred under Diocletian in the hippodrome in Chalcedon. An early church was dedicated to her in Constantinople, and the Council of Chalcedon was held at her sanctuary in Chalcedon in 451. Her relics were later brought to Constantinople by the empress Irene because the saint was considered a friend of the "party of images."[35]

Marina of Antioch in Pisidia was martyred under Diocletian. She was raised by a Christian woman and preached conversion but was disowned by her father and given up for torture to the governor. She was tempted by the devil, whom she trampled, and inspired a mass martyrdom of the people of Pisidia before being beheaded. She wears her customary bright red maphorion; she is protectress of women with children.[36]

Saint Juliana of Nicomedia, a witness to Saint Barbara's torments, was also a beautiful and aristocratic woman devoted to reading the Scriptures. She was martyred along with Barbara when she refused marriage with the governor of Nicomedia, since he would not convert to Christianity. She suffered horrible tortures and was finally beheaded.[37]

Except for Helena and the empress Irene all of the women depicted were martyrs in the early persecutions and carry martyrs' crosses. All the standing figures are haloed, while the roundels serve as haloes for the busts in medallions. According to their written Lives, many of these women were educated and beautiful and suffered tortures and brutal mutilations, described graphically by hagiographers: severed breasts, the rack, burning, beheading, tearing apart by wild beasts. The crowned women, Helena, Irene, and Catherine, stand together as imperial or aristocratic women, while Barbara also has aristocratic status. Marina, Catherine, and Agatha represent protective roles for women.

The themes of the True Cross and the adherence to Orthodoxy it symbolizes are emphasized through the presence of Helena, Anastasia, and Irene and through patriarchal and other crosses held by Constantine and Helena and appearing on their garments. For example, Helena may be juxtaposed with her counterpart in the north lunette, Irene, the Orthodox empress who with her son Constantine VI was considered a "new Helena."[38] Irene is also associated with the Orthodox Council of Nicaea II of 787 and the triumph of Orthodoxy, after which the cult of the cross gained new prominence, especially through its ritual exaltation on September 14.

The holy women on the west wall combine in a chronological and thematic sequence glorifying the cross and Orthodoxy.

Various geographical areas from Sicily to Egypt are represented by the twelve women, and, among other attributes and associations, their number parallels that of the twelve apostles, who are depicted in the intrados and arches of the vaults of the narthex in close proximity to the depictions of the female saints. The holy women also play a role within the program of the rest of the narthex.[39] Four narrative scenes—the Washing of the Feet, Crucifixion, Anastasis, and Incredulity of Thomas—appear in lunettes on the north, east, and south walls of the narthex, forming an abbreviated cycle of the events surrounding Easter.[40] The Washing precedes the Crucifixion, and the Incredulity follows the Anastasis, or Resurrection. On entering the church, the viewer looking upward and to the left sees the image of Christ's death on the cross on the northeast wall of the narthex. This image is diametrically juxtaposed with his conquering of death through the Harrowing of Hell, depicted to the right on the southeast wall. Here, Christ holds up the patriarchal cross like a battle standard. The programmatic use of thematically balanced imagery is evident in the repetition of crosses. The patriarchal cross of the Anastasis is connected visually and topographically with the same type of cross held by Constantine and Helena on the wall directly opposite in a responsive pairing of images and extension of the Passion cycle through the series of female martyrs.

The vaults and remaining lunettes of the narthex broaden the context within which one should understand the female saints. On the lunette over the royal door is the half-length figure of Christ blessing and holding an open Gospel book, expressing the dialogue between image and audience as the worshiper passes into the church proper.[41] In the groin vault before this image are medallion portraits of the Virgin Mary, John the Baptist, and the archangels Michael and Gabriel. Mary and John serve as intercessors between humankind and Christ, for whom the archangels are messengers; their grouped appearance is referred to as a Deesis.[42] Holy men and women, it was believed, served as intercessors for ordinary people in their prayers for salvation, and thus the group of female saints can be seen as participating in the Deesis composition of the narthex on behalf of those addressing prayers to them.

Supporters of the church's mission are represented by the twelve apostles depicted standing or in medallions in the intrados of the four arches spanning the narthex. Thekla may be seen to extend this group of apostles, since she was known as the first female apostle, and a number of the female martyrs were active as teachers or proselytizers for Christianity. The remaining vaults of the north and south bays are occupied by medallion portraits of the *anargyroi,* the healers "without a fee": Cyrus and John, Cosmas and Damian in the north, and Panteleimon, Thalaleus, and Tryphon in the south with the addition of Moccius, an early martyr to whom Constantine dedicated a church in Constantinople. Finally, in the lunette on the west wall over the entrance, and therefore between the two groups of female saints, are medallion portraits of the five martyrs of Persia: Acindynos, Anempodistos, Pegasios, Aphthonios, and Elpidephoros, who were venerated in Constantinople, where their relics were held in special regard. Thus we have in the narthex symmetrically arranged groups, among which are twelve female saints, twelve apostles, eight healers, five martyrs of Persia, a Deesis group, and an abbreviated Passion and Resurrection cycle. Through the narrative scenes and iconic images, the themes of sacrifice, martyrdom, triumph over death, the cross and Orthodoxy, the intercession of the saints, and healing are represented to the viewer.

The exceptional number of female saints at Hosios Loukas might reflect the role of women reported in the Life of the founder of the monastery, Saint Luke of Steiris.[43] We know from the Life that although the monastery was a male institution, women played a prominent role, and that the Katholikon served the surrounding area as well as the crowds of pilgrims and suppliants, both male and female, traveling to the monastery. As in the miracle accounts appended to the *Life of Saint Theodore of Sykeon* discussed in chapter 7, women figure prominently in the accounts of miracles in the *Life and Miracles of Saint Luke of Steiris,* both during the saint's life and post-humously. In one case a woman who is among the "most distinguished citizens of Thebes" was cured by him. In other instances they are poor women who experience miracles at the saint's tomb.[44] The sister of Saint Luke, the nun Kale, also played an important supportive role in his life. She is mentioned several times in the Vita as being engaged in her daily occupations along with her corelegionists and is cited as a source for the narrative of the Life itself, compiled after her brother's death.[45] It is possible even that she belonged to a nunnery in the vicinity, continued to associate herself with the monastery, and helped promote her brother's cult.[46] The exceptional prominence of female saints in the mosaics at Hosios Loukas suggests the possibility that they appear, at least in part, because of the visibility and importance of women in connection with this monastery, indicating the adaptation of the mosaic program to its local setting.[47]

The female saints at Hosios Loukas do not stand alone. Women are prominent also in the frescoes of the middle Byzantine rupestral churches of Cappadocia, in the central plateau of Anatolia, where the sheer density and numbers of figural representations and programs constitute our most plentiful evidence for Byzantine programmatic decoration. Although no individual portraits of female saints are preserved in the other major middle Byzantine programs in mosaic, those at Daphni and Nea Moni on Chios, the Cappadocian frescoes show striking comparisons to Hosios Loukas in selection, arrangement, and iconography.

In the frescoes of Byzantine Cappadocia, dating between the ninth and eleventh centuries, female saints are always depicted in conjunction with Constantine and Helena, who usually appear at the west end of the chapel, near the entrance. For example, at El Nazar, of the late tenth century, the royal pair appear on the right side of the barrel vault inside the entrance, while Saints Catherine, Barbara, and Juliana are identifiable on the wall opposite.[48] At Tokali Kilise, Constantine and Helena appear

*Fig. 32. Interior view of cave Church with female saints: Anastasia, fresco, Church of Kiliçlar Kuşluk, Göreme, Cappadocia, Turkey, eleventh century.*

twice, on the north side of the nave of the Old Church, of the early tenth century, in a row of standing saints who include Catherine, Marina, Anastasia, and Agape, and in the New Church, of the late tenth century, in the intrados of the arch before the sanctuary, while Saints Catherine and Barbara are in the corresponding intrados before the prothesis chamber.[49] At the "Pigeon house" church at Çavuçin, of 965, the imperial pair appear in the main apse itself, supporting the theme of military victory stressed in the program.[50] At the Chapel of the Theotokos, Saint John the Baptist and George, Constantine and Helena are in the center of the row of saints on the north wall, while Catherine and Anastasia stand adjoining the Anastasis image on the entrance wall.[51] In the later "column churches" a slightly different pattern emerges. When the entrance is on the north wall, as at Çaricli Kilise, female saints appear on walls adjacent to the entrance—Paraskeve, Eudocia, Catherine, Barbara, Kiriake, and Irene—while Constantine and Helena appear on the south part of the west wall next to portraits of donors.[52] At Kiliçlar Kuşluk, of the eleventh century, female saints are notably prevalent (pl. 15 and fig. 32); eight half-length figures of female saints appear in the decoration, with Constantine and Helena just below the portraits of donors, man and wife.[53]

In this sampling of depictions of female saints in the Cappadocian churches we see many of the same saints depicted at Hosios Loukas, and they often appear in an analogous placement on the west wall of the church or near an entrance. Constantine and Helena sometimes appear associated with portraits of donors, indicating their intercessory or protective function vis-à-vis those with high status.[54] Among all the saints seen in the Cappadocian churches, Constantine and Helena are the most ubiquitous, and they appear full-length and holding the True Cross between them, as at Hosios Loukas.

A group of painted churches on the island of Cyprus in the eastern Mediterranean serves as a revealing extension of features noted in the preceding examples. Cyprus was part of the Byzantine Empire in the eleventh and twelfth centuries until it was conquered by crusaders in 1190, and then it was ruled until the sixteenth century by a succession of French and Venetian overlords. A tradition of building small family churches existed throughout this period in the Troodos Mountains which form the central spine of the island. A sampling of the evidence for this long tradition shows the survival of Byzantine and Orthodox features and of Greek language, even centuries after the land went out of Byzantine control. In the colorful frescoes of these small Cypriot village and country churches one encounters an internal artistic development in which depictions of female saints appear with great consistency and increasing prominence over time.[55]

Two Cypriot churches of the study group date to the period of Byzantine rule: Asinou and Lagoudera. Even though these are small, modest structures the paintings of their interiors are immediately recognizable as Byzantine in style and program. The Panagia Phorbiotissa of Asinou near Nikitari, of 1106, and the Panagia tou Arakos at Lagoudera of 1192 are painted in a style resembling that used in Byzantine manuscripts. At Asinou, among fifty-two portraits of male saints, are five female saints depicted on the south and east walls: Saint Mary of Egypt (paired with Zosimas), Helena and Constantine, Anna (with Joachim), Ioulitta (with her consort Kyriakos), and Thekla. The paired saints predominate. Mary of Egypt, in contrast to conventional portraits of women, is shown naked except for a rough cloak, emaciated, and with long hair growing on all exposed parts of her body (see fig. 13). Her skeletal appearance and disheveled hair make her a shocking and pitiful sight, clearly intended to provoke a strong response in viewers. Zosimas, who appears on the opposite wall, holds up a liturgical spoon with the communion host. The pair of figures comprises an abbreviated version of the story of the monk's service to this reformed harlot in the desert (see chapter 4). What could this image have meant to twelfth-century viewers?

The royal pair Helena and Constantine appear prominently in a lunette on the south wall at Asinou. Adjacent to them in another lunette are the patron of the church, Nikephoros Magistros, with the Virgin Mary acting as intercessor for him before Christ. Behind Nikephoros is the small figure of his wife, Gephyra. Her name is inscribed along with the date of her death, 1099.[56] In this context the juxtaposition of imperial saints with the donor has several connotations. The rank and wealth of the donor are evoked by the saints' imperial apparel and named status, while funerary associations are evoked by the cross, which serves as a prophylactic symbol of victory over death. The imperial saints may be seen as prototypes and protectors of the aristocratic founder of Asinou and his late wife. At Lagoudera, the son of the Byzantine governor of Cyprus founded a chapel painted in a court style related to the art of Constantinople. The only female saint preserved in this ensemble is Saint Mary of Egypt, whose depiction is similar to the one at Asinou, and is again paired with Zosimas in what was apparently a popular type on Cyprus.

In other churches of the Frankish, or Lusignan, period, we encounter a wider selection of saints. At Moutoullas, dated to 1280, five full-length portraits of female saints appear on the west wall of the naos against a bright red background (fig. 33). On the south wall next to the door to the narthex are Athanasia with her husband, Andronikos, and Mavra; on the north side of the door are Barbara, Marina, and

*Fig. 33. Saints Andronikos, Athanasia, Mavra, Barbara, Marina, and Anastasia, fresco, west wall, Church of the Panagia, Moutoullas, Cyprus, 1280. (Photo by author)*

Anastasia. Athanasia wears dark robes and the monastic hood, a reference to the story of her disguising herself as a monk in order to live near her husband. In contrast, the other sainted women are attired in brightly colored garments, mostly of red and apple-green. Barbara is bedecked with jewels, and her head is swathed in a stylish white veil, referring to her high status. Saint Marina of Antioch is a popular Cypriot saint; according to local beliefs she guards sleeping children and protects lovers. Anastasia, known as the "poison-curer," a female doctor-saint, is associated with powers of healing. Mavra, the Black Saint, is revered locally as a martyr-saint. Of a total of thirteen separate iconic portraits of saints at Moutoullas, eight are of males and five of females. It has been surmised that since the donors, man and wife, are depicted in the sanctuary of the church, their wishes are reflected in the emphasis on saints with healing capacities and local cults.[57]

Perhaps the most impressive array of female saints in any ensemble on Cyprus is found in the Frankish narthex of Asinou, painted around 1333. On the west wall on either side of the entrance are seven full-length figures of female saints, including some we have encountered previously, while the overall program focuses on the Last Judgment and therefore has funerary connotations. On the south side are Anastasia, Irene, and Anna (pl. 16); on the north side of the door are Mavra, with her consort, Timothy, Paraskeve, Eudokia, and Marina. Two of these, Anastasia and Anna, appear with homonymous donatrixes kneeling before them.

Anastasia Saramalina, dressed in light ocher tunic, green cloak with red neck ornament, and intricate veil, supplicates through her gesture Saint Anastasia Pharmako-lytria, the poison-curer, as she is clearly labeled; the saint stands calmly holding her attribute, a long-necked vial (fig. 34). Saint Anna, mother of the Virgin Mary, brightly attired in red mantle and green tunic, stands to the left of a tiny standing donor, also named Anna, who is identified in the inscription as a deaconess (fig. 35); she wears a white tunic with embroidered collar and cuffs, and a black- and white-striped headdress covers her hair. The inscriptions in both panels repeat the formula: "prayer [*deesis*] of the servant of God." The personal wishes of living, contemporary women were responsible for representing Saints Anastasia and Anna, as these two pairs demonstrate.

*Fig. 34. Saint Anastasia Pharmakolytria with donor, Anastasia Saramalina, fresco, detail of pl. 16, Church of Panagia Phorbiotissa, Asinou, Cyprus, 1333. (Photo by author)*

The other saints of the west wall of the Asinou narthex are Mavra and Irene, both with local cults. Paraskeve is the patron saint of Good Friday and, like Constantine and Helena, is associated with the popular cult of the cross. The grouping of female saints on the west wall at Asinou coincides with middle Byzantine usage as it is manifested at Hosios Loukas; however, this instance acquires special significance through the depiction of contemporary women in direct relation with their protecting saints.[58]

Five other Lusignan-period churches of the Troodos Mountains consistently include some of the same selection of female saints as at Moutoullas and the narthex at Asinou.[59] A fine example, the church of the Archangel, or Panagia Theotokos, near Galata, painted in 1514, comes from the period of Venetian occupation. In spite of the church's modest size, its interior was painted with utmost care and skill in a Renaissance version of Byzantine style by Symeon Axentis, working for the Zacharia family. A dedicatory inscription over the north door names the patrons of the church building as Stephanos and his wife, Loiza, and the patrons of the painted decoration as Polos and Madelena and their children. The overall program includes more than fifteen separate narrative scenes and thirty individual portraits of saints in the lower register, eight of which are female saints we have encountered before on Cyprus. On the south side, Saint Mary of Egypt and Zosimas appear on the reveals of the doorway. Barbara, Catherine, and Irene are at the west end of the south wall, while Athanasia appears with Andronikos to one side of the west door, and Paraskeve and Marina to the other (fig. 36).

Constantine and Helena are on the north wall, holding a large True Cross of meticulously detailed wood grain (fig. 37). They appear next to the door over which is the dedication panel of the Zacharia family. Female saints, three of whom occur as parts of pairs, literally surround the worshiper in a wraparound scheme. The donor

*Fig. 35. Detail of pl. 16: Saint Anna with donor,
Anna the Deaconess, fresco, Church of Panagia
Phorbiotissa, Asinou, Cyprus, 1333 (Photo by author)*

portraits in the panel over the north door are carefully rendered and share the same
bright green background as the saints around them.

Kneeling below a Deesis composition is Polos holding a model of the church,
Madelena, their coat of arms, and their four children (figs. 38 and 39). The women
are richly dressed, with gold embroidery on the hem and bands of Madelena's bright
red skirt and pearls on the gold filet in her hair and on her cuffs. The eldest daughter is also stylish, with snooded hair and colorful, wide-sleeved gown, indicating
wealth and high social status. Indeed, Polos was a Cypriot nobleman of Venetian
descent and Madelena a descendant of the royal house of the Lusignans. Madelena
holds a Catholic rosary, while the book held by the eldest daughter indicates she is
Greek Orthodox, for it is inscribed in Greek with the first verse of the Akathistos
hymn. Thus a Hellenized couple of mixed French and Venetian origin sponsored the
decoration of a church strongly in the Byzantine tradition four hundred years after
Asinou and three hundred years after the island passed out of Byzantine control.
The disproportionately large number of female saints at Galata very likely reflects
the wishes of Madelena, who invokes their protection on behalf of herself and her
three daughters.

From this evidence it is clear that there was an increase in the number of holy
women represented in church decoration on Cyprus from the twelfth to the fifteenth
centuries, and that they are no longer confined to the west wall around the entrance
but appear increasingly on the north and south walls. The pairs of saints who appear most widely are Helena and Constantine and Mary of Egypt and Zosimas, holy
pairs of very divergent character. Their popularity on Cyprus is supported by local
and internal developments peculiar to Cyprus, including the numerous village festivals which often incorportated ancient customs. One tradition is that Helena made
a stop here on her way from Jerusalem to Constantinople when she was carrying

*Fig. 36. Saints Barbara, Catherine, Irene, Athanasia, and Andronikos, fresco, south and west walls, Church of the Archangel or Panagia Theotokos, Galata, Cyprus, 1514. (Photo by author)*

*Fig. 37. Saints Constantine and Helena, fresco, north wall, Church of the Archangel, or Panagia Theotokos, Galata, Cyprus, 1514. (Photo by author)*

pieces of the True Cross. Various accounts embroider on this tradition, saying that she built churches and supplied them with relics from the Holy Land. After this, miracles began to take place: the end of a disastrous drought, the cleansing of demons, and a repopulation of the island. Beneficent developments on Cyprus were attributed to the personal influence of Helena.[60]

These and the other paired saints present an intriguing pattern which seems to have proliferated in the Troodos churches. Helena and Constantine are considered to be paradigms of sanctity and therefore serve as appropriate models as well as protectors of aristocratic donors, for they present the prominent image of the True Cross with its evocations of imperial power and victory in battle. The predominance of female saints paired with husbands, mentors, or children may likewise respond to the needs and concerns of families and the maintaining of family groups, the health of children, the protection of marriage ties, and other traditional concerns of women. This interpretation becomes all the more tenable when one considers the numerous instances of the depiction of named donors and their families in dedicatory inscriptions of the churches in which the largest numbers of female saints appear. The selection of certain saints by Cypriot patrons bears out palpable concerns of the donors within their social context. In these tightly knit mountain communities in which family structures and traditions were of great importance, the prioritizing of family is reflected in the popularity of holy pairs of saints.

Female saints also appear individually, without associations with males. They are

*Fig. 38. Deesis composition with donors Polos and Madelena and their children, fresco, north wall, Church of the Archangel, or Panagia Theotokos, Galata, Cyprus, 1514 (Photo by author)*

*Fig. 39. Madelena and her daughters, fresco, detail of figure 38, deesis composition, Church of the Archangel, or Panagia Theotokos, Galata, Cyprus, 1514. (Photo by author)*

sometimes depicted with contemporary women, as in the narthex at Asinou, explicitly expressing the saints' protective roles for those individuals (see figs. 34 and 35). We can therefore assume that female saints were selected, at least on some occasions, to represent the interests or concerns specifically of women, as role models or through their various capacities as intercessors or healers. The frequent appearance of female saints at the west end of the church and near doors can be seen as a reflection of women's place in the church or as an indication of their relatively marginal status compared with males in the eyes of the church. The portraits of female saints express the associations with women in Greek Orthodox society.

This brings me to a consideration of the female saints encountered in the Troodos churches in terms of polarities. Ascetic women such as the emaciated Mary of Egypt and Athanasia in male monastic garb represent self-imposed extremes, through which those women ultimately attained sainthood. Their repeated appearance might stem from an interest in or even fascination with their choices, one shared by men and women alike, for they represent a break from traditional female gender roles. The polarities range from reformed harlot to empress and represent contrasts of social status and condition in life. Their appearances contrast vividly as well, from dark, simple monastic garb to colorful, worldly, and rich attire. Among the Cypriot female saints a balance is also struck between the appearance of saints with local origins or cults, such as Mavra, Athanasia Pharmakolytria, Marina and Paraskeve, and those of more universal appeal, such as Catherine, Barbara, and Thekla. The diverse capacities and connotations of these saints may reflect the range of possible roles available to contemporary women, from the most humble to the most privileged, or the most obedient to the most rebellious.

The numbers, chronological scope, and individual character of these Cypriot paintings help establish a profile for the examples of church programs discussed earlier in the chapter. Cappadocian churches of the ninth to eleventh centuries had already established, at a time soon after the end of iconoclasm, patterns of representing women in the western portions of the cave-chapel or around the entrances. The largest number of holy women in any single church appears at Hosios Loukas of the late tenth or early eleventh century. The Troodos examples, dating from the twelfth to the sixteenth century, extend and expand the trends of the earlier churches and exhibit several consistent patterns. The most popular image in all our examples is that of Helena paired with Constantine. While the origin of the practice of depicting this pair is unknown, it must have become popular in the years after iconoclasm when the cross became associated with the Triumph of Orthodoxy.

In view of the convergences as well as the differences among our examples, I will suggest some interpretations of the presence of female saints in church decoration. Monastic or local churches such as those we have been observing were usually sponsored at least in part by local patronage, by nuns as well as monks, women as well as men, empresses as well as emperors. While all Orthodox citizens of Byzantium venerated the Virgin Mary and Christ through their images and icons, saints, as we have seen from their Lives, have very diverse stories, often stemming from individual circumstance or local history, and hence the reasons for their appeal vary. Female saints had special associations for women and for men, but perhaps more so for women, who shared their dilemmas and sought their singular female properties of providing aid. The gap between ordinary women and sanctity narrowed in the middle Byzantine period, when ordinary women and married women increasingly were adopted as saints.[61] As seen in the saints in the fourteenth-century narthex at Asinou, individual women put themselves under the care of their name-saints or of other female saints and considered these holy women as helping protect and reassure them or guarantee their salvation. Women with illnesses would naturally address healing saints, especially ones associated with their female illnesses or their concerns for the health of their children. For women who had chosen to take the veil, monastic saints would best represent role models for their way of life. From what we have seen of the lives and choices of Byzantine women, female saints and their varied associations represented the diverse circumstances of women in society. We might think of the saints encountered at the back of the church or in the places near the doors as paradigms and supporters for the women who occupied these spaces. As noted above, the relation between viewers of icons and their holy prototypes was one of sympathy as well as communication. The image shared its power with the suppliant; it became the "prayer of the servant of God."

With its systematic placement of imagery and its relation to patterns of Orthodox worship, the fully developed middle Byzantine and post-Byzantine church program reflects the actions and liturgies that were performed repeatedly within its spaces. It evokes for worshipers a timeless ambiance in which they are participants, in the company of holy personages, and bearing witness to sacred events. During the iconoclastic controversy the cross had appeared ubiquitously as an isolated symbol and was considered by iconoclasts the only permissible image for church decoration. Saints Constantine and Helena flanking and holding between them the True Cross frequently appear in posticonoclastic church decoration, indicating they took on new or revived meaning after iconoclasm.

Themes of salvation and resurrection, with a symbolic emphasis on the cross, are repeatedly evoked in the depictions of female saints in conjunction with Constantine and Helena. After the reestablishment of Orthodoxy, the role played by the empresses Irene and Theodora led to a revival of interest in Helena and contributed to the appearance and selection of female saints in middle Byzantine programs. The connotations of military victory and salvation through the salvific cross were attached to the imperial figures of Constantine and Helena after iconoclasm, and this image became the most universally represented from this time on.[62] They may also have prepared the way for the inclusion of other female saints who, like Helena, were paradigms of feminine virtue but emphasized different qualities of women's contributions and therefore served varying functions among members of the church community.[63]

The case of female saints demonstrates the flexibility of the appearance and use of images, especially those associated with the middle Byzantine program of church decoration. Even within the circumscribed practices and imagery of the Orthodox Church each building's images contain an echo of the people who were responsible for the decoration or who worshiped in that church's community, whether it is monastic, urban, or rural. Saintly women, as we have seen in this study, exemplify a feminine ideal and represent symbolically facets of the lives of their living counterparts, holding up a mirror to women in that society. Their depictions in churches were seen in conjunction with their special sympathetic role regarding women. The beliefs, hopes, and fears of women of Byzantium are still recognizable today in Byzantine images of female saints.

## Associated Readings

Carolyn L. Connor, "Female Saints in Church Decoration of the Troodos Mountains in Cyprus," in *Medieval Cyprus: Studies in Art, Architecture, and History in Memory of Doula Mouriki* (Princeton, 1999), 211–28.
———. *Art and Miracles in Medieval Byzantium: The Crypt at Hosios Loukas and Its Frescoes* (Princeton, 1991).

Jan Willem Drijvers, *Helena Augusta: The Mother of Constantine the Great and the Legend of Her Finding of the True Cross* (Leiden, 1992).

Irmgard Hutter, "Das Bild der Frau in der Byzantinischen Kunst," *Byzantios: Festschrift Herbert Hunger zum 70. Geburtstag* (Vienna, 1984).

Henry Maguire, *The Icons of Their Bodies: Saints and Their Images in Byzantium* (Princeton, 1996).

*Pl. 1. Mausoleum of Galla Placidia, Ravenna, Italy, interior, showing Saint Lawrence mosaic; sarcophagi, 425–50. (Copyright Scala/Art Resource, N.Y.)*

*Pl. 2. Mausoleum of Galla Placidia, Ravenna, Italy, interior, showing vault with starry sky, 425–50. (Copyright Scala/Art Resource, N.Y.)*

*Pl. 3. Procession of female saints, mosaic, north wall of nave, Sant' Apollinare Nuovo, Ravenna, Italy, ca. 550. (Copyright Scala/Art Resource, N.Y.)*

*Pl. 4. Vault mosaic, bust surrounded by grapevines, Mausoleum of Santa Costanza, Rome, Italy, ca. 360. (Copyright Scala/Art Resource, N.Y.)*

*Pl. 5. Anicia Juliana with personifications, frontispiece in Dioscurides,* De Materia Medica, *Vienna, Österreichische Nationalbibliothek, cod. med. gr. 1, fol. 6v., ca. 512. (Copyright Austrian National Library, Bildarchiv)*

*Pl. 6. Detail of figure 22, the empress Theodora, Antonina, and Joannina, mosaic, south wall of sanctuary, San Vitale, Ravenna, Italy, ca. 545–47. (Copyright Scala/Art Resource, N.Y.)*

*Pl. 7. Necklace and earrings, gold wire, pearls, carnelian, sapphires, emeralds, Dumbarton Oaks Collection, Washington, D.C., fifth century. (Courtesy Dumbarton Oaks, Byzantine Photograph and Fieldwork Archives, Washington, D.C.)*

*Pl. 8. "Samson Panel," silk, Dumbarton Oaks Collection, Washington, D.C., Egypt, sixth to seventh century. (Courtesy Dumbarton Oaks, Byzantine Photograph and Fieldwork Archives, Washington, D.C.)*

*Pl. 9. Icon of the Triumph of Orthodoxy, British Museum, London, ca. 1400. (Copyright Trustees of the British Museum)*

*Pl. 10. Danielis riding on a litter,* Chronicle of John Skylitzes, *Madrid National Library, Vitr. 26, fol. 102r(a), ca. 1150–75. (Copyright Ministerio de Educación, Cultura y Deporte, Biblioteca Nacional, Madrid)*

*Pl. 11. David composing the Psalms, Paris Psalter, Paris, Bib. Nat. Cod. gr. 139, fol. 1v, mid-tenth century. (Copyright Snark/Art Resource, N.Y.)*

*Pl. 12. Virgin and Child enthroned, detail, apse mosaic, Hagia Sophia, Istanbul, 867.*
*(Copyright Erich Lessing/Art Resource, N.Y.)*

*Pl. 13. Saints Thekla, Constantine and Helena, Agatha, Anastasia, Febronia, and Eugenia, mosaic, west wall of narthex, south bay, Hosios Loukas Katholikon, Greece, late tenth to early eleventh century. (Photo by author)*

*Pl. 14. Saints Irene, Catherine, Barbara, Euphemia, Marina, and Juliana, mosaic, west wall of narthex, north bay, Hosios Loukas Katholikon, Greece, late tenth to early eleventh century. (Photo by author)*

*Pl. 15. Interior view of cave church with female saints, fresco, Church of Kiliçlar Kuşluk, Göreme, Cappadocia, Turkey, eleventh century. (Photo by author)*

*Pl. 16. Saint Anastasia with donor, Saint Irene, Saint Demetrios, and Saint Anna with donor, fresco, narthex, south half, Church of Panagia Phorbiotissa, Asinou, Cyprus, 1333. (Photo by author)*

*Pl. 17. Empress Zoe and Emperor Constantine IX Monomachus with Christ, mosaic panel, Hagia Sophia, Istanbul, Turkey, 1028–42. (Photo by author)*

*Pl. 18. Nicephorus Botaniates and Maria of Alania blessed by Christ,* Homilies of Saint John Chrysostom, *Paris, Bibliothèque Nationale, Ms. gr. Coislin 79, fol. 1 (2bis) v, ca. 1071–81. (Copyright Bibliothèque Nationale de France, BnF)*

*Pl. 19. Initial facing pages of the Lincoln College Typikon, Oxford, Bodleian Library, Cod. gr. 35.* Left: *Constantine Palaeologus and Irene Komnene Branaina, fol. 1v.* Right: *John Synadenos and Theodora Palaeologina, fol. 2r, ca. 1300–1335. (Copyright Lincoln College, Oxford, Ms Gr.35, fol.1v)*

*Pl. 20. Facing pages of the Lincoln College Typikon, Oxford, Bodleian Library, Cod. gr. 35. Left: Theotokos of Sure Hope holding Christ Child, fol. 10v. Right: Theodule and Euphrosyne, fol. 11r, ca. 1300–1335. (Copyright Lincoln College, Oxford, Ms Gr. 35, fols. 10v and 11r)*

*Ten*

# IMPERIAL WOMEN AND MARRIAGE: ZOE

The standard list of Byzantine emperors found in texts about Byzantium makes no reference to the women who coruled as Augustae, who carried out the roles of wife, mother, and empress. Lynda Garland has redressed this omission in her recent book, in which she includes the names of empresses, emperors' mothers, and the children of imperial unions (see also the list of Byzantine emperors and empresses on p. 319 below).[1] A scan of the list reveals that many empresses were foreigners. Some names are striking, for example, Irene the Khazar, wife of Constantine V in the eighth century, and Maria of Alania, wife of Michael VII and of his successor Nicephorus III in the eleventh.[2] The foreign brides continue: Irene of Hungary, Irene of Sulzbach, and Anna of Savoy in the twelfth and Anna, daughter of Basil I of Moscow, in the fifteenth, to name just a few. What did these marriages entail for the women, who were usually very young when they married? The legal age for marriage was twelve for girls and fourteen for boys, but in practice they often married younger. What were the expectations in Byzantine emperors' marriages with foreign women? and, conversely, what preparations were undertaken by Byzantine women entering into unions abroad? Aristocratic and imperial marriages at home are also important, in particular as they affected Byzantine women's roles and when they perpetuated a dynasty through marriage. In this chapter I will consider imperial marriages in Byzantium.

Within the empire, succession to the throne often involved a marriage decision. When an emperor died leaving no son to inherit the throne, a daughter could succeed to power and either rule in her own right or choose a suitable husband from among the civil or military aristocracy to rule as emperor. Such an emperor ruled by virtue of his marriage to the *porphyrogenneta*. Likewise, the widow of a deceased emperor could either rule in her husband's stead or she could remarry, and in so doing secure the future of her dynasty by providing a male head of state. If a usurper killed the emperor in a coup or forced him to abdicate, one way for the usurper to achieve a smooth transition and accession to power was by marrying the wife of his predecessor, by force if necessary. In all these cases it was a woman or a crowned empress who was the legitimizer of male rule through marriage. The empress Zoe is a fascinating case of a woman involved in transfers of power through her marriages.

During a period of twenty-eight years, from 1028 to 1056 a succession of marriages determined a series of six rulers. During this time the imperial princess Zoe and her sister Theodora alternately married or sponsored a ruler or ruled in their own right. The drama of marriage and imperial rule over these twenty-eight years will be the case study for this chapter as we focus on the career of Zoe the empress, including the circumstances under which she shared the palace, and her husband, with his mistress, Skleraina. Our source for Zoe's tempestuous life is the contemporary writings of Michael Psellos, court philosopher, historian, and confidant of the emperor Constantine IX Monomachus, Zoe's third husband. Psellos's well-informed account tells us much about the empress, sometimes couched in conventional, matter-of-fact terms and at other times in brutally frank or biased ones. Through Psellos's vivid narrative, we gain an intimate view of the wishes and priorities of this often-married empress and the conditions of her life of court intrigues and affairs.

Byzantine empresses ruled through birth or marriage according to their individual styles, with different degrees of involvement, or as circumstances dictated. Women who were born or married into the Theodosian house ruled according to a pious but engaged style, especially Galla Placidia, whose second marriage legitimized her rule for and with her son, Valentinian III, for some twenty-five years (see chapter 3). The empress Theodora experienced an abrupt change in status when she married Justinian I, after which she took an active role in making decisions of importance for the state (see chapter 6). Sophia, wife of Justin II, married from within the imperial family and governed for her husband during his lifetime when illness rendered him incompetent. At the time of iconoclasm the deaths of their husbands put Irene and Theodora on the throne as regents for their children; after iconoclasm, Theodora arranged a marriage for her son Michael III through a brideshow, as discussed in chapter 8. Other empresses took a less active role in governing, or their impact simply was never recorded.[3]

The work of governing, which involved primarily military, financial, and administrative decision making and diplomacy was usually the purview of the emperor, while the empress concerned herself with philanthropic, religious, ceremonial, and familial matters. As we have noted, her philanthropic roles were prescribed through a long tradition. The *Book of Ceremonies,* compiled in the tenth century, reflects conventions and public enactments of protocol practiced for hundreds of years, customs in which empresses played a major part. The *gynaikonitis,* or women's quarters, of the palace continued to be the center of the empress's activity, from which she directed a large staff, led by the grand chamberlain, of ladies in waiting and eunuchs. A quality of mystery attached to the gynaikonitis, where plots were hatched and the empress could harbor friends or pursue other activities out of sight of the rest of the world. All of an empress's roles were in fact open to negotiation, and an empress was prepared by her training to assume the work of governing or any of a number of responsibilities, as need be. How were women prepared for such potantially demanding roles, either as incoming or outgoing brides? and how were marriages arranged at home and abroad? As the custom of marrying foreigners increased during these centuries of competing and interacting empires, the ninth through the thirteenth centuries, how did women's roles affect international relations and diplomacy?

Increasingly in the middle Byzantine period, foreign matches were made for princesses of Byzantium, for it was as expedient for foreign dynasties to establish links with the imperial house as it was for the Byzantines to gain leverage with foreign powers. A marriage alliance was potentially more binding and lasting than many of the other forms of international diplomacy, partly because of the children born of the union. The practice of foreign marriage, however, was not condoned initially, at least not in principle. The emperor Constantine VII Porphyrogenitus in his handbook on imperial rule, *De administrando imperio,* expressed disapproval that Byzantine-born princesses should be sent to a foreign country to marry:

> For how can it be admissible that Christians should form marriage associations and ally themselves by marriage with infidels, when the canon forbids it?

After this denunciation of the marriage between Romanus I Lecapenus's daughter Maria and a Bulgarian prince, Peter, he adds,

> But this was no different from giving any other of the ladies of the imperial family, whether more distantly or closely related to the imperial nobility, nor did it make any difference that she was given for some service to the commonweal, or was daughter of the most junior, who had no authority to speak of.(13.174–75).[4]

While Constantine acknowledges that such marriages were of utility politically, being of "some service to the commonweal," he simultaneously villifies Romanos's policy as "unseemly"; it was in some sense beneath the dignity or self-importance of the Byzantines to send women, even not especially highborn women, abroad. An exception, however, was granted the Franks, with whom Constantine I as founder of Byzantium shared his roots.[5]

One of the most ambitious foreign marriages ever planned might have joined the Frankish and Byzantine Empires and reshaped the medieval world. Irene, regent of Constantine VI, arranged in 781 to marry her son to one of Charlemagne's daughters, Rotrud. After negotiations broke down, Irene herself planned a marriage with the widower, Charlemagne.[6] Although neither plan was fulfilled, we gain insights into the preparations through a chronicler's account. The potential alliance was prepared when emmissaries traveled from Byzantium to the Frankish court to arrange the match:

> An agreement having been reached and oaths exchanged, they left the eunuch Elissaios, who was a notary, in order to teach Erythro [Rotrud] Greek letters and language and educate her in the customs of the Roman Empire.[7]

For a foreign-born, incoming princess, knowledge of Greek was a basic prerequisite but more important was knowledge of the customs, which refers to court ceremonial with its traditions and formulae. It is clear that the order, execution, and significance of each gesture, act, and acclamation had to be studied and mastered by those taking part.[8]

For incoming brides, there were several methods of recruitment: by foreign alliance using political criteria, by internal alliance using political criteria, or through a brideshow, when political motives were absent and the beauty of the competitors was apparently the primary criterion.[9] Pictures were part of the initial phase. It is said that the prince Constantine VI was so attached to his fiancée, Rotrud, through a picture which had been sent that he wept when the engagement was broken off.[10] The successful candidate was brought to Byzantium and educated in her role by the empress-mother, for the young fiancée came to live with her future in-laws after the engagement, which sometimes occurred long before the marriage. The couple thus grew up together and often played together as children before assuming royal responsibilities and consummating the marriage. Whether prepared before leaving their native countries or coached after their arrival, foreign brides faced a heavy responsibility at the Byzantine court. From the ninth century on there was increasing international involvement of the Byzantine Empire in what moderns would term world politics, and supporting this involvement were non-Byzantine wives.

We catch glimpses of incoming princesses in the foreign complexions and hairstyles in their images. The idealized beauty of Maria of Alania, daughter of King Bagrat IV of Georgia, is evident, as she appears next to her (second) husband, Nicephorus III Botaniates; both are being blessed by Christ, in the lavish gold-ground frontispieces of a manuscript in Paris, Coislin 79, of 1071–81 (pl. 18).[11] Her red hair is bound by golden clasps close to her neck. She wears a high gold and jeweled crown, loros, and thorakion; her blue, red, and gold silk mantle is set off by her bright red belt and shoes. She carries a thin gold scepter. This empress probably lived at the Byzantine court as a child. She became skilled in maneuvering her way among court politics in her efforts to place her young son in a position to inherit the throne, as I will recount in more detail in chapter 11.

The Komnenian emperors frequently married foreign brides in an attempt to keep enemies at bay. Piriska (or Piroshka), the Hungarian-born wife of John II Komnenos (1118–43), wears traditional imperial garb, including a crown with pendilia, and wears her long, red hair in plaits, as seen in a mosaic dedication panel of ca. 1118 in the southeast gallery of Hagia Sophia in Constantinople (fig. 40). She appears

*Fig. 40. The emperor John II Konmenos and the empress Irene with
the Virgin and Child, mosaic panel, Hagia Sophia, Istanbul, Turkey, ca. 1118.
(Copyright Erich Lessing/Art Resource, N.Y.)*

with her Byzantine name, Irene, inscribed above her head. Irene bore eight children
and jointly founded the Pantocrator monastery with her husband; after her death
in 1134 she was venerated as a saint.[12] The twelfth-century marriages of Bertha of
Sulzbach, sister-in-law of the German emperor Conrad III, and then of Maria of
Antioch, daughter of Raymond of Poitiers and Constance of Antioch, to Manuel I
Komnenos, and then of Anne of Savoy, daughter of Louis VII of France, to Manuel's
son Alexius II were all intended to ease hostilities between Byzantium and the newly
established crusader kingdoms in the East.[13] The utility of these marriages to the Byzantines is self-evident. Should these marriages be considered cruel or an injustice to
the women, since they were planned marriages in which the women had no choice?
Was there a sense of duty, compliance, or adventure that made princesses willing
to leave their childhood homes and cultures and set out to establish themselves in
entirely new circumstances? Is there any reason to believe the incoming princesses
were discontented in fulfilling their roles?

Outgoing Byzantine brides are even more frequently encountered. One finds ample evidence of the practice of princesses raised in the imperial palace marrying monarchs and princes of foreign powers. An ivory plaque in the Musée de Cluny in
Paris dating to the tenth century commemorates the marriage in 972 of an outgoing
Byzantine princess named Theophano to Otto II, heir to the Holy Roman Empire
(fig. 41). The plaque resembles an earlier one, now in the Cabinet des Médailles in
Paris, celebrating the marriage of Romanos II and Eudocia. The Otto and Theophano plaque, a luxury object which was probably admired and prized in the West,
imitated Byzantine artistic practice.[14] The language of divinely blessed union is un-

*Fig. 41. Christ crowning/blessing in marriage Theophano and Otto II, ivory plaque, Musée de Cluny, Paris, ca. 982–93. (Copyright Foto Marburg, Art Resource, N.Y.)*

mistakably expressed by the figure of Christ standing on a high footstool between the two rulers and placing his hands on their heads. Theophano and Otto are shown as being of identical height and dressed in imperial crowns and regalia; their names and titles in Greek and Latin are carved into the ivory above them. No individuality or portrait-like features can be distinguished, further suggesting that the diplomatic role she played and the symbolic function of the ivory were of prime importance. This panel, like its related example, was painted or stained a deep red, adding to its value and emphasizing its imperial connotations.[15]

Theophano traveled to the West in 972 and was married to the future emperor Otto II and crowned in Saint Peter's in Rome. She was contracted in marriage as part of an ongoing effort by Otto I and the emperor John Tzimiskes to build diplomatic relations betweeen the Holy Roman Empire and Byzantium. Theophano was not a porphyrogenneta, but it is thought she was the great niece of the emperor Nicephorus Phokas.[16] She was probably brought up in the imperial palace by her namesake, her godmother, Theophano, empress and wife of Romanos II.[17] The young Theophano did her job well and succeeded in her diplomatic mission, inspiring her son to emulate Byzantium and its long tradition. Numerous objects went with her on her voyage west, spreading examples of Byzantine splendor among foreign peoples. While her training was accomplished at the court of Byzantium, she died in the imperial palace at Nijmegen in 991 and was buried in the church of Saint Pantaleon at Cologne, having raised her child to be the future emperor Otto III.[18]

Sometimes an alliance between a Byzantine princess and head of state had consequences far outlasting the current political advantages. Maria Lekapena, the daughter of Romanos I Lekapenos, mentioned above, married Tsar Peter of Bulgaria in 927, bringing a Christian culture to this rival state.[19] Anna, the daughter of the emperor Romanos II Lekapenos and his wife, Theophano, and sister of the emperor Basil II, was married to Vladimir of Kiev in 988 or 989 on the condition that her husband convert to Christianity. The marriage brought about the Christianization of Russia, which meant not only that Russia entered the sphere of Orthodox Christianity but also that it continued as an important political and military ally of Byzantium. The Byzantine princess Anna herself is said to have helped in the conversion of Rus and sponsored the building of churches in her new land.[20] Such marriage bargains had been taking place with some regularity during the early medieval history of Byzantium, but from the tenth century on they became almost an industry.[21]

A Byzantine princess could expect to marry at around age twelve to fifteen, so her training would take place probably in the two or three preceding years. For outgoing brides, a general training took place within the palace, although it was assumed initially that they could read and write.[22] Literacy, although generally not expected of women, may have been particularly important for Byzantine princesses and porphyrogennetae. Some, we know, were competent scholars and writers. These brides-in-training would be thoroughly versed in Scripture and would be taught all the details of court ceremony and protocol. A woman's acquaintance with material trappings of the court would extend from their maintenance to their creation: jewels, silks, other clothes, bedlinens, rugs, and hangings. The ability to do embroidery, spinning, and weaving were also part of maintaining her proper image and associations with the feminine ideal. Byzantine princesses were expected to present an impressive appearance and maintain the aura of Byzantium as the most wealthy and sophisticated state in Christendom. An outgoing bride would also become familiar with a wide spectrum of the ideological underpinnings of the empire, so as to represent the notions of statecraft and diplomacy to other medieval cultures.[23]

An outgoing princess would be groomed to represent the imperial ideal in dress and manners and would be prepared to preside with her husband at banquets, receptions, and other official duties; also to attend church liturgies and play philanthropic roles such as the distribution of alms and donations to the poor. Her most important role, of course, was to bear children and then to oversee their education. She would be aided in her duties by an entourage, including older women she had brought with her from Byzantium: ladies-in-waiting, a priest, and assistants to tend to her wardrobe, personal effects, and jewelry, for her splendid appearance was part of what made her a desirable match. We know Theophano succeeded admirably in her marriage in the West, but for numerous other princesses there is no record or trace.

Marriages at home also concealed pitfalls and challenges for women. The marriage between Constantine VII Porphyrogenitus and Helena Lecapena, the daughter of Romanus I Lekapenus, in 919 is a good example. An ambitious usurper, the father of the bride, was behind the arrangements. After the marriage, Romanus seized control of the empire in an ostensible joint rule with his son-in-law. He ruled and led the Byzantine armies as Romanus I for twenty-four years, from 920 to 944. In spite of the circumstances of the marriage, the match is said to have been a felicitous one, and Constantine and Helen, while under a kind of house arrest, raised a large, happy family. Protocol or ceremony was an important function for Helen after her husband attained his rightful throne in 945. Ceremonies were performed according to a yearly calendar, as Constantine VII recorded in his *Book of Ceremonies,* but also proper reception of visitors was a standard part of palace protocol. The empress had duties similar to those of the emperor in honoring dignitaries and their wives. For example, on the occasion of the visit of Princess Olga of Kiev to the Byzantine court in 957, it was the duty of Helen to attend to this noble visitor and all her attendants in an elaborate series of banquets and receptions which are described in the *Book of Ceremonies.* The familial nature of these ceremonies is reflected in the extent to which the empress and her household and children participated, with introductions, obeisances, and gifts exchanged in the royal dining halls and reception rooms of the palace. When Olga was baptized on a return trip in 960, so great was her attachment to Helen, her initial hostess, that she took her Christian name, even though Helen was no longer reigning.[24]

For the empress, heading the gynaikonitis of the palace with its myriad details included, of course, the education of her children.[25] If no children issued from a marriage, the result might be the ending of the marriage, as, for example, in the case of the wives of Leo VI (886–912). Leo experienced mismatches and the early deaths of his wives and thus had three wives in eighteen years. His fourth marriage, to Zoe Karbounopsina (Zoe with coal-black eyes), while illegal, was an effort to make their child, Constantine, legitimate heir to the throne. The ensuing "tetragamy scandal" caused a schism in the church and serious divisions in the empire.[26] Rules governing marriage were dictated by canon law, to which even an emperor was forced to adhere or face excommunication. A variety of patterns governed women's marriages within the empire and in cases of both incoming and outgoing brides. In every instance women's preparation and willingness to carry out their roles were crucial in helping stabilize and maintain a system of imperial rule and foreign relations.

In spite of women's demonstrated involvement in the process of maintaining imperial authority in Byzantium, after Edward Gibbon's pronouncements of the 1770s to 1780s history books were all too ready to denigrate imperial women and to belittle their impact, often assigning to them a set of stereotypical vices and assuming their destructive influences and misuses of power. For example, Gibbon dismisses the period of rule of Zoe and her sister Theodora with contempt:

> I have hastily reviewed and gladly dismiss this shameful and destructive period of twenty-eight years, in which the Greeks, degraded below the common level of servitude, were transferred like a herd of cattle by the choice of caprice of two impotent females.[27]

The negative attitude toward Byzantium engendered by Gibbon's categorical denunciation of these women makes it difficult to set the record straight. The testimony of the women themselves is required. Perhaps most tantalizing is the complex case of the middle Byzantine marriage scenarios of Zoe, heiress of the Macedonian dynasty.

# Zoe

A childless woman who inherits the throne inherits not only uncontested rights and powers, but also enormous responsibilities and conflicts. Such was the case with Zoe, the heiress of the Macedonian dynasty in 1028. Even though she never bore children, she survived and maintained her position as legitimate empress through marriage with three successive husbands over a period of twenty-two years, dying before her third husband, Constantine IX Monomachus, in 1050. After Constantine's death, Zoe's sister Theodora was brought out of retirement to rule for another year, from 1055 to 1056.

Through her marriages Zoe perpetuated the Macedonian dynasty, sharing its pride in earlier achievements and conquests, for at the death of her uncle Basil II in 1025 the Byzantine Empire was at its greatest extent and power since the time of Justinian and Theodora. Zoe has been variously described by contemporary authors and modern historians as having pronounced shortcomings, but the most directly engaged and authoritative source is her contemporary Michael Psellos. On examining Psellos's firsthand account of Zoe's career, we will revise the most commonly held notions about her. As we consider the implications of her choices and actions, we affirm that she acted responsibly under the circumstances in which she found herself and that she put her role as porphyrogenneta before all other concerns in her long, unhappy life.

Michael Psellos, the great psychological historian of Byzantine rulers, gives us one of the most thorough and compelling portraits of imperial personages of any time in his *Fourteen Byzantine Rulers,* or *Chronographia,* a history of the rules of emperors from Basil II (976–1025) to Michael VII (1071–78).[28] His access to the inner circle within the palace allowed him to write with an intimate knowledge of his subjects. His account of these reigns is full of details about government, palace life, and anecdotes revealing the personalities of the rulers. In studying his commentary on Zoe, I will take into account Psellos the writer and his expressed opinions, agendas, and biases in order to interpret as clearly as possible the character and motivations of the empress as she deals with the situations brought about by her marriages.

Psellos's self-importance surfaces frequently, for he cannot conceal his pride at being privy to so many secrets and privately conducted episodes of palace life. He readily describes the activity and temperament of the sisters Zoe and Theodora and of everyone else in their immediate circle. His main concern, however, is for his patron, Constantine IX, whose flaws he depicts as stemming from circumstances and his virtues as God-given. He is determined to write history and not encomium, but because his purpose is also to shape a record of Constantine's achievements, a strong male bias is detectable in his writings. His dislike of women with power is also evident, but it is not an obsession with him, as it was with Procopius. Because his depiction of Zoe is not at the center of his narrative, Psellos sometimes conveys a frank and objective view of the empress and sometimes one based on his gendered notion of correct, conventional demeanor for women. The importance of marriages and other social bonds and relationships in the course of his account of these rulers motivated this keen commentator and observer to issue wry judgments, especially when the law was bent to accommodate imperial aims.[29] Through Psellos we get a vivid picture of a woman tossed on the waves of her successive marriages.

Zoe's early years in the imperial palace when her uncle Basil II and father Constantine VIII were ruling can be imagined, for she must have been educated and trained in protocol and diplomacy since childhood. Born around 978 to Constantine VIII and the empress Helena Alypia, she and her two sisters were, according to Psellos, "brought up in the palace and educated in a manner worthy of their exalted rank."[30] In the absence of a son, who would have taken precedence over any female children, the issue of choosing a successor was postponed. The girls remained unmarried in the palace, probably as a potential means of perpetuating the dynastic line when the right time came for forming useful alliances. Zoe apparently was sent to Italy in 1002 at the age of twenty-four as the prospective bride of Otto III, son of the Byzantine princess Theophano and heir to the Holy Roman Empire. The man died before Zoe reached Italy.[31]

By this time Zoe must have been trained in diplomacy and knew the risks and responsibilities of holding power. She was proud to have grown up close to the great emperor Basil II, who ruled from 976 to 1025 and who, according to Psellos, "expressed the strongest affection and love for his nieces."[32] The eldest sister was permitted to join a nunnery, but the second and third sisters, Zoe and Theodora "acquiesced in the ideas of their uncle and father, and made no plans of their own."[33] It was not until the end of the reign of their father, who ruled from 1025 to 1028, that the problem of succession required that one of them step into service:

> When therefore, he [Constantine] felt that the end was near, either persuaded by his counsellors, or through his own recognition of duty, he began to cast round for an heir to the throne, intending to betroth the second of his daughters to the man he chose. (2.9; 58)

In failing health, Constantine made a quick decision for Romanos. But since Romanos was already married, a trick was devised, and his wife was quickly tonsured and put in a nunnery, while Romanos was taken to the palace to marry into the emperor's family.[34] Theodora, the younger daughter, preferred a monastic existence to marriage. So, according to Psellos, it was Zoe who was designated as the bride of Romanos: "The most beautiful of Constantine's daughters was no sooner in his sight than she was made his bride," remarked Psellos.[35] Zoe, the older and more regal in appearance, finally was married to a man she did not know—at age fifty(!).

Romanos III Argyros acquired the right to rule through his marriage to Zoe, but this was more than simple ratification of her father's choice of successor. It was a critical bond to ensure smooth succession, for a dynasty's continuation, more than skillful politics, was considered a divine privilege.[36] Zoe's marriage to Romanos therefore conveyed an indisputable, sanctified right to the new ruler. What did this abrupt change in her life mean to Zoe? When still a young woman she nearly married a young Ottonian prince. Was his death a disappointment? Did she wish for marriage during her following years of late youth and middle age? Did her arranged marriage to Romanos hold any attraction for her now? Her family until this time had been her sisters, two emperors, and other members of the court circle. Did she consider it simply doing her duty, for which she had been trained? One cannot help wondering if she felt bitterness or resignation at her fate, but on this point Psellos is silent.

Soon Zoe did have cause for bitterness. Although she was the legitimizer of her husband's rule, further expectations were that she bear children and an heir to the throne. Romanos had hopes for perpetuating the dynasty through his children, as Psellos recounts:

> Apparently it did not occur to him that Constantine's daughter, with whom he lived after his acclamation, was too old to conceive and already barren (she was in her fiftieth year when she married him). Even in the face of natural incapacity, he clung ever more firmly to his ambitions, led on by his own faith in the future. Hence he ignored the physical prerequisite for conception. (2.5; 65)

At age fifty, Zoe was, not surprisingly, unable to conceive, but nonetheless she had to contend with an unrealistic husband who was bent on participating in practices meant to aid in conception:

> Nevertheless, he did have recourse to the specialists who deal with sexual disorders and claim the ability to induce or cure sterility. He submitted himself to treatment with ointments and massage, and he enjoined his wife to do likewise. In fact, she went further: she was introduced to most of the magical practices, fastening little pebbles to her body, hanging charms about her, wearing chains, decking herself out with the rest of the nonsense. As their hopes were never realized, the emperor at last gave up in despair and paid less attention to Zoe. (2.5; 65)

Zoe participated in Romanos's therapy at the hands of "specialists" and then herself resorted to magic. Wearing of amulets was probably a traditional cure for sterility, and it was customary to seek out advice from magicians on ways to produce conception. Psellos terms the practices "nonsense" and was clearly a skeptic when it came to magical treatments. How much Zoe's efforts were in the public eye can be imagined, if she wore charms and amulets. Her desperation and the sincerity of her efforts must have ended in humiliation as well as disappointment, for not only did all efforts fail but her husband then turned away from her as a result. Whatever emotional support she might have received from her husband was now withheld, and she was rejected and ignored by him.

At a further stage of the marriage Romanos limited the income allotted to Zoe and then took a mistress. Psellos does not mince words in his description of the deteriorating relationship between the imperial pair:

As for the empress, two things more than any other vexed her: the fact that Romanus did not love her, and that she herself was unable to squander money. The treasure-chambers were closed to her, sealed by the emperor's orders, and she was compelled to live on a fixed allowance. Not unnaturally, she was furious with him. (2.6; 66)

Zoe's expenditures are characterized as "squandering," but we are told elsewhere that she liked to give lavish gifts to acquaintances, and that she was liberal in endowing charitable institutions, both of which were acceptable roles of empresses. She must also have been aware that her husband had a mistress, and she was not unaffected by this situation:

[Romanos] came to despise the empress Zoe. Not only did he abstain from sexual intercourse with her, but he was loath to consort with her in any way at all. She, on her side, was stirred to hate him, not only because the blood royal, meaning herself, was treated with such little respect, but, above all considerations, by her own longing for intercourse, and that was due not to her age, but to the soft and sensual manner of her life at the palace. (2.17; 75)

In this frank assessment by Psellos of the underlying cause for Zoe's anger and then hate for Romanus, he says she longed for sexual intercourse. Psellos claims that a postmenopausal woman cannot enjoy sex and assumes that Zoe's desire is for the luxuries and attentions that accompany life at the palace. Later in the *Chronographia*, however, Psellos states that she was having her own affairs at this time. It is clear that Romanos's insults (withholding her funds; taking a mistress) and neglect (disassociating himself from her; no longer sleeping with her) amounted to abuse. Under these circumstances Zoe would have had some personal grounds for retaliation.

Zoe is said to have helped arrange the death of Romanus III. This came about after Michael, the handsome young brother of an ambitious palace functionary, John the Orphanotrophos, was introduced to Zoe. It seems perfectly apparent to Psellos that this was a scheme to gain power for John's family, and Zoe was the vehicle for acquiring power. While the whole court seemed to be aware of Zoe's ensuing affair with Michael, the emperor chose to turn a blind eye. An informant explained to Psellos why this was so:

He told me that Romanus did wish, in a way, to be convinced that she was not Michael's paramour. On the other hand, he knew that she was greatly attracted to the opposite sex, on fire with passion, so to speak. So, to prevent her sharing her favours among many, he was not particularly disgusted at her association with one. Although he pretended not to see it, he allowed the empress to satisfy her desires to the full. (3.23; 79)

The affair was thus perceived by Psellos as sanctioned by the emperor and the rest of the court and as a way of containing Zoe's zeal for sexual relations. The emperor even enlisted Michael's attentions by making him a servant of the bedchamber, requiring him to give foot massages when the two were retired in private and thereby encouraging intimate relations between his wife and her lover.[37] A woman in her fifties, ignored by her husband and still interested in sex, Zoe pursued the handsome Michael. She was in effect being manipulated by John, Michael, and Romanus, while she indulged in an adulterous affair.

Although Psellos is cautious not to accuse Zoe directly of slowly poisoning Romanus, he does describe the illness that befell Romanus in graphic detail and states that when he saw the corpse of the emperor on his bier he noted that the face was reminiscent of men "bloated and pale from drinking poison, so that they appeared absolutely bloodless beneath the cheeks."[38] The death actually came about through drowning, when Romanos was apparently held under water by Michael's friends while swimming in his private swimming pool. Zoe entered the room as Romanus was dying:

> At this an uproar ensued. Several persons came into the room, among them the empress herself, without any bodyguard and apparently stricken with grief. After one look at him, however, she went off, having satisfied herself with her own eyes that he was a dying man. (3.26; 82)

Psellos depicts Zoe's rapid departure as lack of concern for the dying Romanos. But if we look at the facts as recorded by him, she heard of the situation and immediately came to see what was happening, without bothering with formalities. Whatever her reasons, she then quickly departed; we cannot know her emotions at that moment, not even with Psellos's help.

Zoe then made immediate efforts to secure the crown for Michael and was apparently as infatuated with him as she was eager to promote him to the rule, rather than rule in her own right. John the Orphanotrophos advised a quick installation of the new emperor, and she complied:

> Zoe, now completely won over, at once sent for the young man, clothed him in a robe interwoven with gold, placed on his head the imperial crown, and set him down on a magnificent throne, with herself near him in similar dress. (4.2; 88)

The important act of crowning of the new emperor was accomplished by Zoe herself, in a reversal of the customary ceremony in which an emperor crowns his empress.[39] She was aware that the transfer of power from Romanos to Michael had to take place through her agency as the porphyrogenneta, and she acted accordingly. Her choice had to be respected, and the participation of the patriarch in the coronation ceremony was not in this case a necessity, whereas Zoe's participation was.

The new emperor, once installed, soon proceeded to distance himself from Zoe:

> Till now, Michael had played a part: his attitude and the look in his eyes showed love for the empress. It was not long, however, before all this was changed, and her love, as well as her favours to him, were repaid with base ingratitude. I can neither praise nor blame him for it; though I can scarcely commend this hatred for his benefactress or

his behaviour towards her, yet I cannot fail to applaud his fear of the lady, fear lest he too should be involved in catastrophe, like Romanus. (4.6; 89)

Psellos is certain Michael never loved Zoe but merely led her on, with his brother's encouragement, in order to obtain the throne. He also confirms in this passage his suspicion of Zoe's part in Romanus's death. Michael took his job of ruling seriously but also maintained suspicions that just as Zoe had given him power she might betray him. His manner turned from suspicion to hostility, and he had her placed under the equivalent of house arrest: "Permission to leave the palace in her usual way was refused, and she was shut up in the women's quarters" (4.16; 95). No one was allowed to approach her unless carefully screened, and she was isolated and powerless. Zoe's reaction to this treatment is described by Psellos:

> Anyway, she avoided the despicable feminine trait of talkativeness and there were no emotional outbursts. She neither reminded the emperor of the love and belief in her that he had shown in the past, nor did she evince anger against his brothers when they attacked her with their threats and abuse. Not once did she look with bitterness on the captain of the guard or dismiss him from her presence. On the contrary she was gentle to all and like the cleverest orators, adjusted herself to different persons and different conditions. (4.16; 95–6)

Zoe's passive behavior was interpreted by some as resignation and by others as the harboring of possible evil plans; she is described by Psellos as "some lioness which for a while had laid aside her ferocity." [40] We are reminded in this passage of the initial hopefulness that Zoe had experienced in this marriage, and that Michael had been supportive and loving toward her, only to betray her hope and trust.

The marriage further deteriorated not only because Michael did not love her and was suspicious or afraid of her, but also because of his disease. He was ill with leprosy, which now grew worse. As his health declined he feared the embarrassment of being seen by her during one of his epileptic fits. Overcome too by guilt and remorse at his betrayal, he stopped seeing her entirely. [41]

Psellos is close enough to the couple to guess at the psychological reasons behind the emperor's and empress's actions. Let us consider what this treatment might have meant to Zoe. She was now in a situation similar to that she had experienced with Romanos. Her ill husband had no further interest in her, and she was ignored and isolated. According to Psellos, the injustice and cruelty of this treatment are justified because of fear of her capacity to inflict revenge. On this, Psellos is uncompromising, and he evidently had little sympathy for her himself. She was doubtless aware of the aura of fear and suspicion surrounding her and probably felt trapped and hence reacted by withdrawing. Her gentleness and resignation may have been the result of her having fallen into a state of depression. At the very least her sense of pride as empress would have been deeply wounded. Because of her position as heiress of the empire, she now lived only to be manipulated.

Seeing that the emperor's life was going to be short, John addressed his brother to help secure their futures:

> "You know, Sir, that the Empire belongs by inheritance to Zoe, and the whole nation owes greater allegiance to her, because she is a woman and heir to the throne. Moreover, being so generous in her distribution of money, she has won the hearts of the people completely. I suggest, therefore, that we should make her mother to our nephew—if she adopts him it will be more propitious—and at the same time persuade her to promote him to the dignity and title of Caesar. She will not refuse. Zoe is accommodating enough, and in any case she cannot oppose us in any way." (4.22; 100–101)

John was right. He planned to preserve his family's power by persuading Zoe to adopt his nephew, another Michael, so that he would succeed the ailing emperor. When faced with this scheme, Zoe acquiesced. It was a simple matter to win her over because she had no choice, and so she formally proclaimed Michael her adopted son in a ceremony.[42] The passage reveals, however, that Zoe retained a kernel of power, which consisted of her popularity; she had "won the hearts of the people completely" because of her generosity toward the citizens, her imperial philanthropy.

Sensing the end was near, Michael IV sought tonsure and took on the "holy Mantle of Christ" as he retired to a monastery. At hearing the news Zoe reacted with strong emotion:

> When she heard from someone about his tonsure, she dared to leave the women's quarters, overcoming every natural disinclination, and went on foot to see him. But Michael, whether through shame at the evils he had brought upon her, or because in his attention to God he had forgotten her, refused her permission to enter his presence. She returned to the palace.(4.53; 117)

Just as on the death of Romanos, Zoe reacted in an unexpected way, according to Psellos, in rushing to see her dying husband. She may have been hardened to these men because of their abusive treatment of her, but she still felt enough concern or compassion for them to go to them at critical times. One wonders what she might have said or done if she had succeeded in seeing her husband. With Michael IV's death Zoe is again left vulnerable to the plotters.

The empress was the agent in the next transfer of power. Psellos describes the process with undisguised cynicism, as John masterminds, with the assistance of his brothers, the manipulation and flattery of Zoe:

> So with one accord they straightway banded together for the contest. With the artillery of their logic they laid siege to her soul—an easy capture. They reminded her of Michael's adoption, put the young man under the protection of his mother and mistress, and threw him at her feet. Heaping upon her all the flattering names suitable to such a moment, they assured her that their nephew would be emperor only in name, while she, apart from the title, would have, besides, the power that she inherited by

right of descent. If she so desired, she would administer the State in person; if not, she would give her orders to him and use him as a slave-emperor to do her bidding. They took solemn oaths and pledged their loyalty by the Holy Relics, and so made her their prisoner at the first shot. What else, indeed, could she do, bereft as she was of outside assistance and spellbound by their sorcery, or shall I say rather, led astray by their trickery, beguiled by their ruses and converted to their desires? (5.4; 122)

For a witness who did not like Zoe, Psellos describes her victimization by the wily brothers in a surprisingly sympathetic manner. He even compares their scheme metaphorically to the siege of a city. If he disliked Zoe, he had even less regard for John and his opportunistic young nephew, Michael. It is apparent that Zoe had no power to control the outcome at this juncture, and so her adopted son was enthroned as Michael V.

At first Michael showed Zoe a certain respect, but soon, just as in the reign of Michael IV and of Romanos III before him, she was rejected and deprived of power within the palace. Then Michael V went even further. He decided to banish her from the palace and the city.

> When she approached him, he turned a deaf ear; the council-chamber was closed to her, and, worse still, she was denied all access to the imperial treasury. In fact, the empress was held in contempt everywhere. Indeed, I would go further than that—he made her an object of ridicule, for he treated her like a prisoner of war. She was kept under surveillance, in the most ignominious manner, her ladies-in-waiting controlled by the emperor and no corner of her private apartments free from inspection. Not one of the agreements made with her was respected by Michael, and when even these restrictions failed to satisfy him, he brought upon her the final disgrace—nothing less than expulsion from the palace. (5.17; 132)

Zoe's expulsion was accomplished when Michael V concocted a plan to accuse her of trying to poison him; she was convicted and transported to one of the Princess Islands in the Sea of Marmora, Prinkipo. Psellos exclaims in outrage at her arrest that she was driven from her bedchamber: "She who had been born there, driven out by a parvenu! She, the daughter of a most noble family was dispossessed by a man sprung from the gutter."[43] When the gravity of this insult to a porphyrogenneta becomes manifest, Psellos puts into her mouth a dirge apostrophizing the imperial palace and her uncle and ancestors: she addresses Basil II in an expression of nostalgic despair:

> It was you, my uncle and emperor, you who wrapped me in my swaddling clothes as soon as I was born, you who loved me, and honoured me too, more than my sisters, because, as I have often heard them say who saw you, I was like yourself. It was you who said, as you kissed me and held me in your arms, "Good luck, my darling, and may you live many years to be the glory of our family and the most marvellous gift to our Empire!" (5.22; 135)

She prays to the great emperor Basil II to look down from heaven and protect her, as she melodramatically laments her fall from honor and exile. Zoe's plea, which issues from the pen of Michael Psellos, is a skillful piece of rhetoric intended to pursuade a reader or listener of the injustice of her treatment at the hands of Michael. No doubt such a quotation was circulated among the people at this time, when emotions were high and indignation widespread, perhaps by Psellos himself.

At this further affront to the empress, Psellos switches to a reporting of events sympathetic to Zoe:

> She had no intention of meddling in State affairs. Indeed, how could she, spending her life in exile, with one lady-in-waiting? Yet that rascal cherished even more terrible designs against her and trouble was heaped on trouble. In the end, a party was dispatched to cut off her hair—perhaps it would be more correct to say that they were sent to kill her. She was to be offered up, so to speak, as a whole burnt-offering, not to please the Lord maybe, but certainly to appease the wrath of the emperor who gave this order. However, once the design was satisfactorily carried out, he left her alone. (5.23.137)

Zoe survived. The cutting off of her hair, which was usually part of the ceremony of tonsure of a nun—a voluntary part—was in this case a symbolic act meant to humiliate Zoe and eliminate her from public view. Now there followed a social upheaval in the city, and the events are characterized by Psellos as "Divine Justice." At first, the whole city "went into mourning," and then a mob of citizens "ready to lay down their lives for Zoe" formed.[44] The mob consisted not only of men but of women, which astonishes even Psellos as he describes the scene:

> And the women—but how can I explain this to people who do not know them? I myself saw some of them, whom nobody till then had seen outside the women's quarters, appearing in public and shouting and beating their breasts and lamenting terribly at the empress's misfortune but the rest were borne along like Maenads, and they formed no small band to oppose the offender. "Where can she be," they cried, "she who alone is noble of heart and alone is beautiful? Where can she be, she who alone of all women is free, the mistress of all the imperial family, the rightful heir to the Empire, whose father was emperor, whose grandfather was monarch before him—yes and great-grandfather too? How was it this low-born fellow dared to raise a hand against a woman of such lineage?" (5.26; 138–39)

Psellos's description of the women is extraordinary in many respects, as is their lament. He was an eyewitness to the uprising and conveys his own astonishment as vividly as he conveys the scene of rebellion. The appearance of women of distinguished families, since he knew them, and who were normally veiled and confined at home is shocking to him. This banding together of large numbers of women on Zoe's behalf, and in a state he compares to a Bacchic frenzy, is not only a highly unusual event but also breaks the laws of society under which women are not seen in public unveiled.[45] In their lament, the women refer to the empress as noble, beautiful, and free. Her freedom is a function of her lineage and birthright, which are unalterable and unique among women; the empress is exempted from the laws of the state. The women thus act in her defense when she is publicly deprived of her freedom. This gendered reaction of female society, in which women looked to Zoe as representing womenhood, which they shared, and freedom, which they did not share, is enacted in the public sphere. Psellos shares their outrage and articulates Zoe's lament to buttress his own views.

The group protesting Zoe's removal from the city has various constituents. Besides the women, there are men in the mob who are armed with stones and axes, swords, bows, and spears. These men are not of the same class as the women, but more common people, or else Psellos would have mentioned the fact. Psellos, who was standing in front of the palace entrance as the mob approached, may have been afraid for his life. The leaders of this mob go unnamed, but its destructive force is apparent, for the houses of members of the emperor's family were torn down to the ground:

> It was not the hands of strong men in the prime of youth that pulled down the most of it, but young girls and children of either sex lent aid in the work of destruction. (5.29; 140)

A cross section of the populace thus rose spontaneously in defense of the empress. The emperor reacted with alacrity. He recalled Zoe from exile, and in an effort to appease the mob he showed her to the people from the imperial loge in the hippodrome, still clad in her monastic habit. But this did not satisfy them, for they then stormed the Petrion monastery where Zoe's younger sister, Theodora, was encloistered and brought her out by force and proclaimed her empress. Michael Psellos confides that the sisters' relationship had not been amicable and that "jealousy divided the two sisters and kept one in a position of greater importance, the other in an inferior condition."[46]

The "revolution," as Psellos characterizes the uprising, drew to its close in the blinding of Michael V by the mob. Playing the role of moderator, Psellos confronted the emperor and city prefect, who were seeking asylum at the Studios church, while the mob was demanding to take them away. In a dramatic dialogue, Psellos accuses Michael, asking him

> what possible hurt could he have suffered at the hands of his adopted mother and mistress, that he should add such wrongs to her tragic story? (5.41.146)

Psellos sees Zoe's career as empress as a "tragic story." He has enough insight into the actual circumstances of her life and conditions of rule to sympathize with her plight, in spite of his dislike for her. Through it all he has retained his respect for her and for the dynastic inheritance she represents; he sees her abuse as unjust.

The rebellion ended when the emperor was brutally blinded and the two sisters restored to power:

> Each, therefore, had a claim on the Empire. However, the problem was settled for them by Zoe. For the first time, she greeted her sister and embraced her with affection. What is more she shared with her the Empire they both inherited. The question of the government was thus resolved by agreement between them. Next, Zoe brought her to live with herself, escorted by a procession of great magnificence, and made her joint-ruler of the Empire. (5.51; 151)

In spite of the jealousy between the two women, Zoe ended the period of civil unrest and took the necessary measures to restore peace and order in the city. But this did not last for long, for, as Psellos proclaimed, Zoe "would be quite willing to see a stable-lad on the imperial throne rather than let her sister share power with herself."

For awhile, a period of orderly rule prevailed, in which, according to Psellos, reliable supporters of the sisters administered the government, and few changes were made which might prove controversial. The women participate only when necessary, giving instructions in a "calm voice." The temperaments of the two sisters contrasted markedly:

> Zoe was a woman of passionate interests, prepared with equal enthusaism for both alternatives—death or life, I mean. In that she reminded me of sea-waves, now lifting a ship on high and then again plunging it down to the depths. . . . Theodora . . . had a placid disposition, and, in one way, if I may put it so, a dull one. (6.4; 157)

The pun on Zoe's name, which means Life, is intended to emphasize her zesty approach, although Psellos suggests her volatile character amounts to instability in his sea waves metaphor. At this point in his narrative Psellos abruptly changes the tone of his description of the joint rule:

> To put it quite candidly (for my present purpose is not to compose a eulogy, but to write an accurate history) neither of them was fitted by temperament to govern. They neither knew how to administer nor were they capable of serious argument on the subject of politics. For the most part they confused the trifles of the harem with important matters of state. (6.5; 157)

Psellos's scornful statement about the coempresses indicates an ulterior motive. The reason for his change of attitude was an anticipation of a government he preferred: "The affairs of State urgently demanded vigorous and skillful direction, and the country needed a man's supervision."[47] Psellos conveys his preference for a male ruler by denigrating the women's ability to control their desires and to expend the state's financial resources responsibly. He states, "We wanted a man who would make provision for the future and prepare long beforehand against all possible attacks or likely invasions from abroad."[48] The "We" implies there was a movement at the senatorial level or perhaps among close advisors of the women, Psellos among them, to seek a husband who would rule with foresight in military matters. Again Zoe takes action. She ousts her sister and, at age sixty-four, complies with the vote of high officials by marrying Constantine Monomachus, who is crowned Constantine IX on June 11, 1042.

Psellos gives two versions of the election of Constantine. According to one, the choice was not entirely hers, but rather she was the instrument of those controlling the state who voted among viable candidates.[49] She and Constantine had been friends from the time of Romanus's rule, and Zoe had found him attractive, which leads to the other version. In this version, Zoe was in control of the decision:

> Zoe's first reaction, when for the second time she found herself at the head of the Empire, was, as I have already said, to protect herself against any sudden reversal of her good luck in the future. To strengthen her position she proceeded to look for a husband—not a man from abroad, but someone in the court circle. (6.18; 164)

Self-preservation and peaceful rule are, not surprisingly, Zoe's primary concern, and this involves choosing a third husband. She arrived at her choice and "informed the Senate of her plans." This version was probably contrived by Psellos and by the court to make Zoe appear to do the right thing. Psellos, in fact, gives the strategy away by describing the vote which took place "just before." The manipulation of the empresses accomplished the wishes of the court:

> For the empreseses these events marked the end of their authority and personal intervention in the affairs of State; for Constantine, the beginning of his reign. His power was now for the first time established. So, after a joint rule of three months, the sisters retired from public life. (6.21; 165)

Although popular opinion rescued Zoe from exile, the court controls her role in governing. Psellos depicts her as relieved to resign the responsibility of ruling to Constantine and willing to tolerate her sister living near them at court; anything to lead a peaceful existence. Even in this effort, however, she is met with a trying situation.

Constantine already had a mistress, Skleraina, who had been living with him in exile long before he was recalled to the court to marry Zoe. Skleraina was of a noble family and the two might have married, except that both had been married twice previously, and third marriages were forbidden except by special dispensation. Nevertheless, once married to Zoe, Constantine petitioned her to let Skleraina return to Constantinople.

> The empress at once gave her consent. The fact is, Zoe was no longer jealous. She had had her own fill of trouble, and in any case she was now too old to harbour such resentment. (6.53; 182)

From Zoe's point of view, this request might have looked different. She did not want to displease her new husband or risk his enmity toward her, as in her first two marriages, and so her compliance was a practical consideration and part of her efforts to preserve order. To suggest she was not jealous of Skleraina because of her age is another matter.[50] Age has never been known to dull emotions; if anything it heightens them and shows little patience with offense. Of course she was jealous but was left with few alternatives. Zoe once more found herself in a compromised situation in which there was little she could do. Soon Constantine is seen in public with Skleraina and spends much time in visits to her house along with members of the court circle. Even Psellos confesses that the liaison "had a strange air of unreality about it."[51] Finally Constantine asks Zoe to bring Skleraina into the palace and has the relationship ratified in a "treaty of friendship," an "extraordinary contract," witnessed by the Senate:[52]

> What was most astounding was the fact that, although most people were greatly distressed at the way in which Zoe had been deceived and neglected and despised, she herself evinced no emotion whatever, except that she smiled on everyone and apparently was quite pleased with the arrangement. (6.59; 184)

At the same time that he is appalled, Psellos is fascinated by Zoe's apparent lack of concern. He cannot believe she does not appear resentful of Skleraina's presence in the palace. In public processions, the two sisters Zoe and Theodora walk in front of Skleraina. Skleraina's official title was elevated to *sebaste,* or empress, and she participated in official ceremonies, with Zoe "embracing her new partner with unusual warmth."[53] When matters of state are discussed among them, Constantine even tends to take Skleraina's advice over that of the empress.

Psellos's description of this "partnership" between Zoe and Skleraina would lack credibility if he himself did not express dismay and embarrassment at the arrangement. When there should have been jealousy there was instead acceptance, even amity and companionship. While the emperor and the two sisters had adjacent apartments in the palace, Skleraina's quarters were more private, and Zoe only visited the emperor's rooms when Skleraina was "far away." In this intimate detail, Psellos indicates the extent of Zoe's tolerance for the mistress's presence.

When Psellos speaks of Skleraina's manner of relating to the two sisters, he mentions that she gave gifts to each in keeping with her interests. These gifts, he claimed, blunted any cause for resentment between the emperor's mistress and the princesses,

> for Zoe no longer felt jealous of her rival (she was past the age for that) and there was no ill will on her side. As the years passed, too, she had lost her capacity for vehement hatred. And as for Theodora, since her own desires were satisfied, she showed even less resentment than her sister. (6.62; 186)

In this statement Psellos betrays that Zoe did show some resentment when he compares the reactions of the two sisters. If Zoe had a strategy of guarding her real feelings and pretending acceptance, then Psellos reveals it. He appears puzzled himself and is searching for explanations to the contradictory behavior of Zoe. He then turns to a description of Skleraina.

According to Psellos, Skleraina is "not especially remarkable" in appearance,[54] but her cleverness and charm impressed him:

> Her speech was wonderful. It had a delicate beauty of expression, the rhythmic perfection of a scholar. There was in her conversation an unaffected sweetness of diction, an inexpressible grace in her manner of telling a story. She bewitched me. (6.60; 184)

Psellos is charmed by Skleraina because she shares Psellos's intellectual interests. By exchanging learned repartees with him she apparently played up to his own erudition. Psellos openly acknowledges his admiration for her and admits to being under her spell, a gendered compliment to her female charm. Compared to Skleraina's heady company, Zoe appears quite uninteresting to him, and he subtly derides her.

In spite of his derision of Zoe's ability to charm, he finds another side of Zoe more acceptable. Psellos relates the essential facts about Zoe's attachment to an image of Christ, the Christ Antiphonetes, an involvement which gives rise to varying interpretations of her peculiar form of religiosity. Zoe's piety involves the use of rare plants. One use of Zoe's wealth gained from access to the imperial treasury has been the acquisition of expensive plants: "sweet herbs, the purest Indian kind, in particular those that still retained their natural moisture, dwarf olives and the whitest sort of bays."[55] Such imports, in view of contemporary modes of transport, must have been very costly. Their use apparently occupied much of Zoe's time in the palace. Unlike other women, Zoe did not pursue the usual feminine tasks. She "lost all desire to charm" by wearing beautiful dresses, preferring to dress simply and to prepare perfumes and unguents in her private quarters in the palace. Psellos's description is rightly famous:

> Her own private bedroom was not more impressive than the workshops in the market where the artisans and the blacksmiths toil, for all round the room were burning braziers, a host of them. Each of her servants had a particular task to perform: one was allotted the duty of bottling the perfumes, another of mixing them, while a third had some other task of the same kind. In winter, of course, these operations were demonstrably of some benefit, as the great heat from the fires served to warm the cold air, but in the summer-time the others found the temperature near the braziers almost unbearable. Zoe herself, however, surrounded by a whole bodyguard of these fires, was apparently unaffected by the scorching heat. (6.64; 187)

The powerful image he creates here likens Zoe to something between a blacksmith and a sorcerer. He then artfully juxtaposes this image with that of her husband, Constantine, "taking his ease" with Skleraina in her private appartment.

In a series of twists, Psellos imputes a dark side to Zoe, evoking her strange occupations, and then reverses his judgment in an expression of admiration for her greatest redeeming quality, her piety:

> In this she surpassed all others, both women and men. Some men lose themselves in the contemplation of God; their whole being is directed to one perfect object, and on

that object they depend entirely. Others, with still greater devotion, and truly inspired with the Divine Spirit, are even more identified with the object of their worship. So it was with Zoe. Her passionate veneration for the things of God had really brought her into contact, so to speak, with the First and Purest Light. Certainly there was no moment when the Name of God was not on her lips. (6.65; 187)

Ostensibly in direct contrast to her rather sinister and unconventional private occupations, she is deeply religious and in contact with the Light of God's grace. The latter is, in Psellos's view, commendable behavior, suitable to a woman and an empress. How do these two sides of Zoe's personality mesh?

Zoe's occupations in her apartment relate to her piety, as we learn in the description of her image of Christ Antiphonetes. She had had the image made for her personal veneration: "a little figure, embellished with bright metal, appeared to be almost living."[56] This, then, was the object of veneration alluded to by Psellos above. It had special properties of changing color in answer to questions put to it, enabling Zoe to predict the future:

> By changes of colour it answered questions put to it, and by its various tints foretold coming events. . . . If she saw the image turn pale, she would go away crestfallen, but if it took on a fiery red colour, its halo lustrous with a beautiful radiant light, she would lose no time in telling the emperor and prophesying what the future was to bring forth. (6.66; 188)

The image had the capacity of "responding" to Zoe's questions and hence encompassed properties of its prototype, the icon of Christ Antiphonetes, or Christ the Responder. She even believed the icon indicated God's intentions, allowing her to prophesy. Zoe focused her religious zeal on this image, addressing it and treating it as if it were alive:

> I myself have often seen her, in moments of great distress, clasp the sacred object in her hands, contemplate it, talk to it as though it were indeed alive and address it with one sweet term of endearment after another. (6.66; 188)

The great distress Psellos refers to may have been the result of Zoe's neglect by her husband; in any case, her involvement with the image clearly filled an emotional as well as religious need in her life.

In her dedication to the image, Zoe made offerings to it not unlike those associated with pagan practices. Psellos understands the analogy and, while casting her as "by nature perverse," conveys to readers perhaps his most profound perception of the empress:

> She worshipped God in her own way, making no secret of her heart's deep longing and consecrating to Him the things which we regard as most precious and most sacred. (6.67; 188–9)

Later in book 6 he elaborates on this point:

> One thing above all claimed her attention, and on this she expended all her enthu-
> siasm—the offering of sacrifices to God. I am not referring so much to the sacrifice
> of praise, or of thanksgiving, or of penitence, but to the offering of spices and sweet
> herbs, the products of India and Egypt. (6.159; 239)

The perfumes, herbs, and plants Zoe collects and brews are used in her private veneration of the Antiphonetes icon. Far from being magical concoctions, these were
her dedications to God of that which was most rare and precious. In accordance with
the value system within Byzantine culture, Zoe's offering of the most valuable unguents and perfumes made with expensive substances gives the greatest honor possible
to God. The intimacy and reassurance provided by the icon in her private devotions
offer a meaningful source of solace and strength to Zoe. While Zoe is occupied with
her dedications, Constantine continues his infidelities.

After the sudden death of Skleraina, Constantine took as his lover a hostage girl
from Alania, or Georgia, which Psellos explains by stating that "the Empress Zoe
was already past the age for sexual relations," in his now-familiar biological view of
sex. Again, Zoe was no doubt aware of her husband's new preoccupation, which may
have been a more clandestine affair while Zoe was alive, but after her death in 1050
he flaunts his mistress in a garish and vulgar manner described by Psellos.

Zoe was known to Psellos personally only in her declining years. While he focuses
his chronicle on his patron, the emperor Constantine, his occasional descriptions of
the empress make his biases against her evident:

> When she had grown old, she was somewhat lacking in stability. I do not wish to convey
> the impression that she was deranged or out of her right mind, but she was absolutely
> ignorant of public affairs and her judgement was completely warped by the vulgar ex-
> travagance that prevailed in the palace. Whatever intellectual advantages she may have
> enjoyed in the past, her character did not suffer her to preserve even them free from
> insincerity, for a perverse delight in displaying her knowledge showed her for what she
> was—not intellectually honest, but lacking in taste. We will not speak of her reverence
> for God: I cannot find fault with immoderation in that. Surely nobody could surpass
> her in that good quality, for she depended wholly on God, ascribed all events to His
> influence, thought all things were determined by Him. (6.157; 238)

Psellos, the intellectual snob, arrogantly speaks of Zoe's lack of intellectual honesty
and good taste. Since Zoe does not share with Psellos his preoccupation with scholarship and objectivity, a gulf exists in their communication. He then confesses that her
extreme religiosity is a quality with which he cannot find fault; this female stereotype
still characterizes the "good" woman, as it has throughout this book on late ancient
and Byzantine women.

Although cruel and moody at times, Zoe is also cast by Psellos as going to extremes
in her generosity:

She was the most generous of women, and this virtue of generosity, which in her case knew no bounds, led her to pour out all her wealth regardless of all economy. (6.158; 239)

She was also prone to nostalgia:

Any enthusiastic account of the glorious deeds of her family, especially those of her uncle Basil, filled her with delight; the effect on her spirits was instantaneous. (6.158; 239)

Psellos suggests that one way the old woman could be cheered up was by recalling the past glories of her family. Mention of such a natural human reaction helps convince the reader that Psellos's account is after all somewhat objective. He is precise too in his description of the appearance of the aging empress:

Although she had already passed her seventieth year, there was not a wrinkle on her face. She was just as fresh as she had been in the prime of her beauty. It must be admitted, though, that her hands were unsteady; she was subject to tremors too, and her back was bent. (6.158; 239)

In a reversal of his previous expression of scorn for her lack of intellectual pretensions, this touching description shows that Psellos not only admired Zoe's beauty but also had some sympathy for her as a person.

As Zoe ages she chooses not to adorn herself to disguise her age but instead adopts an austere appearance.

As for ornaments about her person, she absolutely despised them: she wore neither cloth of gold, nor diadems, nor lovely things about her neck. Her garments were not of the heavy sort: in fact she clothed herself in thin dresses. (6.158; 239)

Psellos is highly observant, even down to the preferred fabric and modest garb worn by the empress. These descriptions echo Psellos's earlier comment in book 2 on Zoe's appearance:

The second daughter, whom I myself saw in her extreme old age, was very regal in her ways, a woman of great beauty, most imposing in her manner and commanding respect. (2.5; 55)[57]

It was Zoe's whole manner, rather than her facial features or her elegance of dress, that made her beautiful. Psellos recognizes in Zoe qualities he associates with her imperial lineage, both in her deeds of generosity and in her conduct and appearance. He records with accuracy too her largesse when she is at the point of death, a tradition going back to Roman emperors:

Her first thought was for those in prison. Debts were remitted, and an amnesty granted to condemned criminals. She opened up the imperial treasury and allowed the gold kept there to pour forth like a river. So the gold was squandered with all the uncontrolled profusion of a flood, and Zoe, after a short and painful illness, but little change in her outward appearance, departed this life at the age of seventy-two. (6.160; 240)

Psellos's ambivalence is again illustrated in this passage, for while condemning her donations as profligacy, he praises her generosity. Although he did not himself appear greatly affected by the empress's death, he observes Constantine as being "completely heart-broken at the loss." Although frankly acknowledging Zoe's regal qualities and sympathizing with her because of the abuse and manipulation she suffered at the hands of those around her, Psellos also expresses scorn, suspicion, and dislike for her.

Psellos's skillfully crafted insider's account of the rulers resulting from Zoe's marriages conveys an effort at impartiality and objectivitiy, one that partially succeeds in his depiction of Zoe. His bias against powerful, talkative, or emotional women is expressed periodically throughout the work, illustrating the gendered expectations and restrictions he places on women.[58] While his image of Zoe betrays some sympathy, and he admires her for her religious piety, on the whole he is critical of her and subtly undermines her whenever possible. His outrage at her treatment by Michael V and his obvious discomfort caused by the openness of Constantine's liaison with Skleraina are mainly a reaction to the offense to her birth and position, as much a sense of injustice or immorality.

In spite of Psellos's ambivalence, it is possible to discern in his narrative a picture of a woman who because of her lineage carried heavy burdens and anxieties throughout her life. The emotional load of her role as we have gleaned it from the *Chronographia* must have been enormous, and the abuse to which she was subjected demoralizing; she was constantly subject to attacks or manipulation and to the destabilizing effects of adverse circumstances. Her philanthropy and piety, although traditional preoccupations of empresses, appear sincere and no doubt provided a diversion and a refuge from her troubles. She chose not to have a hand in administration, preferring to leave the work of governing to her successive husbands.[59] She won over the people through her deeds of generosity and charity and was genuinely popular.

Zoe made important choices and always acted in the interests of the preservation of the dynasty. She was successful to the extent that she died while still on the throne as empress after a rule of twenty-two years. Psellos makes it evident, however, that she was always handicapped by the prevailing negative attitude of the senators and rest of the court, who carried a ready bias against a woman in power. In spite of her image in the popular imagination as "she who alone of all women is free," in actuality she was more confined by her position as Augusta than she was free to exercise power. Keeping in mind this divided image of Zoe and recalling Psellos's descriptions of her beauty and of her successive marriages, I turn now to her image in the art of mosaic and the messages discernible there.

Zoe's portrait in Hagia Sophia shows her as she appeared when Michael Psellos knew her (see fig. 27 and pl. 17). It is part of a curiously altered mosaic panel, allegorizing the patching together of imperial rule through her successive husbands, combined with her ingenuity and determination as narrated above. The so-called Zoe panel was rediscovered on July 2, 1934, by the Byzantine Institute under the direction of Thomas Wittemore, and the work of uncovering the mosaic and consolidating and cleaning it were completed over the next four years.[60] It is located on the east wall of the south gallery, a space originally reserved for women attending liturgies, and later the meeting place of councils of the church; the gallery had direct access to the imperial palace via an external stair-ramp and was also a place of private imperial liturgical usage, as a tiny domed chapel nearby indicates.[61] The mosaics were planned to be visible not only from within the gallery but also from the western entrance to the nave, or Royal Door, on the main level below. Although damaged in its lower section, the mosaic is largely intact. It represents Christ seated between the standing figures of Constantine Monomachus and the empress Zoe. Christ is significantly larger in scale than the sovereigns, who are slightly over life-size; all are silhouetted against a gold ground.[62]

In the visual language of the mosaic, Christ gives his blessing with a gesture of the right hand, indicating his support and protection of the sovereigns. His abbreviated name is inscribed to the left and right of his head: "Iesous Christos," Jesus Christ. He sits on a jewel-studded, backless throne holding a large book of the Gospels ornamented with a cross and pearls. His heavy robes of deep blue fall in cascades, zigzags, and folds over his body; his ascetic head of thin proportions with flowing brown hair, moustache, and beard has eyes turned to the right. His transparent halo encompasses a gold cross set with jewels and pearls. According to Whittemore, this type of Christ stands at the beginning of a series of similar images whose iconography appears to have originated in Constantinople.[63] His glance to the right might be seen as directing his blessing toward the diminutive figure of the empress Zoe.

Zoe and Constantine both offer objects which they hold in their hands, indicating that the panel commemorates gifts made to the church by the imperial couple. Zoe is turned slightly toward Christ and holds a parchment scroll which indicates a donation to the Great Church; along the length of the scroll is a Greek inscription in red letters with the name of the emperor: "Constantine, in Christ the God, faithful King of the Romans. Monomachos." Her own name appears above her head: "Zoe, the most pious Augusta." Her features are small and delicate in her rosy, round-cheeked face; the color of her cheeks suggests the use of rouge, and the eyelids are elongated and delineated as if darkened with mascara (see fig. 27). Her eyes are yellow-gray and her hair light brown. The mosaic fits Psellos's description of the regal empress who was so well preserved in old age that there was hardly a wrinkle in her face, even at age seventy.

Zoe's splendid garments convey her public role as reigning empress. Although Psellos claims she shunned elaborate clothing, her official portrait shows her with all the attributes of her rank. The double-jeweled bands of the crown are topped by a series of triangular jeweled points, the colors of the glass tesserae probably indicating beryl, garnets, carnelians, emeralds, and pearls; hanging from the crown on either side of her head are pendilia made of gold enamel plates in bright colors, set with more jewels. This crown, the *modiolos,* is far more ornate than the emperor's crown. Her earrings are made of small pearls. Heavy garments all but conceal her body. The *chiton,* or long undergarment, only shows in its jeweled collar; she wears richly woven wristlets and a long, reddish-violet silk mantle, or *divitission,* with gold arrow motifs. Circular ornaments are sewn onto the upper sleeves. A *maniakion* fits over the divitission and is divided into three jewel-studded bands. Beneath the maniakion hangs the heavy, woven, gold-encrusted panel called the *loros,* with clearly indicated large jewels in square and circular settings on violet tissue. Her girdle or ornate, jewel-studded belt is just visible below her hand. Although mosaic tesserae are missing in the lower part of the figure, the colors of the painted setting-bed reveal a large cross studded with and surrounded by jewels in a shield shape, or *thorakion,* on the lower portion of the loros. This ceremonial regalia must have been worn by Zoe during her regular appearances at liturgies in Hagia Sophia, including the times she stood in the gallery in proximity to the portrait.

Constantine stands to Christ's right in the place of honor, and his whole figure leans slightly toward him as he offers the traditional "purse of gold," a leather pouch filled with gold coins, held closed by a red cord secured with a lead seal. Above his haloed head is the inscription, "Constantine, in Christ the God, Autocrat, faithful King of the Romans, Monomachos." His face is round and ruddy, and, unlike the empress's, his complexion gives the impression of a skin tanned by exposure to the outdoors. His eyes, like Zoe's, glance respectfully downward, and his prominent cheekbones are framed by a curving yellow moustache and short beard. His crown, the *stemma,* is surmounted by a cross made of pearls; pearl pendilia ending with clusters of three pear-shaped pearls hang almost to the shoulders. He is vested in chiton, divitission, and loros but worn in a different manner from Zoe. The divitission is reddish violet silk with woven motifs of diagonal rows of gold crosses over a green ground, with round medallions at the upper sleeves. Over the maniakion and divitission is worn a broad loros which has been drawn around and across the body and draped over his left arm where the green silk lining is revealed; it is ornamented with large applied gemstones.

A disturbing feature of the mosaic reveals, however, that the heads of all three figures are replacements. The mosaic tesserae show gaps around the contours of the faces, necks, crowns, and hair, and there is a slight disjunctive quality between the heads and bodies. The tesserae of the replacement heads are also larger than those used for the hands and garments of the figures, indicating less refined workmanship. Thus the bodies of the figures were made when the mosaic as a whole was first installed, and the heads were substituted at some later time. The inscriptions above the heads of Christ and Zoe and the titles accompanying the name of the emperor are original to the time of the creation of the panel. The names maladroitly inscribed above Constantine's head and on the parchment scroll held by Zoe show that these are a substitution for earlier ones, while the titles "In Christ the God, Autocrat, faithful King of the Romans," are original; his family name, Monomachos, has been inserted at the ends of both inscriptions.[64] The mosaic must have been put up under one of Zoe's first two husbands. Later, when Zoe was still empress but with a new consort, all three heads were replaced. The mosaic thus poses intriguing problems. What necessitated the replacements of the heads? Which of Zoe's prior husbands was depicted in the first version of the mosaic? Why were all three heads replaced if only the identity of the emperor changed?

According to Whittemore, the most likely explanation is that Romanus III was the emperor depicted in the first version of the image, along with Zoe. After the accession of her adopted son, Michael V, when Zoe was in exile, the mosaic was defaced. As Psellos explains, Michael trumped up charges that Zoe was trying to poison him, exiled her to Principo and had her hair cut off. Michael took his case to the senate and then to the people, and the verdict was arranged to be sympathetic to the emperor; a legalistic process was followed in order to justify his action against her.[65] The tradition of destruction of portraits of those in disgrace and of usurpation of imperial portraits by successors has a long history in the ancient Near East and Rome; the practice was codified in the fifth century under Theodosius II; it often sufficed to destroy only the head of an image or statue.[66] Whittemore believes Michael V had the mosaic defaced as an act of *damnatio memoriae,* to in effect "erase" Zoe and her former rule. When the mosaic was defaced the surface was gouged out, which removed not only the tesserae but the setting bed as well, suggesting a violent action.[67] While this explains why Zoe's head and that of her husband were effaced and later replaced, it still does not satisfactorily explain why that of Christ was replaced as well.

According to one suggestion, when the mosaic was restored during the rule of Zoe and Constantine Monomachus the head of Christ was reset because of the need for stylistic unity among the three heads, but this is unconvincing. Another suggestion has been made that because emperors were considered Christ's representatives on earth their portraits were made to resemble those of Christ, and that a new emperor would therefore require a revised Christ image.[68] This too lacks credibility because there is, in fact, little resemblance between the two heads. Most recently, the suggestion has been made that the Christ represents a particular type, Christ Antiphonetes. We know of Zoe's devotion to an image of Christ Antiphonetes through Psellos's description, discussed above. A mosaic representing this type might well be attacked because of its close association with the empress.[69] Her burial in the church dedicated to Christ Antiphonites further demonstrates her devotion to this particular image type. Zoe's close association with Christ Antiphonites thus seems a plausible explanation for the destruction of this image, although such an act would still seem to be sacrilegious.

Seen in this light, the history of the mosaic can be divided into three phases. Phase 1 was its installation in the reign of Zoe and Romanus III to commemorate their donation to Hagia Sophia in 1028–34; or possibly it was Zoe's second husband, Michael IV, who had it installed between 1034 and 1041.[70] Phase 2 must have occurred in the days just after Zoe's banishment by Michael V on April 18, 1042, and before the popular revolution which restored her and her sister to power shortly afterward; in an act of damnatio memoriae, Michael ordered the three heads gouged out. The defacing of Zoe's portrait was parallel to her forced removal from the palace and tonsure. The face of Christ Antiphonites, her special protector, was destroyed too, as was the head of whichever emperor was depicted on the left, Romanus III or Michael IV. The names, however, were intentionally left untouched as a public record of Zoe's disgrace. The faceless figures still conveyed a powerful message about the suppression of the empress, renunciation of her protector, and repudiation of the former emperor—but not for long.

In phase 3, Zoe had the mosaic restored after her marriage to Constantine in 1042. The restoration of the image was more about Zoe than it was about a new imperial gift to Hagia Sophia or a new husband.[71] Her restored portrait reasserted her imperial status; the replacement of the Christ Antiphonites head celebrated her special protector; and the head of Constantine properly recorded the name and appearance of her current consort. The youthful or well-preserved face of Zoe was done according to her wishes. Just as Theodora determined her official appearance and company in the panel in San Vitale, as discussed in chapter 6 above, Zoe sponsored the renewal of this panel. Whittemore's attribution of this mosaic some sixty years ago as the "Zoe panel" is all the more appropriate when we consider its phases, which parallel the heights and depths of Zoe's career as empress. The mosaic dramatizes her right by birth to imperial power and confirms her determining role in the making of her image as well as the legitimization of four emperors.

The approach to Zoe through focused readings of Psellos's text and the Hagia Sophia image allows one to read Zoe's story from within its Byzantine context. This approach, I believe, brings new credibility and respect to this otherwise misunderstood and often maligned woman.[72] Following Zoe's death, Constantine continued to rule until his (natural) death in 1055. From 1055 to 1056 Theodora the porphyrogenneta ruled alone, her death in 1056 bringing to a close the rule of one of the most brilliant dynasties in the history of Byzantium. The story of Zoe's long, segmented rule and series of marriages is an extraordinary example of a woman maintaining herself as the pivotal figure in the continuity of power of the Macedonian dynasty.

The episode of her banishment by Michael V reveals much about a cross section of the populace of Constantinople. The people who demanded her return from exile, believing her to be the true and rightful holder of power, included people of all classes of society. This is a rare episode in which we glimpse ordinary women, for girls and married women participated in the riots which destroyed the homes of the emperor's family.[73] Although Psellos frequently expresses skepticism about a woman's right to rule, he still conveys an intimate and well-informed perspective on her eventful life. His most moving portrait is of her way of dealing with the unhappy circumstances of her life, that is, by spending her gold and devoting her time in private to concocting potions of rare and precious plants as offerings to her image of Christ Antiphonites, in a special form of veneration. The *Chronographia* also best explains the Zoe mosaic in Hagia Sophia, with its violent mutilation and subsequent repair. The mosaic depicts Zoe as she herself wished to be seen, and as Psellos himself admittedly admired her. This imperial icon is a visible piece of the history of Zoe's time and speaks of the complicated process of maintaining God-protected power. In part acting to consolidate her dynastic position and in part swept along by others' manipulation of her, she persevered in the difficult role dealt her by her birth.

## Associated Readings

Michael Psellos, *Fourteen Byzantine Rulers: The Chronographia of Michael Psellos,* trans. E. R. A. Sewter (Harmondsworth, 1966).

Barbara Hill, Liz James, Dion Smythe, "Zoe: The Rhythm Method of Imperial Renewal," in *New Constantines: The Rhythm of Imperial Renewal in Byzantium,* ed. Paul Magdalino (Aldershot, England 1994), 215–29.

Judith Herrin, "Theophano: Considerations on the Education of a Byzantine Princess," *The Empress Theophano: Byzantium and the West at the Turn of the First Millennium,* ed. Adelbert Davids (Cambridge, England, 1995), 64–85.

Thomas Whittemore, *The Mosaics of Haghia Sophia at Istanbul: Third Preliminary Report. Work Done in 1935–1938: The Imperial Portraits of the South Gallery* (London, 1942).

*Eleven*

# THE WORLD OF ANNA KOMNENE:
# ANNA'S PASSIONATE VOICE IN THE *ALEXIAD*

The *Alexiad,* written by the imperial princess Anna Komnene, is the story of the dynamic reign of her father, Alexios I Komnenos, from 1081 to 1118.[1] In her writings about the career of this successful military leader and founder of the Komnenian dynasty, she includes her memories of family members and of the society in which she grew up, along with laments about her current circumstances. The work is wonderfully descriptive and evocative of historical events, while also highly subjective in its references to Anna's own experience; we have a continued sense of her presence as a writer throughout the work. The *Alexiad* is often cited as the most accomplished work written by a woman before the Renaissance. I would claim that it is one of the great literary works of any period. It is not only a lively mixture of biography, history, and epic, but also a passionate expression of Anna's complex thoughts and personality.

Born December 2, 1083, in the Porphyra of the imperial palace, she spent her life surrounded by activities of the Byzantine court. She wrote the *Alexiad* late in life, forty to sixty years after the period she is describing, between 1143 and her death in 1153 or 1154, while encloistered—or rather imprisoned—at the convent of the Kecharitomene in Constantinople. Displaying her erudition and superior education, she casts the work in epic terms, using Homeric style and archaizing language. At the same time, Anna encourages our awareness of herelf as the author and frequently interjects first-person soliloquies and asides. Anna's *Alexiad* is written in high-style prose. It also, however, has the intimacy of a personal reminiscence, which is of interest in relation to some literary writing today.[2] Her fascination with people's characters and the twists in courses of action is evident as she skillfully draws the reader into the story with her keen sense of excitement.

It is no wonder one senses Anna's excitement as a writer. For the first forty years of her life she mingled with the most influential and ambitious people in the Byzantine Empire, witnessing or hearing firsthand about the events that were shaping history. Throughout her father's tempestuous reign, she was privy to visits and reports, witnessing the day to day operations, departures, and arrivals from within the imperial palace. This was indeed a momentous time for Byzantium: the rise of the military aristocracy led by the Komnenos family with the support of a band of relatives; threats to the empire from the Normans and Turks, and its own constant internal plots and conflicts; potentially overwhelming clashes with west Europeans, and the consequent needs for cautious diplomacy as Byzantium was drawn into the First Crusade. In spite of her vantage point close to events and her position as favorite daughter of the emperor, she was disappointed in her greatest hope: succeeding her father on the throne. Years later, the pain of this memory drives her narrative as she weaves her father's story in her old age.

Anna's writing style and tone evolved over a lifetime of scholarly pursuits and awareness. The approaches Anna uses as a narrator, describing people and their relationships and accomplishments, stem from her keen intellect combined with her literary education. Her writing often follows ancient conventions and uses formulae ingeniously borrowed from the *Iliad* and the *Odyssey*. At the same time, the vividness of her account reflects her firsthand involvement with the making of history and her nostalgia at remembering an era. Her voice, for she often writes in the first person, conveys her intensity and seriousness as a writer of history. What lent her voice such passion? Since she had failed in her attempt to become empress and was living in exile, what were the possibilities open to her now? She reveals much in her Preface:

> The stream of Time, irresistible, ever moving, carries off and bears away all things that come to birth and plunges them into utter darkness, both deeds of no account and deeds which are mighty and worthy of commemoration. . . . The science of History is a great bulwark against this stream of Time; in a way it checks this irresistible flood, it holds in a tight grasp whatever it can seize floating on the surface and will not allow it to slip away into the depths of Oblivion. (Preface 1.1–10; 17)[3]

Her opening statement in lofty metaphors claims that she will stop the "stream of Time" to preserve her father's story and rescue it from being lost in the "depths of Oblivion." As with Anicia Juliana, who "conquered time," claiming that "oblivion does not wipe out the labours of industrious virtue" (according to her epigram discussed in chapter 5), there is no mistaking both the pride and the melancholy in Anna's words.[4] Anna, however, created not an architectural marvel but a literary monument to recapture the glorious past with which she was associated. Having attained the necessary hindsight and writing from her position in the mid–twelfth century, she pursues her mission with conviction and self-determination. The high-flown language indicates that her task is a matter of personal urgency, as she glorifies not only her father but herself. It is no ordinary voice that she uses for her narrative because if, as the title of the *Alexiad* suggests, it is a recasting of the *Iliad,* then Anna casts herself as a new and immortal Homer.

In the first part of this chapter I will consider the historical context of Anna's life and work, that is, the rule of her father in the last decades of the eleventh century and beginning of the twelfth, as documented by the *Alexiad.* The historical and cultural context is set among the military aristocracy which governed the empire and the scholarly elite associated with the palace; the major events comprise battles and diplomacy, as the dynasty struggles to maintain its territories (see the map on page xvi). Events also often involve the imperial women who were close to Anna and who were highly influential at court. Then, in the second part, I will focus on Anna as an author of the mid–twelfth century, her approach to writing, and her attitudes, interests, and priorities. In considering Anna's voice and presence in the *Alexiad,* in particular her tone and style, we are reminded that she is indeed a "child of her times."

Contemporary twelfth-century literary and intellectual currents help explain why the work is not a strict narration of events, but a synopsis of the deeds of Alexios. The great epic poem *Digenes Akrites,* set in the eleventh to twelfth century, is echoed in Anna's sense of adventure, focus on her "hero," and her visually evocative and, at other times, stylized descriptions.[5] Anna's writing style walks the fine line between adventure narrative and reporting. At this time, as in any time, women's roles varied so greatly that one cannot claim either that Anna is typical of women of her time or that she is an anomaly.[6] Her story forms a part of the *Alexiad,* is told from her unique point of view, and is thoroughly integrated with her experience of contemporary culture.

Anna knows how to tell a good story. She is also very much a participant in her story, and she emerges clearly as a personality through her descriptions of those around her and of events affecting the empire. We learn the facts, but we also become acquainted with Anna's concerns and opinions. Her achievement is of special interest to the current generation of feminists, for Anna follows her own intellectual bents in creating a factual and analytical account. She transcends rather than crosses gender boundaries in her deft handling of subject matter usually associated with male writers, for example, battles and military tactics, while still giving special attention to descriptions of women and female relationships. Her observant, humanitarian approach is attuned to personal character and individuality. The world Anna describes is based in the transitional years after the end of the Macedonian dynasty.

After the death in 1056 of Theodora the empress, sister of Zoe and the last ruler of the Macedonian dynasty, a succession of short rules over the next twenty-five years perpetuated an atmosphere of uncertainty and instability. A disastrous defeat by the Seljuk Turks at Manzikert in 1071 in eastern Anatolia was a major setback for Byzantium; the emperor himself was taken captive and had to be ransomed. In the same year Bari, the last Byzantine stronghold in southern Italy, was taken by the Normans, an aggressive clan installed in southern Italy and Sicily. Roger Guiscard, then his brother Robert, followed later by Robert's son Bohemund threatened the empire from their newly acquired territories with undisguised intent to capture Byzantium. There was a desperate need for military leadership to restore the empire to some semblance of the security it had experienced under Basil II. Alexios I responded to this need.

Alexios's route to the throne was made possible through the combined efforts of his two mothers, first his adoptive mother and then his birth mother.[7] Maria of Alania was the first mother to take his part. She was the daughter of the Georgian king, Bagrat IV, and had married Michael VII Doukas (1071–78) in a politically expedient union, only the second foreign princess to marry an emperor of Byzantium in the eleventh century. Their son, Constantine, born in 1074, was made coemperor with his father at an early age and was betrothed to another foreigner, Helena, the infant daughter of Robert Guiscard, the Norman.[8] Michael Psellos had praised Maria's beauty in his *Chronographia*. It was not her beauty, however, but her efforts to protect her son which now brought her into the forefront of Byzantine politics. In 1078 Nicephorus Botaniates (1078–81) forced Michael to abdicate and retire to a monastery, and then, after the death of his wife, married Maria of Alania. This marriage was considered by many to be adulterous, but it lent continuity and legitimacy to the succession. When Nicephorus refused to name Maria's son coemperor, however, she turned to the two brothers Isaac and Alexios Komnenos. Maria adopted Alexios as her son, and with her support the brothers staged a coup, ousting Nicephorus and forcing him to retire to a monastery. The way was thus cleared for Alexios to take the throne. Maria had helped legitimize Nicephorus as emperor, but when her plans for her son did not materialize, she was instrumental in his removal and the installation of a successor.[9] Maria's maternal as much as her material concerns were behind the change of rule.[10]

Maria's role in the short reigns of two Byzantine emperors is epitomized by her portrait in a manuscript of the Homilies of Saint John Chrysostom, Paris, Coislin 79, folio 1 verso (pl. 18). The manuscript was commissioned when she was married to Michael VII Doukas. In this luxurious frontispiece she appears next to him in a full-length portrait, while a smaller, half-length figure of Christ appears crowning them both. The portraits are painted in luminous colors on the gold foil ground of the page, thus giving the slightly worn and transparent paintings a transcendental quality. The empress is dressed in ceremonial garb of silk brocade mantle and jewel-studded loros with shield-shaped thorakion, very similar to that of Zoe in her mosaic portrait in Hagia Sophia (compare pl. 17). Maria, however, wears a tall, magnificent crown, or stemma, with central red jewel, comparable to or even surpassing that of the emperor. Her name is inscribed above her head, as is that of the emperor beside her.

Michael's name, however, has been rubbed out and replaced by that of Nicephorus III Botaniates. The frontispieces have been cut out and rearranged, and the portraits of Michael have been retouched to make him resemble an older man

(Nicephorus was in his sixties when he married Maria).[11] The manuscript was thus appropriated when Maria was married to her second husband, Nicephorus Botaniates and was altered correspondingly: "Michael" became "Nicephorus," while the empress and her inscribed name remained unchanged. As with the Zoe panel discussed in chapter 10, Maria's legitimizing role in the changes of power—and husband—is reflected in the portraits. Maria's impact on the Komnenians did not end with her boost of Alexios in attaining the throne, for she also had an influence on Alexios's daughter, the young princess Anna Komnene, as we will see.

Now that Alexios was on the throne, familial relationships came into play to assure that he stayed there. His brother Isaac, whom he named *sebastokrator*, a new title indicating he was second only to the emperor, and brother-in-law, George Palaeologus, assumed major responsibilities in administration and remained his staunch supporters throughout his reign. Also important as allies were his mother, Anna Dalassene, and later his wife, Irene Doukaina (see list of rulers on page 320).[12] Maria of Alania, his adoptive mother, continued to play a role for a time. When Alexios moved into the imperial palace as emperor in 1081, he did not initially bring with him his fourteen-year-old wife, Irene Doukaina, whom he had married in 1078, a member of the powerful Doukas family. His mother, Anna Dalassene, was in favor of Alexios putting Irene aside and marrying Maria! Popular sentiment combined with patriarchal support for Irene barely succeeded in persuading the Komnenians to crown Irene as empress. This episode exemplifies the potential for members of the imperial family to bend rules of morality and the laws of church and state if they were set on a politically expedient course of action. In this case, however, Maria lost the possibility of being empress a third time, and Irene was crowned a week after Alexios, thus uniting the Doukas family with the Komnenoi. The episode is described with restraint in book 3 of the *Alexiad*. Maria remained part of the ruling elite, her son Constantine was again named heir to the throne by Alexios, and she was given quarters in the Mangana palace. The engagement between Constantine and Helena, the Norman princess, had been broken off, and so in 1083, after the birth of Alexios's and Irene's first child, a daughter, Constantine was betrothed to her in the expectation that the pair would one day rule Byzantium.[13] This child was Anna Komnene, and this betrothal shaped her expectations throughout her life.

The early years of Alexios's rule involved both successes and failures.[14] After the Norman conquest of Dyrrachium on the Adriatic coast the Byzantines were in need of allies to help resist Norman advances, and Alexios turned to the Venetians. In 1082 a trade agreement with Venice provided the support needed to reconquer Dyrrachium, but in return the Venetians were granted privileges of free trade within the empire; this agreement contributed to the weakening of the Byzantine economy and the eventual conquest of Constantinople by the Fourth Crusade a century later, but at the time Alexios was acting to ensure Byzantium's survival. The rise of a feudal-style aristocracy and a system of grants of *pronoia*, or huge estates, developed, lowering the incentives for local soldiers and landowners to participate in the wars needed to maintain the empire. It became necessary to go to the expense of hiring mercenaries. Dangers erupted along the frontiers in the form of the Pechenegs, then Cumans and Serbs, requiring that Alexios be constantly on the alert or on campaign. During these times he needed a reliable ruler to remain in the capital, so he turned again to a family member, his birth mother, Anna Dalassene.

Anna Dalassene was the most powerful woman of her time, perhaps even more powerful for a time than either her husband or son. Married to John Komnenos, the brother of the emperor Isaac I (1057–59), she had ambitions for her husband which never materialized. After John's death in 1067 she managed a family of eight children, largely by manipulating ties with prominent families to her advantage.[15] After the battle of Manzikert and the rise of the Doukas family she was exiled for plotting against the throne. She and her remaining children were banished to the island of Prinkipo in 1072, and she was tonsured as a nun. This was by no means the end of her career, however, for she returned to the court of Michael VII and succeeded in marrying one son to the empress's cousin. Her second surviving son, Alexios, was married to Irene, the granddaughter of John Doukas, in 1077, when she was twelve years old and he twenty. Four years later in a complicated ruse she took refuge in Hagia Sophia—holding onto the Holy Doors of the sanctuary and refusing to move unless her hands were cut off—in order to obtain a promise from the emperor that would ensure the safety of her family members. The trick (dramatically described in book 2, chapter 5, of the *Alexiad*) worked, and she spent the time encloistered at the monastery of the Petrion, emerging after the successful coup as mother of the reigning emperor.

After Alexios's ascent to the throne Anna Dalassene acted as regent whenever he was absent on campaign, which indicates the extent of Alexios's respect for her intelligence and experience. She was designated to act on his behalf in matters of appointment, promotion, honors, donations, salaries, and taxation.[16] Her administrative skills and intellect made her the most powerful and influential woman of her time; she "drove the imperial chariot," as Anna says, describing her grandmother's leadership.[17] Her piety, also unsurpassed, was aimed at changing the people's perception of the reign to one of modesty and religious devotion, much in the way Pulcheria had done many years earlier (see chapter 3). She determined to do away with the former scandal and immorality of the Zoe regime and "clean up" the palace, as Anna states clearly.[18] Sometime between 1095 and 1100 Anna Dalassene disappears from the record after retiring to the convent she founded, the Pantepoptes, in Constantinople.[19] Alexios had depended on her in the early years of his reign, but later, it appears, he was no longer in need of her help.[20] As we will see, it was now the turn of his wife, Irene Doukaina, to rise in visibility and fully assume the role of coruler with her husband.

The later part of Alexios's reign was spent dealing mainly with crusaders from the West, intermittently with the eastern Seljuk Turks and with a new and formidable aggressor, the Magyars of Hungary. In 1096 the initial waves of the First Crusade reached Constantinople. Through skillful and costly diplomacy Alexios persuaded the crusaders not to linger in the capital, but to be transported across the Bosphorus. As they proceeded on toward the Holy Land he extracted promises and oaths of allegiance. These they broke when, on capturing Antioch and finally Jerusalem in 1099, they set themselves up as rulers in their own right. Relations between the westerners and Byzantium were strained from this time on, as distrust and disdain for these unreliable foreigners, Christian though they were, became ensconced. After the Norman Bohemund was brought under Byzantine sovereignty in 1108, the next threat to the Balkans was the Hungarians. To keep this restless people at bay Alexios relied on negotiation, a part of which was the marriage between his son and heir, John, and the Hungarian princess Irene. The couple appears in a companion panel to the Zoe panel in Hagia Sophia: John II Konmenos and the empress Irene of Hungary, splendidly clad, present gifts to the Virgin and Child (see fig. 40). The bejeweled, formal attire of the empress echoes that of Zoe, but instead of being a diminutive counterpart of the emperor, this foreign bride stands at the same height as her husband and more than equals him in the splendor of her appearance.

Throughout this second period of Alexios's reign, his wife, Irene Doukaina, helped him accomplish his aims. Her family had aided Alexios in his rise to power, and Doukas relatives were a continued presence and source of support on the battlefield as well as at court. Irene bore nine children, two of whom died in infancy. After her childbearing years were over, Irene's influence gradually increased as she became her husband's closest confidant.[21] Of greatest importance for her rising status had been the crowning of her son John in 1092 as coemperor and heir to the throne, replacing Anna Komnene's betrothed, Constantine, who in any case died while still in adolescence. As soon as John was old enough to be left in charge when Alexios was absent from the capital on campaign, Irene accompanied her husband, acting as nurse for his worsening gout and as guardian, especially against poisoning. As her husband grew older he relied on her more and more; even when under attack by Turks, she was with him until her personal galley conducted her away to a safe distance from the action. When the danger passed she rejoined him. She nursed him up until the time of his death.

In addition to performing her role as empress within the palace and on campaigns, Irene was influential in other ways. For example, she was the founder of a large convent in Constantinople, the Kecharitomene, for which the *typikon*, or set of rules, she composed in 1110–16 survives.[22] In it we learn, for example, that women of royal rank, especially her family members, were given privileges and lived in relative comfort in their own "imperial buildings," when they retired to the convent late in life as nuns.[23] She also had an interest in theology and in literature and is known to have requested the writing of pieces by the court poets Prodromos and Kallikles.[24] A history by her son-in-law, Nicephoros Bryennios, was dedicated to her, and it was also she who ordered the writing of a history of Alexios's reign. Her principal influence was cultural rather than administrative, and her membership in the Doukas family helped her maintain her own politically among the other strong women, especially Maria of Alania and Anna Dalassene.

At the death of Alexios in 1118, Irene attempted to divert the succession away from her son John and toward her daughter, Anna Komnene and son-in-law Nicephoros Bryennios. Her motive may have been to extend her own and her family's power by making her daughter empress after her. But the attempt failed and was initially forgiven; she retired to the convent she had founded. Then an assassination plot formed by Anna against her brother forced her into retirement at the Kecharitomene as well.[25] Irene died there around 1123. Anna's husband, Nicephoros Bryennios, continued to support his brother-in-law, the emperor John II, and after him Manual I, conducting successful campaigns in the field. Bryennios's history of the reigns of the Doukas family was completed, but not that of Alexios, for he died in 1137. Anna lived on at the Kecharitomene into the 1150s, and it was she who took up that task, which resulted in the *Alexiad*.

The *Alexiad* is consistently and powerfully written. In the inevitable evaluations and reevaluations to which any history is subjected over time, some have found fault with it. Taken on its own merits, however, there is no question that it is a masterpiece of literature.[26] It could not have been adapted from her husband's notes, as some have suggested, or, much less, written by him and revised by Anna.[27] Anna's own voice in the *Alexiad* is too engaging for the book to be a "laundering" of her husband's text.[28] Since Nicephoros Bryennios died before he could write a history of Alexios's reign, Anna accomplished the task herself.[29] The emperor Constantine VII had written the history of the reign of his grandfather Basil I, founder of the Macedonian dynasty in the tenth century. Michael Psellos wrote the stories of fourteen emperors from the vantage point of a court scholar in the late eleventh century. But no other biography by the scholarly daughter of an emperor exists. In responding as much to her own needs as to the need for a history of Alexios's reign, Anna wrote a work of unique character.

Writing during the reign of Alexios's grandson, Manual I, who came to the throne in 1143, Anna had ample opportunity to draw subtle comparisons between her father's rule and the present one, finding the former superior. Anna's surroundings while writing the *Alexiad* can be deduced from the typikon, or founder's document, of the nunnery in which she was incarcerated. The Kecharitomene nunnery had luxurious quarters for the foundress; the building complex included a chapel, two baths, and courtyards. Anna had life tenure to this complex along with its staff.[30] Her worldview was that of an aristocrat who had received the best education, and even though sequestered or imprisoned for thirty years, her pride remained intact.[31] It was not her mother's directive, but Anna's own choice and determination that produced the *Alexiad*. This work, written in a resounding and passionate voice, became her legacy.

The style chosen by Anna is a composite one and is thoroughly in keeping with her superior birth and education. She uses the elevated epic style of Homer quite naturally, for she was as thoroughly familiar with his poems as she was with ancient philosophy, history, and drama, and she interlards her text with quotations and allusions to Homeric verse. Ancient tragedy finds frequent echoes in the work, along with references to the mythical world of ancient heroes, ever present in Byzantium. She succeeded most surprisingly in combining heroic epic with a mode of first-person observation and psychological description found in Michael Psellos, an author whom she greatly admired. One could say she put Homer's poetic style into Psellos's observant, analytical prose. Into this composite style, she roundly inserts herself, constantly reacting and commenting, occasionally with outbursts of emotion. She is boldly and unapologetically present in her father's story.

Anna's self-conscious use of the heroic style in her writing manifests itself as she considers the need for adequate language to describe her troubles and names potential sources of her style:

> I would need the Siren of Isocrates, the grandiloquence of Pindar, Polemo's vivacity, the Calliope of Homer, Sappho's lyre or some other power greater still. (14.7.4; 459–60)

Evoking ancient writers, orators, and mythical figures is both a display of Anna's erudition and acquaintance with works of antiquity and a frame for her own writing in a comparable elevated, lively style.

Her self-awareness in the writing process is apparent in the middle of a complicated chapter describing battles with Celts and Scyths, ancient names she applies to Normans and Turks. She momentarily focuses the reader's attention on herself and the writing process:

> As I write these words, it is nearly time to light the lamps; my pen moves slowly over the paper and I feel myself almost too drowsy to write as the words escape me. I have to use foreign names and I am compelled to describe in detail a mass of events which occurred in rapid succession; the result is that the main body of the history and the continuous narrative are bound to become disjointed because of interruptions. Ah well, "'tis no cause for anger" to those at least who read my work with good will. Let us go on. (13.6.3; 411–12)

Here, in dynamic contrast to the passage on language quoted above, Anna figuratively turns from her task and addresses the reader in a passage devoid of pretensions. She alludes to the difficult physical and mental circumstances of writing: waning daylight, writer's cramp, drowsiness (she was probably in her sixties), and dogged perseverance. She evokes the mental exercise of dealing with non-Greek words and names and finally apologizes for diverting the reader's attention away from the main war narrative. This disarming passage has the effect of breaking up her account and shifting attention to herself as a writer. At the same time, it echoes Homer in "'tis no cause for anger," as she suggests the reader's possible attitude. This is not simply a case of a writer using license: it is a subtle tour de force in which the author addresses the reader in a personal aside, while assuming the persona of Homer.

Anna's Homeric stance demonstrates that she is indeed firmly in control of her material, as she is in many other similar passages.[32] She made a deliberate choice to relate her father's story in terms of complicated military history because this was the stuff of Homeric epic. In begging for the reader's forbearance in Homeric terms, she seeks to ennoble not only her own task but also that of the reader, who must slog through what is obviously a difficult section of description. Through her request she elevates her audience too. In another Homeric parallel a few lines later, she describes Cantacuzenus's vigilance. She says of the general, "nor did sweet slumber hold back the man," taken from book 2 of the *Iliad,* in which Agamemnon is roused by a dream to lead the Achaeans to battle.[33] Anna's use of Homeric quotation and paraphrase is her primary self-associative literary device throughout the *Alexiad.* Since Homer was well known to every educated person and often quoted in other works of all genres, this familiarity would have served readers of the *Alexiad* too. The association of Anna with Homer in her use of literary conventions would have been inescapable.

Personages in Anna's descriptions of battles often assume heroic proportions. In a passage describing the aggressive, opportunistic archenemy Robert Guiscard, who has taken up the cause of the pretender to the throne, Michael, Anna compares him obliquely to Patroclus in the *Iliad:*

> Having found Michael he had a Patroclus-like excuse and that spark of ambition, hitherto lying hidden beneath the ashes, blazed up into a mighty conflagration. In a terrifying fashion he armed himself to do battle with the Roman Empire. Dromons, triremes, biremes, sermones and other transport vessels in great numbers were made ready. (3.9.1; 124)

The overall tone and content are Homeric as she describes Robert's preparation to move against Alexios. Compare, for example, the general style in a description of Patroclus as he attacks the Paeonians:

> Patroclus whipped the terror in all their hearts
> when he killed the chief who topped them all in battle.
> He rode them off the ships, he quenched the leaping fire,
> leaving Protesilaus' hulk half-burnt but upright still
> and the Trojans scattered back with high, shrill cries. (*Iliad* 16.342–46)[34]

The epic mode of describing the stages of battle was deftly reformulated by Anna so that her father's enemies were depicted as sharing in a heroic struggle in the style of Greeks versus Trojans.

The presence and awareness of the heroic past are characteristic of Byzantine culture. A narrative comprising mainly battles, stratagems, and descriptions of military prowess, therefore, would naturally be cast like the *Iliad;* and clever tricks and unexpected events would be associated with the *Odyssey.* Homeric epithets and quotes are put into the mouths of or are used to describe many characters in the *Alexiad,* even, as we have just noted, those of enemies. The work is therefore as much an epic as it is a history, not a strict account of events but primarily a story of the deeds of its hero, Alexios, who invariably remains in the "compositional center" of the narrative.[35] Alexios is always the source of inspiration and directives; he is respected by allies and enemies alike; he drives the machinery of rule and battle.

Anna's writing is characterized by references to abstract principles at work in the pattern of fate, as in heroic epic, in which the gods are constantly intervening and determining outcomes of conflicts. For example, she refers to Time versus History, to Fortune and Fate being responsible for victory or for the course of events. Robert Guiscard is described as having an advantageous position with regard to western rulers: "In everything Fortune [*Tyche*] worked for him, raised him to power and brought about whatever was to his advantage" (1.13.1; 61). In a similar fashion, speaking of her son's death at the hand of Achilles, Hecuba says, "So this, this is the doom that strong Fate spun out" (*Iliad*, 24.248). Maintaining the epic genre throughout the *Alexiad* was Anna's choice and her literary feat.

Anna's ability as a writer to make us visualize the action of Alexios's campaigns is also very much in the mode of Homer's battle descriptions. Recounting the life of the emperor required an interest in and comprehension of wars and military matters, of which Anna proves herself thoroughly capable. Part of the activity of her father revolves around the Crusades, which cut across the Byzantine territories, causing destruction and anxiety. The detail with which Anna describes the psychology of advantage and of defeat from the Byzantine perspective is astonishing, but it is equally surprising to observe the intimacy of knowledge she acquired of the western or Latin point of view. Anna was fourteen years old when the First Crusade camped outside the walls of Constantinople. Her description is simultaneously personal and subject to literary device:

> It was typical of Alexius: he had an uncanny prevision and knew how to seize a point of vantage before his rivals. Officers appointed for this particular task were ordered to provide victuals on the journey—the pilgrims must have no excuse for complaint for any reason whatever. Meanwhile they were eagerly pressing on to the capital. One might have compared them in number to the stars of heaven or the grains of sand poured out over the shore; as they hurried towards Constantinople they were indeed "numerous as the leaves and flowers of spring," to quote Homer. (10.10.3; 324)[36]

Anna describes the savvy psychology of hospitality to the crusaders factually before shifting smoothly to poetic language, referring to book 2 of the *Iliad*, in which the gathering armies are described:

> So tribe on tribe, pouring out of the ships and shelters,
> marched across the Scamander plain and the earth shook,
> tremendous thunder from under trampling men and horses
> drawing into position down the Scamander meadow flats
> breaking into flower—men by the thousands, numberless
> as the leaves and spears that flower forth in spring. (*Iliad* 2.549–54)[37]

Having used Homeric style to describe the impression the crusaders make, she then changes abruptly to a more personal note, musing over her inability to pronounce their names:

> For all my desire to name their leaders, I prefer not to do so. The words fail me, partly through my inability to make the barbaric sounds—they are so unpronounceable—and partly because I recoil before their great numbers. In any case, why should I try to list the names of so enormous a multitude, when even their contemporaries became indifferent at the sight of them? (10.10.4; 324–5)

Anna's anti-Latin bias is apparent in this passage, as is her snobbish attitude toward these foreigners, who speak languages she cannot understand and have names she cannot pronounce.[38] Her description is colored by her reaction.

The same combination of fact and subjective reaction is used in a description of battle machinery. Anna describes a complicated wooden tower used for Bohemond's siege of Dyrrachium. She has so thoroughly visualized the machine that she sympathizes with the reader, who must try to conjure it up:

> It is hard to picture in words the construction of Bohemond's new weapon; his barbarians devised it as a kind of mantelet with a tower. According to eye-witnesses its appearance was terrifying, and certainly to the Dyrrachines threatened by it it was a most awe-inspiring sight. It was made in the following manner. A wooden tower was built to a considerable height on a four-sided base. So high was it that the city towers were overtopped by as much as five or six cubits. It was essential to make it so, in order that when the landing drawbridges were lowered the enemy ramparts might be easily overrun; . . . The tower was indeed a terrible sight, but it seemed even more terrible in motion. . . . Like some giant above the clouds it was apparently self-propelled. On all sides it had been covered from base to top, and there were many storeys with embrasures of every type all round it from which showers of arrows could be fired. (13.3.9–10; 402–3)

Her description is filled with expressions that react to as much as describe the tower. Her imagination is energetic, and she has the ability to conjure up her subjects in her mind's eye, even though she was not an eyewitness—a gift only of those who have cultivated their visual imaginations over a lifetime. Anna's skill as a descriptive writer of the war machine extends to her portraits of people. This skill comes from her observant nature as much as from her training in ancient literature, rhetoric, and philosophy.

The other major literary influence in Anna's work was Michael Psellos (1018–78), whose mode of biographical narrative we encountered in chapter 10 in his description of Zoe and her husbands. Anna reveals that the *Chronographia* of Psellos was a major inspiration for her approach and that she knew his work well; she cites it eighty-one times in the *Alexiad*.[39] While Psellos is often ambivalent about the subjects of his *Chronographia,* Anna, on the other hand, maintains her father was "immovable and unchangeable" throughout his reign.[40] She describes Psellos as "the famous" Michael Psellos, a person of "native intelligence and quickness of apprehension." She continues,

> He attained the perfection of all knowledge, having an accurate understanding of both Hellenic and Chaldaean science, and so became renowned in those times for his wisdom. (5.8.3; 175)

Anna's admiration is based on Psellos's intelligence and knowledge, and she sees him as her intellectual colleague of several generations preceding. How did she incorporate a Psellan mode into her writing?

Portraits of individuals are particularly striking in Anna's work, as they are in Psellos's. In a long description of Constantine IX, Psellos treats his physical appearance as "a marvel of beauty that Nature brought into being," as he exclaims over the symmetry of his proportions. Then he elevates the description to include mythicheroic and even more transcendent qualities:

> His beauty, we are told, was that of Achilles or Nireus. But whereas, in the case of these heroes the poet's language, having in imagination endowed them with a body compounded of all manner of beauties, barely sufficed for their description, with Constantine it was different, for Nature, having formed in reality and brought him to perfection, with the fine skill of the sculptor shaped him and made him beautiful, surpassing with her own peculiar art the imaginative effort of the poet. And when she had made each limb proportioned to the rest of his body, his head and the parts that go with it, his hands and the parts that go with them, his thighs and his feet, she shed over each of them severally the colour that befitted them. His head she made ruddy as the sun, but all his breast, and his lower parts down to his feet, together with their correspoonding back parts, she coloured the purest white all over, with exquisite accuracy. When he was in his prime, before his limbs lost their virility, anyone who cared to look at him closely would assuredly have likened his head to the sun in its glory, so radiant was it, and his hair to the rays of the sun, while in the rest of his body he would have seen the purest and most translucent crystal. (*Chronographia*, 6.126)[41]

In comparing Constantine's appearance to that of epic heroes, Psellos claims for him the beauty of a statue made by a sculptor. While declaring his actual perfection, he turns to hyperbole, likening him to Phoebus Apollo, with blazing head and hair. Finally the colors are added to the statue's appearance, in keeping with an ideal of male beauty, that of ruddy complexion and flesh the color of crystal. These colors and shining radiance are not only to fill out an accurate picture of beauty but are dictated by the Byzantine aesthetic. The convention of comparing human appearances to those of gods or heroes involved active description. Nature, in creating Constantine, created a work of art. Anna's description of her young fiancé Constantine reveals the influence of Psellos:

The little boy, apart from other considerations, was a lovely child, still quite young (he was not yet seven years old) and no one should blame if I praise my own when the nature of the case compels me. It was delightful enough to hear him speak, but that was not all: his extraordinary agility and suppleness made him unrivalled at games, if one is to believe what his companions in those days said later. He was blond, with a skin as white as milk, his cheeks suffused with red like some dazzling rose that has just left its calyx. His eyes were not light-coloured, but hawk-like, shining beneath the brows, like a precious stone set in a golden ring. Thus seemingly endowed with a heavenly beauty not of this world, his manifold charms captivated the beholder; in short, anyone who saw him would say, "He is like the painter's Cupid." (3.1.3; 104)

Like Psellos's description, Anna's is an *ekphrasis,* a rhetorical description, for it depicts the young boy as a work of art. Although her description is not as elaborate as Psellos's, we detect not only Anna's customary heroic note—Constantine is depicted as having athletic prowess, like a young Greek hero—but also her idealized first love. After their engagement while still children, the two lived in the same household. In this passage Anna reveals her emotional attachment and nostalgia for this handsome young boy whom she never married owing to his early death. The two authors' descriptions of his mother, Maria of Alania, are also revealing. Anna herself draws our attention to Psellos's description of Maria of Alania, which is fairly succinct compared to that of Constantine IX:

> It would be superfluous to praise the empress because of her family, although its wealth and antiquity cannot fail to confer lustre on the highest offices; her own preeminence, not only in virtue, but also in beauty, is commendation enough. If, as the tragic poet says "silence is a woman's glory" then she above all other women is worthy of honour, for she speaks to no one but her husband, and her natural loveliness is far more effective than any artificial adornment dictated by convention. (*Chronographia,* 7.10)[42]

As I noted in chapter 9, Psellos does not like talkative women, although he is impressed by her beauty. Anna's description of Maria is even fuller and shows some similarities to Psellos's description of Constantine IX:

> She was in fact very tall, like a cypress tree; her skin was snow-white; her face was oval, her complexion wholly reminiscent of a spring flower or a rose. As for the flash of her eyes, what mortal could describe it? Eyebrows, flame-coloured, arched above eyes of light blue. A painter's hand has many times reproduced the colours of all the flowers brought to birth each in its own season, but the beauty of the empress, the grace that shone about her, the charming attractiveness of her ways, these seemed to baffle description, to be beyond the artist's skill. Neither Apelles, nor Pheidias, nor any of the sculptors ever created such a work. The Gorgon's head, so they say, turned men who saw her to stone, but a man who saw the empress walking, or who suddenly met her, was stupefied, rooted to the spot where he happened to be and speechless, apparently deprived in that one moment of all feeling and reason. Such was the proportion and

perfect symmetry of her body, each part in harmony with the rest, that no one till then had ever seen its like among human-kind—a living work of art, an object of desire to lovers of beauty. She was indeed Love incarnate, visiting as it were this earthly world. (3.2.4; 107)

Anna's description of Maria is also an *ekphrasis,* in itself a work of art. She expends considerable effort to make Maria visible to the imagination and to express the stunning impact her beauty had on the viewer. In addition, she develops a whole catalogue of features which made up the ideal human body. We again encounter the convention of Nature imitating art: depicting Maria was "beyond the artist's skill." Anna seems to wish to outdo even standard conventions of literary description. She claims Maria had mythical power through her beauty: she was as beautiful as the Gorgon was ugly, but both could turn people to stone; Anna playfully turns the myth of the Gorgon on its head. She goes even further in her literary devices of praise and elevates Maria to divine status, as a goddess who is "visiting this world." Anna's descriptions, like those of Psellos, are meant to encourage visualization.

To help visualize Maria as described by Anna one need only to refer again to the manuscript of the Homilies of Saint John Chrysostom, discussed above, which depicts Maria in her painted portrait (pl. 18). The portrait now offers one, however, an opportunity to juxtapose literary with artistic conventions. The features which Anna refers to, in order—height, skin, shape of face, complexion, eyes, eyebrows—are a kind of checklist for the Byzantine ideal of beauty. The manuscript shows Maria in what may well be regarded as an ideal of female beauty: tall, white-skinned, oval face, blue eyes, and arched eyebrows. Anna's affection for Maria may have been an added incentive to describe her beauty in such lavish terms, for Maria brought Anna up from the time she was eight years old, as Anna tells us. From the time she was betrothed to her son, Constantine, Maria was idealized as a mother and as a beautiful woman.[43] Anna, like Psellos, compares human subjects to works of art.

Anna also takes her cue from Psellos in making frequent interjections in the first person, insisting on the veracity and impartiality of her account. Psellos says, for example,

> Suppose I set aside this project for the moment and undertake to write a history of the lives of the emperors, how, when I leave unsaid things which belong to the province of history, am I to deal with those which are the proper object of eulogy? It would look as if I had forgotten to distinguish its subject-matter and by confusing the role of two forms of literature whose aims are incompatible. (*Chronographia, 6.25*)[44]

Psellos frequently intervenes in his narrative to protest the difficulty of avoiding writing panegyric in place of history. Anna also anticipates criticism by enemies or detractors and even more than Psellos tries at numerous junctures to exonerate herself from writing "mere panegyric:"

Now that I have decided to write the story of his life, I am fearful of an underlying suspicion: someone might conclude that in composing the history of my father I am glorifying myself; the history, wherever I express admiration for any act of his, may seem wholly false and mere panegyric. (Preface, 2.2; 18)

The presence of the author and his high degree of subjectivity are a constant and defining feature of the writing of Michael Psellos, as they are of Anna, who surely modeled herself on her predecessor.

Her concerns that her work might be taken as panegyric also extended to her "portrait" of Anna Dalassene in book 3. There she interjects a disclaimer at the end of a long description of her grandmother's qualities as a leader:

I myself knew her for a short time and admired her. Any unprejudiced witness to the truth knows and, if he cares to, will admit that what I have said about her was not mere empty boasting. Indeed, if I had preferred to compose a panegyric rather than a history, I would have written at greater length, adding more stories about her. (3.8.11; 124)

Anna insists that she writes the truth from firsthand experience, as is required and proper for a history. She is worried about negative opinion and can only interject in her first-person voice in honest defense, "I myself knew her for a short time and admired her." Psellos in similar fashion recounts his meeting with Constantine IX:

As for Constantine, he was affected by a strange feeling of pleasure, as inexplicable as the divinely-inspired utterance of men in a trance. So influenced was he at the first sound of my voice that he almost embraced me. Other men had the right of access to him at set times and for a limited period, but to me his heart's doors were now thrown wide open, and gradually, as I became more intimate with him, he shared with me all his secrets. (*Chronographia*, 6.46)[45]

Modesty does not burden Psellos, as he makes the point that he knew the emperor personally. Both authors let the reader know they were closely connected with their subjects.

It is this very proximity, however, which forces them to defend their honesty. For instance, at the end of the *Alexiad,* after describing her father's bravery and cleverness as a leader, Anna again defends herself:

At this point I must again beg the reader not to rebuke me for being boastful; this is by no means the first time I have defended myself against such an accusation. It is not love for my father which prompts me to these reflections, but the course of events. In any case, there is nothing (as far as truth is concerned) to prevent a person loving his or her father and at the same time respecting veracity. (15.3.4; 478)

Psellos, on the other hand, found it necessary to write a long digression on his own education and contact with the emperor to bolster his credibility:

Now that I have introduced myself with such a wealth of detail into this part of the history, I can assure you that my evidence will avoid all falsehood; whatever is not said, will remain hidden, but none of the things I am going to say will be of doubtful veracity. (*Chronographia* 6.47)[46]

What he omits cannot be held against him, but what he includes will be the truth. Anna does not hedge in this regard but vows that her account is complete as well as truthful. Convention or literary topos though it may be, both express concern about a potentially critical audience, fully aware, of course, that there will always be a critical audience. As a writer, Anna was steeped in the works of great writers, two of whom were particularly influential. Part of Anna's accomplishment is in her skillful synthesis of these influences. Anna in the guise of Homer is complemented by Anna the emulator of Michael Psellos.

The historical sources for Anna's writings are not unknown, for she is clear and insistent about where she got her material. In book 14, near the end of the *Alexiad*, she tells of "men still alive today who knew my father and tell me of his deeds."[47] She sought corroboration for these accounts and obtained it from contemporaries who were alive at the time of the events she describes. But for the bulk of the descriptions, she claims to have been present:

> Most of the time, moreover, we were ourselves present, for we accompanied our father and mother. Our lives by no means revolved round the home; we did not live a sheltered, pampered existence. (14.7.4; 459)

Firsthand observation was her source for much of the material in her work, according to Anna, while other episodes were based on eyewitness accounts and overheard discussions between the emperor and his general, George Palaeologus. Much later, under the reign of Manual I, when she was already encloistered in the convent, she "collected" the greater part of the evidence for her narrative.

> Some of my material is the result of my own observations; some I have gathered in various ways from the emperor's comrades-in-arms, who sent us information about the progress of the wars by people who crossed the straits. Above all, I have often heard the emperor and George Palaeologus discussing these matters in my presence. Most of the evidence I collected myself, especially in the reign of the third emperor after Alexios, at a time when all the flattery and lies had disappeared with his grandfather. (14.7.5; 460)

Anna's collecting spans a long period, from her youth and middle age in the palace to people living under Manual I in her present day.

Anna grieves for the loss of the "three emperors" in her life: her father, her mother, and her husband. She rages at her confinement, for she passes her time in obscurity, devoting herself to her books and to the worship of God. Her mission is made difficult in these circumstances, but she is nonetheless resolved. In her exile, not even unimportant persons are allowed to visit her, so her material had to be gathered from insignificant writings, absolutely devoid of literary pretensions, and from old soldiers who were serving in the army at the time of my father's accession who fell on hard times and exchanged the turmoil of the outer world for the peaceful life of monks. The documents that came into my possession were written in simple language without embellishment; they adhered closely to the truth, were distinguished by no elegance whatever, and were composed in a negligent way with no attempt at style. (14.7.7; 461)

Anna's insistence on the lack of literary pretension in the written documents she used as sources is sworn as an oath. She apparently was able to circulate enough in her exile to talk to elderly monks who had participated in the events she recounts. Since a common pattern for both men and women was to take monastic orders late in life, one important source of information or corroboration for Anna's history could have been other monastics. What she describes is an arduous process of collecting material from disparate sources. No wonder the work is not seamless, as one scholar complained.[48] Whether we choose to take her strictly at her word or not, she undoubtedly had the unique combination of ability and experience to produce her work in the way she describes.

Anna's forthrightness about the sources for her narrative is paralleled by her frankness about her intellectual pretensions. The aspect of her personality that predominates is pride: pride in her birth and pride in her intellectual erudition. Let us start with intellectual concerns, which are connected to the notion of a good education. Education is central to Anna's self-definition. At the beginning of the *Alexiad* she indicates the role learning has had in her life:

I, Anna, Daughter of the Emperor Alexius and the Empress Irene, born and bred in the Purple, not without some acquaintance with literature—having devoted the most earnest study to the Greek language, in fact, and being not unpractised in Rhetoric and having read thoroughly the treatises of Aristotle and the dialogues of Plato, and having fortified my mind with the Quadrivium of sciences (these things must be divulged, and it is not self-advertisement to recall what Nature and my own zeal for knowledge have given me, nor what God has apportioned to me from above and what has been contributed by Opportunity). (Preface 1.2; 17)[49]

Anna received a classical education, the best that could be had, and she was grateful for the opportunity. Behind her accomplishments, however, is not just privilege but her own "zeal for knowledge." Her active role has been enhanced by her natural gifts: "what God has apportioned to me from above." She is thoroughly conscious of her gifts and acknowledges that her native intelligence has been for her as important as her high birth and access to education. How were Anna's intelligence and zeal for knowledge shaped?

The women in her life were fundamental in guiding Anna toward her preoccupation with intellectual pursuits. Anna interrupts her narrative periodically with recollections of her earliest memories, especially those pertaining to her intellectual training and pursuit of a fine education. One reminiscence in book 5 describes her mother's formative influence:

> Many a time when a meal was already served I remember seeing my mother with a book in her hands, diligently reading the dogmatic pronouncements of the Holy Fathers, especially of the philospher and martyr Maximus.

Anna recalls her reaction to her mother's pursuit of philosophical knowledge:

> "How could you of your own accord aspire to such sublimity? For my part, I tremble and dare not give ear to such things even in the smallest degree. The man's writing, so highly speculative and intellectual, makes the reader's head swim."

Her mother's response is sympathetic and empowering:

> "I myself do not approach such books without a tremble. Yet I cannot tear myself away from them. Wait a little and after a close look at other books, believe me, you will taste the sweetness of these." The memory of her words pierces my heart and plunges me into a sea of other reminiscences. But the law of history forbids me: we must return to the affairs of Italos. (5.9.3; 178–79)

The notion of honing the mind, of progressing from accessible to more difficult texts, is instilled in the young Anna. This intimate childhood conversation recurs to Anna as she writes in her place of exile, after her mother's death. The pain Anna feels at this recollection causes an emotional outburst, which only her sense of duty as a historian curbs. Her intellectual curiosity and rationality have sustained her through the disappointments of her life. The origin of Anna's intellectual bent lay with her theologically minded mother.

Another influential woman in Anna's life was Maria of Alania, who raised her from the time she was a child and who, according to Anna, "shared her secrets" with her.[50] Among Anna's female relationships the most influential role, however, was played by her grandmother, Anna Dalassene. Maria and Irene influenced the men around them by supporting them in various ways; Anna Dalassene simply took over men's traditional roles and handled them herself when power was delegated to her by her son. The personal influence of imperial wives and mothers must have varied, and Anna often refers to the role of the *gynaikonitis,* or women's quarters of the palace,[51] but we are left with no doubt that Anna Dalassene played a crucial role in the success of the reign of Alexios I Komnenos. Indeed, she could be said to have ruled through Alexios. Anna's descriptions of all three of these women and their modes of influence at court are intermingled with revelations of Anna's own personality and ambitions. While Maria of Alania and Irene Doukaina are described as "living statues" and are extolled for their beauty, Anna Dalassene is praised for her wisdom and virtue:

> Not only was she a very great credit to her own sex, but to men as well; indeed, she contributed to the glory of the whole human race.(3.8.2; 120)

In this passage Anna acknowledges the differing gender roles of the sexes, while claiming that Anna Dalassene transcends them.[52] She has the exceptional ability to govern, to "drive the imperial chariot," and what gives her this ability Anna also states:

> The truth is that Anna Dalassena was in any case endowed with a fine intellect and possessed besides a really first-class aptitude for governing. (3.6.2; 116)

Intellect is what Anna admires most in men and women, and it is this part of her personality which she comes to depend on most.[53] While Anna Dalassene is seen as outside typical gender roles for the women of her acquaintance, Anna gives no indication that she herself has overstepped expectations for her female gender by having intellectual interests. A superior education was her right by birth. Along with her birth, intellect is what she prized most in herself.

Women can and do break out of traditional gender roles in the *Alexiad*. Anna's alertness to women's potentials in a man's world and their capacity to supersede traditional gender roles is shown in her description of Gaita, the wife of Robert Guiscard. In the middle of her description of the siege of Dyrrachium she recounts an anecdote of how this woman dealt with cowardly soldiers:

> There is a story that Robert's wife, Gaita, who used to accompany him on campaign, like another Pallas, if not a second Athena, seeing the runaways and glaring fiercely at them, shouted in a very loud voice: "How far will ye run? Halt! Be men!" — not quite in those Homeric words, but something very like them in her own dialect. As they continued to run, she grasped a long spear and charged at full gallop against them. It brought them to their senses and they went back to fight. (4.6.4; 147)[54]

Anna admires the image of a woman warrior who dresses in armor and is not only brave but has a loud voice, albeit speaking in a strange dialect; the fact that Gaita is a foreigner perhaps makes her exotic behavior and appearance less surprising—or more credible. Anna no doubt was reminded of Athena's appearance in book 1 of the *Iliad*,[55] or of Hera's in book 5; in the former Athena "cries out with the blast of fifty men, 'Shame! Disgrace! You Argives, you degraded'!" . . . after which she mounts a chariot and spears Ares.[56] Anna's allusion to Gaita also reflects the popularity of contemporary stories of Amazons like Maximo in the epic poem *Digenes Akrites*.[57] For a woman to accompany her husband on campaign was not uncommon, but a woman riding a horse, wielding a spear, and shouting was the stuff of myth or legend. Anna tweaks the reader's sensibilities in her gender-bending story; it is intended to give the reader a good jolt, just as the voice and appearance of Gaita brought the fleeing Normans "to their senses."

Like Gaita, Irene Doukaina accompanied her husband on military campaigns, for Alexios trusted her to protect his interests as he could no other associate. She had her own galley and was brave in the face of danger, taking risks when enemy forces were nearby. Anna admired her mother's bravery:

Alexius immediately gave her permission to return to Byzantium, and she, although distraught, concealed her fear; there was no sign of it in word or manner. She was a brave and resolute woman. Like the famous one praised by Solomon in the Book of Proverbs, she displayed no womanly cowardice—the kind of thing we usually see in women when they hear some dreadful news: their very colour proclaims the timidity of their hearts and from their frequent shrieks and wails you would think the danger was closing in on them already. In this crisis, indeed she acted in a manner worthy of her courage. (15.2.2; 474)

No "womanly cowardice" affects Irene. Gendered expectations of women were hysteria and fear in the face of danger. Bravery under pressure was attached to men. Anna accepts the stereotype but admires her mother for being more like a man in this respect. Anna's tone indicates that she too values self-control and sanguinity in a dangerous situation. She herself must have faced danger when her plot against her brother was discovered, and we can imagine she handled herself with resolute control similar to her mother's. Between the lines describing her mother's reaction to danger, we read Anna's pride in her own ability to display "no womanly cowardice." The influential women in Anna's life, Maria, Anna Dalassene, and Irene are women of strength who, more like the gendered stereotype of men, take an active stance in determining much of what happens to them in their lives.

Anna's intellectual and brave mother also gave her the thing which she valued most, her royal birth. Her birth permeated Anna's consciousness and was her greatest source of pride; it is mentioned even before her zeal for learning in the Preface: "I Anna, daughter of the Emperor Alexios and the Empress Irene, born and bred in the Purple. . . ." She reminds us halfway through the *Alexiad* of her legitimacy and of the fact that she was born first and was therefore a favored child. The occasion comes in a description of the emperor's return from a campaign in 1083:

He found the empress in the throes of childbirth, in the room set apart long ago for an empress's confinement. Our ancestors called it the *porphyra*—hence the world-famous name *porphyrogenitus*. At dawn (it was a Saturday) a baby girl was born to them, who resembled her father, so they said, in all respects. I was that baby.

"I was that baby." In this short sentence Anna sums up the reason for her ambition and for writing the *Alexiad*. Mentioning her resemblance to her father emphasizes how strongly she feels about assimilating herself to him, for she believes she was born to rule. The special bond between her and her parents was established, according to Anna, at the moment of her birth or even before:[58]

I have heard my mother tell how, two days before the emperor's return to the palace . . . she was seized with the pains of childbirth and making the sign of the Cross over her womb, said, "Wait a while, little one, till your father's arrival." . . . but her own command was obeyed—which very clearly signified even in her womb the love that I was destined to have for my parents in the future. (6.8.1; 196)

Anna stresses her bond with her parents when she states, "I had beyond all doubt a great affection for both of them alike." She was likewise part of the ceremonies and observances due the monarchs.

She draws to the reader's attention the ceremonies which accompanied her birth as a royal child:

> I must tell the reader of the events that followed my birth. When all the ceremonies usual at the birth of royal children had been faithfully performed (the acclamations, I mean, and gifts and honours presented to leaders of the Senate and army) there was, I am told, an unprecedented outburst of joy; everyone was dancing and singing hymns, especially the close relatives of the empress, who could not contain themselves for delight. After a determined interval of time my parents honoured me too with a crown and imperial diadem. (6.8.3; 196–97)

Anna's nostalgic recounting of an event which took place when she was too young to remember it reminds the reader of what might have been. We read between the lines her regrets that she was never the center of the festivities welcoming a new empress or the birth of her own children. Her agenda in describing her birth and crowning becomes even clearer as she describes her betrothal to the heir to the throne:

> Constantine, the son of the former emperor Michaell Ducas, who has on many occasions been mentioned in this history, was still sharing the throne with my father; he signed notices of donations with him in purple ink, followed him with a tiara in processions and was acclaimed after him. So it came about that I too was acclaimed and the officers who led the acclamations linked the names of Constantine and Anna. (6.8.3; 197)

At this time, before the birth of the brother who displaced her as heir to the throne, Anna evokes the happy prospect of marrying Constantine, whom she adored, and of ruling with him. Her bitterness that this never happened is one source of her melancholy. It would have been both an expedient and a happy marriage, in Anna's recollection.

Marriage, as we noted especially in chapter 10, was of utmost importance for imperial daughters (*porphyrogennetai*). Anna's marriage might have put her on the throne of Byzantium, for even as the firstborn child of the emperor she could probably not hope to rule successfully alone for long. Nostalgia and melancholy pervade her descriptions of the death of her young fiancé, the prince Constantine Doukas. We recall her description of him as having "a heavenly beauty not of this world," and that "his manifold charms captivated the beholder."[59] Although learned and brave in the face of danger, Anna is deeply sentimental about the ideal marriage that escaped her and about what might have been.

Learning and birth were indeed of greatest importance to Anna. She also affirms her sense of responsibility as a historian, for example, in a brief aside during her description of the Bogomil heresy. In refusing to repeat hearsay in her writing, she pronounces,

> Historian I may be, but I am also a woman, born in the Porphyra, most honoured and first-born of Alexius' children; what was common hearsay had better be passed over in silence. (15.9.1; 500)[60]

Anna states that her role as historian binds her to the truth. She might have failed in her ambition to rule, but her determination to write her father's history will succeed, even though she knows that being a woman and a historian is atypical. Her womanhood further obligates her to fulfill both roles in such a way as to distinguish herself as a woman. She grew up influenced by other virtuous and wise women, and so her position as a singular and privileged woman is to maintain the integrity of the women of her family. In this sense she is indeed a protofeminist.[61] Anna's awareness of these many sides to her personality determines her proud tone and her passionate voice. Her voice is also one of sorrow.

Anna expresses her grief repeatedly throughout her work, so often that it casts a certain sadness over it; indeed, as the translator notes, "Tears came more easily to Anna than laughter."[62] She uses tragic Greek terms to echo her acceptance of Fate. Her melancholy is most palpable at the end of the *Alexiad* in a lament for her own life which she casts in the manner of Euripides:

> Even now I cannot believe that I am still alive and writing this account of the emperor's death. I put my hands to my eyes, wondering if what I am relating here is not all a dream. . . . My life with its great misfortunes . . . I have recorded, but as the tragic playwright says, "There is no suffering, no disaster sent from heaven the burden of which I could not bear." (15.11.21; 513–14)

Remembering Alexios's death some thirty years earlier Anna reflects that this was the beginning of her own disasters. She does not mention her exile or the failed plot against her brother's life which provoked it. She says little of her marriage to Nicephoros Bryennios, and nothing of their four children. Bryennios was apparently unwilling to join in her plot to obtain the throne. She mourns the loss of the rulers, her father and mother, and then of her husband, the Caesar, saying she would prefer to be turned to stone, like the mythical Niobe, than be alive to experience further pain:

> To endure such dangers and to be treated in an abominable way by people in the palace is more wretched than the troubles of Niobe. . . . After the death of both rulers, the loss of the Caesar and the grief caused by these events would have sufficed to wear me out, body and soul, but now, like rivers flowing down from high mountains . . . the streams of adversity united in one torrent flood my house. Let this be the end of my history, then, lest as I write of these sad events I become more embittered. (15.11.23–24; 514–15)

Her voice is deeply despondent in these last lines. Anna's intent here is probably to echo the end of the *Iliad,* where Priam and Achilles together lament their losses, recalling Niobe and her tears, now turned into stone:

> And Niobe, gaunt, worn to the bone with weeping,
> turned her thoughts to food. And now, somewhere
> lost on the crags, on the lonely mountain slopes,
> on Sipylus where, they say, the nymphs who live forever,
> dancing along the Achelous River run to beds of rest —
> there struck into stone, Niobe still broods
> on the spate of griefs the gods poured out to her. (*Iliad* 24.721–27)[63]

Anna casts herself as Niobe overcome with grief, the literary trope merging with her own feelings of despair. She finds it painful enough to recall past calamities, but even more painful considering the helplessness of her current situation. Being treated "in an abominable way by people in the palace" suggests wounds to her pride as an imperial princess. We can surmise that she was not given the respect she felt she deserved by those guarding her; or she may have been curtailed in the funds to which she had access, which would have been an insult to her pride more than a cause of physical hardship. Like Zoe in her lament as she was ferried into exile under the orders of Michael V, Anna rages against the indignity of a person of her royal birth being treated in such a demeaning fashion.

Anna's melancholy state of mind is also evident in the Preface, in which she uses the elements of water and fire to express the intensity of her mental anguish.

> The calamities of the past, in the face of this infinite disaster, I regard as a mere drop of rain compared with the whole Atlantic Ocean or the waves of the Adriatic Sea. They were, it seems, the prelude of these later woes, the warning smoke of this furnace-flame . . . parching my heart imperceptibly, although its flames pierce to the bones and marrow and heart's centre. (Preface 4.3; 21)

What calamity would inspire such rhetorical extremes in describing her present woes, experienced in her monastic retreat? What is the "infinite disaster" to which she refers? Is it loneliness? or some form of physical or emotional abuse? There is much Anna does not tell us, but her tragic voice conveys deep pain. She tries to elicit sympathy from her reader:

> My own lot has been far from fortunate in other ways, ever since I was wrapped in swaddling-clothes in the Porphyra, and I have not enjoyed good luck — although one would not deny that fortune did smile on me when I had as parents an emperor and an empress, and when I was born in the Porphyra. . . . The story of my afflictions would move no one physically to arms or battle, though it would stir the reader to weep with me. (Preface 4.1; 20–21)

Through Anna's account of her father's reign we become acquainted with her as a woman raised to a life of highest privilege, but also as a woman living in emotional pain. For consolation she clings to ideals, stories, and memories of her past but frequently alludes to her present circumstances and bitterness. Her voice is clear and insistent, addressed to the reader and to posterity, and therefore to us. Regardless of how colorful and adventurous her story seems to us almost nine hundred years later, we realize that at the time she was writing, she felt deeply troubled. Her pride and determination resonate throughout her account, in which we learn as much about Anna as about Alexios and his reign. How should we react to her anguish? Should we indeed weep with her?

## Associated Readings

*The Alexiad of Anna Comnena,* trans. E. R. A. Sewter (Penguin, 1969) (English translation).

Lynda Garland, "The Empresses of Alexios Komenos (1981–1118)," chap. 11 in *Byzantine Empresses: Women and Power in Byzantium, AD 527–1204* (New York, 1999), 180–98.

Thalia Gouma-Peterson, ed., *Anna Komnene and Her Times* (New York, 2000).

Barbara Hill, "Alexios I and the Imperial Women," in *Alexios I Komnenos,* ed. Margaret Mullett and Dion Smythe, vol. 1 (Belfast, 1996), 37–54.

Angeliki Laiou, "Introduction: Why Anna Komnene?" in *Anna Komnene and Her Times,* ed. Thalia Gouma-Peterson (New York, 2000), 1–14.

*Part IV*

# LATE BYZANTIUM (1204–1453)

### Introduction: Women's Work

The occupation of Byzantine territories by the Fourth Crusade from 1204 to 1261 ended in the retaking of the capital by Michael VIII Palaeologus and the establishment of the Palaeologan dynasty. While Byzantium would never recover from the damage done by the Latin-speaking westerners, there was now a greater flexibility within Byzantine society, due largely to the necessary opening up of channels to the cultures and countries on the borders of the shrinking empire. The last two hundred years of its existence, however, were marked by civil war and impoverishment of every resource. During this period women's perceptions of their place in society and society's attitude toward them experienced a change, as Donald Nicol has shown in his biographies of twelve aristocratic late Byzantine women.[1] Since Byzantines were conservative, especially in matters regarding traditional social roles, one would expect any change to take place rather slowly or, as in this case, as a result of new and pressing circumstances.[2]

Women's preoccupations continue to be largely with family and children, and their main sphere of influence the management of households, family finances, and their own dowries. However, increasingly women took part in public life, appearing on the street and entering into public disputes, both legal and ecclesiastical. While late Byzantine women continue in the traditional roles we have noted of wife and mother, of monastic founder or celibate nun, and occasionally of scholar, an increase is detected in the power and influence of women, until in the last decades before 1453 a closing down of their circulation in the public sphere seems to presage the end of the empire. With the encroachment of Seljuks, Mongols, and Ottoman Turks, treaties and alliances often involved arranged marriages with aristocratic Byzantine women, which were used to help keep these invaders at bay.

Information about Byzantine women of the twelfth to fifteenth centuries is confined by our sources, which mostly concern noteworthy or influential women rather than ordinary women or peasants. Some observations can be based on legal records of the period, a short treatise by Michael Psellos, and some little-consulted documents which concern women outside the capital. There are changes in the legal rights of ordinary women, in their activity in public financial enterprises, and in their access to education and travel within an increasingly expansive and international framework. Angeliki Laiou describes this new mentality:

> Social realities have changed; and the fear of women, which was still very much evi-
> dent in Psellos (along with a horror of strong-willed women) has been to some degree
> replaced by a tacit acceptance or, in the case of the aristocracy, with some respect.[3]

Although most women were illiterate, there were those well-educated women who belonged to court circles and who had power and influence in political and religious affairs. More research is needed for us to gain a better notion of learned women's roles in the Palaeologan period.[4] In the late Byzantine period women turned increasingly to religion and simultaneously to the maintenance of strong ties among relatives, as the case study of Theodora Synadene and her nunnery shows (see chapter 12). Nunneries were self-sufficient, partly because their holdings were run as businesses, as we will see when we examine the typikon of the convent of the Theotokos of Sure Hope. In chapter 13, the example of another aristocrat, Maria Palaeologina, who became Melania the Nun, reveals the roles of women in diplomacy with the Mongols, as the empire tried to save itself from the waves of invasions. First, however, it is useful to consider some options for women who were not of the higher classes of society.

To what extent were ordinary women who lived in the world engaged in economic enterprise, or what we would call gainful employment, and how were they protected by law? For the declining years before the Ottoman conquest of Constantinople in 1453 we can extrapolate from the records some of the conditions of ordinary women and their occupations.[5] Recent scholarship has been illuminating on the legislation and case studies involving women, and since we are not confined by the problem of possible bias in authorship or of ideals versus realities in considering cases upheld by courts of law, it is possible to focus on what actually happened. The rights of ordinary women as well as aristocratic women were evidently served in this way.

Laws concerning marriage, divorce, dowries, and children continued to be central to the functioning of society. Cases involving women, for example, are a high percentage of those recorded from the eleventh to the fifteenth centuries. Questions which appear in middle and late Byzantine sources involve consanguinity, the age of marriage, and women's property rights in disputes with relatives. Cases involving the accepted number of marriages indicate that while second marriages were discouraged, especially for women, in fact they were extremely common. The accepted age for a girl to marry was twelve, and a woman could be widowed and remarried several times before reaching the age of twenty. Life spans for women averaged around thirty-five years, and for men, forty-two, with the highest number of female deaths occurring between the ages of fifteen and twenty-four, the prime child-bearing years.[6] Widows actually had greater independence and legal rights than married women, and the education and support of their children were their primary responsibility.[7] A woman's ability to bear children remained her most important function, and with high mortality rates and low life expectancies, the law was applied to protect the offspring as well as the institution of marriage and the rights of widowhood.[8]

Of basic economic importance to any marriage was the woman's dowry, which was protected by law. The dowry consisted of goods, properties, or cash in addition to the groom's marriage gift, which was one-half to one-third the value of the contribution on the woman's side.[9] The dowry was designated as the woman's property and served to protect the welfare of her children. It was protected against misuse by the husband and claims by his debtors. The dowry was intended to provide stability to a family and was never intended for risky use. Dowry property could be administered by the husband, in the practice of usufruct, even though it was owned by the wife. In late Byzantium a new pattern emerges, as seen in numerous cases of women taking over the administration of their property. In the Palaeologan period, the dowry became increasingly a liquid asset. Women sometimes took charge of the usufruct of their dowry property, meaning they themselves invested in business enterprises, as, for example, by investing in shipping and trade.[10]

For the vast majority of late Byzantine women, the reality was still that they ran their households, on whatever scale was commensurate with their means. Those who could supplement the family income from their skills also worked outside the home or produced goods for sale. Women in all social groups have been shown to have participated in economic enterprise. Small businesses or trades were among the types of investments managed by women.[11] Ordinary women operated bakeries and sold fruits, vegetables, and other foodstuffs in the markets of Constantinople and participated in other forms of retail trade, thus contributing substantially to the urban economy. As for peasant women's participation in rural agricultural activities, their preparation and marketing of produce must be assumed, but the lack of records leaves this an uncertain issue. Women pursued the occupations of doctor and midwife; they also engaged in money lending.[12] We thus see greater financial activity and economic responsibility taken by women in the late Byzantine period than before. While the image projected by the Byzantines of their society is often that of a static, unchanging continuum, in actuality the situation of women evolved over the centuries.[13]

A traditional occupation of women within the home was the making of cloth, this also being a commonly encountered topos on the work that was considered acceptable for women. Although the usual model of women was that they were not involved in public enterprise, it is likely they produced cloth for sale in the marketplace. Self-sufficency within the household was not always possible or desirable when there was an outside market for women's goods.[14] An associated trade in which women participated outside the household was the manufacture of silk, which was a strictly controlled industry generally, as we learn from the ninth century *Book of the Eparch*.[15] Thebes in Greece was a manufacturing center for silk, and two twelfth-century texts brought to the attention of scholars by Charles Brand testify to the fine quality of their products and to the fate of the Theban weavers after a Norman attack. The women were carried off to Sicily to practice their craft for the Norman king, presumably in Palermo, the Norman capital.[16] Nonetheless, silk continued to be produced in Thebes, and presumably weaving it continued to be primarily a woman's occupation.

Another piece of evidence that women were weavers comes from an earlier, eleventh-century source. One of a series of short treatises by Michael Psellos describes a festival held every year on May 12 in Constantinople called the Agathe. It was celebrated by women who were engaged in the occupations surrounding cloth making.[17] This quasi-religious event involved women who were spinners, weavers, and wool carders, and it included a ceremony at a church in which there were presentations of gifts to icons, processing, singing, and dancing. A series of paintings on the outside of the church is also described. These showed women carding linen and weaving, and various stages of cloth production. They present both successful and unsuccessful workers, including the punishment of young, inept workers. Older, more experienced women who are in charge of the ceremony use the paintings as part of their explication, like a series of do's and don'ts, serving to instruct younger members of the group on proper technique. This description, although somewhat enigmatic, indicates an organized group, perhaps a guild, of women in Constantinople who are engaged in organized cloth production.[18] Such a group may have had much more ancient origins, but it is likely it was still operating in the late Byzantine period. With the possible increasing participation of women in commercial enterprise from the middle into the late Byzantine period, such festivals would have given them greater visibility and thereby an identity outside the home. The Brumalia was another pagan festival, held in the fall and involving the distribution of purple cloth to women.[19] There would have been a sense of female solidarity among ordinary women in such a guild and in such festivals.

Class distinctions gave women in different circumstances varying legal and economic possibilities, and it is as such that I refer to them as working women. Female solidarity could and probably did exist among lower-class women who were members of guilds or who sold flowers in the public market, just as much as it did among the aristocratic women who belonged to a nunnery or an extended family. As we will see in the typikon of Theodora Synadene, managing property and estates was as much a part of an abbess's activities as was providing a core for the interests of the women of her family. When they took up the monastic life, as women did increasingly in late Byzantium, they gave their dowry assets and inheritance, including property, to monasteries, at the same time giving their social group greater visibility and power.[20] Under changed economic and political circumstances, within a foundering empire, it is certain that women of all classes were no longer confined to the home and that they had material capacity to enter into economic enterprise, according to their needs and inclinations. Likewise, women like Maria could be seen as working within the diplomatic sphere when they engineered treaties with Mongol khans.

From the twelfth century on, the gynaeceum was no longer a social reality.[21] In the early period, the better off the family, the less freedom of movement and expression was allowed the women, unless they joined a nunnery. But this does not appear to have applied in late Byzantium. Legal restrictions did continue to affect women, but now as much to protect as to control them and their family interests. Conventions of modest behavior for women, while still the norm in outward appearance, in fact highlight another social reality, one in which they were free to appear and wield more power at all levels of society.[22] In the troubled final centuries, with the empire under siege from various peoples, women were freer in their movements and occupational options, but their work was still centered around the family or its surrogate, the monastery.

## Associated Readings

Angeliki Laiou, "The Role of Women in Byzantine Society," *JOB* 31 (1981): 233–60.

*Twelve*

# FOUNDING MOTHERS AND
# THE TESTIMONY OF THE TYPIKA:
# THEODORA SYNADENE

In this chapter I deal with a rare instance in which a person from the distant past emerges vividly through a single preserved object or work of art. This was the case with Anicia Juliana and her church, discussed in chapter 5, and with Anna Komnene and her *Alexiad,* in chapter 11. It is literally the case for Theodora Synadene, who lived in late thirteenth- and early fourteenth-century Constantinople, and her book known as the Lincoln College Typikon.[1] Preserved in the Bodleian Library in Oxford, the typikon is a complete text of the monastic charter of the nunnery Theodora founded around 1300, including a description of all aspects of its life and administration. She named her foundation *Theotokos tes Bebaias Elpidos,* (Mother of God of Sure Hope,) in reference to its dedication to the Virgin Mary. The foundation document composed by Theodora Synadene, the only evidence for the nunnery's existence, offers a fascinating glimpse of her primary concerns, relationships, and role in its creation, along with details of female monastic life.

Theodora's book, consisting of 12 full-page illuminated frontispieces and 151 pages of text, is factual and precise in its tone and content. It testifies to her wish for association with her large and aristocratic family, as indicated by the series of portraits appearing at the beginning of the manuscript as well as notations about the gifts made by these same personages within the text. Theodora's prime concern as founder, or *ktitor,* and first abbess of the nunnery is her daughter, Euphrosyne, who was dedicated to the Virgin Mary and to Christ when still a child. When Theodora retired to the convent after her husband's death, she took her only daughter with her. The child grew up among the nuns of her mother's foundation and succeeded her as abbess on her death. In an addendum to her mother's typikon Euphrosyne expresses her sympathy and concern for the ordinary women, her fellow nuns who were her companions in her encloistered life, by according them special respect and remembrance. Other addenda refer to the next seventy years of the nunnery's existence. The book thus represents multiple generations of involvement of the women of Theodora's family. It is also informative about monastic women of simple means and ordinary background, who, together with those noblewomen of the Synadene clan, lived in their communal retreat from the world.

In this chapter I will begin with some background, in considering the lifestyle and options available to late Byzantine women within the monastic vocation, both for the aristocracy and for ordinary women, starting with some questions: What is the evidence for the character of late Byzantine nunneries? and how did these foundations come into existence? How were they regulated and what was the normal range of conditions of life in them? Such general questions help inform my study in the second part of the chapter of the Lincoln College Typikon, the nunnery of the Theotokos of Sure Hope to which it pertained, and above all its founder, Theodora Synadene and her daughter, Euphrosyne.

In the Palaeologan period it was customary for women to leave the world late in life and enter a monastery. This custom belongs to a long tradition which took many forms, from late antiquity through early and middle Byzantine times, as we have noted earlier in this book. This chapter might thus be seen as a sequel to two earlier chapters: chapter 1, in which we considered an early female monastic, Macrina, and the nunnery she founded at Annesi in the fourth century, and chapter 7, in which the Life of Saint Irene Abbess of Chrysobalanton served as our window on female monasticism of the ninth and tenth centuries. In the Palaeologan period, entering a convent still meant a certain separation from family and friends; and as the incursions of the Turks in the provinces made life more dangerous for women, it became increasingly sought after as a vocation. A nunnery represented safety from the uncertainties and dangers of the war-worn provinces.[2] Not only virgins and widows but married women and their young daughters sought a religious life behind a convent's walls. Some privileged women maintained access to normal life and even brought their servants with them to make their monastic retreats more comfortable. Other more ordinary women had a life of hard work in return for food, shelter, and the structured life of a community. The ostensible purpose in entering a nunnery was to demonstrate religious commitment and to escape from the world; in practical terms it was a secure home, although not always a happy one, as we will see.

For young women and children, the taking of monastic vows was still regarded as marriage with Christ. The practice of a woman's taking a monastic name—that is, her name in Christ—starting with the first letter of her worldly name continued unchanged from the middle Byzantine period. Since the abbess of a nunnery was overseeing the spiritual union of her "daughters" with Christ, customs associated with the family not surprisingly extended to the monastic vocation. An entrance gift equivalent to a dowry was given to the nunnery by the woman or her family. Strict adherence to the rules of the monastery was necessary to avoid punishment or expulsion, and the abbess was both leader of the community and enforcer of its rules. The symbolic marriage of a woman to Christ involved tensions in the ensuing relationships between this substitute family represented by the nunnery and the family in the world.[3]

Various family functions were fulfilled by the nunnery, which was especially important for women who had no relatives or who came from families too poor to care for them. Family crises of various sorts—the death of a child's parents, an unwanted betrothal, the death of a spouse or child, the loneliness or destitution encountered in sickness or old age—could precipitate the decision to join a nunnery.[4] Unmarried girls who wished to take up a monastic vocation could do so of their own accord. Married women often gave up their spouses and families to join nunneries, sometimes bringing their daughters with them. Widows found solace after their losses as well as relief from financial insecurity. Yet other women took their monastic vows on their deathbeds in the hope that they would find favor with God.[5] Within the nunnery an orderly pattern of life existed, a pattern in many ways resembling the routine within a well-run household. Not only individual spiritual and material concerns were behind women's tonsure, however, for there was within the whole society a sincere, deeply rooted wish to lead an Orthodox, faithful, pious life.

Women often retained their connections with their families even in their monastic retreats. Children headed for a monastic vocation tended to join institutions in which other family members were already encloistered or with which there were other family connections. A given institution thus might become the home of multiple generations of members of the same family. When husbands and wives took monastic vows late in life they often retired to monastic institutions located near each other, retaining at least some geographic proximity in their respective retreats.[6] Ties between parents and children could be problematic, as in the case of Theodora of Thessaloniki, who joined the convent in which her daughter had already been dedicated to God; although emotional ties were forbidden within convents, she could not hide her love for her daughter and was punished by being ordered to live together with her for fifteen years without speaking to her.[7] Familial relationships in life were meant to be abandoned in favor of the monastic family, which made all nuns spiritual sisters regardless of their blood relationships. Connections between nuns and their family members in the outside world were reenforced by more lenient visiting privileges in the late than in the middle Byzantine period. Nuns could leave the convent to visit their families, even unaccompanied, and a father could regularly visit his daughter within the nunnery where she was encloistered.[8]

Unavoidable tensions were created when family members entered monastic life. A woman brought her dowry or legacy with her and donated it when she entered a convent instead of leaving it to relatives or children, thus posing a threat to the family's financial future. In other cases women left their land and other possessions to nunneries in their wills instead of to their relatives. Parents of daughters who took the veil were left without children to care for them in their old age. Children were left without caregivers when their mothers joined convents in despair at the deaths of husbands. Families and nunneries were necessarily interwoven in the many patterns of exclusion and support which existed between them.

After the death of a nun, the monastery continued to play a role in her connections to her family through commemorative practices at her tomb. Proper burial and commemoration after the death of a nun were often specified on her entering the nunnery, and sometimes were spelled out in detail in the typikon of the nunnery. Upper-class women who donated funds or material goods to the foundations they entered were assured burial within the nunnery's cemetery or church, commemoration, and prayers for their perpetual salvation. Burial took place in a monastery chapel or in the main church of the nunnery. Female family members were buried together, and for each there was a service on the anniversary of her death along with certain other observances which could be prescribed: the offering of alms to the poor, the giving of food to beggars, the distribution of *kollyba,* a mixture of grains, nuts, and honey, at the door of the chapel, and the lighting of specified numbers of candles in the church.[9] Commemorative observances were relative to the richness of the gifts or contributions made to the nunnery. Donations of objects used in the liturgies in the monastery church, such as icons, vessels, and fine woven fabrics, also helped ensure commemoration of the giver.

For particularly generous or wealthy donors, funerary chapels, or *parecclesia,* were added to existing churches to house their remains and to accommodate the services of commemoration of their patron. Examples of elegant founders' funerary chapels may still be seen in the late Byzantine parecclesia of the churches of Chora and of the Pammakaristos in Istanbul.[10] On the wall of the niche built to accommodate the sarcophagus was a portrait of the deceased, sometimes depicted along with a spouse or other family members; in some cases these were double portraits, with the deceased shown twice, once as a layperson and again as a monastic.[11] In the Chora church there are remains of fresco portraits of pairs of individuals dressed in elegant clothing, painted in niches on the walls of bays of the narthex in close proximity to their tombs.[12]

Daily life in a nunnery was regulated according to yearly cycles or patterns set by the founder's typikon or by custom, since not all nunneries had written regulatory documents. Of prime importance were the rules of enclosure and segregation of the sexes. Usually nuns were to remain within monastic walls and could leave only for occasional visits with relatives; except for the priest, spiritual confessor, and doctor, men were not admitted.[13] In reality, however, nuns could pursue charitable activities such as visiting prisoners and the sick and could go on pilgrimages to local shrines. Ceremonial occasions, such as the installation of a new abbess, required a visit to the patriarch in his palace. Funerals and commemorative services also sometimes occasioned trips outside the convent's walls. In the late Byzantine period nuns were allowed greater flexibility in visiting and other activities outside the monastery than before.[14]

In general, nuns were offered fewer opportunities for travel than monks, never undertaking, for example, a long journey to the Holy Land. They lived in a cenobitic community, sharing all aspects of life with other nuns, unlike monks, who could live in eremitic solitude in isolated places, enduring a harsh ascetic existence.[15] In the later periods there was no option for extreme isolation for a woman, as in the desert wanderings of Saint Mary of Egypt (see chapter 4). An absence of new female monastic saints in the Palaeologan period is perhaps the result of limitations on women's ability to draw notice to their exemplary virtues or dedication through the practice of extreme asceticism.[16]

Comparatively few typika survive for female monastic communities compared to male ones, but the five that do survive, spanning the twelfth to the fourteenth centuries, give valuable details of their governance.[17] The ideal communal society represented by the nunnery held sisterhood, love, equality, and religious commitment to be basic precepts of everyday life. The superior or abbess (*hegoumene*) acted as spiritual mother to the women, who served as her daughters; obedience was required of all daughters by their abbess, and their equal treatment by her and among one another was mandated by the typikon. All should receive the same food, drink, and clothing, whether they came from an aristocratic or a humble background and regardless of their age.[18] Ostensibly, these self-governing institutions were ideal societies under the control of the women who led and administered them, but such was seldom the case in actuality.

Administrative posts within the nunnery chosen by the hegoumene were the steward, or *oikonomos,* the cellarer, and the treasurer. The sacristan, or *skeuophylakissa,* looked after the holy vessels and church furnishings, disbursed the wax for services, and oversaw the documents concerning the monastery's properties.[19] The cellarer, or *kellaritissa,* maintained control of food supplies and wine. The oikonomos held the highest administrative post inside the monastery, for this position involved supervision of the finances and properties belonging to the nunnery and also of the incomes and produce coming into the monastery from its landholdings outside its walls.[20] The steward also supervised the nunnery's accounts and repairs to the buildings. Caretakers of outside holdings were accountable to her or him, for although in some cases the post was filled by a female, it was usually a male who handled the economic affairs of a nunnery. The *ecclesiarchissa* regulated the daily services with their candles and was in charge of the psalming nuns. A *trapezaria* was in charge of the preparation of the food and dining room, while the *oreiareia* received all foodstuffs, and the *oinokoa* was in charge of the wine.

Although many posts were held by women, those with most responsibility were held by men, such as that of guardian, or *ephoros*.[21] Nunneries were dependent on men as well for the performance of the liturgy and hearing confession, since women were excluded from the priesthood. The nuns were also required to be under the guidance of a spiritual father to whom they had to confess fully; the doctor serving a nunnery was also usually male.[22] Thus in the routine of daily life, female monastics, although led by an abbess, were not exclusively in control of their institutions but depended to a degree on the guidance and authority of men.

The hegoumene had the most extensive duties and responsibilities. If a female aristocrat endowed or founded a nunnery, she usually assumed the role of abbess. Otherwise the abbess would be elected by the nuns at the time of the death of the preceding one. Tremendous wealth could be transferred at the time of the founding of a monastery, including land, buildings, estates, villages, and gold. The incentives for such expenditure were both religious and social. Founding a monastery was a public demonstration of piety and of love of God, perhaps the most important precept underlying Byzantine society. The favor of God and of the Virgin Mary, to whom the institution was often dedicated, assured the founder's ultimate salvation. Prayers of monks and nuns on behalf of the laity were themselves believed to be effective intercession with God. Through the community's prayers, the soul of a founder or an abbess would receive special attention before God. While founding or endowing a nunnery has sometimes been described in modern terms as a financial bargain in which the reward was guaranteed salvation for the soul, such an approach is not in accordance with the more complicated incentives from within the society.

Another motivating factor for aristocratic foundations was that of preserving kinship ties and a sense of family.[23] By providing a place of retirement for her female relatives, the founder attracted large gifts by these women to her institution and in return ensured them and their children of a place of refuge. The conditions of life of the founder's kin would be more comfortable and flexible than those of ordinary nuns.[24] Such assurances contributed to the solidarity and prestige of a family and to the strength of its kinship ties. This beneficial arrangement evidently found favor in late Byzantine society, judging from the five surviving typika alluded to above. Financial benefits outweighed social ones, for funds or properties donated to monasteries were tax exempt, while the founder's family was insured financial security for life.[25] The monastery was a place of retirement for those wishing to leave the world without financial burdens. Even the most humble women who joined nunneries had the security of knowing they would receive decent burial and the prayers of the monastic community.

A reading of the typika makes clear that strict rules and structures characterized monastic life. Within the strict hierarchical system headed by the hegoumene there were two categories of nuns, "church nuns" and "laboring nuns."[26] Church nuns, also called psalming nuns or choir nuns, devoted themselves to the daily services, which included singing the psalms for the daily prayers and liturgies. These nuns had to be able to read and therefore normally came from a higher social background in which an education had been provided for them in childhood. The church nuns likewise held a more prestigious place in the community, and the abbess was usually chosen from among them.[27] Furthermore, a church nun led a more comfortable life than a laboring nun. The laboring nuns were expected to do all the menial tasks, such as working in the gardens, making candles, and serving the other nuns at table. Hard manual labor was performed by laboring nuns in tending the fields and gardens to procure food for the community. The work of cooking, baking, gatekeeping, and infirmary care was also supplied by nuns. Basic housekeeping, cleaning, and working with cloth were performed in the nunnery much as in the home. Spinning, weaving, and embroidery were women's work, whatever the milieu.[28] While equality and diligence were encouraged of all, in reality the laboring nuns had a much harsher life than the church nuns because of the hard physical work.[29]

Strict governance of the dining arrangements by the kellaritissa illustrates the realities of monastic discipline. For example, there were two meals a day, announced by the striking of the *semantron,* a wooden gong. There was to be no conversation during the meal, and a nun must keep her eyes cast downward on her plate alone. Complaining about the food was not tolerated, nor was eating or drinking in secret. Infringements of these rules could result in expulsion. Some wealthier nuns could obtain special consideration in receiving superior food and drink, and others were allowed extra rations because of illness, even though there was a risk of creating jealousy among those without such privileges.[30] Talking was prohibited among the nuns, at work and at meals, as this was considered to undermine the communal spirit of life; one occasion for discussion was the election of a new hegoumene, which could lead to quarrels among the nuns.

Obedience was thus the primary role of the nun. Punishments for the infringements of routine rules consisted of additional genuflections during prayers, standing all night, and withdrawal of food.[31] For laboring nuns without status, life could be difficult. Some of the ordinary women who served as laboring nuns had been sent to nunneries as a correctional measure. Women who were convicted of crimes or who were outcasts, for example, unmarried mothers or women who had been seduced, often spent their lives in nunneries. Women who lacked sufficient dowries for marriage sometimes had no recourse but to join a nunnery.[32] The hardships of monastic life were many, especially for the less privileged or ordinary women in the society, as illustrated by the typika for female monastic institutions.

While nuns found themselves ensconced in monastic institutions for a variety of reasons, many of them were able to pursue their intellectual bents behind monastic walls. The education required to read, write, and study was normally accessible to very few. Women of aristocratic background would have entered the convent with some knowledge of Scripture and often could read and write. Those of higher status, especially abbesses, were sometimes well educated, having been schooled by their fathers or by tutors. We find among Palaeologan abbesses letter writers and poets as well as hymnographers.[33] The choir nuns either came to the convent with the ability to read or were trained to do so within the convent; in addition lay girls sometimes received a basic education within convents. There was much reading aloud of Scripture, especially during meals, as a means of instruction and edification; and the reading aloud of the typikon of that particular nunnery took place on a regular basis.

Books have been ascribed to libraries of convents, some being secular works of classical authors which were owned by aristocratic women, others religious scriptures such as psalters, which were used for study by the nuns. These might have been in the personal collection of an abbess or incoming aristocratic woman; they eventually made up monastic libraries, but very small ones by today's standards. Although nuns have not been established as artists in Byzantium as they have in the medieval West, they have been recognized as authors of typika and of hymns.[34] Women, usually those from the privileged class, did have intellectual pursuits which occupied them as a part of convent life.

While less is known about late Byzantine female monastics than male, a range of sources, including typika, epistolary works, synodal acts, and saints' lives reveal much about nuns of this period. The names of about two hundred Palaeologan nuns and thirty monastic institutions have been gleaned from these sources, and it is clear there were many more. The many lower-class women who entered nunneries and pursued their daily routines are rarely named and their families are unknown.[35]

Among upper-class female monastics, empresses and princesses are naturally the best known and best documented, especially when they themselves leave records telling of their monastic activity, as, for example, in founding religious establishments or serving as their abbesses. Three royal Palaeologan women of around the turn of the foureenth century who took up the monastic vocation left different kinds of records of their activity. Two, Irene Choumnaina and Theodora Palaeologina, will be considered here briefly. The third, Theodora Synadene, will serve as the case study in the second section of the chapter.

Irene-Eulogia Choumnaina Palaeologina, the daughter of Nikephoros Choumnos, chancellor under the emperor Andronicus II, was married in 1303, at age twelve, to the emperor's son. Four years later the prince died, at which time, over the objections of her parents, Irene abruptly took religious vows and retired from the world. Using her fortune, she rebuilt the convent of Philanthropos Soter in Constantinople, which she entered as its abbess, taking the monastic name of Eulogia.[36] Her spiritual director, or mentor, was Theoleptus of Philadelphia, and although her letters to him have been lost, five of his letters to her have survived. His reply in one letter suggests her state of mind: "Having Christ, you have every blessing. What is it that you miss and you are complaining? What is it that you lack and you are upset?"[37] It was apparently not easy for Eulogia to be a patient, acquiescent nun; it is clear from Theoleptus's letters that she was impetuous and proud.[38] As the advisor dictates to Eulogia her duties and courses of action, we can sense her residual feelings of attachment to her family and possessions.

After the death of Theoleptus another spiritual advisor took his place. Her dependence on the unnamed successor for fifteen years is evident in her surviving eight letters to him and his fourteen letters to her.[39] Their correspondance gives an intimate view of her unhappy life. Especially moving is her plea for the intellectual stimulation sparked by his visits to her:

I am fond of learning and cling to it. For this reason I seek your conversation; for it is not only to my spiritual [benefit] and edification . . . but is also most erudite. . . .

I wait for your voice like the thirsty earth for the rain. . . .

I beg you for the sake of Christ Himself do not let me drown. . . . I have been thrown again deeper into the sea to drown. I have written this not with ink but with my tears.[40]

Desperation and melancholy emanate from these few phrases.

Eulogia was finally granted monthly meetings with her advisor. The princess must have found the routines of her life as an abbess intellectually stultifying as well as frustrating. Her intellectual needs were not met until she threw herself in with the Hesychast movement, a politico-religious conflict of the mid–fourteenth century, becoming one of its most passionate defenders. Although her theological position gained her enemies, she died in 1355 with an aura of sanctity, as miracles were said to take place at her grave.[41] Eulogia's correspondence affords an intimate glimpse of some of the realities of the life of an aristocratic woman who pursued her vocation in monasticism for more than fifty years and was able to affect controversy within the greater society. They also reveal that in spite of her reputation for learning Eulogia's literary training was poor. The letters are filled with mistakes of grammar and syntax, reflecting the relatively low standards of education offered even a favored and talented daughter.[42]

Another aristocratic woman active in religious matters was the empress Theodora Doukaina Komnene Palaeologina.[43] Born about 1240, she lived an active life in two phases, her first thirty years as the wife of the emperor Michael VIII Palaeologos, who ruled from 1259 until his death in 1282, during which she bore seven children, and the last twenty, from 1282 to 1303, as dowager empress, during which time she devoted her energies to charitable works, in particular the refurbishing of monasteries. Theodora's name occurs on the seals of administrative documents of monasteries around the empire, showing that she took a special interest in endowing religious institutions; more are preserved for her than for any other empress.[44] After her husband's death and the accession of her son as the emperor Andronicus II Palaeologus, she undertook the renovation of the monastery of Lips in Consantinople, or Fenari Isa Camii, as the mosque complex is called today.

The monastery had been founded in the tenth century, and Theodora undertook to rebuild and refound it as a nunnery, adding her own church dedicated to Saint John the Baptist. We know of Theodora's activity from the typikon of the associated nunnery dedicated to the Theotokos.[45] The typikon of the nunnery of Lips, dated between 1294 and 1301, was drafted according to her instructions and gives specifications as to the numbers and roles of the nuns. Fifty nuns were specified by the typikon, of whom thirty were to be choir sisters; the remaining twenty were to perform menial chores. A new church dedicated to Saint John the Baptist was built adjacent to the preexisting church of the Theotokos, and two priests were assigned to each. The emperor was designated as the protector of the nunnery, and the positions of treasurer, church director, and sacristan were given to nuns, while the steward was to be a layman. Attached to the complex was a hospital for the treatment of laywomen; a further charitable activity was to dispense food to the poor.[46]

The church of Saint John the Baptist was planned as the mausoleum for Theodora's family, and she allotted funds for the memorial services for herself and her descendants. Her own tomb was constructed before her death in a niche on the south side of the church.[47] She anticipated that her children and their spouses and her mother and brother would all be buried and commemorated there, making this a dynastic mausoleum comparable to that at the Comnenian-sponsored Pantocrator monastery built two centuries earlier. The typikon also specified a number of properties she donated for the maintenance of the nunnery, from villages to a fish hatchery, indicating how great was the wealth accumulated by this dowager empress. An appendix to this typikon specifies the restoration of the convent of Saints Cosmas and Damian in Constantinople as a sister institution housing thirty nuns and served by two priests.[48] Thus at least two religious foundations depended on the support of Theodora.

A monody written by the statesman and scholar Theodore Metochites and recited on the occasion of Theodora's death in 1303 offers further information on Theodora's activity. In it he mentions the numerous books and objects Theodora had commissioned during her lifetime for the churches and monasteries she restored: "careful ornaments of holy scriptures and books," "vessels and cups perfect in their purity."[49] He also mentions that Theodora herself took the monastic habit before her death and with it the name Eugenia. Her coffin is said to have been carried with ceremony through the muddy streets of Constantinople in a sleet storm.[50] No doubt there were splendid candlelit services in the church of Saint John as the former empress was buried as the nun Eugenia, attended by her son, the emperor, and the highest court officials.

## Theodora Synadene

Theodora Komnene Palaeologina Synadene, monastic founder, abbess, and author, was the niece of the emperor Michael VIII, whose wife, the empress Theodora Palaeologina, was just discussed above. The strands of her life have been pieced together partly from historical records and partly from her account in the surviving typikon of her monastery, today in the Bodleian Library.[51] A series of twelve images at the beginning of the typikon subtly affirm and lend nuance to her story, while the text, although formal and precise and based on an earlier tradition of monastic typika, reveals the conditions of life for Theodora, her daughter, and the nuns of the convent of the Theotokos of Sure Hope.[52] The woman, the text of her typikon, and its images are inseparably linked.

Born around 1265, Theodora lost her parents at an early age and was brought up in the family of the emperor, who served as her guardian. She was married in 1281 at the age of fifteen to a prominent aristocrat and military leader in the emperor's service, John Synadenos; this planned marriage was a distinguished one, for it joined five imperial families.[53] With John Synadenos, Theodora had three children: a daughter, Euphrosyne, born around 1285, and then two sons, Theodore and John. In 1290 John Synadenos died after a distinguished military career, having taken the monastic habit some time before his death. He left his twenty-five-year-old wife with three young children.

Around 1285 Theodora founded the nunnery of Theotokos tes Bebaia Elpidos, and work must have commenced soon after on this large complex of monastic buildings, which included a church, monastic dwellings, a funeral chapel of Saint Nicholas, and a bell tower. From this time on the nunnery was the prime association with the family, with much prestige accruing to the Synadenoi through it. Completed between 1295 and 1300, the convent initially accommodated thirty nuns, and Theodora joined the community, after taking the monastic name of Theodule. With her she brought her daughter, whom she had dedicated to the Virgin Mary at birth. Now, at around ten years of age, the child became the votive, or gift to God, that she had been designated. She joined the community of nuns, never having been given any name other than her monastic name, Euphrosyne. She spent the rest of her life in the nunnery, becoming abbess herself after her mother's death, when she was around forty-seven years old. The date of her death is unknown.

About 1300, after mother and daughter had left the world to live in the convent of the Theotokos of Sure Hope, Theodora composed the typikon, making provision for every detail of its daily life and administration. Her love and concern for her daughter are evident, as is her concern for eternal and proper commemoration of herself and her family members after their deaths. Family concerns outweigh all others and are her great source of pride.[54] Over the following three decades the nunnery prospered and became, through Theodora's efforts and cultivation, the "spiritual center of the family."[55]

Theodora revised and completed her typikon about 1330, bringing it up to date with commemorations of deceased relatives. Great prominence is given to provisions for commemoration of recently deceased family members in the text of the completed typikon. At this time, it has been hypothesized, she also had a luxury edition of the volume made for her son, Theodore, who served as the ephor of the nunnery, complete with a series of thirteen finely painted miniatures depicting family members, herself and her daughter in monastic garb, and the community of nuns. Shortly after Theodora's death around 1332, her daughter, Euphrosyne, now the abbess, wrote her own revisions to the typikon.[56] About 1335, probably also at Euphrosyne's instigation, a text of her mother's original typikon and her own addendum were combined and headed by thirteen portrait pages copied from the luxury edition made for Theodore. In the following generations up to the end of the century other family members added brief notices to this typikon, finally making up the manuscript we have today in Oxford. There is reason to believe that the Lincoln College Typikon was the very copy kept at the nunnery, probably in Euphrosyne's possession, where it was frequently referred to and read and the illuminated pages often handled.

As Irmgard Hutter emphasizes, this manuscript is not a luxurious edition of the typikon, but a utilitarian one. The oldest text portion, dating back to ca. 1300, was written by several hands and is filled with changes and erasures, awkwardly drawn initials, and inconsistencies. It lacks the trim appearance of Gospel manuscripts, for example. It is thought even that the nuns were the calligraphers and designers of the ornamental letters heading the various chapters, thus constituting a rare example of female scribing.[57] We do not know how long this copy was kept at the nunnery or how long the nunnery continued to function, but the last date mentioned in it is 1402. The volume was still in Constantinople in 1540 when it was copied in its entirety, but at some later time it made its way to Athens, where it was acquired by the traveler Sir George Wheler in 1676.[58] He in turn willed it to his Oxford college on his death in 1723; it was deposited in the Bodleian in 1892.

A close examination of this manuscript is rewarding. It is a small and intimate object of high artistic quality and a superb example of late Byzantine style and painting technique. Also, in its close connection with Theodora Synadene, it is highly evocative of the context and way of life she prescribes and within which this book functioned. Since images and text functioned in synergy with one another, let us consider the book as a whole. The covers of the manuscript measure 24 by 17.5 cm (9.5 by 7 inches) and are of dark reddish-brown, tooled leather stretched over wooden boards .8 cm thick. The binding has come loose from the gatherings of pages, and the little volume is worn and shiny from use. The parchment folios measure 23 by 16.5 cm (9 by 6.5 inches), and the ends, like the outside edges and corners of most leaves, are darkly stained. The volume is 7.5 cm (3 inches) thick and is easily held in one's hand, weighing no more than a pound and a half. Its appearance is unremarkable, until one encounters a blaze of color on opening to the initial folios.

On the first facing pages, folios 1 verso and 2 recto, are brightly costumed, crowned pairs of figures, man and wife (pl. 19). Each couple is silhouetted against a gleaming gold field outlined in red and measuring 7.5 by 5 inches. On 1 verso, the man on the left is dressed in tunic and mantle with a bold pattern of double-headed eagles in cinnabar-red and gold, while the woman on the right wears a long brocaded tunic and overmantle with sleeves touching the ground. His crown is an imperial stemma, and she wears a wide, ornate jeweled crown with pendilia and large gold hoop earrings. Their names and titles are inscribed beside their heads in white ink: "Constantine Komnenos Palaeologos, the all-effective sebastocrator, and father of the foundress"; "Irene Komnene Branaina Palaeologina, the sebastocratorissa and mother of the foundress."[59] These formal portraits depict the aristocratic parents of Theodora Synadene. Hovering in the air between them is the half-length figure of the Virgin holding the Christ Child. The Virgin Mary is clad in a deep reddish-brown maphorion over a blue tunic and veil. The child is clad in light brown, and the garments of both mother and son glitter with gold highlights in the sharp patterning known as chrysography. Their names are inscribed in red. The gestures of all figures indicate the interrelationship among them: Irene gestures to her right, indicating her husband; Constantine gestures upward to the Virgin and Child; and the Child, held close by his mother, blesses the pair with outstretched arms. The parents of Theodora are seen as blessed and protected by the Virgin and Christ.

The faces of the regal couple are finely but conventionally painted, with arched brows, pursed lips, and aquiline noses; the pupils of their eyes are cast slightly upward. Irene's complexion is a delicate shade of pinkish white, and Constantine's a slightly darker, tawnier hue. Individual hairs were used to paint the beard and hair of Constantine and for the modeling of Irene's cheeks. The faces of the Virgin and Child are painted in a very different style and tonality from those of the royal couple. Underpainting in deep green underlies olive-brown complexions, with contrasting dashes of red, white, and black in their expressively highlighted features and side-glancing eyes. Two distinct artistic conventions of portraiture are clearly in evidence here, the one for formal human portraits, and the other for divine figures. The entire ground is gold, with the figures painted on the gold leaf.

The page just described sets the standard for the couples depicted on the facing page and six more folios, with minor variations: 8r, 3r, 5r, 6r, 4r, and 9r. The order of the folios, which was disturbed in a rebinding, has been reconstructed. The correct order of the illuminations by category and subject is the following:[60]

| | | |
|---|---|---|
| Parents: | Irene Branaina and Constantine Palaeologos | 1v |
| Founders: | Theodora Palaeologina and John Synadenos | 2r |
| | Theodora/Theodule, John/Joacheim, Euphrosyne | 7r |
| Sons and wives: | Eudokia and Theodore Synadenos | 8r |
| | Irene and John Synadenos | 3r |
| Granddaughters and spouses: | Anna Doukaina and Manuel Asan | 5r |
| | Euphrosyne Doukaina and Constantine Palaeologos | 6r |
| | Anna Kantakouzene and Michael Philanthropenos | 4r |
| | Irene Kantakouzene and Michael Asan | 9r |
| Dedication pages: | The Virgin and Child, *Theotokos e Beaia Elpis* | 10v |
| | Theodoule and Euphrosyne presenting gifts | 11r |
| | Community of Nuns | 12r |

As this list indicates, the miniatures fall into five separate categories: parents, founders, sons and their spouses, granddaughters and their spouses, and a series of three dedication pages which depict, respectively, the Virgin of Sure Hope, the founder and her daughter, and the community of nuns. It is important to explore the content of these frontispieces, not only for their artistic subtlety, but also because of their relationship to the text of the typikon and its emphasis on family connections, monastic vocations for the women, and the protection of the Virgin and Christ.

*Fig. 42. Joacheim the Monk and Theodule the Nun, with the Child Euphrosyne Between Them, Lincoln College Typikon, Bodleian Library, Oxford, Cod. gr. 35, fol. 7r., ca. 1300–1335. (Copyright Lincoln College, Oxford, Ms Gr.35, fol.7r)*

Facing the page with the foundress's parents is a similar pair of lavishly dressed figures labeled "Ioannes Konmenos Doukas Synadenos and Megas Stratopedarches and Founder" (pl. 19, right side). He wears a red robe known as the *kabbadion,* a gold belt from which hangs a ceremonial handkerchief, and a headdress called the *skaranikon* depicting an enthroned emperor. The woman is labeled "Theodora . . . [names are too rubbed to be legible] and Foundress." She wears the same red and gold outfit as her mother on the facing page, a two-piece robe consisting of a long tunic over which is worn a long, wide-sleeved garment with a tasseled fringe. Between them is the half-length figure of the Virgin and Child labeled "Mother of God, the Sure Hope." The founders are protected by the Virgin with the special epithet, "Sure Hope," after whom they named their foundation.

Keeping in mind that the pages are not in their original order, we skip to 7r, the page which would have followed that showing the founders. This page presents an altogether different impression. In stark contrast to the bright colors of the preceding couples, this page shows two individuals, man and woman, clad in black monastic garb from head to toe (fig. 42). The gold ground seen in the preceding pages is lacking here, and the black robes are painted directly on the parchment, giving an inkier quality to these garments. Both figures gesture to a half-length Virgin and Child, "The Sure Hope," with one hand, and with the others they present a small child who stands between them. She wears a long, reddish-brown tunic and has light brown hair. Flaking of the pigment of the dress reveals that this figure, unlike the parents, is painted over gold ground. The woman leads the child by the wrist, and the man places his hand protectively on the child's head. The man is labeled "Joacheim, monk, the founder"; the inscription above the woman's head is too badly rubbed and flaked to be legible. Above the child's head can be discerned only ". . . daughter of the founders." This miniature alludes to the dedication of the daughter of John and Theodora as a child to the Virgin and Christ, The founders, now seen as Joacheim the monk and Theodule the nun, are hooded and cloaked in monastic garb, and the

*Fig. 43. Theodule and Euphrosyne, detail of color plate 20, Lincoln College Typikon, Bodleian Library, Oxford, Cod. gr. 35, fol. 11r., ca. 1300–1335. (Copyright Lincoln College, Oxford, Ms Gr.35, fol.11r)*

child is bareheaded and in the brown dress of a novice. The miniature is too badly damaged to compare the facial features with the ceremonial portraits in 2r. The page has clearly been much handled and the names abraded, probably when they were pointed out and repeatedly touched for emphasis.

The following six pages in reconstructed order show the two sons of the founders and their wives, then the four granddaughters of the founders and their husbands. The titles in each case are lengthy and, with the exception of the two sons, indicate the relationship to the foundress only, as in "daughter-in-law of the foundress," "granddaughter of the foundress," "niece of the foundress," "nephew of the foundress."

The final three folios in the series of frontispieces are grouped as two facing pages and one recto: The Virgin of Sure Hope is on 10v, facing a striking mother-daughter portrait of Theodule and Euphrosyne on 11r (see pl. 20 and fig. 43). This striking juxtaposition shows a full-length Virgin wearing her distincitve blue tunic and brown maphorion and holding a brown-clad Child. The gleaming gold background dominates the page; the footstool on which the Virgin stands is gold and studded with jewels surrounded by gold. The robes of both figures are a web of lines indicating folds and highlights which are not painted over the colored garments as one would expect, but instead scratched through the painted surfaces to reveal the gold ground underneath.[61] The Virgin wears red shoes, and the blue of her tunic is of a brilliance which indicates the pigment is most likely ground lapis lazuli. In contrast her voluminous maphorion is a dull reddish brown. The Virgin's maphorion is characteristically dark blue, and this change from the customary iconography must indicate her special role in this monastic context by the use of a modest hue associated with monastic practice; she is a "monastic" Virgin. As in the hovering half-length figures on the preceding pages, the faces are deeply shadowed in tones of olive green and brown with sharp white highlights. The Virgin's expression of gravity and concern and the expansive gesture of her left hand indicate the mother and daughter on the facing page.

On 11r, Theodora and Euphrosyne in their black, hooded monastic robes turn slightly toward the Virgin, producing the same jarring contrast as did the founders' portraits in fol. 3r, to the surrounding pages (see pl. 20, right side, and detail in fig. 43). In this case, however, there is a subtle and calculated interplay between the subjects and the color schemes across the facing pages. The mother is simply labeled "Theodule, nun and foundress." She is swathed in blackish-gray tunic and black maphorion and stares directly out at the viewer. Her face is that of an ascetic and is much paler and more elongated than in her portrait as the wife of John Synadenos in fol. 2r (compare pl. 19). The modeling in fine brushstrokes indicates her hollow cheeks. Balanced on her right arm she holds a model of the church of her nunnery which she symbolically presents to the Virgin and Child. The masonry of the little round, domed structure is pinkish-beige, and the roofs of the dome and ambulatory glow with the same lapis blue pigment as the Virgin's tunic. A prominent door with apsed recesses above and to the left is perpendicular to the main axis; a red-roofed apse and narthex are shown on left and right sides respectively. This highly colorful, decorative structure contrasts with the black of the presenter's clothing but corresponds with the color scheme of the Virgin to whom it is offered.

With her left hand Theodora grasps the wrist of her now-grown daughter, on her right, leading her forward as a second presentation to the Virgin. This nun is labeled more fully: "Euphrosyne, nun, Komnene Doukaina Palaeologina and daughter of the founders." Euphrosyne's distinguished lineage makes Theodora's gift all the more valuable before the Virgin and Christ. The younger woman, slightly shorter than her mother, has full lips and a rounded, rosy face. She carries in her left hand a bound book which she in turn presents as her gift to the Virgin. There is a blue diamond-shaped motif on its pinkish-brown cover, and the pages are blue-gray in color. This book is, of course, the typikon itself.

The book depicted within the book points to the central role played by the typikon in the lives of these two women. The ascetic and pious Theodora is demonstrably the key figure and originator of the dedications of church, child, and typikon. The Virgin holding her child, whom she offers as a sacrifice, is hailed by Theodora, who in turn offers her child as a dedication. Her gifts of the child, the church/nunnery, and the book are juxtaposed with the infant Christ in Mary's arms. Most precious to her, Theodora's aristocratic, titled daughter is presented as the "Bride of Christ." The church building she holds represents the convent and symbolizes Theodora's Sure Hope for the Virgin's protection and the salvation of her soul.[62] The book held by Euphrosyne symbolizes the way of life espoused by mother, daughter, and community. It also represents a hefty financial investment in craftsmanship, materials, and artistry, as we noted in the refinement of technique of its frontispieces, which were surely commissioned from the best available artists. Visually the two pages with their contrasting and corresponding colors, gestures, and facial expressions dramatize the roles and relationships shared among the women, human and divine beings, and tangible objects.

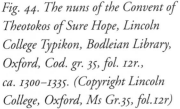

*Fig. 44. The nuns of the Convent of Theotokos of Sure Hope, Lincoln College Typikon, Bodleian Library, Oxford, Cod. gr. 35, fol. 12r., ca. 1300–1335. (Copyright Lincoln College, Oxford, Ms Gr.35, fol.12r)*

The final frontispiece in the series forms an adjunct to the dedication pages just discussed. Fol. 12r depicts the community of nuns, in a rare monastic "group portrait" (fig. 44).[63] Forming a compact phalanx, the black clad and veiled figures of twenty-seven adult nuns can be distinguished, for some are visible only as the tops of foreheads in the rear. Their garb is depicted in subtly modulated shades of black and black-brown, with fine white lines and doubled lines indicating edges of veils, contours of shoulders, and folds. Standing in front of the elder nuns are five smaller members of the community who wear various kinds of dress; the first and third from the left wear brown tunics with white veils, the second wears a black tunic and veil, the fourth a black tunic and no headcovering, and the fifth a brown tunic and black veil. These must be the novices who from early childhood proceed through various stages, each with its distinctive garb, before being fully initiated and tonsured as nuns. The brown dress with buttons up the front worn by three of these youngsters corresponds to the dress worn by the child Euphrosyne in the family portrait on 3r. In that portrait she, like the novice who is the second from the right, does not yet wear a veil, probably indicating the youngest group of the novitiate.

The group portrait, then, is an accurate record of the various ages and stages of the monastic vocation as they existed in Theodora's nunnery. The children are given special prominence in their placement in front of the elder nuns; a nun on the right bends over them as if indicating they are her special charges. All but one of the nuns in the group portrait incline their heads to the left, and many raise their hands in a gesture of prayer. The second nun from the left in the front row of elders gestures with her right hand and holds with her left a brown staff—the staff of the abbess.

The group portrait, in its orientation toward the left, echoes the attention directed toward the Virgin and Child by the mother and daughter on the preceding folio; like them, the monastic community as a whole looks to the Virgin as their Sure Hope. The implication of their gestures is that the nuns, led by their abbess, pray to her for her intercession on behalf of those souls deemed worthy of her attention. They function as a community of Brides of Christ whose prayers are constantly offered to the Virgin and Christ. In the language of images and order and positioning of the manuscript's illuminations, the group portrait turns back toward the founders and their many family members, expressing the assurance of perpetual remembrances and prayers of the community of nuns, particularly on behalf of the founders and their family members depicted on the preceding pages, and thus encompassing the whole series of portraits. The illuminated pages thus function in a series of complex and subtle interrelationships expressing visually the hopes and beliefs of those contributing to the welfare of the nunnery.

The language and themes of the text of the typikon relate to the initial pages. Theodora begins her founder's typikon with a series of thirteen paragraphs in which she states her aims, introduces her family and her rationale and motives for founding the nunnery, and expresses the basic precepts for life within its walls. Then begins the main body of the work, which is divided into twenty-four chapters. Paragraphs are numbered by the editor for convenience throughout the document: there are 145 paragraphs; a second typikon of seven chapters, written by Euphrosyne, runs from paragraph 146 to 156, followed by some late additions (157 to 159).[64]

The table of contents of the founder's typikon is ornamented with a twisted band in red and green at the top, large red and green initial letters, and writing in two columns. The last item in the list is written in lines of decreasing length down the middle of the page, forming a V-shape (13). The whole list is apparently written by a nonprofessional scribe, possibly Theodora/Theodule or one of the nuns. It has been suggested that the ornament and initial letters were added after the pages had been bound, instead of beforehand, as is the usual practice.[65] The manuscript's irregular appearance emphasizes the compiled, utilitarian character of the volume: alterations are apparent throughout; a number of pages have been cut out; and the text was evidently written in stages. It was clearly heavily used. The book's condition represents a physical link with those women of the convent who consulted, discussed, showed, read aloud, and worked over this volume.

Theodora's introduction begins with a statement about the virtue of monastic foundation:

It seems to me that there are many fine and great ways to show our pure love for the Creator and our ardent passion for him; but nothing, I think, is better than to construct for him from the foundations divine sanctuaries and holy dwellings, sparing no expense, and to demonstrate attentive eagerness and generosity "with all one's soul (Matt. 22:37) and hands."(1)

Although phrased in the abstract, the passage serves to point out the magnitude of Theodora's contribution, for to construct buildings "from the foundations" requires greater initiative than the renovation of existing buildings, which was also a frequent practice. The ultimate achievement is to construct both a church (*theia temene*) and monastic dwellings (*oikous hierous*). Her project of constructing the buildings essential to a monastery is already an ambitious one, but Theodora performs the task "sparing no expense." She aims to produce the best money can buy. Such an act of generosity honors God, to be sure, but it also honors the donor, who thereby demonstrates her great piety in tangible form.

The convent is, however, not her only gift:

Since in some obscure fashion I conceived in the womb of my heart and gave birth to this truly good and holy and divine love and desire, I decided to construct a holy dwelling for my all-pure Lady the Mother of God, and in addition to build from the foundations a convent. It was to be a secure refuge for women who have chosen the ascetic way of life, and it was also for me and my dearly beloved and most true daughter, whom I consecrated not only from infancy, but almost from the momeent of her very birth to the all-holy Virgin and Mother of God, and through her to the God of all. (4)

Theodora's intent from the start was to provide a retreat for ascetic women recruits, for herself, and for her young daughter, whom she consecrated to the Virgin close to the time of her birth. Convent and daughter thus have parallel origins. The plan was "conceived" and "given birth" in order to honor the Virgin Mary, just as her daughter was born and dedicated to the Virgin. The dedication of both daughter and convent suggests the additional parallel: Mary's conception and dedication of "the God of all" for the salvation of humankind. The language is filled with word play and constructs concerning divine and human love and motherhood, all expressed by Theodora in the first person, as she relates the origin and fruition of her plan.

The writing of this passage of the typikon apparently takes place when she has seen her hopes realized:

I have now accomplished this task and brought to light and realization that deep-felt and old desire of mine." (4)

In the following section, Theodora terms her dedications "repayment" of her debts to the Virgin; she expresses her gratitude to her for the fortunate life she has led and for her noble and virtuous parents. Her pride is evident as she refers to their distinguished lineage, her father's title of sebastocrator given him by his brother, the emperor, and then to her marriage into another aristocratic family. The initial portraits of the typikon's frontispieces are evoked here, including the titles with family names and displaying the insignia of wealth and privilege in the portraits of her parents and herself and her husband, John Synadenos.

Theodora was orphaned when very young, and from this time the emperor served as her guardian. Imperial and family connections and titles are the focus of her reminiscences in this paragraph, which suggests she was brought up in the palace with the expectation that her eventual marriage would form an alliance useful to the emperor, as discussed in chapter 10. She seems to have accepted these circumstances, for she treats them as a blessing. Her marriage placed her in a position to make some choices. Saying little about her husband of ten years, she quickly turns to her resolution to take up monastic life:

> But when my husband died (such are the inscrutable judgments of God!), I was left alone in life, anchoring my hopes on one daughter, who is exceptionally dear to me above all others, and on my two young sons. I then decided not to remain any longer in the world, nor to live in a worldly fashion nor attach myself to its dreams, nor struggle in vain with its shadows and fantasies, but with the help of God rather to break loose from the world and be mortified to all life, and to adopt this monastic yoke. (8)

Theodora's reaction to widowhood is to decide, at the age of twenty-five, to give up her life in the world and become a nun. Disappointment with what she had hoped to do in life is evident as she mentions, "dreams," "shadows," and "fantasies." Her solace in this retreat is her daughter:

> Therefore, disregarding all delights and abandoning from my heart all the beguiling pleasures of this enjoyable and delightful life, I brought myself to this convent, and I also brought my only daughter who is good and fine in all respects, the pleasant and charming light of my eyes, my sweetest love, the flame of my heart, my breath and life, the hope of my old age, my refreshment, my comfort, my consolation. With joyful and leaping soul I dedicated her to the Mother of God and through her to Christ. . . . If she who is mystically wed to him should prove fit to please and satisfy and refresh the Bridegroom, this will be a great mercy for me in accordance with my hopes and prayers to the Mother of God, this will be the chief of her blessings on me, this will be the height of her many great instances of succor. (9)

Theodora's intense expression of love for her daughter reflects her motherly affection and delight in her child and at the same time explains her wish to see her married not in the world but to Christ, the Bridegroom. Her most precious possession is her most meaningful gift to God. Instead of seeing her daughter married as she herself had been, she prefers to take her out of circulation, and keep the child close to her as a Bride of Christ. The ancient term for the woman who leaves the world to be a monastic is still in use after a millennium.

Theodora's fondest hope is that her daughter will prove a fitting "sacrifice" and that her mystical wedding will prove pleasing to Christ. The child was so young when the decision was made that she had no awareness or understanding of the decision. The image on folio 7r (3) of the typikon showing Theodora and Joacheim clad as monastics with their little daughter between them clad in the tunic of a novice is evoked in this passage (see fig. 42); in the image the Virgin holding Christ hovers overhead, reinforcing the notion expressed here of a dedication pleasing to her and to God. The love of parents and the love of God are juxtaposed in the typikon passage as they are in the family group of the miniature. The image refers retrospectively to the decision of the parents to leave the world and to ensure the same fate for their daughter.

Having spoken of her gifts, Theodora now speaks of her expectations:

> But in this way and for these reasons the entire convent together with this divine church was constructed from the foundations and established in honor of the Mother of God. Through her powerful intercessions and protection may it be fruitful as a vineyard, having virgins and nuns within like flourishing and beautiful vine branches, teeming with numerous large and excellent bunches of grapes, to the glory of Christ and to the glory of his wholly undefiled Mother, and for the eradication of my unspeakable sins, which I have committed inasmuch as I am human and of changeable and fallible nature, and therefore I incited and provoked my Creator to anger (would that I had not!). (11)

In a conventional allusion to her sins Theodora includes the wish that the Virgin will intercede with Christ to obtain forgiveness for her human failings; she also prays for the protection of the convent and its success, using the metaphor of a fruitful vineyard. Likewise, the typikon's three dedication frontispieces on folios 10v to 12r showing the Virgin of Sure Hope, Theodule and her daughter, and the community of nuns evoke visually this relationship of protection and intercession of the Virgin for the women of the convent (see fig. 44 and pl. 20). The Virgin's gesture encompasses them all, and since she is the mother of God her power to intercede with him on behalf of the women is persuasive, providing Sure Hope for their salvation. It is in her capacity as intercessor that the Virgin's title is meaningful for the convent; she is *e bebeia elpis*, the Sure Hope.

Theodora then turns to the set of rules and regulations (*hypotyposis kai diataxis*) which she expects will be strictly maintained within the convent, not only while she is alive but for all time:

> It is time then for me to turn to my purpose towards which I was eagerly hastening. This is for me to set down a sort of rule for this convent, prescribing the exact regulations and authorized observance of all behavior and every situation therein, which our teachers received from their elders long ago. They preserved these regulations by observing them themselves well and in a manner pleasing to God, and handed them on in exact fashion to their successors as was fitting in word and deed. . . . My dear

women, if you follow these rules and regulations in the conduct of your lives and in your behavior, I know well that first of all you will act in accordance with the approval and good will of my Lady who is praised by all, and you will then act in accordance with my wishes, and in accordance with what I do and strive for most eagerly and desire.(12)

Theodora couches her rule in tradition, referring to the "elders long ago" who originated it; she assures the nuns that those who follow these rules will be obeying not only the founder but the Virgin herself. Addressing the nuns directly, she assures them that the reward for their obedience will be public praise as well as God's approval, as they set an example to others of the "angelic way of life" (12). The rules are written, she states, for the abbess and the nuns:

> This set of rules and regulations is to be a kind of reminder of pastoral administration and supervision for your superior and common teacher, and for her disciples a law of genuine submission and a lesson in pure obedience. The Mother of God herself is to be the guardian of her rules, and, as she knows best, is to wisely inspire spiritual perfection, and whatever guides and leads to the promised blessedness. (13)

While the abbess's role is meant to resemble that of a shepherd tending her flock, the nuns are reminded that they are subject to a set of laws which they must obey. The Theotokos is evoked as the overseer and inspiration behind the rules; as divine leader she supports the mortal one.

The proscriptions appearing in the rules reveal great concern about the autonomy of the convent. It is to remain "completely free and unenslaved of any power and authority here one earth" (14), implying that some monastic institutions were taken over and run by individuals, probably for their profit. She is even more specific about who might offer a threat to the convent's independence:

> Even he who is most holy patriarch at the time should take only that which he is commanded to take by the holy canons, should be content with these things alone and perforce keep his hands off the rest. (16)

The patriarch himself, head of the Orthodox Church, is cited as one who might interfere with the running of a convent or act "tyrannically and by force and for base gain" (16); the warning of this possible incursion is meant to fend off the eventuality. If someone does interfere, however, the typikon invokes the Virgin as avenger:

> He will be subject to the worst curses, and will greatly provoke divine hostility, and will find the Mother of God herself opposing him, as an avenger of such injustice and boldness. (17)

The typikon threatens retaliation for abuses. Methods ranging from curses to the maledictions of the Virgin Mary will deal with any usurper. The convent is under the powerful protection of the Mother of God

Seeking for her convent the most powerful worldly protectors as well, Theodora names her sons as its ephors or guardians:

> On occasion the frail nature of women requires the *ephoreia* and guardianship of men, to drive away to the best of their ability the insolent and greedy who are likely to attack them from time to time, through the envy and rage and cooperation of the devil who is always indignant at and envious of the good, so that the nuns may be completely liberated from troublesome and bothersome people. . . .
>
> Who else is dearer and closer and, as I have said, is better disposed to me than my dearly beloved sons, who, just as they are the heirs and successors of the family and of my other possessions, are also the heirs of the things which I have strived to accomplish to the glory of God and the salvation of souls. Therefore let the eldest of my sons be the first *ephoros* and first guardian; and after him, my second son. Then whoever of their descendants is abundantly endowed by heaven above with grace and foresight and succor, and thus by far surpasses his other relatives in power and title, and in all other ways of prosperity appears much more distinguished and notable than the others. (18, 19)

Theodora cannily specifies that the important role of ephor is to remain within the family; she names her sons as first holders of the position, then after them the criteria for choosing officeholders are family (hers), money, and distinction. She implies that the bonds of family take precedence over all other ties when it comes to guaranteeing diligence and loyalty, and that a man will prove stronger and more dependable than a woman in filling this responsible position.

As for the number of nuns in the convent, Theodora states that it should remain at thirty, and she has her reasons:

> This number [thirty] should never be exceeded nor diminished and reduced. For this number is sufficient for the demands of a cenobitic community, and does not require any increase, which would be superfluous and useless. Some of the nuns are to perform their pious duties at church offices and services, each in accordance with her knowledge and age and piety and discipline, with one of themselves as their leader. Another nun will be assigned as a prudent and faithful steward of their common property, and to care for physical necessities, another will be entrusted with the important charge of the storeroom. As for the others, the superior will assign them with much care and testing to different duties for the common good, with the cooperation and advice of the preeminent and better nuns here, not to say all of them, just as the fathers of old have taught us. (23)

The allotment of tasks allows for the efficient running of the community by thirty nuns. Theodora specifies first a leader of the church nuns, an ecclesiarchissa, and another as steward to look after property and stores. Other duties will also be assigned, with the abbess taking into account the advice of the most preeminent nuns, probably the most aristocratic women. This allocation of duties is traditional for monastic administration, stemming from ancient practice according to the "fathers of old." The abbess should be elected by the nuns and be of exemplary character and wisdom:

> It is fitting that their superior be capable of instructing the others in the noble teachings of divine philosophy, and to guide them in good works and lead them along the path of virtue. She should persuade them, not force them, teaching them a little about virtue through words, but teaching them much more with good actions, wondrously matching her words to her deeds, thus guiding and leading her followers steadily towards salvation. (24)

Qualified to teach by example, the abbess should be superior in all respects to the other nuns. The gravity of her responsibility is impressed on the community as well as on the abbess-elect, as she is officially installed by the patriarch and receives from him "the blessing and grace of authority as well as the pastoral staff" (26). A male figure again plays the principal role at an important juncture for the institution. From this time on, the community of nuns owes the new abbess unfailing obedience.

The abbess's protective role in her community is described in battle metaphors, as the typikon issues its directives to her:

> Spiritual mother, do not labor only to teach and instruct your charges all the time about this frightful war, and after arming them securely and fortifying them on all sides lead them forth to the fierce battle against demons; you should also strive to fight in their front ranks, to protect and shield them . . . through psalmody, prayer, vigil, abstinence, contrition, tears, all the other weapons of the Holy Spirit. Thus you will defeat the enemy with all your strength and utterly vanquish them, and will render your disciples invulnerable to the wounds of arrows, and make them completely safe, and totally remove them from all danger. (28)

The abbess is to act as a prophylactory. Just as the Virgin was called upon to avenge any incursions on the monastery's autonomy, the abbess takes on a military role comparable to that of a competent general with his host of effective weapons, in this case, against demons. The old image of the godly war against infidel demons is evoked in the typikon's language. After she has applied the metaphor of the general in addressing the superior, Theodora now applies a very different one, that of master artist, with language borrowed from a letter of Saint Basil:[66]

> Like a a skillful and master artist, you should look often at the lives of the most blessed and "holy" female saints, as if they were "living images" and "efficacious and inspiring figures," and examine them very clearly; thus you will make your own way of life an accurate model of them, and will adorn it with all the imperishable flowers and colors of the virtues, and thus you will make their goodness and their fair beauty your own through exact imitation. (30)

This passage depends on a principle linking Byzantine art and practice, that imitation of an image is necessary to capture and transfer the essence of an original or prototype; the highest aspiration of an icon painter or artist was likewise faithful copying of a model. In this passage filled with the language of artistic production, Theodora similarly urges the abbess to remember the virtuous qualities of female saints, and through exact imitation (*ekmimeseos*) of an accurate model (*akribeia . . . metagrapheis*) to compose her life to be like one of these "living images" (*eikonas emphyxous*). Life should imitate art in adorning itself symbolically with the beauty of virtue's imperishable "flowers and colors" (*anthesi te kai chromasi*), for color (as noted in chapter 9 above) also had spiritual value and meaning within this society.

According to Theodora's use of the metaphor of abbess as artist, the best example is what is perceived visually, translated through inspiring stories into a language of color and beauty of form in painting. Images of female saints thus make a more effective model than words. She may have been thinking of portraits of female saints painted on the interior walls of her church or of pictures seen elsewhere in portable icons, similar to the images discussed in chapter 9. By the same token, she arranged for the skillfully executed and colorful frontispieces of her manuscript, images illustrating the virtues and piety of her family and of herself and her daughter, as "efficacious and inspiring figures."

The metaphor continues as Theodora urges the nuns to make the abbess the model for their own lives:

> In the same way the nuns under our direction should look at and regard your stead-
> fast and orderly conduct and your dignified way of life as the perfect archetype, and
> should scrupulously transform their own conduct, and model their own images after
> the original charater of your goodness and virtue. Thus the many different types of
> conduct will resemble each other, and thus in a similar fashion the good character of
> life will shine upon the entire community, just as, if several artists were to paint the
> representation of one model, all the images would resemble each other. (31)

As in artistic practice, the nuns should imitate the character and virtues of the abbess in the formation of their own images (*eikonas mimetikos*). The result is similar to numerous artists (*zographoi*) painting copies of the same prototype, for the images will all resemble the model and their natures will all be comparable to that of the original, the abbess. Verisimilitude is the aim of the nun, as of the artist. These references show Theodora's awareness of the precepts associated with art within the culture, for if she sponsored a church and its embellishment and a book with lavish illustrations, she understood the functioning of images in relation to their human counterparts. In commissioning the originals of her series of frontispieces she was creating a visual and artistic parallel to the aims and accomplishments of the individuals referred to in its text.

In prescribing the abbess's relationship with the nuns she speaks metaphorically once more, this time in reference to her body:

> You will set forth this example, if you love and cherish the entire assembly of nuns
> equally and like your own limbs, as if they were your organs. As is reasonable, you

should show more honor to the nuns who are the most useful and distinguished; but you should radiate your love and sympathy equally, like the rays of the sun, not more or less, since we naturally love the limbs of our body equally, but we consider some to be more honorable than others. For we love our eyes and feet equally, but we do not deem them both worthy of the same honor, nor do we protect them in the same way, although the pain of both affects us in the same way. Therefore in accordance with this line of thought, you should care for and watch over these nuns as a true mother looks after her own daughters, and cares for them like her own limbs and organs.(35)

Theodora's maternal care for the nuns is compared to attention to her own limbs and organs. Although we know that one precept of ascetisicm was to neglect the body, Theodora here reflects on her belief that all parts of the body are important. Favoritism for some more "honorable" nuns nuances her comparison to honoring some parts of the body more than others; the eyes are presumably considered more precious to her than her feet, and so disproportionate attention to some nuns is justified, while all are loved equally. Who were these "more honorable" nuns, and how were they treated? This becomes clear later in the typikon.

The typikon stresses the nuns' obedience and through it the road to "immortality and eternal life" (39). In return the nuns can rely on the abbess to carry all their burdens and more:

She will carry your burdens, she will be your judge, your leader, your guide, your corrector, your steward, your guardian, she will be everything to you, she will substitute for your father, your mother, your brothers and sisters, your other relatives and acquaintances and friends, she will substitute for everything else; she will be your teacher, your counselor, your doctor, your consolation, your exhortation, your cure, your refreshment, your encouragement; and perhaps I should mention the greatest and most important point, that she, in imitation of Christ, "will lay down her life for you" (John 13.37) and on the Day of Judgment she will give an accounting for you to Christ, who judges all our actions impartially. (38)

The totality of worldly relationships is subsumed in the abbess's care of her "daughters of God," and in addition, she takes responsibility for divine care of the eternal soul. In return for her obedience, each nun is assured by the abbess "immortality and eternal life" (39). Just as total is the renunciation of all personal preoccupations:

Banish from your midst every rivalry and dispute, whispers and slanders and jealousies and the evil fruits of envy and hatred. Preserve with great care the most perfect communal life, in which all private property will be abolished, and every disagreement will be banished, and private friendships will be meaningless. Meaningless, too, will be the expressions "mine" and "yours," everything private, every personal possession will cease to exist, rather the principle will strongly prevail that you have everything in common, your souls, thoughts, bodies, food and other physical necessities. . . . For you have many separate bodies, but you all have one indivisible soul; you have many bodies, but the bodies are instruments of the same purpose. (46)

This longest portion of the typikon is devoted to obedience, ten chapters spelling out the ways in which a nun should give up her individuality and become instead an instrument of a higher purpose under the direction of the abbess.

After the abbess, the ecclesiarchissa, has the most authority and importance. This nun is chosen jointly by the abbess and other nuns, and Theodora specifies what qualities are desirable or necessary for this post. She should be an example of virtue, wisdom, and piety, but she needs an additional qualification:

> She should be a nun who is able to sing and chant in tune, and with skill, and is much more familiar than the others with the ecclesiastical office and rite [50]. . . . She is to assign the proper place and position to each of the choir sisters, with the knowledge and approval of the superior [51]. . . . The young nuns who devote all their efforts and zeal exclusively to chanting and to learning their letters will be under her authority and will be assigned to obey her, so that these offices may thus be performed in good order. (53)

The ecclesiarchissa bears a heavy responsibility for orchestrating the church services of the convent, on which the rhythm of life depends. The young nuns who are schooled within the convent look to her for guidance and direction; she decides the parts they will sing, their "place and position," in the orderly services in the church. Corresponding to this description is the group portrait of the nuns on folio 12r (see fig. 44) of the typikon showing the five younger nuns lined up in front of the greater assembly, with one older nun bending over them in an attitude of caring. This is probably the ecclesiarchissa shown in relation to her young charges.

Along with the ecclesiarchissa, the oikonomos plays a central role in the convent administration. Unlike the former, the steward should be a nun who "first of all has passed through youth and middle age and is already elderly, not so much in terms of actual years, but with respect to her wisdom and character." This should be a woman "with experience in practical affairs" (54). Her duty is economic management, not only of internal properties but also of external estates owned by the nunnery. The income of the nunnery depends on her shrewd administration, and the storerooms for agricultural products are entrusted to her. Record keeping, which would require mathematical skills, is her responsibility, and valuable objects of gold and silver which have come into the possession of the nunnery are to be stored in a safe place known to her and to the abbess.

Having dealt with these two important roles, Theodora distinguishes the roles of the two classes of nuns, the choir sisters and the working nuns. The choir sisters have "as their sole occupation the offices celebrated in the church" (56). Theodora instructs them to attend to their duties without regard for the sisters who wait upon them and serve them and "are thus distracted and concerned for your comfort, and for this reason are absent from the communal offices and prayers" (58). The implication here is of radical inequality in the expectations placed on the two classes of nuns. The choir nuns attend to their singing, while the working nuns serve them, enduring "every toil and labor." In terms of job difficulty, the working nuns are perceived to have a harder life than the choir nuns. While we are not told specifically what they do, we can imagine the physical labor involved in the everyday running of the nunnery. Theodora's main concern is that these working nuns should not absent themselves from the services in the church: "nor should you hear the singing of the holy hymns only from a distance" (60). She instructs them as follows:

> But when you have free time and complete leisure from your work, and it is time for an office and the wooden semantron is struck for the holy office, summoning the nuns to the service, then you should hasten as fast as possible to the sacred precincts. (61)

The working nuns are chided for working during hours "specially dedicated and consecrated to God" (63) at the same time that they are excused from attending all the services because of the demands of their physical work. These nuns perform the menial labor in lieu of servants. A third class of nuns is suggested by the passage in paragraph 61, a group that should be summoned to the service, which is presumably already attended by the singing nuns. What was this third group which was not responsible either for doing chores or for singing at the services?

Nuns who do not attend to their duties, who demonstrate "carelessness and slackness," or who break the strict rules are disciplined by the abbess:

> She should discipline and punish them, sometimes with genuflections, at other times with fasting or drinking only water, sometimes by standing vigils, and at other times other remedies appropriate to the fault. . . . the superior will expediently discipline and punish not only those who are careless and lazy, but also all the others who engage in untimely and inappropriate conversations with each other. (65)

Exhibiting laziness or carelessness or talking with another nun both merit punishment. The ban on conversation must have meant that utterances consisted mainly of singing, praying, and reading aloud from Scripture. Otherwise the nun was admonished to keep silent.

Duties of the keeper of the storeroom and the cellarer are described as those of minor officials necessary to the smooth functioning of the nunnery. The keeper of the storeroom guards and dispenses items of everyday use:

> She is to receive all the cloaks and tunics, and all the shoes, and the covers and bedding, and everything else which you assuredly need. She is also to receive all the fruit. She is to take the delivery of all these items when they come from some outside source, and after she receives them she is to keep them all with precise accounts. (68)

In this passage there is a distinction between those items produced within the nunnery and those coming from outside. The clothing and bedding were probably woven or sewn within the nunnery by the nuns, while shoes may have been made outside. Fruit is singled out as a commodity requiring special treatment, perhaps because it spoiled unless carefully stored in a cool place. The cellarer, on the other hand, is the keeper of food and wine, making sure supplies are dispensed in appropriate quantities and are served in the refectory:

> Other nuns should assist her in her duties. Of necessity she will be assisted by the nun in charge of the refectory and waiting on the sisters, who will serve the dishes and remove them again and perform other services for the pleasure and refreshment of the nuns seated in the refectory. [69]
>
> She will not be the only assistant, but also the nuns who have the task of making and distributing the communal bread, as well as the cook. (70)

In addition to the cellarer herself, a whole staff is distinguishable in this description of the management of food and meals in the refectory, for food is naturally a central concern. There are those who cook, bake, and serve. Those who prepare the food are distinct from those who serve and clear; yet another group is "seated" in the refectory and takes "pleasure and refreshment." Is this the group or class of nuns we discerned above, who have less onerous responsibilities and who serve neither as working nuns nor as choir nuns?

Finally, the gatekeeper serves as the guard of the convent. This nun keeps the keys to gates and doors; she receives them from the abbess in the morning and returns them to her in the evening, opening the gates only for essential needs and only with permission from the abbess. Theodora adds, "If security is maintained here in this way, none of the nuns will suffer any spiritual harm, nor can any monastic property at all be secretly stolen" (72). This responsibility should be filled by a person who is neither too youthful nor too old.

All the above officials of the convent are to be elected by the body of nuns, after which a solemn investment ceremony takes place, presided over by a priest:

> After the *trisagion* and a general prayer, your spiritual father, who is perforce a priest, will make the concluding prayer. Then the nun who has thus been elected to the needful service, pressing her head to the ground, she will prostrate herself three times before the all-holy icon of the Mother of God, and beg with all her soul to receive her assistance in the duties assigned to her. (74)

The investiture includes prostration before an icon of the Theotokos. The particular type of the Theotokos venerated at the nunnery was that "Of Sure Hope," the type illustrated and labeled on folio 10v (see pl. 20) among the frontispieces of the manuscript. The page showing the Virgin and Child, with the Virgin clad in a brown maphorion, the monastic type, thus exemplifies a type probably depicted in icons at the convent. It was very likely an icon with such an image of the Theotokos which was referred to in the typikon's description of the investiture ceremony. Once again, images and text work in a complementary fashion.

After procedures for investing the necessary officials, Theodora deals with another area of special concern in the daily life of the convent: visits. The correct procedures for receiving visits from relatives and for going out on visits are described in some detail. Relatives may visit with a nun if they meet in the area "between the two gates," presumably an area clearly visible to the abbess; even so, the nuns should be accompanied by a venerable elderly nun, for security (76). If a younger nun wishes to make a visit to her relatives at home "for the sake of a little relaxation," she is to be accompanied by two nuns who are to be constantly with her, and the nun who has made the visit to her family must return before nightfall and must relate every detail of the visit to the abbess (77):

> She should tell her what she was thinking about all day, and what her soul was thinking and meditating, and what words were spoken, and what matters occurred perhaps contrary to her wish, and if she remained in fear of God for the entire day, and if she was tempted to violate any of the customary rules, either because she slipped and was led into this as a result of her own indolence and laziness, or because she was carried along unwillingly by disorders and circumstances beyond her control. (77)

Accounting to the abbess for any time spent away from the convent is meant to keep a nun's life beyond reproach. The text suggests, however, that some violation of a nun's vows was suspected or anticipated on such visits. Theodora's readiness to correct any such "slips" served as a warning to those who made subsequent visits. We are not told what the punishments were for various forms of trespass. Her concern, however, manifested itself as a form of tight control.

Theodora prescribes clearly in chapter 16 that in the liturgical cycle of everyday services and prayers, the convent is to follow the Sabas Typikon, or Jersualem Typikon, the oldest and most revered pattern of observances, already established in the sixth or seventh century.[67] As a companion to Theodora's aristocratic founder's typikon, we must assume there was a companion volume, the liturgical typikon, which was consulted daily. The antiquity of this liturgical rule makes it more venerable. According to its instructions, the services and vigils should be performed by a priest who is mature, married, and dependable, for priests could be married in Byzantium. Theodora summarizes some of the prescriptions in the liturgical typikon regarding meals and fasts, especially during the Lenten season.

Diet, as we have noted earlier in the text, is of great concern, and Theodora insists on absolute equality of treatment for all the nuns regarding the quantity and quality of their nourishment (83). Meals are to be communal and an occasion for instruction:

> Sacred writings should be appointed to be read aloud. For only the book is to speak and to teach, while all of you alike are with great reverence to maintain the utmost silence, and to listen to the readings with the proverbial "pricked ears." Thus you will nourish your body with these material foods on an equal basis, and also nourish your soul equally with the incorporeal sustenance of the spiritual readings.(85).

Not only silence but also visual isolation is to be guarded:

> No one at table will be allowed to raise her eyes and look at her neighbor to see how she eats and food set before her, and what has been served her. Each nun should not only have eyes for herself alone and focus her attention on the food set before her, but should concentrate to an even greater extent on the sacred readings. (86)

The attitude to food is as controlled as are the tongue and the eyes:

> For taking of nourishment has one purpose, the satisfaction of one's needs, and moderation means to stop eating when one is still a little hungry.
> . . . you should not make eating a pleasurable end in itself, but only a means of survival, renouncing undisciplined pleasure. (86, 87)

The strict regimen outlined here with regard to food exemplifies Theodora's principle of self-deprivation, not only physically but emotionally, for the suppression of pleasure of any kind is central to her rule.

The health of the nuns overrides Theodora's strict rules, for if a nun becomes ill every effort is made to restore her to good health, including eating "healthy foods," "being taken to the bath to bathe," and the administering of "medical remedies" (90). In the context of maintenance of health we encounter special treatment of some privileged nuns:

> The superior should treat not only ailing nuns in the manner which I have described, but also women of noble families, who have been accustomed to a luxurious life in the world, if they should enter the convent, in order to dwell with you and share a communal life. If she wishes to make concessions and treat them more sympathetically for a time, and give them a modest degree of comfort, in accordance with her discretion, she has permission to do so. . . .
>   The superior should not only provide these comforts, but should also grant permission if any of them should ask to have one servant only to provide a modest amount of service and ease. But she is to make this exception only for those women who come here from a life of privilege, and in no case for anyone else. (93, 94)

The abbess may use her discretion to provide comforts and service for nuns in a special category, noble nuns. What are the circumstances under which these nuns entered the convent? Could a nun earn this privilege?

If noble nuns are treated more sympathetically (*sympathesteron*), then does the abbess consider her treatment of the other nuns less sympathetic? The harshness of the life of the nuns may be seen in contrast to that offered noblewomen. Was this strict control by the abbess a way of maintaining her authority? or was it simply traditional for the ascetic vocation? Does Theodora feel regret or compassion about the hard life she imposes on the majority of nuns of her community?

Work on behalf of the community is assumed by the abbess for all nuns. A particular kind of work is associated with the rules on clothing:

Thus all of you alike should work on behalf of the community, and with such intent you should take your work materials from the common stores. When the nun in charge of the common stores distributes these materials to you, you should keep your hands on your work, and pray aloud when this is possible. . . .

The nun in charge of the common stores will furnish you with the essential garments, providing them out of your common toil and labors, and will distribute them to you as follows. . . .

Every year each nun should receive two white tunics, worn next to the body, and also one black tunic, which we wear over the other clothes and usually call "himation." In the same way each nun is to be provided with shoes suitable for women like yourselves, two new pairs annually, and when they are worn out they should be repaired from the common stores and made new again. . . .

In addition to the garments described above, a cloak and two vests thick enough to insulate and warm the body and protect it sufficiently against the bitter cold of winter. Each nun will receive not only these items from the common stores but everything she needs to cover her head. (96, 97, 98, 99)

These simple garments are made by hand, stored, and distributed by the nuns for their own use: tunic, black himation (cloak), shoes, vest, and veil. The community of nuns depicted on 12r (see fig. 44) of the manuscript shows them dressed all in black, with the novices wearing brown tunics, which are not mentioned here. The abbess, her daughter, and the older nuns wear a high headpiece over which their veils are fastened. It is in Theodora's description in the typikon that we learn what constitutes the nuns' garb, and in the frontispieces on folios 7r, 11r, and 12r (see figs. 42–44) that we see it in use.

Mundane details are also included in the typikon. The nuns are provided with niter to wash their clothing (100) and linseed oil to light their cells; those who wish to bathe are given permission to do so four times a year. (101)

The importance of daily confession is stressed, and the choice of a spiritual father is expected of all the nuns, "a man who knows exactly how to provide wisely for your salvation" (111). Just as a priest is required for celebrations of the liturgy on Tuesday, Thursday, Saturday, and Sunday (79) and for the investiture of nuns into special offices, a male confessor attends to the spiritual direction of each of the nuns. While the abbess maintains strict control of all aspects of daily life, males are relied upon for assuming important roles within the nunnery.

On August 15, at the liturgical feast of the Dormition of the Virgin, elaborate services are held at the nunnery Of Sure Hope in honor of its divine protector and name saint, the Virgin Mary (112). The celebration includes all-night vigils and lavish illumination. Six candelabra filled with candles are lit on this day, along with other smaller chandeliers. The entire church is decorated, and incense is offered. All the nuns are given wax candles to hold during the vigil. The expense of celebrating this feast is not limited to the liturgy, for wax and oil and incense were expensive commodities, but also more expensive food than usual was consumed, and bread and wine were given to the poor at the gate. At this time, the typikon specifies, the usual priest is to be the only one to officiate at the all-night vigil, and no other priest "from outside" is to be invited. In such details, Theodora sees that every precaution is taken against intrusion and possible violation of the strict rules of closure.

In the final chapters, Theodora designates the exact arrangements for commemorations of the deceased founders and donors to the convent. Her parents are mentioned first, but their titles are not mentioned here, only their monastic names, Kallinikos and Maria (113). The service of commemoration includes a number of steps: the church is decorated, the six candelabra are prepared, the *kollyba*, a dish of sweetened grain and rasins, is made for offering in memory of the departed, eleven priests from outside are invited—but the singing nuns are not to be allowed to sing and stand together with these priests. An all-day series of services and ceremonies then takes place on the day, terminating in a costly meal in the refectory. The poor are offered bread and wine at the gate of the nunnery (114–15).

Theodora then designates the same commemoration on the anniversary of her husband, the monk Joacheim's, death as for herself. For her daughter, she designates commemorations "more lavish and splendid than those of her parents on whatever day she is transported from this life . . . in accordance with her dying instructions" (118). The two sons of the foundress and their wives are to be given the same commemorative honors as their parents at their deaths (119). The stipulations for commemoration are associated with the subjects of the most prominent portraits among the frontispieces. Theodora then turns to her bequests, which occupy all of chapter 23.

Foremost among her bequests, according to Theodora, is the typikon itself. To ensure adherence to its prescriptions regarding all matters, she instructs that it be read aloud:

> You should read this typikon aloud in the refectory more often than any other book, with all of you listening, and you should read it attentively and read it at the beginning of each month. For if my written instructions are always resounding in your ears, they will not permit forgetfulness to do her work, making you forget these instructions from reading them infrequently, and they will enable my divine purpose to be realized by you. So first of all I bequeath this typikon to you instead of great wealth and any other rich inheritance, the finest and most valuable of all my possessions. I bequeath it as a great benefit for your souls through the grace of Christ and the support and compassion of my Mother of God, for the procuring of salvation, for your greater edification, and greater security. Thus I bequeath it to my beloved sisters in Christ. (120)

By placing the book and the way of life it prescribes first in her list of bequests Theodora prioritizes the nunnery and what it represents. The nuns as heirs are the living guarantee that the book's contents will continue to be heard and respected. The book prescribes the reading of itself as perpetuation of itself, for Theodora's properties and other possessions can be preserved only if the institution survives. Likewise, her memory and those of her relatives will remain palpable only if commemorations are carried out as she has ordained. Thus Theodora's own memory, the community of nuns, the conventual possessions, and the book itself are inextricably linked.

Of her possessions she leaves half to the nuns and retains half for her own discretion:

> For your physical needs and suppport I leave you half of my entire ancestral estate called Pyrgos whatever this half might be, whether arable land or a vineyard . . . ; but the other half will be mine for now, and will be managed by me personally for the maintenance and modest comfort of myself and my dearly beloved daughter.(121)

Half of the income from the Pyrgos estate subsidizes the running of the convent, and the other half is retained by the founder and her daughter. If both women were encloistered, what expenses did they encounter that required funds equal to those needed to support the entire convent? Other possessions are divided similarly: a village called Ainos, vineyards at Selokaka, Mesomphalos, and Kanikleion and near Kosmidion; another village, Morokoumoulou (122). Her ancestral vineyard and another vineyard, both at Pegai "beyond the Queen of Cities" (Constantinople), are bequeathed in the same way. Some of the possessions listed were gifts to the nunnery from relatives, some her own inheritance. Theodora's concern that they remain consecrated to the nunnery is backed up by threats to anyone who should confiscate them, for that person will "bring down upon himself the most terrible curses and judgments, which have been brought from of old against everyone who trampled on and disobeyed the holy laws of truth and justice" (123).

Theodora reiterates those properties retained in part for her own use, mentioning in addition a "garden called Gymnou" (124). The reason for the extensive needs on her part and that of her daughter is hinted at:

> On account of the weakness of my human nature and for the care of my daughter who is most dear in every respect, and for the modest comfort and relief of her many serious illnesses, I have retained personally for myself the following properties. (124)

Theodora's "human nature" and her daughter's "many serious illnesses" (*pollon te kai megalon arrostematon*) merited the special food, bathing, and other living conditions prescribed for noble nuns earlier in the typikon and for those who were ill. What was Euphrosyne's illness? We are never told, but it is likely these women lived with personal servants, superior food and drink, and in relatively commodious appartments, perhaps even with indoor sanitary facilities, within the convent walls. Theodora guarantees her daughter a life of comfort by bequeathing her these possessions, which are in turn to be donated to whatever purpose Euphrosyne wishes at her death (124).

The agrarian character of all Theodora's possessions is evident. Farming villages and gardens must have produced the staples of the convent's diet, but what about the vineyards? The predominance of vineyards poses the question of whether the wine that was produced was all consumed by the nuns at table in the convent and on feast days, or whether the convent was running its vineyards as a business, for profit.

In closing, Theodora reminds the nuns of their predecessors who

> mocked at and crushed the satanic forces and ranks as easily as pitiable sparrows. The heroic conduct and wondrous lives of these holy women are preserved in writing for the benefit of their successors in the discourses of wise men and sacred books. (132)

Keeping the textual images of holy or saintly women, written by men, before them as their models, the nuns should emulate these female predecessors. The books which preserve their stories are revered as the keepers of an ancient tradition, and tradition was clearly expected to hold great persuasive power. Theodora's careful instructions and hortatory comments addressed to the nuns end with the prayer

> that through the precise observance of this typikon . . . in the world to come you will accompany the wise virgins into the pure and celebrated bridal chambers to rule together and be glorified together with your greatly beloved Bridegroom. (133)

As in her opening lines, she ends with the ancient reference to nuns as brides of Christ.

Theodora's appendix on commemorations of her relatives is revealing about patterns of bequest, inheritance, and monastic practice. For those who are already deceased among her "blood brothers, sisters and relatives" she specifies on what days of the year and how their individual commemorations should take place. For example, she writes of her daughter-in-law,

> On February 11 should be commemorated my beloved daughter-in-law, I mean the wife of my dearest son lord John Palaeologos, the *megas konostaulos*, lady Thomaïs Komnene Doukaina Laskarina Kantakouzene Palaeologina, who took the monastic name of Xene. The illumination should be more lavish than usual, and there should be four liturgies for her soul. For she donated the vineyard at Kanikleion of [blank] modioi. Refreshment should also be served in the nuns' refectory. (135)

Thomaïs was apparently the first wife of her son, John. His current wife, Irene, is depicted on folio 3r of the typikon with the same family names as this deceased wife—and a distinguished and aristocratic string of names they are! Did he marry his first wife's sister? Lady Thomaïs was a major donor of land, a vineyard, to the convent; before her death she took vows, probably at the convent of Sure Hope, as the nun Xene. All the women mentioned in the commemorative prescriptions took monastic names, presumably when entering Theodora's convent.

Another woman, Theodora's granddaughter and namesake, is commemorated even though she did not make a donation to the convent. She is excused from this obligation, apparently, because, as the typikon mentions, her father "will make further donations in the future" on her behalf. Perhaps she died young, but she still took a monastic name, Theodosia, before her death (136). Theodora's sister, Maria Komnene Branaina Laskarina Doukaina Tornikina Palaeologina, not mentioned otherwise, is similarly recorded as having made a donation; she took the monastic name of Mariamne before her death and received commemoration with "seven liturgies for her soul, with two candelabra" (139). There is a direct connection between gifts and commemorations in most cases, but the family ties of individuals take precedence even over their ability to make a substantial contribution.

Through the commemorative notices we receive an impression of the richness of some objects donated to the nunnery. For example, a nephew gave

> a gold icon of the all-holy Mother of God, all decorated with pearls, and with eight precious stones, four red, the other four light blue, together with a veil all covered with pearls, what they call *syrmatinon*, bearing an image of my all-holy Mother of God. (142)

The frame around the painted, gold-ground icon must have been inset with pearls and jewels. A pearl-studded veil covered the image and was drawn aside to reveal it at appropriate times. The revealing of images normally hidden under veils is occasionally mentioned in Byzantine sources. The most famous is the regular Friday unveiling of the Virgin's icon at the church of the Virgin in the Blachernai palace. Mention of this veiled icon indicates that at Theodora's church too there was a staged appearance, and disappearance, of the holy presence of the Virgin icon. It is even possible to associate a similar veiling and unveiling with Theodora's typikon itself.

On close examination of the manuscript of the typikon, I noted a peculiarity among several of the frontispiece pages. Along the tops of these pages, with their colorfully clad couples and monastic portraits, are the remains of stitching in heavy red silk, especially noticable on folios 3, 4, 5, and 11. Where the stitches themselves have disappeared on other folios, the holes remain at the tops of the pages. Curtains were apparently once sewn onto each page covering each of the images, perhaps simply as a protective measure, but there is another plausible explanation.[68] Just as the icon given by the nephew had its own veil, the colorfully gleaming frontispieces of the typikon had their own silk veils, which were parted or lifted when the manuscript was viewed. This evidence suggests that the portraits were part of private liturgical dramas as they were revealed to show to donors, and as the Virgin and Child of Bebaia Elpis were revealed to offer reassurance to the nuns of the convent or other more important visitors. Such a practice is supported by the physical evidence of the manuscript's pages.

The bejeweled icon donated to the convent by Theodora's nephew represented the Virgin and Child. We have noted that the portraits of the Virgin and Child occurring on many of the frontispieces of the typikon in half-length figures, and in the full-length figure on folio 10v, were painted in a style and technique which differ markedly from that of the worldly and monastic portraits. The faces of Virgin and Child are modeled through a deep olive green for underpainting and a convention of highlights utilizing sharp dashes of bright color; chrysography is abundant in the robes of these figures and relies on scratching through the paint layer to the gold ground. This technique is encountered in and was probably developed for painted icons on wooden panels. The divine portraits in the typikon were very likely painted by an icon painter who worked on wooden panels as well as on parchment. This technical detail further demonstrates the likelihood that the frontispiece pages of the book functioned in a similar fashion to veiled icons painted on panels.

Theodora is as precise in her description of the boundaries, or *periorismos,* of her convent as she is of the donors' gifts. On folios 156 and 157 she traces the properties abutting the boundary wall, going counterclockwise around its periphery, starting at and ending with the "great gate" of the convent; the land enclosed within the wall appears quite extensive, as it shares boundaries with not only single buildings, such as a bakery and the house of a tailor, but also with at least five other monastic houses, gardens, and vineyards (145). Her own apartments and garden occupied a separate sector at the far edge of the convent. Alterations were apparently made in the text to reflect changes in the definitions of the circuit wall. The manuscript of the typikon has a page cut out after folio 156, and the second page of the periorismos is very different in character from the first: it is unruled and written in an untidy hand, indicating a change in the boundaries or ownership of land abutting the convent. Great care and precision were applied to this copy of the typikon throughout the book's history.

Following Theodora's typikon proper, the list of commemorations, and boundary description are sections which were added after the principal text. These begin with the so-called second typikon" (*hupotyposis deutera*), written after her mother's death by Euphrosyne. This short section includes eight chapters and runs from folios 146 to 157. In it we learn the concerns of the now-grown woman who was dedicated when still a child and who joined the monastic community at around the age of ten. At the time of the writing of her typikon, Euphrosyne was around forty-four years old and was abbess of the convent.[69] Her revisions focus on the nuns of the community.

The prescribed number of nuns, which was set out in Theodora's typikon at thirty, is changed by Euphrosyne to fifty. The number had apparently already grown while her mother was still alive, and Euphrosyne is recording formally what already existed in practice:

> But while she was still alive, inasmuch as she was of a loving and compassionate disposition, she yielded to the entreaties of certain people and allowed the number to be increased to fifty. (146)

Euphrosyne firmly directs that this number is not to be exceeded in the future—but why was it raised? The nunnery must have been prosperous to allow such substantial growth in the number of its nuns. As we have noted, the section on commemorations indicates a large number of family members who made contributions to the nunnery. The "certain people" who entreated Theodora, then, may have been relatives who were taking the veil. A disproportionately large number of aristocratic ladies entering the convent may have required a larger community of choir nuns and working nuns to accommodate their needs. The growing practice of noblewomen of her family retiring to the nunnery may have necessitated the change in numbers.

Euphrosyne's next ordinance is also cast in strict terms. She excludes lay children from receiving an education at the nunnery:

> I absolutely forbid the admission of lay children for the sake of being educated and learning their letters or anything else. For I find that it is a pernicious influence on the morals and habits of the nuns. For anyone who has renounced the world once and for all, and then comes into contact again with laypeople and assumes responsibilities incongruous with our vows, and thus causes confusion within himself and obscures the light of understanding . . . should not have entered a monastery nor donned monastic habit in the first place. . . . But if certain girls should wish to be enrolled among the nuns, but want first to be educated, and learn lessons which contribute to the monastic rule, with the intention of being tonsured years later and numbered among the nuns, I fully approve and consent. (148)

Euphrosyne's insistent tone indicates that this is a matter of passionate concern to her. What caused her to change the previous policy? The nunnery must initially have taken in lay girls to give them an education, but this proved to be a source of confusion to the girls who had made a longer term commitment to the nunnery. She is very likely referring to her own experience, her own initial lack of understanding of the implications of monastic closure. Perhaps Euphrosyne herself envied these girls for having alternatives she never had, for how could a young girl have comprehended her own dedication as a sacrifice? Remembering her own fear and confusion when exposed to girls who lived in the outside world may have prompted her to change the policy on the education of girls. Her personal experience and desire to protect other young nuns from similar confusion may have been at the root of this restriction. She then turns to another aspect of monastic practice which requires a change.

Commemoration, which so preoccupied Theodora, is of concern to Euphrosyne too, but commemoration regarding not aristocratic family members, but her sisters in monastic enclosure:

> When my holy lady and mother set down instructions about the commemorations of my holy lords and ancestors, of my holy father, who was a founder, and herself, and of my dearest masters and brothers and other members of our family, she left no instructions at all about the commemorations for all of you my dearly beloved sisters and mothers. . . . Whenever any of you departs to the Lord, I order that one liturgy be celebrated daily for her soul for forty days, and forthwith her portion of food should

be distributed daily to the needy at the gate of the convent, and afterwards the deceased nun should be commemorated once a year on the anniversary of her death in perpetuity. (149)

Euphrosyne feels that honor should be paid not only to those who have made donations to the convent and who have the luxury of "their own dwellings" or apartments in it. The ordinary nuns, she believes, also merit commemoration and respect because they "endure every labor" (149) for the good of the community. This prescription makes up for the apparent neglect of commemoration of ordinary nuns prior to this time. Euphrosyne further mandates that at the great feast of the Virgin on August 15, when the founders are habitually commemorated, there should also be a separate commemoration of all the deceased nuns, her "mothers and sisters" (150). At this time, either on the feast day itself or the day after

> the illumination should be more lavish than usual, with two candelabra, and there should be refreshment for the nuns in the refectory, and three liturgies on their behalf, and a distribution to the poor at the gate of one *annonikos modios* of bread and one measure of wine. (150)

Although not as elaborate as the observances for family members, the observances for the ordinary nuns were to take place as part of the yearly liturgical pattern. In addition, offerings of consecrated bread were to be made for each of the deceased ordinary nuns on the Saturdays of Meatfare and Pentecost (151). Euphrosyne exhorts the monastic community to maintain these practices which she has instituted "out of extraordinary desire" for their salvation and as a "deed of kindness" to them. (152). On the other hand, she does not write detailed instructions for her own commemoration, merely asking that this not be performed "carelessly and indifferently and superficially"; she would, however, give instructions at the time of her death (153). The instructions, however, were not recorded in this copy of the typikon.

While deathbed vows and instructions at the end of a donor's or founder's life were ritualized in monastic practice, ordinary nuns depended on the wishes and generosity of their abbess for the rewards of commemoration. In her typikon, Euphrosyne shows sincere compassion for her sisters in enclosure, for she had spent her life from childhood among them and been taught, nurtured, and served by them. Her mother, Theodora, one surmises, was occupied to a large extent with the administration of her institution and its landholdings, leaving her daughter's care and companionship to the nuns. Euphrosyne, however, was not as involved in financial matters and materialistic concerns as her mother. She developed a different set of sensitivities and was keenly aware that the lives of her fellow nuns were harder than hers. She therefore made an effort to maintain in practice the equality among the sisters stressed in principle at the beginning of her mother's typikon. In the group portrait on folio 12 of the frontispieces, the principle of equality of the senior nuns is stressed in their almost identical appearance, along with concern for the young nuns, shown at varying stages of novitiate and subtly differentiated from one another. In its factuality and immediacy, this page, which was probably executed at Euphrosyne's request, reflects the attitude of its sponsor.

Notices of a few further gifts and commemorations comprise the remainder of the typikon. The final pages with paragraphs 157 to 159 were evidently added to the volume periodically during the fourteenth century, the last of these being dated 1402. Euphrosyne herself probably compiled the typikon up to paragraph 157 around 1335. The text of her section of the typikon, paragraphs 155 and 148 to 154, now bound out of order, is worn and abraded, although the prickings and rulings made to guide the scribe are fresh and clear. Erasures are especially notable in some of the upper margins, indicating changes and additions, and comments are written in the margins in red ink. The numbers and headings of all seven chapters of her short typikon appear not within the text, but as inscriptions in the upper, lower, and side margins, keyed to the place in the text where each chapter begins. This section of the typikon appears even messier than the preceding, longer section with its added initials with their smudged offsets. The fine cursive handwriting in the margins is likely that of Euphrosyne, who, in supervising the compiling of the frontispieces, main typikon, and her second typikon at the end, wished for greater clarity in the headings. Instead of having the document recopied, she added them herself.

The utilitarian and at times makeshift character of the Lincoln College Typikon and the relation between text and images make it a particularly informative document about late Byzantine monasticism. Although the twenty-four chapters of the first and principal typikon and twelve folios of frontispieces were produced at least thirty years apart, they complement one another perfectly. The logic of their being bound together by Euphrosyne along with her typikon for use at the convent is evident. The document represents an example of female patronage and authority in the creation, regulation, and changes to a monastic institution. Of the fifty founders' charters of monastic institutions which survive, dating from the ninth to the fifteenth century, only five female charters (for nunneries) exist and are written by women. None has illuminations that approach this one in quality or which complement so cogently the intentions of those responsible for its production.

The typikon and its miniatures are eloquent in announcing Theodora's distinguished and elite ties between her family, the nunnery, and its donors, and we are reminded continually of the close relation between text and miniatures in the subtle but precise function of the images. The language evoking the abbess as artist and the images of female saints as examples for imitation by the nuns indicate a refined awareness of the interaction between art and viewer. Viewed as both a beautifully crafted object and a text composed and compiled with great care, the Lincoln College Typikon tells an otherwise forgotten story of women's dedication, leadership, and carefully modulated use of imagery.

# Associated Readings

"Bebaia Elpis: Typikon of Theodora Synadene for the Convent of the Mother of God Bebaia
Elpis in Constantinople," in *Byzantine Monastic Foundation Documents,* trans. Alice-Mary
Talbot, ed. John Thomas and Angela Constantinides Hero (Washington, D.C., 2000),
4:1512–78.

Irmgard Hutter, "Die Geschichte des Lincoln College Typikons" *JÖB* 45 (1995): 79–114.

Iohannis Spatharakis, *The Portrait in Byzantine Illuminated Manuscripts* (Leiden, 1976), 191–
207 and pls. 141–55.

*Thirteen*

# EPILOGUE: THE "LADY OF THE MONGOLS"

From Thekla of Iconium and the success of her text in the earliest Christian times to Theodora Synadene in her fourteenth-century monastic retreat, we have noted that sources concerning women depict Christianity as a defining factor in their lives. Throughout late antiquity and the long history of the Byzantine Empire, Christian beliefs, attitudes, pursuits, and personal models appear to have been central to women's identities or at least to the definitions they were given by others within the context of a patriarchal society. In texts written by men, women's qualities were defined in a manner that kept them contained within a paradigm; men reinforced women's gendered roles and kept them from competing in a male-dominated hierarchy of power and influence. Women, however, also recognized and used their intellectual capacities and, like men, were capable of wielding power. Although female sanctity is the most consistent paradigm for women, notable exceptions such as Anicia Juliana, Theodora the empress, and Anna Komnene acted independently and with integrity and strong resolve to accomplish their objectives. Their sense of themselves surmounted society's constraints on women generally, and their actions and voices demonstrate how women could and did achieve greatness outside the patriarchal order.

Athough the evidence we have examined for women takes a multiplicity of forms and has been subject to biases and topoi on the part of authors and to conventionality on the part of artists, we still derive an impression of how women actually lived and, more important, how they thought of themselves within Byzantine society. Although most of our evidence is drawn from testimonies not intended to convey historical truth as we know it today, when seen as a continuum, the multifaceted story of women who were part of Byzantine society takes on shape and clarity. With perseverance, the modern scholar is rewarded by a composite view of these distant but not forgotten persons; with continued alertness to the possibilities, the process of inquiry will continue.

The stories gathered in this book come not from direct reporting, as in an interview or an oral history, but by more circuitous routes; they are initially obscure in their meaning, as, for example, the pursuits of the female celebrants of the festival of the Agathe discussed in the introduction to part 4 or the strange peregrinations of Mary of Egypt (see chapter 4). Recorded law cases concerning women's rights to their property are an altogether different kind of evidence, for women could and did claim what what theirs and were protected by law, especially in claims affecting their children. Because the evidence for women is sporadic and variable, and a woman's place relatively marginal, it is all the more important to channel one's efforts into investigating the historical problem of their roles through direct accounts and material remains. In this endeavor one discovers the benefits of weaving together diverse kinds of evidence and applying it by means of an eclectic and empirical method. As we have discovered, there is no lack of material and physical evidence concerning women.

Women emerge as real people who left behind varied types of records, not as representations or constructs within theorized ideologies, although these approaches also are useful. As the case studies reveal, it is possible to discover individual women and how they pursued their lives, both ordinary women and the better-documented aristocratic and imperial women. Across the spectrum of class, it is true that there is far more to marvel at, or to find scandalous, in considering royal princesses or empresses than when we extrapolate, for example, some realities of the lives of laboring nuns in the convent of Bebaia Elpidos or women of the countryside who came to the tomb of Luke of Steiris seeking to be healed. I have tried to recognize the activity of women of all walks of life, anonymous as well as named and titled, from harlots to saints, provincial women as well as cosmopolitan women of the capital. They are present and their activity is discernible—as in the case of the women who raised the child Theodore of Sykeon—if one teases out their record from the text.

Women's voices are rarely heard in first-person accounts, but listening to those that do survive helps understand specific women's concerns. Their stories provide a catalyst for imagining what women in comparable circumstances might have experienced. As in Theodora's speech during the Nika riots, even with all its difficulties of interpretation, or Zoe's lament as she is carried into exile, these voices are filtered through the agendas of male authors. In the case of Anna Komnene, on the other hand, one hears a learned woman's voice in highly stylized form intermixed with cries of frustration. Euphrosyne Synadene speaks insistently for the perpetual remembrance of the anonymous nuns in her convent in her addendum to its typikon, and Anicia Juliana urgently vaunts her family's distinction through the prolix metrical lines of her epigram inscribed in Hagios Polyeuktos. Even though the styles and modes of speaking are varied and problematic, one hears and values these voices all the more because of the overwhelming silence of women in Byzantine and medieval sources.

Art offers another kind of filter. In the artistic media with which I have dealt—mosaics, frescoes, sculpture, goldsmithing, enameling, and manuscript illumination—more varied kinds of messages are expressed about women than could ever find articulation in words. Indirect messages concerning paradigms of sanctity are found in the staring portraits of female saints in the painted churches of Cyprus, while pragmatic messages are palpable in the awe-inspiring imperial panels in Hagia Sophia in Istanbul. Multiple layers of meaning reside in the mosaics at San Vitale in Ravenna, whose paired male and female images of authority are visualized with all the badges and trappings of their exalted rank, as upholders of an Orthodox society. Much in the Byzantines' conception of images involves a visual lineage of "quotations," as well as the repetition of standard types, most of which cannot be traced because of the great losses of artworks over time. The types of depictions of women encountered in art have their own long tradition, as in the images of female saints and those of donors in Theodora Synadene's typikon. Art and imagery present a meaningful cipher for women's beliefs and prescribed roles in life and society.

Sponsorship of art by women conveys a remote but linked set of messages in various media, expressing who these women were and how they wished to be remembered, through their expenditure of wealth. Galla Placidia, Anicia Juliana, Theodora Synadene, and others sponsored projects which reveal much about them, but they do so only after close scrutiny of sources, investigation of various media, and synthesis of the evidence.

I have utilized many modes of inquiry to extract from diverse kinds of records information about Byzantine women. By examining various kinds of textual and visual evidence, each in a manner appropriate to its genre, I have intentionally created a patchwork design rather than a regular fabric and avoided the limitations of compressing the evidence into a single approach. In the process, I have determined a useful modality of approach. The resulting impression is comprehensive chronologically and contextually while eclectic in application. Women's stories perceived through the lens of literature and art, from the earliest years of Christianity in Roman antiquity through the rise of Byzantium and up to the final centuries of the empire, resonate over almost fifteen hundred years of civilization. Contextualizing the evidence according to cogent themes in four historical periods, arbitrary though these dates may be, helps provide a frame for observing changes over time. The range of topics and of individual women studied has made possible a nuanced understanding of how and where to find and recognize evidence about women. The list of associated readings at the end of each chapter illustrates possibilities for further inquiry. I have tried to demonstrate the need for maintaining an open mind and imagination, and fresh and flexible thinking about diverse kinds of testimonia. The reward is the rediscovery of specific individuals within their Byzantine contexts.

In conclusion, and as a final example of the perplexing nature of evidence about

*Fig. 45. Deesis mosaic, east wall of inner narthex, Kariye Djami, Istanbul, Turkey, 1313–20. (Courtesy Dumbarton Oaks, Byzantine Photograph and Fieldwork Archives, Washington, D.C.)*

women, I will consider Maria Palaeologina, who apparently took both routes commonly open to women of Byzantium, the conventional one of a marriage convenient to her family and then a later life in religion and religious patronage. For Maria, however, we have no informative document as we did for Macrina or Irene of Chrysobalanton, only a poem and a fragmentary mosaic. Her story, as intriguing as it is incomplete, poses the question of what it meant to be sent as a bride to live among the Mongols. A mosaic in the church of Kariye Djami in Istanbul invites us to reflect on Maria's choices and on her fate.

In the inner and outer narthexes of the well-preserved monastery church of the Chora in Istanbul, known as Kariye Djami, is an extensive series of carefully balanced and planned compositions in mosaic which have been shown by scholars to reflect the aims and designs of the founder, Theodore Metochites.[1] This elegant, jewel-like church, restored and enlarged in the years between 1316 and 1321, is an expression not only of Theodore's religious piety, but also of his pride and success as finance minister for the emperor Andronicus II Palaeologus, his artistic taste and sophistication, and his legitimate position in the succession of distinguished founders, or *ktetors,* who had embellished the monastery in previous centuries. A mosaic composition in the inner narthex of the church poses questions through its inclusion of a small image of a nun (see figs. 45 and 46).

*Fig. 46. Melane the Nun, mosaic, detail of deesis Mosaic, figure 45, Kariye Djami, Istanbul, Turkey, 1313–20. (Courtesy Dumbarton Oaks, Byzantine Photograph and Fieldwork Archives, Washington, D.C.)*

In an imposing lunette on the east wall of the inner narthex, in a prominent position adjacent to the entry door into the naos, the two principal holy personages of Byzantine Orthodoxy, Christ and the Virgin Mary, are depicted along with two smaller figures in attitudes of prayer (fig. 45).[2] Christ and the Virgin are represented in a standing position, more than twice life-size; they tower over the viewer standing in the relatively constricted space of the inner narthex. The two main figures form an abbreviated Deesis composition, with Christ standing frontally and the Virgin turned toward him in an attitude of supplication, expressing her intercessory role for those on earth. Christ is labeled with the epithet "Chalkites," linking him to a type seen over the Chalke Gate, the grand entranceway to the imperial palace of the emperors. Further imperial associations are evident in the two small figures down closer to eye level. On the left is a crowned, richly attired standing figure who is identified by his inscription: "The son of the most high emperor Alexius Comnenus, Isaac the Porphyrogennitus." Isaac Comnenus looks upward and across at Christ. This third son of Alexius I (1081–1118) and younger brother of Anna Komnene founded the Kosmosotira monastery in Constantinople; his mother, Maria Doukaina, founded the Kecharitomene monastery, as noted in chapter 11, and was also a patron of the Chora monastery. Isaac had requested that he be buried there, and although this did not happen, Isaac's portrait is a reference to the former location of his tomb as it was set up in an earlier, twelfth-century phase of restoration at the Chora. The emphasis on his imperial lineage is his principal association in this fourteenth-century context.[3]

Another phase of patronage is indicated by the kneeling figure to the right and even lower down in the composition. Her black garb, with high, black, veiled headpiece, indicates that she is a nun, but the label above her head is more problematic. The inscription, whose initial word is missing reads, ". . . of Andronicus Palaeologos, the Lady of the Mongols, Melane the nun"[4] (fig. 46). The mosaic has barely survived, for most of the mosaic cubes have been scraped away, leaving only the outline of her figure in the painted setting-bed. The tesserae of her face with its rapt expression, however, remain intact; she gazes upward toward the Virgin, who returns her gaze. It has recently been argued that Melane's special female concerns are expressed through the pictorial language of the lunette and surrounding mosaic compositions of the vaults.[5] We are concerned, however, with her designation as *kyra ton Mougoulion,* "Lady of the Mongols." Through this image we confront the experience of a Byzantine woman sent as a bride to the khan of the Mongols.

Two Byzantine women named Maria were married to Mongol khans in the thirteenth century, which generalizes their situation and makes their example more indicative. The practice of arranged foreign marriages, which I examined in chapter 10, was increasingly common in the final centuries of the empire. The two most likely candidates for this Lady of the Mongols are the illegitimate daughter of Michael VIII Palaeologus and half-sister of the emperor Andronicus II Palaeologus and the illegitimate daughter of Andronicus II, both of whom were named Maria Palaeologina. As we know, it was customary on retiring to a nunnery to adopt a monastic name beginning with the same letter or letters as one's given name; hence Maria could have become Melane. Whichever Maria/Melane is represented here, her relationship with the emperor Andronicus II Palaeologus is stressed as part of the overall imperial connotations of the mosaic.[6] Because of the missing name in the mosaic inscription and the lack of other records, we do not know for certain whether it was "sister" or "daughter." The two options involve a brief consideration of Byzantine relations with the Mongols.

The Mongols, a seminomadic people who originated in what is today northern China and were led by Ghengis Khan (d. 1227), made their way across the vast deserts and steppes of Russia invading and destroying all in their path, changing patterns of life and taking over the lands of various peoples. In 1240 they conquered Kievan Rus and by 1258 had conquered the Seljuk Empire and occupied the capital in Baghdad. In 1265, to help ensure good relations with the Persian Mongols, Michael VIII Palaeologus of Byzantium sent his illegitimate daughter Maria to Karakorum to marry the Ilkhan Hulagu. The khan died before Maria reached his court, and so she married his son, Abaga, instead. This alliance affirmed the Mongols' loyalty to the Byzantine Christians as opposed to the Moslem Turks or the Mamluks of Egypt.[7] But since the Mamluks maintained friendly relations with another, geographically closer Byzantine threat, the Tatars, or Mongols of the Golden Horde in southern Russia, it was necessary also to negotiate, around 1272, another marriage between the khan of the Golden Horde, Nogaj, and another of Michael's illegitimate daughters, Euphrosyne.[8] The Mongol threat was multiplied when the Persian Mongols turned against the empire along with their vassals the Seljuk Turks.

After the arrival of the Ottoman Turks in Asia Minor, the Persian Mongols offered one means of diverting this new and powerful enemy. It is thought that Maria, who had returned to Constantinople in 1285 after her husband Abaga's death, may have tried to persuade his successor, the Ilkhan Gazan, to help the Byzantines by sending his troops against the Turks. In the early years of the fourteenth century she played an important diplomatic role because of her ties to the Mongols. As the Turks closed in on western Asia Minor, Maria was sent to Nicaea to assure the people that help was on the way from the allied Mongols, but shows of support by the Mongols only delayed the eventual capture of these territories by the Ottoman Turks. Maria was patron at this time of the monastery of the Theotokos Panagiotissa in Constantinople, which was also known as Theotokos Mouchliotissa, St. Mary of the Mongols (whose church is still functioning), for it was dedicated to the "Virgin of the Mongols."[9] Maria/Melane was known to the Byzantines as Despina Mougoulion, or the Lady of the Mongols, and to the Mongols as Despina Khatoun.[10]

Another Maria, illegitimate daughter of Andronicus II, married Tokhtu, the Mongol khan of the Golden Horde of southern Russia, in 1297.[11] When he died she was sent out again to marry his son in 1307, but this marriage did not take place. It is thought by scholars that the earlier Maria/Melane is the one who is depicted in the narthex of the Chora church, although there is some disagreement.[12] Further marriages preserved friendly relations with the Mongols of Russia; for example, Michael VIII married one of his daughters to Ozbeg, the khan of the Golden Horde. These Mongols of South Russia remained generally sympathetic to the Byzantine cause, and marriages kept them from aligning themselves against Byzantium with either the Bulgarians, the Mongols of Persia, or the Mamluks of Egypt.[13] The upheaval caused by the Mongols was immense, and Byzantine brides were part of the diplomatic maneuvers to preserve the empire.

After her return from the Persian Mongols to Constantinople and before taking vows as Melane the nun, probably in the second decade of the fourteenth century, Maria Palaeologina, sister of the emperor Andronicus II, donated a precious Gospel Book to the Virgin of Chora, as recorded in a poem by the court poet Manuel Philes.[14] The poem is written as if spoken by a woman named Maria Palaeologina addressing her prayer to the Virgin. While the poem has been cited as evidence for the renewed devotion to the cult of the Virgin in late Byzantine times, it has not been considered as evidence about Maria's life. It was apparently meant to be recited at the time of presentation of a precious book as a gift to the Chora monastery, a thank-offering, by Maria, who says,

> It was appropriate [for me] to bring, yet with great affection,
> a gift of royal character, as if to an empress,
> for recompensation of the goods [*chariton*] I enjoyed from her [the Virgin]
> for recompensation of the innumerable dangers I am saved from
> by the alliance and the mighty strength
> of the all-powerful and ever-praised Maiden . . .

She hopes in return for her gift to receive salvation:

... I, Maria, your genuine maid-servant,
descended from the family of the Palaiologoi,
I, the empress of the whole Orient.
But with favor toward me, Empress of all, pay attention
to what I bring you with burning heart,
although at present it is not of equal value.
And make me come to dwell in the heavenly mansions,
in the never-ageing house of Eden.[15]

Through the poem Maria expresses her thanks for the benefits and salvation from dangers which she personally experienced, having been "empress of the whole Orient." This statement probably refers to the risks she undertook in traveling and living far from her home, among the Mongols of central Asia.[16]

At the time Maria dedicated the book and poem, Metochites was working on the restoration of the Chora monastery, which was also to house the famous library assembled by the statesman. Soon after, she must have taken her vows, for when Metochites commissioned the final stage of his project, he had her depicted as the Lady of the Mongols, Melane the nun in mosaics executed between 1313 and 1321. Not only was she the emperor's sister and also related to Theodore by marriage, but she was a patroness of the monastery's library, making her a fitting participant in the Deesis composition in Theodore's church.[17] Contemporaries who viewed this mosaic would have known of her eventful career before taking monastic vows. Melane's attitude of prayer toward the Virgin in the mosaic commissioned by Metochites echoes visually Philes' poem to the Virgin of Chora written in Melane's voice, as an expression of her thanks for her salvation from "innumerable dangers." Although we can only imagine what she saw and experienced as the wife of the Ilkhan Abaga and in her diplomatic negotiations in Anatolia, at least we have this fragile record indicating that Melane's work in this world was finally done.

## Associated Readings

Natalia Teteriatnikov, "The Place of the Nun Melania (the Lady of the Mongols) in the Deesis Program of the Inner Narthex of Chora, Constantinople," *CA* 43 (1995): 163–80.

David Morgan, *The Mongols* (Oxford and New York, 1986).

Robert Ousterhout, *The Art of the Kariye Camii* (London, 2002).

Ihor Sevcenko, *Theodore Metochites, the Chora, and the Intellectual Trends of His Time*, in *The Kariye Djami* (New York-Princeton, 1975), 4:19–33.

*Appendix 1. Genealogy*

# SIMPLIFIED FAMILY TREE SHOWING CONNECTIONS
# AMONG THEODOSIAN WOMEN

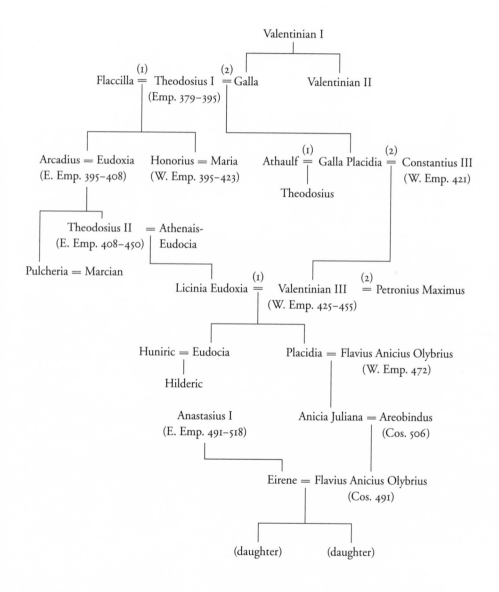

# LIST OF BYZANTINE EMPERORS AND EMPRESSES MENTIONED IN THE TEXT

306–337 Constantine I (mother: Helena) m. Fausta
daughters: Constantina, Helena
361–3 Julian m. Helena (daughter of Constantine I)

| *West* | | *East* | |
|---|---|---|---|
| 375–83 | Gratian | 379–95 | Theodosius I m. Flaccilla; Galla |
| 383–92 | Valentinian II | | daughter: Galla Placidia |
| 395–423 | Honorius | 395–408 | Arcadius m. Eudoxia |
| 421 | Constantius III m. Galla Placidia | 408–450 | Theodosius II (sister: Pulcheria) |
| | son: Valentinia III | | m. Athnais-Eudocia |
| 425–55 | Valentinian III m. Licinia Eudoxia | | daughter: Licinia Eudoxia |
| | daughters: Placidia, Eudoxia | 450–457 | Marcian and Pulcheria |
| 472 | Olybrius m. Placidia | 457–74 | Leo I m. Verina |
| | daughter: Anicia Juliana | | daughter: Ariadne |
| 475–6 | Romulus Augustulus | 474–91 | Ariadne m. Zeno |
| | (Last emperor in the West) | | |

491–518 Ariadne m. Anastasius I
518–27 Justin m. Euphemia,
527–65 Justinian I m. Theodora
565–78 Justin II m. Sophia
610–41 Heraclius m. Eudocia; Martina

717–41 Leo III m. Maria
775–80 Leo IV m. Irene
780–97 Constantine VI
797–802 Irene (widow of Leo IV; mother of Constantine VI)
829–42 Theophilus m. Theodora

842–67 Michael III m. Eudokia Dekapolitissa

867–86 Basil I the Macedonian m. Maria; Eudokia Ingerina

886–912 Leo VI m. wife #4: Zoe Karbounopsina (mother of Constantine VII)

913–59 Constantine VII m. Helena (daughter of Romanos I Lekapenos)

920–44 Romanos I Lekapenos

959–63 Romanos II m. Eudokia; Theophano

963–9 Nikephoros II Phokas m. Theophano

969–76 John I Tzimiskes m. Maria Skleraina; Theodora
    (daugher of Constantine VII)

976–1025 Basil II

1025–8 Constantine VIII, brother of Basil II m. Helena Alypia
    (daughters: Zoe, Theodora)

1028–34 Romanos III Argyros m. Zoe

1034–41 Zoe m. Michael IV Paphlagon (adopted son: Michael V Kalaphates)

1041–2 Michael V Kalaphates

1042 Zoe and Theodora (daughters of Constantine VIII and Helena Alypia)

1042–55 Zoe m. Constantine IX Monomachos (mistress: Maria Skleraina)

1055–6 Theodora (again)

1071–8 Michael VII Doukas m. Maria of Alania

1078–81 Nikephoros III Botaneiates m. Maria of Alania
    (adopted Isaac and Alexios Komnenos)

1081–1118 Alexios I Komnenos (mother Anna Dalassene) m. Irene Doukaina
    daughter: Anna Komnene

1118–43 John II Komnenos m. Irene of Hungary

1143–80 Manuel I Komnenos m. Irene of Sulzbach; Maria of Antioch


1259–82 Michael VIII Palaeologos m. Theodora Doukaina Komnene Palaeologina

1282–1328 Andronikos II Palaeologos m. Anne of Hungary; Irene of Montferrat

# NOTES

## Abbreviations

| | |
|---|---|
| *AB* | *Art Bulletin* |
| *Age of Spirituality* | Kurt Weitzmann, ed., *The Age of Spirituality: Late Antique and Early Christian Art, Third to Seventh Century* (New York, 1979) |
| *Anal.Bol.* | *Analecta Bollandiana* |
| Beckwith, *Art* | John Beckwith, *Early Christian and Byzantine Art* (1970; reprint, Penguin, 1970) |
| *BF* | *Byzantinische Forschungen* |
| *Byzance* | *L'art byzantine dans les collections publiques françaises* (Paris, 1992) |
| *Byzantion* | *Byzantion: Revue Internationale des Études Byzantines* |
| *BZ* | *Byzantinische Zeitschrift* |
| *CP* | *Classical Philology* |
| *DOP* | *Dumbarton Oaks Papers* |
| *Glory of Byzantium* | *The Glory of Byzantium: Art and Culture of the Middle Byzantine Era A.D. 843–1261*, ed. Helen Evans and William Wixom (New York, 1997) |
| *GRBS* | *Greek, Roman and Byzantine Studies* |
| *JOB* | *Jahrbuch der Österreichische Byzantinistik* |
| *JRS* | *Journal of Roman Studies* |
| Krautheimer, *Architecture* | Richard Krautheimer, *Early Christian and Byzantine Architecture* (Penguin, 1965) |
| Mango, *Art* | Cyril Mango, *The Art of the Byzantine Empire 312–1453* (Sources and Documents Series) (Toronto and London, 1986) |
| *ODB* | *Oxford Dictionary of Byzantium* |
| Ostrogorsky, *History* | George Ostrogorsky, *History of the Byzantine State* (New Brunswick, 1969) |
| *PG* | *Patrologiae cursus completus, Series Graeca*, ed. J. P. Migne (Paris, 1857–66) |
| *PL* | *Patrologiae cursus completus, Series Latina*, ed. J. P. Migne (Paris, 1844–80) |

| | |
|---|---|
| *REB* | *Revue des Etudes Byzantines* |
| *Synax. CP* | *Synaxarium Ecclesiae Constantinopolitanae*, ed. H. Delehaye, in *Propylaeum ad Acta Sanctorum Novembris* (Brussels, 1902) |
| Volbach, *Art* | W. R. Volbach, *Early Christian Art* (New York, 1979) |

## Introduction

1. Joan W. Scott, in her article "Gender: A Useful Category of Historical Analysis," in *Gender and the Politics of History* (New York, 1988), 28–50, states that gender "becomes a way of denoting 'cultural constructions'—the entirely social creation of ideas about appropriate roles for women and men"; women are gendered because they represent "the relational aspect of normative definitions of femininity," that is, they are defined through contrasts with men (32). Women may be seen within a given pattern as differentiated from the norm through binary polarities, oppositions with other women, or, as in Michel Foucault's approach aimed at deciphering a regime of power, as breaking through barriers in a process of empowerment; see Michel Foucault, *The History of Sexuality* (New York, 1978), esp. 135–59. Peter Brown's recognition of exemplars in those who shed common standards in striving for a Christlike perfection is also an essential model; see P. R. L. Brown, "The Saint as Exemplar," *Representations* I (1983): 1–25.

2. Angeliki E. Laiou, "Observations on the Life and Ideology of Byzantine Women," *BF* 9 (1985): 59–102, esp. 60.

## Introduction to Part 1: Late Antiquity

1. See in general Jean LaPorte, *The Role of Women in Early Christianity* (New York and Toronto, 1982). See also Ross S. Kraemer, *Her Share of the Blessings: Women's Religions among Pagans, Jews, and Christians in the Greco-Roman World* (New York and Oxford, 1992), esp. chap. 12, "Women's Leadership and Offices in Christian Communities," 174–90. My parallel constructions of gender for women and female saints were first presented in the paper "Byzantine Female Sanctity and Gender Construction: The Case of Thekla," *Byzantine Studies Conference, Abstracts* (Princeton, 1993), 73.

2. See *ODB*, s.v. "Thekla," 2033–34.

3. On Thekla, the writings about her, and her cult, see Stephen J. Davis, *The Cult of Saint Thecla: A Tradition of Women's Piety in Late Antiquity* (Oxford, 2001).

4. References to the *Acts of Thekla* will be made by paragraph number. The translation used is in Ross S. Kraemer, *Maenads, Martyrs, Matrons, Monastics* (Philadelphia, 1988), 280–88. The fullest edition is in *Acta Apostolorum Apocrypha*, ed. R. A. Lipsius and M. Bonnet (Leipzig, 1891). For a Greek version, see *Vie et Miracles de Sainte Thècle*, ed. Gilbert Dagron (Brussels, 1978).

5. See Kraemer, *Maenads,* 407, also Kraemer, *Blessings,* 181.

6. Kraemer, *Maenads,* 407; Stevan L. Davies, *The Revolt of the Widows: The Social World of the Apocryphal Acts* (Carbondale, 1980), 95–109.

7. For the cult, most useful and up-to-date is Davis, *Thecla,* esp. 3–80, 15–18, and notes 55 and 56, for the tradition of women's storytelling in antiquity.

8. See Davis, *Thecla;* on the material evidence, see *Age of Spirituality,* 326–27.

9. Kansas City, Nelson Gallery, Atkins Museum, no. 48.10; see *Age of Spirituality,* cat.

no. 513, p. 574. The roundel, 64.7 cm (25.5 in.) in diameter, probably served as sculptural orna-ment in a church, but its architectural context is undocumented.

10. Paris, Louvre, MNC 1926; see ibid., cat. no. 516, pp. 576–77. For a catalogue of published ampullae with Saint Thekla, see Davis, *Thecla*, 195–200.

11. *The Martyrdom of Saints Perpetua and Felicitas,* an early third-century narrative, is writ-ten primarily by the martyr Perpetua herself and demonstrates the emergence of a female view-point in conjunction with a male testimony to the factuality of her account; see Rosemary Rader, trans., in Patricia Wilson-Kastner, *A Lost Tradition: Women Writers of the Early Church* (Washington, 1981), 19–32. See also Kraemer, *Maenads,* 96–107.

12. See G. Dagron, ed., *Vie et Miracles de Sainte Thècle* (Brussels, 1978). For more on the women's participation in the Miracles, see Davis, *Thecla,* 40–41, 48–80.

13. *PG,* Symeon Metaphrastes, 821–46. The Synaxarium is a church calendar of fixed feasts with appropriate lections for each and brief notices on each saint; See also *ODB,* s.v. "Synaxarion of Constantinople,"

14. On the social role of hagiography, see most recently Peter Brown, "Arbiters of the Holy: The Christian Holy Man in Late Antiquity," in *Authority and the Sacred: Aspects of the Chris-tianization of the Roman World* (Cambridge, 1995), 55–78, 85–87.

## Chapter 1: Ascetic Women and Religious Life in Early Christianity

1. See Ramsay MacMullen, *Christianizing the Roman Empire A.D. 100–400* (New Haven, 1984), and Peter R. L. Brown, *The World of Late Antiquity A.D. 150–750* (1971; rpt. London, 1978) in general for the changes accompanying the advent of Christianity. With the exception of the period of Julian the Apostate's rule, from 361 to 363, the fourth century supported the shift to Christianity.

2. Glen W. Bowersock, "From Emperor to Bishop: The Self-Conscious Transformation of Political Power in the Fourth Century A.D.," *CP* 8 (1986): 288–307.

3. See Ross S. Kraemer, *Her Share of the Blessings: Women's Religions among Pagans, Jews, and Christians in the Greco-Roman World* (New York and Oxford, 1992), 156.

4. On asceticism, see Jo Ann McNamara, *Sisters in Arms: Catholic Nuns Through Two Mil-lennia* (Cambridge, Mass., 1996), esp. chap. 3, "The Discipline of the Desert," 61–88. See also Susanna Elm, *Virgins of God: The Making of Asceticism in Late Antiquity* (Oxford, 1994), esp. 13. See also P. Brown, "Daughters of Jerusalem: The Ascetic Life of Women in the Fourth Century," in *The Body and Society: Men, Women and Sexual Renunciation in Early Christianity* (New York, 1988), 259–84. On food and fasting among ascetic women in the medieval West, see Caroline Walker Bynum, *Holy Feast and Holy Fast: The Religious Significance of Food to Medieval Women* (Berkeley, 1987).

5. See *The Lives of the Desert Fathers: The Historia Monachorum in Aegypto,* trans. Norman Russell, intro. Benedicta Ward (London and Oxford, Cistercian Publications, 1981); the Lausiac History of Palladius is a similar compendium of ascetic lives; see Robert T. Meyer, *Palladius: The Lausiac History,* Ancient Christian Writers 34 (New York, 1964). See also Derwas J. Chitty, *The Desert a City: An Introduction to the Study of Egyptian and Palestinian Monasticism under the Christian Empire* (Crestwood, N.Y., 1966). See also *Sayings of the Desert Fathers: The Apophtheg-mata Patrum,* trans. Benedicta Ward (Kalamazoo, 1975).

6. *Lives,* Russell and Ward, 24.

7. Ibid., 67.

8. On the appeal of Christian Lives as ideological and literary exemplars, see Averil Cameron, *Christianity and the Rhetoric of Empire* (Berkeley, 1991), 141–54.

9. *Lives,* Russell and Ward, 4–10. On monasticism in general, see *ODB,* s.v. "Monasticism," 1392–94.

10. For an overview of this movement, see Averil Cameron, *The Mediterranean World in Late Antiquity A.D. 395–600* (London and New York, 1993), esp. 148–51.

11. See McNamara, *Sisters,* 48.

12. See Elizabeth A. Clark, *Women in the Early Church* (Wilmington, Del., 1983), 15–17.

13. See Paul Veyne, ed., *A History of Private Life,* vol. 1, *From Pagan Rome to Byzantium* (Cambridge, Mass., 1985), 20; on marriage, see also Gillian Cloke, *"This Female Man of God": Women and Spiritual Power in the Patristic Age, A.D. 350–450* (London, 1995), 100–111.

14. See Cloke, *Female Man of God,* 109–111.

15. Veyne, *Private Life,* 33.

16. Ibid., 40.

17. Clark, *Women in the Early Church,* 18.

18. On virginity, see McNamara, *Sisters,* esp. chap. 2, "Cult and Countercult," 34–60.

19. See Brown, "Daughters of Jerusalem," 258–84.

20. Ibid., 261.

21. See Elm, *Virgins of God,* 26–28.

22. On *parthenoi,* or virgins, within their families, see ibid., 34–36.

23. McNamara, *Sisters,* esp. chap. 3, "The Discipline of the Desert," 61–88.

24. See Brown, "Daughters of Jerusalem," 280–84. On Olympias, see esp. Elizabeth A. Clark, "Authority and Humility: A Conflict of Values in Fourth-Century Female Monasticism," *BZ* 9 (1985): 17–33.

25. See Arnaldo Momigliano, "The Life of St. Macrina by Gregory of Nyssa," in *The Craft of the Ancient Historian: Essays in Honor of Chester G. Starr,* ed. John W. Eadie and Josiah Ober (Lantham, England, 1985), 443–58, esp. 447; see also Clark, *Women in the Early Church,* 204–43.

26. See Elizabeth A. Clark, "Ascetic Renunciation and Feminine Advancement: A Paradox of Late Ancient Christianity," *Anglican Theological Review* 63 (1981): 240–57.

27. Veyne, *Private Life,* 263–87.

28. See Ross S. Kraemer, *Maenads, Martyrs, Matrons, Monastics* (Philadelphia, 1988), 241–42; also Kraemer, *Blessings,* 171–73.

29. See Aideen Hartney, "Manly Women and Womanly Men: The *subintroductae* and John Chrysostom," in *Desire and Denial in Byzantium,* ed. Liz James (Aldershot, England, 1999), 41–48.

30. The English translation used here is by Kevin Corrigan, *The Life of Saint Macrina by Gregory, Bishop of Nyssa* (Toronto, 1989). For the original Greek version, see *Grégoire de Nysse, Vie de Sainte Macrine,* ed. and trans. Pierre Maraval (Paris, 1971), or *PG* 46:959–1000. For *On the Soul and the Resurrection,* see *Nicene and Post-Nicene Fathers* (Grand Rapids, 1954), vol. 5, Gregory of Nyssa, 430–67. Quotations in this chapter will cite first the chapter and line from Maraval's Greek edition, and then page number in Corrigan's English translation, in order to make the sources easily accessible to all readers; a similar citation practice will be followed throughout this book.

31. See Patricia Wilson-Kastner, "Macrina: Virgin and Teacher," *Andrews University Seminary Studies* 17 (1979): 105–17, esp. 117.

32. Ibid., 108.

33. See Cloke, "Female Man of God," 82–86, on widows. For the precedent for the decision to remain "by herself," see Elm, *Virgins of God,* 44.

34. For the ascetic family in connection with Macrina, see ibid., 39.

35. On Basil's rules for the female ascetic community, see ibid., 68–72; on the relations between male and female communities, 75.

36. For the double monastery, see ibid., 80–102.

37. For a discussion of Western medieval writings by males concerning female saints, and the associated detectable biases and questions of differentiation of the male voice from that of the female subject, see Carolyn Walker Bynum, "Foreword," in Catherine M. Mooney, ed., *Gendered Voices: Medieval Saints and Their Interpreters* (Philadelphia, 1999), ix–xi; see also in ibid., Catherine M. Mooney, "Voice, Gender and the Portrayal of Sanctity," 1–15.

38. Elm, *Virgins of God,* 383.

## Chapter 2: Pilgrimage

1. See *ODB,* s.v. "Pilgrimage," 1676–77. For articles relevant to this chapter, see Robert Ousterhout, ed., *The Blessings of Pilgrimage,* Illinois Byzantine Studies I (Urbana, 1990). See also Alice-Mary Talbot, "Female Pilgrimage in Late Antiquity and the Byzantine Era," *Acta Byzantina Fennica,* n.s. 1 (2002): 73–88.

2. Susanna Elm, *Virgins of God: The Making of Asceticism in Late Antiquity* (Oxford, 1994), 280.

3. See John Wilkinson, "Jewish Holy Places and the Origins of Christian Pilgrimage," in Ousterhout, *Blessings of Pilgrimage,* 41–53, esp. 44–45.

4. For a study of modern Jewish pilgrimage to holy tombs, see Susan S. Sered, *Women as Ritual Experts: The Religious Lives of Elderly Jewish Women in Jerusalem* (New York, 1992), esp. 114–20. On martyria, see E. D. Hunt, *Holy Land Pilgrimage in the Later Roman Empire, A.D. 312–460* (Oxford, 1982), 101.

5. See also Sabine MacCormack, "The Organization of Sacred Topography," in Ousterhout, *Blessings of Pilgrimage,* 7–39, esp. 18.

6. For later descriptions of surviving relics, see George P. Majeska, *Russian Travelers to Constantinople in the Fourteenth and Fifteenth Centuries* (Washington, D.C., 1984).

7. See *ODB,* s.v. "Xenodocheion," 2208.

8. See Hunt, *Holy Land Pilgrimage,* esp. chap. 3, "The Journey," 50–82.

9. On pilgrim souvenirs, see Cynthia Hahn, "Loca Sancta Souvenirs: Sealing the Pilgrim's Experience," in Ousterhout, *Blessings of Pilgrimage,* 85–96, esp. 88.

10. Gary Vikan, *Byzantine Pilgrimage Art* (Washington, D.C., 1982), 13. See also Gary Vikan, "Byzantine Pilgrims' Art," in Linda Safran, ed., *Heaven on Earth: Art and the Church in Byzantium* (University Park, Penn., 1998), 229–66.

11. See Kenneth Holum, "Hadrian and St. Helena: Imperial Travel and the Origins of Christian Holy Land Pilgrimage," in Ousterhout, *Blessings of Pilgrimage,* 66–84, esp. 67.

12. See Elizabeth A. Clark, *Women in the Early Church* (Wilmington, Del., 1983), esp. 184–86, for excerpts by Socrates Scholasticus about Helena and the legend of the finding of the True Cross.

13. See Krautheimer, *Architecture,* 77–78.

14. For female pilgrims and the wish to follow female models, see Elm, *Virgins of God*, 273.

15. For the *Life of Constantine,* see E. C. Richardson, *A Select Library of Nicene and Post-Nicene Fathers,* vol. 1 (1971; rpt. Oxford and New York, 1980), 481–540. See also *ODB,* s.v. "Vita Constantini," 2181. See Dominic Janes, *God and Gold in Late Antiquity* (Cambridge, U.K., 1998), on the use of church art to further the aims of Christianity.

16. For a summary with extracts from the journal of the Bordeaux Pilgrim, see John Wilkinson, ed. and trans., *Egeria's Travels,* 3d ed., (Warminster, England, 1999), 22–34; for the spring on Mount Syna and fertility miracles, see line 585; the well at Sychar, line 588; the tomb of Rachel, line 598; and the tombs at Hebron, line 599.

17. Holum, "Hadrian and St. Helena," 76.

18. See Elm, *Virgins of God,* 274: Poemenia "was accompanied by several ships carrying, among others, her enunchs, Moorish slaves and the bishop Diogenes."

19. See Elizabeth A. Clark, *The Life of Melania the Younger: Introduction, Translation, and Commentary* (New York and Toronto, 1984), 50, 52, 64, 68–70.

20. Ibid., chap. 36, p. 52.

21. Ibid., chap. 41, p. 55.

22. See Elm, *Virgins of God,* 332–34.

23. Clark, *Life of Melania,* chap. 37, p. 52.

24. Ibid., chap. 39, pp. 53–54.

25. From *The Sayings of the Desert Fathers: The Apophthegmata Patrum,* trans. Benedicta Ward (Kalamazoo, 1975): "Arsenius," chap. 28, pp. 13–14.

26. See Clark, *Women in the Early Church,* 197–203; she notes that for women, "the stimulating world of travel was sanctioned as pilgrimage" (203).

27. See Wilkinson, *Egeria's Travels.*

28. See Patricia Wilson-Kastner, ed. and trans., *A Lost Tradition: Women Writers of the Early Church* (Washington, D.C., 1981), "Egeria," 71–134; on Egeria's name, see 72.

29. For an introduction to the work with informative maps, plans, associated documents, and reconstruction drawings, see Wilkinson, *Egeria's Travels.* The text of *Egeria's Travels* is on 107–64.

30. See MacCormack, "Sacred Topography," 22–23.

31. The translation used and quoted here is Wilson-Kastner because it is, as she herself states, in the conversational tone appropriate to a journal account; see Wilson-Kastner, *A Lost Tradition,* 80–81, on her translation. The narrative on pages 71–134 is organized by chapter. References to quotations are by chapter number and line(s).

32. For Evagrius's sixth-century description of the complex in his *Historia Ecclesiastica,* see Mango, *Art,* 30.

33. On pilgrims and the liturgy, see Hunt, *Holy Land Pilgrimage,* 107–27.

34. See in general for this display by the church, Janes, *God and Gold,* esp. 139–52.

35. See Gary Vikan, "Pilgrims in Magi's Clothing: The Impact of Mimesis on Early Byzantine Pilgrimage Art," in Ousterhout, *Blessings of Pilgrimage,* 97–107, esp. 100.

## Chapter 3: Female Imperial Authority: Empresses of the Theodosian House

1. See *ODB,* s.v. "Empress," 694–95. See also Michael McCormick, *Eternal Victory: Triumphal Rulership in Late Antiquity, Byzantiun and the Early Medieval West* (Cambridge, 1986). For the Theodosian dynasty, see Kenneth G. Holum, *Theodosian Empresses: Women and Im-*

*perial Dominion in Late Antiquity* (Berkeley, 1982); this work has been of great utility in the writing of this chapter.

2. See J. B. Bury, *The Imperial Administrative System in the Ninth Century, with a Revised Text of the Kletorologion of Philotheos* (1911; repr. New York, n.d.). On eunuchs, see Shaun F. Tougher, "Byzantine Eunuchs: An Overview, with Special Reference to Their Creation and Origin," in *Women, Men and Eunuchs: Gender in Byzantium*, ed. Liz James (London and New York, 1997), 168–84; see also Kathryn M. Ringrose, *The Perfect Servant: Eunuchs and the Social Construction of Gender in Byzantium* (Chicago, 2002).

3. Warren Treadgold, "The Bride-shows of the Byzantine Emperors," in *Byzantion* 49 (1979): 395–413.

4. An unusually large number of portraits of this influential empress survive, in ivory and marble; see *Age of Spirituality*, 30–32, nos. 24 and 25, and fig. 7 in this book.

5. For a history of the Theodosian dynasty, see A. H. M. Jones, *The Later Roman Empire 284–602*, vol. 1 (Norman, 1964), esp. 154–73.

6. For the speech and its implications, see Holum, *Theodosian Empresses: Women and Imperial Dominion in Late Antiquity* (Berkeley, 1982), 22–44.

7. Ibid., 24.

8. Ibid., 31.

9. Anne S. Robertson, *Roman Imperial Coins in the Hunter Coin Cabinet, University of Glasgow*, vol. 5, *Diocletian to Leo* (Oxford, 1982), pl. 87:2.

10. For references to further instances of illustrations and points of disagreement on these coin types and on hairstyles, see Holum, *Theodosian Empresses*, 32–34.

11. For the Themistius text on these statues in the Senate house, see Holum, *Theodosian Empresses*, 41; the statue of Flaccilla is referred to as an *agalma*, or a pleasure-producing artwork, a word used to describe works of art in ancient Greece. The sum effect of seeing the statues was described as follows: "Thus will the majesty of their dances be increased by the partnership *[koinonia]*"; see n. 107.

12. Paris, Bibliothèque nationale, Cabinet des Médailles, no. 13. See *Byzance*, cat. no. 4, p. 36.

13. See Robertson, *Roman Imperial Coins*, for coins of Constantinople, Cyzicus, and Antioch, 426–27, nos. 7, 9, 13, 14; also pl. 87: F7 and F13.

14. See Holum, *Theodosian Empresses*, 41.

15. Ibid., 58–65, esp. 65 on Saint John Chrysostom's praise for her humility.

16. See Hugh Goodacre, *A Handbook of the Coinage of the Byzantine Empire* (London, 1967), 26–27, pl. on p. 27. See also the tables on the coins minted for fifth-century empresses in Philip Grierson and Melinda Mays, *Catalogue of Late Roman Coins in the Dumbarton Oaks Collection and in the Whittemore Collection: From Ardadius and Honorius to the Accession of Anastasius* (Washington, D.C., 1992), table 2 on p. 8; also of emperors and their consorts in table 1 on p. 4; pl. 11:273.

17. Holum, *Theodosian Empresses*, 69–77.

18. John Chrysostom, *Hom. cum ir. in exil.*: see Holum, *Theodosian Empresses*, 77.

19. For the story of her clash with Chrysostom, see Holum, *Theodosian Empresses*, 69–79.

20. Ibid., 90–93.

21. Grierson and Mays, *Catalogue of Late Roman Coins in the Dumbarton Oaks Collection*, pl. 17:437–40; 443.

22. See Kenneth Holum, "Pulcheria's Crusade A.D. 421–22 and the Ideology of Imperial Victory," *GRBS* 18 (1977): 153–72.

23. For a discussion of these coin types in connection with the notion of God-ordained victory, see ibid., esp. 157; for the testimony of Sozomon on Pulcheria's political influence, see ibid., 158–59.

24. Ibid., 165–66.

25. See W. F. Volbach, *Elfenbeinarbeiten der Spätantike und des frühen Mittelalters*, Römisch-germanisches Zentralmuseum zu Mainz, Katalog VII, 3d ed. (Mainz, 1976), no. 143. For a summary of the scholarship, see Beckwith, *Art*, 172 and pl. 74.

26. Kenneth Holum and Gary Vikan, "The Trier Ivory, *Adventus* Ceremonial, and the Relics of St. Stephen," *DOP* 33 (1979): 113–33. For another study with much incisive observation, see Suzanne Spain, "The Translation of Relics Ivory, Trier" *DOP* 31 (1977): 279–304. See also Leslie Brubaker, "Iconoclasm and the Trier Ivory," *Abstracts of the Byzantine Studies Conference* 25 (1999): 83–84, for a much later dating.

27. For the Vienna leaf with Ariadne seated, see also *Age of Spirituality*, cat. no. 25, pp. 31–32. The seated Ariadne gestures with her right hand in the same manner as the female figure on the Trier ivory. Also, on the Vienna leaf, her robe has many traces of color and the background is purple, indicating the original polychrome appearance. These ivories have also been associated with marble portrait heads of the empress, with which they share physiognomic features.

28. See Holum and Vikan, "The Trier Ivory," 125–26, and, for the authoritative study, Cyril Mango, *The Brazen House: A Study of the Vestibule of the Imperial Palace of Constantinople* (Copenhagen, 1959).

29. The passage is from an encomium of Saint Stephen found among Saint John Chrysostom's spurious writings, found in *PG* 63:933. For a discussion, see Holum and Vikan, "The Trier Ivory," 131.

30. See *The Chronicle of Theophanes Confessor*, trans. Cyril Mango and Roger Scott (Oxford, 1997), 86: 26–87 line 5; see also ibid., 127 and n. 69. For the continuing role of Pulcheria as a collector of relics and a sponsor of churches to house them, see Holum, *Theodosian Empresses*, 136–37.

31. See Holum and Vikan, "The Trier Ivory," 132.

32. Holum, *Theodosian Empresses*, 141.

33. Ibid., 142–43.

34. See Norman Baynes, "The Supernatural Defenders of Constantinople," *Anal.Bol.* 67 (1949): 165–77; repr. in N. Baynes, ed., *Byzantine Studies and Other Essays* (London, 1955), 248–60, esp. 257–58. See also Averil Cameron, "The Theotokos in Sixth-Century Constantinople: A City Finds Its Symbol," in *The Journal of Theological Studies* 29 (1978): 79–108; repr. in *Continuity and Change in Sixth-Century Byzantium* (London: Variorum Reprints, 1981), xvi.

35. The sixth-century account of John Malalas gives the elements of the story in book 14, lines 352–56 (E. Jeffreys, M. Jeffreys, and R. Scott, eds., *The Chronicle of John Malalas* [Melbourne, 1986], 191–93).

36. For Holum's views on her origins and the politics which brought her into the palace, see Holum, *Theodosian Empresses*, 112–46, esp. his interpretation of Olympiodorus of Thebes's *History*. For a criticism of Holum's theories, see Alan Cameron, "The Empress and the Poet: Paganism and Politics at the Court of Theodosius II," *Yale Classical Studies* 27 (1982): 217–83, esp. 276–77, 283–84.

37. Grierson and Mays, *Catalogue of Late Roman Coins in the Dumbarton Oaks Collection*, pl. 18:454–56; for the cross within a wreath type, see pl. 18:448–52 and 460–74.

38. See Ostrogorsky, *History,* 56.

39. See Holum, *Theodosian Empresses,* esp. 126.

40. Alan Cameron believes that Eudocia's literary activity was aimed not at asserting pagan ideals but at converting pagans to Christianity by using language adapted from the pagan classics; see "Empress and the Poet," 284.

41. For a discussion of her writings and a translation of the "Life of St. Cyprian," see G. Ronald Kastner, "Eudocia," in *A Lost Tradition: Women Writers of the Early Church* (Washington, D.C., 1981), ed. Patricia Wilson-Kastner et al, 135–71.

42. Ibid. "The Martyrdom of St. Cyprian," introduction, 140–47; translation, 149–69; a resumé of the "Martyrdom" survives in the *Bibliotheka* of Photius.

43. Kastner, "Eudocia," 155.

44. Ibid., 156–57.

45. Cameron, "Empress and the Poet," 277.

46. Kastner, "Eudocia," 145–46.

47. Although Nestorious recognized Christ as the Son of God, under his theology Mary could only be called Mother of Christ, not Mother of God. The teachings of Nestorius appeared to undermine the unity of Christ's person and imply that there were actually two sons, the divine Son of God and the human son of Mary. This position was unacceptable to Orthodox Christians. On the urging of Cyril, patriarch of Alexandria, the council met and resolved the dispute, the result of which was that Nestorius was deposed and Mary was declared to be Theotokos.

48. See Cameron, "Empress and the Poet," 278, for the cooperation of the two Augustae in the acquisition and housing of relics. Also, the positions of the two empresses on religious matters are noted in the ecclesiastical histories by Sozomon and Socrates; Sozomon eulogizes Pulcheria, and Socrates, Eudocia (265). We know from the literary evidence of the *Palatine Anthology* that Eudocia founded at least two churches in Constantinople, as discussed below in chapter 5.

49. Jeffreys, Jeffreys, and Scott, *Chronicle of John Malalas,* book 14, lines 356–58, pp. 193–94.

50. For an analysis of dating and versions of the apple story and surrounding intrigue, including the birth of Eudocia's son, whose father may have been Paulinus, see Cameron, "Empress and the Poet," 259–69.

51. According to the Monophysites, the divine nature of Christ subordinated the human nature so completely that Christ had a single divine nature. The Orthodox position asserted a combined human and divine nature "without confusion or change, division or separation." This position prevailed only after much division and enmity within the church. See *ODB,* s.v. "Monophysitism," 1398–99.

52. See Pères Hughes Vincent and F.-M. Abel, *Jérusalem: Recherches de topographie, d'archéologie et d'histoire* (Paris, 1926), 2:777, for archaeological evidence of her tomb, and 801–02 for a discussion of the occupants of the tombs as Eudocia and Eudocia the Younger.

53. See Holum, *Theodosian Empresses,* 208 and n. 163.

54. Robertson, *Roman Imperial Coins,* 485:2 and pl. 94.

55. Holum, *Theodosian Empresses,* 213 and n. 186.

56. See Stewart Irvin Oost, *Galla Placidia Augusta: A Biographical Essay* (Chicago, 1968), 244 and n. 128.

57. Ibid., 244. See also Grierson and Mays, *Late Roman Coins,* 245–46.

58. J. P. C. Kent, *The Roman Imperial Coinage: The Divided Empire and the Fall of the West-ern Parts AD 395–491* (London, 1994) 10:164–65 and pl. 49:2016, 2023; Grierson and Mays, *Late Roman Coins,* 244–45 and pl. 34:870.

59. Oost, *Galla Placidia,* 304–06.

60. See *ODB,* s.v. "Galla Placidia," 818.

61. In this section I will refer frequently to Oost, *Galla Placidia Augusta,* an important and invaluable scholarly work for understanding this woman's role in late ancient society. For a summary of her life and a bibliography on major works written about Galla Placidia, see also Grierson and Mays, *Late Roman Coins,* 229–30.

62. Oost, *Galla Placidia,* 49.

63. Ibid., 55.

64. Ibid., 56.

65. Ibid., 61.

66. Mark J. Johnson, "On the Burial Places of the Theodosian Dynasty," *Byzantion* 61 (1991): 330–39, esp. 330.

67. Oost, *Galla Placidia,* 63–64.

68. See Johnson, "Burial Places," 334.

69. Oost, *Galla Placidia,* 122.

70. Ibid., 128–29.

71. Ibid., 137.

72. Ibid., 156–61.

73. Ibid., 162.

74. See Grierson and Mays, *Late Roman Coins,* 230–31, pl. 32:824.

75. See ibid. for Galla Placidia: pl. 32:824–34; for Justa Grata, pl. 34: 866–69.

76. Oost, *Galla Placidia,* 191. See Grierson and Mays, *Late Roman Coins,* 32:817.

77. See Grierson and Mays, *Late Roman Coins,* 12, on the *vota* series; see also pl. 32:824.

78. For this rare example in Paris, Bibliothèque Nationale, see Oost, *Galla Placidia,* pl. 1, op. p. 222.

79. See Amy Richlin, "Julia's Jokes, Galla Placidia, and the Roman Use of Women as Po-litical Icons," in *Stereotypes of Women in Power: Historical Perspectives and Revisionist Views,* ed. B. Garlick, S. Dixon, and P. Allen (Westport, Conn., 1992), 65–91, esp. 82–83.

80. For this remark by Cassiodorus, see Oost, *Galla Placidia,* 195.

81. Ibid., 196–97.

82. Ibid., 220, 246.

83. Ibid., 245.

84. Ibid., 257.

85. Ibid., 265.

86. Ibid., 269 and fig. 8.

87. For the subjects of the mosaics and a description by Merobaudes, see Frank M. Clover, "Merobaudes, Ravenna's St. John Evangelist and the Survival of Theodosius' House," *Abstracts of the Byzantine Studies Conference* 24 (1998): 63–64. On Galla Placidia's sponsorship of build-ings and the tradition of women's "matronage" going back to Helena, mother of Constantine, see Leslie Brubaker, "Memories of Helena: Patterns in Imperial Female Matronage in the Fourth and Fifth Centuries," in *Women, Men and Eunuchs,* ed. James, 52–75, esp. 53–55 and 61.

88. Oost, *Galla Placidia,* 274–75.

89. Ibid., 276–77.

90. For a new interpretation of the Saint Lawrence lunette in connection with Galla Placidia's sponsorship, see Gillian Mackie, "New Light on the So-Called Saint Lawrence Panel at the Mausoleum of Galla Placidia, Ravenna," *Gesta* 29 (1990): 54–60.

91. See Beckwith, *Art,* 35–37 and figs. 20, 21. For the best color plates showing the building and its mosaics, see *Il Mausoleo di Galla Placidia a Ravenna* (The Mausoleum of Galla Placidia Ravenna), ed. Clementina Rizzardi (Modena, 1996; Mirabilia Italiae series), 15–112.

92. See Gillian Mackie, "The Mausoleum of Galla Placidia: A Possible Occupant," *Byzantion* 65 (1995): 396–404.

93. See ibid., 402 and nn. 25 and 26.

94. See ibid., 402–03, for the chain of evidence that convincingly claims that the burial is correctly identified as that of Galla Placidia and Theodosius.

95. Oost, *Galla Placidia,* 270 and pl. 8.


Introduction to Part 2: The Problematic for a Study of Byzantine Women

1. Judith Herrin, "In Search of Byzantine Women: Three Avenues of Approach," in *Images of Women in Antiquity,* ed. Averil Cameron (Detroit and London, 1983), 167–89. See also the excellent overview title "Women" by Alice-Mary Talbot, in *The Byzantines,* ed. Gugliolmo Cavallo, trans. Thomas Dunlap, Teresa Lavender Fagan, and Charles Lambert (Chicago and London, 1997), 117–43.

2. Talbot, "Women," in Cavallo, ed., *The Byzantines,* 167.

3. Ibid.

4. Some recent titles are Liz James, ed., *Women, Men and Eunuchs: Gender in Byzantium* (London, 1997), Lynda Garland, *Byzantine Empresses: Women and Power in Byzantium* (London and New York, 1999), Judith Herrin, *Women in Purple: Rulers of Medieval Byzantiun* (Princeton, 2001), Alice-Mary Talbot, ed., *Holy Women of Byzantiun: Ten Saints' Lives in English Translation* (Washington, 1996), Alice-Mary Talbot, *Women and Religious Life in Byzantium* (Variorum Collected Studies, 2001), Barbara Hill, *Imperial Women in Byzantium 1025–1204: Power, Patronage and Ideology* (Harlow, Essex, 1999), Donald M. Nicol, *The Byzantine Lady: Ten Portraits, 1250–1500* (Cambridge and New York, 1994), Thalia Gouma-Peterson, ed., *Anna Komnene and Her Times* (New York and London, 2000), Anne McClanan, *Representations of Early Byzantine Empresses: Image and Emnpire,* New Middle Ages Series (Palgrave, forthcoming), Ioli Kalavrezou, ed., *Byzantine Women and Their World,* Catalogue of an Exhibition at the Arthur M. Sackler Museum, Harvard University, Oct. 2002–Mar. 2003 (Cambridge, Mass., 2003).

5. See James A. Brundage, *Law, Sex and Christian Society in Medieval Europe* (Chicago and London, 1987), chap. 3, "Sex and the Law in the Christian Empire, from Constantine to Justinian," 77–123, esp. 87–89 and 113–23.

6. See Gillian Clark, *Women in Late Antiquity: Pagan and Christian Life-styles* (Oxford, 1993).

7. Herrin, "In Search of Byzantine Women," 171–78. The subtitle to chapter 4 above, "Women at Risk," is derived from this source (172).

8. On deaconesses, see Ross Shepard Kraemer and Mary Rose D'Angelo, eds., *Women and Christian Origins* (Oxford, 1999), 312–19.

9. Herrin, "In Search of Byzantine Women," 179, 185.

10. See R. Cormack, *Writing in Gold,* 158–59; for the role of the Virgin Mary in society as revealed through art, see 168–78.

11. See Averil Cameron, "Images of Authority: Elites and Icons in Late Sixth-Century Byzantium," *Past and Present* 84 (1979): 3–35, esp. 5–6.

12. See the important study by Averil Cameron, "The Theotokos in Sixth-Century Constantinople: A City Finds Its Symbol," in A. Cameron, *Continuity and Change in Sixth-Century Byzantium* (London, 1981), 79–108, esp. 80, for the appearance by the mid–sixth century of Romanos's Akathistos hymn as a liturgically adopted tribute to the Virgin Mary and her protective role, and 82–83 for the reverence shown the Virgin in Corippus's poem on the accession of Justin II in 566. See also Cameron, "Elites and Icons." The Council of Ephesus of 431 made Mary officially the Mother of God, or Theotokos, which gave impetus to the formation of her cult and made her the symbol of Orthodox belief. See also, *ODB,* s.v. "relics," 1779–81.

13. See Cameron, "Theotokos," 101. See Herrin, *Women in Purple;* see also Robin Cormack, "Women and Icons, and Women in Icons," in James, ed., *Women, Men and Eunuchs,* 24–51.

## Chapter 4: Sinners and Saints: Women at Risk

1. Benedicta Ward, "St. Mary of Egypt: The Liturgical Icon of Repentance," in *Harlots of the Desert: A Study of Repentance in Early Monastic Sources,* ed. Benedicta Ward (Kalamazoo, 1987), 7; Mary Magdalene appears in all four Gospel accounts of the burial and Resurrection; she is also identified as the prostitute in Luke 7.36–50.

2. Sebastian P. Brock and Susan A. Harvey, *Holy Women of the Syrian Orient* (Berkeley, 1987), 13.

3. Ibid., 3; for a similar approach to Western saints' lives, see also Jane T. Schulenburg, *Forgetful of Their Sex: Female Sanctity and Society ca. 500–1100* (Chicago, 1998).

4. Brock and Harvey, *Holy Women of the Syrian Orient,* and Alice-Mary Talbot, ed., *Holy Women of Byzantium: Ten Saints' Lives in English Translation* (Washington, 1996).

5. See Schulenburg, *Forgetful,* chap. 1, "Saints' Lives as a Source for the History of Women, ca. 500–1100," 17–57; see esp. 21–22 on sanctity and the collective memory of a community and the formulating of a public cult.

6. See Susan A. Harvey, "Sacred Bonding: Mothers and Daughters in Early Syriac Hagiography," *Journal of Early Christian Studies* 4 (1996): 27–56.

7. See II Timothy 4.7 as a model for the language of ancient competitive events and winning of crowns by victors in athletic struggles.

8. Schulenburg, *Forgetful,* 28–34.

9. See Catherine M. Mooney, "Voice, Gender, and the Portrayal of Sanctity," in *Gendered Voices: Medieval Saints and Their Interpreters,* ed. Catherine M. Mooney (Philadelphia, 1999), 1–15, esp. 3.

10. Brock and Harvey, *Holy Women of the Syrian Orient,* 22.

11. Ibid., 26.

12. See Schulenburg, *Forgetful,* 22–24. See also *ODB,* s.v. "Canonization," 372.

13. As in previous chapters, the section or paragraph will be cited along with the page number in the most accessible or readable translation; citations from the "Life of Pelagia of Antioch" are from Brock and Harvey, *Holy Women of the Syrian Orient,* 40–62; for the Greek editions, see ibid., 40, nos. 1 and 2.

14. See Margaret Miles, "'Becoming Male': Women Martyrs and Ascetics," in *Carnal Know-*

ing: *Female Nakedness and Religious Meaning in the Christian West* (Boston, 1989), 53–77, esp. 70–72, for Pelagia and the dangers of elaborate or seductive dress in women; some early writers even urged women to neglect their appearance.

15. See Lynda L. Coon, *Sacred Fictions: Holy Women and Hagiography in Late Antiquity* (Philadelphia, 1997), chap. 4, "God's Holy Harlots: The Redemptive Lives of Pelagia of Antioch and Mary of Egypt," 77–84, esp. 81, in which Pelagia is compared to the bride in the Song of Songs 1.10 and 4.9 or to the Whore of Revelation 17.4.

16. See Evelyne Patlagean, "L'Histoire de la femme déguisée en moine et l'évolution de la sainteté féminine à Byzance," *Studi Medievali*, ser. 3, 17 (1976): 597–623.

17. Ibid., 607–08. Patlagean asserts, "L'histoire de la femme déguisée en moine propose un modèle de sainteté qui transgresse, dans les versions les plus radicales, tant la hiérarchie du couple et de la famille que l'ordre du monde monastique, et qui abolit, en tout état de cause, les deux catégories constituantes de l'humanité" [The story of the woman disguised as a monk presents a model of sanctity which in the most radical versions transgresses as much the hierarchy of the couple and the family as the ordering of the monastic world and which abolishes, in any case, the two categories which make up the human race] (615).

18. On prostitution in Byzantium, see José Grosdidier de Matons, "La femme dans l'empire Byzantin," in *Histoire Mondiale de la Femme*, Pierre Grimal, ed. (Paris, 1974), 11–43, esp. 23–26.

19. Ibid., 26.

20. The most comprehensive treatment of the subject of women and the law appears in Joëlle Beaucamp, *Le Statut de la femme à byzance (4e-7e siècle)*, vols. 1 and 2 (Paris, 1990 and 1992); on prostitution, see esp. 1:122–32.

21. Gillian Clark, *Women in Late Antiquity: Pagan and Christian Lifestyles* (Oxford, 1993), 28–38.

22. Ibid., 36.

23. Ibid., 31–33.

24. Ibid., 37–38.

25. See Procopius, *Secret History* (Ann Arbor, 1963), 17.5.

26. Nicholas Constas, trans., "Life of St. Mary/Marinos," in Alice-Mary Talbot, ed., *Holy Women of Byzantium: Ten Saints' Lives in English Translation* (Washington, 1996), 1–12.

27. Ibid., 12.

28. See Kathy L. Gaca, "The Sexual and Social Dangers of *Pornai* in the Septuagint Greek Stratum of Patristic Christian Greek Thought," in *Desire and Denial in Byzantium*, ed. Liz James (Brookfield, Vt., 1999), 40.

29. See Miles "Women Martyrs," esp. 67, on women "becoming male" as a way to avoid traditional roles, that of dressing like a man being one way of escaping from marriage: "In Orthodox Christianity two roles were acceptable for women — virginity or motherhood. Women could 'become male' by living in ascetic virginity, or they could, according to 1 Timothy 2:15, be 'saved in childbearing.'" Of the two roles, virginity was the more prized.

30. Ward, "St. Mary of Egypt," 8.

31. Alice-Mary Talbot, ed., *Holy Women of Byzantium: Ten Saints' Lives in English Translation* (Washington, 1996), x, xi.

32. For a lucid account of the changes to the Arian mosaics from the time of Theodoric, resulting in the processions of male and female saints we see today, see Thomas F. Mathews, *The Clash of Gods* (Princeton, 1993), 168–69 and fig. 131. See also figs. 130–32.

33. For an interpretation of these mosaics in the context of the liturgy, see Otto Von Simson,

*Sacred Fortress: Byzantine Art and Statecraft in Ravenna* (Princeton, 1987), esp. 83–110; see also pls. 39, 42, 43. For women's dress, see *ODB*, s.v. "Costume," esp. 539.

34. "In Sant' Apollinare Nuovo, however, the identification between onlooker and image was designed to be not moral but mystical. The congregation assembled in the basilica knew these saints to be with them in the hour of the mystery" (Von Simson, *Sacred Fortress*, 99). ·

35. Ibid., 102.

36. Ward, "St. Mary of Egypt," 7.

37. For a discussion of these distinctions, see Gaca, "Sexual and Social Dangers," 36–40, esp. 36.

38. See E. Schwartz, trans., *Kyrillos von Skythopolis* (Leipzig, 1939), the "Life of Kyriakos," 222–35; 233–34 tells Mary's story. See also Ward, "St. Mary of Egypt," 28–32.

39. Maria Kouli, trans., "Life of St. Mary of Egypt," in Talbot, ed., *Holy Women of Byzantium,* introduction, 64–69; Life, 70–93, esp. 67.

40. Ward, "St. Mary of Egypt," 32–34; for Ward's translation of the Life, see 35–56.

41. The original in Greek is published in the series *PG* 87:3693–3726. The Latin text, translated by Paul the Deacon from the Greek of Sophronius, is in *PL* 73:671–90. The translation used here is by Maria Kouli in Talbot, *Holy Women of Byzantium*, 70–93.

42. Citations in the text will refer to paragraph and then to page in Kouli, "Life of St. Mary."

43. For nakedness as a form of virginity, see Miles, "Women Martyrs," 64–67.

44. Ibid., 41; Talbot, *Holy Women of Byzantium*, 93.

45. Kouli, "St. Mary of Egypt," 68.

46. See Carolyn L. Connor, "Female Saints in Church Decoration of the Troodos Mountains in Cyprus," in *Medieval Cyprus: Studies in Art, Architecture, and History in Memory of Doula Mouriki,* ed. Nancy P. Ševčenko and Christopher Moss (Princeton, 1999), 211–28, esp. 224–26, and nn. 74–76.

47. Ibid., 224.

48. Ibid., fig. 3.

49. Ibid., 217 and n. 31.

50. Ward, "St. Mary of Egypt," 34.

51. *The Lenten Triodion,* trans. Mother Mary and Kallistos Ware (London, 1978): Canon of St. Mary of Egypt, 447–48.


## Chapter 5: Women and Artistic Patronage

1. The issues of patronage discussed in this chapter will not extend to female financial support of individuals and their missions and religious or political agendas but will apply instead to concrete productions in various media. For the former definition of patronage, see, for example, Ross S. Kraemer, *Her Share of the Blessings: Women's Religions among Pagans, Jews, and Christians in the Greco-Roman World* (New York and Oxford, 1992), esp. "Women's Leadership and Offices in Christian Commninties," 174–81.

2. In his work on Justinian's projects, *De Aedificiis (On the Buildings),* Procopius credits Justinian, and to a lesser extent Theodora, with the sponsorship of buildings all over the empire. Most of these have disappeared, but Justinian's most famous church, Hagia Sophia, is described in detail along with his role in designing and building it, including the names of the architects.

3. For a view of late ancient sponsorship of buildings by women, sometimes called "matro-

nage," see Leslie Brubaker, "Memories of Helena: Patterns in Imperial Female Matronage in the Fourth and Fifth Centuries," in *Women, Men and Eunuchs: Gender in Byzantium,* ed. Liz James (London and New York, 1997), 52–75. For introductions and overviews of art and artifacts of the period, see *Age of Spirituality;* Volbach, *Art;* Beckwith, *Art;* and Krautheimer, *Architecture.*

4. For the most cogent discussion of art, its aesthetic impact, and symbolic messages in this period, see Dominic Janes, *God and Gold in Late Antiquity* (Cambridge, 1998).

5. See *Age of Spirituality,* 610, cat. no. 546.

6. On silver stamps, see Marlia Mango, "The Purpose and Places of Byzantine Silver Stamping," in Susan A. Boyd and Marlia M. Mango, eds., *Ecclesiastical Silver Plate in Sixth-Century Byzantium* (Washington, D.C., 1992), 203–15.

7. See Mango, *Art,* 72.

8. For the capitals of Hagia Sophia and their monograms, see numerous views in Roland Mainstone, *Hagia Sophia: Architecture, Structure and Liturgy of Justinian's Great Church* (New York, 1988), esp. figs. 57 and 68.

9. For the inscriptions on the Obelisk of Theodosius, see Linda Safran, "Points of View: The Theodosian Obelisk in Context," *GRBS* 34 (1993): 409–35, esp. 409–10 and pls. 4 and 5; for the still undetermined patronage of the Imperial Palace floor mosaic, see James Trilling, "The Soul of the Empire: Style and Meaning in the Mosaic Pavement of the Imperial Palace in Constantinople," *DOP* 43 (1989): 27–72, a masterful investigation of the evidence of the mind and the money behind this great mosaic.

10. See Boyd and Mango, eds., *Ecclesiastical Silver Plate,* part 1, "The Sion Treasure," 3–93.

11. See Susan Boyd, "A 'Metropolitan Treasure' from a Church in the Provinces: An Introduction to the Study of the Sion Treasure," in Boyd and Mango, eds., *Ecclesiastical Silver,* 5–38, see esp. 20, cat. no. 5.

12. Boyd and Mango, eds., *Ecclesiastical Silver,* 29, cat. no. 45 and figs. S45.1–2.

13. Ibid., 47.

14. Ibid., 23.

15. Ibid., 16.

16. Ibid., 14.

17. See Marlia M. Mango, *Silver from Early Byzantium: The Kaper Koraon and Related Treasures* (Baltimore, 1986), 3–36, for a reconstruction of the Kaper Koraon treasure from four known hoards: Hama, Stuma, Riha, and Antioch.

18. Ibid., 10–11.

19. Boyd, "A Metropolitan Treasure," 133 and note 110.

20. See Mango, *Silver from Byzantium,* no. 35 on 165–70, fig. 35.3: Dumbarton Oaks Collection no. 24.5; see 166 for inscription.

21. Ibid., 9.

22. Ibid., 108, cat. no. 15.

23. Ibid., 246, cat. no. 73. See nos. 79, 81, 83.

24. Ibid., 266–67.

25. For a wide range of artifacts associated with women, see the catalogue of the first exhibition entirely devoted to this subject: *Byzantine Women and Their World:* An Exhibition at the Arthur M. Sackler Museum, Harvard University, 26 October 2002 to 23 March, 2003, ed. Ioli Kalavrezou (Cambridge, Mass., 1993).

26. See *Age of Spirituality,* pl. 8 and 319–21 (cat. no. 296).

27. See Gary Vikan, "Byzantine Pilgrims' Art," in Linda Safron, ed., *Heaven on Earth: Art and the Church in Byzantium* (University Park, Penn., 1998), 229–66, esp. 252 and fig. 8.30, an amuletic armband with *locus sanctus* scenes.

28. See ibid., 283–84 (cat. no. 262); also M. C. Ross, *Catalogue of the Byzantine and Early Mediaeval Antiquities in the Dumbarton Oaks Collection,* vol. 2, *Jewelry, Enamels, and Art of the Migration Period* (Washington, D.C., 1965), cat. no. 38, 37–39, pl. 30–32 and color plate A. For an almost identical marriage belt in the Louvre Museum in Paris, see *Byzance,* cat. no. 89, pp. 133–34, whose inscription is, "Wear this in good health," thus indicating the common female concern for health and the hope that such jewelry would serve a protective function.

29. *Age of Spirituality,* 496 (cat. no. 446); see also Ross, *Jewelry,* cat. no. 69, plates 43, 44, and color plate E.

30. See *Age of Spirituality,* 634–36 (cat. no. 574).

31. Ross, *Jewelry,* cat. no. 6E, pl. 14.

32. See *Byzance,* cat. nos. 88, 133.

33. See in general Roger Ling, *Ancient Mosaics* (Princeton, 1998).

34. Michelle Piccirillo, *The Mosaics of Jordan* (Amman, Jordan, 1993), esp. 47, for the unusually large number of mosaicists named in these mosaics.

35. Ibid., 96–106, pls. 78, 80, and 95.

36. Ibid., 128, pl. 141.

37. Ibid., 165, pls. 213, 215. For a floor mosaic from the church of Saint Elias, Gerare/Orda with two female donors, one named Kyra Silthous, depicted as offering objects and coins in donation, see R. Cohen, "A Byzantine Church and Mosaic Floor Near Kissufim," *Qadmoniot* 12 (1979): 19–29, and plate on p. 21 (reproduced in Mango, *Silver from Byzantium,* 11, fig. 1.2).

38. For illustrations of the mosaics, see Robin Cormack, "The Mosaic Decoration of S. Demetrios, Thessaloniki: A Re-examination in the Light of the Drawings of W. S. George," *Annual of the British School at Athens* 64 (1969): 17–52. For a brief discussion and illustrations of these mosaics, see R. Cormack, *Writing in Gold: Byzantine Society and Its Icons* (New York, 1985), 86–89 and figs. 27–30. See also Henry Maguire, *The Icons of Their Bodies: Saints and Their Images in Byzantium* (Princeton, 1996), 101–03 and figs. 83–85. I wish to acknowledge the excellent work done on these mosaics by Sarah Levin-Richardson in her senior thesis, "Women in the Mosaics of the Church of Saint Demetrius in Thessaloniki" (March 2003).

39. See Mark J. Johnson, "Late Antique Imperial Mausolea" (Ph.D. diss., Princeton University, 1986), 73–79.

40. Ibid., 91–101.

41. See Gillian Mackie, "A New Look at the Patronage of Santa Costanza, Rome," *Byzantion* 67 (1997): 383–406, esp. 391–92.

42. Ibid., 397.

43. The identities of these portraits have been much discussed, with suggestions ranging from Bacchus to portraits of Constantina and her husband. See ibid., 400–03, for a review of the theories about these portraits and for her persuasive interpretation of the mosaics as Constantina and Helena. For the mosaics and the mausoleum, see Volbach, *Art,* 318–19 and pls. 28–35.

44. See Stewart Irvin Oost, *Galla Placidia Augusta: A Biographical Essay* (Chicago, 1968), 269–78.

45. See Raymond Janin, *Constantinople Byzantine: Développement urbain et répertoire topo-*

*graphique* (Paris, 1964), for sources on *ta Ioulianes* (360–61) and *ta Olybriou* (398–99), probably the same district of the city in which were located the church of Saint Euphemia and her family's palace, a construction that may have been part of her mother, Placidia's, dowry, and occupied by her father, Olybrius. For Anicia Juliana, see also William Smith and Henry Wace, *Dictionary of Christian Biography* (London, 1882), 3:469.

46. For general information and sources on Juliana, see *ODB*, s.v. "Anicia Juliana," 99–100. See also J. R. Martindale, *The Prosopography of the Later Roman Empire*, vol 2, *AD 395–527* (Cambridge, 1980), 635–36.

47. See *ODB*, s.vv. "Akakios patriarch, Akakian Schism," 42–43, "Anicia Juliana," 99–100, and "Henotikon," 913. See also Theophanes, who refers to the standoff between Juliana and the emperor Anastasius together with his monophysite patriarch Timothy; he states, "Juliana . . . was so firm in her support of the Synod of Chalcedon that even the emperor, who devised many traps for her, was unable to persuade her to be in communion with Timothy. And though Timothy himself often visited her, he was unable to persuade her" (*The Chronicle of Theophanes Confessor,* trans. Cyril Mango and Roger Scott [Oxford, 1997], AM 6005 ([239]). Juliana met with Saint Sabas, who came from Palestine to Constantinople to support the Chalcedonian cause; the two corresponded with Pope Hormisdas, aiding in affecting the final reconciliation (ibid., 242 and n. 9).

48. For an excellent synopsis of the history of this time, see John W. Barker, *Justinian and the Later Roman Empire* (Madison, 1977). See also J. A. S. Evans, *The Age of Justinian: The Circumstances of Imperial Power* (London and New York, 1996). For a biased but informative contemporary text, see *Procopius, Secret History,* trans. R. Atwater (Ann Arbor, 1963).

49. For an introduction and catalogue of the excavated remains of the church of Hagios Polyeuktos, see Martin Harrison, *Excavations at Saraçhane in Istanbul,* vol 1, *The Excavations, Structures, Architectural Decoration, Small Finds, Coins, Bones, and Molluscs* (Princeton, 1986), hereinafter referred to as Harrison, *Saraçhane*. For a summary of the excavation results and highly readable overview of the monument's significance, see Martin Harrison, *A Temple for Byzantium: The Discovery and Excavation of Anicia Juliana's Palace-Church in Istanbul* (Austin, 1989).

50. See M. Harrison, "Anicia Juliana's Church of Saint Polyeuktos," *JOB* 32 (1981): 435–42: "The building was provided with curvilinear open exedrae and appears to have been a domed basilica; it was certainly for a handful of years the largest church in Constantinople, and Justinian's church of Saint Sophia is best regarded as a deliberate response to it" (435).

51. These ideas were presented in two papers by Carolyn Connor: "The Epigram on the Church of Hagios Polyeuktos in Istanbul and Its Byzantine Response," *Abstracts of the Byzantine Studies Conference,* 23 (Madison, 1997), 47, and "The Church of Hagios Polyeuktos in Constantinople as Anicia Juliana's Burial Church," *Congrès international des études byzantines* (Paris, 2001), 303.

52. See *Greek Anthology,* Loeb Classical Library Edition, vol. 1, trans. W. R. Paton, book 1, epigram 10, pp. 6–11, for the Greek text and English translation; for Harrison's translation of the inscription, see also his *Saraçhane,* 5–10. For the initial discovery, see C. Mango and I. Ševčenko, "Remains of the Church of Saint Polyeuktos at Constantinople," *DOP* 15 (1961): 243–47. For wider connotations and implications of the inscription in relation to the archaeological finds, see Carolyn Connor, "The Epigram in the Church of Hagios Polyeuktos in Constantinople and Its Byzantine Response," *Byzantion* 69 (1999): 479–527.

53. See Harrison, *Temple for Byzantium,* 53 and plan in fig. 48; also Harrison, *Saraçhane,* 406–08, for an assessment of the architecture.

54. For the excavation results regarding architectural sculpture, see Harrison, *Saraçhane,* 414–18; for the mosaics see 182–84.

55. For a discussion of the scholia and their placement and implications, see Connor, "Epigram," 479–527, esp. 494–97 and n. 37.

56. See Harrison, *Saraçhane,* chap. 5, "The Marble Carving," 117–67, and Harrison, *Temple for Byzantium,* chap. 3, "The Decorations," 77–124, for a catalogue and analyses of these details.

57. See Henry Maguire, *Earth and Ocean: The Terrestrial World in Early Byzantine Art* (University Park, Penn., and London, 1987), 60–61, and 39 on the meaning of the peacock; fig. 51, a painted tomb in Nicaea, and figs. 69 and 71, mosaic floors with frontal and profile peacocks depicted in a context of grapevines.

58. See Volbach, *Art,* pls. 34 and 35, and Maguire, *Earth and Ocean,* fig. 51.

59. See Thelma K. Thomas, *Late Antique Egyptian Funerary Sculpture: Images for This World and the Next* (Princeton, 2000): niche head with spread peacock tail from the monastery of Apa Jeremias, fig. 24; Dionysus among grapevines from Hieracleopolis, fig. 40.

60. For the polyvalence of such images, see Maguire, *Earth and Ocean,* 8–10 and figs. 3, 4, 69, 71.

61. See Ling, *Ancient Mosaics,* 106, fig. 76.

62. For the mosaics of Santa Costanza, see Volbach, *Art,* fig. 32; for the sarcophagus, see Robert Milburn, *Early Christian Art and Architecture* (Los Angeles, 1988), 60–61 and fig. 31.

63. See Milburn, *Early Christian Art and Architecture,* 78 and fig. 45, for the sarcophagus of Archbishop Theodore, sixth century, in Sant' Apollinare in Classe.

64. See Maguire, *Earth and Ocean,* 32, for the meanings given the vine in the sermons of Saint Basil.

65. It is known as Vienna, Österreichische Nationalbibliothek, cod. med. gr. 1. For an introduction and reproduction of several pages from this manuscript, see K. Weitzmann, *Late Antique and Early Christian Book Illumination* (New York, 1977), 60–71. See also A. Von Premerstein, "Anicia Juliana im Wiener Dioskorides-Kodex," *Jahrbuch der Kunsthistorischen Sammlungen des Allerh. Kaiserhauses* 24 (1903): 105–24. The facsimile edition is Hans Gerstinger, *Dioscurides Codex Vindobonensis Med Gr. 1, der Österreichischen Nationalbibliothek* (Graz, 1965–70), 2 vols.

66. See Von Premerstein, "Anicia Juliana," esp. 111. This epigram is too complicated grammatically to render the translation in poetic setting.

67. For an assessment of the initiative behind this manuscript, see Kathy Jo Wetter, "Anicia Juliana and the Patronage of the Vienna Dioscorides" (M.A. thesis, University of North Carolina, 1993).

68. Theophanes mentions her as "the most noble Juliana who founded the sacred church of the Mother of God at Honoratoi," Mango and Scott, eds., *Chronicle of Theophanes Confessor,* AM 6005 (239).

69. The *Greek Anthology* records six inscriptions from a church of Saint Euphemia "ta Olybriou" refurbished by Anicia Juliana, and, like Hagios Polyeuktos, built by generations of women of her line. See Paton, *Greek Anthology,* vol. 1, nos. 12–15. They are similar in tone and language to the epigrams in the Dioscurides manuscript and in Hagios Polyeuktos. For a

comparative analysis of these epigrams, see Connor, "Epigram," 479–527. For Saint Euphemia en Oblibriou, see Raymond Janin, *La Géographie ecclèsiastique de l'empire Byzantin, I et III, Les Eglises et les monastères* (Paris, 1969), 120–30, esp. 124–26. For the Honoratae Church, see Theophanes, *Chronographia,* AM 6005 (de Boor 157, rr 34 ss), and Janin, *Géographie,* 121–23; for a church of Saint Stephen *en Konstantinianais,* founded by Anicia Juliana, who built it to house the saint's relics which she had brought from Jerusalem, see Janin, *Géographie,* 475–76; the parallel with Athenais Eudocia is evident.

70. For a discussion of the peacock as Juliana's symbol, see Connor, "Epigram," esp. 509 and n. 64.

71. For the Greek epigram and its English translation by Martin Harrison, see Harrison, *Saraçhane,* 5–7; see also Paton, *Greek Anthology,* book 1, epigram 10. The lines will be noted after each excerpt. As with the manuscript's epigram, the language of this epigram is too complicated grammatically to render the translation in poetic setting.

72. See Brubaker, "Memories of Helena," esp. 56 on Juliana's place in the tradition of church-building women.

73. For a fuller analysis of the metrical inscription, see Connor, "Epigram."

74. The church of Hagia Euphemia also had a series of epigrams inscribed in its interior, as mentioned above; it is also possible the Vienna Dioscurides epigram was inscribed in the church at Honoratae, and that Anicia Juliana was the author of all these prominently exhibited inscriptions.

75. If one is to believe, even in part, the allegations by Procopius about the greed and corruption of Justinian and his associates, she would have had good reason to fear for her family and her fortune; see Procopius, *Secret History,* trans. R. Atwater (Ann Arbor, 1966).

76. The story and quotations are taken from the English translation of the text excerpted from *De gloria martyrum, PL,* 71, cols. 793–95), in Harrison, *Saraçhane,* 8–9.

77. The story told by Gregory of Tours that Anicia Juliana had her wealth made into gold plates to cover the roof (or ceiling) of Hagios Polyeuktos is revealing about the fate of much private wealth in Justinian's time; the fortune in gold revetment necessary to cover the ceiling of Hagios Polyeuktos has been estimated at 331 Roman pounds; see Marlia Mango, "The Monetary Value of Silver Revetments and of Objects Belonging to Churches, A.D. 300–700," in *Ecclesiastical Silver Plate,* ed. Boyd and Mango, 126.

78. See chapter 3, p. 62 and note 52, for a discussion of the detailed report of the excavation of this church in Pères Hughes Vincent and F.-M. Abel, *Jérusalem: Recherches de topographie, d'archéologie et d'histoire* 2:743–925.

79. See Mark Johnson, "On the Burial Places of the Theodosian Dynasty," *Byzantion* 61 (1991): 330–39, esp. 334.

## Chapter 6: The Challenge of Theodora

1. The best photographic plates of the San Vitale ensemble are published in *La Basilica di San Vitale a Ravenna; The Basilica of San Vitale Ravenna,* ed. Patrizia Angiolini Martinelli (Modena, Italy, 1997), *Atlas,* vol. 1; for the Theodora panel, see plates 434–40, esp. details 436–37. See also the hand-retouched plates in André Grabar, *Byzantine Painting* (New York, 1953), 60–70.

2. See Averil Cameron, *Procopius and the Sixth Century* (Berkeley, 1985), chap. 5, "Proco-

pius and Theodora," 67–83, esp. 67, n. 1, for the titles of novels and plays with titles such as "Empress of the Dusk" or "Theodora and the Emperor." See also Anne McClanan, "The Empress Theodora and the Tradition of Women's Patronage in the Early Byzantine Empire," in *The Cultural Patronage of Medieval Women,* ed. June Hall McCash (Athens, Ga., 1996), 57, in which she states that such books demonstrate "the ready acceptance of Procopius's slander."

3. I first presented the introductory material in this chapter in my paper "Theodora's Challenge"; see *Abstracts of the Byzantine Studies Conference* 18 (1991): 22. The problematic depiction of Theodora in the *Secret History* is summarized in Pauline Allen, "Contemporary Portrayals of the Byzantine Empress Theodora (A.D. 527–548)," in *Stereotypes of Women in Power: Historical Perspectives and Revisionist Views,* ed. B. Garlick, S. Dixon, and P. Allen (Westport, Conn., 1992), 93–104. For an excellent assessment of this problem, see Elizabeth A. Fisher, "Theodora and Antonina in the *Historia Aracana:* History and/or Fiction?" *Arethusa* 11 (1978): 253–79.

4. The best histories of the period are John W. Barker, *Justinian and the Later Roman Empire* (Madison, 1977), and J. A. S. Evans, *The Age of Justinian: The Circumstances of Imperial Power* (New York, 1996). See also Warren Treadgold, *A History of the Byzantine State and Society* (Stanford, Calif., 1997), esp. on Justinian's reign, chap. 6, 174–218. Also John Julius Norwich, *The Early Centuries* (New York, 1989), is a readable, well-informed popular version.

5. See Cameron, *Procopius,* 3–18, for an introduction to the problem of Procopius, his background, and his works.

6. See Glanville Downey, "Justinian as Builder," *AB* 32 (1950): 262–6.

7. See Geoffrey Greatrex, "The Dates of Procopius' Works," *BMGS* 18 (1994): 101–14, in which he agrues for a date of 550–51 for books 1–7 of the *Wars,* 550–51 for the *Secret History,* 554 for book 8 of the *Wars,* and 554 for the *Buildings;* Procopius died in 554.

8. See Janet Fairweather, "Fiction in the Biographies of Ancient Writers," *Ancient Society* 5 (1974): 231–75; see esp. on conventions of invective, 245–47.

9. The English translation used is Richard Atwater, *Procopius, Secret History* (Ann Arbor, 1963) because of its easily readable prose. For the Greek, see H. B. Dewing, *Procopius, Secret History* (Cambridge, Mass., 1998). Passages from the *Secret History* are followed by references to chapter and line for ease of access to any Greek or English edition.

10. See, for example, *Secret History,* chap. 4.25: "he [Belisarius] was not conscious that he had once been a man."

11. See, for example, esp. chap. 17.

12. When in chapter 10 Procopius claims that the law made it possible not only for Justinian to marry Theodora but also for "anyone else to marry a courtesan," this twists the actual import of the law, for only a former actress that had been made a patrician would qualify, a rarefied category indeed. See also Garland, *Byzantine Empresses,* 14–16, for more on Justinian's laws governing marriage, inheritance, and rape.

13. See, for example, Bernard Stolte, "Desires Denied: Marriage, Adultery and Divorce in Early Byzantine Law," in *Desire and Denial in Byzantium,* ed. Liz James (Brookfield, Vt., 1999), 77–86, esp. 80–82. See also David Daube, "The Marriage of Justinian and Theodora: Legal and Theological Reflections," *Catholic University of America Law Review* 16 (1967): 380–99, esp. 388–89, 392. The law pardons not only penitent actresses: a further paragraph in the law says that a woman promoted to the Patriciate is also rid of blemish (391). That this was designed as personal protection for Justinian and Theodora in case they had children or an heir is established by Daube (393).

14. See, for example, chap. 17.7ff, in which she arranges marriages for women with men who are far below their social class.

15. Theodora's efforts at managing profitable and advantageous marriages for her own family show her concern for those related to her, especially in her arranging intermarriage with the house of the emperor Anastasius and propelling her own niece, Sophia, into a marriage with her nephew, Justin. She never knew she succeeded in an alliance that eventually put Justin and Sophia on the throne of Byzantium. See Garland, *Byzantine Empresses,* 37–38, and A. Cameron, "The House of Anastasius," *GRBS* 19 (1978): 259–76. For the success of the marriage connections engineered by Theodora, see Cameron, *Procopius,* 80–81.

16. See P. Allen, "Contemporery Portrayals of the Empress Theodora (A.D. 527–548)," in B. Garlick et al. *Stereotypes of Women in Power,* 93–103. Allen claims, "However, the exaggerated and prurient account of her exploits by Procopius must be seen as pertaining to that stereotype that links female power with rampant sexuality, that attempts to blacken both the prominent woman and those associated with her" (95).

17. Compare this with a formulaic rhetorical and somewhat fawning description in the *Buildings* of her statue on a purple column near the Arcadianae baths: "The statue is indeed beautiful, but still inferior to the beauty of the Empress," *Buildings* 1.11.9.

18. See Charles Pazdernik, "'Our Most Pious Consort Given Us by God': Dissident Reactions to the Partnership of Justinian and Theodora, A.D. 525–548," *Classical Antiquity* 13 (1994): 256–81, esp. 263. See also McClanan, "Empress Theodora and the Tradition of Women's Patronage," in Cash, ed., *Cultural Patronage of Medieval Women,* 50–72, esp. 59. See also, in the same volume, Allen, "Portrayals of Theodora," 94.

19. See *Secret History* 15.10.

20. *Wars* 1.24.33; see also J. A. S. Evans, "The 'Nika' Rebellion and the Empress Theodora," *Byzantion* 54 (1984): 380–82, for the ambiguities intended by Procpius in relating this story; see also the discussion of this episode in Garland, *Byzantine Empresses,* 32–33.

21. See *ODB,* s.v. "Demons," 609.

22. *Secret History* 22.27.

23. It is noteworthy that Justinian is accused by Procopius of the opposite misdemeanor: he didn't spend enough time sleeping, but "hardly ever slept" (15.11).

24. *Secret History* 16.1.

25. When on campaign with Belisarius Procopius must have been kept informed of all details of diplomacy and tactics; not surprisingly, he was constantly frustrated while in residence in the palace in Constantinople at not having access to all the information he would have liked.

26. See Procopius, *Buildings* 1.2.17; 1.11.24–35 on hospices built by Theodora in the center of the city. See also McClannan "Empress Theodora," 61, on Theodora's patronage of buildings in Antioch and, 62, in Jerusalem. See *The Chronicle of John Malalas,* trans. Elizabeth Jeffreys, Michael Jeffreys, and Roger Scott (Melbourne, 1986), esp. 17.18 and 18.23–28. See also Garland, *Byzantine Empresses,* 21.

27. *Buildings* 1.9.5–6.

28. John Malalas mentions Theodora's crackdown on brothel keepers and her "freeing the girls from the yoke of their wretched slavery" in book 18, chap. 24 (Jeffreys et al., eds., *Chronicle of John Malalas,* 255.) For Theodora's acts of philanthropy and patronage, see the works of John of Ephesus, John Malalas, and John Lydus, as discussed in McClanan, "Empress Theodora and the Tradition of Women's Patronage," in McCash, ed., *Cultural Patronage of Medieval Women,* 50–

72; see esp. 57 on the founding of Repentance as a punitive act vs. a consolitory one. Theodora evidently cosponsored numerous buildings around the empire; her personal initiative is difficult to substantiate, although the presence of her monogram with Justinian's at Hagia Sophia, for example, and her inclusion in dedicatory inscriptions, such as that at Saints Sergius and Bacchus, indicate some involvement.

29. *Secret History* 17.24–6.

30. As Averil Cameron points out, she was still represented as a patron and commemmoree in Orthodox churches, such as Hagia Sophia and Saints Sergius and Bacchus in Constantinople and at the monastery at Sinai (Cameron, *Procopius,* 80).

31. John of Ephesus, *Lives of the Eastern Saints,* ed. and trans. E. W. Brooks, *Patrologia Orientalis,* vol. 18, fasc. 4 (Paris, 1924), 525–681. For an assessment of Theodora's Monophysite activity, see Garland, *Byzantine Empresses,* "Theodora and the Church," 23–29; as Garland states, "Theodora was at the centre of a complex nexus directly responsible for the spread of monophysitism as a dynamic faith" (29).

32. See Cameron, *Procopius,* 76–77, 80; and John of Ephesus, *Lives of the Eastern Saints,* in *Patrologia Orientalis* 17 (1924).

33. Garland believes that Justinian was partially won over to support of Monophysitism, or at least that he permitted her involvement in the movement (*Byzantine Empresses,* 29).

34. See *Wars* 1.25.4. For the Law Code, see Daube, "The Marriage of Justinian and Theodora," 380–99, esp. 397, on this confesssional statement by Justinian in Novel 74.4.

35. See Pazdernik, "Our Most Pious Consort Given Us by God," 256–81, esp. 266 on Novel 8.1 of 535 AD.

36. See Cameron, *Procopius,* 67–83, esp. 81–83. Overall, Procopius is thoroughly biased as a source on Theodora, for example: "Deeply suspicious of women, especially if they have acquired power, Procopius was hostile to Theodora from the beginning" (81).

37. See Pazdernik, "Our Most Pious Consort Given Us by God," 256–81, esp. 267.

38. See Averil Cameron, "The Empress Sophia," *Byzantion* 45 (1975): 5–21; repr. in *Continuity and Change in Sixth-Century Byzantium* (London, 1981), xi.

39. For an excellent assessment of women in Procopius's writings, see Fisher, "Theodora and Antonina," 260.

40. Ibid., 261–66, 272.

41. Ibid., 275.

42. Ibid., 276.

43. See Charles Barber, "The Imperial Panels at San Vitale: A Reconsideration," in *BMGS* 14 (1990): 19–42 and n. 1 on p. 19 for the extensive bibliography on these panels.

44. See T. F. Mathews, *The Early Churches of Constantinople: Architecture and Liturgy* (University Park, Md., 1971), 146–47.

45. For a brilliant interpretation of the mosaics, see Otto Von Simson, *Sacred Fortress: Byzantine Art and Statecraft in Ravenna* (Chicago, 1948), 23–39; for the dating, see 29. Where mosaics depicting patronage were not installed, the presence of monograms, such as those of Justinian and Theodora in Hagia Sophia in Constantinople, would serve a similar purpose; the dedicatory inscription in Saints Sergius and Bacchus evokes Theodora's generosity in the building of this church.

46. See Martinelli, *San Vitale,* vol. 1, pls. 434–40. For details of Theodora, 436–37; for details of Antonina and Joannina, 438.

47. *Secret History,* 10.11.

48. Vienna Kunsthistorisches Museum, Antikensammlung, X39; see *Age of Spirituality,* no. 25, 31–32, and Richard Delbrueck, *Die Consulardiptychen und verwandte Denkmäler* (Berlin and Leipzig, 1929), no. 52.

49. Procopius, *Buildings,* 1.11.1–9.

50. Procopius, *Buildings,* 1.10.16–19.

51. The senatorial entourage in the Chalke mosaic may have resembled that on the Theodosian obelisk still standing in the hippodrome of Constantinople. Note that the hippodrome base does not include the empress Flaccilla, while the Chalke mosaic did include Theodora, perhaps indicating a change in the public image of imperial consorts in the 150-year interval between the production of the two images.

52. While Barber asserts that in the Ravenna mosaic Theodora is "transgressing male boundaries" by wearing "adapted male clothing" and that she is "of both sexes and of neither" (37–39), I would prefer to see Theodora's images as representing the concept of female imperal rule; rather than transgressing gender boundaries, the image reaffirms her authority as both woman and empress, which was certainly not a new concept in Byzantium.

53. See *Secret History,* 17.24–26.

54. See Irina Andreescu-Treadgold and Warren Treadgold, "Procopius and the Imperial Panels of S. Vitale," *Art Bulletin* 79 (1997): 708–23. See also Irina Andreescu-Treadgold and Warren Treadgold, "Dates and Identities in the Imperial Panels of San Vitale," *Abstracts of the Byzantine Studies Conference* 16 (1990): 52–54.

55. *Secret History,* 4.17.

56. See ibid., chaps. 4 and 5.

57. See Martinelli, *San Vitale,* vol. 1, pls. 434–40 (Theodora panel) and pls. 421–27 (Justinian panel). See also Von Simson, *Sacred Fortress,* pls. 2 and 18.

58. Belisarius fell into disgrace and was recalled to Constantinople in 548, providing a terminus ante quem for the mosaics. Andreescu-Treadgold and Treadgold believe they were installed in late 544 to early 545 ("Imperial Panels," 721).

59. *Secret History,* 5.19.

60. See Andreescu-Treadgold and Treadgold, "Imperial Panels" 720.

61. Von Simson, *Sacred Fortress,* 39, originally made the case that the panels were intended to represent the presence of the sovereigns in Ravenna: "In these awe-inspiring images the sovereigns, though far away in Byzantium, had actually set foot on the soil of Italy." My interpretation lends a double purpose to this transported presence. The case made by Thomas Mathews for the liturgical representation being the Little Entrance ceremony as it took place in Hagia Sophia might be pushed one stage further, for the ceremony envisioned now extends to a liturgy in Hagia Sophia which will culminate in an imperial marriage. Since Justinian and Theodora never visited Ravenna, it has been suggested by F. W. Deichmann that the portraits in San Vitale were copies of *laureia,* ceremonial pictures, that were sent from Constantinople to Ravenna, and that this is the means by which vivid personal likenesses were achieved.

62. On Roman jewelry, see Ann Stout, "Jewelry as a Symbol of Status in the Roman Empire," in *The World of Roman Costume,* ed. Judith Sebesta and Larissa Bonfante, (Madison, 1994), 77–100; Stout claims, "Jewelry thus played a prominent role in Roman society in distinguishing one's rank and state. Among Roman citizens it indicated whether you were an aristocrat, whether or not you had imperial favor, or whether you were married or betrothed. In all periods

it spoke of one's wealth" (83). For numerous examples of women wearing jewelry in the Fayuum portraits, see Euphrosyne Doxiadis, *The Mysterious Fayum Portraits: Faces from Ancient Egypt* (New York, 1995).

63. Stout, "Jewelry," 83.

64. The crown with pendilia worn by Theodora is consistent with those worn by Theodosian empresses in the coin portraits discussed in chapter 3 above. The first was Flaccilla, who had the same large forehead jewel as her husband, Theodosius I; she wears the chlamys and the three-pendant brooch as well.

65. See *Glory of Byzantium*, figs. on 187.

66. Inv. VII B 307: see Stout, "Jewelry," 87 and fig. 5.14.

67. See *Age of Spirituality*, cat. no. 294, 317–18.

68. Metropolitan Museum inv. 95.15.115; see ibid., cat. nos. 275, 302–03.

69. See M. C. Ross, *Byzantine and Early Mediaeval Antiquities in the Dumbarton Oaks Collection*, vol 2, *Jewelry, Enamels, and Art of the Migration Period* (Washington, D.C., 1965), D.O. no. 28.9, cat. no. 1B, E, 1–4, and pl. B.

70. Ibid., D.O. no. 28.12, cat. no. 4A, fig. 5.17; see also *Age of Spirituality*, cat. no. 286, 312.

71. Antikenmuseum, Berlin State Museums, inv. 30219.505. See Stout, "Jewelry," 89 and fig. 5.18, and K. R. Brown, "Necklace," in *Age of Spirituality*, 310–11 and fig. 284.

72. Metropolitan Museum, inv. 17.190.1670.1671; see *Age of Spiritualilty*, cat. nos. 300, 323–24. For early Byzantine jewelry, see ibid., 297–301.

73. Milan, Castello Sforzesco, Civico Museo d'Arte Antica, 755. See Stout, "Jewelry," 94–95 and figs. 5.30–32; see also *Age of Spirituality*, cat. no. 27, 33. See also ibid., cat. nos. 25 and 26 on pp. 31 and 32, an ivory diptych showing Ariadne and a bronze bust of Euphemia with very similar hairstyles and crowns.

74. This top-of-the-head ornament on the Milan head may have consisted of attached jewels, just as the use of now-lost attachments is assumed in the statuette tentatively identified as Flaccilla in the Cabinet des Médailles in Paris (fig. 4 in this book). The crown and snooded hair covering are also seen in the ivory Ariadne diptych of ca. 500 in the Kunsthistorisches Museum, Antikensammlung, in Vienna (Stout, *Jewelry*, 96 and fig. 5.33, and *Age of Spiritualility*, cat. nos. 25, 31–32). For hairstyles and headdresses in Byzantium, see Melita Emmanuel, "Some Notes on the External Appearance of Ordinary Women in Byzantium; Hairstyles, Headdresses: Texts and Iconography," in *Stephanos: Byzantinoslavica* 56 (1995): 769–78, and esp. M. Emmanuel, "Hairstyles and Headdresses of Empresses, Princesses and Ladies of the Aristocracy in Byzantium," in *Deltion tis Christ. Arch. Het.* 17 (1993–94): 113–20.

75. The story of the smuggling of silkworms into Byzantium in the staffs of men posing as itinerant monks, described in Procopius, *Wars* 8.17.1–8, is well known. This was to have taken place ca. 554.

76. See Adele La Barre Starensier, *An Art Historical Study of the Byzantine Silk Industry* (Ann Arbor, 1982), esp. 130. For the color purple and its symbolism, use in textiles, and dyeing from the murex molusk, see *ODB*, s.v. "Purple," 1759–60.

77. Starensier, *Silk Industry*, 116–31.

78. See *Byzance*, cat. no. 104, 154, of the fifth to sixth century. For other figural designs on silks (in color), see, for example, nos. 101, 103, 195, 284, 285.

79. For examples of Christian scenes in woven textiles, see *Age of Spirituality*, cat. nos. 390–92, 412–13, 477, 494.

80. See Starensier, *Silk Industry*, 116–20. See also *Byzance*, cat. no. 281, 374–75; for informative introductions to the silks in this catalogue, see *Byzance*, Marielle Martiniani-Reber, "Textiles," 148–51, and "Les Textiles IX^e–XII^e Siècles," 370–73.

81. See *Handbook of the Byzantine Collection*, Dumbarton Oaks (Washington, D.C., nd), D.O. no. 34.1, fig. 371.

82. See Starensier, *Silk Industry*, 134.

83. Ibid., 133.

84. See *Byzance*, cat. no. 280, 374.

85. Stout, "Jewelry," 96–98; she claims that as time went on, the maxim for wearing of jewelry was "the showier the better" (98).

## Chapter 7: Ordinary Women in the Orbit of Theodore of Sykeon

1. *Three Byzantine Saints: Contemporary Biographies of St. Daniel the Stylite, St. Theodore of Sykeon and St. John the Almsgiver*, translated from the Greek by Elizabeth Dawes and Norman H. Baynes (Crestwood, N.Y., 1977), is a partial translation. For the full Greek text and translation (French), see André-Jean Festugière, ed. and trans., *Vie de Théodore de Sykeon*, Subsidia Hagiographica, 48, 2 vols. (Brussels, 1970). *The Life of St. Theodore of Sykeon* will be referred to in the text as *Life of Theodore;* individual passages are quoted from the Dawes and Baynes translation. In parentheses after each passage, chapter and line refer to the Greek edition, for the convenience of readers of either the Greek or English version. For the location of Sykeon, see Festugière, *Vie de Théodore*, 2, 168.

2. See Robin Cormack, *Writing in Gold: Byzantine Society and Its Icons* (New York, 1985), chapter 1, "Theodore of Sykeon: The Visible Saint," 9–49, for a commentary on the Life, especially for the "accuracy" of such a text, 18–20. See also *Life of Theodore*, chaps. 22 and 148 (Festugière, 1–2, 22, 170) for the author's self-introduction, dating of the saint's life, and for his invocation of God's prayers for his salvation.

3. Festugière, *Vie de Théodore*, 1–2.

4. *Life of Theodore*, 4.

5. See Peter Brown, "The Rise and Function of the Holy Man in Late Antiquity" *JRS* 61 (1971): 80–101; repr. in *Society and the Holy in Late Antiquity*, ed. Peter Brown (Berkeley, 1982), 103–53; also, Peter Brown, "Arbiters of the Holy: The Christian Holy Man in Late Antiquity," in *Authority and the Sacred: Aspects of the Christianisation of the Roman World* (Cambridge, Mass., 1995), 55–78.

6. I owe this quantitative analysis to my student Lisa Clifford, whose tables provided useful profiles of Theodore's miracles.

7. For a study of the relationships between mothers and daughters as found in hagiographies, see Susan A. Harvey, "Sacred Bonding: Mothers and Daughters in Early Syriac Hagiography," *Journal of Early Christian Studies* 4 (1996): 27–56. See also S. Harvey, "Women in Early Byzantine Hagiography: Reversing the Story," in *That Gentle Strength: Historical Perspectives on Women in Christianity*, ed. Lynda L. Coon, Katherine J. Haldane, and Elisabeth W. Sommer (Charlottesville and London, 1990).

# Introduction to Part 3: Women, the Faith in Icons, and the Triumph of the Orthodoxy

1. For the relationship between image and viewer in the period after iconoclasm, see Thomas F. Mathews, "The Sequel to Nicaea II in Byzantine Church Decoration," *Perkins Journal* 41 (1988): 11–21.

2. For a convenient collection of excerpts of the *horoi* of the Council of 787 and from theologians who helped define these distinctions, see Mango, *Art,* esp. 165–77. See also *ODB,* s.vv. "Icons," 977–78, and "Iconoclasm," 975–77.

3. For an in-depth study of the period of iconoclasm and the three female rulers who affected the outcome, see Judith Herrin, *Women in Purple: Rulers of Medieval Byzantium* (Princeton, 2001).

4. See Lynda Garland, *Byzantine Empresses: Women and Power in Byzantium, AD 527–1204* (London and New York, 1999), chap. 4, "Irene," 73–94, esp. 80, 92–93; also Herrin, *Women in Purple,* chap. 2, "Irene: The Unknown Empress from Athens," 51–129.

5. See Herrin, *Women in Purple,* 104–05.

6. See Garland, *Byzantine Empresses,* 90, for Irene's exile by Nicephorus I. For the revival of iconoclasm, see Herrin, *Women in Purple,* 153. For the Life of Irene the Empress, who became a saint, see Warren T. Treadgold, "The Unpublished Saint's Life of the Empress Irene (BHG 2205)," *BF* 8 (1982): 237–51; and for the Greek, see François Halkin, "Deux Impératrices de Byzance, I: La Vie de l'impératrice sainte Irène et le second concile de Nicée en 787," *AB* 106 (1988): esp. 5–27.

7. See ibid., 92.; Cyril Mango, *The Brazen House: A Study of the Vestibule of the Imperial Palace of Constantinople* (Copenhagen, 1959), 150. See also Marie-France Auzépy, "La destruction de l'icone du Christ de la Chalcé par Léon III: Propagande ou réalité?" *Byzantion* 60 (1990): 445–92, esp. 449.

8. See A. P. Kazhdan ad Alice-Mary Talbot, "Women and Iconoclasm," *BZ* 84–85 (1991–92): 391–408; according to an entry in the *Synaxarium of Constantinople,* Theodosia led a group of women in resistance to the order, and they were executed in the Forum of the Ox; in an alternate version the woman's name was Maria (392 and n. 4).

9. Auzépy, "La destruction de l'icone du Christ," 445–92, esp. 481–82. As Auzépy suggests, the legend "became history" (491). See Robin Cormack, "Women and Icons, and Women in Icons," in *Women, Men and Eunuchs: Gender in Byzantium,* ed. Liz James (London and New York, 1997), 39–43, for a summary of the evidence and the evolution of Maria into Theodosia and the invention of propaganda by the iconophiles after iconoclasm.

10. See Cormack, "Women and Icons," 24–51, esp. 24, 35–43. That this story is part of the polemics of the iconoclast side, thereby villainizing women, is dealt with by Cormack's assessment of the origin and agendas of the sources; the complexity of the interpretation of such stories is evident.

11. Auzépy, "La destruction de l'icone du Christ," 462.

12. See *Kassia: The Legend, the Woman and Her Work,* ed. and trans. Antonia Tripolitis (New York and London, 1992).

13. See ibid.: Thekla (4–5), Pelagia (6–7), Barbara (12–13), Agatha (42–43), Eudocia of the Samarians (44–45), Mary of Egypt (48–49), and Christina of Tyre (56–65). She also composed hymns to Mary Magdalene and the Virgin Mary.

14. See Garland, *Byzantine Empresses,* 100–101.

15. Ibid. 102–03; for the epigram inscribed beside the Chalke icon, see 103.

16. Ibid., 104–08.

17. See Judith Herrin, "Public and Private Forms of Religious Commitment among Byzantine Women," 181–203, in *Women in Ancient Societies: An Illusion of the Night,* ed. Leonie J. Archer, Susan Fischler, and Maria Wyke (London, 1994); see also Judith Herrin, "Women and the Faith in Icons in Early Christianity," in *Culture, Ideology and Politics,* ed. Raphael Sammuel and Gareth Stedman Jones (London, 1982), 56–83, esp. 69–70.

18. See Herrin, "Women and the Faith in Icons," 72: The cult of icons provided a suitable vehicle for the expression of female religiosity, being a very personal one which could be practiced privately either at church or at home.

19. Herrin, "'Femina Byzantina': The Council in Trullo on Women," *DOP* 46 (1992): 97–105.

20. Herrin, "Public and Private," 191–99.

21. Judith Herrin, "Women and the Church in Byzantium," *Bulletin of the British Association of Orientalists* 11 (1980): 8–14, esp. 9.

22. Lynda Garland, "The Life and Ideology of Byzantine Women: A Further Note on Conventions of Behaviour and Social Reality as Reflected in Eleventh- and Twelfth-Century Historical Sources," *Byzantion* 58 (1988): 361–93.

23. See Charles M. Brand, "Some Byzantine Women of Thebes—and Elsewhere," *To Hellenikon: Studies in Honor of Speros Vryonis, Jr.* (New York, 1993), 1:59–68.

24. See Garland, *Byzantine Empresses,* on Zoe, chap. 8, 136–55, and on Theodora, chap. 9, 161–67.

25. Garland, "Life and Ideology," 387–89.

26. Ibid., 392.

## Chapter 8: Women's Monasticism

1. London, British Museum, M&LA 1988, 4–11,1 (National Icon Collection, no. 18); see D. Buckton, ed., *Byzantium: Treasures of Byzantine Art and Culture From British Collections* (London, 1994), cat. no. 140, 129–31, and pl. 140.

2. Her Life by Constantine Acropolites is edited in *PG* 140, col. 921c, although she is thought to be legendary; see Marie-France Auzépy, "La destruction de l'icone du Christ de la Chalcé par Léon III: Propagande ou réalité?" *Byzantion* 60 (1990): 445–492, esp. 481–82.

3. On punishments, see Alexander P. Kazhdan and Alice-Mary Talbot, "Women and Iconoclasm," *BZ* 84–85 (1991–92): 391–408, esp. 404.

4. On brideshows in the eighth and ninth centuries, see W. T. Treadgold, "The Bride-shows of the Byzantine Emperors," *Byzantion* 49 (1979): 395–413, esp. 404–06.

5. See Alice-Mary Talbot, "A Comparison of the Monastic Experience of Byzantine Men and Women," *Greek Orthodox Theological Review* 30 (1985): 1–20. See also, in general, Alice-Mary Talbot, "Byzantine Women, Saints' Lives, and Social Welfare," in *Through the Eye of a Needle: The Judaeo-Christian Roots of Social Welfare,* edd. E. A. Hanawalt, C. Lindbergh (Kirksville, Mo., 1994), 105–22; see also Dorothy Abrahamse, "Women's Monasticism in the Middle Byzantine Period: Problems and Prospects," *BF* 9 (1985): 35–58. For the collected articles by Alice-Mary Talbot, see *Women and Religious Life in Byzantium* (Washington, D.C., 2001).

6. For a study of the typika, see Catia Galatariotou, "Byzantine Ktetorika Typika: A Comparative Study," *Revue des Etudes Byzantines* 5 (1987): 77–138. For a discussion of the types of founders' typika, see Alice-Mary Talbot, "The Byzantine Family and the Monastery," *Dumbarton Oaks Papers* 44 (1990): 119–29, esp. 128. See also the important work, John Philip Thomas, *Private Religious Foundations in the Byzantine Empire* (Washington, D.C., 1987).

7. See Talbot, "Byzantine Women, Saints' Lives, and Social Welfare," esp. 117–19.

8. For these two basic types and associated terms, see *ODB*, s.vv. "Typikon, Liturgical," 2131–32, and "Typikon, Monastic," 2132.

9. See Alice-Mary Talbot and Catia Galatariotou, "Byzantine Women's Monastic Communities: The Evidence of the Typika," *JOB* 38 (1988): 263–90. For studies and translations of monastic typika, see *Byzantine Monastic Foundation Documents,* ed. John Thomas and Angela C. Hero, 5 vols. (Washington, D.C., 2000).

10. See Talbot, "A Comparison of the Monastic Experience," 6, 13–14.

11. For the text, see Thomas and Hero, *Byzantine Monastic Foundation Documents,* vol. 2, *"Kecharitomene: Typikon of Empress Irene Doukaina Komnene for the Convent of the Mother of God Kecharitomene in Constantinople,"* trans. Robert Jordan, 649–724. See also Talbot and Galatariotou, "Monastic Communities," 263–64, n. 2. See also Angeliki Laiou, "Observations on the Life and Ideology of Byzantine Women," *BF* 9 (1985): 59–102, esp. 68ff and n. 28.

12. See Abrahamse, "Women's Monasticism," 46.

13. See Judith Herrin, "'Femina Byzantina': The Council in Trullo on Women," *Dumbarton Oaks Papers* 46 (1992): 97–105, esp. 105.

14. See Alice-Mary Talbot, "Late Byzantine Nuns: By Choice or Necessity?" *BF* 9 (1985): 103–17.

15. See Talbot, "Byzantine Women, Saints' Lives and Social Welfare," 120–21.

16. Ibid., 122.

17. See Talbot, "A Comparison of the Monastic Experience," esp. tables on 18–20.

18. Ibid., 5.

19. See Claudia Rapp, "Figures of Female Sanctity: Byzantine Edifying Manuscripts and Their Audience," *DOP* 50 (1996): 313–32, esp. 316.

20. See, for example, Barskij's drawings of the monastery of Nea Moni on the island of Chios, which still survives today, in Charalambos Bouras, *Nea Moni on Chios: History and Architecture* (Athens, 1982), fig. 15 on p. 49.

21. For a documentation of the monastery in recent color photographs, see Nano Chatzidakis, *Wall Mosaics and Frescoes: Hosios Loukas* (Athens, 1996); see also C. L. Connor, *Art and Miracles in Medieval Byzantium: The Crypt at Hosios Loukas and Its Frescoes* (Princeton, 1991).

22. See Lyn Rodley, *Cave Monasteries of Byzantine Cappadocia* (Cambridge, 1985).

23. See Talbot, "Byzantine Family and the Monastery," esp. 122.

24. On the different reasons women joined monasteries, see Talbot, "Late Byzantine Nuns," 103–17.

25. See Abrahamse, "Women's Monasticism," esp. 50.

26. See Alice-Mary Talbot, "Bluestocking Nuns: Intellectual Life in the Convents of Late Byzantium," *Okeanos, Essays Presented to Ihor Ševčenko on His Sixtieth Birthday by his Colleagues and Students = Harvard Ukranian Studies* 7 (1983): 604–18; see also Abrahamse, "Women's Monasticism," 53.

27. See Talbot, "Late Byzantine Nuns," 112.

28. This category of cross-dressing women has been the subject of a separate study; see Evelyne Patlagean, "L'histoire de la femme déguisée en moine et l'évolution de la sainteté féminine à Byzance," *Studi Medievali* 17 (1976): 597–623.

29. See Evelyne Patlagean, "Sainteté et Pouvoir," in *The Byzantine Saint* (Birmingham, 1981), 88–105, esp. 91–92, for a tabulation of preserved lives of middle Byzantine female saints, their dates, and oldest known text.

30. These recurring aspects of saints' lives are discussed in Patlagean, "Sainteté et Pouvoir," 92–105.

31. See *Holy Women of Byzantium: Ten Saints' Lives in English Translation,* ed. Alice-Mary Talbot (Washington, D.C., 1996), esp. vii. For a study of the process of sanctification of Theodora of Thessalonike, see Alice-Mary Talbot, "Family Cults in Byzantium: The Case of St. Theodora of Thessalonike," *Leimon: Studies Presented to Lennart Rydèn on His Sixty-Fifth Birthday,* ed. Jan Olof Rosenqvist (Uppsala, 1996), 49–69. See also, A.-M. Talbot, *ODB,* s.v. "Canonization," 372. Thanks to a new computerized database of information gleaned from middle Byzantine saints' lives there will soon be a means for social historians and hagiographers to use these texts as a tool. The Dumbarton Oaks Hagiography Project is launching a series which will focus on the Greek Lives of holy men and women of the eighth to fifteenth centuries. The first volume of the series has been published: Talbot, ed., *Holy Women of Byzantium.* The most complete list of Byzantine sources available in translation is found in E. A. Hanawalt, *An Annotated Bibliography of Byzantine Sources in English Translation* (Brookline, Mass., 1982). For comparable western medieval hagiographical studies, see R. M. Bell, *Saints and Society: The Two Worlds of Western Christendom, 1000–1700* (Chicago, 1982).

32. *The Life of St. Irene Abbess of Chrysobalanton: A Critical Edition with Introduction, Translation, Notes and Indices,* Jan Olof Rosenqvist (Uppsala, 1986). Because of conflicting numerations of sections within the Greek text, citations after quoted passages will refer to chapter, according to Rosenqvist's edition, and page in his English translation, for greatest utility to the reader. For the audiences of saints' lives among, respectively, men and women see Rapp, "Figures of Female Sanctity," 312–32.

33. Rosenqvist, *Life of Irene,* 13.

34. The name Chrysobalanton, meaning "golden purse," stems from a story that Irene of Bithynia, needing the funds to complete her monastery, had a dream that she would find what she needed in a place near the church of the Holy Apostles. Going there, she discovered the purse and named the monastery accordingly. The monastery was located north of the Holy Apostles on the heights; see Raymond Janin, *Constantinople Byzantine: Développement urbain et répertoire topographique* (Paris, 1964), 330–31.

35. For the audience and its expectations, see Rapp, "Figures of Female Sanctity."

36. See Alexander Kazhdan, "Byzantine Hagiography and Sex in the Fifth to Twelfth Centuries," *DOP* 44 (1990): 131–43, esp. 140–42 for demons and magic in provoking sexual temptation.

37. Keeping things secret is particularly prominent in the Gospel of Mark. I owe this comment to William Race.

38. This is the only topographic allusion helping to locate the convent, as its remains have not been found. The cistern of Aspar is in the northwest sector of Constantinople, on the fifth hill, north of the Church of the Holy Apostles (see map of Constantinople on p. xvii above).

39. See Rosenqvist, *Life of Irene,* xxvi–xxvii.

## Chapter 9: Women in Art: The Byzantine Image of Female Sanctity

1. This investigation stems from my work on portraits, first reported on in "The Portrait of the Holy Man in Middle Byzantine Art," International Congress of Byzantine Studies, Washington, D.C., 1986, *Abstracts of Short Papers,* 72. See also Carolyn L. Connor, *Art and Miracles in Medieval Byzantium: The Crypt at Hosios Loukas and Its Frescoes* (Princeton, 1991), 58–63 on style. A further stage, "Female Saints in Byzantine Monumental Decoration," was presented at the Byzantine Studies Conference, published in *Abstracts* 17 (1991): 48–49. See also Carolyn L. Connor, "Female Saints in Church Decoration of the Troodos Mountains in Cyprus," in *Medieval Cyprus: Studies in Art, Architecture, and History in Memory of Doula Mouriki,* Monographs of the Department of Art and Archaeology, ed. Nancy P. Ševčenko and Christopher Moss (Princeton, 1999), 211–28.

2. See Henry Maguire, *Glory of Byzantium,* 210–12, with color plates.

3. See ibid., 210, for the interpretations given by modern scholars, including the possibility of the Islamic origins of the dancing figures. Since they, like the figures on two further plaques showing female personifications of Humility and Truth, wear thin diadems or filets around their haloed heads, it is possible they also are allegorical figures associated with the imperial personae, or that they are motifs associated with the pleasures of courtly entertainment.

4. Madrid, National Library, *Chronicle of John Skylitzes,* Vitr. 26–2, fol. 102r (a), dating to ca. 1150–75. See André Grabar and M. Manoussacas, *L'illustration du manuscrit de Skylitzès de la bibliothèque nationale de Madrid* (Venice, 1979), 62–63, fig. 110 and pl. 19.

5. For a detailed assessment of developments in imagery, see Hans Belting, *Likeness and Presence: A History of the Image Before the Era of Art* (Chicago, 1994), esp. chap. 7, "Image Devotion, Public Relations, and Theology at the End of Antiquity," 115–43, and chap. 8, "Church and Image: The Doctrine of the Church and Iconoclasm," 144–63.

6. Vatican Library, Vat. Pal. gr 431, sheet 12. For the standard work, and examples of classical models, see Kurt Weitzmann, *The Joshua Roll: A Work of the Macedonian Renaissance,* Studies in Manuscript Illunination 3 (Princeton, 1948). For color illustrations, see *Glory of Byzantium,* 239. On the Macedonian Renaissance, see Kurt Weitzmann, "The Character and Intellectual Origins of the Macedonian Renaissance," in *Studies in Classical and Byzantine Manuscript Illumination* (Chicago and London, 1971), 176–223.

7. Paris, Bibliothèque Nationale, ms. gr. 139, fol. 1v. See H. Omont, *Miniatures des plus anciens manuscrits grecs,* 2d ed. (Paris, 1929), pl. 1.

8. Paris, Bibliothèque Nationale, ms. gr. 139, fol. 5v. See H. Omont, *Miniatures des plus anciens manuscrits grecs,* 2d ed. (Paris, 1929), pl. 5. See Weitzmann, "Macedonian Renaissance," 203 and fig. 184.

9. See Irmgard Hutter, "Das Bild der Frau in der Byzantinischen Kunst," *Byzantios: Festschruft für H. Hunger zum 70, Geburtstag* (Vienna, 1984), 163–74.

10. *Kg.* 54:219. See *Glory of Byzantium,* no. 157 on p. 234. The Adam and Eve plaque is on one side of this rosette casket, a characteristic type. All the other plaques display the same puppet- or doll-like quality.

11. On naming, see Henry Maguire, *The Icons of Their Bodies: Saints and Their Images in Byzantium* (Princeton, 1996), esp. chap. 3, "Naming and Individuality," 100–145; on individual aspects of female saints, see 28–34.

12. See Connor, *Art and Miracles,* 58–63, on the iconography of style.

13. For a study of these qualities and their priorities, see Liz James, *Light and Colour in Byzantine Art* (Oxford, 1996).

14. St. Gregory of Nyssa, *Laudatio S. Theodori,* in Mango, *Art,* 37.

15. Photius, Homily 17, in Mango, *Art,* 189 .

16. Mango, *Art,* 187 (Photius, Homily 17); see also Cyril Mango, trans., *The Homiles of Photius Patriarch of Constantinople* (Washington, D.C., 1958), 286–96, esp. 296. See also Robin Cormack, *Writing in Gold: Byzantine Society and Its Icons* (New York, 1985), chap. 4, "Afer Iconoclasm: The Illusion of Tradition," 141–78, esp. 146–57 on the mosaic in Hagia Sophia. See also Hans Belting, "The Holy Image in Church Decoration and New Policy of Images," in Belting, *Likeness and Presence,* 164–83.

17. For a useful elaboration and illustration of this system, see Henry Maguire, "The Cycle of Images in the Church," in *Heaven on Earth: Art and the Church in Byzantium,* ed. Linda Safran (University Park, Penn., 1998), 121–51.

18. See Liz James, who rightly argues that the use of art, in particular selections of saints' portraits, is as individual as the circumstances behind each religious foundation ("Monks, Monastic Art, the Sanctoral Cycle and the Middle Byzantine Church," in *The Theotokos Evergetis and Eleventh-Century Monasticism,* ed. M. Mullett and A. Kerby [Belfast, 1994], 162–75).

19. For the revisions by Symeon Metaphrastes, see *ODB,* s.vv. "Menologion," 1341, "Synaxarion," 1991, and esp. "Symeon Metaphrastes," 1983–84; see also Nancy Patterson Ševčenko, *Illustrated Manuscripts of the Metaphrastian Menologion* (Chicago and London, 1990).

20. See Carolyn L. Connor and W. Robert Connor, trans., *The Life and Miracles of Saint Luke of Steiris, Text, Translation and Commentary* (Brookline, Mass., 1994), referred to hereafter as *Vita,* chapter 59.

21. See Connor, *Art and Miracles;* see also Carolyn L. Connor, "Hosios Loukas as a Victory Church," *GRBS* 33 (1992): 293–308. See Maguire, "The Cycle of Images," 125. For good color plates, see Nano Chatzidakis, *Mosaics and Frescoes: Hosios Loukas* (Athens, 1997).

22. The *Painter's Manual* by Dionysius of Fourna, an eighteenth-century guide to church decoration and icon painting written by a monk-artist, specifies that Constantine and Helena are to be placed to the right inside the doors of the naos and the holy women to the left: see *Ermeneia tes zographikes technes,* ed. A. Papadopoulos-Kerameus (St. Petersburg, 1909), 273.

23. See Claudia Rapp, "Figures of Female Sanctity: Byzantine Edifying Manuscripts and Their Audience," *DOP* 50 (1996): 313–32, esp. 332 for observations on the lack of gender-specific preferences in the audience for writings about monastic lives. Since art might be juxtaposed with literature in terms of appearances of women versus men, I would suggest that the distinct groupings of men versus women in art, rather than mixed groupings, must have meant something to the audience, and that this evidence does indeed suggest gender-specific concerns.

24. See William Tronzo, "Mimesis in Byzantium," *RES* 25: *Archaeology and Aesthetics* (1994): 61–76.

25. Brigitte Cazelles, *The Lady as Saint: A Collection of French Hagiographic Romances of the Thirteenth Century* (Philadelphia, 1991); Carolyn W. Bynum, *Fragmentation and Redemption: Essays on Gender and the Human Body in Medieval Religion* (New York, 1992), esp. 17, 27–51.

26. See Averil Cameron and Judith Herrin, eds., *Constantinople in the Early Eighth Century: The Parastaseis Syntomoi Chronikai* (Leiden, 1984), chap. 34, which mentions statues of Constantine and Helena on the roof of the Milion, seen with a cross (95), and chap. 52, which notes,

"In the Forum Bovis a silver gilt cross was set up and likenesses of Constantine and Helena, the hands of both . . . holding the cross" (127).

27. See Maguire, *Icons of Their Bodies*, 32–33.

28. See *ODB*, s.v. "Commendatio Animae," 488. See also S. Davis, *The Cult of Saint Thecla: A Tradition of Women's Piety in Late Antiquity* (Oxford, 2001).

29. See *Kassia: The Legend, the Woman, and Her Work*, ed. and trans. Antonia Tripolitis (New York and London, 1992), 42–43.

30. See *The Lives of the Holy Women Martyrs*, trans. and compiled from the Greek of *The Great Synaxaristes of the Orthodox Church* (Buena Vista, Col., 1991), 39–52.

31. See Sebastian Brock and Susan Harvey, *Holy Women of the Syrian Orient* (Berkeley, 1987), 150–76.

32. See *Lives of the Holy Women Martyrs*, 563–90.

33. See *ODB*, s.v. "Catherine of Alexandria," 392–93.

34. See *Lives of the Holy Women Martyrs*, 528–42.

35. See ibid., 369–80; also *ODB*, s.v. "Euphemia of Chalcedon," 747–48.

36. See *Lives of the Holy Women Martyrs*, 236–50. On Marina and her images, see also Jaroslav Folda, "The Saint Marina Icon: Maniera cypria, Lingua Franca, or Crusader Art?" in Bertrand Davezac, ed., *Four Icons in the Menil Collection*, (Austin, 1992), 107–33.

37. See ibid., 545–54.

38. See Judith Herrin, *Women in Purple: Rulers of Medieval Byzantium* (Princeton, 2001), 88–89: At the council of Nicaea of 787 Irene and her son were proclaimed, in imitation of Constantine I at the first Council of Nicaea in 325, the new Constantine and Helena.

39. Doula Mouriki stresses that portraits in monumental decoration must be seen as integrated in meaning with narrative scenes; see *The Mosaics of Nea Moni on Chios* (Athens, 1985), 207.

40. See Eustathius Stikas, *To Oikodomikon Xronikon Tes Mones Osiou Louka Fokidos* (Athens, 1970), pls. G, D and fig. 3b; see also Chatzidakis, *Wall Mosaics and Frescoes*, figs. 19–24.

41. See Robert S. Nelson, "The Discourse of Icons, Then and Now," *Art History* 12 (1989): 144–57, esp. 147–49.

42. For the role of angels in early Christian and Byzantine iconography, see Glen Peers, *Subtle Bodies: Representing Angels in Byzantium* (Berkeley, 2001).

43. See G. Kremos, *Fokika*, vol. 1 (Athens, 1874), 25–62, and Connor and Connor, *Saint Luke of Steiris*. See also the new edition with modern Greek translation by Demetrios Z. Sophianos, *Osios Loukas, O Bios tou: prolegomena—Metafrase—Kritike Ekdose tou Keimenou* (Athens, 1993).

44. See *Vita*, chaps. 61, 69–72.

45. See *Vita*, chap. 2.

46. For evidence of a burial society which included female members and functioned in association with Hosios Loukas, see J. Nesbitt and J. Wiita, "A Confraternity of the Comnenian Era," *BZ* 68 (1975): 360–84.

47. It has been suggested that women stood in the narthex during church services and at burials and that this custom is one explanation for the placement of their portraits in this location. A similar case of shared liturgical practices and location of images is represented by the mosaics of the Washing of the Feet which appear on the north walls of the narthex at Hosios Loukas, Daphni, and Nea Moni on Chios. The space in front of this wall was used for the ritual

foot washing performed at the monasteries as part of the Good Friday observances; see Tronzo, "Mimesis."

48. See Marcell Restle, *Die Byzantinische Wandmalerei in Kleinasien* (Recklinghausen, 1967), vol. 2, fig. 15.

49. Ibid., vol. 2, figs. 77, 82 and plan X.

50. Ibid. vol. 3, plan XXVI; see also Nicole Thierry, "Une image du triomphe impérial dans une église de Cappadoce: L'église de Nicéphore Phocas à Çavuşin," *Bulletin de la Société Nationale des Antiquaires de France* (1985): 28–35, esp. 31.

51. Restle, *Byzantinische Wandmalerei,* vol. 2, figs. 124 and plan XII.

52. Ibid., vol. 2, fig. 194 and plan XXI.

53. Ibid., vol. 2, figs. 279–301 and plan XXV; see esp. 295–99 for the half-length orant figures of female saints.

54. The popularity of the True Cross in Cappadocian church decoration is discussed by Nicole Thierry, "La Croix en Cappadoce: Typologie et Valeur Représentative," in *Le Site monastique copte des Kellia: Sources historiques et explorations archéologiques* (Geneva, 1987), 197–212, esp. 206. Before and during the iconoclast era, the cult of the cross was widespread in Cappadocia, and the cross appeared as the principal symbol of Christian sacrifice and victory in church decoration. After iconoclasm the image of Constantine and Helena holding the True Cross between them appeared, in response to the popularity of the relic of the True Cross. The cross symbol was suppressed as having iconoclast connotations but continued to appear in funerary contexts as a sign of Christ's victory over death; on imperial and military connotations of the cross, see also Nicole Thierry, "Le culte de la croix dans l'empire byzantine du VIIe siècle au Xe dans ses rapports avec la guerre contre l'infidèle," *Rivista di Studi Byzantini e Slavi; Miscellanea Agostino Pertusi* 1 (1981): 205–228. Thierry, whose studies have illuminated the practices and character of the Cappadocian frescoes, has established that there was a school of painting in the neighborhood of Maçan near Göreme. For the church of Meryemana kilise, she concludes that certain female saints—Barbara, Paraskevi, Marina, Eudoxia, Anastasia, Eupraxia—appear as privileged and that this choice is without doubt that of the donatrix, who was probably the benefactor of a female monastery: see "Un atelier cappadocien du XIe siècle à Maçan-Göreme," *Cahiers Archéologiques* 44 (1996): 117–40, esp. 123, 137. For the "nachleben" and reception of Constantine and Helena in the sources and in art, see Jan Willem Drijvers, *Helena Augusta: The Mother of Constantine the Great and the Legend of Her finding of the True Cross* (New York, 1992); see also Jan Willem Drijvers, "Marutha of Maipherqat on Helena Augusta, Jerusalem and the Council of Nicaea," *Studia Patristica* 34 (2001): 51–64, esp. 51–52. See also Stephen Bann, "Legends of the True Cross," in *The True Vine: On Visual Representation and the Western Tradition* (New York, 1989), 216–43.

55. This material was published initially in Connor, "Female Saints in Church Decoration," 211–28.

56. Ibid., 215–16 for the inscription, and fig. 5.

57. See Doula Mouriki, "The Wall Paintings of the Church of the Panagia at Moutoullas, Cyprus," in *Byzanz und der Westen: Studien zur Kunst des europäischen Mittelalters,* ed. Irmgard Hutter (Vienna, 1984), 171–213, esp. 199.

58. Other donors, both male and female, are depicted in relation to saints and compositions, including the Virgin Mary elsewhere in the complex decoration of the narthex. For Asinou,

see M. Sacopoulo, *Asinou en 1106 et sa contribution à l'icongraphie* (Brussels, 1966), and for the Cypriot churches more generally, J. Stylianou and A. Stylianou, *The Painted Churches of Cyprus: Treasures of Byzantine Art* (London, 1985).

59. See Connor, "Female Saints in Church Decoration," 219–20.

60. See ibid., 222–24.

61. See, for example, the "Pious Housewives" St. Mary the Younger and St. Thomais of Lesbos, whose Lives were written in the tenth century and whose popularity must have been shared among ordinary women. See "Life of St. Mary the Younger," trans. Angeliki Laiou, and "Life of St. Thomais of Lesbos," trans. Paul Halsall, in *Holy Women of Byzantium: Ten Saints' Lives in English Translation,* ed. Alice-Mary Talbot (Washington, D.C., 1996), 239–90 and 291–322, respectively.

62. See Natalia Teteriatnikov, "The True Cross Flanked by Constantine and Helena: A Study in the Light of the Post-iconoclastic Re-evaluation of the Cross," *Deltion* (1995): 169–88. In a rare instance in the medium of ivory, for example, individual saints represent the interests of the female donor or donor's wife; on the front of the Crucifixion Triptych in London the name saint of the patron, Anna, and Joachim appear juxtaposed in medallions, while two other female saints, Barbara and Thekla, appear in medallions below; see A. J. Goldschmidt and K. Weitzmann, *Die byzantinischen Elfenbeinskulpturen des X.-XIII. Jahrhunderts, I Kästen* (Berlin, 1930), no. 38, p. 37, pl. 15b. Constantine and Helena appear on several triptychs of the Crucifixion, either paired in one of the wings, as on an example in Berlin, or actually standing at the foot of the cross, as in an example in Paris: ibid. no. 72a, p. 46, pl. 28, and no. 39, p. 37, pl. 16 (Cabinet des Médailles).

63. A ninth-century manuscript also shows the use of saints we have encountered as visual commentary; see Leslie Brubaker, "Politics, Patronage, and Art in Ninth-Century Byzantium: The Homilies of Gregory of Nazianzus in Paris," *Dumbarton Oaks Papers* 41 (1987): 10 and pl. 7; on fol. 285r is a visual commentary in the form of portraits of Helena and Paraskeve which accompany the scene of Habbakuk's Vision. The women refer to Helena's discovery of the "saving tomb of Christ," cited in a sermon by the patriarch Photius, and therefore to the Resurrection; on fol. 440r Helena is shown once discovering the True Cross and again sitting enthroned.

## Chapter 10: Imperial Women and Marriage

1. Lynda Garland, *Byzantine Empresses: Women and Power in Byzantium AD 527–1204* (New York, 1999), table I: "Byzantine Emperors and Empresses," 229–31.

2. Mary of Alania was only the second Byzantine empress of the eleventh century to be chosen from outside Byzantium's borders.

3. Those women who were born or received imperial power have often been suppressed in the history books; persistence is required to gather their stories or to learn anything about them at all. Some will always remain unknown except for their names. About Ariadne very little is known. Sophia, Martina, Irene, and Theodora Restorer of Orthodoxy are the subjects of chapters in Lynda Garland, *Byzantine Empresses,* in which these relatively less known empresses have received sound attention. Irene, Euphrosyne, and Theodora are given detailed treatment in Judith Herrin, *Women in Purple: Rulers of Medieval Byzantium* (Princeton, 2001). It is ironic that in the case of marriages of Byzantine emperors with nonimperial women these women often developed more autonomy and individuality of action than those who came as a result of

dynastic marriages, and, just as ironically, women whose marriges made rulers of their husbands sometimes gave up their own personal influence.

4. See Deno John Geanakoplos, *Byzantium: Church, Society, and Civilization Seen Through Contemporary Eyes* (Chicago, 1984), 122–23. See also *Constantine Porphyrogenitus, de Administrando Imperio,* ed. G. Moravcsik (Washington, D.C., 1967), 73–75.

5. See Judith Herrin, "Theophano: Considerations on the Education of a Byzantine Princess," in *The Empress Theophano: Byzantium and the West at the Turn of the First Millennium,* ed. Adelbert Davids (Cambridge, 1995), 64–85, esp. 68.

6. See W. T. Treadgold, "The Bride-shows of the Byzantine Emperors," *Byzantion* 49 (1979): 396 and n. 3. See also Adelbert Davids, "Marriage Negotiations between Byzantium and the West and the Name of Theophano in Byzantium (Eighth to Tenth Centuries), in *The Empress Theophano: Byzantium and the West at the Turn of the First Millennium,* ed. Adelbert Davids (Cambridge, 1995), 99–120, esp. 104. See also Garland, *Byzantine Empresses, 76.*

7. See *The Chronicle of Theophanes Confessor: Byzantine and Near Eastern History AD 284–813,* trans. and commentary by Cyril Mango and Roger Scott (Oxford, 1997), 628. See also Herrin, "Education," 70.

8. See Herrin, "Education," 71 and n. 23.

9. Ibid., 66–67.

10. See ibid., 66, for a discussion of the source for this information in *Theophanes' Chronographia.*

11. Bibliothèque Nationale, Ms. Gr. Coislin 79, Fol 1(2bis)v: see *Glory of Byzantium,* cat. no. 143, 207–09 and pl. on 182.

12. See Garland, *Byzantine Empresses,* 199.

13. See ibid., 199–202. See also *Oxford Illustrated History of the Crusades,* ed. Jonathan Riley-Smith (Oxford, 1995), 189ff.

14. For the Otto II and Theophano plaque, see *Byzance,* cat. no. 160, 247–49, which is attributed to Constantinople or the court of Otto II in ca. 982–83; the donor is depicted on the lower left. For the Romanos and Eudocia plaque, see *Byzance,* cat. no. 148, 232–33, which is attributed to Constantinople in 945–99; for alternate suggestions for dating, see 233. The two plaques reflect a standard Byzantine genre of the time, for they are also related generally to the type of commemorative plaque represented by the ivory with Constantine VII's Coronation by Christ in the National Library in Moscow; see *Glory of Byzantium,* cat. no. 140, and pl. on 203.

15. See Carolyn L. Connor, *The Color of Ivory: Polychromy on Byzantine Ivories* (Princeton, 1998), 18 and fig. 5.

16. Herrin, "Education," 79.

17. Ibid., 79–80.

18. On Theophano, see the series of studies Davids, ed., *Empress Theophano.* See also *ODB,* s.v. "Theophano," 2065.

19. See J. Shepard, "A Marriage too Far?: Maria Lekapena and Peter of Bulgaria," chap. 7 in Davids, ed., *Empress Theophano.*

20. See Herrin, "Education," 69.

21. See Ruth Macrides, "Dynastic Marriages and Political Kinship," in *Byzantine Diplomacy,* ed. J. Sheperd and S. Franklin (Aldershot, 1992), 263–80, esp. 266–70.

22. Herrin, "Education," 76.

23. Ibid., 78.

24. See D. Obolensky, "The Baptism of Princess Olga of Kiev: The Problem of the Sources," *Philadelphie et autres études* (Paris, 1984), 159–76, esp. 161–62, 171. For a modern interpretation of the *Book of Ceremonies,* see also Averil Cameron, "The Construction of Court Ritual: The Byzantine Book of Ceremonies," in *Rituals of Royalty: Power and Ceremonial in Traditional Societies,* ed. David Cannadine and Simon Price (Cambridge, 1987), 106–36.

25. See Herrin, "Education," 72.

26. For the wives of Leo VI, see Garland, *Byzantine Empresses,* chap. 6, "The Wives of Leo VI (886–919)," 109–35.

27. Edward Gibbon, *The Decline and Fall of the Roman Empire,* vol. 2, *395–1185 A.D.* (New York, 1932), 904.

28. *Fourteen Byzantine Rulers: The Chronographia of Michael Psellos,* ed. and trans. E. R .A. Sewter (London, 1953); for the original Greek, with French translation, see E. Renauld, *Chronographie,* 2 vols (Paris, 1926–28).

29. For more on Psellos's stance in writing of Zoe's marriages, see Angeliki Laiou, "Imperial Marriages and Their Critics in the Eleventh Century: The Case of Skylitzes," *DOP* 46 (1992): 165–76, esp. 165–73.

30. Psellos, *Chronographia,* 2.4; Sewter, *Fourteen Byzantine Rulers,* 55. References to the *Chronographia* will be according to book and chapter, and to the page number in the Sewter translation, for ease of access to readers.

31. Garland, *Byzantine Empresses,* 137 and nn. 5 and 6.

32. Psellos, *Chronographia,* 2.4; Sewter, *Fourteen Byzantine Rulers,* 55.

33. Psellos, *Chronographia,* 2.5; Sewter, *Fourteen Byzantine Rulers,* 56.

34. For a discussion of Zonaras and Skylitzes on Zoe's marriages, see Angeliki Laiou, "Imperial Marriages and Their Critics in the Eleventh Century: The Case of Skylites," *DOP* 46 (1992): 165–76, esp. 166–73.

35. Psellos, *Chronographia,* 2.10; Sewter, *Fourteen Byzantine Rulers,* 59.

36. See Barbara Hill, Liz James, Dion Smythe, "Zoe: The Rhythm Method of Imperial Renewal," in *New Constantines: The Rhythm of Imperial Renewal in Byzantium, 4th–13th Centuries,* Magdalino, P., ed. (Aldershot, 1994), 215–29.

37. Psellos, *Chronographia,* 3.21; Sewter, *Fourteen Byzantine Rulers,* 78.

38. For the illness see Psellos, *Chronographia,* 3.24–5; Sewter, *Fourteen Byzantine Rulers,* 80–81. For the dead man, see Psellos, *Chronographia,* 4.4–6; Sewter, *Fourteen Byzantine Rulers,* 89. A number of other authors claimed Zoe was poisoning Romanos and that he was drowned by followers of Michael; see Milton V. Anastos, "The Coronation of Emperor Michael IV in 1034 by Empress Zoe and Its Significance," *To Hellenikon: Studies in Honor of Speros Vryonis, Jr.* (New York, 1993), 1:23–43, esp. 26.

39. Although the patriarch resisted performing the marriage ceremony, he and other clergy performed it after a gift of one hundred pounds of gold was made. See Anastos "Coronation of Emperor Michael IV," 29.

40. Psellos, *Chronographia,* 4.17; Sewter, *Fourteen Byzantine Rulers,* 96.

41. Ibid.

42. Psellos, *Chronographia,* 4.23; Sewter, *Fourteen Byzantine Rulers,* 101.

43. The bedchamber must be the *Porphyra,* the room where imperial children were born and the site of elaborate ceremonals. Psellos, *Chronographia,* 5.21; Sewter, 134–35.

44. Psellos, *Chronographia,* 5.25; Sewter, *Fourteen Byzantine Rulers,* 138.

45. The event is reminiscent of the reaction of women during the supposed rebellion at the Chalke Gate, dealt with in the Introduction to Part Three.

46. Psellos, *Chronographia*, 5.34; Sewter, *Fourteen Byzantine Rulers*, 143.

47. Psellos, *Chronographia*, 6.10; Sewter, *Fourteen Byzantine Rulers*, 159.

48. Ibid.

49. Psellos, *Chronographia*, 6.13; Sewter, *Fourteen Byzantine Rulers*, 161.

50. Psellos insists on Zoe's lack of resentment being due to her old age again later in the chapter, in 6.62, suggesting a rather defensive attitude on his part and a weak effort to justify what was clearly an insult to the empress.

51. Psellos, *Chronographia*, 6.56; Sewter, *Fourteen Byzantine Rulers*, 183.

52. Psellos, *Chronographia*, 6.58; Sewter, *Fourteen Byzantine Rulers*, 183.

53. Psellos, *Chronographia*, 6.59; Sewter, *Fourteen Byzantine Rulers*, 184.

54. Psellos relates the anecdote about Sklerain's flatterer shorty later, indicating she must have been attractive enough to justify comparison to Helen of Troy (Psellos, *Chronographia*, 6.61; Sewter, *Fourteen Byzantine Rulers*, 185).

55. Psellos, *Chronographia*, 6.62; Sewter, *Fourteen Byzantine Rulers*, 185–86.

56. Psellos, *Chronographia*, 6.66; Sewter, *Fourteen Byzantine Rulers*, 188.

57. Psellos, *Chronographia*, 2.5; Sewter, *Fourteen Byzantine Rulers*, 55.

58. The notion of gendered and restrictive ideology is circumscribed by the person who is doing the talking/writing and what his or her particular anxieties or biases happen to be. To speak of a whole society sharing the same ideology regarding women's roles, while convenient, is counterproductive as well as tenuous at best, for it neutralizes what is most natural in any social group, the coexistence of different ways of treating the same phenomenon, with no one way being dominant. The dangers of imposing our own twenty-first century definitions of ideology on Byzantine society are apparent if one takes as an example Psellos's account of the rule(s) of Zoe. Psellos changes his attitude in every successive paragraph; it seems more productive to look at the text and its author rather than trying to apply our own theoretical frame in order to simplify or classify such complex material. Hill, "Imperial Women and the Ideology of Womanhood," suggests that "a viable explanation of the ambiguity of the historians' opinions on powerful women . . . is made possible only by investigating ideology as a tool before approaching the historical evidence" (94). I would propose that we consider the evidence *before* framing it within our contemporary notion of ideology (see Barbara Hill, "Imperial Women and the Ideology of Womanhood in the Eleventh and Twelfth Centuries," in *Women, Men and Eunuchs: Gender in Byzantium,* ed. Liz James [New York, 1987], 76–99, esp. 76–77; and Lynda Garland, "The Life and Ideology of Byzantine Women: A Further Note on Conventions of Behaviour and Social Reality as Reflected in Eleventh- and Twelfth-Century Historical Sources," *Byzantion* 58 [1988]: 361–93). Inheritance by blood does not overrule female gender roles, as claimed by Hill in "Imperial Women and the Ideology of Womanhood," who claims, "One ideology was gendered and restrictive but there was another one that could be mobilised to justify a woman in power in her own right: the ungendered ideology of blood inheritance" (82). Is there a need to suppose an ideology in order to assert that women could rule through their blood inheritance of imperial authority?

59. See Lynda Garland on Zoe's choices as opposed to those of her sister, Theodora's, in "Zoe Porphyrogenneta," 157.

60. See Thomas Whittemore, *The Mosaics of Haghia Sophia at Istanbul: Third Preliminary*

*Report. Work Done in 1935–1938: The Imperial Portraits of the South Gallery* (Boston, 1942), esp. chap. 1, "The Zoe Panel," 9–20 and pls. 3–19.

61. Ibid., 29.

62. The dimensions of the panel are 2.40 m in width by 2.44 m in height. Zoe's head, for example, from the lower edge of her crown to the tip of her chin measures 16 cm.

63. Ibid., 30–31.

64. The squeezing of the letters of Constantine's name(s) into the space occupied by the original emperor's name and the careless worksmanship in comparison with the original letters may be clearly seen in the details published in Whittemore's survey in *Mosaics of Hagia Sophia,* pls. 2–19, esp. 16 and 18. The poor quality of the inscription suggests haste rather than lack of ability of the craftsman.

65. See Psellos, *Chronographia,* 5.23.

66. Whittemore, *Mosaics,* 17–20.

67. Whittemore notes that in the cases of the three heads, the surface is concave, even though the tesserae used are larger than in the rest of the mosaic (Whittemore, *Mosaics,* 42, 48, 53). This must indicate that there was a hole that was not filled adequately in the course of the repairs to bring the new surface up to the level of the original one.

68. Robin Cormack, "Interpreting the Mosaics of S. Sophia at Istanbul," *Art History* 4 (1981): 131–47, esp. 144–45.

69. See Hill, James, and Smythe, "Zoe: The Rhythm Method," 215–29, esp. 225 and n. 31.

70. See Natalia Teteriatnikov, "Hagia Sophia: The Two Portraits of the Emperors with Moneybags as a Functional Setting," *Arte Medievale* 10 (1996): 47–66.

71. See Robin Cormack, "Paradise Sought: The Imperial Use of Art," in *Writing in Gold: Byzantine Society and its Icons* (New York, 1985), 179–214, esp. 178–89, for another interpretation of the mosaic; Cormack posits Constantine's agency in its renovation as an expression of his superior donation to that of his predecessor but does not deal with the question of the rationale behind the replacements of the heads of Christ and Zoe.

72. For example, ideology is the focus of Barbara Hill's article, in which she stresses the need for women to assume one ideology or another but not two at once; see "Imperial Women and the Ideology of Womanhood," esp. 76–82. Lynda Garland is also ambivalent in her assessment of the empress but goes to some lengths to give her a modern cast by stressing her egotism, materialism and profligacy; see "Zoe Porphyrogenneta," 136–57.

73. Another instance of public participation of women is described by Psellos. See Angeliki Laiou, "The Festival of 'Agathe': Comments on the Life of Constantinopolitan Women," in *Byzantium: Tribute to Andreas N. Stratos,* vol. 1, *History—Art and Archaeology* (Athens, 1986), 111–22, esp. 118–19 on the women who participated in the riots to restore Zoe to power. In this article Laiou suggests that the existence of this female festival shows that women formed professional groups, perhaps formed a guild or guilds, and that their public festival with its processions, singing, and representations of their tasks (carding, spinning, and weaving) shows women's participation in the economic system of the city. Thus it was the public appearance of women who were not of the class of the guild workers that shocked Psellos the most.

## Chapter 11: The World of Anna Komnene

1. In this chapter, in order to accommodate readers, I follow the current trend in scholarship of transliterating Greek spellings (including spelling *Komnenian* with a *K* rather than a *C*)

instead of using the traditional, Anglicized (or Latinized) spellings of names, as elsewhere in this book.

2. Take, for example, David McCullough's biographical novel *John Adams* (New York, 2001) and its effective quoting of the historical documents, consisting mainly of the letters written between John and his wife, Abigail.

3. For the English translation, see *The Alexiad of Anna Comnena,* trans. E. R. A. Sewter (Penguin, 1969); for the Greek (with French translation), see *Anne Comnène: Alexiade,* trans. Bernard Leib, 3 vols. (Paris, 1967). Citations will be by book, chapter, and section and also by page in the Sewter translation, for the reader's convenience.

4. *Greek Anthology,* Loeb Classical Library Edition, vol. 1, trans. W. R. Paton, book I, epigram 10, lines 47 and 29.

5. See, for the most recent translation, *Digenis Akritis,* ed. and trans. Elizabeth Jeffreys (Cambridge, 1998).

6. See Angeliki Laiou, "Introduction: Why Anna Komnene?" in *Anna Komnene and Her Times,* ed. Thalia Gouma-Peterson (New York, 2000), 1: "But is our interest in her primarily because she was a child of her age, capturing the spirit of an epoch? Or is it because she was atypical, an exception, a figure who by her very singularity transcends in some ways her historical milieu and speaks to perennial concerns?"

7. Lynda Garland, "The Empresses of Alexius I Komnenos (1081–1118)," chap. 11 in *Byzantine Empresses: Woman and Power in Byzantium, AD 527–1204* (New York, 1999), 180–98, esp. 183.

8. Ibid., 180. Her given name at birth was Olympias, but when she was brought by Maria of Alania to be educated in Constantinople she was renamed Helena.

9. Ibid., 183.

10. See Barbara Hill, "Alexios I and the Imperial Women," in *Alexios I Komnenos,* ed. Margaret Mullett and Dion Smythe (Belfast, 1996), 1:37–54, esp. 38–39.

11. See Iohannis Spatharakis, *The Portrait in Byzantine Illuminated Manuscripts* (Leiden, 1976), 107–17, esp. 108–10. See 114 for the theory of the reuse and alteration of the portraits.

12. For the Komnenos family, their family alliances, and cultural role, see in general: *ODB,* s.v. "Komnenos," 1143–44, and the genealogical chart on 1145.

13. For an account of these events, see Garland, *Byzantine Empresses,* 184–85.

14. For an overview of military and cultural events, see Laiou, "Introduction," esp. 2–3; see also Robert Browning, *The Byzantine Empire* (Washington, 1992), 157–66.

15. Ibid., 186–93.

16. Ibid., 190.

17. *Alexiad,* 3.7.1; Sewter, *The Alexiad of Anna Comnena,* 118.

18. *Alexiad,* 3.8.2; Sewter, *The Alexiad of Anna Comnena,* 120: "The women's quarters in the palace had been the scene of utter depravity ever since the infamous Constantine Monomachos had ascended the throne and right up to the time when my father became emperor had been noted for foolish love intrigues, but Anna effected a reformation."

19. For an architectural and photographic survey of the monastery, of which the church survives, see Thomas F. Mathews, *The Byzantine Churches of Istanbul: A Photographic Survey* (University Park, Penn., and London, 1976), "Church of Christ the All-Seeing," 59–70.

20. See Hill, "Alexios I and the Imperial Women," 53–54.

21. Garland, *Byzantine Empresses,* 193–98.

22. See Robert Jordan, translation and commentary: "*Kecharitomene:* Typikon of Empress

Irene Doukaina Komnene for the Convent of the Mother of God Kecharitomene in Constanti-nople," in *Byzantine Monastic Foundation Documents,* ed. John Thomas and Angela Constantini-des Hero (Washington, 2000), 2:649–724, esp. 710. For a French translation, see P. Gautier, "Le typikon de Theotokos Kécharitomène," *REB* 43 (1985): 5–165.

23. See Angeliki Laiou, "Observations on the Life and Ideology of Byzantine Women," *BF* 9 (1985): 59–102, esp. 75–77.

24. Garland, *Byzantine Empresses,* 196.

25. Ibid., 198. For a discussion of the two women's quarters at the Kecharitomene, see Laiou, "Observations," 76.

26. For a summary of reactions to the *Alexiad,* see Jakov Ljubarskij, "Why Is the Alexiad a Masterpiece of Byzantine Literature?" in Gouma-Peterson, ed., *Anna Komnene and Her Times,* 169–85.

27. See James Howard-Johnston, "Anna Komnene and the Alexiad," in *Alexios I Komnenos,* Papers of the Second Belfast Byzantine International Colloquium, 14–16 April 1989, ed. Margaret Mullett and Dion Smythe (Belfast, 1996), 260–301.

28. Ibid., 275, 294. Here as in numerous other instances, Howard-Johnston denigrates Anna's handling of material; for example, he says she "cuts out military material" (285), and, re-garding the telling of anecdotes, she "had no special aptitude for this genre of writing" (286–87); he calls Byzantine statecraft as depicted as lapsed by Anna a "travesty" (297), and her diatribes against foreigners have "shallow diplomatic perspective" (299). One wonders what his model for a more satisfactory [to him] writing of history is, whereas the literary aspects of the work—and it is a literary work as much as a historical one—seem to be lost on him.

29. *Alexiad,* preface 2.3; Sewter, *The Alexiad of Anna Comnena,* 19–20.

30. See Howard-Johnston, "Anna Komnene and the Alexiad," 263–64 and n. 9.

31. See Laiou, "Introduction," 6–7.

32. Ruth Macrides refutes the claims of Howard-Johnston that Nicephorus Brennius was the actual author of the *Alexiad:* "My reading of the *Alexiad* gives choice back to Anna. She did not have to make her history of her father's reign about war because that was the material her husband provided. She wanted to make her history about war because this subject was true to her father's reign, true to the *ethos* of the Komnenoi, and true to the hero her father was. Hers was a true history"; see R. Macrides, "The Pen and the Sword: Who Wrote the *Alexiad*?" in Gouma-Peterson, ed., *Anna Komnene and Her Times,* 63–82, esp. 69.

33. *Iliad* 2.85.

34. *Homer: The Iliad,* trans. Robert Fagles (Penguin, 1990), 422.

35. For the connections between persons in Anna's narrative to Homeric and mythical char-acters, see Ljubarskij, "Alexiad," 172–73; according to him there are fifty-eight references to the *Iliad* and nine to the *Odyssey* (n. 11). See also Macrides, "Pen and Sword," 68–69, for Anna's modeling of Alexios after Odysseus.

36. The quotation is derived from *Iliad,* 2.468, and *Odyssey,* 9.51.

37. Fagles, *Iliad,* 114–15.

38. For Anna's assessment of the Latin race her blunt statements earlier in the chapter suf-fice: "The Latin race at all times is unusually greedy for wealth" (10.6.4; Sewter, *The Alexiad of Anna Comnena,* 312); she compares them to a plague of locusts and has no illusions that they have any other motive than seizing Constantinople (10.6; Sewter, *The Alexiad of Anna Comnena,* 311).

39. Ljubarskij, "Alexiad," 176 and n. 23.

40. Ibid., 178.

41. *Fourteen Byzantine Rulers: The Chronographia of Michael Psellus*, trans. E. R. A. Sewter, 6.126; Sewter, *The Alexiad of Anna Comnena*, 221.

42. Sewter, *Chronographia*, 372.

43. See *Alexiad*, 3.1; Sewter, *The Alexiad of Anna Comnena*, 105. According to Byzantine custom, a betrothed woman lived with her fiancé's family from childhood; thus a couple could play together as children before attaining the age of marriage, which was usually twelve years for girls.

44. Sewter, *Chronographia*, 167.

45. Ibid., 178.

46. Ibid., 179.

47. *Alexiad* 14.7.4; Sewter, *The Alexiad of Anna Comnena*, 459.

48. Howard-Johnston, "Anna Komnene," in one of his many derisive comments on Anna as author, criticizes her for her "shallow diplomatic perspective" (299); here, as in many other instances, he seems to forget that Anna was not trying to write according to a twentieth-century notion of historical narrative.

49. Compare this speech to that of Michael Psellos: "At the time I was in my twenty-fifth year and engaged in serious studies. My efforts were concentrated on two objects: to train my tongue by rhetoric, so as to become a fine speaker, and to refine my mind by a course of philosophy. I soon mastered the rhetoric enough to be able to distinguish the central theme of an argument and logically connect it with my main and secondary points. I also learnt not to stand in complete awe of the art, nor to follow its precepts in everything like a child, and I even made certain contributions of a minor character myself. Then I applied myself to the study of philosophy, and having acquainted myself thoroughly with the art of reasoning, both deductive, from cause to immediate effect, and inductive, tracing causes from all manner of effects, I turned to natural science and aspired to a knowledge of the fundamental principles of philosophy through mathematics" (*Chronographia*, 6.37; Sewter, 173). This passage on his education continues for another ten chapters. Anna's self-praise of her talents is comparable to his in this passage.

50. See *Alexiad*, 3.1; Sewter, *The Alexiad of Anna Comnena*, 105.

51. See, for example, *Alexiad*, 2.1; Sewter, *The Alexiad of Anna Comnena*, 74.

52. See Thalia Gouma-Peterson, "Passages to the Maternal in Anna Komnene's *Alexiad*," in *Anna Komnene and Her Times*, 107–24, esp. 116, where she says of the passage below that it "reveals a woman who in the twelfth century was more acutely aware of gendered categories and their implications than many twentieth-century historians and critics."

53. As Macrides has concluded, Anna is "bound more to her family, her times, and her genre than to her sex" ("Pen and Sword," 75). She refers to other scholars' preoccupation with Anna's personality being particularly related to her gender but finds this a less important matter for concern.

54. In an earlier passage Anna notes that Gaita "went on campaign with her husband and when she donned armour was indeed a formidable sight" (1.15.1; Sewter, *The Alexiad of Anna Comnena*, 66).

55. *Iliad*, 1.242–43; Fagles, trans., *The Iliad*, 84.

56. *Iliad*, 5.971–90; Fagles, trans., *The Iliad*, 192.

57. *Digenis Akritis*, ed. and trans. Elizabeth Jeffreys (Cambridge, 1998), book 6, 152–201, esp. lines 550–785.

58. See Gouma-Peterson, "Passages to the Maternal," 117–18.

59. *Alexiad*, 3.1.3; Sewter, *The Alexiad of Anna Comnena*, 104.

60. See also on this passage, Gouma-Peterson, "Passages to the Maternal," 120.

61. See Barbara Hill, "Actions Speak Louder Than Words: Anna Komnene's Attempted Usurpation," in Gouma-Peterson, *Anna Komnene and Her Times*, 45–62, esp. the section "Was Anna Komnene a Feminist?" 56–58.

62. Sewter, *The Alexiad of Anna Comnena*, 16.

63. *Iliad*, 24.21–27; Fagles, trans., *The Iliad*, 608.


## Introduction to Part 4: Women's Work

1. See Donald M. Nicol, *The Byzantine Lady: Ten Portraits, 1250–1500* (Cambridge, 1996). Nicol chose to work on biographies pertaining to upper-class women because they are better documented and, as he claims, "more interesting," for the "wives and daughters of farmers, shepherds and country priests led hard and generally dull lives" (2). This tongue-in-cheek statement aside, I nevertheless maintain that these ordinary women make fascinating subjects in the rare cases in which their activity can be discerned.

2. For this late period of Byzantine history, see D. M. Nicol, *The Last Centuries of Byzantium, 1261–1453* (Cambridge, 1993).

3. Angeliki Laiou, "The Role of Women in Byzantine Society," *JOB* 31 (1981): 233–60, esp. 259.

4. Ibid., 257.

5. See, for example, the pioneering study of Angeliki Laiou, *Peasant Society in the Late Byzantine Empire: A Social and Demographic Study* (Princeton, 1977).

6. See Alice-Mary Talbot, "Old Age in Byzantium," *BZ* (1984): 267–78.

7. See Joëlle Beaucamp, "La situation juridique de la femme à Byzance," *Cahiers de civilisation médiévale* 20 (1977): 145–76, esp. 165. She examines the treatment of women under the law, for example, in cases of rape (153) and adultery (156–17), noting that women's long hair was a traditional sign of their submission (150).

8. See Laiou, "Role of Women," 234–36.

9. Ibid., 237.

10. Ibid., 241.

11. Ibid., 237–41.

12. Ibid., 245–47.

13. See Beaucamp, "Situation juridique," 145–76. See also Laiou, "Role of Women," 234, for a table indicating numbers of legal cases involving women.

14. Laiou, "Role of Women," 245.

15. See *Roman Law in the Later Roman Empire: Byzantine Guilds, Professional and Commercial,* trans. Edwin H. Freshfield (Cambridge, 1938), esp. 17–27.

16. See Charles Brand, "Some Byzantine Women of Thebes—and Elsewhere," *To Hellenikon: Studies in Honor of Speros Vryonis, Jr.* (New York, 1993), 1:59–68, esp. 59–60. The probable sweatshop conditions he suggests do not paint a happy picture of this female occupation.

17. See A. Laiou, "The Festival of "Agathe"; Comments on the Life of Constantinopolitan Women," *Byzantium: Tribute to Andreas N. Stratos* (Athens, 1986), 1:111–22. The specifically female nature of the festival is indicated in the title of the treatise (see citation below). The

names for the different workers in the process are technical and must refer to groups with spe-
cific functions (see 112, n. 4). For the Greek text, see *Michael Psellos, Historical Writings and
Letters,* vol. 5, ed. C. N. Sathas (Paris, 1876), "Peri tes en Byzantio gunaikeias panegureos tes
Agathes," 527–31.

18. Ibid. Laiou is cautious in interpreting the text but rightly takes it as evidence of a mid-
eleventh-century organized women's guild representing the handicrafts, *banausiai,* of spinning
and weaving.

19. See Theophanes Continuatus, 139ff., in Mango, *Art,* 165.

20. See Laiou, "Role of Women," table on 239.

21. Ibid., 249. Laiou is mainly concerned with aristocratic women. Simply because most surviving sources deal with this class, however, does not mean that the trends she outlines should
not be extended generally to women of the middle and lower classes as well.

22. See Lynda Garland, "Life and Ideology of Byzantine Women: A Further Note on Conventions of Behaviour and Social Reality as Reflected in Eleventh- and Twelfth-Century Historical Sources," *Byzantion* 58 (1988): 361–93, esp. 392–93 for her interesting reference to the
concept of "double-think" which characterized Byzantine society.

## Chapter 12: Founding Mothers and the Testimony of the Typika

1. The manuscript, owned by Lincoln College, Oxford University, is MS Lincoln College Gr. 35, and it is housed in the Duke Humphrey reading room of the Bodleian Library in
Oxford, England. I am indebted to Martin Kaufmann, curator of manuscripts, for generously
facilitating my examination of this manuscript.

2. See Alice-Mary Talbot, "Late Byzantine Nuns: By Choice or Necessity?" *BF* 9 (1985):
103–17, esp. 110.

3. Alice-Mary Talbot, "The Byzantine Family and the Monastery," *DOP* 44 (1990): 119–29;
for gifts in lieu of dowries, see esp. 121. See also Talbot, "Late Byzantine Nuns" 103–17.

4. Talbot, "Byzantine Family," 121.

5. See Talbot, "Late Byzantine Nuns," generally for the reasons women joined nunneries;
see esp. 117 on the spiritual decision leading women to monasticism.

6. Talbot, "Byzantine Family," 122–23.

7. See ibid., 123.

8. Ibid., 123.

9. Ibid., 124.

10. See Hans Belting, Cyril Mango, Doula Mouriki, *The Mosaics and Frescoes of St. Mary
Pammakaristos (Fethiye Camii) at Istanbul* (Washington, D.C., 1978); the Pammakaristos parec-
clesion was commissioned by a woman, Maria-Martha Glabaina, for her late husband, Michael
Tarchaneiotes Glabas (died 1305). See also Robert G. Ousterhout, *The Architecture of the Kariye
Camii in Istanbul* (Washington, D.C., 1987); Paul A. Underwood, *The Kariye Djami,* 4 vols.
(New York, 1966; Princeton, 1975).

11. For an example, see the double portrait of the emperor John VI Cantacuzenos (1347–
54) in a manuscript containing his theological treatises, Paris gr. 1242; he appears on fol. 123v as
emperor on the left and as the monk Joasaph on the right: Iohannis Spatharakis, *The Portrait
in Byzantine Illuminated Manuscripts* (Leiden, 1976), 135 and fig. 87.

12. For the remnants of funerary portraits in the outer narthex of Kariye Djami, see Under-

wood, *Kariye Djami,* vol. 1, *Sepulchral Monuments,* 269–99, and vol. 3, *Plates,* 533–53; for the tomb of Irene Raoulaina Palaeologina, see 540; for a pair of portraits, of a monk and a nun, see 542.

13. Alice-Mary Talbot, "The Monastic Experience of Men and Women," *Greek Orthodox Theological Review* 30 (1985): 1–20, esp. 13.

14. See Talbot, "Byzantine Family," 125.

15. Talbot, "Monastic Experience," 16; see tables 1 and 2 on pp. 18–20 for a tabulation of male vs. female monasteries around the Byzantine Empire.

16. Talbot, "Monastic Experience," 17.

17. Catia Galatariotou, "Byzantine Women's Monastic Communities: The Evidence of the Typika," *JOB* 38 (1988): 263–90. Out of fifty surviving typika, five were written by women for women's monasteries: Eirene Doukas, for the monastery of Theotokos Kecharitomene (c. 1118); Theodora Palaeologina, for the monastery of Lips (late thirteenth century); Theodora Palaeologina, for the monastery of Sts. Anargyroi, Constantinople (late thirteenth century); Eirene Laskarina Palaeologina, for the monastery of Christ Phlanthropinos, Constantinople (1312); and Theodora Palaeologina Synadene, for the Theotokos Babaia Elpidos, Constantinople (c. 1300–35). On the rise of self-governing monasteries and their typika, see John P. Thomas, "The Rise of the Independent and Self-Governing Monasteries as Reflected in the Monastic Typika," *Greek Orthodox Theological Review* 30 (1985): 21–30.

18. Galatariotou, "Monastic Communities," 265–67.

19. Ibid., 270.

20. Ibid., 284.

21. See Talbot, "Monastic Experience," 11.

22. Galatariotou, "Monastic Communities," 287.

23. Ibid.: "The desire to strengthen and preserve the ties of kinship found expression in the foundation of monasteries whose purpose was to constitute a material and eternal bond between the founder or foundress and his or her kin" (279).

24. Ibid., 280–81.

25. Ibid., 279.

26. Ibid., 271.

27. Ibid., 272.

28. Talbot, "Monastic Experience," 12.

29. Galatariotou, "Monastic Communities," 273–4.

30. Ibid., 274–75.

31. Ibid., 275.

32. Ibid., 276. See also Talbot, "Late Byzantine Nuns," 103–17.

33. Alice-Mary Talbot, "Bluestocking Nuns: Intellectual Life in the Convents of Late Byzantium," *Okeanos, Harvard Ukranian Studies VII* (1983): 604–18, esp. 607.

34. Annemarie Weyl Carr, "Women and Monasticism in Byzantium: Introduction from an Art Historian," *BF* 9 (1985): 1–15, and Annemarie Weyl Carr, "Women Artists in the Middle Ages," *Feminist Art Journal* 5 (1976): 5–9, 26.

35. Talbot, "Late Byzantine Nuns," 104.

36. The remnants of this typikon, which is based on that of the Kecharitomene by Irene Doukaina Komnene, are published in *Byzantine Monastic Foundation Documents,* ed. John Thomas and Angela C. Hero (Washington, D.C., 2000), 4:1383–88, trans. and commentary by

Alice-Mary Talbot. On Eulogia, see Angela Hero, "Irene-Eulogia Choumnaina Palaeologina, Abbess of the Convent of Philanthropos Soter in Constantinople," *BZ* 9 (1985): 119–147.

37. Hero, "Irene-Eulogia," 129.

38. Ibid., 125.

39. Ibid., 134.

40. Ibid., for letters 9, 11 and 15, see nn. 54–56 on pp. 137–38.

41. Ibid., 143–44.

42. Ibid., 135 and n. 48; 147.

43. Alice-Mary Talbot, "Empress Theodora Palaiologina, Wife of Michael VIII," *DOP* 46 (1992): 295–303.

44. Ibid., 297.

45. See ibid., 298–301. The typikon appears in *Byzantine Monastic Foundation Documents*, vol. 3, *Typikon of Theodora Palaiologina for the Convent of Lips in Constantinople*," trans. Alice-Mary Talbot, 1254–86. The typikon, much damaged, is preserved in the British Library, Add. 22748.

46. Thomas and Hero, "Typikon of Theodora," 1265–82.

47. Talbot, "Empress Theodora," 300.

48. Ibid., 300–301.

49. Ibid., 301.

50. Ibid., 303.

51. For a recent study of the manuscript, see Irmgard Hutter, "Die Geschichte des Lincoln College Typikons," *JOB* 45 (1995): 79–114. For a full publication of the manuscript, see Irmgard Hutter, *Corpus der Byzantinischen Miniaturenhandschristen: Oxrord College Libraries*, vols. 5.1 (text) and 5.2 (plates) (Stuttgart, 1997), 56–62. For the text, see Alice-Mary Talbot, trans. and introduction, "Bebaia Elpis: Typikon of Theodora Synadene for the Convent of the Mother of God Bebaia Elpis in Constantinople," in Thomas and Hero, eds., *Byzantine Monastic Foundation Documents* 4:1512–78. My research for this chapter was first presented in a paper, "A Sense of Family: Monastic Portraits in the Lincoln College Typikon," Byzantine Studies Conference, Harvard University, Cambridge, Mass., *Abstracts* 26 (2000): 107–08.

52. This typikon has been shown to follow in general the model set by the eleventh-century Evergetis Typikon. See Talbot, "Bebaia Elpis," 1513.

53. See Hutter, "Geschichte des Lincoln College Typikons," 82.

54. See Angeliki Laiou, "Observations on the Life and Ideology of Byzantine Women," *BF* 9 (1985): 59–102, esp. 70–75.

55. Hutter, "Geschichte des Lincoln College Typikons," 104: ". . . das geistliche Zentrum der Familie."

56. Ibid., 105.

57. Ibid., 107–08. See also Hutter, *Corpus der Byzantinischen Miniaturenhandschristen*, 56–62, esp. 57–58.

58. See Hutter, *Corpus der Byzantinischen Miniaturenhandschristen*, 57.

59. For the Greek transcriptions of these labels and those on the following pages, see Hutter, *Corpus der Byzantinischen Miniaturenhandschristen*, 59–61.

60. This order was first established by Iohannis Spatharakis, *The Portrait in Byzantine Illuminated Manuscripts* (Leiden, 1976), 191–92.

61. This technique is also applied to the small figures of the Virgin and Child as well as to Christ Emmanuel appearing in the family members' portraits on the preceding folios.

62. For visual parallels to this image of the offering of a church building by a donor, see the mosaic of the southeast vestibule of Hagia Sophia, dating to the tenth century, in which Justinian offers a model of Hagia Sophia to the Virgin and Child. In another example dating to ca. 1320, Theodore Metochites offers his foundation of the Chora Church to an enthroned Christ in a mosaic lunette over the door from the inner narthex into the naos (see Underwood, *Kariye Djami*, vol. 2, plate 3, pp. 26–29.

63. A similar instance of a monastic group portrait appears on the east entrance wall of the crypt of the monastery of Hosios Loukas in Greece. Probably dating to the tenth or early eleventh century or later, this damaged fresco shows a group of monks in several tiered rows, standing behind a foremost figure, presumably the hegoumenos. All have their hands raised in a gesture of prayer or intercession, while Christ appears in an aureole over their heads; see Carolyn L. Connor, *Art and Miracles in Medieval Byzantium: The Crypt at Hosios Loukas and Its Frescoes* (Princeton, 1991), fig. 79.

64. For the Greek text, see Hippolyte Delehaye, "Deux Typica Byzantins de l'époque des Paléologues," *Mémoires de l'Académie royale de Belgique, Classe des Lettres, 2e série, t. XIII, no. 4* (Brussels, 1931), 18–105; repr. in *Synaxaires byzantins, ménologes, typica* (Variorum, 1977). The translation into English by Alice-Mary Talbot appears in *Byzantine Monastic Foundation Documents* 4:1523–68; this translation from the Greek has been used here for quotations, to which references are made by paragraph number.

65. Martin Kaufmann of the Bodleian Library suggested that these portions were ornamented after the book was bound, causing the offsets in red on many of the facing pages, such as on 45r and 77r.

66. See Talbot, *Bebaia Elpis,* 1531 and note 17.

67. See *ODB*, s.v. "Sabaitic Typika," 1823.

68. In response to my inquiry, Martin Kaufmann of the Bodleian Library suggested that the pages probably once had their own cloth coverings sewn onto the parchment above each miniature. I am grateful for this information.

69. See Hutter, "Geschichte des Lincoln College Typikons," III.


## Chapter 13: Epilogue: The "Lady of the Mongols"

1. See Ihor Sevcenko, "Theodore Metochites, the Chora, and the Intellectual Trends of His Time," in Paul Underwood, *The Kariye Djami* (New York-Princeton, 1975), 4:19–33.

2. See Underwood, *Kariye Djami* 1:45, 2:36, fig. 6; pls. 36–41.

3. See Robert S. Nelson, "The Chora and the Great Church: Intervisuality in Fourteenth-Century Constantinople," *BMGS* 23 (1999): 67–101, esp. 74–75 for the intended connotations of these images.

4. See Underwood, *Kariye Djami* 1:45, vol. 2, pls. 36–41.

5. See Natalia Teteriatnikov, "The Place of the Nun Melania (the Lady of the Mongols) in the Deesis Program of the Inner Narthex of Chora, Constantinople," *CA* 43 (1995): 163–80.

6. See Nelson, "Chora," for the agenda of Theodore Metochites in commissioning this mosaic with its imperial connotations and echoes of mosaic compositions in Hagia Sophia.

7. See Donald. M. Nicol, *The Last Centuries of Byzantium: 1261–1453* (New York, 1972),

86. This Mongol is proposed as the wife of Melanie by Robert Ousterhout, *The Art of the Kariye Camii* (London, 2002), 23.

8. Ibid.

9. For the tradition that Maria Palaeologina, daughter of Michael VIII, refounded the monastery of the Theotokos Panaiotissa in Constantinople, see Raymond Janin, *Constantinople Byzantine: La Géographie ecclésiastique de l'empire Byzantine, I, III: Les Eglises et les monastères* (Paris, 1969), 213–14. For the church's remains in Istanbul, see Thomas Mathews, *The Byzantine Churches of Istanbul* (University Park, Penn., 1976), 366–75; it is called Theotokos Panagia Mougliotissa (Mother of God of the Mongols).

10. Ibid. 147–48; *ODB*, s.v. "Mongols," 1395.

11. Nicol, *Last Centuries,* 210.

12. See Underwood, *Kariye Djami* 1:46–47, for the later Melane, and Paul. A. Underwood, "The Deesis Mosaic in the Kariye Djami at Istanbul," *Late Classical and Medieval Studies in Honor of A. M. Friend, Jr.* (Princeton, 1955), 254–60; see also Nelson, "Chora," 76, and Natalia Teteriatnikov, "The Dedication of the Chora Monastery in the Time of Andronikos II Palaeologos," *Byzantion* 66 (1996): 188–207, esp. 198, for the earlier Melane; see also ibid., 197, n. 18, on Melane's identity.

13. *ODB,* s.v. "Mongols," 1395.

14. See Teteriatnikov, "Dedication," 193–207.

15. For the original Greek and translation by Asdracha and Sherry, see Teteriatnikov, "Dedication," 194–96.

16. Philes himself would have known of these dangers, for in 1297 he traveled to the court of the Tatars to arrange the marriage for Andronicus II's daughter Maria with the khan, Tochtai (see Teteriatnikov, "Dedication," 199); these are different Mongols, however, from the ones among whom Andronicus's sister lived.

17. Ibid., 200.

# GLOSSARY

| | |
|---|---|
| abbess | head of a nunnery; superior; *hegumene* |
| acrostic | word formed from the first letters of the first words of successive lines in a poem |
| *Akathistos* | name of a famous poetic hymn to the Virgin Mary |
| amphitheater | area or racetrack surrounded by tiers of seating on a circular or elliptical plan |
| ampulla(ae) | vial or flask made of clay or lead, used to hold a substance (*eulogia*) gathered at a holy site |
| *Anastasis* | Resurrection, often depicted as Christ pulling Adam and Eve from their coffins; Easter image of the Orthodox Church |
| apocrypha | texts not accepted as canonical |
| apotactite | virgin; religious woman |
| apotropeia | protective or amuletic objects or symbols |
| apse | vaulted semicircular room, located at east end of a church |
| arena | *see* amphitheater; area for fights or races in Roman and Byzantine cities |
| Arian, Arianism | heretical brand of Christianity which undermines the divinity of Christ |
| ascetic | person who adopts a self-depriving or harsh way of life |
| Augusta | empress; a title conferred on imperial women |
| *basileia* | royalty, power, majesty |
| bay | a unit or compartment of an architectural space, defined by vaulting or wall elements |
| bezel | the top face of a ring |

| | |
|---|---|
| catechumens | those who are preparing for baptism |
| C.E. | Common Era, equivalent to A.D. (*Anno Domini*) |
| cenobitic | style of monastic life in which individuals live together in a group |
| Chalke | name of gate at the main entrance into the imperial palace in Constantinople |
| *chiton(es)* | tunic; a basic shift or undergarment |
| *chlamys* | a cloak fastened by a fibula; standard element of court costume |
| ciborium | free-standing canopy or cover over a sacred place or altar |
| *clavus(i)* | ornamental stripe applied to a tunic |
| cloisonné | metalworking technique in which wires (cloisons) of metal are soldered to a base, forming compartments which hold the colors in enamels |
| crypt | space under the main floor of a church, usually for burial or to house saints' relics |
| dalmatic | tunic |
| deaconess | ecclesiastical title given to women in the church |
| *deesis* | prayer, entreaty |
| *Deesis* | figural composition in which the Virgin Mary and Saint John the Baptist are shown supplicating Christ |
| *dextrarum iunctio* | joining of right hands in marriage |
| diptych | two hinged panels or leaves; lists of the names of the living and dead |
| *ecclesiarchissa* | nun in charge of church services and of singing nuns and their training |
| *ekphrasis* | rhetorical description of a work of art, often set as a poem |
| encomium | literary work praising a person; panegyric |
| entablature | architectural members carried on piers or columns, often supporting the superstructure or gallery of a church; architrave, frieze, and cornice above supporting columns or piers |
| *ephoros; ephoreia* | guardian of a monastery; guardianship |
| eremitic | pertaining to solitary life or life as a hermit |
| eschatological | dealing with last things: death, judgment, heaven, and hell |
| *eulogia(ai)* | token, blessing; substance believed to have amuletic powers |
| eunuch | castrated male |
| *eusebeia* | piety |

| | |
|---|---|
| *ex voto* | an offering made in fulfillment of a vow |
| fibula | pin or brooch |
| fresco | technique of painting on wet plaster which when dry is long-lasting; used in decorating walls of churches |
| frontispiece | initial page or pages of a manuscript |
| gallery | upper level of a church, above the side-aisles and open to the nave |
| *gynaeceum; gynaikonitis* | women's quarters of a house or palace |
| *gynaikeia* | galleries or place in a church reserved for women |
| hagiography | writing about saints' lives |
| *hegumene* | abbess |
| hieratic | stiff, formal, frontal, as in a portrait or group portrait; as in an icon |
| *himation* | long mantle |
| hippodrome | an arena for horse racing and popular entertainment |
| *hosios* | holy man; saint |
| *hypotyposis* | set of rules of a monastery |
| icon (from *eikon(es)*) | image; picture or portable panel with sacred use and connotations |
| iconoclast | destroyer of images; opposed to images |
| iconoclasm | movement of the eighth and ninth centuries that denied the holiness of images |
| iconodule | servant of images; in favor of images; iconophile |
| intrado(s) | inner surface or an arch or doorway |
| katholikon | principal church of a monastic complex |
| *kellariotissa* | nun in charge of dining at a monastery |
| *ktitor* | founder |
| *largesse* | generosity in the form of gifts or favors |
| *latreia* | worship |
| liturgy; liturgical | any repeated performance or observance; a rite, usually within the church |
| *locus(a) sanctus(a)* | holy place, a site visited by pilgrims associated with a sacred event or saint's remains |
| loros | a jeweled scarf worn by imperial figures |
| *maniakion* | a wide, jeweled ceremonial collar or necklace |
| *maphorion* | veil or shawl worn over the head; typical costume of the Virgin Mary |
| martyrium | building at a place where a person or event bore witness to God's grace |
| medallion | portrait used for painted or mosaic decoration having a round frame |

| | |
|---|---|
| medium | material of which something is made, as in gold, glass or wood |
| *Menaia* | books or readings pertaining to saints commcmorated according to the monthly calendar |
| *menologium* | collection of notices of saints' lives (*vitae*) arranged by month according to their feast days in the church calendar |
| Metaphrastes | name of a compiler and regularizer of saints' lives in the late tenth century |
| monastery (male or female community) | community of nuns or monks living in a walled enclosure and segregated from the rest of society |
| Monophysitism | heretical brand of Christianity which claimed that the divinity of Christ outweighed his humanity |
| mosaic | costly technique of setting individual colored cubes, or tesserae, of stone or glass into a plaster surface to form decorative images on the walls of churches |
| *naos* | nave or central space of a church; main worship space, under the dome |
| narthex | porch or vestibule before the entrance to a church |
| nave | see *naos* |
| Nestorianism | heresy in which the unity of Christ's person was undermined and which implied that there were actually two sons, the divine Son of God and the human son of Mary |
| niello | a shiny black, bituminous substance used, for example, to fill engraved letters of inscriptions on silver liturgical objects |
| *oikonomos* | financial manager of a monastery; steward |
| Orthodox(y) | Christianity as defined by correct beliefs, as determined at the seven ecumenical councils of the church |
| obverse | front or main surface of a coin |
| *paludamentum* | cloak |
| *Panagia* | most holy; usually refers to the Virgin Mary |
| panegyric | encomium; work praising someone or something |
| Pantocrator | all-powerful; creator of all |
| parecclesion | funerary chapel adjacent to a church |
| *parresia* | free speech or communication with God |
| *parthenos(oi)* | virgin(s) |
| paten | flat dish used to hold the eucharistic bread on the altar |
| Patriarch | head of the church at one of the principal sees of Eastern Christianity, Rome, Alexandria, Antioch, Jerusalem and Constantinople |

| | |
|---|---|
| *pendilia,* or *prependulia* | pendant ornaments on an imperial crown |
| *philandreia* | fecundity |
| *philanthropeia* | love of mankind, generosity |
| *philoparthenos* | a friend of virgins |
| *Porphyra* | chamber in the imperial palace with red stone (porphyry) walls where the empress gave birth to children |
| *porphyrogennetos; porphyrogenneta(ai);* also *porphyrogenitus (a)* | a child born in the Porphyra of the imperial palace |
| porphyry | hard, reddish-purple stone quarried in Egypt, reserved for imperial use |
| prophylactory | protective device |
| *proskynesis* | act of reverence, veneration |
| *putto(i)* | in art, a small, naked child with wings, associated with symbolic or allegorical subjects |
| register | horizontal row of decoration |
| relief | carving on a block of stone that stands out from the ground |
| reverse | back surface of a coin |
| rotunda | round building, usually with spherical domed roof |
| roundel | image in carved, painted, or mosaic decoration with a round frame |
| *sebastokrator* | title given to the second in authority after the emperor; commander-in-chief |
| senate | group of officials or dignitaries carrying out mainly ceremonial roles |
| senmurv | Sassanian mythical beast, combined bird and lion, often appearing as a design on textiles |
| snood | hair net |
| *solidus(i)* | gold coin weighing 1/72 of a pound; *nomisma* |
| *stemma* | a type of imperial crown |
| *strategos* | military governor or general |
| *superior* | *abbess; hegumene;* head of a nunnery |
| *synaxis* | liturgy or celebration honoring an event or person, usually a saint |
| *synaxarium* | church calendar with readings for fixed feast days; collection of hagiographical texts |
| *tableion* | ornamental patch sewn onto a cloak indicative of rank; badge of office |

| | |
|---|---|
| *tabula ansata* | oblong frame with "handles" carrying an inscription, often appearing above the head of an individual in a portrait, as on a consular diptych or a sarcophagus |
| *tapeinophrosyne* | humility |
| tessera(ae) | individual cubes of stone, glass, or terracotta (or glass with a layer of silver or gold) used in mosaic technique |
| theophany | a divine appearance, as in a manifestation of God; an epiphany |
| Theotokos | "God-bearer"; refers to the Virgin Mary, or Mother of God |
| *thorakion* | a shield-shaped motif found on the front of an empress's ceremonial garb |
| *topos(oi)* | the place(s); a conceit referring to a particular type of event or pattern of life found repeatedly in poems, saints' lives or other highly constructed texts |
| Triumph of Orthodoxy | final defeat of iconoclasm in 843, celebrated on the first Sunday in Lent |
| *typikon* | regulatory document or foundation charter of a monastery, of two types, founders and liturgical |
| *univira* | the right to one marriage and no more |
| *Vita(ae)* | life, lives; referring to hagiographic texts, saints' lives |
| *xenodocheion* | an inn or hospice for travelers (strangers) or for the sick |

# BIBLIOGRAPHY

## Primary Sources

*The Alexiad of Anna Comnena.* Translated by E. R. A. Sewter. Harmondsworth, 1969.

*Anne Comnène: Alexiade.* Translated by Bernard Leib. 3 vols. (Greek with French translation). Paris, 1967.

Brock, Sebastian, and Susan Harvey. *Holy Women of the Syrian Orient.* New York, 1992.

Brock, Sebastian, and Harvey, Susan, trans. "Pelagia of Antioch." In Sebastian P. Brock and Susan A. Harvey, *Holy Women of the Syrian Orient,* 40–62. Berkeley, 1987.

Clark, Elizabeth A. *The Life of Melania the Younger: Introduction, Translation and Commentary.* New York and Toronto, 1984.

Connor, Carolyn L., and W. Robert Connor, introduction and trans. *The Life and Miracles of Saint Luke of Steiris, Text, Translation, and Commentary.* Brookline, Mass., 1994.

Constas, Nicholas, trans. "Life of St. Mary/Marinos." In *Holy Women of Byzantium: Ten Saints' Lives in English Translation,* ed. Alice-Mary Talbot, 1–12. Washington, D.C., 1996.

Corrigan, Kevin, trans. *The Life of Saint Macrina By Gregory, Bishop of Nyssa.* Toronto, 1987.

Dagron, Gilbert, ed., *Vie et Miracles de Sainte Thècle.* Greek, fifth-century version. Brussels, 1978.

Dawes, Elizabeth, and Norman H. Baynes, ed. and trans. *The Life of Theodore of Sykeon.* In *Three Byzantine Saints,* 88–185. Crestwood, N.Y., 1977.

Delehaye, Hippolyte, ed. and trans. "Deux Typika byzantins de l'époque des Paléologues." *Mémoires de l'Académie Royale de Belgique, Classe des Lettres, 2e série, t. XIII, no. 4,* 1–213. Brussels, 1921. Repr. *Synaxaires byzantins, ménologues, typica* 6:18–105. London, 1977.

*Digenis Akritis.* Edited and translated by Elizabeth Jeffreys. Cambridge, 1998.

*Ermeneia tes zographikes technes.* Edited by A. Papadopoulos-Kerameus. St. Petersburg, 1909.

Festugière, André-Jean, ed. and trans. *Vie de Théodore de Sykeon.* Subsidia Hagiographica 48. Brussels, 1970.

Freshfield, Edwin H., trans. *Roman Law in the Later Roman Empire: Byzantine Guilds, Professional and Commercial.* Cambridge, 1938.

*Grégoire de Nysse, Vie de Sainte Macrine.* Edited and translated by Pierre Maraval. In Greek. Paris, 1971.

Hennecke, E., and W. Schneemelcher. *New Testament Apocrypha.* 2 vols. Philadelphia, 1963–65.

Hero, Angela C. *A Woman's Quest for Spiritual Guidance: The Correspondence of Princess Irene Eulogia.* Brookline, Mass., 1986.

James, M. R., ed. and trans. *Acts of Paul and Thekla.* In *The Apocryphal Gospels, The Apocryphal New Testament,* 272–81. Oxford, 1924.

Jeffreys, Elizabeth, Michael Jeffreys, and Roger Scott, trans. *The Chronicle of John Malalas.* Melbourne, 1986.

*Kassia; the Legend, the Woman and Her Work.* Edited and translated by Antonia Tripolitis. New York and London, 1992.

Kouli, Maria, trans. "Life of St. Mary of Egypt." In *Holy Women of Byzantium: Ten Saints' Lives in English Translation,* ed. Alice-Mary Talbot, 64–93. Washington, D.C., 1966.

Kraemer, Ross S., ed. "Thekla of Iconium: An Ascetic Christian and the Prototypical Convert." In *Maenads, Martyrs, Matrons, Monastics.* English translation of the *Acts,* 280–88. Philadelphia, 1988.

*The Lives of the Holy Women Martyrs.* Translated and compiled from the Greek of *The Great Synaxaristes of the Orthodox Church.* Buena Vista, Colo., 1991.

Mango, Cyril, trans. *The Homiles of Photius, Patriarch of Constantinople.* Washington, D.C., 1958.

Mango, Cyril, and Roger Scott, trans. and comp. *The Chronicle of Theophanes Confessor: Byzantine and Near Eastern History, AD 284–813.* Oxford, 1997.

Paton, W. R., trans. "The Epigram from Hagios Polyeuktos." In *Greek Anthology,* vol. 1, book I, epigram 10, Greek text with facing English translation, 6–11. 1916; reprint Cambridge, 1993.

Procopius. *Secret History.* Translated by Richard Atwater. Ann Arbor, 1963.

Procopius. *Secret History, Wars, Buildings.* Translated by H. B. Dewing. 1914–40; reprint Loeb Classical Library, Cambridge, Mass., 1998. Greek text and English translation.

Psellus, Michael. *Chronographia.* Edited and translated by E. Renauld. 2 vols. Paris, 1926–28. Greek text and French translation.

———. *Psellus.* In *Fourteen Byzantine Rulers: The Chronographia of Michael Psellus.* Translated by E. R. A. Sewter. Harmondsworth, 1966.

Rosenqvist, Jan Olof, ed. *The Life of Saint Irene Abbess of Chrysobalanton: A Critical Edition with Introduction, Translation, Notes and Indices.* Uppsala, 1986.

Russel, Norman, trans., and Benedicta Ward, intro. *The Lives of the Desert Fathers: The Historia Monachorum in Aegypto.* London and Oxford, 1981.

*Synaxarium Ecclesiae Constantinopolitanae.* Edited by H. Delehaye. In *Propylaeum ad Acta Sanctorum,* 75–78, on Saint Thekla. Brussels, 1902. Greek.

Talbot, Alice-Mary, trans. and intro. "Bebaia Elpis: Typikon of Theodora Synadene for the Convent of the Mother of God Bebaia Elpis in Constantinople." In *Byzantine Monastic Foundation Documents,* edited by John Thomas and Angela Constantinides Hero, 4:1512–78. Washington, D.C., 2000.

Ward, Benedicta, trans. *Sayings of the Desert Fathers: The Apophthegmata Patrum*. Kalamazoo, 1975.

Ware, Mother Mary, and Kallistos, trans. *The Lenten Triodion*. London, 1978.

## Secondary Sources

Abrahamse, Dorothy. "Women's Monasticism in the Middle Byzantine Period: Problems and Prospects." *BF* 9 (1985): 35–58.

Auzépy, Marie-France. "La destruction de l'icone du Christ de la Chalcé par Léon III: Propagande ou réalité?" *Byzantion* 60 (1990): 445–92.

Allen, Pauline. "Contemporary Portrayals of the Byzantine Empress Theodora (A.D. 527–548)." In *Stereotypes of Women in Power: Historical Perspectives and Revisionist Views,* edited by Barbara Garlick, S. Dixon, and P. Allen, 93–103. New York, 1992.

Anastos, Milton V. "The Coronation of Emperor Michael IV in 1034 by Empress Zoe and Its Significance." In *To Hellenikon: Studies in Honor of Speros Vryonis, Jr.* 1:23–43. New York, 1993.

Andreescu-Treadgold, Irina, and Warren Treadgold. "Procopius and the Imperial Panels of S. Vitale." *Art Bulletin* 79 (1997): 708–23.

Bann, Stephen. "Legends of the True Cross." In *The True Vine: On Visual Representation and the Western Tradition,* 216–43. New York, Port Chester, Melbourne, Sydney, 1989.

Barber, Charles. "The Imperial Panels in San Vitale: A Reconsideration." *Byzantine and Modern Greek Studies* 14 (1990): 19–41.

Baynes, Norman. "The Supernatural Defenders of Constantinople." *Anal.Bol.* 67 (1949): 165–77. Reprinted in N. Baynes, ed., *Byzantine Studies and Other Essays,* 248–60. London, 1955.

Beaucamp, Joëlle. *Le Statut de la femme à Byzance (4e-7e siècle)*. Volume 1: *Le Droit Impérial*. Volume 2: *Les Pratiques sociales*. Paris, 1990, 1992.

———. "La situation juridique de la femme à Byzance." *Cahiers de civilisation médiévale* 20 (1977): 145–76.

Beckwith, John. *Early Christian and Byzantine Art.* 1979; reprint New York, 1986.

Bell, R. M. *Saints and Society: The Two Worlds of Western Christendom, 1000–1700.* Chicago, 1982.

Belting, Hans. *Likeness and Presence: A History of the Image Before the Era of Art.* Chicago, 1994.

Belting, Hans, Cyril Mango, and Doula Mouriki. *The Mosaics and Frescoes of St. Mary Pammakaristos (Fethiye Camii) at Istanbul.* Washington, D.C., 1978.

Boyd, Susan, and Marlia Mango, eds. *Ecclesiastical Silver Plate in Sixth-Century Byzantium.* Washington, D.C., 1992.

Brock, Sebastian, and Susan Harvey, eds. *Holy Women of the Syrian Orient.* Berkeley, 1987.

Brand, Charles M. "Some Byzantine Women of Thebes—and Elsewhere." In *To Hellenikon: Studies in Honor of Speros Vryonis, Jr.,* 1:59–68. New York, 1993.

Brown, Peter. "Arbiters of the Holy: The Christian Holy Man in Late Antiquity." In *Authority and the Sacred: Aspects of the Christianization of the Roman World* 1:55–78, 85–87. Cambridge, 1995.

———. "Aspects of the Christianization of the Roman Aristocracy." *JRS* 51 (1961): 1–11.

———. "Bodies and Minds: Sexuality and Renunciation in Early Christianity." In *Before Sexuality: The Construction of Erotic Experience in the Ancient Greek World,* edited by David M. Halperin, John J. Winkler, and Froma I. Zeitlin, 479–93. Princeton, 1990.

———. *The Body and Society: Men, Women, and Sexual Renunciation in Early Christianity.* New York, 1988.

———. "Daughters of Jerusalem: The Ascetic Life of Women in the Fourth Century." In *The Body and Society: Men, Women and Sexual Renunciation in Early Christianity,* 259–84. New York, 1988.

———. "The Rise and Function of the Holy Man in Late Antiquity." *JRS* 61 (1971): 80–101. Reprinted in *Society and the Holy in Late Antiquity,* 103–52. Berkeley, 1982.

———. "The Saint as Exemplar in Late Antiquity." *Representations* 1/2 (1973): 1–25. Reprinted in J. S. Hawley, ed., *Saints and Virtues,* 3–14. Berkeley, 1987.

———. *The World of Late Antiquity, AD150–750.* London, 1978.

Browning, Robert. *The Byzantine Empire.* Washington, D.C., 1992.

———. *Justinian and Theodora.* London, 1971.

Brubaker, Leslie. "Memories of Helena: Patterns in Imperial Female Matronage in the Fourth and Fifth Centuries." In *Women, Men and Eunuchs: Gender in Byzantium,* ed. Liz James, 52–75. London and New York, 1997.

Brundage, James A. *Law, Sex and Christian Society in Medieval Europe,* esp. chap. 3, "Sex and the Law in the Christian Empire, from Constantine to Justinian," 77–123. Chicago and London, 1987.

Bowersock, Glen W. "From Emperor to Bishop: The Self-Conscious Transformation of Political Power in the Fourth Century A.D." *Classical Philology* 8 (1986): 298–307.

Buckton, D., ed. *Byzantium: Treasures of Byzantine Art and Culture From British Collections.* London, 1994.

Bury, J. B. *The Imperial Administrative System in the Ninth Century, with a Revised Text of the Kletorologion of Philotheos.* 1911; reprint New York, n.d.

Bynum, Caroline Walker. *Holy Feast and Holy Fast: The Religious Significance of Food to Medieval Women.* Berkeley, 1987.

———. *Fragmentation and Redemption: Essays on Gender and the Human Body in Medieval Religion.* New York, 1992.

Cameron, Alan. "The Empress and the Poet: Paganism and Politics at the Court of Theodorius II." *Yale Classical Studies* 27 (1982): 217–83.

Cameron, Averil, *Christianity and the Rhetoric of Empire: The Development of Christian Discourse.* Berkeley, 1991.

———. "The Construction of Court Ritual: The Byzantine Book of Ceremonies." In *Rituals of Royalty: Power and Ceremonial in Traditional Societies,* ed. David Cannadine and Simon Price. Cambridge, 1987.

———. "The Empress Sophia." *Byzantion* 45 (1975): 5–21.

———. "Images of Authority: Elites and Icons in Late Sixth-Century Byzantium." *Past and Present* 84 (1979): 3–35.

———. *The Mediterranean World in Late Antiquity AD 395–600.* London and New York, 1993.

———. *Procopius and the Sixth Century.* Berkeley, 1985.

———. "The Theotokos in Sixth-Century Constantinople: A City Finds Its Symbol." *Jour-

*nal of Theological Studies* 29 (1978): 79–108. Reprinted in *Continuity and Change in Sixth-Century Byzantium.* London, 1981.

———. "The Virgin's Robe: An Episode in the History of Early Seventh-Century Constantinople." In Averil Cameron, *Continuity and Change in Sixth-Century Byzantium,* 42–56. London, 1981.

Cameron Averil, and Judith Herrin, eds. *Constantinople in the Early Eighth Century: The Parastaseis Syntomoi Chronikai.* Leiden, 1984.

Capizzi, Carmelo. "Anicia Giuliana (462ca–530ca): Ricerche Sulla Sua Famiglia e la sua Vita." *Rivista di Studi Byzantini* 5 (15) (1968): 191–226.

Carr, Annemarie Weyl. "Women as Artists in the Middle Ages: 'The Dark Is Light Enough.'" In *Dictionary of Women Artists,* ed. Delia Gaze, 1:3–21. On Byzantium, see 14–17.

———. "Women and Monasticism in Byzantium: Introduction from an Art Historian." *BF* 9 (1985): 1–15.

Cazelles, Brigitte. *The Lady as Saint: A Collection of French Hagiographic Romances of the Thirteenth Century.* Philadelphia, 1991.

Chatzidakis, Nano. *Wall Mosaics and Frescoes: Hosios Loukas.* Athens, 1996.

Chitty, Derwas J. *The Desert a City: An Introduction to the Study of Egyptian and Palestinian Monasticism under the Christian Empire.* Crestwood, N.Y., 1966.

Clark, Elizabeth A. *Ascetic Piety and Women's Faith: Essays on Late Ancient Christianity.* Studies in Women and Religion 20. Lewiston, N.Y., 1986.

———. "Ascetic Renunciation and Feminine Advancement: A Paradox of Late Ancient Christianity." *American Theological Review* 63 (1981): 240–57.

———. "Authority and Humility: A Conflict of Values in Fourth-Century Female Monasticism." *BZ* 9 (1985): 17–33.

———. "Devil's Gateway and Bride of Christ: Women in the Early Christian World." In *Ascetic Piety and Women's Faith: Essays on Late ancient Christianity,* 23–60. Lewiston, N.Y., 1986.

———. "Early Christian Women: Sources and Interpretation." In *That Gentle Strength: Historical Perspectives on Women in Christianity,* ed. Lynda L. Coon, Katherine J. Haldane, and Elisabeth W. Sommer, 19–35. Charlottesville, Va., 1990.

———. "Claims on the Bones of Saint Stephen: The Partisans of Melania and Eudocia." *Church History* 51 (1982): 141–56.

———. *Women in the Early Church.* Wilmington, Del., 1983.

Clark, Elizabeth A., and Herbert Richardson. *Women and Religion: A Feminist Sourcebook of Christian Thought.* New York, 1977.

Clark, Gillian. *Women in Late Antiquity: Pagan and Christian Life-styles.* Oxford, 1993.

Cloke, Gillian, *"This Female Man of God": Women and Spiritual Power in the Patristic Age, AD 350–450.* London, 1995.

Connor, Carolyn L. *Art and Miracles in Medieval Byzantium: The Cyprt at Hosios Loukas and Its Frescoes.* Princeton, 1991.

———. "The Epigram in the Church of Hagios Polyeuktos in Constantinople and Its Byzantine Response." *Byzantion* 69 (1999): 479–527.

———. "Female Saints in Church Decoration of the Troodos Mountains in Cyprus." In *Medieval Cyprus: Studies in Art, Architecture, and History in Memory of Doula Mouriki,* ed. Nancy P. Ševčenko and Christopher Moss, 211–28. Princeton, 1999.

———. "Hosios Loukas as a Victory Church." *GRBS* 33 (1992): 293–308.

Coon, Lynda L., Katherine J. Haldane, and Elisabeth W. Sommer. *That Gentle Strength: Historical Perspectives on Women in Christianity.* Charlottesville, Va., 1990.

Coon, Lynda L. "God's Holy Harlots: The Redemptive Lives of Pelagia of Antioch and Mary of Egypt." In *Sacred Fictions: Holy Women and Hagiography in Late Antiquity,* 71–94. Philadelphia, 1997.

———. *Sacred Fictions: Holy Women and Hagiography in Late Antiquity.* Philadelphia, 1997.

Cormack, Robin. "Interpreting the Mosaics of S. Sophia at Istanbul." *Art History* 4 (1981): 131–47.

———. "The Mosaic Decoration of S. Demetrios, Thessaloniki: A Re-examination in the Light of the Drawings of W. S. George." *Annual of the British School at Athens* 64 (1969): 17–52.

———. "Woman and Icons, and Women in Icons." In *Women, Men and Eunuchs: Gender in Byzantium,* ed. Liz James, 24–51. London and New York, 1997.

———. *Writing in Gold: Byzantine Society and Its Icons,* esp. chap. 1, "Theodore of Sykeon: The Visible Saint," 9–49; chap. 5: "Paradise Sought: The Imperial Use of Art," 179–214. New York, 1985.

Cutler, Anthony, and Paul Magdalino. "Some Precisions on the Lincoln College Typikon." *CA* 27 (1978): 179–98.

Daube, David. "The Marriage of Justinian and Theodora: Legal and Theological Reflections." *Catholic University of America Law Review* 16 (1967): 380–99.

Davids, Adelbert, ed. *The Empress Theophano: Byzantium and the West at the Turn of the First Millennium.* Cambridge, 1995.

———. "Marriage Negotiations between Byzantium and the West and the Name of Theophano in Byzantium (Eighth to Tenth Centuries)." In *The Empress Theophano: Byzantium and the West at the Turn of the First Millennium,* edited by Adelbert Davids, 99–120. Cambridge, 1995.

Davis, Stephen J. *The Cult of Saint Thecla: A Tradition of Women's Piety in Late Antiquity.* Oxford, 2001.

Delbrueck, Richard. *Die Consulardiptychen und verwandte Denkmäler.* Berlin and Leipzig, 1929.

Drijvers, Jan Willem. *Helena Augusta: The Mother of Constantine the Great and the Legend of Her Finding of the True Cross.* Leiden, 1992.

———. "Marutha of Maipherqat on Helena Augusta, Jerusalem and the Council of Nicaea." *Studia Patristica* 34 (2001): 51–64.

Diehl, Charles. "Theodora." In *Byzantine Empresses,* 44–64. 1927; reprint London, 1963.

Downey, Glanville. "Justinian as Builder." *AB* 32 (1950): 262–66.

Doxiadis, Euphrosyne. *The Mysterious Fayum Portraits: Faces from Ancient Egypt.* New York, 1995.

Elm, Susanna. *"Virgins of God": The Making of Asceticism in Late Antiquity.* Oxford, 1994.

Emmanuel, Melita. "Hairstyles and Headdresses of Empresses, Princesses and Ladies of the Aristocracy in Byzantium." In *Deltion tis Christ. Arch. Het.* 17 (1993–94): 113–20.

———. "Some Notes on the External Appearance of Ordinary Women in Byzantium; Hairstyles, Headdresses: Texts and Iconography." *Stephanos: Byzantinoslavica* 56 (1995): 769–78.

Evans, Helen C., and William D. Wixom, eds. *The Glory of Byzantium: Art and Culture of the Middle Byzantine Era A.D. 843–1261.* New York, 1997.

Evans, J. A. S. *The Age of Justinian: The Circumstances of Imperial Power.* New York, 1996.

———. *Procopius.* New York, 1972.

Fairweather, Janet. "Fiction in the Biographies of Ancient Writers." *Ancient Society* 5 (1974): 231–75.

Fentress, James, and Chris Wickham. *Social Memory.* Oxford, 1992.

Fiorenza, E. Schüssler. *In Memory of Her: A Feminist Theological Reconstruction of Christian Origins.* New York, 1983.

———. "Word, Spirit and Power: Women in Early Christian Communities." In *Women of Spirit: Female Leadership in the Jewish and Christian Traditions,* edited by R. Reuther and E. McLaughlin, 29–70. New York, 1979.

Fisher, Elizabeth A. "Theodora and Antonina in the *Historia Aracana:* History and/or Fiction?" *Arethusa* 11 (1978): 253–79.

Folda, Jaroslav. "The Saint Marina Icon: Maniera Cypria, Lingua Franca, or Crusader Art?" In *Four Icons in the Menil Collection,* edited by Bertrand Davezac, 107–33. Austin, 1992.

Gaca, Kathy L. "The Sexual and Social Dangers of *Pornai* in the Septuagint Greek Stratum of Patristic Christian Greek Thought." In *Desire and Denial in Byzantium,* ed. Liz James, 36–40. Brookfield, Vt., 1999.

Galatariotou, Catia. "Byzantine Ktetorika Typika: A Comparative Study." *REB* 5 (1987): 77–138.

———. "Byzantine Women's Monastic Communities: The Evidence of the Typika." *JOB* 38 (1988): 263–90.

Gardner, Jane F. *Women in Roman Law and Society.* London and Sydney, 1986.

Garland, Lynda. *Byzantine Empresses: Women and Power in Byzantium, AD 527–1204.* New York, 1999.

———. "The Empresses of Alexios Komenos (1081–1118)." In *Byzantine Empresses: Women and Power in Byzantium, AD 527–1204,* edited by Lynda Garland, 180–98. New York, 1999.

———. "The Life and Ideology of Byzantine Women: A Further Note on Conventions of Behaviour and Social Reality as Reflected in Eleventh- and Twelfth-Century Historical Sources." *Byzantion* 58 (1988): 361–93.

———. "Theodora, Wife of Justinian (527–48)." In *Byzantine Empresses: Women and Power in Byzantium, AD 527–1204,* edited by Lynda Garland, 11–39. New York, 1999.

———. "Zoe Porphyrogenneta." In *Byzantine Empresses: Women and Power in Byzantium, AD 527–1204,* edited by Lynda Garland, 136–57. London, 1999.

Geanakoplos, Deno John. *Byzantium: Church, Society, and Civilization seen Through Contemporary Eyes.* Chicago, 1984.

Gibbon, Edward. *The Decline and Fall of the Roman Empire.* Volume 2: *395–1185 A.D.* New York, 1932.

Goodacre, Hugh. *A Handbook of the Coinage of the Byzantine Empire.* London, 1967.

Gouma-Peterson, Thalia, ed. *Anna Komnene and Her Times.* New York, 2000.

———. "Passages to the Maternal in Anna Komnene's Alexiad." In *Anna Komnene and Her Times,* 107–24. New York, 2000.

Grabar, André. *Byzantine Painting.* Skira, 1953.

Grabar, André, and M. Manoussacas. *L'illustration du manuscrit de Skylitzès de la bibliothèque nationale de Madrid.* Venice, 1979.

Greatrex, Geoffrey. "The Dates of Procopius' Works." *BMGS* 18 (1994): 101–14.

Grierson, Philip, and Melinda Mays. *Catalogue of the Late Roman Coins in the Dumbarton Oaks Collection and in the Whittemore Collection: From Arcadius and Honorius to the Accession of Anastasius.* Washington, D.C., 1992.

Grosdidier de Matons, José. "La femme dans l'empire Byzantin." In *Histoire Mondiale de la Femme,* edited by Pierre Grimal, 11–43. Paris, 1974.

Hahn, Cynthia. "Loca Sancta Souvenirs: Sealing the Pilgrim's Experience." In *The Blessings of Pilgrimage,* edited by R. Ousterhout, 85–96. Illinois Byzantine Studies 1. Urbana, 1990.

Halkin, François. "Deux Impératrices de Byzance." *AB* 106 (1988): 5–34.

Hanawalt, Emily A. *An Annotated Bibliography of Byzantine Sources in English Translation.* Brookline, Mass., 1982.

*Handbook of the Byzantine Collection.* Dumbarton Oaks. Washington, D.C., nd.

Harrison, Martin. *Excavations at Saraçhane in Istanbul.* Volume 1: *The Excavations, Structures, Architectural Decoration, Small Finds, Coins, Bones, and Molluscs.* Princeton, 1986.

———. "A Source for Anicia Juliana's Palace-Church." *Philadelphie et autres études* (1984): 141–42.

———. *A Temple for Byzantium: The Discovery and Excavation of Anicia Juliana's Palace Church in Istanbul.* Austin, 1989.

Hartney, Aideen. "Manly Women and Womanly Men: The *subintroductae* and John Chrysostom." In *Desire and Denial in Byzantium,* ed. Liz James, 41–48. Brookfield, Vt., 1999.

Harvey, Susan Ashbrook. *Asceticism and Society in Crisis: John of Ephesus and the Lives of the Eastern Saints,* esp. chap. 6, "Some Implications: The Case of Women," 108–33. Berkeley, 1990.

———. "Sacred Bonding: Mothers and Daughters in Early Syriac Hagiography." *Journal of Early Christian Studies* 4 (1996): 27–56.

———. "Women in Early Byzantine Hagiography: Reversing the Story." In *That Gentle Strength: Historical Perspectives on Women in Christianity,* ed. Lynda L. Coon, Katherine J. Haldane, and Elisabeth W. Sommer, 36–59. Charlottesville, Va., 1990.

Heffernam, Thomas J. *Sacred Biography: Saints and Their Biographers in the Middle Ages.* New York, 1988.

Hero, Angela. "Irene-Eulogia Choumnaina Palaeologina, Abbess of the Convent of Philanthropos Soter in Constantinople." *BZ* 9 (1985): 119–47.

Herrin, Judith. "'Femina Byzantina': The Council in Trullo on Women." *DOP* 46 (1992): 97–105.

———. "In Search of Byzantine Women: Three Avenues of Approach." In *Images of Women in Antiquity,* edited by A. Cameron and A. Kuhrt, 167–89. Detroit and London, 1983.

———. "Public and Private Forms of Religious Commitment Among Byzantine Women." In *Women in Ancient Societies: "An Illusion of the Night,"* edited by L. Archer, S. Fischler, S. Wyke, and M. Wyke. New York, 1994.

———. "Theophano: Considerations on the Education of a Byzantine Princess." In *The Empress Theophano: Byzantium and the West at the Turn of the First Millennium,* edited by Adelbert Davids, 64–85. Cambridge, 1995.

———. "Women and the Church in Byzantium." *Bulletin of the British Association of Orientalists* II (1980): 8–14.

———. "Women and the Faith in Icons in Early Christianity." In *Culture, Ideology and Politics,* edited by Raphael Sammuel and Gareth Stedman Jones, 56–83. London, 1982.

———. *Women in Purple: Rulers of Medieval Byzantium.* Princeton, 2001.

Hill, Barbara. "Actions Speak Louder Than Words: Anna Komnene's Attempted Usurpation." In *Anna Komnene and Her Times,* edited by Thalia Gouma-Peterson, 45–62. New York, 2000.

———. "Alexios I and the Imperial Women." In *Alexios I Komnenos,* edited by Margaret Mullett and Dion Smythe, 1:37–54. Belfast, 1996.

———. "Imperial Women and the Ideology of Womanhood in the Eleventh and Twelfth Centuries." In *Women, Men and Eunuchs: Gender in Byzantium,* edited by Liz James, 76–99. New York, 1987.

Hill, Barbara, Liz James, and Dion Smythe. "Zoe: The Rhythm Method of Imperial Renewal." In *New Constantines: The Rhythm of Imperial Renewal in Byzantium,* edited by Paul Magdalino, 215–29. London, 1994.

Holum, Kenneth. "Hadrian and St. Helena: Imperial Travel and the Origins of Christian Holy Land Pilgrimage." In *The Blessings of Pilgrimage,* edited by R. Ousterhout, 66–84. Illinois Byzantine Studies I. Urbana, 1990.

———. *Theodosian Empresses: Women and Imperial Dominion in Late Antiquity.* Berkeley, 1982.

———. "Pulcheria's Crusade A.D. 421–22 and the Ideology of Imperial Victory." *GRBS* 18 (1977): 153–72.

Howard-Johnston, James. "Anna Komnene and the Alexiad." In *Alexios I Komnenos,* Papers of the Second Belfast Byzantine International Colloquium, 14–16 April 1989, edited by Margaret Mullett and Dion Smythe, 260–301. Belfast, 1996.

Hunt, E. D. *Holy Land Pilgrimage in the Later Roman Empire, AD 312–460.* Oxford, 1982.

Hutter, Irmgard. "Das Bild der Frau in der Byzantinischen Kunst." *Byzantios: Festschrift Herbert Hunger zum 70. Geburtstag.* Vienna, 1984.

———. *Corpus der Byzantinischen Miniaturenhandschriften.* Volume 5.1 (text), 6–62; Volume 5.2 (plates), 85–109. Stuttgart, 1997.

———. "Die Geschichte des Lincoln College Typikons." *JOB* 45 (1995): 79–114.

James, Liz. *Light and Colour in Byzantine Art.* Oxford, 1996.

———. "Monks, Monastic Art, the Sanctoral Cycle and the Middle Byzantine Church." In *The Theotokos Evergetis and Eleventh-Century Monasticism,* edited by M. Mullett and A. Kerby, 162–75. Belfast, 1994.

———, ed. *Women, Men and Eunuchs: Gender in Byzantium.* London and New York, 1997.

Janes, Dominic. *God and Gold in Late Antiquity.* Cambridge, 1998.

Janin, Raymond. *Constantinople Byzantine: Développement urbain et répertoire topographique.* Paris, 1964.

———. *La Géographie ecclésiastique de l'empire Byzantine, I, III: Les Eglises et les monastères.* Paris, 1969.

Johnson, Mark J. "Late Antique Imperial Mausolea." Ph.D. diss., Princeton University, 1986.

———. "On the Burial Places of the Theodosian Dynasty." *Byzantion* 61 (1991): 330–39.

Jones, A. H. M. *The Later Roman Empire, 284–602*. Volume 1. Norman, Okla., 1964.

Jordan, Robert. "*Kecharitomene:* Typikon of Empress Irene Doukaina Komnene for the Convent of the Mother of God Kecharitomene in Constantinople." In *Byzantine Monastic Foundation Documents*, translated, annotated, and edited by John Thomas and Angela Constantinides Hero, 2:649–724. Washington, D.C., 2000.

Kalavrezou, Ioli, et al., eds. *Byzantine Women and Their World*. Catalogue of the Exhibition at the Arthur M. Sackler Museum, Harvard University, 26 October 2002 to 23 March, 2003. New Haven, 2003.

Kastner, G. Ronald. "Eudocia." In *A Lost Tradition: Women Writers of the Early Church*, edited by Patricia Wilson-Kastner et al., 135–71. Washington, D.C., 1981.

Kazhdan, Alexander P., and Alice-Mary Talbot. "Women and Iconoclasm." *BZ* 84–85 (1991–92): 391–408.

Kazhdan, Alexander. "Byzantine Hagiography and Sex in the Fifth to Twelfth Centuries." *DOP* 44 (1990): 131–43.

Kent, J. P. C. *The Roman Imperial Coinage: The Divided Empire and the Fall of the Western Parts AD 395–491*. Volume 10. London, 1994.

Kraemer, Ross S. *Her Share of the Blessings: Women's Religions Among Pagans, Jews, and Christians in the Greco-Roman World*. New York and Oxford, 1992.

———, ed. *Maenads, Martyrs, Matrons, Monastics: A Sourcebook on Women's Religions in the Greco-Roman World*. Philadelphia, 1988.

Krautheimer, Richard. *Early Christian and Byzantine Architecture*. Harmondsworth, 1979.

Laiou, Angeliki. "Addendum to the Report on the Role of Women in Byzantine Society." *Akten: XVI Internationale Byzantinistenkongress*, part 2, volume 1, 198–204. Vienna, 1982.

———. "The Festival of "Agathe"; Comments on the Life of Constantinopolitan Women." In *Byzantium: Tribute to Andreas N. Stratos*, 1:111–22. Athens, 1986.

———. "Imperial Marriages and Their Critics in the Eleventh Century: The Case of Skylitzes." *DOP* 46 (1992): 165–76.

———. "Introduction: Why Anna Komnene?" In *Anna Komnene and Her Times*, edited by Thalia Gouma-Peterson, 1–14. New York, 2000.

———. *Marriage, Amour et Parenté à Byzance zus XIe-XIIIe Siècles*. Paris, 1992.

———. "Observations on the Life and Ideology of Byzantine Women." *BF* 9 (1985): 59–102.

———. *Peasant Society in the Late Byzantine Empire: A Social and Demographic Study*. Princeton, 1977.

———. "The Role of Women in Byzantine Society." *JOB* 31 (1981): 233–60.

LaPorte, Jean. *The Role of Women in Early Christianity*. Studies in Women and Religion 7. New York and Toronto, 1982.

Ling, Roger. *Ancient Mosaics*. Princeton, 1998.

Ljubarskij, Jakov. "Why Is the Alexiad a Masterpiece of Byzantine Literature?" In *Anna Komnene and Her Times*, edited by Thalia Gouma-Peterson, 169–85. New York, 2000.

Lowden, John. *The Octateuchs: A Study in Byzantine Manuscript Illustration*. University Park, Penn., 1992.

MacCormack, Sabine. "The Organization of Sacred Topography." In *The Blessings of Pilgrimage*, edited by R. Ousterhout, esp. p. 18. Illinois Byzantine Studies 1. Urbana, 1990.

MacDonald, Dennis Ronald. *The Legend and the Apostle*. Philadelphia, 1983.

Mackie, Gillian. "The Mausoleum of Galla Placidia: A Possible Occupant." *Byzantion* 65 (1995): 396–404.

———. "New Light on the So-Called Saint Lawrence Panel at the Mausoleum of Galla Placidia, Ravenna." *Gesta* 29 (1990): 54–60.

———. "A New Look at the Patronage of Santa Costanza, Rome." *Byzantion* 67 (1997): 383–406.

MacMullen, Ramsay. *Christianizing the Roman Empire AD 100–400.* New Haven, 1984.

Macrides, Ruth. "Dynastic Marriages and Political Kinship." In *Byzantine Diplomacy,* edited by J. Shepard and S. Franklin, 263–80. Aldershot, 1992.

———. "The Pen and the Sword: Who Wrote the Alexiad?" In *Anna Komnene and Her Times,* ed. Thalia Gouma-Peterson, 63–82. New York, 2000.

Maguire, Henry. *Art and Eloquence in Byzantium.* Princeton, 1981.

———. *Byzantine Magic.* Cambridge, Mass., 1995.

———. "The Cycle of Images in the Church." In *Heaven on Earth: Art and the Church in Byzantium,* ed. Linda Safran, 121–51, and plates III–V. University Park, Penn., 1998.

———. *Earth and Ocean: The Terrestrial World in Early Byzantine Art.* University Park, Penn., and London, 1987.

———. *The Icons of Their Bodies: Saints and Their Images in Byzantium.* Princeton, 1996.

Mainstone, Rowland J. *Hagia Sophia: Architecture, Structure and Liturgy of Justinian's Great Church.* New York, 1988.

Majeska, George P. *Russian Travelers to Constantinople in the Fourteenth and Fifteenth Centuries.* Washington, D.C., 1984.

Mango, Cyril. *The Brazen House: A Study of the Vestibule of the Imperial Palace of Constantinople.* Copenhagen, 1959.

Mango, Marlia M. *Silver from Early Byzantium: The Kaper Koraon and Related Treasures.* Baltimore, 1986.

Martinelli, Patrizia Angiolini, ed. *La Basilica di San Vitale a Ravenna; The Basilica of San Vitale Ravenna.* Mirabilia Italiae series. Atlas, volume 1 for plates. Modena, Italy, 1997.

Mathews, Thomas F. *The Byzantine Churches of Istanbul: A Photographic Survey.* University Park, Penn., and London, 1976.

———. *The Clash of Gods.* Revised edition. Princeton, 1993.

———. *The Early Churches of Constantinople: Architecture and Liturgy.* University Park, Pa., 1971.

———. "The Sequel to Nicaea II in Byzantine Church Decoration." *Perkins Journal* 41 (1988): 11–21.

McClanan, Anne. "The Empress Theodora and the Tradition of Women's Patronage in the Early Byzantine Empire." In *The Cultural Patronage of Medieval Women,* ed. June Hall McCash, 50–72. Athens, Ga., 1996.

———. *Representations of Early Byzantine Empresses: Image and Empire.* New Middle Ages Series. Palgrave, 2002.

McCormick, Michael. *Eternal Victory: Triumphal Rulership in Late Antiquity, Byzantiun and the Early Medieval West.* Cambridge, 1986.

McNamara, Jo Ann. *Sisters in Arms: Catholic Nuns Through Two Millennia,* esp. chap. 3, "The Discipline of the Desert," 61–88. Cambridge, Mass., 1996.

———. *A New Song: Celibate Women in the First Three Christian Centuries.* New York, 1983.

Milburn, Robert. *Early Christian Art and Architecture.* Los Angeles, 1988.

Miles, Margaret. "'Becoming Male': Women Martyrs and Ascetics." In *Carnal Knowing: Female Nakedness and Religious Meaning in the Christian West,* 53–77. Boston, 1989.

Momigliano, Arnaldo. "The Life of St. Macrina by Gregory of Nyssa." In *The Craft of the Ancient Historian: Essays in Honor of Chester G. Starr,* edited by John W. Eadie and Josiah Ober, 443–58. Lantham, England, 1985.

Mooney, Catherine M., ed. *Gendered Voices: Medieval Saints and Their Interpreters.* Philadelphia, 1999.

———. "Voice, Gender, and the Portrayal of Sanctity." In *Gendered Voices: Medieval Saints and their Interpreters,* ed. Catherine M. Mooney, 1–15. Philadelphia, 1999.

Morgan, David. *The Mongols.* Oxford and New York, 1986.

Mouriki, Doula. *The Mosaics of Nea Moni on Chios.* Athens, 1985.

———. "The Wall Paintings of the Church of the Panagia at Moutoullas, Cyprus." In *Byzanz und der Westen: Studien zur Kunst des europäischen Mittelalters,* edited by Irmgard Hutter, 171–213. Vienna, 1984.

Mullett, Margaret, and Dion Smythe, eds. *Alexios I Komnenos,* vol. 1, Papers of the Second Belfast Byzantine International Colloquium, 14–16 April 1989. Belfast, 1996.

Nelson, Robert S. "The Chora and the Great Church: Intervisuality in Fourteenth-Century Constantinople." *BMGS* 23 (1999): 67–101.

———. "The Discourse of Icons, Then and Now." *Art History* 12 (1989): 144–57.

Nicol, Donald M. *The Byzantine Lady: Ten Portraits 1250–1500.* Cambridge, 1994.

———. *The Last Centuries of Byzantium, 1261–1453.* Cambridge, 1993.

Obolensky, D. "The Baptism of Princess Olga of Kiev: The Problem of the Sources." *Philadelphie et autres études,* 159–76. Paris, 1984.

Omont, H. *Miniatures des plus anciens manuscrits grecs.* 2d ed. Paris, 1929.

Oost, Stewart Irvin. *Galla Placidia Augusta: A Biographical Essay.* Chicago, 1968.

Ostrogorsky, George. *History of the Byzantine State.* New Brunswick, 1969.

Ousterhout, Robert G. *The Art of the Kariye Camii.* London, 2002.

———. *The Architecture of the Kariye Camii in Istanbul.* Washington, D.C., 1987.

———, ed. *The Blessings of Pilgrimage.* Illinois Byzantine Studies 1. Urbana, 1990. See also articles by author.

Patlagean, Evelyne. "Ancient Byzantine Hagiography and Social History." In *Saints and Their Cults, Studies in Religious Sociology, Folklore and History,* edited by S. Wilson, 101–21. Cambridge, 1983.

———. "L'Histoire de la femme déguisée en moine et l'évolution de la sainteté féminine à Byzance." *Studi Medievali,* ser. 3, 17 (1976): 597–623.

———. "Sainteté et Pouvoir." In *The Byzantine Saint,* University of Birmingham Fourteenth Spring Symposium of Byzantine Studies, ed. Sergei Hackel, 99–105. London, 1981.

Pazdernik, Charles. "'Our Most Pious Consort Given Us by God': Dissident Reactions to the Partnership of Justinian and Theodora, A.D. 525–548." *Classical Antiquity* 13 (1994): 256–81.

Piccirillo, Michelle. *The Mosaics of Jordan.* Amman, Jordan, 1993.

Peers, Glen. *Subtle Bodies: Representing Angels in Byzantium.* Berkeley, 2001.

Pelikan, Jaroslav. *Christianity and Classical Culture: The Metamorphosis of Natural Theology in the Christian Encounter with Hellenism.* New Haven, 1993.

Power, Eileen. "The Position of Women," In *The Legacy of the Middle Ages,* edited by C. G. Crump and E. F. Jacob, 401–33. Oxford, 1926.

Ranft, Patricia. *Women and the Religious Life in Premodern Europe.* New York, 1996.

Rapp, Claudia. "Figures of Female Sanctity: Byzantine Edifying Manuscripts and Their Audience." *DOP* 50 (1996): 313–32.

Restle, Marcell. *Die Byzantinische Wandmalerei in Kleinasien.* Recklinghausen, 1967.

Richlin, Amy. "Julia's Jokes, Galla Placidia, and the Roman Use of Women as Political Icons." In *Stereotypes of Women in Power: Historical Perspectives and Revisionist Views,* edited by B. Garlick, S. Dixon, and P. Allen, 65–91. Westport, Conn., 1992.

Ringrose, Kathryn M. *The Perfect Servant: Eunuchs and the Social Construction of Gender.* Chicago, 2002.

Rizzardi, Clementina, ed. *Il Mausoleo di Galla Placidia a Ravenna; The Mausoleum of Galla Placidia Ravenna.* Mirabilia Italiae series. Modena, Italy, 1996.

Robertson, Anne S. *Roman Imperial Coins in the Hunter Coin Cabinet, University of Glasgow.* Volume 5: *Diocletian to Zeno.* Oxford, 1982.

Ross, M. C. *Catalogue of the Byzantine and Early Mediaeval Antiquities in the Dumbarton Oaks Collection.* Volume 2: *Jewelry, Enamels, and Art of the Migration Period.* Washington, D.C., 1965.

Sacopoulo, M. *Asinou en 1106 et sa contribution à l'iconographie.* Brussels, 1966.

Safran, Linda, ed. *Heaven on Earth: Art and the Church in Byzantium.* University Park, Penn., 1998.

Schulenburg, Jane Tibbetts. *Forgetful of Their Sex: Female Sanctity and Society ca. 500–1100.* Chicago, 1998.

Sered, Susan S. *Women as Ritual Experts: The Religious Lives of Elderly Jewish Women in Jerusalem.* New York, 1992.

Ševčenko, Ihor. "Theodore Metochites, the Chora, and the Intellectual Trends of His Time." In *The Kariye Djami* 4:19–33. New York and Princeton, 1975.

Ševčenko, Nancy Patterson. *Illustrated Manuscripts of the Metaphrastian Menologion.* Chicago and London, 1990.

Smith, William, and Henry Wace, eds. *A Dictionary of Christian Biography.* London, 1882.

Spatharakis, Iohannis. *The Portrait in Byzantine Illuminated Manuscripts,* 191–207 and pls. 141–55. Leiden, 1976.

Starensier, Adele La Barre. "An Art Historical Study of the Byzantine Silk Industry." Ph.D. diss., Columbia University. Reproduced by UMI, Ann Arbor, 1982.

Stikas, Eustathius. *To Oikodomikon Xronikon Tes Mones Osiou Louka Fokidos.* Athens, 1970.

Stolte, Bernard. "Desires Denied: Marriage, Adultery and Divorce in Early Byzantine Law." In *Desire and Denial in Byzantium,* edited by Liz James, 77–86. Ashgate, 1999.

Stout, Ann. "Jewelry as a Symbol of Status in the Roman Empire." In *The World of Roman Costume,* edited by Judith Sebesta and Larissa Bonfante, 77–100. Madison, 1994.

Stylianou, J. and A. Stylianou. *The Painted Churches of Cyprus: Treasures of Byzantine Art.* London, 1985.

Talbot, Alice-Mary. "Bluestocking Nuns: Intellectual Life in the Convents of Late Byzantium." *Okeanos, Harvard Ukranian Studies* 7 (1983): 604–18.

———. "The Byzantine Family and the Monastery." *Dumbarton Oaks Papers* 44 (1990): 119–29.

———. "Byzantine Women, Saints' Lives, and Social Welfare." In *Through the Eye of a Needle: The Judaeo-Christian Roots of Social Welfare,* edited by E. A. Hanawalt and C. Lindbergh, 105–22. Kirksville, Mo., 1994.

———. "A Comparison of the Monastic Experience of Byzantine Men and Women." *Greek Orthodox Theological Review* 30 (1985): 1–20.

———. "Empress Theodora Palaeologina, Wife of Michael VIII." *DOP* 46 (1992): 295–303.

———. "Family Cults in Byzantium: The Case of St. Theodora of Thessaloniki." In *Leimon: Studies Presented to Lennart Rydén on His Sixty-Fifth Birthday,* edited by Jan Olof Rosenqvist, 49–69. Uppsala, 1996.

———. "Female Pilgrimage in Late Antiquity and the Byzantine Era." *ABzF* 1 (2002): 73–88.

———, ed. *Holy Women of Byzantium: Ten Saints' Lives in English Translation.* Washington, 1996.

———. "Late Byzantine Nuns: By Choice or Necessity?" *BF* 9 (1985): 103–17.

———. "Old Age in Byzantium." *BZ* (1984): 267–78.

———. "Women." In *The Byzantines,* edited by Guglielmo Cavallo, translated by Thomas Dunlap, Teresa Lavender Fagan, and Charles Lambert, 117–43. Chicago and London, 1997.

———. *Women and Religious Life in Byzantium.* Washington, D.C., 2001. (Not consulted; reprints of most of the articles cited here appear in this volume.)

Talbot, Alice-Mary, and Galatariotou, Catia. "Byzantine Women's Monastic Communities: The Evidence of the Typika." *JOB* 38 (1988): 263–90.

Teteriatnikov, Natalia. "The Dedication of the Chora Monastery in the Time of Andronikos II Palaiologos." *Byzantion* 66 (1996): 188–207.

———. "The Place of the Nun Melania (the Lady of the Mongols) in the Deesis Program of the Inner Narthex of Chora, Constantinople." *CA* 43 (1995): 163–80.

———. "The True Cross Flanked by Constantine and Helena: A Study in the Light of the Post-iconoclastic Re-evaluation of the Cross." *Deltion* 18 (1995): 169–88.

———. "Hagia Sophia: The Two Portraits of the Emperors with Moneybags as a Functional Setting." *Arte Medievale* 10 (1996): 47–66.

Thierry, Nicole. "Un atelier cappadocien du XIe siècle á Maçan-Göreme." *Cahiers Archéologiques* 44 (1996): 117–40.

———. "La Croix en Cappadoce: Typologie et Valeur Representative." In *Le Site monastique copte des Kellia: Sources historiques et explorations archéologiques,* Actes du Colloque de Genève, 13–15 August 1984, Mission suisse d'archéologie copte de l'université de Genève, 197–212. Geneva, 1986.

———. "Le culte de la croix dans l'empire byzantine du VIIe siècle au Xe dans ses rapports avec la guerre contre l'infidèle." *Rivista di Studi Byzantini e Slavi; Miscellanea Agostino Pertusi* 1 (1981): 205–28.

———. "Une image du triomphe impérial dans une église de Cappadoce: L'église de Nicéphore Phocas à Çavuşin." *Bulletin de la Société Nationale des Antiquaires de France* (1985): 28–35.

Thomas, John Philip. *Private Religious Foundations in the Byzantine Empire.* Washington, D.C., 1987.

———. "The Rise of the Independent and Self-Governing Monasteries as Reflected in the Monastic Typika." *Greek Orthodox Theological Review* 30 (1985): 21–30.

Thomas, John Philip, and Angela C. Hero, eds. *Byzantine Monastic Foundation Documents.* 5 volumes. Dumbarton Oaks Studies 35. Washington, D.C., 2000.

Thomas, Thelma K. *Late Antique Egyptian Funerary Sculpture: Images for This World and the Next.* Princeton, 2000.

Tougher, Shaun F. "Byzantine Eunuchs: An Overview, with Special Reference to their Creation and Origin." In *Women, Men and Eunuchs: Gender in Byzantium,* ed. Liz James, 168–84. London and New York, 1997.

Treadgold, Warren, T. "The Bride-shows of the Byzantine Emperors." *Byzantion* 49 (1979): 395–413.

———. "The Unpublished Saint's Life of the Empress Irene (BHG 2205)." *BF* 8 (1982): 237–51.

Trilling, James. "The Soul of the Empire: Style and Meaning in the Mosaic Pavement of the Imperial Palace in Constantinople." *DOP* 43 (1989): 27–72.

Tronzo, William. "Mimesis in Byzantium." *RES* 25: *Archaeology and Aesthetics* (1994): 61–76.

Underwood, Paul A. *The Kariye Djami.* 4 volumes. New York and Princeton, 1966; Princeton, 1975.

———. "The Deesis Mosaic in the Kariye Djami at Istanbul." In *Late Classical and Medieval Studies in Honor of A. M. Friend, Jr.,* 254–60. Princeton, 1955.

Veyne, Paul, ed. *A History of Private Life: From Pagan Rome to Byzantium.* Cambridge, 1987.

Vikan, Gary. *Byzantine Pilgrimage Art.* Washington, D.C., 1981.

———. "Byzantine Pilgrims' Art." In *Heaven on Earth: Art and the Church in Byzantium,* edited by Linda Safran, 229–66. University Park, Penn., 1998.

———. "Pilgrims in Magi's Clothing: The Impact of Mimesis on Early Byzantine Pilgrimage Art." In *The Blessings of Pilgrimage,* edited by R. Ousterhout, 97–107. Illinois Byzantine Studies 1. Urbana, 1990.

Vikan, Gary, and Kenneth Holum. "The Trier Ivory." *DOP* 33 (1979): 115–33.

Vincent, Père Hughes, and Père F.-M. Abel. *Jérusalem: Recherches de topographie, d'archéologie et d'histoire.* Volume 2. Paris, 1926.

Volbach, Wolfgang F. *Early Christian Art.* 1962; reprint New York, 1979.

———. *Elfenbeinarbeiten der Spätantike und des frühen Mittelalters.* Römisch-germanisches Zentralmuseum zu Mainz, Katalog VII, 3d ed. Mainz, 1976.

Von Premerstein, A. "Anicia Juliana im Wiener Dioskorides-Kodex." *Jahrbuch der Kunsthistorischen Sammlungen des Allerh. Kaiserhauses* 24 (1903): 106–24.

Von Simson, Otto. *Sacred Fortress: Byzantine Art and Statecraft in Ravenna,* esp. chap. 2, "San Vitale," 23–39. 1948; repr. Princeton, 1987.

Ward, Benedicta. *Harlots of the Desert.* Kalamazoo, 1987.

———. "St. Mary of Egypt: The Liturgical Icon of Repentance." In *Harlots of the Desert: A Study of Repentance in Early Monastic Sources,* 26–56. Kalamazoo, 1987.

Weitzmann, Kurt. "The Character and Intellectual Origins of the Macedonian Renaissance." In *Studies in Classical and Byzantine Manuscript Illumination,* ed. Herbert L. Kessler, 176–223. Chicago and London, 1971.

———. *The Joshua Roll: A Work of the Macedonian Renaissance.* Studies in Manuscript Illumination 3. Princeton, 1948.

Whittemore, Thomas. *The Mosaics of Haghia Sophia at Istanbul: Third Preliminary Report. Work Done in 1935–1938: The Imperial Portraits of the South Gallery.* Boston, 1942.

Wilkinson, John. *Egeria's Travels*. London, 1971.

———. "Jewish Holy Places and the Origins of Christian Pilgrimage." In *The Blessings of Pilgrimage,* edited by R. Ousterhout, 41–53. Illinois Byzantine Studies 1. Urbana, 1990.

Wilson-Kastner, Patricia. "Macrina: Virgin and Teacher." *Andrews University Seminary Studies* 17 (1979): 105–17.

Wilson-Kastner, Patricia, et al., eds. *A Lost Tradition: Women Writers of the Early Church.* Washington, D.C., 1981.

# INDEX

abbess, 161, 167, 172, 175, 179, 269–78, 289–307
adoption, imperial succession and, 221–22
adultery, 83–84; in the empress Zoe's marriages, ch. 10 *passim*
Aelia, as honorific title, 54
Agathe, festival of, 266
agriculture, women and, 155–57
*Alexiad* of Anna Komnene, ch. 11 *passim*
Amalasuntha, 128
ampullae, 9–10
amuletic objects, 100–102
Anastasia, saint, 176
Anicia Juliana, 96, 105–15
Anna, wife of Vladimir of Kiev, 212–13
Anna Dalassene, 242–45, 253–58
Anna Komnene, ch. 11 *passim*; anti-Latin bias of, 255–57; assassination plot of, 245, 260; education of, 255–57; Homeric stance of, 246–47; influence of Michael Psellus on, 249–50; writing style of, 239–59
anti-Latin bias, 249
Antonina, wife of Belisarius, 119–21, 138
Apostolic Constitutions, 19
apotactite, 41

Ariadne, empress, 48–49, 57
Arian heresy, 69
art, expenditure and, 95; patronage and, ch. 5 *passim*
ascetic life, 283, 293
asceticism, 174, 177; ch. 1 *passim*, 203
ascetics, secret, 172, 177
Athenais Eudocia, empress, 49, 55, 59, 60–61, 106, 115
"athlete of Christ," 24–25
Augusta, 45–46
authorship, female, 180, 238, 245

baptism, 7, 90
Basil the Great, 20
baths and bathing, 127
battered wives, 171
beauty, Byzantine ideal of, 252
betrothal, 23, 48, 122–23, 138–39
body, assembly of nuns as, 292
*Book of Ceremonies,* 208, 214
"brides of Christ," 15, 86, 283, 287
brideshow, 47–48, 167, 173–74
Brumalia festival, 266
burial, 170, 179
Byzantine style in art, 182–87

liturgical calendar, 173
liturgical objects, 96, 97–100
*loca sancta,* 30–32

Macrina, saint, ch. 1 *passim*
magic and sorcery, 127, 176–77; to aid
    conception, 217
Manzikert, battle of, 240, 243
Maria Lekapena, 212
Maria of Alania, 210, 241–42, 245, 251–52,
    256, pl. 18
Maria Palaeologina/Melane the Nun,
    312–16, figs. 45, 46; identity of, 314–15
marriage, 16, 20, 122–23, 125, 139; im-
    perial, ch. 10 *passim;* imperial suc-
    cession through, 207, 216–20, 226;
    interdictions of, 209; legal age of, 207,
    213; legal number of, 214; preparation
    of brides for, 207–14; with foreigners,
    207–9, 211
marriage belt, 101, fig. 16
martyrdom, language of, 14
martyria, 30
Mary Magdalene, 78
Mary of Egypt, 87–93, 198–203
Mary/Marinos, 84
mausolea, 104–5
Melane the Nun, 312–16, figs. 45–46
Melania the Elder, 18
Melania the Younger, 32, 61
Michael Psellus, 208, 215–37, 241, 245–46,
    249–50, 252–54, 264, 266
miracles, 26, 27, 155–57, 173, 176–80
monasteries, 75, 163, 170; administration
    of, 272–74; buildings in, 171; fami-
    lies and, 270, 273, 278, 302–4; female,
    23–26; founding of, 273, 278; in late
    Byzantium, 268–77, 289–307; lay
    children and, 305; life in, 168–71, 175,
    ordinary women and, 264–65, 269,
    273–75, 306–7; as prisons, 172; reasons
    for entering, 171; size of, 170
monasticism, female, 159–80; types of, 15
monazontes, 41
Mongols, 263, 267, 312–16

Monophysite heresy, 131; Athenais Eudo-
    cia and, 62
Mother of God of Sure Hope monastery,
    264, 268–69, 277–307
Mount Sinai, 30, 36–38

names, of women in inscriptions, 98–105
naming, of nuns, 275–78; in monasticism,
    168
New Rome. *See* Constantinople
Nika riots, 118, 126
Normans of Sicily, 240–42, 244, 247, 249,
    257
nunneries. *See* monasteries
nuns, 19, 312–16; categories of, 273–74,
    294–307; health of, 298; names of, 275;
    privileged, 274–75; roles of, 294–307;
    status of, 170

*Odyssey,* 239, 247
Olympias, 18, 19
ordinary women, 79, 83–85, 88, ch. 7
    *passim,* 163, 171, 223–24, 236
Ottoman Turks, 263–64, 314–16

painter (artist), 179
*Painter's Manual,* 191
palace, imperial, 46–47
Palaeologan dynasty, 263–65, 269
Pantepoptes monastery, 243
Pantocrator monastery, 211
*parecclesia. See* funerary chapels
*parresia. See* intercession
*parthenoi,* 17, 41
patronage, women and, ch. 5 *passim*
Paula, 18
peacocks, meaning and symbolism of,
    108–12
Pelagia of Antioch, 80–84, 86
perfumes, empress Zoe and, 228
personifications, 110
Petrion monastery, 243
*Philanthropeia,* 50
Philanthropos Soter monastery, 275–76
philanthropy, women and, 153–54